Adobe® Creative Suite Web Premium All-in-One For Dummies®

Common Menu Options

Option	How It's Used
New	Cr…
Open	Op… …r hard drive or a disk to …
Close	Closes the current document; if you have unsaved changes, you're prompted to save those changes first.
Save	Saves the changes you've made to the current document.
Save As	Saves a new copy of the current document.
Place or Import	Imports a file, such as an image or a sound file, into the current document.
Export	Exports the current data to a specified file format. You can sometimes select several different kinds of file formats to save the current data in.
Copy	Copies the currently selected data onto the computer's Clipboard.
Paste	Pastes the data from the Clipboard into the current document.
Undo	Undoes the most recent thing you did in the program.
Redo	Redoes the steps that you applied the Undo command to.
Zoom In	Magnifies the document so that you can view and edit the contents closely.
Zoom Out	Scales the view smaller so that you can see more of the document at once.
Help	Opens the help documentation for the current program.

Common Keyboard Shortcuts

Command	Windows Shortcut	Mac Shortcut
New	Ctrl+N	⌘+N
Open	Ctrl+O	⌘+O
Save	Ctrl+S	⌘+S
Undo	Ctrl+Z	⌘+Z
Redo	Shift+Ctrl+Z	Shift+⌘+Z
Copy	Ctrl+C	⌘+C
Paste	Ctrl+V	⌘+V
Print	Ctrl+P	⌘+P
Preferences (General)	Ctrl+K	⌘+K
Zoom In	Ctrl++ (plus sign)	⌘++ (plus sign)
Zoom Out	Ctrl+ – (minus sign)	⌘+ – (minus sign)
Help	F1 or sometimes Ctrl+?	F1 or sometimes ⌘+?

For Dummies: Bestselling Book Series for Beginners

Adobe® Creative Suite® 4 Web Premium All-in-One For Dummies®

Cheat Sheet

Common Panels

- **Color:** Use the Color panel to select or mix colors for use in the current document. Choose different color modes, such as RGB and CMYK, from the panel menu.

- **Info:** The Info panel shows you information about the document itself or a particular selection you've made. The Info panel includes information on size, positioning, and rotation of selected objects. You can't enter data into the Info panel — use the Transform panel to make modifications.

- **Swatches:** You can use the Swatches panel to create a library of color selections, which you can save and import into other documents or other programs. You can store colors and gradients that you use repeatedly in the Swatches panel.

- **Tools:** The Tools panel (commonly called the toolbar) isn't available in all the Creative Suite programs, but it's a very important panel in the programs it does exist in. A program's toolbar contains the tools used in that program.

- **Layers:** The Layers panel is used to display and select layers. The Layers panel also enables you to change layer order and helps you select items on a particular layer.

- **Align:** The Align panel enables you to align selected objects to each other or align them in relation to the document itself. This panel makes it easy to do precise alignment with multiple objects.

- **Stroke:** The Stroke panel allows you to select strokes and change stroke attributes, such as color, width/weight, style, and caps (ends). The program you're using determines what attributes you can change.

- **Transform:** The Transform panel is used to display and change the *shear* (skew), rotation, position, and size of a selected object in the document. You can enter new values for each of these transformations.

- **Character:** The Character panel is used to select fonts, font size, character spacing, and other settings related to using type in your documents.

Common Tools

Tool	What It Does
Selection	Selects elements in the document.
Marquee	Selects elements in a document using a rectangular or oval shape.
Lasso	Makes freehand selections in a document.
Magic Wand	Selects similar adjoining colors in a document.
Pencil	Makes freehand solid marks (with a hard edge) in the document.
Pen	Creates vector paths in a document.
Brush	Creates painterly brush marks in the document; brushes vary in size, shape, and pattern.
Text	Adds text to the document.
Shape	Creates various shapes in the document.
Scale	Increases or decreases the *scale* (size) of an element in the document.
Hand	Moves the contents of the document for viewing purposes.
Zoom	Changes the magnification of the document.

Copyright © 2009 Wiley Publishing, Inc. All rights reserved. Item 1407-1.

For more information about Wiley Publishing, call 1-800-762-2974.

For Dummies: Bestselling Book Series for Beginners

Adobe® Creative Suite® 4 Web Premium
ALL-IN-ONE
FOR
DUMMIES®

by Jennifer Smith, Christopher Smith, and Fred Gerantabee

Wiley Publishing, Inc.

Adobe® Creative Suite® 4 Web Premium All-in-One For Dummies®

Published by
Wiley Publishing, Inc.
111 River Street
Hoboken, NJ 07030-5774

www.wiley.com

Copyright © 2009 by Wiley Publishing, Inc., Indianapolis, Indiana

Published by Wiley Publishing, Inc., Indianapolis, Indiana

Published simultaneously in Canada

For general information on our other products and services, please contact our Customer Care Department within the U.S. at 877-762-2974, outside the U.S. at 317-572-3993, or fax 317-572-4002.

For technical support, please visit www.wiley.com/techsupport.

Wiley also publishes its books in a variety of electronic formats. Some content that appears in print may not be available in electronic books.

Library of Congress Control Number: 2009920040

ISBN: 978-0-470-41407-1

Manufactured in the United States of America

10 9 8 7 6 5 4 3 2 1

WILEY

About the Authors

Jennifer Smith is the co-founder and Vice President of Aquent Graphics Institute (AGI). She has authored numerous books on Adobe's software products, including development of many of the Adobe *Classroom in a Book* titles. She regularly speaks at conferences and seminars, including the CRE8 Conference. Jennifer has worked in all aspects of graphic design and production, including as an art director of an advertising agency. Jennifer combines her practical experience and technical expertise as an educator. She has developed training programs for Adobe Systems and for all types of designers involved in creating print, Web, and interactive solutions, along with designers creating fashion and apparel. Her teaching and writing style show the clear direction of a practiced designer with in-depth knowledge of the Adobe Creative Suite applications. When she's not speaking or teaching, she can be found in suburban Boston, Massachusetts, with her husband and five children. You can read about Jennifer's seminar and conference appearances at www.agitraining.com.

Christopher Smith is co-founder and President of Aquent Graphics Institute (AGI), the training and professional development division of Aquent that serves creative and marketing organizations. An Adobe Certified Expert for multiple Adobe products, he has worked as part of the Adobe Creative Team to develop many of the Adobe *Classroom in a Book* series and has authored numerous books on both InDesign and Acrobat. Christopher manages content for the CRE8 Conference for creative professionals and also the Adobe Acrobat & PDF Conference. He has also served as an elected member of the School Board in his hometown in suburban Boston, Massachusetts, where he lives with his wife and children.

Fred Gerantabee is an Emmy-award winning interactive designer, author, and educator with more than 13 years of experience in Web and interactive design, development, and consulting.

Most recently, Fred was an interactive producer with Walt Disney Interactive/ ABC television, creating synchronous, Flash-based applications and interactive games for major television events, such as the 2004 Presidential Elections, the Academy Awards, and *Extreme Makeover: Home Edition*.

Fred is an Adobe Certified Instructor and ACE (Adobe Certified Expert) for Flash, Dreamweaver, and Flash Lite, and is the author of several books on Flash and Dreamweaver, including *Flash CS4 Digital Classroom* and *Dreamweaver CS4 Digital Classroom* (Wiley), and the *Adobe CS4 Design Premium All-In-One For Dummies* and *Adobe CS4 Web Premium All-In-One For Dummies* with Jennifer and Christopher Smith. He is a training manager and instructor at Aquent Graphics Institute, and can be found as a guest speaker at several industry conferences and events.

Dedication

Jennifer and Christopher Smith: To our parents, Ed and Nancy Smith, along with Mary Kelly. In loving memory of Jennifer's father, Joseph Kelly, the best teacher of all. Also to our perfect children, Kelly, Alex, Grant, Elizabeth, and Edward.

Fred Gerantabee: Love and thanks to my wonderful wife Samantha for all her support and love, and, my mom Francine for her never-ending support and encouragement. Thanks to Cindy and Michael Urich, my friends and family, my colleagues at Aquent Graphics Institute, and Jennifer Smith for the opportunity to work with her on these great books. In memory of my loving grandmother, Yolande Gray, and my father, Michael Nas Gueran, who inspires me to this day.

Authors' Acknowledgments

Thanks to all our friends and colleagues at Adobe Systems for their support and the many product team members who responded to our questions throughout the writing process. Extra thanks to Ron Friedman and Lori Defurio of Adobe Systems for their inspiration and encouragement.

To the highly professional instructional staff at Aquent Graphics Institute (AGI), we appreciate your great insight into the best ways to help others discover creative software applications.

Thanks to all at Wiley Publishing and to our technical editor Cathy Auclair for her great insight.

Grant, Elizabeth, and Edward — thanks for putting up with our long hours in front of the keyboard night after night.

Thanks to all of Kelly and Alex's friends for permission to use their photos.

Publisher's Acknowledgments

We're proud of this book; please send us your comments through our online registration form located at http://dummies.custhelp.com. For other comments, please contact our Customer Care Department within the U.S. at 877-762-2974, outside the U.S. at 317-572-3993, or fax 317-572-4002.

Some of the people who helped bring this book to market include the following:

Acquisitions and Editorial

Project Editor: Rebecca Huehls

Acquisitions Editor: Amy Fandrei

Copy Editor: Jennifer Riggs

Technical Editor: Cathy Auclair

Editorial Manager: Leah P. Cameron

Editorial Assistant: Amanda Foxworth

Sr. Editorial Assistant: Cherie Case

Cartoons: Rich Tennant
(www.the5thwave.com)

Composition Services

Project Coordinator: Patrick Redmond

Layout and Graphics: Sarah Philippart, Ronald Terry, Christine Williams

Proofreaders: Melissa Cossell, Bonnie Mikkelson

Indexer: Ty Koontz

Publishing and Editorial for Technology Dummies

Richard Swadley, Vice President and Executive Group Publisher

Andy Cummings, Vice President and Publisher

Mary Bednarek, Executive Acquisitions Director

Mary C. Corder, Editorial Director

Publishing for Consumer Dummies

Diane Graves Steele, Vice President and Publisher

Composition Services

Gerry Fahey, Vice President of Production Services

Debbie Stailey, Director of Composition Services

Contents at a Glance

Table of Contents

Introduction

Adobe software has always been highly respected for creative design and development. Adobe creates programs that allow you to produce amazing designs and creations with ease. The Adobe Creative Suite 4 (CS4) Web Premium is one of the company's latest release of sophisticated and professional-level software that bundles many separate programs together as a suite. Each program in the suite works individually, or you can integrate the programs together by using *Version Cue,* Adobe's work management software that helps keep track of revisions and edits, and *Adobe Bridge,* an independent program that helps you control file management with thumbnails, metadata, and other organizational tools.

You can use the Adobe CS4 Web Premium programs to create a wide range of products, from Web graphics, Web sites, and interactive applications to photographic manipulations. Integrating the CS4 programs extends your possibilities as a designer. Don't worry about the programs being too difficult to figure out — just come up with your ideas and start creating!

About This Book

Adobe Creative Suite 4 Web Premium All-in-One For Dummies is written in a thorough and fun way to show you the basics on how to use each of the programs included in the suite. You find out how to use each program individually and how to work with the programs together, letting you extend your projects even further. You find out just how easy it is to use the programs through simple steps so that you can discover the power of the Adobe software. You'll be up and running in no time!

Here are some things you can do with this book:

✦ Manipulate photographs by using filters and drawing or color correction tools with Photoshop.

✦ Make illustrations by using drawing tools with Illustrator.

✦ Create Web pages and post them online with Dreamweaver.

✦ Create Web images, rollovers, image maps, and slices with Fireworks.

✦ Record and edit audio in Soundbooth, whether it's simple narration or a multitrack file with vocals and instruments.

✦ Create animations and videos with Flash.

✦ Create PDF (Portable Document Format) documents with Adobe Acrobat or other programs.

✦ Discover how to collaborate with others by using Contribute to maintain a site, whether as an administrator or as a user.

You discover the basics of how to create all these different kinds of things throughout the chapters in this book in fun, hands-on examples and clear explanations, getting you up to speed quickly!

Foolish Assumptions

You don't need to know much before picking up this book and getting started with the Web Premium suite. All you have to know is how to use a computer in a very basic way. If you can turn on the computer and use a mouse, you're ready for this book. A bit of knowledge about basic computer operations and using software helps, but it isn't necessary. We show you how to open, save, create, and manipulate files by using the CS4 programs so that you can start working with the programs quickly. The most important ingredient to have is your imagination and creativity — we show you how to get started with the rest.

Conventions Used in This Book

Adobe CS4 Web Premium is available for both Windows and the Macintosh; both platforms are covered in this book. Where the keys you need to press or the menu choice you need to make differs between Windows and the Mac, we let you know by including instructions for both platforms. For example:

✦ Press the Alt (Windows) or Option (Mac) key.

✦ Choose Edit➪Preferences➪General (Windows) or Dreamweaver➪Preferences➪General (Mac).

The programs in Web Premium Suite often require you to press and hold down a key (or keys) on the keyboard and then click or drag with the mouse. For brevity's sake, we shorten this action by naming the key you need to hold down and adding click or drag, as follows:

✦ Shift-click to select multiple files.

✦ Move the object by Ctrl+dragging (Windows) or ⌘+dragging (Mac).

Here are the formatting conventions used in this book:

✦ **Bold:** We use **bold** to indicate when you should type something or to highlight an action in a step list. For example, the action required to open a dialog box appears in bold in a step list.

✦ `Code font`**:** We use this computerese font to show you Web addresses (URLs), e-mail addresses, or bits of HTML code. For example, you type a URL into a browser window to access a Web page, such as `www.google.com`.

✦ *Italic:* We use *italic* to highlight a new term, which we then define. For example, *filters* may be a new term to you. The word itself is italicized and is followed by a definition to explain what the word means.

What You Don't Have to Read

This book is pretty thick; you may wonder whether you have to read it from cover to cover. You don't have to read every page of this book to discover how to use the programs in the Web Premium Suite. Luckily, you can choose bits and pieces that mean the most to you and will help you finish a project you may be working on. Perhaps you're interested in creating a technical drawing and putting it online. You can choose to read a couple chapters in Book III on Illustrator and then skip ahead to Book IV on Dreamweaver and just read the relevant chapters or sections on each subject. Later, you may want to place some associated PDF documents online, so read a few chapters in Book VIII on Acrobat or Book II on exporting Web graphics. Find out how to create animations for the Web and video in Book VII, which covers Flash.

You don't have to read everything on each page, either. You can treat many of the icons in this book as bonus material. Icons supplement the material in each chapter with additional information that may interest or help you with your work. The Technical Stuff icons are great if you want to find out a bit more about technical aspects of using the program or your computer, but don't feel that you need to read these icons if technicalities don't interest you.

How This Book Is Organized

Adobe Creative Suite 4 Web Premium All-in-One For Dummies is split into eight quick-reference guides, or minibooks. You don't have to read these minibooks sequentially, and you don't even have to read all the sections in any particular chapter. You can use the Table of Contents and the index to find the information you need and quickly get your answer. In this section, we briefly describe what you find in each minibook.

Book I: Adobe Creative Suite 4 Basics

Book I shows you how to use the features in Web Premium programs that are similar across all the programs described in this book. You discover the menus, panels, and tools that are similar or work the same way in most of the CS4 programs. You also find out how to import, export, and use common commands in each program. If you're wondering about what shortcuts and common tools you can use in the programs to speed up your workflow, this part has tips and tricks you'll find quite useful. The similarities in all the programs are helpful because they make using the programs that much easier.

Book II: Photoshop CS4

Book II on Photoshop CS4 is aimed to help you achieve good imagery, starting with basics that even advanced users may have missed along the way. In this minibook, you find out how to color correct images like a pro and use tools to keep images at the right resolution and size, no matter whether the image is intended for print or the Web.

This minibook also shows you how to integrate new features in Photoshop, such as the new Adjustments panel and Masks panel, as well as informs you of the new 3D tools. By the time you're finished with this minibook, you'll feel like you can perform magic on just about any image.

Book III: Illustrator CS4

Book III starts with the fundamentals of Adobe Illustrator CS4 to help you create useful and interesting illustrations. Check out this minibook to discover how to take advantage of features that have been around for many versions of Illustrator, such as the Pen tool, as well as new and exciting features, such as vector tracing. See how to take advantage of the Appearance panel and save time by creating graphic styles, templates, and symbols. Pick up hard-to-find keyboard shortcuts that can help reduce the time spent mousing around for menu items and tools.

Book IV: Dreamweaver CS4

Book IV shows you how creating a Web site in Dreamweaver CS4 can be easy and fun. Take advantage of the tools and features in Dreamweaver to make and maintain a very clean and useable site. Discover how to take advantage of improved Cascading Style Sheets (CSS) capabilities, as well as how to use exciting rollover and action features that add interactivity to your site. In the past, these functions required lots of hand-coding and tape on the glasses, but now you can be a designer and create interactivity easily in Dreamweaver — no hand-coding or pocket protectors required.

Book V: Fireworks CS4

Fireworks CS4 offers you the capabilities you need to create virtually any sort of Web graphic. With Fireworks, you can optimize (prepare for the Web) images and graphics, as well as create cool rollover effects and sliced graphics. Find out in Book V how to spice up your Web site with buttons, image maps, and more!

Book VI: Soundbooth CS4

Adobe Soundbooth CS4 software gives Web designers, video editors, and other creative professionals the tools to create and edit multiple tracks of audio, customize music, add sound effects, and much more. Spice up your interactive documents and Web sites by taking advantage of this incredible application.

Book VII: Flash CS4

Find out how to create interactive animations for the Web and video with Flash CS4. Start with the basics, such as creating simple animations with tweening, all the way up to animations that allow for user interaction. This Timeline-based program may be different than anything that you've ever worked with, but Flash is sure to be an exciting program to discover.

Book VIII: Acrobat 9.0

Adobe Acrobat 9.0 is a powerful viewing and editing program that allows you to share documents with colleagues, clients, and production personnel, such as printers and Web-page designers. Book VIII shows you how you can save time and money previously spent on couriers and overnight shipping by taking advantage of annotation capabilities. Discover features that even advanced users may have missed along the way and see how you can feel comfortable about using PDF as a file format of choice.

Book IX: Contribute CS4

Adobe Contribute CS4 software allows you to collaboratively author, review, and publish Web content while maintaining a site's integrity. Better yet, you can do it without having to figure out HTML (HyperText Markup Language).

In Contribute CS4, you can now edit and publish Web pages, created as Dreamweaver templates, within your browser.

Icons Used in This Book

What's a *For Dummies* book without icons pointing you in the direction of really great information that's sure to help you along your way? In this section, we briefly describe each icon we use in this book.

The Tip icon points out helpful information that is likely to make your job easier.

This icon marks a generally interesting and useful fact — something that you may want to remember for later use.

The Warning icon highlights lurking danger. With this icon, we're telling you to pay attention and proceed with caution.

When you see this icon, you know that there's techie stuff nearby. If you're not feeling very technical, you can skip this info.

You can use the Adobe CS4 programs together in many different and helpful ways to make your workflow more efficient. Throughout this book, we explain just how you can implement integration wherever it's pertinent to the discussion at hand. We highlight these tidbits with the Integration icon — you won't want to miss this information.

Where to Go from Here

Adobe Creative Suite 4 Web Premium All-in-One For Dummies is designed so that you can read a chapter or section out of order, depending on what subjects you're most interested in. Where you go from here is entirely up to you!

Book I is a great place to start reading if you've never used Adobe products or if you're new to design-based software. Discovering the common terminology, menus, and panels can be very helpful for the later chapters that use the terms and commands regularly!

Book I
Adobe Creative Suite 4 Basics

The 5th Wave — By Rich Tennant

"Just how accurately should my Web site reflect my place of business?"

Contents at a Glance

Chapter 1: Introducing Adobe Creative Suite 4

In This Chapter

✔ Introducing Photoshop CS4

✔ Drawing with Illustrator CS4

✔ Creating Dreamweaver CS4

✔ Getting fired up with Fireworks CS4

✔ Adding noise with Soundbooth

✔ Getting into Flash CS4

✔ Getting started with Acrobat 9.0

✔ Getting to know Contribute

✔ Putting Adobe Bridge into your workflow

✔ Integrating the programs in Adobe CS4

With the Adobe Creative Suite 4 (CS4) Web Premium release, you get the tools you need to be creative for Web and interactive projects, from an interactive e-commerce Web site to an interactive application. Each piece of software in the Adobe Creative Suite works on its own as a robust tool. Combine all the applications, including Adobe Bridge, and you have a dynamic workflow that just can't be matched.

In this minibook, you discover the many features that are consistent among the applications in the suite. You find consistencies in color, file formats, and text editing, as well as general preferences for rulers and guides throughout all the applications in CS4. This minibook also shows you where to find the new features and how to save time by taking advantage of them.

In this chapter, you meet each of the components in Adobe CS4 Web Premium and discover what you can create with each of these powerful tools.

Getting Started with Photoshop CS4

Photoshop is the industry-standard software for Web designers, video professionals, and photographers who need to manipulate bitmap images. Photoshop allows you to manage and edit images by correcting color, editing photos by hand, and even combining several photos together to create interesting and unique effects. Alternatively, you can use Photoshop as a painting program, where you can artistically create images and graphics. Photoshop even includes a file browser that lets you easily manage your images by assigning keywords or allowing you to search the images based on metadata.

Photoshop allows you to create complex text layouts by placing text along a path or within shapes. You can edit the text after it's been placed along a path; you can even edit the text in other programs, such as Illustrator CS4. Join text and images together into unique designs or page layouts.

Sharing images from Photoshop is very easy to do. You can share multiple images in a PDF file, create an attractive photo gallery for the Web with a few clicks of the mouse, or upload images to an online photo service. You can pre-view multiple filters (effects) at once without having to apply each filter separately. Photoshop CS4 also supports various artistic brush styles, such as wet and dry brush type effects and charcoal and pastel effects. Photoshop also has some great features for scanning. You can scan multiple images at once, and Photoshop can straighten each photo and save it as an individual file.

It's hard to believe that Photoshop can be improved upon, but Adobe has done it again in Adobe Photoshop CS4. Find these new features and many more in Book II.

There's much more to see in Photoshop CS4. Book II shows you the diverse capabilities of Photoshop. From drawing and painting to image color correction, Photoshop has many uses for print and Web design alike. Read Book II, Chapter 1 to discover all the new features in Photoshop CS4, including new and improved adjustment layers and new 3D tools and features.

Using Illustrator CS4

Adobe Illustrator is the industry's leading vector-based graphics software. Aimed at everyone from graphics professionals to Web users, Illustrator allows you to design layouts, logos for print, or vector-based images that can be imported into other programs, such as Photoshop, Dreamweaver, Flash, and Fireworks. Adobe also enables you to easily and quickly create files by saving Illustrator documents as templates (so that you can efficiently reuse designs) and using a predefined library and document size.

Illustrator also integrates with the other products in the Adobe Creative Suite by allowing you to create PDF, PNG, GIF, and SWF documents easily within Illustrator. Illustrator allows you to beef up your rich interactive documents by introducing Flash features that give you the tools you need to build exciting interactive designs in Flash.

Here are some of the things you can create and do in Illustrator:

✦ Create technical drawings (floor plans, architectural sketches, and so on), logos, illustrations, posters, packaging, and Web graphics.

✦ Add effects, such as drop shadows and Gaussian blurs, to vector images.

✦ Enhance artwork by creating your own custom brushes.

✦ Align text along a path so that it bends in an interesting way.

✦ Create charts and graphs with graphing tools.

✦ Create gradients that can be imported and edited in other programs, such as InDesign.

✦ Create documents quickly and easily by using the existing templates and included stock graphics in Illustrator.

✦ Save a drawing in almost any graphic format, including Adobe's PDF, PSD, EPS, TIFF, GIF, JPEG, and SVG formats.

✦ Save your Illustrator files for the Web by using the Save for Web & Devices dialog box, which allows you to output HTML, GIF, and JPEG.

✦ Save Illustrator files as secure PDF files with 128-bit encryption.

✦ Export assets as symbols to Flash.

There are many new features for you to investigate, many of them integrated in the chapters in Book III. Find out about new tools, including the improved Appearance panel, guides that help you work more accurately, and improved isolation features that help you focus on your artwork, quickly and easily. Find additional features by reading Book III, Chapter 1.

Introducing Dreamweaver CS4

Dreamweaver CS4 is used to create professional Web sites quickly and efficiently, without the need to know or understand HTML (HyperText Markup Language). You can work with a visual authoring workspace (commonly known as a *Design view*), or you can work in an environment where you work with the code. Dreamweaver enables you to set up entire Web sites of multiple pages on your hard drive, test them, and then upload them to a Web server. With Dreamweaver's integration capabilities, you can create pages easily that contain imagery from Adobe Illustrator, Photoshop, and Flash.

Dreamweaver also has built-in support for CSS (Cascading Style Sheets). *CSS* is a language that allows you to format your Web pages and control text attributes, such as color, size, and style of text. CSS gives you control over the layout of the elements on your Web pages.

Go to Book IV to find out how to use Dreamweaver CS4 to create exciting Web sites that include text, images, and multimedia. Read Book IV, Chapter 1 to discover all the new features in Dreamweaver, including a better interface, faster CSS integration, and improved Spry widget features.

Welcoming you to Fireworks CS4

In the Web Premium suite, you now have a new tool for creating Web graphics! Fireworks is a much-needed tool in the Creative Suite package because it offers features that were available in ImageReady in the CS2 suite.

You may wonder why Fireworks is included in the Web Premium suite when it already includes two other image editing programs, Photoshop and Illustrator. Among other things, Fireworks is great for mocking up Web page designs, making it quick and easy to design a Web page layout and Web applications. Fireworks also enables you to edit both bitmap and vector images.

Use Fireworks for the following tasks:

✦ Compare file formats before exporting Web graphics.

✦ Create animations, rollovers, and pop-up windows.

✦ Create sliced images that use HTML tables or CSS (Cascading Style Sheets).

✦ Make wireframes, or mock up a Web site by using the template and pages features.

Find out more about the helpful Web creation tools in Fireworks in Book V.

Recording and Editing Audio in Soundbooth

You can take command of your online audio needs with Adobe Soundbooth software. With Soundbooth, you can easily add sound to videos, Flash files, and other online presentations.

Although Soundbooth includes controls that satisfy audio professionals, Soundbooth also provides new tools that video editors, designers, and others need to add sound to their files.

With Soundbooth, you can

✦ Arrange audio files on multiple tracks

✦ Match volume levels with a single command

✦ Remove unwanted noises and background sounds

✦ Improve voice-overs

✦ Add effects and filters

Moving into Flash CS4

Flash combines stunning motion graphics, visual effects, and interactivity that have made it the industry standard for creating Web sites, CD-ROM presentations, and interactive learning tools.

Create graphics and type in Flash with its comprehensive set of drawing tools and then put them in motion with Timeline-based animation, movie clips, and interactive buttons. Add photos, sound, and video for an even richer experience or use Flash's built-in scripting language, *ActionScript,* to create complex interactive environments that stand out.

The most recent versions of Flash have continued to revolutionize the way Web sites, presentations, and rich Internet applications are built. With improved drawing tools, advanced video features, effects filters, and further improvements on ActionScript, Flash CS4 promises to continue its place as the "king of all media."

Turn to Book VII to discover how to use Flash to create drawings and animations, to use ActionScript to create interactive Web pages, and more.

Working with Acrobat 9.0

Acrobat 9.0 Professional is aimed at both business and creative professionals and provides an incredibly useful way of sharing, security, and reviewing the documents you create in your Web Premium Suite applications.

Portable Document Format (PDF) is the file format used by Adobe Acrobat. It's used primarily as an independent method for sharing files. This format allows users who create files on either Macintosh or PC systems to share files with each other, and with users of hand-held devices or UNIX computers. PDF files generally start out as other documents — whether from a word processor or a sophisticated page layout and design program.

Although PDF files can be read on many different computer systems with the free Adobe Reader, users with the Professional or Standard version of Adobe Acrobat can do much more with PDF files. With your version of Acrobat, you can create PDF documents, add security to them, use review and commenting tools, edit the documents, and build PDF forms.

Use Acrobat to perform any of the following tasks:

✦ Create interactive forms that can be filled out online.

✦ Allow users to embed comments within the PDF files to provide feedback. Comments can then be compiled from multiple reviewers and viewed in a single summary.

✦ Create PDF files that can include MP3 audio, video, SWF, and even 3D files.

✦ Combine multiple files into a single PDF and include headers and footers, as well as watermarks.

✦ Create secure documents with encryption.

✦ Take advantage of a new, intuitive user interface. You can now complete tasks more quickly with a streamlined user interface, new customizable toolbars, and a Getting Started page to visually direct you to commonly used features. In other words, you get an interface more in line with what you may see in the rest of the Creative Suite products.

✦ Combine multiple files into a searchable, sortable PDF package that maintains the individual security settings and digital signatures of each included PDF document.

✦ Use auto-recognize to automatically locate form fields in static PDF documents and convert them to interactive fields that can be filled electronically by anyone using Adobe Reader software (Windows only).

✦ Manage shared reviews — without IT assistance — to allow review participants to see one another's comments and track the status of the review. Shared reviews are possible through Acrobat Connect, formerly Breeze.

✦ Enable advanced features in Adobe Reader to enable anyone using free Adobe Reader software to participate in document reviews, fill and save electronic forms offline, and digitally sign documents.

✦ Permanently remove metadata, hidden layers, and other concealed information and use redaction tools to permanently delete sensitive text, illustrations, or other content.

✦ Save your PDF to Microsoft Word. This feature is a treasure! You can now take advantage of improved functionality for saving Adobe PDF files as Microsoft Word documents, retaining the layout, fonts, formatting, and tables.

✦ Enjoy improved performance and support for AutoCAD. Those of you using AutoCAD can now more rapidly convert AutoCAD drawing files into compact, accurate PDF documents, without the need for the native desktop application.

Want to discover other great Acrobat improvements? Read Book VIII to find out all about Acrobat and PDF creation.

Collaborating with Contribute

Adobe Contribute CS4 software enables users, who might not know HTML, to collectively author, review, and publish Web content while maintaining site integrity.

With Contribute, you can

✦ **Edit in your browser:** The new full-featured in-browser editor in Contribute CS4 provides a powerful interface for editing and publishing Web pages within your browser.

✦ **Use Dreamweaver templates:** Easily edit advanced HTML layouts with Adobe Dreamweaver templates, which provide editable regions within protected areas of the page.

✦ **Use rich media support:** Easily drag and drop your images, FLV and SWF files, or PDF documents into your Contribute pages. Contribute automatically uploads the dependent files to the Web server when the pages are published.

✦ **Auto save:** Protect contributors' ongoing edits with the new Auto Save feature. The Auto Save feature allows you to specify how frequently updated drafts are saved.

Crossing the Adobe Bridge

Adobe Bridge is really an incredible application, especially with the CS4 release because the processing speed is greatly improved and new features are available.

Bridge CS4 is a separate application that you can access through the Creative Suite applications. It allows you to quickly access and manage multiple documents (such as images, text files, and Adobe stock photos), which you can use in all the CS4 applications. Bridge CS4 also has a home area where users can get updates and tips and tricks about all programs in the Creative Suite.

Integrating Software

With so many great pieces of software in a single package, it's only natural that you'll want to start using the programs together to build exciting projects. You may want to design a book by using InDesign (with photos edited in Photoshop and drawings created in Illustrator) and then create a Web site for that content in Dreamweaver. Similarly, you may want to take a complex PDF file and make it into something that everyone can view online. Or you might create a symbol or Flash text in Illustrator and complete the animation in Flash. All the tools in the Adobe Creative Suite are built to work together, and achieving these tasks suddenly becomes much easier to do because the products are integrated.

Integrating software is typically advantageous to anyone. Integration allows you to streamline the workflow among programs and sometimes among team members. Tools exist that allow you to drop native images into Dreamweaver, InDesign, Illustrator, and Flash. With Adobe Bridge, you can view your files and investigate specifics about the file, such as color mode and file size, before selecting them for placement.

Chapter 2: Using Common Menus and Commands

In This Chapter

✓ Discovering common menus and dialog boxes

✓ Addressing CS4 alerts

✓ Working with common menu options

✓ Understanding contextual menus

✓ Speeding up your workflow with shortcuts

✓ Changing preferences

When you work with Adobe Creative Suite 4 Web Premium, you may notice that many menus, commands, and options are similar among its various programs. Discovering how to use menus and dialog boxes is essential to using the programs in the Creative Suite.

You may already be familiar with using dialog boxes and menus from other software packages. The way you use these elements is pretty much the same for any program. Some specific keyboard shortcuts are the same across programs, even ones made by different software companies. This consistency makes finding out how to use the commands and options very easy. This chapter provides an overview of some of the common menus, dialog boxes, options, commands, and preferences that exist in most or all the programs in Adobe CS4 Web Premium.

Discovering Common Menus

When you work with programs in Adobe CS4 Web Premium, you probably notice that many of the menus in the main menu bar are the same. And then you probably see that these menus often contain many of the same commands across each program. These menus are somewhat similar to other graphics programs you may have used. Similar functionality makes finding certain commands easy, even when you're completely new to the software you're using.

Menus contain options and commands that control particular parts or functions of each program. You may have the option of opening a dialog box, which is used to input settings or preferences or to add something to a document. A menu may also contain commands that perform a particular action. For example, you may save the file as a result of selecting a particular command in a menu. Menus that commonly appear in the CS4 programs are

- ✦ **File:** Contains many commands that control the overall document, such as creating, opening, saving, printing, and setting general properties for the document. The File menu may also include options for importing or exporting data into or from the current document.

- ✦ **Edit:** Contains options and commands for editing the current document. Commands include copying, pasting, and selecting, as well as options for opening preferences and setting dialog boxes that are used to control parts of the document. Spell check and transforming objects are also common parts of the Edit menu.

- ✦ **View:** Contains options for changing the level of magnification of the document. The View menu also sometimes includes options for viewing the workspace in different ways, showing rules, grids, or guides, and turning on and off snapping.

- ✦ **Window:** Contains options that are primarily used to open or close whatever panels are available in the program. You can also choose how to view the workspace and save a favorite arrangement of the workspace.

- ✦ **Help:** Contains the option to open the Help documentation that's included with the program. This menu may also include information about updating the software, registration, and tutorials.

Adobe Web Premium on the Mac also has an additional menu that bears the name of the program itself. This menu includes options for showing or hiding the program on the screen, opening preferences, and opening documents that provide information about the software.

Figure 2-1 shows a menu in Photoshop that contains many common options to control the program.

Notice that more menus are available in the programs than are in the previous list. Each program has additional program-specific menus that are determined by the specific needs of whatever software you're using. For example, Photoshop has an Image menu that enables you to resize the image or document, rotate the canvas, and duplicate the image, among other functions. What additional menus exist in each program is determined by what the software is designed to do; we discuss these menus where appropriate throughout the book.

Figure 2-1:
Menus in
Photoshop
allow you
to choose
and control
different
options.

Using Dialog Boxes

A *dialog box* is a small window that contains a combination of options formatted as drop-down lists, panels, lists, text fields, option buttons, check
boxes, and buttons that enable you to make settings and enter information
or data as necessary. The dialog boxes enable you to control the software or
your document in various ways. For example, when you open a new file, you
typically use the Open dialog box to select a file to open. When you save a
file, you use a Save As dialog box to select a location to save the file in, name
it, and execute the Save command.

Some dialog boxes also include tabs. These dialog boxes may need to contain many settings of different types that are organized into several sections,
using tabs. Dialog boxes typically have a button that executes the particular
command and one that cancels and closes the dialog box without doing anything. Figure 2-2 shows a common dialog box.

A dialog box in Windows is a lot like a dialog box you find on the Mac. Dialog boxes perform similar functions and include the same elements to enter or select information. For example, some of the functions that dialog boxes perform include the following:

✦ Save a new version of a file.

✦ Set up your printing options or page setup.

✦ Set up the preferences for the software you're using.

✦ Check spelling of text in a document.

✦ Open a new document.

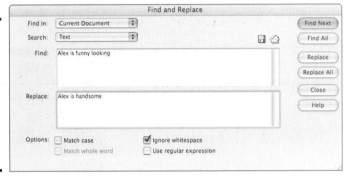

Figure 2-2: An example of a dialog box for finding and replacing text in Dream-weaver CS4.

When you have a dialog box open in the program you're using, the window pops up on the screen. Before you can begin working with the program again, you have to close the dialog box. You can close the dialog box either by making your choices and clicking a button (such as Save or OK) when you're finished, or clicking the Cancel button to close the dialog box without making any changes. You can't use the program you're working with until the dialog box is closed.

Encountering Alerts

Alerts are common on any operating system and in most programs. *Alerts* are similar to dialog boxes in that they're small windows that contain information. However, alerts are different from dialog boxes because you can't edit the information in an alert. Alerts are designed to simply tell you something and give you one or more options made by clicking a button. For example, you may encounter an alert that indicates you can't select a particular option. Usually you see an OK button to click to acknowledge and close the alert. You may have other buttons on the alert that will cancel what you were doing or a button that opens a dialog box. Figure 2-3 shows a typical alert.

Figure 2-3:
An alert
in Adobe
Illustrator
CS4.

Alerts are also sometimes used to confirm actions before executing them. Sometimes these alert windows also offer the option (typically in the form of a check box) of not showing the alert or warning again. You may want to select this option if you repeatedly perform an action that shows the warning and you don't need to see the warning each and every time.

Using Common Menu Options

Various menu options are typically available in each of the CS4 Web Premium programs. However, within each of these menus, several other options are available. Some of the options open dialog boxes, and those options are typically indicated by an ellipsis that follows the menu option, as shown in Figure 2-4.

Figure 2-4:
If an ellipsis
follows
a menu
option, a
dialog box
appears
when
selected.

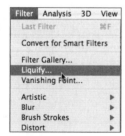

The following menu options are found in several of the CS4 programs, and these commands either perform similar (or the same) functions or they open similar dialog boxes:

✦ **New:** Creates a brand new document in the native file format. For example, in Illustrator, a new *AI* (the extension for Adobe Illustrator documents) file is created by choosing File➪New➪Document. You can sometimes choose what type of new file you want to create.

✦ **Open:** Opens a dialog box where you can choose a (supported) file on your hard drive or a disc to open.

✦ **Close:** Closes the current document. If you have unsaved changes, you're prompted to save those changes first.

✦ **Save:** Saves the changes you've made to the current document.

✦ **Save As:** Saves a new copy of the current document.

✦ **Import:** Imports a file into the current document, such as an image or sound file.

✦ **Export:** Exports the current data to a specified file format. You can sometimes select several different kinds of file formats to save the current data in.

✦ **Copy:** Copies the currently selected data onto the computer's Clipboard.

✦ **Paste:** Pastes the data from the Clipboard into the current document.

✦ **Undo:** Undoes the most recent thing you did in the program. For example, if you just created a rectangle, the rectangle is removed from the document.

✦ **Redo:** Redoes the steps that you applied the Undo command to. For example, if you removed that rectangle you created, the Redo command adds it back to the document.

✦ **Zoom In:** Magnifies the document so that you can view and edit the contents closely.

✦ **Zoom Out:** Scales the view smaller so that you can see more of the document at once.

✦ **Help:** Opens the Help documentation for the current program.

About Contextual Menus

Contextual menus are available in all kinds of programs; they're an incredibly useful, quick way to make selections or issue commands. Contextual menus include some of the most useful commands you may find yourself choosing over and over again.

A *contextual menu* is similar to the menus that we describe in the previous sections; however, it's context sensitive and opens when you right-click (Windows) or Control-click (Mac) something in the program. *Contextual* means that what options appear in the menu depends on what object or item you right-click (Windows) or Control-click (Mac). For example, if you open a contextual menu when the cursor is over an image, commands involving the image are listed in the menu. However, if you right-click (Windows) or Control-click (Mac) the document's background, you typically see options that affect the entire document rather than just a particular element within it. This means that you can select common commands specifically for the item that you've selected. Figure 2-5 shows a contextual menu that appears when you right-click (Windows) or Control-click (Mac) an object in Photoshop.

Figure 2-5:
Open a contextual menu in Windows by right-clicking an image or object.

Keep in mind that the tool you select in the toolbox may affect which contextual menus you can access in a document. You may have to select the Selection tool first to access some menus. If you want to access a contextual menu for a particular item in the document, make sure that the object is selected first before you right-click (Windows) or Control-click (Mac).

If you're using a Mac, you can right-click to open a contextual menu if you have a two-button mouse hooked up to your Mac. Otherwise, Control-click to open a contextual menu.

Using Common Shortcuts

Shortcuts are key combinations that enable you to quickly and efficiently execute commands, such as saving, opening, or copying and pasting objects. Many of these shortcuts are listed in the menus discussed in the previous sections. If the menu option has a key combination listed next to it, you can press that key combination to access the command instead of using the menu to select it. Figure 2-6 shows associated shortcuts with a menu item.

For example, if you open the File menu, next to the Save option is Ctrl+S (Windows) or ⌘+S (Mac). Instead of choosing File➪Save, you can press the shortcut keys to save your file. This is a very quick way to execute a particular command.

Some of the most common shortcuts in the Adobe Creative Suite 4 Web Premium programs are listed in Table 2-1.

Table 2-1	Common Keyboard Shortcuts	
Command	*Windows Shortcut*	*Mac Shortcut*
New	Ctrl+N	Ô+N
Open	Ctrl+O	Ô+O
Save	Ctrl+S	Ô+S
Undo	Ctrl+Z	Ô+Z
Redo	Shift+Ctrl+Z	Shift+Ô+Z
Copy	Ctrl+C	Ô+C
Paste	Ctrl+V	Ô+V
Print	Ctrl+P	Ô+P
Preferences (General)	Ctrl+K	⌘+K
Help	F1 or sometimes Ctrl+?	F1 or sometimes ⌘+?

Many additional shortcuts are available in each program in the CS4 programs, and they're not all listed in the menus. You can find these shortcuts throughout the documentation provided with each program. Memorizing the shortcuts can take some time, but the time you save in the long run is worth it.

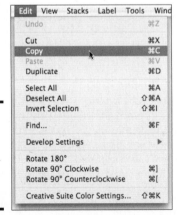

Figure 2-6: Shortcuts are shown next to their associated commands.

Changing Your Preferences

Setting your preferences is important when you're working with new software. Understanding what the preferences can do for you gives you a good idea about what the software does as well. All the programs in the Web Premium Suite have different preferences; however, the way that the Preferences dialog box works in each program is the same.

The Preferences dialog box for each program can be opened by choosing Edit➪Preferences (Windows) or *Program Name*➪Preferences➪General (Mac). The Preferences dialog box opens, as shown in Figure 2-7.

The Preferences dialog box contains a great number of settings you can control by entering values into text fields, using drop-down lists, buttons, check boxes, sliders, and other similar controls. Preferences can be quite detailed. However, you don't have to know what each preference does or even change any of them. Most dialog boxes containing preferences are quite detailed in outlining what the preferences control and are therefore intuitive to use. Adobe also sometimes includes a Description area near the bottom of the dialog box. When you mouse over a particular control, a description of that control appears in the Description area.

Figure 2-7:
Click an
item in
the list on
the left
side of the
Preferences
dialog box
to navigate
from one
topic to
the next.

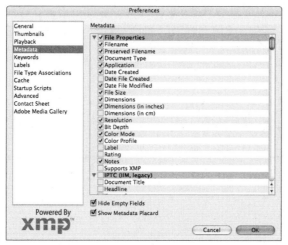

In some Preferences dialog boxes, the left side of the dialog box has a list box containing the different categories of preferences that you can change. When you're finished changing the settings in that topic, select a new topic from the list and change the settings for another topic.

In some programs, not all the settings you can modify are in the Preferences dialog box. For example, in Illustrator, you can change your color settings by choosing Edit⇨Color Settings to open the Color Settings dialog box. What is very useful about this dialog box is that when you mouse over particular drop-down lists or buttons, a description of that control appears at the bottom of the dialog box.

By launching Adobe Bridge and choosing Edit⇨Creative Suite Color Settings, you can change the color settings preferences across all the Web Premium programs at once, as shown in Figure 2-8.

Figure 2-8: The Suite Color Settings dialog box in Adobe Bridge.

In many CS4 programs, you have an option for setting up the main preferences for the overall document, such as setting up the page dimensions, the number of pages in the document, or the orientation (landscape or portrait) of the pages. In Dreamweaver and Photoshop, these kinds of options are available by choosing File⇨Page Setup; in Acrobat and Illustrator, choose File⇨Document Setup. Figure 2-9 shows a Document Setup dialog box.

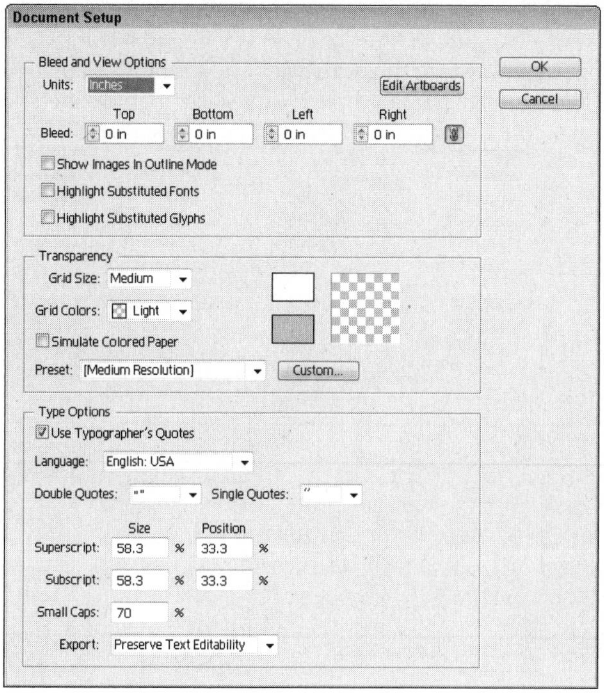

Figure 2-9: The Illustrator Document Setup dialog box.

Chapter 3: Exploring Common Panels

In This Chapter

✔ **Exploring the synchronized workspace**

✔ **Manipulating panels in the workspace**

✔ **Discovering different kinds of panels**

✔ **Getting to know the common panels in Adobe CS4**

*P*anels are an integral part of working with most of the programs in Adobe Creative Suite 4 (CS4) because they contain many of the controls and tools that you use when you're creating or editing a document.

The basic functionality of panels is quite similar across the programs in the Adobe Creative Suite, and the purpose of all panels is the same. Panels offer you a great deal of flexibility in how you organize the workspace and what parts of it you use. What you use each program for and the level of expertise you have may affect what panels you have open at a given moment. This chapter gives you an overview of how to work with the panels you find in Adobe CS4.

Understanding the Synchronized Workspace

One thing that you immediately notice when opening the applications in the Creative Suite is the synchronized workspace. All the applications look very similar and have the same set of features to help you organize your workspace.

The tools in Flash, Illustrator, and Photoshop appear as a space-saving, single-column toolbar, and panels are arranged in convenient, self-adjusting docks that can be widened to full size or narrowed so that the panels are collapsed to icons.

Here are some pointers to help you navigate the workspace in the Creative Suite applications:

✦ Expand your tools in Illustrator and Photoshop to two columns by clicking the right-facing double arrows in the gray bar on top of the tools.

✦ Collapse the tools in Illustrator and Photoshop to a single column by clicking the left-facing double arrows in the gray bar on top of the tools.

✦ To expand a docked panel, simply click the icon in the docking area. The panel that you selected expands, but goes away when you select a different panel.

   If you're having difficulty identifying the panel, you can choose the panel you want from the Window menu.

✦ Expand all the docked panels by clicking the left-facing double-arrow icon at the top of the docking area; put them away by clicking the right-facing double-arrow icon in the gray bar above the panels.

✦ To undock a panel, simply click the tab (where the panel name is located) and drag it out of the docking area. You can re-dock the panel by dragging the panel back into the docking area.

Using Panels in the Workspace

Panels are small windows in a program that contain controls, such as sliders, menus, buttons, and text fields, that you can use to change the settings or attributes of a selection or of the entire document. Panels may also include information about a section or about the document itself. You can use this information or change the settings in a panel to modify the selected object or the document you're working on.

Whether you're working on a Windows machine or on a Mac, panels are very similar in the way they look and work. Here are the basics of working with panels:

✦ **Opening:** Open a panel in one of the Creative Suite programs by using the Window menu; choose Window and then select the name of a panel. For example, to open the Swatches panel (which is similar in many programs in the suite), choose Window⇨Swatches.

✦ **Closing:** If you need to open or close a panel's tab or panel altogether, just choose Window⇨*Panel's Tab Name*. Sometimes a panel contains a close button (an X button in Windows or the red button on a Mac), which you can click to close the panel.

✦ **Organizing the workspace:** All the programs in the Creative Suite now offer options for workspace organization. You can return to the default workspace, which puts panels back in their original location, by choosing Window➪Workspace➪Default. You can also open the frequently used panels, position them where you want, and save a customized workspace by choosing Window➪Workspace➪Save Workspace. Name the workspace and click OK; the saved workspace is now a menu item that you can open by choosing Window➪Workspace➪*Your Saved Workspace's Name.*

You can also choose from a wide range of included presets that are designed for a variety of specialized tasks.

✦ **Accessing the panel menu:** Panels have a panel menu, which opens when you click the arrow in the upper-right corner of the panel, as shown in Figure 3-1. The panel menu contains a bunch of options you can select that relate to the tab currently selected when you click the panel menu. When you select one of the options in the panel menu, it may execute an action or open a dialog box. Sometimes a panel menu has very few options, but particular panels may have a whole bunch of related functionality and therefore many options in the panel menu.

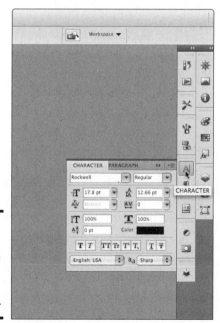

Figure 3-1:
Click the arrow in the upper right to see the panel menu.

✦ **Minimizing/maximizing:** All you need to do to minimize a selected panel is to click the Collapse to Icons double-arrow button in the title bar of the panel (if it's available). If the panel is undocked, you can also double-click the tab itself (of an undocked panel) in the panel. This will either partially or fully minimize the panel. If it only partially minimizes, double-clicking the tab again fully minimizes the panel. Double-clicking the active tab when it's minimized maximizes the panel again.

Panels that partially minimize give you the opportunity to work with panels that have differing amounts of information. This simplifies the workspace while maximizing your screen real estate.

Most panels contain tabs, which help organize information and controls in a program into groupings. Panel tabs contain a particular kind of information about a part of the program; a single panel may contain several tabs. The name on the tab usually gives you a hint about the type of function it controls or displays information about, and it is located at the top of the panel (refer to Figure 3-1). Inactive tabs are dimmed.

Moving panels

You can move panels all around the workplace, and you can add or remove single tabs from a panel. Each panel snaps to other panels, which makes it easier to arrange panels alongside each other. Panels can overlap each other as well. To snap panels to each other, drag the panel to a new location on-screen, as shown in Figure 3-2; you see the top bar of the panel become shaded, indicating that it's becoming part of another panel's group.

Grouping similar tabs by moving them into a single grouped panel is a good idea — it makes accessing the different functions in your document a lot easier because you have less searching to do to find related functions for a task if similar panels are grouped together.

You can hide all panels by pressing the Tab key. Press the Tab key again to reveal all the panels you've hidden.

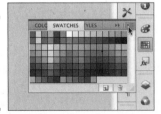

Figure 3-2:
To move a
panel, drag
the panel
by its tab.

Looking at common panels

Many panels are similar across programs in the Creative Suite. Although each panel doesn't have exactly the same contents in each of the programs it's included in, many are extremely similar in what they contain. You use these panels in very similar ways, no matter what program or operating system you're using.

Acrobat doesn't contain numerous panels like the other programs in the Creative Suite. Instead, Acrobat relies mainly (but not entirely) on a system of menus and toolbars filled with buttons and drop-down lists. In Acrobat, you can open dialog boxes that contain a bunch of settings you can enter for your documents.

The following panels aren't available in *all* the programs in the Creative Suite. However, you find them in most of the programs:

✦ **Color:** The Color panel is used to select or to mix colors for use in the document you're currently working on. You can use different color modes and several ways of mixing or choosing colors in the Colors panel.

✦ **Info:** The Info panel shows you information about the document itself or a particular selection you've made. The Info panel includes information on size, positioning, and rotation of selected objects. You can't enter data into the Info panel. The Info panel only displays information instead of accepting it, so you'd have to use the Transform panel (described in a bit) to make these modifications, if necessary.

✦ **Swatches:** The Swatches panel can be used to create a swatch library, which can be saved and imported into other documents or other programs. You can store colors and gradients that you use repeatedly in the Swatches panel.

✦ **Tools:** The Tools panel (commonly called the *toolbox*) isn't available in all the Creative Suite programs, but it's a very important panel in the programs it does exist in. The toolbox is used to select tools, such as the Pencil, Brush, or Pen tool, that you use to create objects in a document.

✦ **Layers:** The Layers panel is used to display and select layers. The Layers panel also enables you to change layer order and helps you select items on a particular layer.

✦ **Align:** The Align panel enables you to align selected objects to each other or align them in relation to the document itself. This enables you to arrange objects in a precise way.

✦ **Stroke:** The Stroke panel allows you to select strokes and change the attributes of those strokes, such as the color, width/weight, style, and cap. The program you're using determines what attributes you can change.

✦ **Transform:** The Transform panel is used to display and change the *shear* (skew), rotation, position, and size of a selected object in the document. You can enter new values for each of these transformations.

✦ **Character:** The Character panel is used to select fonts, font size, character spacing, and other settings related to using type in your documents.

Chapter 4: Using Common Extensions

In This Chapter

✔ Discovering the real purpose of filters and extensions

✔ Using common filters and plug-ins in Adobe CS4

*E*xtensions (also known as plug-ins) are pieces of software that you install or save on your computer that work as add-ons to existing programs. For example, an extension may enable you to integrate with a different program, or it may help add functionality to the program (such as the ability to create 3D text). Extensions may allow you to change the appearance of an object in your software or add a 3D effect to a video file. Filters are used to change parts of a document. Even if you haven't used Photoshop, you're probably already familiar with some of the popular Photoshop filters, such as the filters used for artistic effects, like the Watercolor and Emboss filters. This chapter shows you common plug-ins, extensions, and filters, as well as how to use them in the Creative Suite.

Looking at Common Extensions and Filters

Extensions are sometimes used for similar tasks in several programs and are designed to enhance a program's existing capabilities. Extensions and filters can also dramatically speed up the creative process. At the mere click of a button, you can add an amazing effect to your project that may have taken many hours to accomplish without the plug-in.

Additional filters and plug-ins for the programs are available or linked from the Adobe Web site. It's also very easy to find plug-ins on the Web for download as well. A search yields many results for these packages. A good place to start is at the Adobe Exchange, located at www.adobe.com/cfusion/exchange/index.cfm. This site includes a wealth of tools that you can download and install for the all the applications in the Creative Suite.

Filters for Photoshop are probably the most common kind of add-on you find online. You have to purchase many filters before you can download and use them; however, some filters are offered for free.

Installing extensions

Extensions can be installed in a few different ways. Sometimes they're installed by using an executable file: You double-click the file on your hard drive, and it automatically installs the software. This is a lot like installing any other program on your computer, such as the programs in the Creative Suite itself.

Sometimes you're given individual files that need to be placed in a folder first. In this case, you need to find the Plug-Ins folder on your computer in the install directory of the program the plug-in or filter is for. For example, if your plug-in is for Photoshop on the Mac, you need to find this folder on your hard drive: `Applications\Adobe Photoshop CS4\ Plug-Ins`. You then copy and paste or move the files into this folder.

If you're installing extensions for Flash or Dreamweaver, you can also take advantage of the Adobe Extension Manager CS4 application that installs automatically with the default CS4 installation. Locate the Extension Manager in your Programs (Windows) or Applications (Mac) folder and double-click to launch it. Select the application that you want to install the extension into, click the Install button to locate the extension you want to install, click the Select button, and you're on your way!

If it's not clear how to install a plug-in, locate instructions for the software that explain how to install it on your computer. You can find instructions on the manufacturer's Web site, or instructions may be bundled with the plug-in file itself in a text file (usually `readme.txt`).

Adding on to Photoshop

Photoshop has a lot of plug-ins and filters already included with the program when you install it that give more functionality to the program. Not only can you find additional filters, but you can also find plug-ins to add new features that can inevitably add some interesting effects to your documents. You can also find a plug-in that installs a great number of filters into Photoshop. The kinds of filters and plug-ins you can find for Photoshop create the following effects:

✦ Remove blemishes and scratches from photos, using special tools.

✦ Create 3D text, objects, and effects by using several different plug-ins. Effects include drop shadows, bevels, and embosses that go beyond what's already available in Photoshop.

✦ Use special masking tools to create amazing selections of difficult items like fur and hair.

✦ Use one of thousands of special effects made by many companies to enhance, modify, and add to your images.

✦ Add a frame from a library to place around your favorite images.

These are only some of the many Photoshop plug-ins (which are commonly a set of many filters bundled together) available.

Many plug-ins have custom interfaces that you can use to make your settings. These interfaces include sliders, text fields, and buttons, and usually a thumbnail preview of how the filter is affecting the image. These interfaces vary greatly in style and features, but they're usually fairly intuitive and easy to use.

Using Illustrator plug-ins

You can find many tools to extend the capabilities of Illustrator. Plug-ins are available that enable you to take 3D illustration farther than the standard 3D features allow. You can create forms from your drawings and also take your 3D files and turn them into line drawings. Other plug-ins, ranging from simple to very complex, allow you to

+ **Create multipage documents.**

+ **Organize your font sets.**

+ **Add common symbols (such as road signage) to use in your documents.** The symbols are organized into libraries that you can use right in the Illustrator workspace.

+ **Import CAD (Computer-Aided Design) files into a document.**

+ **Create interactive documents.**

+ **Handle patterns geared at creating textures and backgrounds.**

You can enhance Illustrator's capabilities after you download and install a few plug-ins. Simple projects become much more interesting or complex by merely entering a value and clicking a button.

Some fun things to download and install into Illustrator are custom brushes. This means that you can have a wider array of brushes available to work with when you create drawings and illustrations. Styles can also be installed into Illustrator and are usually obtained for free. You can also download and install custom brushes for Photoshop.

Adding on capabilities to Acrobat

Acrobat has several plug-ins available that help speed up and diversify your project workflow. Some plug-ins available for Acrobat are designed to help you

+ Add new stamps to the documents.

+ Add features, such as page numbering and watermarks.

+ Streamline productivity by offering solutions for batch processing.

+ Convert file formats to diversify what kinds of documents you can create from Acrobat.

+ Work with and fix the PDF (Portable Document Format) in prepress quickly and efficiently.

Many of the plug-ins available for Acrobat enable you to batch process the pages in a document. This means that all the pages are processed at one time. Many plug-ins for Acrobat help save you a lot of time when you're creating PDF files. Plug-ins are usually designed to be very easy to use and can thus save you from having to perform a tedious and repetitive task.

Plug-ins for Acrobat are available from the Adobe Web site, as well as from numerous third-party Web sites.

Extending Dreamweaver

Dreamweaver offers you a quick and easy way to make Web pages, but you can add more tools to Dreamweaver to diversify what the program can do. These extensions (essentially, plug-ins) also speed up the process of creating Web sites. Some of the available plug-ins are described in the following list:

+ Add e-commerce modules to a Web site automatically.

+ Create professional DHTML (Dynamic HTML) and CSS (Cascading Style Sheets)-based vertical and horizontal menus.

+ Add a calendar popup.

+ Add PayPal to your Web site.

Dreamweaver also allows you to use behaviors in the program. *Behaviors* are premade JavaScript scripts that can be added to your Web sites for additional interactivity or interest. You can also use premade templates for your sites, many of which are available at www.adobe.com/cfusion/exchange.

Using Filters or Plug-Ins

You can install plug-ins or filters into your Creative Suite programs. For example, a filter can enhance an existing photo in a very exciting way. After you install a plug-in into Photoshop or Illustrator that includes a bunch of additional filters, check out what the filter can do to your photos.

Install some filters for Photoshop (or Illustrator or any other program in the suite). After you complete the installation and restart your computer, if necessary, open Photoshop and locate the Effects menu option (the new filters are available in this menu).

To use a filter or plug-in after installing it, follow these steps:

1. **Open a file in the appropriate program so that you can try your new filter or plug-in.**

For example, if you downloaded a Photoshop plug-in that added a new filter, open an interesting photo that you want to apply an effect to in Photoshop. Choose a photo that has many colors or a lot of contrast to work with.

2. **Choose a filter from the Effects menu.**

   Select a filter that you've installed from the Effects menu. You may also find that a plug-in created a new menu item in the program — in that case, use the new menu item to apply the effect.

3. **Modify the filter's (or plug-in's) settings, if necessary, and click OK to apply the effect.**

   Sometimes, you have a thumbnail preview to assess how the filter changes the image. For some filters and plug-ins, you even use a custom interface to manipulate the document. You can then change the settings accordingly until you're happy with the modifications that will be applied.

4. **Look at the image or document after you choose and apply the filter or plug-in.**

   Your image or file is updated immediately. If you're unhappy with the results, you can either undo your changes by choosing Edit⇨Undo, or you can apply the filter or plug-in again.

Filters add a great deal of interest and variety to a document. However, you can easily go overboard when using filters and plug-ins. You can use filters in many different ways in the Web Premium Suite — and some of these ways you use filters (and the filters themselves) are considered better than others. Going into filter overload is easy, particularly when you first start using filters. This is okay when you're experimenting with filters; just make sure that you don't use too many filters on one part of an image when you're creating a final project. For example, if you bevel and emboss a particular letter in a few different ways, that character can become illegible. Similarly, adding a huge drop shadow can distract the eye from other parts of the text.

The trick is knowing what you intend to accomplish with your document before you actually go about creating it. If you set out to create your project with a particular design in mind, you can sometimes achieve better results. Try drawing your ideas on paper first, writing down some notes about what you want to achieve, and thinking about the plug-ins you want to use to achieve it. Use one filter at a time and make sure that you like the results before moving on to the next. The alternative is to continue adding filter upon filter to achieve a particular result when you aren't quite sure what you're after or how to get there. You can end up with a picture with too many filters applied and an unpleasant result. With a clear idea of what you want out of a picture, and what filters you need to achieve that effect, you'll use filters in a much more successful way.

Chapter 5: Importing and Exporting

In This Chapter

✔ **Integrating Adobe Bridge into your workflow**

✔ **Importing content**

✔ **Moving files from one CS4 application to another**

✔ **Exporting content out of your documents**

✔ **Exporting content from CS4 programs**

*I*mporting and exporting content are important tasks for much of the creative process you experience while using programs in the Creative Suite. You commonly find yourself importing content to work within your documents. You may want to import text composed by a designated writer into a Dreamweaver document so that you can include the content in a page layout. Or you may want to import a 3D design into an Illustrator document so that you can use the image in a design. Importing is necessary in all kinds of circumstances during a typical workflow.

Exporting content from each program is sometimes necessary when you want to save the document as a different file format. You may want to do this for compatibility reasons: Your audiences, or those you're working with, need a different file format in order to open your work, or you may need to export to a different file format in order to import the work into a different program.

Discovering the Adobe Bridge Application

With this version of the Creative Suite, Adobe has dramatically enhanced the Adobe Bridge application. The *Adobe Bridge* application helps you organize and manage your assets, such as pictures, text, movie and audio files, as well as non-Adobe applications like Word or Excel files to name a few. Adobe Bridge acts like a hub for the Creative Suite; for example, by choosing to open files by using the Bridge interface, you can browse directories quickly and see thumbnail previews of your files, as shown in Figure 5-1. You can even use the Filter panel to help you find files and view metadata to your file, including important information such as keywords and copyright information.

Figure 5-1:
The Adobe
Bridge
workspace.

Not only does Bridge make a great deal of information accessible; you can use Bridge as a central resource for all your Help needs.

Not all Adobe Bridges are the same. If you installed your Adobe programs separately (not using the Creative Suite installer), you may be lacking some features. If you notice some features are mentioned in this chapter that you don't have access to, check to see if all the CS4 applications are installed or run the CS4 installer again.

Accessing the Bridge software

Knowing where to locate the Adobe Bridge application is helpful. The Bridge application should already be in your system if you went through a standard installation of the entire Creative Suite. Otherwise, go back and choose to install the Bridge software with your installation CDs. After you install the Bridge software, you can open it in the following two ways:

✦ Access the Bridge software with the directory system of your computer. Choose `C:\Programs\Adobe\Adobe Bridge\Bridge` (Windows) or `Hard Drive\Applications\Adobe Bridge\Bridge` (Mac).

✦ Select the Launch Bridge button in the Application bar, as shown in Figure 5-2. If you don't see the Launch Bridge icon, you can choose File⟹Browse in Bridge. You can launch into Bridge from any of the applications included in the Creative Suite.

Importing and
Exporting

Figure 5-2:
Access
the Bridge
application
with the
Launch
Bridge
button.

Navigating in Adobe Bridge

To navigate Bridge, simply use the Folders panel in the upper left to choose the folder you want to view. Watch in amazement as previews are created and automatically replace the standard file format icon.

Adobe Bridge may take a fair amount of time to build the preview the first time you use it, so be patient. You can choose Tools⇨Cache⇨Build and Export Cache to save this data, or choose Tools⇨Cache⇨Purge Cache to free up file space.

Select an individual file by clicking it once (twice opens it), or select multiple files by Ctrl-clicking (Windows) or ⌘-clicking (Mac).

With one or more files selected, you can do the following:

✦ **Relocate the file(s) to another location by dragging it to a folder in the Folders panel in the upper-left corner.** Use Bridge as a central filing system. With the commands in the File menu, you can create new folders and delete or move files or groups of files.

✦ **Read metadata in the Metadata panel in the lower-right corner.** This includes information, such as Camera, Flash, F-stop, and more. See Figure 5-3.

✦ **Enter your own metadata for any item listed by clicking the pencil icon to the right.**

✦ **Use the Keywords panel, as shown in Figure 5-4, to enter your own keywords to help you find your images later.**

✦ **Choose Edit⇨Find or use the Filter panel to locate your files within the Bridge by entering criteria, such as Keywords, Description, Date Created, and more.**

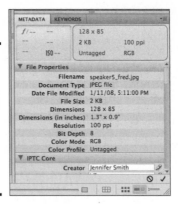

Figure 5-3:
Use the
Metadata
panel to find
important
information
about your
selected
image.

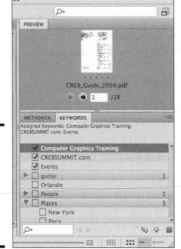

Figure 5-4:
The
Keywords
panel can
help you
locate
images.

✦ **Create image stacks.** You can select many files in Bridge by holding
down the Ctrl key (Windows) or ⌘ key (Mac) and clicking multiple
files. You can then choose Stacks⇨Group as Stack, or use the keyboard
shortcut Ctrl+G (Windows) or ⌘+G (Mac). This stacks the images into
one compact thumbnail, as shown in Figure 5-5. The number of images
in the stack is shown in the upper left of the image stack. To reopen
the stack, click the stack number; to close it, click the stack number
again. If you decide you don't want the stack any more, you can choose
Stacks⇨Ungroup from Stack, or use the keyboard shortcut Ctrl+Shift+G
(Windows) or ⌘+Shift+G (Mac).

Figure 5-5:
Stack
similar
images
together
to help
keep files
organized.

✦ **Check under the Tools menu for application-specific tools, such as** *Photomerge* **(merging panoramic images together),** *Live Trace* **(tracing images as vector images), and PDF Presentation.**

Managing color

Using Bridge for color management is a timesaver and a production boost! The color settings that you use to set in each individual application can be set across the board in all Creative Suite applications. Create consistent color choices in all the Creative Suite applications with the synchronized color management controls that Adobe Bridge offers.

Choose Edit⇨Creative Suite Color Settings to choose a color management setting that remains consistent through all your Creative Suite applications, as shown in Figure 5-6. Read more about what these settings mean in Book II, Chapter 7.

The setting for Joe's Press (see Figure 5-6) was created in Adobe Photoshop. If your printer can send you the Joe's Press color settings, you can load them by using the Suite Color Settings dialog box in Photoshop, and then make them accessible to all your CS4 applications by selecting the settings in Adobe Bridge.

Figure 5-6:
Synchronize
your color
management
policies by
setting color
settings
in Adobe
Bridge.

Importing Files into a Document

Importing files works similarly, no matter what program you're working with. Importing content is more important in some programs than others. In this section, we take a look at importing content into each program.

Adding content to a Photoshop file

In Photoshop, you can choose to open an image to work with or you can import content into a document that's open already. Choose File⇨Place to import PDF, AI, EPS, or PDP files. These files import onto a new layer in the document, and you can then use tools to manipulate the imported content, as shown in Figure 5-7.

Figure 5-7:
Imported
content
is placed
on a new
layer; in this
example,
the
Illustrator
file has been
placed and
converted
to a Smart
Object.

As a default, your placed Illustrator file embeds into the Photoshop file. This is the Smart Object feature that you can read about in Book II, Chapter 9. Double-click the placed artwork layer to open and edit the embedded Illustrator file. After the file's been saved, the changes are immediately reflected in Photoshop! Note that your original file isn't changed.

Want to import images from your digital camera right into Adobe Bridge? Choose File➪Get Photos.

Placing files into Illustrator

Illustrator allows you to place images and other forms of data in a new document. You can import Photoshop, PDF, image, and vector files by choosing File➪Place. The Place dialog box appears, allowing you to choose a file to import. Click Place to import the file. An Import dialog box may appear at this point, depending on the type of file you're importing. This dialog box offers you several options for choosing a way to import the content into Illustrator. For example, you can sometimes choose between flattening layers or retaining layers when you import a document containing layers.

EPS (Encapsulated PostScript) is a commonly used file format for saving vector drawings (although it can be used for other file types as well). Because this file format is used in many programs, you may find other people giving you these files to work with. To import an EPS document, you also choose File➪Place; after you import an EPS document into Illustrator, the file is converted to Illustrator objects, but it isn't editable. To edit the EPS object, choose File➪Open to open the file.

You can also import text files into Illustrator. Microsoft Word, TXT (text only), RTF (rich text format), and Unicode, among other text documents, are all supported by Illustrator, and you can import them by choosing File➪Place. When you import the text file, you're prompted to choose the character set used for the text.

Not only can you use the Place command for importing files, but you can also copy and paste from other programs. You can select part of an image in Photoshop and copy it onto the Clipboard by pressing Ctrl+C (Windows) or ⌘+C (Mac), and then pasting it into the Illustrator document.

Use the Place command whenever possible to avoid losing quality in the content you're importing. Also, transparency isn't supported from one application to another when you copy and paste, but it is when Place is used.

When you have particular plug-ins installed, you can import additional file types, such as CAD files, into Illustrator.

Adding to Acrobat

Adobe Acrobat is primarily a tool for sharing completed documents — you'll do most of your document construction and editing in other programs, such as Illustrator. However, you can import several kinds of data into PDF documents, and you can do some creative things when you place data into PDF files as well:

✦ **Comments:** Probably the most useful and common items to import into an Adobe PDF file are comments made by using the review and markup tools provided by Adobe Acrobat. By importing comments into a PDF file, you can consolidate suggestions and input from several reviewers (those editing a document) into a single document. This feature helps the reviewing process when many people are working on a single document. To import someone's comments into a PDF, choose Comments⇨Import Comments. If you're reviewing a document, you can also export only the comments rather than send the document owner the entire PDF file.

✦ **Form data:** You can import form data into a PDF document by choosing Forms⇨Manage Form Data⇨Import Data. The data that you import can be generated by exporting the form data from another PDF form, or it can come from a delimited text file. This allows you to share form data between forms or from a database.

✦ **Trusted identities:** If you share digitally signed files or secured files with other Acrobat users, you can import the public version of their signature file into your list of trusted users with whom you share files. To import the identity of a user, choose Advanced⇨Manage Trusted Identities, and in the Manage Trusted Identities dialog box that appears, click the Add Contacts button.

✦ **Multimedia files:** If you've ever had the urge to add a movie or sound file into your PDF documents, you're in luck. By using the Sound tool or Movie tool, you can identify the location on the page where you want the file to appear, and then choose whether to embed the multimedia file (compatible with Acrobat 6 or later) or create a link to the file (compatible with Acrobat 5 and earlier).

✦ **Buttons:** Creating buttons to turn pages, print a document, or go to a Web site makes your PDF files easier to use. Adding custom button images, such as pictures of arrows or a printer icon, makes your document unique. Use the Button tool to create the location of the button and then select the graphic file that will be used as the image on the button. The image file that you use must first be converted to a PDF graphic.

✦ **Preflight information:** If you're creating a PDF file that will be sent to a commercial printer for reproduction, you may want to preflight the file to check that it meets the specifications and needs of the printer. If your printer has supplied a preflight profile for Acrobat, you can import the profile to ensure that Acrobat checks for the things your printer has requested, such as certain font types or color specifications. Import a preflight profile by choosing Advanced⇨Print Production⇨Preflight, and in the Preflight window that opens, choose Options⇨Import Preflight Profile.

Importing into Dreamweaver

In Dreamweaver, you can import several different kinds of files into a site you're creating:

✦ **Insert images and other media, such as Flash, FlashPaper, and Flash Video with the Insert menu item.**

✦ **Cut and paste a layered file in Photoshop.** Simply choose Edit⇨Copy Merged and paste it right into Dreamweaver. An Image Preview window appears (see Figure 5-8), allowing you to optimize the image for the Web. Choose your settings and click OK. (You can read about the best settings for Web imagery in Book II, Chapter 10.)

Figure 5-8: The Image Preview window appears when a native PSD file is pasted onto a Dream-weaver page.

Exporting Your Documents

Exporting content from your Adobe Creative Suite documents is important if you're working with importing the content into another program, placing the document where it's publicly available and where it needs to be interpreted on other computers. Similarly, you may be working with a team of individuals who need your document to be readable on their machines when it's imported into other programs. Exporting your document as a different file format helps solve these issues, and the Adobe Creative Suite offers you the flexibility of allowing you to export your document as many different file formats.

Other programs sometimes accept native Adobe documents as files that you can import. For example, Adobe Flash CS4 can import Illustrator AI files, Photoshop PSD files, and PDF documents.

Exporting content from Photoshop

Photoshop can export paths in a document to Illustrator (an AI file). This means that your work in Photoshop is easy to manipulate after you open it with Illustrator.

You have another option, though: You can export your Photoshop file with the Zoomify feature. This great feature can export a large file to a smaller, more compact SWF file. This file can be easily sent via e-mail and opened with the free Flash Player that most everyone already has installed.

To use Zoomify, do the following:

1. **Choose File⇨Export⇨Zoomify.**
2. **Click Folder in the Output Location section of the Zoomify dialog box and choose a folder location to save your SWF file to.**
3. **Choose the quality and size and then click OK.**

   The Zoomify Preview window appears. Use this window to zoom in to see detail.

   You can then retrieve the files that were created in your destination folder and post them online, or attach them to an e-mail message.

Exporting Illustrator files

Illustrator supports exporting to many different file formats. You can export files in a long list of image formats. Choose File⇨Export, and the Export dialog box opens. Click the Save as Type (Windows) or Format (Mac) drop-down list to view the exportable file formats.

After you choose a file type to export to, a second dialog box may appear, allowing you to enter a bunch of settings for the exported file.

Try choosing the Flash SWF file format when you export a file. A second dialog box opens that includes many settings, such as options to generate an HTML page, save each layer as a separate SWF document, and preserve editability (when possible). The options that are available when you export a document depend on the type of file format to which you're exporting.

Exporting Acrobat content

Acrobat allows you to export certain parts of a PDF document that you're working on. For example, you may be using *form data* — the data that's filled into a form made of text fields and so on — in one of your files. You can export this data from Acrobat and then send it online, which is great because PDF documents tend to be rather large for the Web. Therefore, only a small amount of formatted data is sent online rather than a huge PDF file.

You can also export parts of an Acrobat document to use in other programs. You can export comments in a PDF to a Microsoft Word file that was used to create the PDF by choosing Comments⇨Export Comments⇨To Word. You can also export comments to an AutoCAD file (assuming that it was used to create the PDF). In both cases, you need the original document that was used to generate the PDF file in order to successfully import the comments.

Similarly, you can export all comments from a PDF file by choosing Comments⇨Export Comments⇨To File and then import them into another version of the same document. You can use this option to consolidate comments from multiple reviewers, or overlay comments from a draft with a final version to confirm that all edits were completed.

Exporting Dreamweaver content

In Dreamweaver, you can export your sites so that they're prepared for publishing and ready to be placed on a live Web site. The site you're working on in Dreamweaver is exported onto your hard drive before you put it somewhere on a server. The HTML styles used in a site you're working on can be exported and saved as an XML document, which in turn can be reused if necessary. These files can then be imported into another Dreamweaver project you're working on.

Chapter 6: Handling Graphics, Paths, Text, and Fonts

Graphics, paths, text, and fonts are all integral parts of creating documents with Adobe Creative Suite. You must know how to handle each element in your documents and how to work with these elements together. Discovering the different ways you can work with images, text, and drawing is the fun part!

Whether you're designing Web sites or creating an interactive document, you can use these elements on their own or together, and it's likely you'll find out something new each time you work with them. A layout can include text, images, and drawings, but sometimes the layout includes more. If you're creating documents for the Web or you're creating PDF (Portable Document Format) files with multimedia elements, you may be working with sound, animation, and video alongside text, images, and illustrations.

Using Graphics in Your Documents

A *graphic* can be an image, a drawing, or a vector graphic. You can create graphics manually by making marks on a page, or you can create them electronically with software. Graphics can be displayed in many formats, such as on a computer screen, projected onto a wall, or printed in a magazine or book.

Computer graphics come in many forms, grouped by the way they're created electronically. Bitmap and vector graphics are formed in different ways to achieve the end result that you use in your documents.

Working with bitmap images

Bitmap images are pictures that are made up of many tiny squares, or *bits,* on an invisible grid. When these dots are next to each other, the picture is formed, depending on where and how the colors are arranged on the grid. The dots are also called *pixels,* and if you zoom in far enough, you can even see the blocky pixels that make up the image. At 400 percent zoom, notice how the image in Figure 6-1 is made of large squares. However, when you just look at most bitmap images at actual size, you don't even see the pixels.

Figure 6-1:
A bitmap image is created from pixels.

Bitmaps are a great way to display photographs and apply effects to text. When you paint or create detailed graphics, you frequently use bitmaps. However, remember that you can lose some quality if you *scale* (change the size of) the image. Resizing the small pixels causes the image to lose definition and quality. Most problems occur when an image is enlarged. Common kinds of bitmap files are JPEG, GIF, TIFF, BMP, and PICT. You can read more about bitmaps in Book II.

Discovering vector graphics

A *vector image* (or graphic or drawing) is very different from a bitmap image. A vector image is created by a series of mathematical calculations or code that describes how the image should be formed. These calculations tell the computer how the lines should display and render on the page.

Vector images are usually smaller in file size than bitmap graphics. This is because the information that's required to make the calculations that create the vector image are usually smaller in file size than the information that it takes to make up each pixel of a bitmap. Compression can lessen a bitmap's file size, but they're usually larger and slower to display.

For this reason, and also because vectors are great when it comes to scaling an image, as shown in Figure 6-2, these graphics are well suited for the Web.

Figure 6-2:
A vector
image is
smooth at
any zoom
level.

Scaling is easy to do when you're using vectors because the program needs to modify the calculations only slightly to make the image larger or smaller. This means that the file size won't change, and the scaling is very quick. You can scale the image on a Web page to fill the browser window, whatever size it is, or make the image huge for a large banner. The quality won't degrade, and the file size remains the same.

Vectors aren't always perfect for the Web though. A bitmap is frequently the best way to display a photograph because if you change a bitmap image into a vector drawing (which is possible through the use of tools), you lose too much of the photograph's detail for many purposes. Also, certain effects, such as drop shadows, are best displayed as a bitmap image.

Working with Paths and Strokes

Paths are the vector lines and outlines that you create in a document. You can use paths to outline an image, separate areas of text, or be part of an illustration you create. You typically make paths with a Line tool or a Pen tool, or the Shape tools. You can use these tools to create paths of different shapes and sizes. You also can use tools to modify the color and size of *strokes* (the actual line that makes up a path).

You can use paths to create clipping paths and paths for text. *Clipping paths* are used to mask (or *hide*) elements on a page. You define that mask with paths to create a shape for that area you need to hide. Clipping paths can even be saved in a file and imported into a different design pattern. A common workflow is to create an image in Photoshop CS4 with a clipping path and import that image into Illustrator. Illustrator can interpret the clipping path, meaning that you can automatically remove the area you want to mask.

When you want to create text that flows along a path, begin by creating a new path and then use the Type On a Path tool to type text directly onto that path. For example, in Illustrator, you'd create a path with the Pen tool and then select the Type On a Path tool in the toolbox. If you click the tool on the path you created, you can type new text along that path.

A *stroke* is the color, width, and style of the line that makes up the path you create. You might draw a line with the Pen tool, and the line making up that path is the stroke. However, that path can also have no stroke (represented as a diagonal line in the Tools panel), which means you won't see the path itself. However, you may see a color or pattern filling that stroke (the *fill*), as shown in Figure 6-3.

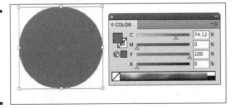

Figure 6-3: This path has a fill but no stroke applied to it.

You can change the color, width, style (or *type*), and shape of a stroke with controls and tools in the toolbox and the Stroke panel in Illustrator. This means that you can create dashed or solid strokes of different patterns that are wide or narrow.

Adding Text

You may add text to your projects for different reasons. Text is frequently used to educate and inform people who read it, and this kind of document is a lot different from those that use text for artistic purposes only. For example, if you're creating an article, you may place the text in columns on the page with a large title at the top. Other times, you may use text as a creative element, or even as an object rather than a letter. Alternatively, you may be laying out a Web page and use the text for both a creative element in an animation and the content on pages that make up the Web site.

You can add text to a document by using the Text tool or by importing the text from another source, such as Microsoft Word. You can create a single line of text in a text field, or large blocks of text with or without columns. Text fields can be rotated and resized, and you can change the color, font face, orientation, and character size of the text.

Text can also be placed on a path, as we mention briefly in the preceding section, "Working with Paths and Strokes." This allows you to add text to your documents in a different way because you can draw a path and have the text follow it. Paths are particularly useful for headings on a page, footers, and artistic works that use text as one of the elements.

Using fonts

A *font* refers to the typeface of a set of characters. You can set the font to be a number of sizes, such as a miniscule size of 2 or a gargantuan size of 200. Fonts are given names, such as *Times New Roman* or *Comic Sans*.

You may also hear about *glyphs,* which refers to an actual character itself. For example, S is a glyph. A set of glyphs makes up a font. You can view glyphs in the Glyph panel in Illustrator (choose Window⇨Type⇨Glyphs), which is especially useful when you're using fonts like Wingdings that are made of pictures instead of letters and numbers.

What fonts you use can make a huge difference to the look, feel, and style of your documents. Whether you're working on a layout for a magazine article or creating a digital piece of art, the kinds of fonts you use help the feel of the work.

Two major groupings for fonts exist:

✦ **Serif:** Characters have a small line that intersects the end of each line in a character, such as the feet on "rif" in *serif.*

✦ **Sans-serif:** Characters don't have the small intersecting lines at the end of a line in a character.

Sometimes sans-serif fonts feel more modern, whereas serif sometimes looks more historical, formal, or literary. (This, of course, is all a matter of opinion.) Take a moment to look around the Web and how text is used in your books, magazines, advertisements, and even the newspaper. How text is commonly used greatly affects how other people view your work and find the overall *feel* of it. Finding an appropriate font is sometimes a challenging design task, but it can also be fun.

Discovering types of fonts

Although you can find a gadzillion fonts for free on the Internet, be concerned about the quality of your finished product. Typically, those in the professional graphics industry use PostScript fonts, and preferably OpenType fonts, which are more reliable when printing, as compared to TrueType fonts, which may reflow when outputting to different resolutions.

TrueType

Like other digital typefaces, the *TrueType* font file contains information, such as outlines, hinting instructions, and character mappings (which characters are included in the font). Available for both the Mac and Windows formats, there are slight differences in the TrueType fonts designed for each OS; therefore, Mac and Windows users can't share TrueType fonts.

PostScript (Type 1)

PostScript is a scalable font system that's compatible with PostScript printers; it allows users to see fonts on the screen the same way they'd be printed. Type 1 font files consist of two files — a screen font with bitmap information for on-screen display and a file with outline information for printing. For high-end printing, both parts of the Type 1 font files (Printer and Screen fonts) must be included with the file. Due to differences in their structure, Mac and Windows PostScript Type 1 fonts aren't cross-platform compatible.

OpenType

OpenType is font technology that was created in a joint effort between Adobe and Microsoft and is an extension of the TrueType font format that can also contain PostScript data. OpenType fonts are *cross-platform* — the same font file works under both Macintosh and Windows operating systems. This digital type format offers extended character sets and more-advanced typographic controls. Like TrueType, a single file contains all the outline, metric, and bitmap data for an OpenType font. Although any program that supports TrueType fonts can use OpenType fonts, not all non-Adobe programs can access the full features of the OpenType font format. You can find the symbols in the Font menus of many of the CS4 programs representing the type of font.

Using text and fonts on the Web

Using text and fonts on the Web is a difficult task at times. When you use fonts in a Web page, system fonts are used to display text. You'll usually specify a font or a group of fonts to use on each page, and the fonts that are installed on the visitor's computer are used to display the text. The problem arises if you use (or want to use) fonts that aren't installed on the visitor's computer. If you choose to use the Papyrus font and the visitor doesn't have that font, a different font is substituted and the page looks completely different as a result.

When you're using Dreamweaver to create Web sites, you can establish a set of fonts that you want to use on each page. These fonts are similar in how they look, and if one of the fonts isn't available, the next font is used instead. Among the fonts in the set, at least one of them should be installed on the visitor's computer. Having a set of fonts ensures that your pages will look very similar to your original layout when displayed on your visitors' computers.

You can use Photoshop and Illustrator to create an image by using any font that is installed on your computer and then save that image for the Web (choose File➪Save for Web & Devices). Then you can place that image in your Web page with Dreamweaver. This option is best used for small amounts of text — say, for buttons in a navigation bar, headings to separate areas of text, or a customized banner at the top of your Web page.

Exploring Web Page Layout Fundamentals

Page layout incorporates the many elements that we discuss in previous sections of this chapter, mainly text and images (and sometimes other forms of multimedia), to create a design on a page. When you're creating a page design, you must think about how people view a layout, such as how the eye moves across the page to take in the flow of information. Also consider how the elements are arranged and how much empty space is around them.

Image manipulation for the Web is frequently done with Photoshop. Photoshop is also the standard program for manipulating and correcting images intended for print. However, you have to make certain considerations when you put something online. Navigation, usability, file size, dimensions, and computer capabilities are considerations for the Web that aren't a concern when you're working for print. However, resolution, colors, and cropping (to name a few) are considerations of someone designing a piece for print, which aren't concerns for the Web.

Layout for the Web is quite different from layout for print. However, many of the same issues arise in both print and Web layout, such as keeping your text legible and flowing across the page (or screen) in an intelligent way. In Web layouts, navigation and usability open up a few doors for things you should consider when planning a Web page:

- ✦ **Usability:** A useable site is accessible to most, if not all, of your visitors. This means that visitors can access your content easily because the text is legible, the file formats work on their computers, and they can find content on your site. Also, if the visitor has a challenge, such as a sight or reading disability, he or she can use software on the computer so that the site is read or described aloud.

- ✦ **Size:** File size should always be kept to a minimum, which may mean changing your layout to accommodate for this. If many parts of your design require large images, you may need to change the design completely to reduce your file size. Also, you need to design the page with monitors in mind. If a visitor has his or her monitor set to a resolution of 800 x 600, your site scrolls horizontally if it's designed any larger than 780 pixels wide. Most Web surfers dislike scrolling horizontally, so the dimensions of the visitor's display should be considered when designing sites.

- ✦ **Navigation:** Users have to navigate between pages on your site. To accommodate your users, you need to create links to those pages by using buttons, text links, menus, and so on. Making that navigation easy to find and use takes some forethought and planning. Be sure that navigation is a big part of your plans when designing the layout of your site.

Not only do you have to think about usability and navigation, but you also have to account for the different kinds of computers accessing the page and how people from all over the world may try to access your page. If you need your page to be universal, you may need to translate it into different languages and use different character sets. (This is true of print as well, if you're designing a page that requires a special character set other than the ones you regularly use.)

Because you may be using multimedia (such as images and animation) alongside text, you're constrained to the dimensions and color limitations of a computer monitor and have to think about both file size and scrolling.

There are many differences between preparing a layout for the Web and for print; however, you'll find that you use many of the same tools for both, and a great deal of information crosses over between the two mediums.

Chapter 7: Using Color

In This Chapter

✓ **Discovering color modes**

✓ **Finding out about swatches**

✓ **Using color on the Web**

*U*sing color in your documents is probably one of the most important considerations you can make in your projects. The colors you use, the mode that you use them in, and even the way you select colors make a difference in the way you create a document and the final output of that document. Even though you can create a document that looks the same on a monitor in different color modes, how that file prints onto paper is a different matter. Color is a very broad subject, and in this chapter, you find out the basics of how color affects the projects you work on.

Figuring out what kinds of colors you're using is important, and this decision is greatly determined by what kind of output you've planned for the document. Different color modes are appropriate for work for the Web and work that you're having professionally printed. Monitors and printers have different modes for color, which means that you need to work with your files in different color modes (although you can change the mode after you start working on a file, if necessary). You may also find yourself in situations where very particular colors are required in your work. You may be working with specific colors that a company needs to match its logo, or creating an image that replicates how a building should be painted with specific colors of paint. You may need to use particular Pantone colors or color mixes, if not for the printing process, for the purpose of matching a client's needs.

In this chapter, we introduce you to the different color modes and how to use them. You discover new terminology and how to find, mix, and add colors to your documents in the Creative Suite.

Looking at Color Modes and Channels

Several different color modes are available for use in the Creative Suite applications. When you start a new document in Photoshop and Illustrator, you can choose the color mode you want to work in. In fact, both Photoshop and Illustrator help you by allowing you to choose the color mode in the New Document dialog box. The choice you make affects how colors are created. You can change your color mode later by choosing File⇨Document Color Mode in Illustrator or Image⇨Mode in Photoshop. If you're working with print, generally you use CMYK mode. If you're working on files that are to be displayed on a monitor, RGB is the choice.

Using RGB

RGB (Red, Green, Blue) is the color mode used for on-screen presentation, such as an image displayed on the Web or a broadcast design for TV. Each of the colors displayed on-screen has a certain level (between 0 and 100 percent) of red, green, and blue to create the color. In a color panel, you can either use sliders to set the level in values, as shown in Figure 7-1, or you can enter a percentage into a text field (such as in CMYK color mode).

Figure 7-1:
Creating colors with the sliders in RGB mode.

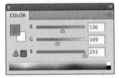

Note the exclamation point on the color panel, which indicates that this color wouldn't reproduce correctly in CMYK mode. You can click the CMYK warning exclamation point to convert to a color that's suitable for the CMYK gamut. Color is discussed in the Book II, Chapter 3, including more details about how you can adjust the Color Settings dialog box.

When you create a Web page, the color is represented as a hexadecimal number. A *hexadecimal number* starts with a pound sign (#) followed by three pairs of letters and numbers (A–F and 0–9) — the first pair for red, the second pair for green, and the last pair for blue. The lowest value (the least amount of the color) in a hexadecimal number is 0 (zero), and the highest value (the greatest amount of the color) is F. For example, #000000 is black, #FFFFFF is white, #FF0000 is red, and #CCCCCC is a light gray. To see what a particular hexadecimal color looks like, go to Webmonkey at www.webmonkey.com/reference/Color_Charts.

Looking at color channels

When you work with an image in Photoshop, the image has at least one (but typically more) color channels. A *color channel* stores information about a particular color in a selected image. For example, an RGB image has three color channels: one that handles the reds (R), one for handling green information (G), and the last for information about the blues (B). See Figure 7-2.

Figure 7-2:
This RGB
file is
created
from a Red,
Green,
and Blue
channel.

In addition to each of the color channels, you can have an alpha channel. An *alpha channel* can hold the transparency information about a particular image. If you're working with a file format that supports transparency, you can add and use the alpha channel to save alpha information.

You can also use an alpha channel to save a selection. By choosing Select➪Save Selection in Photoshop, you create an alpha channel with your selection saved to it. You can choose Select➪Load Selection and choose the channel to reload your selection at any time.

In Photoshop, you can access the channels in your image by choosing Windows➪Channels. When the Channels panel opens, you can toggle visibility of each icon by clicking the eye icon next to each channel (refer to Figure 7-2).

Choosing Colors

When you create a document, you may have to consider what colors you use, or you may have the freedom to use an unlimited number of colors. If you print your documents, you can choose a specific set of colors to use. You may be restricted to only the two colors in a company logo, or you may have to print in grayscale. So finding the colors you need to use in each program is important and then figuring out how to access those colors repeatedly in a document saves you a great deal of time.

Using swatches

Swatches are a good way to choose a color, particularly when you intend to print the document. The Swatches panel in the Creative Suite programs contains colors and sometimes gradients. (The Swatches panel, as shown in Figure 7-3, is from Illustrator.) You can create libraries of swatches that contain colors that you can use repeatedly across several documents.

Figure 7-3:
The
Swatches
panels are
similar in
most CS4
applications.

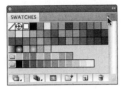

You can choose libraries of swatches from the panel menu or you can load and save swatch libraries. You can customize a swatch library by adding or deleting colors.

Mixing colors

A color mixer is found in the Color panel, and it helps you choose colors. You can use the Eyedropper tool to choose a color, or you can enter values for each hue or percentages if you prefer that instead. You can use one of several different color modes in the programs that you use, which offers you a lot of flexibility for all your projects.

Follow these steps to choose a color in a specified color mode:

1. **In a program that has a Color panel, choose Window⇨Color to open the Color panel (if it's not open already).**

2. **Click the Color panel menu to choose a new color mode.**

   Open this menu by clicking the arrow button in the upper-right corner of the Color panel.

3. **Choose the RGB color mode from the panel menu that opens.**

   The panel switches to RGB color mode.

4. **In the Color panel, click either the Fill box (solid square) or the Stroke box (hollow square) to choose what color you want to change.**

   If you click the Fill box, you can modify the color of a *fill* (the color inside a shape). If you click the Stroke box, you can modify the color of a *stroke* (the outline of a shape or a line).

5. **Use the sliders in the Color panel to change the color values.**

   You can also change the percentage values to the right of each slider.

6. **After you choose a color that you're happy with, return to your document and create a new shape that uses that color.**

Hold down the Shift key when adjusting any one-color slider, and the other color sliders adjust proportionally to provide you with various tints from your original.

Using Color on the Web

In the past, you had to be very conscious of what colors you used on the Web. Some computer monitors were limited in the number of colors they could display. Nowadays, color monitors are much more advanced and can handle a full range of colors, so images on the Web are much more likely to be properly displayed.

It doesn't have to do with color, but Macintosh and Windows computers usually display your work differently because of gamma differences on these machines. Generally speaking, colors on a Mac appear lighter, and colors on a PC look darker. You can account for this difference by making a Mac version of your site, videos, and so on look darker so that both are the same (or you can make the Windows version lighter), but these changes aren't usually necessary.

Even though most computers can handle a full range of colors, you may have to consider color limitations. If you're designing a site specifically targeted at old computers or a certain user base, you may have to limit your colors to the 256 Web-safe colors, which means that any other colors used are approximated, which can look poor. If it's likely that your site will be viewed by users with older computers, consider the following:

+ Use a Web-safe palette of 216 colors to design your Web sites so that you specifically design with those older displays in mind and know what the pages will look like. This number is 216 rather than 256 because the lower number is compatible with both Mac and Windows computers. This panel is usually called the *Web-Safe Palette* or *Web-Safe RGB*, and you can access it from the Swatches panel menu in Photoshop and Illustrator.

+ Avoid using gradients if possible because they use a wide range of colors (many unsupported in a limited Web panel).

+ If a color is approximated because it can't be handled by someone's computer, that color is *dithered* — the computer tries to use two or more colors to achieve the color you specified, causing a typically displeasing granular appearance. So a limited number of colors can have a negative affect on an image; notice the granular appearance on what should be the shape of a face in Figure 7-4.

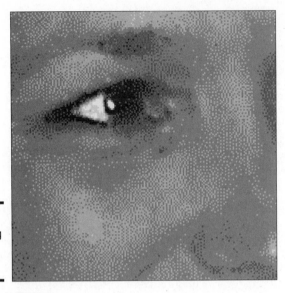

Figure 7-4:
The shading
in the face
is dithered.

If you keep the preceding elements in mind, you're ready to start designing for the Web! Remember also that you don't have to worry about using the Web-safe palette of colors if you're designing primarily for more up-to-date computers.

Book II
Photoshop CS4

Contents at a Glance

Chapter 1: Exploring New Features in Photoshop CS4

In This Chapter

✔ Working with the improved panel workspace

✔ Experimenting with nondestructive adjustment layers

✔ Experimenting with 3D

*P*hotoshop CS4 includes significant improvements to the workspace, editing tools, and 3D tools. In this chapter, you take a quick tour of some of the most exciting new capabilities. The features you see depend on the version of Photoshop CS4 that you have (Standard or Extended).

This quick rundown of what's new and exciting in Photoshop CS4 is a help to you when you start experimenting with the new tools and features.

If you really want to dive into the new features, choose Window➪Workspace➪ What's New in CS4. Instantly, all the new features are highlighted in the menus! (We have to say that not all the highlighted features are totally new — many existed in CS3. Maybe Adobe thinks that users missed them!)

An Improved Workspace Helps You Find the Tools You Need

You have to give it to the Adobe Photoshop engineers; they hear the pleas of the average users and they're trying to help. Help with what you ask? Understanding the Photoshop terminology and unique names of their tools and controls. Many people who have been using Photoshop for years feel quite at ease with the unique terminology, but new users seem to have a more difficult time finding the tools and options that they want to use.

Palettes are now *panels,* like the rest of the CS4 applications. The panels are collapsed to a compact view and represented by space-saving icons. This workspace makes focusing on the images easier, and the tools become a natural extension of your work.

Photoshop continues to make extensive use of panels. To activate a panel in this new version, simply click the appropriate panel icon. If you select another panel icon, its panel is brought to the front of the display. You can return panels to icons by clicking the Collapse to Icons bar at the top of the panel docking area. When an icon is dragged to the work area, it automatically expands and then returns to an icon when dragged back into the docking area.

Showing and hiding all your tools and panels is easy. Press the Tab key to hide all your tools and panels. To cause them to reappear, move your cursor over the left or right side of your screen and pause when you see the vertical gray bar appear — the toolbar or panels then appear!

Other improvements to the workspace include

+ **Tool options are easier to find.** This is partly because some of the tools and panels now have relevant names. For example, the Control palette in earlier versions is now more appropriately the Options panel. If you want to make your brush bigger or smaller, or change the color of your text, simply choose Window⇨Options.

+ **You can change the one-column toolbar to two columns by clicking the gray bar at the top of the toolbar.**

+ **You can select layer features, such as Auto Align and Auto Blend right from the Layer menu (choose Layer⇨Auto Align or Layer⇨Auto Blend).**

Adjustments Panel

The new Adjustments panel makes non-destructive editing changes quick and easy. Use the new Adjustments panel to apply one new adjustment layer after another to your image, without affecting the original image. Adjustment layers have been a fabulous feature that's existed in the last several versions of Photoshop. Far too few people seem to take advantage of them, but when you do, it'll be hard to imagine using any other method to change your image.

Here's an overview of how to use the new Adjustments panel in Photoshop CS4:

1. **Open an image in Photoshop.**

2. **If the Layers panel isn't open, choose Windows⇨Layers.**

3. **Click the Create New Fill or Adjustment Layer button, and select an adjustment that you want to apply to the active layer (which can also include the layers below), as shown in Figure 1-1.**

The Adjustments panel appears, as shown in Figure 1-2.

Figure 1-1:
Select a
new layer
from the
Layers
panel.

Figure 1-2:
Choose
Adjustments
for your
layers from
the new
Adjustments
panel.

For this example, the Black & White adjustment was selected because it shows a drastic change to the underlying layers,

4. **Choose a preset from the Preset drop-down list or make your changes with the sliders.**

A new adjustment layer is added on top of the last active layer.

To experiment with color to black-and-white conversions, click your image or a color that you want to appear lighter (when converted to black and white) and then drag to the right. Click a color that you want to appear darker and then drag to the left. Photoshop figures out what sliders need to be adjusted automatically!

Adjustment layers affect only the layers beneath them in the layer stacking order.

Turn off the visibility icon to the left of the new adjustment layer in the Layers panel, and the adjustment no longer occurs. Double-click the adjustment layer, and the Layer Style dialog box appears so that you can make changes. Drag the adjustment layer to the trash can, and it's like you never did anything to the image.

Make Your Layers Go 3D!

In earlier versions of Photoshop, you could open and make some slight editing changes on 3D files. Now, in CS4 you not only can open 3D files, but you can also take standard layers in Photoshop and convert them to 3D layers. This gives you the opportunity to convert virtually anything into a 3D image.

To experiment, open any image in Photoshop to experiment with the different methods of converting to 3D layers. Choose 3D⇨Create 3D Shape and then choose a method. For example, the image in Figure 1-3 was created by choosing 3D⇨Create 3D Shape⇨Soda Can. This method wraps your image around a soda can!

Figure 1-3: Create a 3D object from an image.

Rotate and revolve your 3D layer by using two new tools that are added to the toolbar — the 3D Rotate and 3D Orbit tools, as shown in Figure 1-4.

Figure 1-4:
Use the new
3D tools to
rotate 3D
layers.

By double-clicking the icon in the 3D layer in the Layers panel, you can edit the 3D layer, and experiment with different texture and lighting rendering methods.

We could write an entire book on just the new 3D options, but the reality is that for the scope of this book, we'll just have to recommend that you experiment . . . a lot! The 3D options are definitely worthy new features.

Kuler System Comes to Photoshop

Advanced color users in Illustrator could take advantage of the Kuler feature since CS3, but now Photoshop can use this incredible color themed-based application. With Kuler, you can easily generate color combinations to experiment and apply to your artwork. Whether you're creating Web sites, brochures, patterns, or logos, you can experiment quickly with color variations.

ConnectNow

Adobe ConnectNow is a free Web conferencing solution that allows users to share ideas, discuss details, and complete work together while online. By choosing File➪Share Your Screen, you can collaborate through chat, a whiteboard, and a shared notes Connections panel.

Chapter 2: Getting Into Photoshop CS4 Basics

In This Chapter

✔ Discovering the Photoshop tools

✔ Navigating your work area

✔ Changing screen modes

✔ Performing basic tasks in Photoshop CS4

*N*avigating the work area in Photoshop can be slightly cumbersome at first, especially if you've never worked in a program that relies so heavily on panels. In this chapter, we introduce you to Photoshop CS4. We introduce you to the work area, show you what the Photoshop CS4 tools are all about, and reveal how to neatly organize and hide panels. We also show you how to do basic tasks, such as opening, cropping, and saving an image.

Getting to Know the Tools

Tools are used to create, select, and manipulate objects in Photoshop CS4. When you open Photoshop, the Tools panel appears along the left edge of the workspace (see Figure 2-1), and panels appear on the right side of the screen. (We discuss panels in the upcoming section, "Navigating the Work Area.")

In the Tools panel, look for the name of the tool to appear in a ToolTip when you hover the cursor over the tool. Following the tool name is a letter in parentheses, which is the keyboard shortcut command that you can use to access that tool. Simply press the Shift key along with the key command you see to access any hidden tools. In other words, pressing P activates the Pen tool, and pressing Shift+P activates the hidden tools under the Pen tool in the order that they appear. When you see a small triangle at the lower-right corner of the tool icon, you know that this tool contains hidden tools.

Figure 2-1:
Photoshop
CS4
workspace
includes the
Tools panel.

Table 2-1 lists the Photoshop tools, what each is used for, and in what chapter you can find more about each.

Table 2-1		Photoshop CS Tools	
Button	**Tool**	**What It Does**	**Chapter in This Minibook**
	Move (V)	Moves selections or layers	Chapter 4
	Marquee (M)	Selects image area	Chapter 4
	Lasso (L)	Makes freehand selections	Chapter 4
	Quick Selection Tool (New) (W)	Selects similar pixels	Chapter 4
	Crop (C)	Crops an image	Chapter 2
	Slice (K)	Creates HTML slices	n/a

Button	Tool	What It Does	Chapter in This Minibook
	Spot Healing Brush (J)	Retouches flaws	Chapter 8
	Brush (B)	Paints foreground color	Chapter 8
	Clone Stamp (S)	Copies pixel data	Chapter 8
	History Brush (Y)	Paints from selected state	Chapter 8
	Eraser (E)	Erases pixels	Chapter 8
	Gradient (G)	Creates a gradient	Chapter 8
	Blur (R)	Blurs pixels	Chapter 8
	Toning (O)	Dodges, burns, saturates	Chapter 8
	Pen (P)	Creates paths	Chapter 5
	Type (T)	Creates text	Chapter 9
	Path Selection (A)	Selects paths	Chapter 5
	Vector Shape (U)	Creates vector shapes	Chapter 9
	3D Rotate (K)	Rotates 3D objects	Chapter 9
	3D Orbit (N)	Rotates 3D objects	Chapter 9
	Hand (H)	Navigates page	Chapter 9
	Zoom (Z)	Increases, decreases view	Chapter 2

Book II
Chapter 2

Getting Into
Photoshop CS4
Basics

Looking for the Magic Wand tool? Click and hold on the Quick Selection tool in the Tools panel to access it.

Navigating the Work Area

Getting around in Photoshop isn't much different from getting around in other Adobe applications. All Adobe applications make extensive use of panels, for example. In the following sections, we cover the highlights on navigating in Photoshop.

Docking and saving panels

Panels, panels everywhere . . . do you really need them all? Maybe not just yet, but when you increase your skill level, you'll take advantage of most (if not all) of the Photoshop panels. The panels give you easy access to important functions. Book I, Chapter 3 provides a lot of basic information about using panels in the Adobe Creative Suite, so check out that chapter if you need a refresher on using panels. We add only a few things here that are specific to using the panels in Photoshop.

When you work in Photoshop, keep in mind these two key commands:

+ Press Tab to switch between hiding and showing the tools and panels.

+ Press Shift+Tab to hide the panels, leaving only the Tools panel visible.

If you find that you're always using the same panels, hide the panels that you don't need and arrange your other panels on-screen where you want them. Then follow these steps to save that panel configuration:

1. **Choose Window➪Workspace➪Save Workspace.**

2. **In the Save Workspace dialog box that appears, name your workspace and click Save.**

3. **Any time you want the panels to return to your saved locations, choose Window➪Workspace➪***Name of Your Workspace* **(where** *Name of Your Workspace* **is the name you supplied in Step 2).**

Choose Window➪Workspace➪Reset Panel Locations to put the panels back in the same order they were upon the initial installation.

Taking advantage of new workspace features

Photoshop CS4 includes many new saved workspaces that you can take advantage of to streamline workspaces and open the panels you need for specific tasks. These new workspaces include those that can be used for Web design, painting and retouching, and color and tonal correction, to name a few.

Increase your work area by turning your panels into icons, as shown in Figure 2-2. Do so by either right-clicking the tab of a panel and selecting Collapse to Icons or clicking the Auto Collapse gray bar at the top of the *panel drawer*. Yes, you read it correctly — the area where the panels are located is actually a drawer that can be adjusted in or out by clicking and dragging on the vertical pane to the left of the panels.

Zooming in to get a better look

What looks fine at one zoom level may actually look very bad at another. You'll find yourself zooming in and out quite often while you work on an image in Photoshop. You can find menu choices for zooming in the View menu; a quicker way to zoom is to use the keyboard commands listed in Table 2-2.

Book II
Chapter 2

Getting Into
Photoshop CS4
Basics

Table 2-2	Zooming and Navigation Keyboard Shortcuts	
Command	*Windows Shortcut*	*Mac Shortcut*
Actual size	Alt+Ctrl+0 (zero)	⌘+1
Fit in window	Ctrl+0 (zero)	⌘+0 (zero)
Zoom in	Ctrl++ (plus sign) or Ctrl+spacebar	⌘++ (plus sign) or ⌘+spacebar
Zoom out	Ctrl+– (minus) or Alt+spacebar	⌘+– (minus) or Option+spacebar
Hand tool	Spacebar	Spacebar

Here are a few things to keep in mind while you work with the Zoom tool to get a better look at your work:

✦ **100-percent view:** Double-clicking the Zoom tool in the Tools panel puts you at 100-percent view. Do this before using filters to see a more realistic result of your changes.

✦ **Zoom marquee:** Drag from the upper left to the lower right of the area you want to zoom to. While dragging, a marquee appears; when you release the mouse button, the marqueed area zooms up to fill the image window. The Zoom marquee gives you much more control than just clicking the image with the Zoom tool. Zoom out again to see the entire image by pressing Ctrl+0 (Windows) or ⌘+0 (Mac). Doing so fits the entire image in the viewing area.

✦ **Zoom with the keyboard shortcuts:** If you have a dialog box open and you need to reposition or zoom to a new location on your image, you can use the keyboard commands without exiting the dialog box.

✦ **A new window for a different look:** Choose Window➪Arrange➪New Window to create an additional window for your front-most image. This technique is helpful when you want to see the entire image (say, at actual size) to see the results as a whole, yet zoom in to focus on a small area of the image to do some fine-tuning. The new window is linked dynamically to the original window so that when you make changes, the original and any other new windows created from the original are immediately updated.

✦ **Cycle through images:** Press Ctrl+Tab (Windows) or ⌘+Tab (Mac) to cycle through open images.

Figure 2-2: Turn your panels into icons.

Choosing Your Screen Mode

You have a choice of three screen modes in which to work. Most users start and stay in the default (standard screen mode) until they accidentally end up in another. The modes are

✦ **Standard mode** is the typical view, where you have an image window open but can see your desktop and other images open behind.

✦ **Maximized screen mode** displays a maximized document window that fills all available space between docks and that resizes when dock widths change.

✦ **Full-screen mode with menu** view surrounds the image out to the edge of the work area with a neutral gray. This mode not only prevents you from accidentally clicking out of an image and leaving Photoshop, but also from seeing other images behind your working image.

✦ **Full-screen mode, no menu** is a favorite with multimedia types. This mode shows your image surrounded by black and also eliminates the menu items from the top of the window. Press Tab to hide all tools, and you have a very clean work environment.

Getting Started with Basic Tasks in Photoshop CS4

Unless you use Photoshop as a blank canvas for painting, you may rarely create a new file in Photoshop. This is because you usually have a source image that you start with. This image may have been generated by a scanner, digital camera, or stock image library.

**Book II
Chapter 2**

The following sections show you how to open an existing image file in Photoshop, create a new image (if you want to use Photoshop to paint, for example), crop an image, and save your edited image.

Getting Into
Photoshop CS4
Basics

Opening an image

You can open existing Photoshop images by choosing File➪Open, selecting the file in the Open dialog box, and then clicking the Open button.

You can also open your file by choosing File➪Browse. By selecting Browse instead of Open, you launch the Adobe Bridge application. Read more about Adobe Bridge later in this section and also in Book I, Chapter 5.

Photoshop can open a multitude of file formats, even if the image was created in another application, such as Illustrator or another image-editing program, but you have to open the image in Photoshop by choosing File➪Open, or with Adobe Bridge, you can select an image and drag it to the Photoshop icon in the taskbar (Windows) or Dock (Mac). If you double-click an image file (one that wasn't originally created in Photoshop, or from different versions) in a directory, the image may open only in a preview application.

If you're opening a folder of images that you want to investigate first, choose File➪Browse to open *Adobe Bridge,* the control center for Adobe Creative Suite. You can use Adobe Bridge to organize, browse, and locate the assets you need to create your content. Adobe Bridge keeps native PSD, AI, INDD, and Adobe PDF files, as well as other Adobe and non-Adobe application files, available for easy access.

Adobe Bridge is a standalone application that you can access from all applications in the Creative Suite by choosing File➪Browse or by clicking the Go to Bridge icon in the upper-right corner of the application window. Use the Bridge interface to view your images as thumbnails and look for metadata information.

Creating a new file

If you're creating a new file, you may be doing so to create a composite of existing files or to start with a blank canvas because you're super creative.

Discover Camera Raw

If you haven't discovered the Camera Raw capabilities in Adobe Photoshop, you'll want to give them a try. Camera Raw is a format available for image capture in many cameras. Simply choose the format in your camera's settings as Raw instead of JPEG or TIFF. These Raw files are a bit larger than the standard JPEG files, but you capture an enormous amount of data with the image that you can retrieve upon opening. (See www.adobe.com for a complete list of cameras supporting Camera Raw.)

A Camera Raw file contains unprocessed picture data from a digital camera's image sensor, along with information about how the image was captured, such as the camera and lens used, the exposure settings, and the white balance setting. When you open the file in Adobe Photoshop CS4, the built-in Camera Raw plug-in interprets the Raw file on your computer, making adjustments for image color and tonal scale.

When you shoot JPEG images with your camera, you're locked into the processing done by your camera, but working with Camera Raw files gives you maximum control over your image, such as controlling the white balance, tonal range, contrast, color saturation, and image sharpening. Cameras that can shoot in Raw format have a setting on the camera that changes its capture mode to Raw. Instead of writing a final JPEG, a Raw data file is written, which consists of black-and-white brightness levels from each of the several million pixel sites on the imaging sensor. The actual image

hasn't yet been produced, and unless you have specific software, such as the plug-in built into Adobe Photoshop, opening the file can be very difficult, if not impossible.

To open a Camera Raw file, simply choose File⇨Browse. Adobe Bridge opens, and you see several panels, including the Folders, Content, Preview, and Metadata panels. With the Folders panel, navigate to the location on your computer where you've saved your Camera Raw images; thumbnail previews appear in the Content panel. Think of Camera Raw files as your photo negative. You can reprocess the file at any time to achieve the results you want.

Starting in Photoshop CS3, you can right-click (Windows) or Control+click (Mac) a JPEG or TIFF file and choose Open in Camera Raw from the contextual menu. This is a great way to experiment with all the cool features that are available with this plug-in, but your results aren't as good as if you used an actual Raw file.

If Adobe Photoshop CS4 doesn't open your Raw file, you may need to update your Raw plug-in. (See www.adobe.com for the latest plug-in.) The plug-in should be downloaded and placed in this location in Windows: `C:\Program Files\Common Files\Adobe\Plug-Ins\CS4\File Formats`, and this location on the Macintosh: `Library\Application Support\Adobe\Plug-Ins\CS4\File Formats`.

For whatever reason, note that when you choose File⇨New, you have a multitude of basic format choices that you can select from the Preset menu. They range from basic sizes and resolutions, such as U.S. Paper or Photo, to other final output such as the Web, Mobile Devices, or Film.

Keep in mind that you're determining not only size but also resolution in your new file. If your new file is to contain images from other files, make sure the new file is the same resolution. Otherwise, you may get unexpected size results when cutting and pasting or dragging images into your new file. Choose Image⇨Image Size to see the document dimensions.

Cropping an image

A simple but essential task is to crop your image. *Cropping* means to eliminate all that isn't important to the composition of your image.

Cropping is especially important in Photoshop. Each pixel, no matter what color, takes up the same amount of information, so cropping eliminates unneeded pixels and saves on file size and processing time. Because of that, you want to crop your image before you start working on it.

You can crop an image in Photoshop CS4 in two ways:

+ Use the Crop tool.

+ Select an area with the Marquee tool and choose Image⇨Crop.

To crop an image by using the Crop tool, follow these steps:

1. **Press C to access the Crop tool and drag around the area of the image that you want to crop to.**

2. **If you need to adjust the crop area, drag the handles in the crop-bounding area.**

3. **When you're satisfied with the crop-bounding area, double-click in the center of the crop area or press the Return or Enter key to crop the image.**

4. **If you want to cancel the crop, press the Esc key.**

Ever scan in an image crooked? When using the Crop tool, if you position the cursor outside any of the handles, a rotate symbol appears. Drag the crop-bounding area to rotate it and line it up how you want it cropped. When you press Return or Enter, the image is straightened out.

Saving images

Save an image file by choosing File⇨Save. If you're saving the file for the first time, the Save As dialog box appears. Notice in the Format drop-down list that you have plenty of choices for file formats. The different file formats are discussed in more detail in Chapter 10 of this minibook. You can always play it safe by choosing the Photoshop (PSD) file format. The native Photoshop format supports all features in Photoshop. Choosing some of the other formats may eliminate layers, channels, and other special features.

Many users choose to save a native Photoshop file as a backup to any other file formats. It's especially important to have a backup or original file saved as a native Photoshop file (PSD) when you increase in capabilities and start taking advantage of layers and the other great capabilities of Photoshop. Keep in mind that as a Creative Suite user, the native file format for Photoshop (.psd) can be used in all the other Creative Suite applications.

Chapter 3: Messing with Mode Matters

In This Chapter

✔ Editing pixels in bitmap images

✔ Understanding Photoshop image modes

✔ Working in black and white, RGB, or CMYK

*B*efore diving into Photoshop, you must know what image mode you should be working in and how important color settings are. So no matter whether you're doing a one-color newsletter, a full-color logo, or something in between, this chapter can help you create much better imagery for both the Web and print.

Working with Bitmap Images

You may have already discovered that Photoshop works a little differently than most other applications. In order to create those smooth gradations from one color to the next, Photoshop takes advantage of pixels. *Bitmap images* (or *raster images*) are based on a grid of pixels. The grid is smaller or larger depending on the resolution that you're working in. The number of pixels along the height and width of a bitmap image are the pixel dimensions of an image, which are measured in pixels per inch (ppi). The more pixels per inch, the more detail in the image.

Unlike *vector graphics* (mathematically created paths), bitmap images can't be scaled without losing detail. (See Figure 3-1 for an example of a bitmap image and a vector graphic.) Generally, it's best to use bitmap images at or close to the size that you need. If you resize a bitmap image, it can become jagged on the edges of sharp objects: On the other hand, you can scale vector graphics and edit them without degrading the sharp edges.

Bitmap   Vector

Figure 3-1:
Bitmap
versus
vector.

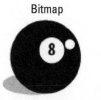

Photoshop has the capability to work on both bitmap and vector art. (See the path line around the vector shape layer and notice that the path isn't pixilated.) It gives you, as a designer, incredible opportunities when combining the two technologies.

For information on changing and adjusting image resolution, see Chapter 6 of this minibook.

Choosing the Correct Photoshop Mode

Choose Image➪Mode to view the image mode choices you can choose from. Selecting the right one for an image is important because each mode offers different capabilities and results. For example, if you choose the Bitmap mode, you can work only in black and white . . . that's it. No shades of color, not even gray. Most features are disabled in this Bitmap mode. This is fine if you're working on art for a black-and-white logo, but not for most images. If, instead, you work in the RGB (Red, Green, Blue) mode, you have full access to Photoshop's capabilities. Read on to see what image mode is best for your needs. When you're ready to make your mode selection, open a file and choose a selection from Image➪Mode. You can read descriptions of each image mode in the following sections.

Along with a description of each image mode, we include a figure showing the Channels panel set to that mode. A *channel* is simply the information about color elements in the image. The number of default color channels in an image depends on its color mode. For example, a CMYK image has at least four channels — one each for cyan, magenta, yellow, and black information. Grayscale has one channel. If you understand the printing process, think of each channel representing a plate (color) that, when combined, creates the final image.

Bitmap

Bitmap mode offers little more than the ability to work in black and white. Many tools are unusable, and most menu options are grayed out in this mode. If you're converting an image to bitmap, you must convert it to grayscale first.

Grayscale

Use Grayscale mode, as shown in Figure 3-2, if you're creating black-and-white images with tonal values, specifically for printing to one color. Grayscale mode supports 256 shades of gray in the 8-bit color mode. Photoshop can work with grayscale in 16-bit mode, which provides more information, but may limit your capabilities when working in Photoshop.

When you choose Image➪Mode➪Grayscale to convert to Grayscale mode, you get a warning message confirming that you want to discard all color information. If you don't want to see this warning every time you convert an image to grayscale, select the option to not show the dialog box again before you click Discard.

Figure 3-2:
Grayscale supports 256 shades of gray.

Using the Black & White adjustment is the best way to get a good grayscale image. Simply click and hold on the Create New Fill or adjustment button at the bottom of the Layers panel and choose Black & White. Set the sliders to achieve the best black-and-white image and then choose Image➪Mode➪ Grayscale.

Duotone

Use Duotone mode when you're creating a one- to four-color image created from spot colors (solid ink, such as Pantone colors). You can also use the Duotone mode to create Monotones, Tritones, and Quadtones. If you're producing a two-color job, duotones create a beautiful solution to not having full color.

The Pantone Matching color system helps to keep printing inks consistent from one job to the next. By assigning a numbered Pantone color, such as 485 for red, you don't risk one vendor (printer) using fire-engine red and the next using orange-red for your company logo.

To create a Duotone, follow these steps:

1. **Choose Image➪Mode➪Grayscale.**

2. **Choose Image➪Mode➪Duotone.**

3. **In the Duotone dialog box, choose Duotone from the Type drop-down list.**

   Your choices range from *Monotone* (one-color) up to *Quadtone* (four-color). Black is assigned automatically as the first ink, but you can change that if you like.

4. **To assign a second ink color, click the white swatch immediately under the black swatch to open the Color Libraries dialog box, as shown in Figure 3-3.**

5. **Now comes the fun part: Type (quickly!) the Pantone or PMS number that you want to access and then click OK.**

   There's no text field for you to enter the number in, so don't look for one. Just type the number while the Color Libraries dialog box is open.

   Try entering **300** for an easy one. That selects PMS 300. You can already see that you've created a tone curve.

6. **Click the Curve button to the left of the ink color to further tweak the colors.**

7. **Click and drag the curve to adjust the black in the shadow areas, perhaps to bring down the color overall; experiment with the results.**

Figure 3-3:
Click the white swatch to open the Color Libraries dialog box.

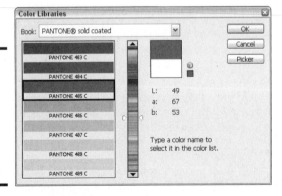

8. **(Optional) If you like your Duotone settings, store them by clicking the Save button.**

   Click the Load button to find your customized presets and to find preset Duotones, Tritones, and Quadtones supplied to you by Adobe.

Duotone images must be saved in the Photoshop Encapsulated PostScript (EPS) format in order to support the spot colors. If you chose another format, you risk the possibility of converting your colors into a build of CMYK (Cyan, Magenta, Yellow, and Black).

9. **Click OK when you're finished.**

Index color

You may not work in Index color, but you probably have saved a file in this mode. The Indexed Color mode (see Figure 3-4) uses a color look-up table (CLUT) in order to create the image.

Book II
Chapter 3

Messing with Mode Matters

Figure 3-4:
Index color uses a limited number of colors to create an image.

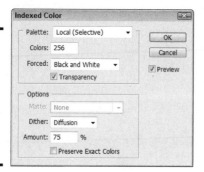

A *CLUT* contains all the colors that make up your image, such as a box of crayons used to create artwork. If you have a box of eight crayons and only those crayons are used to color an image, you have a CLUT of only eight colors. Of course, your image would look much better if you used the 64-count box of crayons with the sharpener on the back, but those additional colors increase the size of the CLUT and the file size.

The most colors that can be in index mode are 256. When saving Web images, you often have to define a color table. We discuss the Save for Web & Devices feature (which helps you to more accurately save an index color image) in Chapter 10 of this minibook.

Choose Image⇨Mode⇨Color Table to see the color table making up an image.

RGB

RGB (Red, Green, Blue), as shown in Figure 3-5, is the standard format that you work in if you import images from a digital camera or you scan images on a scanner in RGB mode. For complete access to features, RGB is probably the best color mode to work in. If you're working on images for use on the Web, color copiers, desktop color printers, and on-screen presentations, stay in the RGB mode.

Figure 3-5:
RGB creates
the image
from red,
green,
and blue.

If you're having your image printed on a press (for example, if you're having the image professionally printed), it must be separated. Don't convert images to CMYK mode until you're finished with the color correction and you know that your color settings are accurate. A good print service may want the RGB file so that it can do an accurate conversion.

CMYK

CMYK (Cyan, Magenta, Yellow, Black) is the mode used for final separations for the press. Use a good magnifying glass to look closely at anything that has been printed in color, and you may see the CMYK colors that created it. A typical four-color printing press has a plate for each color and runs the colors in the order of cyan, magenta, yellow, and then black.

Don't take converting an image into this mode lightly. You need to make decisions when you convert an image to CMYK, such as where the file will be printed and on what paper stock, so that the resulting image is the best it can be. Talk to your print provider for specifications that are important when converting to CMYK mode.

Lab color

Lab (Lightness, A channel, and B channel) is a color mode that many high-end color professionals use because of its wide color range. With Lab, you can make adjustments to *luminosity* (lightness) without affecting the color. In this mode, you can select and change an *L* (Lightness or Luminosity) channel without affecting the *A* channel (green and red) and the *B* channel (blue and yellow).

Lab mode is also a good mode to use if you're in a color-managed environment and want to easily move from one color system to another with no loss of color.

Some professionals prefer to sharpen their images in Lab mode because they can select just the Lightness channel and choose Filter⇨Sharpen⇨ Unsharp Mask to sharpen only the gray matter of the image, leaving the color noise-free.

Multichannel

Multichannel is used for many things; sometimes you end up in this mode, and you're not quite sure how you got there. Deleting a channel from an RGB, CMYK, or Lab image automatically converts the image to Multichannel mode. This mode supports multiple spot colors.

Bit depth

You have more functionality in 16-bit and even 32-bit mode. Depending upon your needs, you may spend most of your time in 8-bit mode, which is more than likely all that you need.

Bit depth, or *pixel depth* or *color depth,* measures how much color information is available to display or print each pixel in an image. Greater bit depth means more available colors and more accurate color representation in the digital image. In Photoshop, this increase in accuracy does also limit some of the features available, so don't use it unless you have a specific request or need for it.

To use 16-bit or 32-bit color mode, you also must have a source to provide you with that information, such as a scanner or camera that offers a choice to scan at 16-bit or 32-bit.

**Book II
Chapter 3**

**Messing with
Mode Matters**

Chapter 4: Creating a Selection

In This Chapter

✔ Discovering the selection tools

✔ Painting selections the easy way

✔ Giving transformed selections a try

✔ Feathering away

✔ Keeping selections for later use

✔ Using the Vanishing Point feature

*U*sing Photoshop to create compositions that may not actually exist and retouching images to improve them is common. What you don't want is obvious retouching or a composition that looks contrived. (The exception is if you intend an image to be humorous, such as putting baby Joey's head on Daddy's body.)

That's where the selection tools come in. In this chapter, you discover several selection methods and how to use the selection tools to make your images look as though you *haven't* retouched or edited them. Even if you're an experienced Photoshop user, this chapter provides a plethora of tips and tricks that can save you time and help make your images look absolutely convincing.

Getting to Know the Selection Tools

You create selections with the selection tools. Think of *selections* as windows in which you can make changes to the pixels. Areas that aren't selected are *masked,* which means that these unselected areas are unaffected by changes, much like when you tape around windows and doors before you paint the walls. In this section, we briefly describe the selection tools and show you how to use them. You must be familiar with these tools in order to do *anything* in Photoshop.

As with all the Photoshop tools, the Options bar (viewed across the top of the Photoshop window) change when you choose different selection tools. The keyboard commands you read about in this section exist on the tool Options bar and appear as buttons across the top.

If you move a selection with the Move tool, pixels move as you drag, leaving a blank spot in the image. To *clone* a selection (that is, to copy and move the selection at the same time), Alt+drag (Windows) or Option+drag (Mac) the selection with the Move tool.

The Marquee tool

 The Marquee tool is the main selection tool; by that, we mean that you'll use it most often for creating selections. The exception, of course, is when you have a special situation that calls for a special tool — the Lasso, Magic Wand tool, or the new Quick Selection tool. Throughout this section, we describe creating (and then deselecting) an active selection area; we also provide you with tips for working with selections.

The Marquee tool includes the Rectangular Marquee (for creating rectangular selections), Elliptical Marquee (for creating round or elliptical selections), and Single Row Marquee or Single Column Marquee tools (for creating a selection of a single row or column of pixels). You can access these other Marquee tools by holding down on the default, Rectangle Marquee tool in the Tools panel.

To create a selection, select one of the Marquee tools (remember you can press M) and then drag anywhere on your image. When you release the mouse button, you create an active selection area. When you're working on an active selection area, whatever effects you choose are applied to the whole selection. To deselect an area, you have three choices:

 ✦ Choose Select➪Deselect.

 ✦ Press Ctrl+D (Windows) or ⌘+D (Mac).

 ✦ While using a selection tool, click outside the selection area.

How you make a selection is important because it determines how realistic your edits appear on the image. You can use the following tips and tricks when creating both rectangular and elliptical selections:

 ✦ Add to a selection by holding down the Shift key; drag to create a second selection that intersects the original selection (see the left image in Figure 4-1). The two selections become one big selection.

 ✦ Delete from an existing selection by holding the Alt (Windows) or Option (Mac) key and then drag to create a second selection that intersects the original selection where you want to take away from the original selection (on the right in Figure 4-1).

 ✦ Constrain a rectangle or ellipse to a square or circle by Shift+dragging; make sure that you release the mouse button before you release the Shift key. Holding down the Shift key makes a square or circle only when there are no other selections. (Otherwise, it adds to the selection.)

✦ Make the selection from the center by Alt+dragging (Windows) or Option+dragging (Mac); make sure that you release the mouse button before the Alt (Windows) or Option (Mac) key.

✦ Create a square or circle from the center out by Alt+Shift+dragging (Windows) or Option+Shift+dragging (Mac). Again, make sure that you always release the mouse button before the modifier keys.

✦ When making a selection, hold down the spacebar before releasing the mouse button to drag the selection to another location.

Figure 4-1:
You can
add and
delete from
selections.

 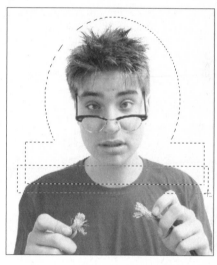

Fixed size

If you've created an effect that you particularly like — say, changing a block of color in your image — and you want to apply it multiple times throughout an image, you can do so. To make the exact same selection multiple times, follow these steps:

1. **With the Marquee tool selected, select Fixed Size from the Style drop-down list on the Options bar.**

You can also select Fixed Ratio from the Style drop-down list to create a proportionally correct selection, but not fixed to an exact size.

2. **On the Options bar, type the Width and Height values into the appropriate text fields.**

You can change ruler increments by choosing Edit⇨Preferences⇨Units and Rulers (Windows) or Photoshop⇨Preferences⇨Units and Rulers (Mac).

3. **Click the image.**

   A selection sized to your values appears.

4. **With the selection tool, drag the selection to the location that you want selected.**

Shift+drag a selection to keep it aligned to a straight, 45-degree, or 90-degree angle.

Floating and nonfloating selections

As a default, when you're using a selection tool, such as the Marquee tool, your selections are *floating*, which means that you can drag them to another location without affecting the underlying pixels. You know that your selection is floating by the little rectangle that appears on your cursor (see the left image in Figure 4-2).

If you want to, however, you can move the underlying pixels. With the selection tool of your choice, just hold down the Ctrl (Windows) or ⌘ (Mac) key to temporarily access the Move tool; the cursor changes to a pointer with scissors, denoting that your selection is nonfloating. Now, when you drag, the pixel data comes with the selection (as shown on the right in Figure 4-2).

Hold down Alt+Ctrl (Windows) or Option+⌘ (Mac) while using a selection tool and drag to clone (copy) pixels from one location to another. Add the Shift key, and the cloned copy is constrained to a straight, 45-degree, or 90-degree angle.

Figure 4-2: The Float icon is used on the left, and the Move icon is used on the right.

 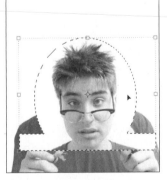

The Lasso tool

Use the Lasso tool for *freeform selections* (selections of an irregular shape). To use the Lasso tool, just drag and create a path surrounding the area to be selected. If you don't return to your start point to close the selection before you release the mouse button, Photoshop completes the path by finding the most direct route back to your starting point.

Just like with the Marquee tool, you can press the Shift key to add to a lasso selection and press the Alt (Windows) or Option (Mac) to delete from a lasso selection.

Hold down on the Lasso tool to show the hidden Lasso tools, the Polygonal Lasso and the Magnetic Lasso tool. Use the Polygonal Lasso tool by clicking a start point and then clicking and releasing from point to point until you come back to close the selection. Use the Magnetic Lasso tool by clicking to create a starting point and then hovering the cursor near an edge in your image. The Magnetic Lasso tool is magnetically attracted to edges; as you move your cursor near an edge, the Magnetic Lasso tool creates a selection along that edge. Click to manually set points in the selection; when you get back to the starting point, click to close the selection.

You may find that the Polygonal Lasso and the Magnetic Lasso tools don't make as nice of a selection as you want. Take a look at the upcoming section, "Painting with the Quick Mask tool," for tips on making finer selections.

The Quick Selection tool

The Quick Selection tool was introduced in CS3. This incredible tool lets you quickly "paint" a selection with a round brush tip of adjustable size. Click and drag and then watch as the selection expands outward and automatically follows defined edges in the image. A Refine Edge command lets you improve the quality of the selection edges and visualize the selection in different ways for easy editing.

Follow these steps to find out how you can take advantage of this new tool:

1. **Open a file that requires a selection.**

You can find sample images in Windows at `C:\Program Files\Adobe\Adobe Photoshop CS4\Extras\Samples` and on the Mac at `Applications\Adobe\Adobe Photoshop CS3\Extras\Samples`.

2. **Select the Quick Selection tool.**

3. **Position the cursor over the area that you wish to select. Notice the brush size displayed with the cursor; click and drag to start painting the selection.**

You can adjust the size of the painting selection by pressing [to make the brush size smaller or] to make the brush size larger.

With the Add to Selection or Subtract from Selection buttons in the Options bar, you can paint more of the selection or deselect active areas (see Figure 4-3).

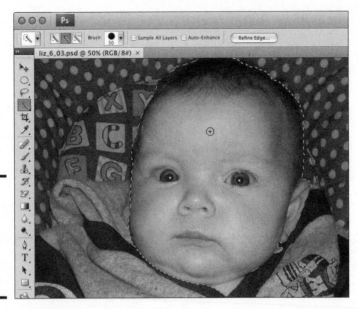

Figure 4-3:
The Quick
Selection
tool allows
you to
paint your
selection.

 ## The Magic Wand tool

The Magic Wand tool is particularly helpful when you're working on an image of high contrast or with a limited number of colors. This tool selects individual pixels of similar shades and colors. Select the Magic Wand tool, click anywhere on an image, and hope for the best — the Magic Wand tool isn't magic at all. You decide how successful this tool is. What we mean by that is that you control how closely matched each pixel must be in order for the Magic Wand tool to include it in the selection. You do so by setting the tolerance on the Options bar.

When you have the Magic Wand tool selected, a Tolerance text field appears on the Options bar. As a default, the tolerance is set to 32. When you click with a setting of 32, the Magic Wand tool selects all pixels within 32 shades (steps) of the color that you clicked. If it didn't select as much as you want, increase the value in the Tolerance text field (all the way up to 255). The amount that you enter really varies with each individual selection. If you're selecting white napkins on an off-white tablecloth, you can set as low as 5 so that the selection doesn't leak into other areas. For colored fabric with lots of tonal values, you might increase the tolerance to 150.

 Don't fret if you miss the entire selection when using the Magic Wand tool. Hold down the Shift key and click in the missed areas. If the tool selects too much, choose Edit⇔Undo (step backward) or press Ctrl+Z (Windows) or ⌘+Z (Mac), reduce the value in the Tolerance text field, and try again.

Painting with the Quick Mask tool

If you have fuzzy selections (fur, hair, or leaves, for example) or you're having difficulty using the selection tools, the Quick Mask tool can be a huge help because it allows you to paint your selection uniformly in one fell swoop.

To enter into Quick Mask mode, create a selection and then press Q. (Pressing Q again exits you from Quick Mask mode.) You can also click the Quick Mask button at the bottom of the Tools panel. If you have a printing background, you'll notice that the Quick Mask mode, set at its default color (red), resembles something that you may want to forget: rubylith and amberlith. (Remember slicing up those lovely films with Exacto blades before computer masking came along?) In Quick Mask mode, Photoshop shows your image as it appears through the mask. The clear part is selected; what's covered in the mask isn't selected.

Book II
Chapter 4

Creating a Selection

To create and implement a quick mask, follow these steps:

1. **Press Q to enter Quick Mask mode.**

2. **Press D to change the foreground and background color boxes the default colors of black and white.**

3. **Select the Brush tool and start painting with black in the clear area of the image in Quick Mask mode.**

It doesn't have to be pretty; just get a stroke or two in there.

4. **Press Q to return to the Selection mode.**

You're now out of Quick Mask mode. Notice that where you painted with black (it turned red in the Quick Mask mode), the pixels are no longer selected.

5. **Press Q again to re-enter the Quick Mask mode and then press X.**

This step switches the foreground and background colors (giving you white in the foreground, black in the background).

6. **With the Brush tool, paint several white strokes in the red mask area.**

The white strokes turn clear in the Quick Mask mode.

7. **Press Q to return to the Selection mode.**

Where you painted white in the Quick Mask mode is now selected.

When in Quick Mask mode, you can paint white over areas you want selected and black over areas that you don't want selected. When painting in the Quick Mask mode, increase the brush size by pressing the] key. Decrease the brush size by pressing the [key.

In the Selection mode, your selection seems to have a hard edge; you can soften those hard edges by using a softer brush in the Quick Mask mode. To make a brush softer, press Shift+[; to make a brush harder, press Shift+].

Because the Quick Mask mode makes selections based on the mask's values, you can create a mask by selecting the Gradient tool and dragging it across the image in Quick Mask mode. When you exit Quick Mask mode, it looks as though there's a straight-line selection, but actually the selection transitions as your gradient did. Choose any filter from the Filters menu and notice how the filter transitions into the untouched part of the image to which you applied the gradient.

If you're working in Quick Mask mode, choose Window⇨Channels to see that what you're working on is a temporary alpha channel. See the later section, "Saving Selections," for more about alpha channels.

Manipulating Selections with Refine Selection

After you master creating selections, you'll find that working with the selections — painting, transforming, and feathering them — can be easy and fun.

Transforming selections

Don't deselect and start over again if you can just nudge or resize your selection a bit. You can scale, rotate, and even distort an existing selection. Follow these steps to transform a selection:

1. **Create a selection and then choose Select⇨Transform Selection.**

You can use the bounding box to resize and rotate your selection.

- Drag the handles to make the selection larger or smaller. Drag a corner handle to adjust width and height simultaneously. Shift+drag a corner handle to size proportionally.

- Position the cursor outside the bounding box to see the Rotate icon; drag when it appears to rotate the selection. Shift+drag to constrain to straight, 45-degree, or 90-degree angles.

- Ctrl+drag (Windows) or ⌘+drag (Mac) a corner point to distort the selection, as shown in Figure 4-4.

2. **Press Enter or Return or double-click in the center of the selection area to confirm the transformation; press Esc to release the transformation and return to the original selection.**

Figure 4-4:
Distort, resize, and rotate a selection with the Transform Selection feature.

Feathering

Knowing how to retouch an image means little if you don't know how to make the retouching discreet. If you boost up the color using curves to the CEO's face, do you want it to appear like a pancake has been attached to his cheek? Of course not — that isn't discreet at all (or very wise). That's where feathering comes in. *Feathering* a selection blurs its edges, so as to create a natural-looking transition between the selection and the background of the image.

To feather an image, follow these steps:

1. **Create a selection.**

For the nonfeathered image shown on top in Figure 4-5, we used the Elliptical Marquee tool to make a selection. We then copied the selection, created a new, blank image, and pasted the selection into the new image.

To create the feathered image on the bottom in Figure 4-5, we used the Elliptical Marquee tool to select the same area on the original image and went on to Step 2.

2. **Choose Select➪Modify➪Feather.**

3. **In the Feather dialog box that appears, type a value in the Feather Radius text field and then click OK.**

For example, we entered **20** in the Feather Radius text field. (We then copied the selection, created a new image, and pasted the feathered selection into the new image to create the image on the bottom of Figure 4-5.) *Voilà!* The edges of the image are softened over a 20-pixel area, as shown on the bottom of Figure 4-5. This technique is also referred to as a *vignette* in the printing industry.

Figure 4-5: The top image doesn't have feathering, whereas the second has feathering applied.

The results of the feathering depend upon the resolution of the image. A feather of 20 pixels in a 72-ppi (pixels per inch) image will be a much larger area than a feather of 20 pixels in a 300-ppi image. Typical amounts for a nice vignette on an edge of an image would be 20 to 50 pixels. Experiment with your images to find what works best for you.

This feathering effect created a nice soft edge to your image, but it's also useful when retouching images:

1. **Using any selection method, create a selection around a part of an image that you want to lighten.**

2. **Choose Select⇨Modify⇨Feather; in the Feather dialog box that appears, enter 25 in the Feather Radius text field and click OK.**

   If you get an error message stating, "No pixels are more than 50% selected," click OK and create a larger selection.

3. **Choose Image⇨Adjustments⇨Curves.**

4. **Click in the center of the curve to add an anchor point and drag up to lighten the image.**

   This step lightens the midtones of the image.

Notice how the lightening fades out so that there's no definite edge to the correction. You can have more fun like this in Chapter 7 of this minibook, where we cover color correction.

More fun with selections

Like to experiment, but also want a preview of exactly what your changes to the selection are actually doing? Then you'll love the Refine Edge feature. The Refine Edge feature was introduced in Photoshop CS3 and is available in the Options bar across the top of the Photoshop window whenever you have any selection tool active.

To use the Refine Edge feature, follow these steps:

1. **Make a selection.**

2. **With any selection tool active, click the Refine Edge button in the Options bar at the top of the Photoshop window.**

   The Refine Edge dialog box appears, as shown in Figure 4-6.

3. **Choose a preview method by clicking the icons across the bottom of the Refine Edge dialog box.**

   On White is the default setting, and it shows your selection as it would appear on a white background.

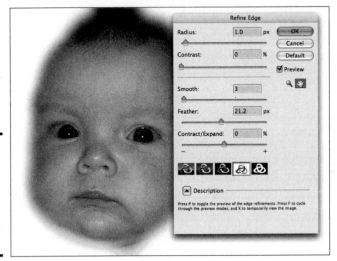

Figure 4-6:
Tweak the edges of a selection with the Refine Edge dialog box.

Don't worry! The rest of your image hasn't been removed; this preview helps you to better see the effects of this feature.

Here are the selections that you can choose from in the Refine Edge dialog box:

- *Radius:* Radius determines the size of the region around the selection boundary in which edge refinement occurs.

- *Contrast:* Contrast sharpens selection edges and removes fuzzy artifacts.

- *Smooth:* Smooth reduces irregular areas in the selection boundary.

- *Feather:* Feather creates a soft-edged transition between the selection and its surrounding pixels.

- *Contract/Expand:* Use Contract/Expand to shrink or enlarge the selection boundary.

4. **When you're happy with the results, click OK.**

Saving Selections

The term *alpha channel* sounds pretty complicated, but it's simply a saved selection. Depending upon the mode you're in, you already have several channels to contend with. A selection is just an extra channel that you can call on at any time.

To create an alpha channel, follow these steps:

1. **Create a selection that you want to save.**

2. **Choose Select⇨Save Selection.**

3. **Name the Selection and click OK.**

An additional named channel that contains your selection appears in the Channels panel.

To load a saved selection, follow these steps:

1. **Choose Select⇨Load Selection.**

The Load Selection dialog box appears.

2. **Select your named channel from the Channel drop-down list.**

If you have an active selection and then choose to load a selection, you have additional options. You can do the following with an active selection when loading a channel by selecting one of the following options:

- *New Selection:* Eliminate the existing selection and create a new selection based upon the channel you select.

- *Add to Selection:* Add the channel to the existing selection.

- *Subtract from Selection:* Subtract the channel from the existing selection.

- *Intersect with Selection:* Intersect the channel with the existing selection.

3. **Click OK.**

Other Adobe applications, such as InDesign, Illustrator, Premiere, and After Effects, can also recognize alpha channels.

Using the Improved Vanishing Point Feature

This incredible new feature lets you preserve correct perspective in edits of images that contain perspective planes, such as the sides of a building. You can do so much with this feature, and we provide you with a simple introduction. Try experimenting with multiple planes and copying and pasting items into the Vanishing Point window for even more effects. Follow these steps:

1. **Open a file that you want to apply a perspective filter to.**

If you don't have an appropriate image handy, try using a `Vanishing Point.psd` file. You can find the file in Windows at `C:\Program Files\ Adobe\Adobe Photoshop CS3\Extras\Samples` and on the Mac at `Applications\Adobe\Adobe Photoshop CS3\Extra\Samples`.

2. **Create a new blank layer by clicking the Create a New Layer button at the bottom of the Layers panel.**

   If you create a new layer each time you use Vanishing Point, the results appear on a separate layer. Putting the Vanishing Point results in a separate layer and also preserves your original image, as you can delete the result of the vanishing point filter and still retain your original layer.

3. **Choose Filter⇨Vanishing Point.**

   A separate Vanishing Point window appears. If you receive an error message about an existing plane, click OK.

   If you're using a sample file from Photoshop, it will have a perspective plane already created for you. To help you understand this feature better, delete the existing plane by pressing the Delete or Backspace key.

4. **Select the Create Plane tool and define the four corner nodes of the plane surface.**

   Try to use objects in the image to help create the plane. In Figure 4-7, the planks of wood were used to make the perspective plane.

   After the four corner nodes of the plane are created, the tool automatically is switched to the Edit Plane tool.

Figure 4-7:
Use objects in an image to build a perspective plane.

5. **Select and drag the corner nodes to make an accurate plane.**

The plane grid should appear blue, not yellow or red, if it's accurate.

After creating the plane, you can move, scale, or reshape the plane. Keep in mind that your results depend on how accurately the plane lines up with perspective of the image.

You can use your first Vanishing Point session to simply create perspective planes and then click OK. The planes appear in subsequent Vanishing Point sessions when you choose Filter⇨Vanishing Point. Saving perspective planes is especially useful if you plan to copy and paste an image into Vanishing Point and need to have a ready-made plane to target.

6. **Choose the Stamp tool in the Vanishing Point window and then choose On from the Heal drop-down list in the Options bar.**

You'll love where this is going. In the example image, `Vanishing Point.psd`, we simply clone the blue broom, but it should get your brain working about all the ways that you can apply this greatly improved feature.

7. **With the Stamp tool still selected, cross over part of the area or part of the image you want to clone and Alt-click (Windows) or Option-click (Mac) to define it as the source that's to be cloned.**

In the image `Vanishing Point.psd`, we clicked the middle part of the blue broom.

8. **Without clicking, move toward the back of the perspective plane (you can even clone outside the plane) and then click and drag to reproduce the cloned part of the image.**

Notice in Figure 4-8, it's cloned as a smaller version, in the correct perspective for its new location.

9. **Start from Step 7 and clone any region of an image up closer to the front of the perspective pane.**

The cloned region is now cloned as a larger version of itself.

You can use the Marquee tool options (Feather, Opacity, Heal, and Move Mode) at any time, either before or after making the selection. When you move the Marquee tool, the Stamp tool, or the Brush tool into a plane, the bounding box is highlighted, indicating that the plane is active.

10. **Click OK.**

To preserve the perspective plane information in an image, save your document in PSD, TIFF, or JPEG format.

Book II
Chapter 4

Creating a Selection

Figure 4-8:
Cloning in
perspective.

Chapter 5: Using the Photoshop Pen Tool

In This Chapter

🖊 **Putting shape layers to work**

🖊 **Working with a path as a selection**

🖊 **Creating clipping paths**

The Pen tool is the ultimate method to make precise selections. You can also use it to create vector shapes and clipping paths (silhouettes). In this chapter, you discover how to take advantage of this super multitasking tool. This chapter also shows you how to apply paths made with the Pen tool as shapes, selections, and clipping paths. If you're interested in the fundamentals of creating paths with the Pen tool in Illustrator, check out Book III, Chapter 5, where we cover the Pen tool in more detail.

We recommend that you use the Pen tool as much as you can to truly master its capabilities. If you don't use it on a regular basis, it will seem awkward, but it does get easier! Knowing how to effectively use the Pen tool puts you a grade above the average Photoshop user, and the quality of your selections will show it. Read Chapter 9 of this minibook to find out how to use the Pen tool to create layer masks and adjustment layers.

Using Shape Layers

As a default, when you start creating with the Pen tool, Photoshop automatically creates a *shape layer,* which is useful for adding additional elements, but is frustrating if you're attempting to create just a path with the Pen tool. Select the Pen tool and note the default setting on the left side of the Options bar. You can choose from the following options:

✦ **Shape layers:** Creates a new shape layer, a filled layer that contains your vector path.

✦ **Paths:** Creates a path only; no layer is created.

✦ **Fill pixels:** Creates pixels directly on the image. No editable path or layer is created. This option may not be useful to new users, but some existing users prefer to use this method because it's the only way to access the Line tool from earlier versions.

Shape layers can be very useful when the goal of your design is to seamlessly integrate vector shapes and pixel data. A shape layer can contain vector shapes that you can then modify with the same features of any other layer. You can adjust the opacity of the shape layer, change the blending mode, and even apply layer effects to add drop shadows and dimension. Find out how to do this in Chapter 9 of this minibook.

Create a shape layer with any of these methods:

✦ **Create a shape with the Pen tool.** With the Pen tool, you can create interesting custom shapes and even store them for future use. We show you how in the following section.

✦ **Use a Vector Shape tool, as shown in Figure 5-1.** *Vector shapes* are premade shapes (you can even create your own!) that you can create by dragging on your image area with a shape tool.

✦ **Import a shape from Illustrator.** Choose File⇨Place and choose an .ai file; when the Options window appears, choose to place as a shape layer or a path. This imports an Illustrator file as a shape layer or path into Photoshop.

Figure 5-1:
The Vector
Shape tools.

Creating and using a custom shape

Perhaps you like the wave kind of shape (see Figure 5-2) that's been cropping up in design pieces all over the place.

Figure 5-2:
A custom
wave shape
integrated
with an
image in
Photoshop.

You can copy and paste shapes right from Illustrator CS4 into Photoshop CS4. Simply select your shape in Adobe Illustrator, choose Edit⇨Copy, switch to the Photoshop application, and with a document open, choose Edit⇨Paste.

You can create a wavy shape like that, too. With an image or blank document open, just follow these steps:

1. **Click and drag with the Pen tool to create a wavy shape.**

Don't worry about the size of the shape. The shape is vector, so you can scale it up or down to whatever size you need without worrying about making jagged edges. Just make sure that you close the shape (return to the original point with the end point).

When you create the shape, it fills in with your foreground color. Try to ignore it if you can; the next section shows you how to change the fill color, and Chapter 8 of this minibook covers how to change it to a transparent fill.

2. **With the shape still selected, choose Edit⇨Define Custom Shape, name the shape, and press OK.**

After you save your custom shape, you can re-create it at any time. If you don't like the shape, choose Windows⇨Layers to open the Layers panel and then drag the shape layer you just created to the Trash Can in the lower-right corner of the panel. If you want to experiment with your custom shape now, continue with these steps.

3. **Click and hold on the Rectangle tool to access the other hidden vector tools; select the last tool, the Custom Shape tool.**

When the Custom Shape tool is selected, a Shape drop-down list appears on the Options bar at the top of the screen, as shown in Figure 5-3.

You have lots of custom shapes to choose from, including the one you've just created. If you just saved a shape, yours is in the last square; you have to scroll down to select it.

Book II
Chapter 5

Using the Photoshop
Pen Tool

Figure 5-3:
A Shape drop-down list appears in the Options bar when the Custom Shape tool is active.

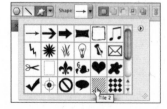

4. **Select your custom shape; click and drag in the image area to create your shape.**

   You can make it any size that you want.

5. **To change the shape's size, choose Edit⇨Free Transform Path, press Ctrl+T (Windows) or ⌘+T (Mac), grab a bounding box handle, and drag.**

   Shift+drag a corner handle to keep the shape proportional as you resize it.

Because a shape is created on its own layer, you can experiment with different levels of transparency and blending modes in the Layers panel. Figure 5-4 shows shapes that are partially transparent. Discover lots of other features you can use with shape layers in Chapter 9 of this minibook.

Figure 5-4:
Experiment with blending modes and opacity changes on shape layers.

Changing the color of the shape

When you create a shape with a shape tool, the shape takes the color of your present foreground color. To change the color of an existing shape, open the Layers panel by choosing Window⇨Layers; notice that the Vector Shape tool creates a new layer for every shape you make. Creating a new layer is a benefit when it comes to creating special effects because the shape layer is independent of the rest of your image. (Read more about using layers in Chapter 9 of this minibook.)

To change a shape's color, double-click the color thumbnail on the left in the shape layer, or click the Set Color box in the Options bar across the top of the Document window. The Color Picker appears, as shown in Figure 5-5. To select a new color, drag the Hue slider up or down or click in the large color pane to select a color with the saturation and lightness that you want to use. Click OK when you're done.

With the Color Picker open, you can also move outside the picker dialog box and sample colors from other open images and objects.

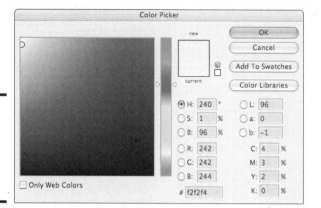

Figure 5-5:
Select a
new color
for the
shape
layer's fill.

Editing a shape

Like Adobe Illustrator, Photoshop provides both a Path Selection tool and a Direct Selection tool. The Direct Selection tool is hidden under the Path Selection tool. To move an entire shape on a layer, choose the Path Selection tool and drag the shape.

To edit the shape, deselect the shape (while using the Path Selection or Direct Selection tool, click outside the shape). Then select the Direct Selection tool. With the Direct Selection tool, click individual anchor points and handles to edit and fine-tune the shape, as shown in Figure 5-6.

Figure 5-6:
Edit
individual
anchor
points with
the Direct
Selection
tool.

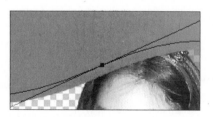

Removing a shape layer

Because the Pen tool now has multiple options, you may find yourself unexpectedly creating a shape layer. Delete a shape layer by dragging the layer thumbnail to the Trash Can in the lower-right corner of the Layers panel.

If you want to keep your path but throw away the shape layer, choose Window➪Paths. Then drag the shape vector mask to the New Path icon, as shown in Figure 5-7, which creates a saved path. Now you can throw away the shape layer.

Figure 5-7:
Save your path by dragging the shape path to the Create New Path icon.

Using a Path as a Selection

You can use the Pen tool to create precise selections that would be difficult to create with other selection methods. The Pen tool produces clean edges that print well and can be edited using the Direct Selection tool. Before using the Pen tool, make sure that you click the Paths button on the Options bar.

To use a path as a selection (which is extremely helpful when you're trying to make a precise selection), follow these steps:

1. **Open any file or create a new blank file.**

2. **With the Pen tool (make sure that the Paths button is selected on the Options bar or else you'll create a shape layer), click to place anchor points.**

3. **Drag to create a curved path around the image area that you want selected and completely close the path by returning to the start point (see Figure 5-8).**

   Use the techniques that we discuss in Book III, Chapter 4 to perform this step. A circle appears before you click to close the path.

4. **Choose Window➪Paths.**

   In the Paths panel, you can create new and activate existing paths, apply a stroke, or turn paths into selections by clicking the icons at the bottom of the panel (see Figure 5-9).

5. **Click and drag the Work Path down to the Create New Path icon at the bottom of the Paths panel.**

   The path is now named Path 1 and is saved. You can also double-click to rename the file if you like.

Figure 5-8:
Make sure that you select the Paths button to create only the path, not a shape layer.

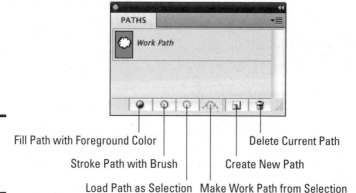

Figure 5-9:
The Paths panel and its options.

Fill Path with Foreground Color

Stroke Path with Brush

Load Path as Selection

Delete Current Path

Create New Path

Make Work Path from Selection

6. Click the Load Path as Selection icon.

The path is converted into a selection.

TIP

Use this quick and easy method for turning an existing path into a selection: Ctrl-click (Windows) or ⌘-click (Mac) the path thumbnail in the Paths panel.

Clipping Paths

If you want to create a beautiful silhouette that transfers well to other applications for text wrapping (see Figure 5-10), create a clipping path.

Figure 5-10:
Clipping
paths
allow you
to create
silhouettes
in other
applications.

Creating a clipping path is easy when you have a good path! Just follow these steps:

1. **Use the Pen tool to create a path around the image area that's to be the silhouette.**

2. **In the Paths panel, choose Save Path from the panel menu (click the triangle in the upper-right corner of the panel to access this menu), as shown in Figure 5-11, and then name the path.**

   If Save Path is grayed out, your path has already been saved; skip to Step 3.

3. **From the same panel menu, choose Clipping Path.**

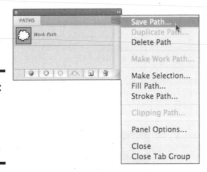

Figure 5-11:
Convert
your work
path to a
saved path.

4. **In the Clipping Paths dialog box, choose your path from the drop-down list if it's not already selected; click OK.**

   Leave the Flatness Device Pixels text field blank unless you have a need to change it. The flatness value determines how many device pixels are used to create your silhouette. The higher the amount, the less points are created, thereby allowing for faster processing time. This speed does come at a cost, though; set the flatness value too high, and you may see (you'd have to look really close) straight edges instead of curved edges.

5. **Choose File⇨Save As and in the Format drop-down list, select Photoshop EPS; in the EPS Options dialog box that appears, accept the defaults and click OK.**

If you get PostScript errors when printing, choose Clipping Path from the panel menu and up the value to 2 pixels in the Flatness Device Pixels text field. Keep returning to this text field and upping the value until the file prints, or give up and try printing your document with another printer.

If you're placing this file in other Adobe applications, such as InDesign, you don't need to save the file as EPS; you can leave it as a Photoshop (.psd) file.

Here's an even faster method that you can use to create a clipping path that can be used in other Adobe applications, such as InDesign and Illustrator:

1. **Create a path around the item that you wish to keep when the clipping path is created.**

Make sure that you're working on a layer and not the Background layer. To convert the Background layer to a layer, hold down the Alt key (Windows) or the Option key (Mac) and double-click the Background layer. The Background layer is now Layer 0.

2. **In the Layers panel, click the Add Layer Mask button and then click the Add Layer Mask button again.**

A layer vector mask is created, and everything outside the path becomes transparent, as shown in Figure 5-12.

Figure 5-12: Creating a clipping path the easy way, with layers.

You can still edit the path by using the Direct Selection tool.

3. **Save the file in the .psd format.**

4. **Choose File⇨Place to put the image, with its clipping path included, into other Adobe applications.**

Chapter 6: Thinking about Resolution Basics

In This Chapter

✔ **Understanding resolution basics**

✔ **Adjusting file size**

✔ **Applying the Unsharp Mask filter to your image**

Something as important as getting the right resolution for your images deserves its own chapter, but fortunately, the topic isn't all that complex. In this chapter, you discover the necessary resolution for various uses of Photoshop imagery (from printing a high-resolution graphic to e-mailing a picture of your kids to Mom), how to properly increase the resolution, and how to adjust image size.

Having the proper resolution is important to the final outcome of your image, especially if you plan to print that image. Combine the information here with using the correction tools that we show you in the Chapter 7 of this minibook, and you should be ready to roll with great imagery.

Creating Images for Print

To see and make changes to the present size and resolution of an image in Photoshop, choose Image⇨Image Size. The Image Size dialog box appears.

The Width and Height text fields in the Pixel Dimensions area of the Image Size dialog box are used for on-screen resizing, such as for the Web and e-mail. The Width and Height text fields in the Document Size area show the size at which the image will print. The Resolution text field determines the resolution of the printed image; a higher value means a smaller, more finely detailed printed image.

Before you decide upon a resolution, understand what some of the resolution jargon means:

✦ **dpi (dots per inch):** The resolution of an image when printed.

✦ **lpi (lines per inch):** The varying dot pattern that printers and presses use to create images (see Figure 6-1). This dot pattern is referred to as the lpi, even though it represents rows of dots. The higher the lpi, the finer the detail and the less of the dot pattern or line screen you see.

✦ **Dot gain:** The spread of ink as it's applied to paper. Certain types of paper will wick a dot of ink farther than others. For example, newsprint has a high dot gain and typically prints at 85 lpi; a coated stock paper has a lower dot gain and can be printed at 133–150 lpi and even higher.

Human eyes typically can't detect a dot pattern in a printed image at 133 dpi or higher.

Figure 6-1: The dot pattern used to print images is referred to as lpi (lines per inch).

Deciding the resolution or dpi of an image requires backward planning. If you want to create the best possible image, you should know where it'll print *before* deciding the resolution. Communicate with your printer service if the image is going to press. If you're sending your image to a high-speed copier, you can estimate that it will handle 100 lpi; a desktop printer will handle 85 lpi to 100 lpi.

The resolution formula

When creating an image for print, keep this formula in mind:

$$2 \times lpi = dpi \text{ (dots per inch)}$$

This formula means that if your image is going to press using 150 lpi, have your image at 300 dpi. To save space, many people in production use 1.5 x lpi because it reduces the file size significantly and you get very similar results; you can decide which works best for you.

Changing the resolution

Using the Image Size dialog box is only one way that you can control the resolution in Photoshop. Even though you can increase the resolution, do so sparingly and avoid it if you can. The exception is when you have an image that is large in dimension size but low in resolution, like those that you typically get from a digital camera. You may have a top-of-the-line digital camera that produces 72 dpi images, but at that resolution, the pictures are 28 x 21 inches (or larger)!

To increase the resolution of an image without sacrificing quality:

1. Choose Image⇨Image Size.

The Image Size dialog box appears.

2. Deselect the Resample Image check box.

This way, Photoshop doesn't add additional pixels.

3. Enter the desired resolution in the Resolution text field.

Photoshop keeps the *pixel size* (the size of the image on-screen) the same, but the *document size* (the size of the image when printed) decreases when you enter a higher resolution.

4. If the image isn't the size that you need it to be, select the Resample Image check box and type the size in the Width and Height text fields in the Document Size section.

Note that it's best to reduce the size of a bitmap image, such as a digital photo, rather than increase it.

You can also deselect the Resample Image check box and essentially play a game of give and take to see what the resolution will be when you enter the size you want your image printed at in the Width and Height text fields in the Document Size area.

Images can typically be scaled from 50 to 120 percent before looking jagged (to scale by a percentage, select Percent from the drop-down lists beside the Width and Height text fields). Keep this in mind when placing and resizing your images in a page layout application, such as InDesign.

 5. Click OK when you're finished; double-click the Zoom tool in the Tools panel to see the image at actual size on-screen.

 To increase the resolution *without* changing the image size, follow these steps. (This situation isn't perfect because pixels that don't presently exist are created by Photoshop and may not be totally accurate. Photoshop tries to give you the best image, but you may have some loss of detail.)

1. Choose Image⇨Image Size.

2. When the Image Size dialog box appears, make sure that the Resample Image check box is selected.

Note that Bicubic is selected in the Method drop-down list. This method is the best, but slowest, way to reinterpret pixels when you resize an image. With this method, Photoshop essentially looks at all the pixels and takes a good guess as to how the newly created pixels should look, based upon surrounding pixels.

3. Enter the resolution that you need in the Resolution text field, click OK, and then double-click the Zoom tool to see the image at actual size.

**Book II
Chapter 6**

**Thinking about
Resolution Basics**

Determining the Resolution for Web Images

Did you ever have somebody e-mail you an image, and, after spending ten minutes downloading it, you discover that the image is so huge that all you can see on the monitor is your nephew's left eye? Many people are under the misconception that if an image is 72 dpi, it's ready for the Web. Actually, pixel dimension is all that matters for Web viewing of images; this section helps you make sense of this.

Most people view Web pages in their browser windows in an area of about 640 x 480 pixels. You can use this figure as a basis for any images you create for the Web, whether the viewer is using a 14-inch or a 21-inch monitor. (Remember, those people who have large monitors set to high screen resolutions don't necessarily want a Web page taking up the whole screen!) If you're creating images for a Web page or to attach to an e-mail message, you may want to pick a standard size to design by, such as 600 x 400 pixels at 72 dpi.

To use the Image Size dialog box to determine the resolution and size for on-screen images, follow these steps:

1. **Have an image open and choose Image⇨Image Size.**

   The Image Size dialog box appears.

2. **To make the image take up half the width of a typical browser window, type** 300 **(half of 600) in the top Width text field.**

   If a little chain link is visible to the right, the Constrain Proportions check box is selected, and Photoshop automatically determines the height from the width that you entered.

3. **Click OK and double-click the Zoom tool to see the image at actual size on-screen.**

   That's it! Whether your image is 3,000 or 30 pixels wide doesn't matter; as long as you enter the correct dimensions in the Pixel Dimension area, the image works beautifully.

Applying the Unsharp Mask Filter to an Image

When you resample an image in Photoshop, it can become blurry. A good practice is to apply the Unsharp Mask filter. This feature sharpens the image based upon levels of contrast, while keeping the areas that don't have contrasting pixels smooth. You do have to set up this feature correctly to get good results. Here's the down-and-dirty method of using the Unsharp Mask filter:

1. **Choose View⇨Actual Pixels or double-click the Zoom tool.**

When you're using a filter, view your image at actual size to best see the effect.

2. **Choose Filter⇨Sharpen⇨Unsharp Mask.**

In the Unsharp Mask dialog box that appears, set these three options:

- *Amount:* The Amount value ranges from 0 to 500. The amount that you choose has a lot to do with the subject matter. Sharpening a car or appliance at 300 to 400 is fine, but do this to the CEO's 75-year-old wife, and you may suffer an untimely death because every wrinkle, mole, or hair will magically become more defined. If you're not sure what to use, start with 150 and play around until you find an Amount value that looks good.

- *Radius:* The Unsharp Mask filter creates a halo around the areas that have enough contrast to be considered an edge. Typically, leaving the amount between 1 to 2 is fine for print, but if you're creating a billboard or poster, increase the size.

- *Threshold:* This option is the most important one in the Unsharp Mask dialog box. The Threshold setting is what determines what should be sharpened. If left at zero, you'll see noise throughout the image, much like the grain that you see in high-speed film. Bring it up to 10, and this triggers the Unsharp Mask filter to apply only the sharpening when the pixels are ten shades or more away from each other. The amount of tolerance ranges from 1 to 255. Apply too much, and no sharpening appears; apply too little, and the image becomes grainy. A good number to start with is 10.

To compare the original state of the image with the preview of the Unsharp Mask filter's effect in the preview pane of the Unsharp Mask dialog box, click and hold on the image in the Preview pane; this shows the original state of the image. When you release the mouse button, the Unsharp Mask filter is previewed again.

3. **When you've made your choice, click OK.**

The image appears to have more detail.

Once in a while, stray colored pixels may appear after you apply the Unsharp Mask filter. If you feel this is a problem with your image, choose Edit⇨Fade Unsharp Mask immediately after applying the Unsharp Mask filter. In the Fade dialog box, select the Luminosity blend mode from the Mode drop-down list and then click OK. This step applies the Unsharp Mask filter to the grays in the image only, thereby eliminating sharpening of colored pixels.

Book II
Chapter 6

Thinking about
Resolution Basics

Note that you can also choose Filter⇨Convert for Smart Filters before you apply the Unsharp Mask filter. Smart filters allow you to undo all or some of any filter, including sharpening filters that you apply to a layer. Find out how by reading Chapter 9 in this minibook.

Chapter 7: Creating a Good Image

In This Chapter

✔ Understanding the histogram

✔ Getting ready to correct an image

✔ Making a good tone curve

✔ Editing adjustment layers

✔ Testing your printer

*W*ith all the incredible things you can do in Photoshop, you can easily forget the basics. Yes, you can create incredible compositions with special effects, but if the people look greenish, it detracts from the image. Get in the habit of building good clean images before heading into the artsy filters and fun things. Color correction isn't complicated, and if done properly, it'll produce magical results in your images. In this chapter, you discover how to use the values you read in the Info panel and use the Curves panel to produce quality image corrections.

Reading a Histogram

Before making adjustments, look at the image's *histogram,* which displays an image's tonal values, to evaluate whether the image has sufficient detail to produce a high-quality image. In Photoshop CS4, choose Window⇨Histogram to display the Histogram panel.

The greater the range of values in the histogram, the greater the detail. Poor images without much information can be difficult, if not impossible, to correct. The Histogram panel also displays the overall distribution of shadows, midtones, and highlights to help you determine which tonal corrections are needed.

Figure 7-1 shows a good full histogram that indicates a smooth transition from one shade to another in the image. Figure 7-2 shows that when a histogram is spread out and has gaps in it, the image is jumping too quickly from one shade to another, producing a posterized effect. *Posterization* is an effect that reduces tonal values to a limited amount, creating a more defined range of values from one shade to another. Great if you want it, yucky if you want a smooth tonal change from one shadow to another.

Figure 7-1:
A histogram showing smooth transitions from one color to another.

Figure 7-2:
A histogram showing a lack of smoothness in the gradation of color.

So how do you get a good histogram? If you're scanning, make sure that your scanner is set for the maximum amount of colors. Scanning at 16 shades of gray gives you 16 lines in your histogram . . . not good!

If you have a bad histogram, we recommend that you rescan or reshoot the image. If you have a good histogram to start with, keep the histogram good by not messing around with multiple tone correction tools. Most professionals use the Curves feature . . . and that's it. Curves (choose Image⇨Adjustments⇨ Curves), if used properly, do all the adjusting of levels (brightness and contrast) and color balance, all in one step. You can read more about curves in the section "Creating a Good Tone Curve," later in this chapter.

Figure 7-3 shows what happens to a perfectly good histogram when someone gets a little too zealous and uses the entire plethora of color correction controls in Photoshop. Just because the controls are there doesn't mean that you have to use them.

Figure 7-3:
Tonal
information
is broken up.

Book II
Chapter 7

Creating a Good
Image

If you see a Warning icon appear while you're making adjustments, double-click anywhere on the histogram to refresh the display.

Breaking into key types

Don't panic if your histogram is smashed all the way to the left or right. The bars of the histogram represent tonal values. You can break down the types of images, based upon their values, into three key types:

✦ **High key:** A very light-colored image, such as the image shown in Figure 7-4. Information is pushed toward the right in the histogram. Color correction has to be handled a little differently for these images to keep the light appearance to them.

✦ **Low key:** A very dark image, such as the image shown in Figure 7-5. Information is pushed to the left in the histogram. This type of image is difficult to scan on low-end scanners because the dark areas tend to blend together with little definition.

✦ **Mid key:** A typical image with a full range of shades is considered mid key, such as the image shown in Figure 7-6. These images are the most common and easiest to work with. In this chapter, we deal with images that are considered mid key.

Setting up the correction

To produce the best possible image, try to avoid correcting in CMYK (Cyan, Magenta, Yellow, Black) mode. If your images are typically in RGB (Red, Green, Blue) or LAB mode (L for lightness, and A and B for the color-opponent dimensions), keep them in that mode throughout the process. Convert them to CMYK only when you're finished manipulating the image.

Don't forget! Press Ctrl+Y (Windows) or ⌘+Y (Mac) to toggle on and off the CMYK preview so that you can see what your image will look like in CMYK mode without converting it!

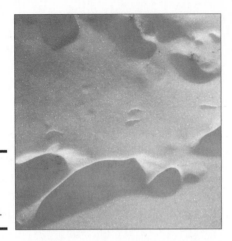

Figure 7-4:
A high key image is a light image.

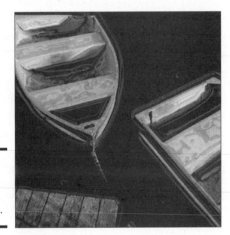

Figure 7-5:
A low key image is a dark image.

Figure 7-6:
A typical image with a full range of values is a mid key image.

Set up these items before starting any color correction:

1. **Select the Eyedropper tool; on the Options bar, change the sample size from Point Sample to 3 by 3 Average in the Sample Size drop-down list.**

This setting gives you more accurate readings.

2. **If the Histogram panel isn't already visible, choose Window➪Histogram.**

3. **If the Info panel isn't already visible, choose Window➪Info to show the Info panel so that you can check values.**

4. **Make sure that your color settings are correct.**

If you're not sure how to check or set up color settings, see Chapter 3 of this minibook.

Creating a Good Tone Curve

A *tone curve* represents the density of an image. To get the best image, you must first find the highlight and shadow points in the image. An image created in less-than-perfect lighting conditions may be washed out or have odd color casts. See Figure 7-7 for an example of an image with no set highlight and shadow. Check out Figure 7-8 to see an image that went through the process of setting a highlight and shadow.

To make the process of creating a good tone curve more manageable, we've broken the process into four parts:

+ Finding the highlight and shadow

+ Setting the highlight and shadow

+ Adjusting the midtone

+ Finding a neutral

Even though each part has its own set of steps, you must go through all four parts to accomplish the task of creating a good tone curve (unless you're working with grayscale images, in which case you can skip the neutral part). In this example, an adjustment layer is used for the curve adjustments. The benefit is that you can turn off the visibility of the adjustment at a later point or double-click the adjustment layer thumbnail to make ongoing edits without destroying your image.

Figure 7-7:
The image is murky before defining a highlight and shadow.

Figure 7-8:
The tonal values are opened after highlight and shadow have been set.

Finding and setting the highlight and the shadow

In the non-computer world, you'd spend a fair amount of time trying to locate the lightest and darkest parts of an image. Fortunately, you can cheat in Photoshop by using some of the features in the Curves panel. Here's how you access the panel:

1. **With an image worthy of adjustment — one that isn't perfect already — choose Window⇨Layer (if the Layers panel isn't already open).**

2. **Click and hold on the Create New Fill or Adjustment Layer button at the bottom of the Layers panel and select Curves.**

   The Adjustments panel appears with the Curves panel active, as shown in Figure 7-9.

Notice the grayed-out histogram behind the image in the Curves panel. The histogram aids you in determining where you need to adjust the image's curve.

If you're correcting in RGB (as you should be!), the tone curve may be opposite of what you think it should be. Instead of light to dark displaying as you'd expect, RGB displays dark to light. Now think about it: RGB is generated with light, and no RGB means that there's no light and you therefore have black. Turn all RGB on full force, and you create white. Try pointing three filtered lights, one red, one green, and one blue. The three lights pointed in one direction really do create white.

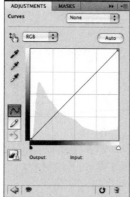

Figure 7-9: Access the Curves panel with the Create New Fill or Adjustment Layer button.

Book II
Chapter 7

Creating a Good Image

If working with RGB confuses you, simply select Curve Display Options from the panel menu in the upper-right corner of the Adjustments panel. When the Curves Display dialog box appears, as shown in Figure 7-10, select the Pigment/Ink % radio button and click OK.

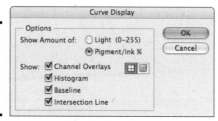

Figure 7-10: View the curve using light or pigment.

If you need a little more space in the Curves panel, click the Expanded View button at the bottom of the Curves panel. The panel enlarges.

Note that in the Curves panel, you see a Preset drop-down list that offers quick fixes using standard curves for certain corrections. These settings are great for quick fixes, but for the best image, create a custom curve.

The first thing you need to do in the Curves panel is determine the lightest and the darkest parts of the image, which is referred to as locating the highlight and shadow:

1. **Before starting the correction, click once on the Set Black Point eyedropper (as shown in Figure 7-11).**

Set Gray Point

Set Black Point   Set White Point

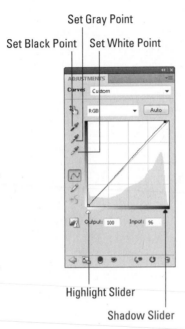

Figure 7-11: The critical tools on the Curves panel.

Highlight Slider

Shadow Slider

2. **Hold down the Alt (Windows) or Option (Mac) key and click the shadow input slider, as shown in Figure 7-11.**

   When you Alt/Option+click, the clipping preview turns on, revealing the darkest area of the image.

   If you don't immediately see a dark area in the clipping preview, you can drag the shadow input slider to the left while holding down the Alt/Option key.

3. **While still holding down the Alt/Option key, hold down the Shift key and click directly on the image in that dark region.**

   This drops a color sampler on the image that will help you reference that point later.

4. **Repeat Steps 1–3 with the highlight input slider. Select the Set White Point eyedropper in the Curves panel.**

5. **Hold down the Alt/Option key and click the highlight input slider.**

Again, you can drag the slider toward the right if the lightest point doesn't immediately show up.

When you locate the lightest point, as indicated by the lightest point in the clipping preview, you can (still holding down on the Alt/Option key) Shift+click it to drop a second color sampler. See Figure 7-12.

Figure 7-12:
With the Set White Point eyedropper selected, you can Alt/Option+ Shift-click to drop a color sampler.

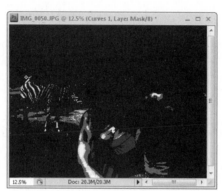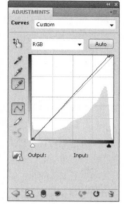

Setting the highlight and shadow values

Now that you've determined the lightest and darkest points in the image, set their values:

1. **Set the highlight values by double-clicking the Set White Point eyedropper (the white eyedropper on the left side of the Curves panel).**

When you double-click the Set White Point eyedropper, the Color Picker dialog box appears.

2. **Enter a generic value for the lightest point in your image: Type 5 into the Cyan text box, type 3 into the Magenta text box, type 3 into the Yellow text box, leave the Black text box at 0 (zero), and then click OK.**

The Black value helps to correct most images for print and online.

3. **With the Set White Point eyedropper still selected, click once on the color sampler that you dropped on the image, indicating the lightest point in the image.**

Now, set your shadow point.

4. **Double-click the Set Black Point eyedropper.**

The Color Picker dialog box appears.

5. **Type** 65 **in the Cyan text box, type** 53 **in the Magenta text box, type** 51 **in the Yellow text box, type** 95 **into the Black text box, and then click OK.**

   As with the highlight value, the Black value is a generic value that works for most print and online images.

6. **With the Set Black Point eyedropper still selected, click once on the color sampler that you dropped on the image, indicating the darkest point in the image.**

Adjusting the midtone

You may have heard the statement, "Open up the midtones." This phrase essentially means that you're lightening the midtonal values of an image. In many cases, opening up the midtones is necessary to add contrast and bring out detail in your image.

To adjust the midtones, follow these steps:

1. **In the Curves panel, click the middle of the curve ramp to create an anchor point; drag up slightly.**

   The image lightens. (If you're in Pigment/Ink % mode, drag down to lighten the image.) Don't move a dramatic amount and be very careful to observe what's happening in your Histogram panel (which you should always have open when making color corrections).

   Because you set highlight and shadow (see preceding section) and are now making a midtone correction, you see the bars in the histogram spreading out.

2. **To adjust the three-quarter tones (the shades around 75 percent), click halfway between the bottom of the curve ramp and the midpoint to set an anchor point.**

   Use the grid in the Curves panel to find it easily. (In Pigment/Ink %, the three-quarter point is in the upper section of the color ramp.) Adjust the three-quarter area of the tone curve up or down slightly to create contrast in the image. Again, keep an eye on your histogram!

   If you're working on a grayscale image, your tonal correction is done.

   If you're working on a color image, keep the Curves panel open for the final steps, which are outlined in the next section.

Finding a neutral

The last steps in creating a tone curve apply only if you're working on a color image. The key to understanding color is knowing that equal amounts of color create gray. By positioning the mouse cursor over gray areas in an image and reading the values in the Info panel, you can determine what colors you need to adjust.

1. **With your Curves panel open, position it so that you can see the Info panel.**

   If the Info panel is buried under another panel or a dialog box, choose Window➪Info to bring it to the front.

2. **Position your cursor over your image and, in the Info panel, look for the RGB values in the upper-left section.**

   You see color values and then forward slashes and more color values. The numbers before the slash indicate the values in the image before you opened the Curves panel; the numbers after the slash show the values now that you've made changes in the Curves panel. Pay attention to the values after the slashes.

3. **Position the cursor over something gray in your image.**

   It can be a shadow on a white shirt, a counter top, a road — anything that's a shade of gray. Look at the Info panel. If your image is perfectly color balanced, the RGB values following the forward slashes should all be the same.

4. **If your color isn't balanced, click the Set Gray Point eyedropper in the Curves panel and click the neutral or gray area of the image.**

   The middle eyedropper (Set Gray Point) is a handy way of bringing the location that you click closer together in RGB values, thereby balancing the colors.

Curves can be as complex or as simple as you make them. As you gain more confidence using them, you can check neutrals throughout an image to ensure that all unwanted color casts are eliminated. You can even individually adjust each color's curve by selecting it from the Channel drop-down list in the Curves panel.

When you're finished with color correction, using the Unsharp Mask filter on your image is a good idea. Chapter 6 of this minibook shows you how to use this filter.

Editing an Adjustment Layer

You may go through a curve adjustment only to discover that some areas of the image are still too dark or too light. Because you used an adjustment layer, you can turn off the correction or change it over and over again with no degradation to the quality of the image. Here are the steps you can take if you still have additional adjustments to make to an image, such as lightening or darkening other parts of the image:

1. **Select the area of the image that needs adjustments.**

   See Chapter 4 of this minibook if you need a refresher on how to make selections in Photoshop.

Book II
Chapter 7

Creating a Good Image

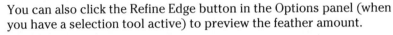

2. **Choose Select⇨Modify⇨Feather to soften the selection.**

   The Feather dialog box appears.

3. **Enter a value into the Feather dialog box.**

   If you're not sure what value will work best, enter **15** in the Feather Radius text field and click OK.

   You can also click the Refine Edge button in the Options panel (when you have a selection tool active) to preview the feather amount.

4. **If the Layers panel isn't visible, choose Windows⇨Layers; click and hold on the Create New Fill or Adjustment Layer icon and select Curves.**

5. **In the Curves panel, click the middle of the curve ramp to create an anchor point; drag up or down to lighten or darken your selected area.**

   Notice in the Layers panel (see Figure 7-13) that your adjustment layer, Curves 1 by default, has a mask to the right of it. This mask was automatically created from your selection. The selected area is white; unselected areas are black.

Figure 7-13: Paint on the adjustment layer mask.

6. **With your adjustment layer selected in the Layers panel, use the Brush tool to paint white to apply the correction to other areas of the image; paint with black to exclude areas from the correction.**

   You can even change the opacity with the Brush tool in the Options bar at the top to apply only some of the correction!

Testing a Printer

If you go through all the work of making color corrections to your images and you still get printed images that look hot pink, it may not be you! Test your printer by following these steps:

1. **Create a neutral gray out of equal RGB values (double-click the Fill Color swatch in the Tools panel).**

2. **Create a shape, using your neutral gray as the fill color.**

   For example, you can use the Ellipse tool to create a circle or oval.

3. **Choose File⇨Print and click OK to print the image from your color printer.**

If you're seeing heavy color casts, adjust your printer; cleaning or replacing the ink cartridge may fix the problem. Check out Chapter 10 of this minibook for more about printing your Photoshop files.

**Book II
Chapter 7**

Creating a Good
Image

Chapter 8: Working with Painting and Retouching Tools

In This Chapter

✔ Working in the Swatches panel

✔ Getting to know foreground and background colors

✔ Introducing painting and retouching tools

✔ Discovering blending modes

✔ Saving presets for tools

*T*his chapter shows you how to use the painting and retouching tools in Photoshop. If you're unsure about how good the painting you're about to do will look, create a new layer and paint on that. (See Chapter 9 of this minibook to find out how to create and use layers.) That way, you can delete the layer by dragging it to the Trash Can (at the bottom of the Layers panel) if you decide that you don't like what you've done. Don't forget to make the Eraser tool your friend! You can also repair painting or retouching mistakes by Alt+dragging (Windows) or Option+dragging (Mac) with the Eraser tool selected to erase the last version saved or present history state.

Have fun and be creative! Because Photoshop is pixel-based, you can create incredible imagery with the painting tools. Smooth gradations from one color to the next, integrated with blending modes and transparency, can lead from super-artsy to super-realistic effects. In this chapter, you discover painting fundamentals, and we show you how to use retouching tools to eliminate wrinkles, blemishes, and scratches. Don't you wish you could do that in real life?

Using the Swatches Panel

Use the Swatches panel to store and retrieve frequently used colors. The Swatches panel allows you to quickly select colors. The Swatches panel also gives you access to many other color options. By using the panel menu, you can select from a multitude of different color schemes, such as Pantone or Web-safe color sets. These color systems are converted to whatever color mode in which you're working.

To sample and store a color for later use, follow these steps:

1. **To sample a color from an image, select the Eyedropper tool in the Tools panel and click a color in the image.**

   Alternatively, you can use any of the paint tools (the Brush tool, for example) and Alt-click (Windows) or Option-click (Mac).

   The color you click becomes the foreground color.

2. **If the Swatches panel isn't already open, choose Window➪Swatches.**

3. **Store the color in the Swatches panel by clicking the New Swatch button at the bottom of the Swatches panel.**

Anytime you want to use that color again, simply click it in the Swatches panel to make it the foreground color.

Choosing Foreground and Background Colors

At the bottom of the Tools panel reside the foreground and background color swatches. The *foreground color* is the color that you apply when using any of the painting tools. The *background color* is the color that you see if you erase or delete pixels from the image.

Choose a foreground or background color by clicking the swatch, which opens the Color Picker dialog box. To use the Color Picker, you can either enter values in the text fields on the right, or you can slide the hue slider.

Pick the *hue* (color) that you want to start with and then click in the color panel to the left to choose the amount of light and saturation (grayness or brightness) you want in the color. Select the Only Web Colors check box to choose one of the 216 colors in the Web-safe color palette. The hexadecimal value used in HTML documents appears in the text field in the lower right of the Color Picker.

If you want to quickly save a color, click the Add to Swatches button right in the Color Picker.

The Painting and Retouching Tools

Grouped together in the Tools panel are the tools used for painting and retouching. The arrow in the lower right of a tool icon indicates that the tool has more related hidden tools; simply click and hold on the tool icon to see additional painting and retouching tools. In this chapter, we show you how to use the Spot Healing Brush, Healing Brush, Patch, Red Eye, Brush, Clone Stamp, History Brush, Eraser, and Gradient tools. You also discover ways to fill shapes with colors and patterns.

Changing the brush

As you click to select different painting tools, note the Brush menu (second from the left) on the Options bar, as shown in Figure 8-1. Click the arrow to open the Brushes Preset picker. You can use the Master Diameter slider to make the brush size larger or smaller, as well as change the hardness of the brush.

The hardness refers to how "fuzzy" the edges are; a softer brush is more feathered and soft around the edges, whereas a harder edge is more definite (see Figure 8-2).

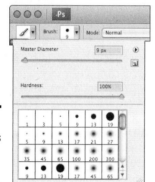

Figure 8-1:
The Brushes
Preset
picker.

Figure 8-2:
A soft edge
(left) as
compared to
a hard edge
(right) brush
stroke.

Don't feel like accessing the Brushes Preset picker every time you want to make a change? Press the right bracket] several times to make your brush diameter larger or press the left bracket [to make the brush diameter smaller. Press Shift+] to make the brush harder or Shift+[to make the brush softer.

Choose Window➪Brushes to see a list of brush presets, plus more brush options that you can use to create custom brushes. You can also choose other brush libraries with the panel menu. When you select an additional library, a dialog box appears, asking whether you want to replace the current brushes with the brushes in the selected library. Click the Append button to keep existing brushes and add the library to the list, or click OK to replace the existing brushes.

Access the Brushes Preset picker while you're painting by right-clicking (Windows) or Control-clicking (Mac) anywhere in the image area. Double-click a brush to select it; press Esc to hide the Brushes Preset picker.

The Spot Healing Brush tool

The Spot Healing Brush tool is destined to become everyone's favorite. Who wouldn't love a tool that can remove years from your face and any blemishes, too?

The Spot Healing Brush tool quickly removes blemishes and other imperfections in your images. Click a blemish and watch it paint matching texture, lighting, transparency, and shading to the pixels being healed. The Spot Healing Brush tool doesn't require you to specify a sample spot. The Spot Healing Brush automatically samples from around the retouched area.

The Healing Brush tool

You can use the Healing Brush tool for repairs, such as eliminating scratches and dust from scanned images. The difference between the Spot Healing Brush tool and the Healing Brush tool is that a sample spot is required before applying the Healing Brush. Follow these steps to use this tool:

1. **Select the Healing Brush tool in the Tools panel (it's a hidden tool of the Spot Healing Brush tool).**

2. **Find an area in the image that looks good and then Alt-click (Windows) or Option-click (Mac) to sample that area.**

   For example, if you'll eliminate wrinkles on a face, choose a wrinkle-free area of skin near the wrinkle. (Try to keep it relatively close in skin tone.)

3. **Position the mouse cursor over the area to be repaired and start painting.**

   The Healing Brush tool goes into action, blending and softening to create a realistic repair of the area.

4. **Repeat Steps 2 and 3 as necessary to repair the blemish, wrinkles, or scratches.**

The Patch tool

Hidden behind the Healing Brush tool in the Tools panel is the Patch tool. Use the Patch tool to repair larger areas, such as a big scratch or a large area of skin, by following these steps:

Book II
Chapter 8

Working with
Painting and
Retouching Tools

1. **Click and hold the Healing Brush tool to select the Patch tool; on the Options bar, select the Destination radio button.**

   You can either patch the source area or the destination. The preference is really up to you. We recommend taking a good source and dragging it over the area that needs repaired.

2. **With the Patch tool still selected, drag to create a marquee around the source that you want to use as the patch.**

   The source is an unscratched or wrinkle-free area.

3. **After you create the marquee, drag the selected source area to the destination that's to be repaired.**

   The Patch tool clones the selected source area while you drag it to the destination (the scratched area); when you release the mouse button, the tool blends in the source selection and repairs the scratched area!

Make the patch look better by choosing Edit⬎Fade Patch Selection immediately after you apply the patch. Adjust the opacity until no tell-tale signs show that you made a change.

The Red Eye tool

So you finally got the group together and shot the perfect image, but red eye took over! *Red eye* is caused by a reflection of the camera's flash in the retina of your photo's subject(s). You see it more often when taking pictures in a dark room because the subject's irises are wide open. If you can, use your camera's red-eye reduction feature. Or, better yet, use a separate flash unit that you can mount on the camera farther away from the camera's lens.

You'll love the fact that red eye is extremely easy to fix in Photoshop. Just follow these steps:

1. **Select the Red Eye tool (hidden behind the Spot Healing Brush tool).**

2. **Click and drag to surround the red eye.**

   You should see a change immediately, but if you need to make adjustments to the size or the darkness amount, you can change options in the Options bar.

The Brush tool

Painting with the Brush tool in Photoshop is much like painting in the real world. What you should know are all the nifty keyboard commands that you can use to be much more productive when painting. These shortcuts are really great, so make sure that you try them while you read about them. By the way, the keyboard commands you see in Table 8-1 work on all the painting tools.

Table 8-1	Brush Keyboard Shortcuts	
Function	*Windows*	*Mac*
Choose the Brush tool	B	B
Increase brush size	]	]
Decrease brush size	[	[
Harden brush	Shift+]	Shift+]
Soften brush	Shift+[	Shift+[
Sample color	Alt-click	Option-click
Switch foreground and background color	X	X
Change opacity by a given percentage	Type a number between 1 and 100	Type a number between1 and 100

If you're really into the brushes, you have lots of great options available in the Brushes panel (choose Window⇨Brushes to open the panel), as shown in Figure 8-3.

You have several choices of attributes, most of which have dynamic controls in the menu options that allow you to vary brush characteristics by tilting or applying more pressure to a stylus pen (if you're using a pressure-sensitive drawing tablet), among other things.

A warning sign indicates that you don't have the appropriate device attached to use the selected feature, such as a pressure-sensitive drawing tablet.

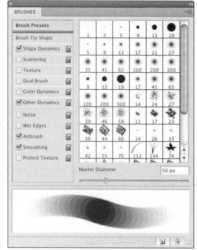

Figure 8-3:
Additional
options are
available for
painting in
the Brushes
panel.

The following options are available in the Brushes panel:

✦ **Brush Tip Shape:** Select from these standard controls for determining brush dimensions and spacing.

✦ **Shape Dynamics:** Change the size of the brush as you paint.

✦ **Scattering:** Scatter the brush strokes and control brush tip count.

✦ **Texture:** Choose from pre-existing patterns or your own.

Create a pattern by selecting an image area with the Rectangular Marquee tool. Choose Edit⇨Define Pattern, name the pattern, and then click OK. The pattern is now available in the Brushes panel's Texture choices.

✦ **Dual Brush:** Use two brushes at the same time.

✦ **Color Dynamics:** Change the color as you paint.

✦ **Other Dynamics:** Change the opacity and flow.

Here's what these attributes available in the Options bar do:

✦ **Noise:** Adds a grainy texture to the brush stroke.

✦ **Wet Edges:** Makes the brush stroke appear to be wet by creating a heavier amount of color on the edges of the brush strokes.

✦ **Airbrush:** Gives airbrush features to the Brush tools. Enable the Airbrush feature by clicking the Airbrush button and adjusting the pressure and flow on the Options bar.

If you click and hold with the Brush tool on the image area, the paint stops spreading. Turn on the Airbrush feature and notice that when you click and hold, the paint keeps spreading, just like with a can of spray paint. You can use the Flow slider on the Options bar to control the pressure.

✦ **Smoothing:** Smoothes the path created with the mouse.

✦ **Protect Texture:** Preserves the texture pattern when applying brush presets.

In addition to the preceding options, you can also adjust the jitter of the brush. The *jitter* specifies the randomness of the brush attribute. At 0 percent, an element doesn't change over the course of a stroke; at 100 percent, a stroke will totally vary from one attribute to another. For example, if you select Other Dynamics in the Brushes panel and then change the Opacity Jitter to 100 percent, the opacity will vary from 0 to 100 percent while you're painting.

After going through all the available brush options, you may want to start thinking about how you'll apply the same attributes later. Saving the Brush tool attributes is important as you increase in skill level.

The Clone Stamp tool

The Clone Stamp tool is used for pixel-to-pixel cloning. It's different from the Healing Brush tool in that it does no automatic blending into the target area. You can use the Clone Stamp tool for removing a product name from an image, replacing a telephone wire that is crossing in front of a building, or duplicating an item.

Here's how you use the Clone Stamp tool:

1. **With the Clone Stamp tool selected, position the cursor over the area that you want to clone and then Alt-click (Windows) or Option-click (Mac) to define the clone source.**

2. **Position the cursor over the area where you want to paint the cloned pixels and start painting.**

   Note the cross hair at the original sampled area, as shown in Figure 8-4. While you're painting, the cross hair follows the pixels that you're cloning.

When using the Clone Stamp tool for touching up images, it's best to resample many times so as to not leave a seam where you replaced pixels. A good clone stamper Alt-clicks (Windows) or Option-clicks (Mac) and paints many times over until the retouching is complete.

Choose Window⇨Clone Source to open the Clone Source panel, as shown in Figure 8-5. With this handy little panel, you can save multiple clone sources to refer to while working. Even better, you can scale, preview, and even rotate your clone source . . . before you even start cloning!

Figure 8-4: A cross hair over the source shows what you're cloning.

Figure 8-5: Additional options in the Clone Source panel.

The Clone Source panel can be extremely helpful with difficult retouching projects that involve a little more precision.

Follow these steps to experiment with this fun and interactive panel:

1. **If the Clone Source panel isn't visible, choose Window⇨Clone Source.**

   Note the Clone Source icons across the top. These are yet to be defined. The first stamp is selected as a default.

2. **Alt-click (Windows) or Option-click (Mac) in the image area to record the first clone source.**

3. **Click the second Clone Source icon at the top of the Clone Source panel and then Alt-click (Windows) or Option-click (Mac) somewhere else on the page to define a second clone source.**

   Repeat as needed to define more clone sources. You can click the Clone Source icons at any time to retrieve the clone source and start cloning.

4. **Enter any numbers you want in the Offset X and Y, W and H, and Angle text boxes in the center section of the Clone Source panel to set up transformations before you clone.**

5. **Select the Show Overlay check box to see a preview of your clone source.**

   Whatever you plan on doing, it's much easier to see a preview *before* you start cloning. If you don't use the Clone Source panel for anything else, use it to see a preview of your clone source before you start painting. If it helps to see the clone source better, select the Invert check box.

   You see an *overlay* (or preview) prior to cloning. This helps you to align your image better, which is great for precision work. If you want the preview to go away after you start cloning, select the Auto Hide check box.

The History Brush tool

Choose Window⇨History to see the History panel. You could work for weeks playing around in the History panel, but this section gives you the basics.

At the top of the History panel is a snapshot of the last saved version of the image. Beside the snapshot is an icon noting that it's the present History state.

 By default, when you paint with the History Brush tool, it'll paint back to the way the image looked at the last saved version, but you can click the empty square to the left of any state in the History panel to make it the target for the History Brush tool. Use the History Brush tool to fix errors and add spunk to images.

The Eraser tool

 You may not think of the Eraser tool as a painting tool, but it can be! When you drag on the image with the Eraser tool, it rubs out pixels to the background color. (Basically, it paints with the background color.) If you're dragging with the Eraser tool on a layer, it rubs out pixels to reveal the layer's transparent background. (You can also think of using the Eraser tool as painting with transparency.)

The Eraser tool uses all the same commands as the Brush tools. You can make an eraser larger, softer, and more or less opaque. But even better, follow these steps to use the Eraser tool creatively:

1. **Open any color image and apply a filter.**

   For example, we chose Filter⇨Blur⇨Gaussian Blur. In the Gaussian Blur dialog box that appeared, we changed the blur to 5 and then clicked OK to apply the Gaussian Blur filter.

2. **Select the Eraser tool and press 5 to change it to 50 percent opacity.**

   You can also use the Opacity slider on the Options bar.

3. **Hold down the Alt (Windows) or Option (Mac) key to paint back 50 percent of the original image's state before applying the filter.**

4. **Continue painting in the same area to bring the image back to its original state!**

   The original sharpness of the image returns where you painted.

Holding down the Alt (Windows) or Option (Mac) key is the key command to erase to the last saved version (or history state). This tool is incredible for fixing mistakes or removing applied filters.

The Gradient tool

Choose the Gradient tool and click and drag across an image area to create a gradient in the direction and length of the mouse motion. A short drag creates a short gradient; a long drag produces a smoother, longer gradient.

With the Options bar, you also can choose the type of gradient that you want: Linear, Radial, Angle, Reflected, or Diamond.

As a default, gradients are created using the current foreground and background colors. Click the arrow on the Gradient button on the Options bar to assign a different preset gradient.

To create a gradient, follow these steps:

1. **Choose the Gradient tool and click the Gradient Editor button on the Options bar.**

   The Gradient Editor dialog box appears. At the bottom of the gradient preview, you see two or more stops. The *stops* are where new colors are inserted into the gradient. They look like little house icons. Use the stops on the top of the gradient slider to determine the opacity.

2. **Click a stop and click the color swatch to the right of the word Color to open the Color Picker and assign a different color to the stop.**

3. **Click anywhere below the gradient preview to add more color stops.**

4. **Drag a color stop off the Gradient Editor dialog box to delete it.**

5. **Click the top of the gradient preview to assign different stops with varying opacity, as shown in Figure 8-6.**

6. **When you're finished editing the gradient, name it and then click the New button.**

   The new gradient is added to the preset gradient choices.

7. **To apply your gradient, drag across a selection or image with the Gradient tool.**

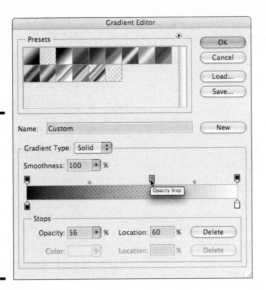

Figure 8-6:
Assigning
varying
amounts
of opacity
using the
stops on
top of the
gradient
slider.

Blending Modes

You can use blending modes to add flair to the traditional opaque paint. Use blending modes to paint highlights or shadows that allow details to show through from the underlying image or to colorize a desaturated image. You access the blending modes for paint tools from the Options bar.

You really can't get a good idea of how the blending mode works with the paint color and the underlying color until you experiment. (That's what multiple undos are for!) Alternatively, you can copy the image you want to experiment with onto a new layer and hide the original layer; see Chapter 9 of this minibook for more about layers.

The following list describes the available blending modes:

✦ **Normal:** Paints normally, with no interaction with underlying colors.

✦ **Dissolve:** Gives a random replacement of the pixels, depending on the opacity at any pixel location.

✦ **Behind:** Edits or paints only on the transparent part of a layer.

✦ **Darken:** Replaces only the areas that are lighter than the blend color. Areas darker than the blend color don't change.

✦ **Multiply:** Creates an effect similar to drawing on the page with magic markers. Also looks like colored film that you see on theater lights.

+ **Color Burn:** Darkens the base color to reflect the blend color. If you're using white, no change occurs.

+ **Linear Burn:** Looks at the color information in each channel and darkens the base color to reflect the blending color by decreasing the brightness.

+ **Darker Color:** Compares the total of all channel values for the blend and base color and displays the lower value color.

+ **Lighten:** Replaces only the areas darker than the blend color. Areas lighter than the blend color don't change.

+ **Screen:** Multiplies the inverse of the underlying colors. The resulting color is always a lighter color.

+ **Color Dodge:** Brightens the underlying color to reflect the blend color. If you're using black, there's no change.

+ **Linear Dodge:** Looks at the color information in each channel and brightens the base color to reflect the blending color by increasing the brightness.

+ **Lighter Color:** Compares the total of all channel values for the blend and base color and displays the higher value color.

+ **Overlay:** Multiplies or screens the colors, depending on the base color.

+ **Soft Light:** Darkens or lightens the colors, depending on the blend color. The effect is similar to shining a diffused spotlight on the artwork.

+ **Hard Light:** Multiplies or screens the colors, depending on the blend color. The effect is similar to shining a harsh spotlight on the artwork.

+ **Vivid Light:** Burns or dodges the colors by increasing or decreasing the contrast.

+ **Linear Light:** Burns or dodges the colors by decreasing or increasing the brightness.

+ **Pin Light:** Replaces the colors, depending on the blend color.

+ **Hard Mix:** Paints strokes that have no effect with other Hard Mix paint strokes. Use this mode when you want no interaction between the colors.

+ **Difference:** Subtracts either the blend color from the base color or the base color from the blend color, depending on which has the greater brightness value. The effect is similar to a color negative.

+ **Exclusion:** Creates an effect similar to, but with less contrast than, the Difference mode.

✦ **Hue:** Applies the hue (color) of the blend object onto the underlying objects but keeps the underlying shading or luminosity intact.

✦ **Saturation:** Applies the saturation of the blend color but uses the luminance and hue of the base color.

✦ **Color:** Applies the blend object's color to the underlying objects but preserves the gray levels in the artwork. This mode is great for tinting objects or changing their colors.

✦ **Luminosity:** Creates a resulting color with the hue and saturation of the base color and the luminance of the blend color. This mode is the opposite of the Color mode.

Painting with color

This section provides an example of using the blending modes to change and add color to an image. A great example of using a blending mode is tinting a black-and-white (grayscale) image with color. You can't paint color in Grayscale mode, so follow these steps to add color to a black-and-white image:

1. **Open an image in any color mode and choose Image⇨Mode⇨RGB.**

2. **If the image isn't already a grayscale image, choose Image⇨ Adjustments⇨Desaturate.**

This feature makes it appear as though the image is black and white, but you're still in a color mode with which you can apply color.

3. **Choose a painting tool (the Brush tool, for example) and, with the Swatches panel, choose the first color that you want to paint with.**

4. **On the Options bar, select Color from the Mode drop-down list and then use the Opacity slider to change the opacity to 50 percent.**

You could also just type **5**.

5. **Start painting!**

The Color Blending mode is used to change the color of the pixels, while keeping the underlying grayscale (shading) intact.

Another way to bring attention to a certain item in an RGB image (like those cute greeting cards that have the single rose in color and everything else in black and white) is to select the item you want to bring attention to. Choose Select⇨Modify⇨Feather to soften the selection a bit (5 pixels is a good number to enter in the Feather Radius text field). Then choose Select⇨ Inverse. Now with everything else selected, choose Image⇨Adjustments⇨ Desaturate. Everything else in the image looks black and white, except for the original item that you selected.

Filling selections

If you have a definite shape that doesn't lend itself to being painted, you can fill it with color instead. Make a selection and choose Edit➪Fill to access the Fill dialog box. From the Use drop-down list, you can choose from the following options to fill the selection: Foreground Color, Background Color, Color (to open the Color Picker while in the Fill dialog box), Pattern, History, Black, 50% Gray, or White.

If you want to use an existing or saved pattern from the Brushes panel, you can retrieve a pattern by selecting Pattern in the Fill dialog box as well. Select History from the Use drop-down list to fill with the last version saved or the history state.

 If you'd rather use the Paint Bucket tool, which fills based upon the tolerance set on the Options bar, it's hidden in the Gradient tool. To use the Paint Bucket tool to fill with the foreground color, simply click the item that you want to fill.

Saving Presets

All the Photoshop tools allow you to save presets so that you can retrieve them from a list of presets. The following steps show you an example of saving a Brush tool preset, but the same method can be used for all other tools as well:

1. **Choose a brush size, color, softness, or anything!**

2. **Click the Tool Preset Picker button on the left side of the Options bar.**

3. **Click the triangle in the upper-right corner to access the fly-out menu and then choose New Tool Preset.**

   The New Tool Preset dialog box appears.

4. **Type a descriptive name in the Name text field (leave the Include Color check box selected if you want the preset to also remember the present color) and then click OK.**

5. **Access the preset by clicking the tool's Preset Picker button and choosing it from the tool's Preset Picker list.**

Each preset that you create is specific to the tool that it was created in, so you can have a crop preset, an eraser preset, and so on. After you get in the habit of saving presets, you'll wonder how you ever got along without them!

Chapter 9: Using Layers

In This Chapter

✔ **Discovering layers**

✔ **Using text as a layer**

✔ **Implementing layer masks**

✔ **Organizing layers**

✔ **Using Smart Objects**

✔ **Using 3D layers to create 3D objects**

✔ **Merging and flattening a layered image**

*L*ayers are incredibly helpful in production. By using layers, you can make realistic additions to an image that you can remove, edit, and control with blending modes and transparency. Unfortunately, to show you all the features of layers goes beyond what we can cover in this chapter. This chapter covers layer basics to get you started working with layers in Photoshop. We show you how to create composite images using easy layer features — just enough knowledge to get yourself into a pretty complex mess of layers! Even if you're an experienced Photoshop user, read this chapter to discover all sorts of neat key commands that can help you in your workflow.

If you're a video professional, you can open videos in Photoshop CS4. Photoshop Extended automatically creates a Movie layer, and with the Timeline, you can do pixel editing frame by frame!

New in Photoshop CS4 Extended, you can make regular layers into 3D files! Though many of the 3D features are beyond the scope of this book, you can discover enough to be dangerous in the "Experimenting with 3D Files" section.

Have fun with layers and don't worry if you mess up; you can always press F12 to revert the image to the state it was in at the last time you saved it.

Creating and Working with Layers

Layers make creating *composite images* (images pieced together from many other individual images) easy because you can separate individual elements of the composite onto their own layers. Much like creating collages by cutting pictures from magazines, you can mask out selections on one image and place them on a layer in another image. When pixel information is on its own layer, you can move it, transform it, correct its color, or apply filters just to that layer, without disturbing pixel information on other layers.

The best way to understand how to create and use layers is to, well, create and use layers. The following steps show you how to create a new, layered image:

1. **Choose File⇨New to create a new document.**

   The New dialog box appears.

2. **Select Default Photoshop Size from the Preset Sizes drop-down list, select the Transparent option from the Background Contents area, and then click OK.**

   Because you selected the Transparent option, your image opens with an empty layer instead of a white background layer. The image appears as a checkerboard pattern, which signifies that it's transparent.

   If you don't like to see the default checkerboard pattern where there's transparency, choose Edit⇨Preferences⇨Transparency and Gamut (Windows) or Photoshop⇨Preferences⇨Transparency and Gamut (Mac). In the Preferences dialog box that appears, you can change the Grid Size drop-down list to None to remove the checkerboard pattern entirely. If you don't want to totally remove the transparency grid, you can change the size of the checkerboard pattern or change the color of the checkerboard.

   When you open an existing document (say a photograph), this image is your background layer.

3. **Create a shape on the new image.**

   For example, we created a black square by using the Rectangular Marquee tool to create a square selection; we then filled the selection with black by double-clicking the Foreground color swatch, selecting black from the Color Picker, and clicking in the selection with the Paint Bucket tool (hidden under the Gradient tool).

   After you select the color, you can also use the key command Alt+Delete (Windows) or Option+Delete (Mac) to fill the selected area with color.

4. **To rename the layer, double-click the layer name (Layer 1) in the Layers panel and type a short, descriptive name.**

   A good practice is to name your layers based on what they contain; for this example, we named the layer we created in Step 3 with the catchy name *square*.

5. **Create a new layer by Alt-clicking (Windows) or Option-clicking (Mac) the New Layer button at the bottom of the Layers panel.**

   The New Layer dialog box appears.

6. **Give your new layer a descriptive name and then click OK.**

7. **Create a shape on the new layer.**

   We created a red circle by using the Elliptical Marquee tool and filling the selection with red.

   The new shape can overlap the shape on the other layer, as shown in Figure 9-1.

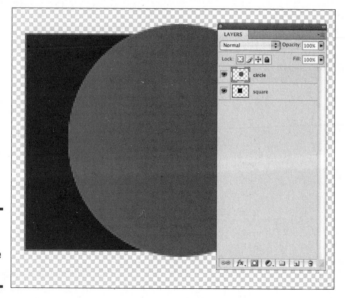

Figure 9-1:
The circle
overlaps the
square.

Duplicating a layer

Perhaps you want to create a duplicate of a layer for your composite. This technique can be helpful for do-it-yourself drop shadows, as well as adding elements to an image, such as more apples in a bowl of fruit.

Alt+drag (Windows) or Option+drag (Mac) a layer to the New Layer button at the bottom of the Layers panel to duplicate it. Again, by holding down Alt (Windows) or Option (Mac), you can name the layer while you create it.

Selecting a layer

When you start working with layers, you may find yourself moving or adjusting pixels, only to discover that you accidentally edited pixels on the wrong layer. Select the layer that you plan to work on by clicking the layer name in the Layers panel.

Unlike previous versions of Photoshop, Photoshop CS4 represents a selected layer by simply highlighting the layer in the Layers panel. The indicator paintbrush icon is gone in this version.

Here are some tips to help you select the correct layer:

✦ Select the Move tool and then right-click (Windows) or Control-click (Mac) to see a contextual menu listing all layers that have pixel data at the point you clicked and to choose the layer that you want to work with.

✦ Get in the habit of holding down the Ctrl (Windows) or ⌘ (Mac) key while using the Move tool and when selecting layers. This technique temporarily turns on the Auto Select feature, which automatically selects the topmost visible layer that contains the pixel data that you clicked.

✦ Press Alt+[(Windows) or Option+[(Mac) to select the next layer down from the selected layer in the stacking order.

✦ Press Alt+] (Windows) or Option+] (Mac) to select the next layer up from the selected layer in the stacking order.

Controlling the visibility of a layer

Hide layers that you don't immediately need by clicking the Eye icon in the Layers panel. To see only one layer, Alt-click (Windows) or Option-click (Mac) the eye icon of the layer you want to keep visible. Alt-click (Windows) or Option-click (Mac) the Eye icon again to show all layers.

Rearranging the stacking order

Layers are like clear pieces of film lying on top of each other. Change the stacking order of the layers in the Layers panel by dragging a layer until you see a black separator line appear, indicating that you're dragging the layer to that location. You can also use these great commands to help you move a layer:

Command	Windows Shortcut	Mac Shortcut
Move selected layer up	Ctrl+]	⌘+]
Move selected layer down	Ctrl+[	⌘+[

Creating a Text Layer

When you create text in Photoshop, the text is created on its own layer. By having the text separate from the rest of your image, applying different styles and blending modes to customize the type, as well as repositioning the text, is simplified.

To create a text layer, choose the Type tool and click the image area. You can also click and drag to create a text area. The Options bar, as shown in Figure 9-2, gives you the controls to change font, size, blending mode, and color of the text.

When you're finished typing you must confirm your text entry by selecting the check box (on the right of the Options bar) or pressing Ctrl+Enter (Windows) or ⌘+Return (Mac)

Toggle the Character and Paragraph Panels

Font
Family

Font
Size

Left, Center,
and Right Align

Figure 9-2:
The Text
tool options.

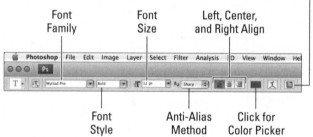

Font
Style

Anti-Alias
Method

Click for
Color Picker

 ## Warping text

When you click the Create Warped Text button on the Options bar, the Warp Text dialog box appears. This dialog box enables you to apply different types of distortion to your text.

You can still edit text that's been warped. To remove a warp, click the Create Warp Text button again and select None from the Style drop-down list.

Fine-tuning text

For controls such as leading, baseline shift, and paragraph controls, click the Toggle the Character and Paragraph Panels icon near the right end of the Options bar.

Use the keyboard commands in Table 9-1 to fine-tune text in Photoshop. Make sure that you have text selected when you use these shortcuts.

Table 9-1	Helpful Typesetting Key Commands	
Function	*Windows*	*Mac*
Increase font size	Shift+Ctrl+>	Shift+⌘+>
Decrease font size	Shift+Ctrl+<	Shift++⌘+<
Increase kerning (cursor must be between two letters)	Alt+→	Option+→
Decrease kerning (cursor must be between two letters)	Alt+←	Option+←
Increase tracking (several letters selected)	Alt+→	Option+→
Decrease tracking (several letters selected)	Alt+←	Option+←
Increase or decrease leading (several lines selected)	Alt+↑ or Alt+↓	Option+↑ or Option+↓

To change the font, drag over the font family name on the Options bar and then press the up-arrow key (↑) to go up in the font list or the down-arrow key (↓) to go down in the font list.

After you're finished editing text, confirm or delete the changes by clicking the buttons on the right of the Options bar.

If you'd rather use key commands to confirm or delete your changes, press the Esc key to cancel text changes; press Ctrl+Enter (Windows) or ⌘+Return (Mac) to commit text changes (or use the Enter key on the numeric keypad).

Using Layer Masks

In this section, we show you how to create a layer mask from a selection or a pen path. A *layer mask* covers up areas of the image that you want to make transparent and exposes pixels that you want visible. Masks can be based upon a selection that you've created with the selection tools, by painting on the mask itself, or by using the Pen tool to create a path around the object you want to keep visible.

Creating a layer mask from a selection

You need to have two images open to follow these steps where we show you how to create layer masks from a selection:

1. **When combining images, choose Image⇨Image Size to make sure that the images are approximately the same resolution.**

   Otherwise, you may create some interesting, but disproportional, effects.

2. **With the Move tool, click one image and drag it to the other image window.**

A black border appears around the image area when dropping an image into another image window. By dragging and dropping an image, you automatically create a new layer on top of the active layer.

Hold down the Shift key when dragging one image to another to perfectly center the new image layer in the document window.

3. **With any selection method, select a part of the image that you want to keep on the newly placed layer and choose Select⇨Modify⇨Feather to soften the selection (5 pixels should be enough).**

4. **Click the Layer Mask button at the bottom of the Layers panel.**

A mask is created off to the right of your layer, leaving only your selection visible, as shown in Figure 9-3.

5. **If you click the Layer thumbnail in the Layers panel, the mask thumbnail shows corner edges, indicating that it is activated.**

While the layer mask is active, you can paint on the mask.

6. **Press D to return to the default black-and-white swatch colors in the Tools panel.**

Figure 9-3: Click Layer Mask to create a custom mask from an active selection.

7. **Select the Brush tool and paint black while the mask thumbnail is selected to cover up areas of the image that you don't want to see; press X to switch to white and paint to expose areas on the image that you do want to see.**

You can even change the opacity while you paint to blend images in with each other.

To create a smooth transition from one image to another, drag the Gradient tool across the image while the layer mask is selected in the Layers panel.

Creating a vector mask from a pen path

A *vector mask* masks a selection, but it does so with the precision that you can get only from using a path. The following steps show you another, slightly more precise, way to create a layer mask by using a pen path:

1. **Use the Pen tool and click from point to point to make a closed pen path.**

   If you already have a path, choose Windows⇨Paths and click a path to select it.

   See Chapter 5 of this minibook for more about working with the Pen tool.

2. **On the Layers panel, click the Layer Mask button and then click it again.**

   Wow! A mask from your pen path! Anything that wasn't contained within the path is now masked out. Use the Direct Selection tool to edit the path, if necessary.

If you no longer want a vector mask, drag the thumbnail to the Trash Can in the Layers panel. An Alert dialog box appears, asking if you want to discard the mask or apply it. Click the Discard button to revert your image to the way it appeared before applying the mask or click the Apply button to apply the masked area.

Organizing Your Layers

As you advance in layer skills, you'll want to keep layers named, neat, and in order. In this section, we show you some tips to help you organize multiple layers.

Activating multiple layers simultaneously

Select multiple layers simultaneously by selecting one layer and then Shift-clicking to select additional layers. The selected layers are highlighted. Selected layers will move and transform together, making repositioning and resizing easier than activating each layer independently.

Select multiple layers to keep their relative positions to each other and take advantage of alignment features. When you select two or more layers and choose the Move tool, you can take advantage of alignment features on the Options bar (see Figure 9-4). Select three or more layers for distribution options.

Align Horizontal Centers

Align
Bottom

Distribute
Bottom Edges

Distribute
Top
Edges

Distribute
Horizontal
Centers

Figure 9-4:
Align
layers with
the Move
tool align
options.

Align
Top

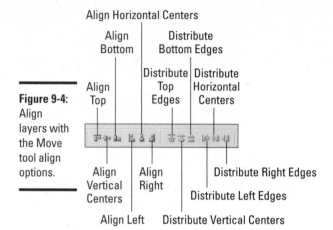

Align
Vertical
Centers

Align
Right

Distribute Right Edges

Distribute Left Edges

Align Left   Distribute Vertical Centers

Auto-Align Layers tool

Ever have multiple shots of a group, one with the guy's eyes shut, and the girl looking the other way? Or maybe you like the smile in one better than in another. With the auto-alignment feature, you can pull the best parts of multiple images into one "best" image.

To use this new tool, simply have the Move tool active, select multiple layers, and then click the Auto-Align Layers button to the right of the alignment tools. The Auto-Align Layer dialog box appears, as shown in Figure 9-5; make your selection and click OK.

Figure 9-5:
The new
Auto-Align
Layers
feature can
help create
a better
composite.

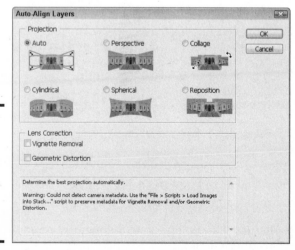

Layer groups

After you start using layers, you'll likely use lots of them, and your Layers panel will become huge. If you find yourself scrolling to navigate from one layer to another, take advantage of *layer groups,* which essentially act as folders that hold layers that you choose. Just like a folder you use for paper, you can add, remove, and shuffle around the layers within a layer group. Use layer groups to organize your layers and make the job of duplicating multiple layers easier.

To create a layer group, follow these steps:

1. **After creating several layers, Shift-click to select the layers that you want to group together in a set.**

2. **Choose New Group from Layers from the Layers panel menu, name the group, and then click OK.**

   That's it. You've created a layer group from your selected layers.

With the Blending Mode drop-down list in the Layers panel, you can change all the layers within a group to a specific blending mode, or you can use the Opacity slider to change the opacity of all layers in a group at once. *Pass through* in the blending mode indicates that no individual blending modes are changed.

After you create a layer group, you can still reorganize layers within the group or even drag additional layers in or out. You can open and close a layer group with the arrow to the left of the group name.

Duplicating a layer group

After you create a layer group, you may want to copy it. For example, you may want to copy an image, such as a button created from several layers topped off with a text layer. The most efficient way to make a copy of that button is to create a layer group and copy the entire group. To copy an image made up of several layers that aren't in a layer group would require you to individually duplicate each layer — how time-consuming!

To duplicate a layer group, follow these steps:

1. **Select a group from the Layers panel.**

2. **From the panel menu, choose Duplicate Group.**

   The Duplicate Group dialog box appears.

3. **For the destination, choose the present document or any open document or create a new document.**

   Be sure to give the duplicated set a distinctive name!

4. **Click OK.**

Using Layer Styles

Layer styles are wonderful little extras that you can apply to layers to create drop shadows, bevel and emboss effects, apply color overlays, gradients, patterns and strokes, and more.

Applying a style

To apply a layer style (for example, the drop shadow style, one of the most popular effects) to an image, follow these steps:

1. **Create a layer on any image.**

For example, you could create a text layer to see the effects of the layer styles.

**Book II
Chapter 9**

2. **With the layer selected, click and hold the Layer Style button at the bottom of the Layers panel; from the menu options, choose Drop Shadow.**

In the Layer Style dialog box that appears, you can choose to change the blending mode, color, distance spread, and size of a drop shadow. You should see the style has already applied to your text. Position the cursor on the image area and drag to visually adjust the position of the drop shadow.

Using Layers

3. **When you're happy with the drop shadow, click OK to apply it.**

To apply another effect and change its options, click and hold the Layer Style button in the Layers panel and choose the name of the layer style from the menu that appears — Bevel and Emboss, for example. In the dialog box that appears, change the settings to customize the layer style and click OK to apply it to your image. For example, if you choose Bevel and Emboss from the Layer Styles menu, you can choose from several emboss styles and adjust the depth, size, and softness.

Here are some consistent items that you see in the Layer Style dialog box, no matter what effect you choose:

✦ **Contour:** Use contours to control the shape and appearance of an effect. Click the arrow to open the Contour fly-out menu to choose a contour preset or click the contour preview to open the Contour Editor and create your own edge.

✦ **Angle:** Drag the cross hair in the angle circle or enter a value in the Angle text field to control where the light source comes from.

✦ **Global light:** If you aren't smart about lighting effects on multiple objects, global light makes it seem as though you are. Select the Use Global Light check box to keep the angle consistent from one layer style to another.

✦ **Color:** Whenever you see a color box, you can click it to select a color. This color can be for the drop shadow, highlight, or shadow of an emboss, or for a color overlay.

Creating and saving a style

If you come up with a combination of attributes that you like, click the New Style button in the upper right of the Layer Style dialog box. Name the style, and it's now stored in the Styles panel. After you click OK, you can retrieve the style at any time by choosing Window➪Styles. If it helps, click the panel menu button and choose either Small or Large List to change the Styles panel to show only the name of the styles.

After you apply a layer style to a layer, the style is listed in the Layers panel. You can turn off the visibility of the style by turning off the Eye icon or even throw away the layer style by dragging it to the Layers panel's Trash Can.

Thinking about opacity versus fill

In the Layers panel, you have two transparency options — one for opacity and one for fill. Opacity affects the opacity of the entire layer, including effects. Fill, on the other hand, affects only the layer itself, but not layer styles. Figure 9-6 shows what happens when the Bevel and Emboss style is applied to text and the fill is reduced to 0 percent — it looks like the text was embossed onto the image. You can do lots of neat stuff with the Layer Fill feature!

Figure 9-6: A text layer with styles applied and the fill reduced to 0 percent.

Smart, Really Smart! Smart Objects

Choose File➪Place and place an image, illustration, or even a movie into a Photoshop document and discover that, as always, a new layer is created, but even better than that, a Smart Object is created. The icon in the lower right of the layer thumbnail indicates that this layer is a Smart Object.

What does being a Smart Object mean? It means that you have much more flexibility with the placement of your images. Have you ever placed a logo, to find out later you need it to be three times the size? Resizing is no longer an issue, as the Photoshop Smart Object is linked to an embedded original. If the original is vector, you can freely resize the image over and over again without worrying about poor resolution. Want to change the spelling of your placed Illustrator logo? Just double-click the Smart Object, and the embedded original is opened right in Adobe Illustrator. Make your changes, save the file, and *violá* . . . the file's automatically updated in the Photoshop file.

What could be better than this? Smart Filters, of course. You can apply Smart Filters to any Smart Object layer, or even convert a layer to use Smart Filters, by choosing Filters➪Convert for Smart Filters. After a layer's been converted to a Smart Object, you can choose filters, any filters, and apply them to the layer. If you want to paint out the effects of the filter on the layer, simply paint with black on the Filter Effects thumbnail. Paint with different opacities of black and white to give an artistic feel to the filter effect, as shown in Figure 9-7. You can even turn off the filters by turning off the visibility on the Filter Effects thumbnail by clicking the Eye icon to the left of the Filter Effects thumbnail.

**Book II
Chapter 9**

Using Layers

Figure 9-7:
Cover the filter effects by painting on the Filter Effects thumbnail.

Experimenting with 3D Files

As previously mentioned, working with 3D files is beyond the scope of this book, but even a 3D novice can experiment with the new 3D features implemented in Photoshop CS4. Follow these steps to try out some 3D features on your own:

1. **Create a new Photoshop document.**

   You can choose the Default Photoshop Size, but make sure that the Background Contents drop-down list is set to Transparent.

2. **Select the Type tool, click in the image area, and type any word.**

   In this example, we typed **3D**.

3. **Select the Move tool.**

4. **Choose 3D⇨Create New 3D Postcard from Layer.**

   The image looks like it's now on a perspective plane. Also, note that the type layer now has a 3D icon on the layer thumbnail in the Layers panel, as shown in Figure 9-8, indicating that this is now a 3D layer.

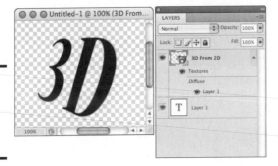

Figure 9-8: Creating a 3D layer in Photoshop CS4.

5. **Experiment with angle and positioning by clicking and dragging on your 3D layer with the 3D Rotate tool and the 3D Orbit tool.**

   Notice that these tools have additional options available in the Options bar across the top of your Photoshop document.

Merging and Flattening the Image

Merging layers combines several selected layers into one layer. *Flattening* is when you reduce all layers to one background layer. Layers can increase your file in size, thereby also tying up valuable processing resources. To keep file size down, you may choose to merge some layers or even flatten the entire image down to one background layer.

Merging

Merging layers is helpful when you no longer need every layer to be independent, like when you have a separate shadow layer aligned to another layer and don't plan on moving it again, or when you combine many layers to create a composite and want to consolidate it to one layer.

To merge layers (in a visual and easy way), follow these steps:

1. **Turn on the visibility of only the layers that you want merged.**

2. **Choose Merge Visible from the Layers panel menu.**

    That's it. The entire image isn't flattened, but the visible layers are now reduced to one layer.

To merge visible layers onto a *target* (selected) layer that you create while keeping the visible layers independent, do the following: Create a blank layer and select it. Hold down Alt (Windows) or Option (Mac) when choosing Merge Visible from the panel menu.

Flattening

If you don't have to flatten your image, don't! Flattening your image reduces all layers to one background layer, which is necessary for certain file formats, but after you flatten an image, you can't take advantage of blending options or reposition the layered items. (Read more about saving files in Chapter 10 of this minibook.)

If you absolutely must flatten layers, keep a copy of the original, unflattened document for additional edits in the future.

To flatten all layers in an image, choose Layer⇨Flatten Image or choose Flatten Image from the panel menu on the Layers panel.

**Book II
Chapter 9**

Using Layers

Chapter 10: Saving Photoshop Images for Print and the Web

In This Chapter

✔ Determining the correct file formats for saving

✔ Preparing your images for the Web

✔ Discovering the color table

✔ Saving your settings

A productive workflow depends on you choosing the proper format in which to save your Photoshop files. Without the correct settings, your file may not be visible to other applications, or you may delete valuable components, such as layers or saved selections. This chapter provides you with the necessary information to save the file correctly for both print and the Web. We cover the file format choices before moving on to the proper use of the Save for Web & Devices feature (for saving in the GIF, JPEG, PNG, and WBMP file formats).

 Saving files in the correct file format is important not only for file size, but in support of different Photoshop features, as well. If you're unsure about saving in the right format, save a copy of the file, keeping the original in the PSD format (the native Photoshop format). Photoshop alerts you automatically when you choose a format in the Save As or the Save for Web & Devices dialog box that doesn't support Photoshop features. When you choose a format that doesn't support some of the features you've used, such as channels or layers, a yield sign appears when a copy is being made. Now with the ability of all the Adobe applications (and even non-Adobe applications) to read native Photoshop (.psd) files, it's wise to keep files in this native file format unless there's a compelling reason not to.

Choosing a File Format for Saving

When you choose File➪Save for the first time (or you choose File➪Save As to save a different version of a file), you see at least 18 different file formats that you can choose from in the Save as Type drop-down list. We don't cover each format in this chapter (some are specific to proprietary workflows), but we do show you which formats are best for the typical workflow that you may face.

Wonderful and easy Photoshop PSD

If you're in an Adobe workflow (you're using any Adobe products), you can keep the image in the native Photoshop PSD format. By choosing this format, transparency, layers, channels, and paths are all maintained and left intact when placed in the other applications.

If compatibility with older versions of Photoshop is an issue, choose Edit➪Preferences➪File Handling (Windows) or Photoshop➪Preferences➪File Handling (Mac). Choose Always from the Maximize PSD and PSB File Compatibility drop-down list. This choice saves a *composite* (flattened) image along with the layers of your document. (PSB is a format used for saving large Photoshop documents over 30,000 by 30,000 pixels in size.)

Leaving the Maximize PSD and PSB File Compatibility drop-down list set to Always creates a larger file. If file size is an issue, leave the drop-down list set to Ask and only use the feature when you need to open the Photoshop file in older versions of Photoshop.

Photoshop EPS

Virtually every desktop application accepts the EPS (Encapsulated PostScript) file format. The EPS format is used to transfer PostScript-language artwork between various applications. It supports vector data, duotones, and clipping paths.

When you choose to save in the EPS format, an EPS Options dialog box appears. Leave the defaults and click OK.

Alter the settings in the EPS Options dialog box *only* if you're familiar with custom printer calibration, or if you need to save your image to a specific screen ruling. Screen rulings (*lpi,* lines per inch) are usually set in a page layout application, such as Adobe InDesign or QuarkXPress.

Photoshop PDF

If compatibility is an issue, save your file in the Photoshop PDF (Portable Document Format) format. PDF files are supported by more than a dozen platforms when viewers use Acrobat or Adobe Reader. (Adobe Reader is available for free at www.adobe.com.) What a perfect way to send pictures to friends and family! Saving your file in the Photoshop PDF format supports your ability to edit the image when you open the file by choosing File➪Open in Photoshop.

If you're planning to send a layered file by e-mail, it's a good idea to select Layer⇨Flatten Layers before choosing to save the file as a PDF. This cuts the file size considerably.

TIFF

TIFF (Tagged Image File Format) is a flexible bitmap image format that's supported by most image-editing and page-layout applications widely supported by all printers. TIFF supports layers and channels, but it has a maximum size of 4GB. We hope your files aren't that large!

DCS

The Photoshop DCS (Desktop Color Separation) 1.0 and 2.0 formats are versions of EPS that enable you to save color separations of CMYK (Cyan, Magenta, Yellow, Black) or multichannel files. Some workflows require this format, but if you've implemented spot color channels in your image, using the DCS file format is required to maintain them.

Choose the DCS 2.0 format unless you received specific instructions to use the DCS 1.0 format — for example, for reasons of incompatibility in certain workflows.

Saving for the Web and Devices

To access the maximum number of options for the GIF, JPEG, PNG, and WBMP file formats, save your image by choosing File⇨Save for Web & Devices. The Save for Web & Devices dialog box appears, which allows you to optimize the image as you save it. This procedure may sound big, but it's just the process of making the image as small as possible while keeping it visually pleasing.

Saving images for the Web is a give-and-take experience. You may find yourself sacrificing perfect imagery to make the image small enough in size that it can be downloaded and viewed quickly by users. Read the upcoming sections on GIF and JPEG formats to see how you can best handle creating Web images.

The following sections describe the differences between GIF, JPEG, PNG, and WBMP. Choose the appropriate format based upon the type of image you're saving.

TIP

Having the image size correct before you save the file for the Web is a good practice. If you need to read up on resizing images, see Chapter 6 of this minibook. Generally speaking, you want to resize the image to the right pixel dimensions. Choose Filter⇨Sharpen⇨Unsharp Mask to gain back some of the detail lost when resizing the image and then save the image for the Web.

GIF

Supposedly, the way you pronounce GIF (Graphics Interchange Format) is based on the type of peanut butter you eat. Is it pronounced like the peanut butter brand (Jiff), or with a hard G, like gift? Most people seem to pronounce it like gift (minus the T).

Use the GIF format if you have large areas of solid color, such as a logo like the one shown in Figure 10-1.

Figure 10-1:
An image with lots of solid color makes a good GIF.

The GIF format isn't *lossy* (it doesn't lose data when the file is compressed in this format), but it does reduce the file size by using a limited number of colors in a color table. The lower the number of colors, the smaller the file size. If you've ever worked in the Index color mode, you're familiar with this process.

Transparency is supported by the GIF file format. Generally, GIFs don't do a good job with anything that needs smooth transitions from one color to another because of its poor support of anti-aliasing. *Anti-aliasing* is the method that Photoshop uses to smooth jagged edges. When an image transitions from one color to another, Photoshop produces multiple colors of pixels to create an even blend between the two colors.

Because anti-aliasing needs to create multiple colors for this effect, GIF files are generally not recommended. In fact, when you reduce a GIF in size, you're more apt to see *banding* because the anti-aliasing can't take place with the limited number of colors available in the GIF format.

You can, of course, dramatically increase the number of colors to create a smoother transition, but then you risk creating monster files that take forever to download.

Saving a GIF

When you choose File⇨Save For Web & Devices, you first see the available GIF format options. The GIF options may be more clear to you if you have an image (with lots of solid color) open.

To save a file for the Web as a GIF, follow these steps:

1. **Choose File⇨Save for Web & Devices.**

    The Save for Web & Devices dialog box appears.

2. **At the top, click the 2-Up tab.**

    You see the original image on the left and the optimized image on the right (or top and bottom, depending upon the proportions of your image).

    In the lower portion of the display, you see the original file size compared to the optimized file size, as well as the approximate download time. This time is important! Nobody wants to wait around for a Web page to load; most people won't wait more than ten seconds for the entire Web page to appear, so try to keep an individual image's download time down to five seconds or less. Remember, all the images on a page can add up to one monstrous wait time for the viewer!

    Change the download speed by choosing from the Preview menu (it's the arrow on the upper-right side of the Save for Web & Devices dialog box). The Preview menu isn't labeled, so look for the ToolTip to appear when you hover your cursor over the arrow icon.

3. **Choose GIF 32 No Dither from the Preset drop-down list.**

    You may see a change already. Photoshop supplies you with presets that you can choose from, or you can customize and save your own.

4. **Choose whether you want dithering applied to the image by selecting an option from the Specify the Dither Algorithm drop-down list.**

    This choice is purely personal. Because you may be limiting colors, Photoshop can use dithering to mix the pixels of the available colors to simulate the missing colors. Many designers choose the No Dither option because dithering can create unnatural color speckles in your image.

5. **If your image is on a transparent layer and you want to maintain that transparency on a Web page, select the Transparency check box.**

Using the color table in the Save for Web & Devices dialog box

When you save an image as a GIF using the Save for Web & Devices dialog box, you see the color table for the image on the right side of the dialog box. The color table is important because it not only allows you to see the colors used in the image, but also enables you to customize the color table by using the options at the bottom of the color table.

You may want to customize your color table by selecting some of your colors to be Web safe and locking colors so that they're not bumped off as you reduce the amount of colors.

To customize a color table, follow these steps:

1. **If your image has only a few colors that you want to convert to Web-safe colors, choose the Eyedropper tool from the left of the Save for Web & Devices dialog box and click the color, in the Optimized view.**

   The sampled color is highlighted in the color table.

2. **Click the Web Safe button at the bottom of the color table.**

   A ToolTip appears when you cross over this button with the text Shifts/Unshifts Selected Colors to Web panel.

   A diamond appears, indicating that the color is now Web safe.

3. **Lock colors that you don't want to delete as you reduce the number of colors in the color table.**

   Select a color with the Eyedropper tool or choose it in the color table and then click the Lock Color button. A white square appears in the lower-right corner, indicating that the color is locked.

   If you lock 32 colors and then reduce the color table to 24, some of your locked colors are deleted. If you choose to add colors, those locked colors are the first to return.

How is the color table created? Based upon a color reduction algorithm method that you choose, the Save for Web & Devices feature samples the number of colors that you indicate. If keeping colors Web safe is important, select the Restrictive (Web) option for the method; if you want your image to look better on most monitors but not necessarily be Web safe, choose the Adaptive option.

4. **Use the arrows to the right of the Colors combo box or enter a number to add or delete colors from the color table.**

5. **If your image uses transparency, select the Transparency check box.**

   Remember that transparency is counted as one of your colors in the color table.

6. **Select the Interlaced check box only if your GIF image is large in size (25K or larger).**

   Selecting this option causes the image to build in several scans on the Web page, a low-resolution image that pops up quickly to be refreshed with the higher resolution image when it's finished downloading. Interlacing gives the illusion of the download going faster but makes the file size larger, so use it only if necessary.

7. **Click Save.**

   Now the image is ready to be attached to an e-mail message or used in a Web page.

JPEG

JPEG (Joint Photographic Experts Group) is the best format for continuous tone images (those with smooth transitions from one color to another, as in photographs), like the image shown in Figure 10-2.

The JPEG format is lossy, so you shouldn't save a JPEG, open it, edit it, and save it again as a JPEG. Because the JPEG compression causes data to be lost, your image will eventually look like it was printed on a paper towel. Save a copy of the file as a JPEG, keeping the original image in the PSD format if you need to later edit the image, open the original PSD, make your changes, save the PSD, and then save a copy of the edited file as a JPEG.

The JPEG format does *not* support transparency, but you can cheat the system a little by using matting.

Figure 10-2: Images with smooth transitions from one color to another are good candidates for the JPEG file format.

A good image to save in the JPEG format is a typical photograph or illustration with lots of smooth transitions from one color to the next. To save an image as a JPEG, follow these steps:

1. **Choose File⇨Save for Web & Devices and then click the 2-Up tab to view the original image (left) at the same time as the optimized image (right).**

2. **Choose one of the JPEG preset settings from the Settings drop-down list.**

   You can choose Low, Medium, High, or customize a level in between the presets by using the Quality slider.

3. **Leave the Optimized check box selected to build the best JPEG at the smallest size.**

   The only issue with leaving this check box selected is that some very old browsers won't read the JPEG correctly. (This is probably not an issue for most of your viewers.)

4. **Leave the Embed Color Profile check box deselected unless you're in a color-managed workflow and color accuracy is essential.**

   Leaving this check box deselected dramatically increases the file size, and most people aren't looking for *exact* color matches from an image on the monitor.

5. **If you have to have the file size even smaller, use the Blur slider to bring down some detail.**

   It's funny, but one JPEG that's the exact same pixel dimensions as another may vary in file size because the more detailed an image, the more information is needed. So an image of lots of apples will be larger than an image the same size that has a lot of clear blue sky in it. The blur feature does blur the image (surprise!), so you may want to use this for only a Low Source image in Dreamweaver.

6. **(Optional) Choose a matte color from the Matte drop-down list.**

   Because JPEG doesn't support transparency, you can flood the transparent area with a color that you choose from the Matte drop-down list. Choose the color that you're using for the background of your Web page by choosing Other and entering the hexadecimal color in the lower portion of the Color Picker.

7. **Click Save.**

PNG

PNG (Portable Network Graphics) is almost the perfect combination of JPEG and GIF. Unfortunately, PNG isn't yet widely supported . . . note, as well, that PNG-24 images have file sizes that can be too large to use on the Web.

PNG supports varying levels of transparency and anti-aliasing. This variation means that you can specify an image as being 50-percent transparent, and it will actually show through to the underlying Web page! You have a choice of PNG-8 and PNG-24 in the Save for Web & Devices dialog box. As a file format for optimizing images, PNG-8 doesn't give you any advantage over a regular GIF file.

PNG files are *not* supported by all browsers. In older browsers, a plug-in may be required to view your page. Ouch . . . by choosing PNG, you could shoot yourself in the foot because not all your viewers can view the PNG.

If you're saving a PNG file, you have a choice of PNG-8 or PNG-24. The PNG-8 options are essentially the same as the GIF options; see the "Saving a GIF" section, earlier in this chapter, for details.

**Book II
Chapter 10**

PNG-24 saves 24-bit images that support *anti-aliasing* (the smooth transition from one color to another). They work beautifully for continuous-tone images but are much larger than a JPEG file. The truly awesome feature of a PNG file is that it supports 256 levels of transparency. In other words, you can apply varying amounts of transparency in an image, as shown in Figure 10-3, where the image shows through to the background.

Saving Photoshop Images for Print and the Web

Figure 10-3: A PNG-24 file with varying amounts of transparency.

WBMP

WBMP (Wireless BitMap) is a format optimized for mobile computing, has no compression, is one-bit color (just black and white, no shades!), and is one-bit deep. WBMP images aren't necessarily pretty, but they're functional (see Figure 10-4). You do have dithering controls to show some level of tone value.

If you're creating images for mobile devices, know that WBMP is part of the Wireless Application Protocol, Wireless Application Environment Specification Version 1.1.

TIP

Click the Preview in Default Browser button at the bottom of the Save for Web & Devices dialog box to launch your chosen Web browser and display the image as it will appear with the present settings. If you haven't set up a browser, click the down arrow and choose Other from the drop-down list. Browse to locate a browser that you want to preview your image in.

Want to see how your mobile content will look on specific devices? Click the Device Central button in the lower right of the Save for Web & Devices dialog box.

Figure 10-4: The WBMP format supports black and white only.

Matte

Matting appears as a choice in the JPEG, GIF, and PNG format options. Matting is useful if you don't want ragged edges appearing around your image. Matting looks for pixels that are greater than 50-percent transparent and makes them fully transparent; any pixels that are 50 percent or less transparent become fully opaque.

Even though your image might be on a transparent layer, there will be some iffy pixels, the ones that aren't sure what they want to be . . . to be transparent or not to be transparent. Choose a matte color to blend in with the transparent iffy pixels by selecting Eyedropper, White, Black, or Other (to open the Color Picker) from the Matte drop-down list in the Save for Web & Devices dialog box.

Saving Settings

Whether you're saving a GIF, a JPG, or a PNG file, you probably spent some time experimenting with settings to find what works best for your needs. Save your selected options to reload at a later time by saving the settings. Do so by clicking the arrow to the right of the Preset drop-down list. Choose Save Settings from the menu that appears and give your settings a name. Your named, customized settings then appear in the Preset drop-down list.

Book III
Illustrator CS4

Contents at a Glance

Chapter 1: What's New in Illustrator CS4

Yes, Adobe has done it again — the developers have created an even better Adobe Illustrator, and you can discover the best new features in this chapter. This chapter breezes through the new features to open your eyes to exciting new work methods. Don't forget to look for references to where you can get more in-depth knowledge in other locations in this minibook.

Finally! Multiple Artboards

For those of you who wished that you could produce multiple page documents in Illustrator, your wish has come true. Something should be said about the new multiple artboard feature because Illustrator isn't really the creation tool that you want to use to make multiple page documents, such as catalogs and books, but it's handy to be able to add artboards to spec sheets and technical drawings.

In the past, adding pages was done using a rather convoluted method of making a large artboard and then tiling the pages. Now you can create multiple artboards (up to 100!) as soon as the New Document dialog box appears.

Creating a document with multiple artboards

To create a document with multiple artboards, follow these steps:

1. **Launch Adobe Illustrator CS4 and choose File⇨New.**

   The New Document dialog box appears, as shown in Figure 1-1.

2. **Choose how many artboards you want to start with by entering a number in the Number of Artboards text box.**

3. **Click a grid icon to the right of the Number of Artboards text box to determine how you want the artboards laid out.**

With these grid boxes, you can set how many rows and columns you wish to use and you can also change the direction of the layout from left to right or right to left.

4. **Enter an amount in the Spacing text box to determine how far apart the artboards will be.**

Enter **0** (zero) if you want the artboards butting against each other or a higher value if you want some space between them.

5. **Click OK to create your new document.**

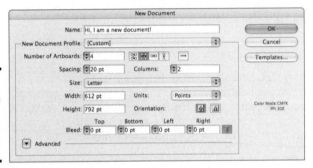

Figure 1-1:
Add multiple artboards right from the start.

Don't worry if you need to edit the artboards at a later time. You can edit them by choosing File➪Document Setup and then clicking the Edit Artboards button in the upper-right corner in the Document Setup dialog box. You can also click the Document Setup button on the Control Panel to get to this same dialog box, as shown in Figure 1-2.

Printing a document with multiple artboards

Pay close attention before you print a document with multiple artboards, or you may print needless pages. Here's how you can control the artboards that print:

1. **Choose File➪Print.**

The Print dialog box appears, as shown in Figure 1-3.

2. **Below the Preview box in the lower-left corner, click the arrows to preview the artboards.**

3. **After you determine which artboards you want to print, enter them into the Range text box.**

If you want to print all the artboards, make sure the All radio button is selected; otherwise enter a consecutive range, such as **1–3** in the Range text box. You can also print non-consecutive pages by separating them with a comma — enter **1, 5, 7** to print only artboards 1, 5 and 7.

4. **Click the Print button to print your selected artboards.**

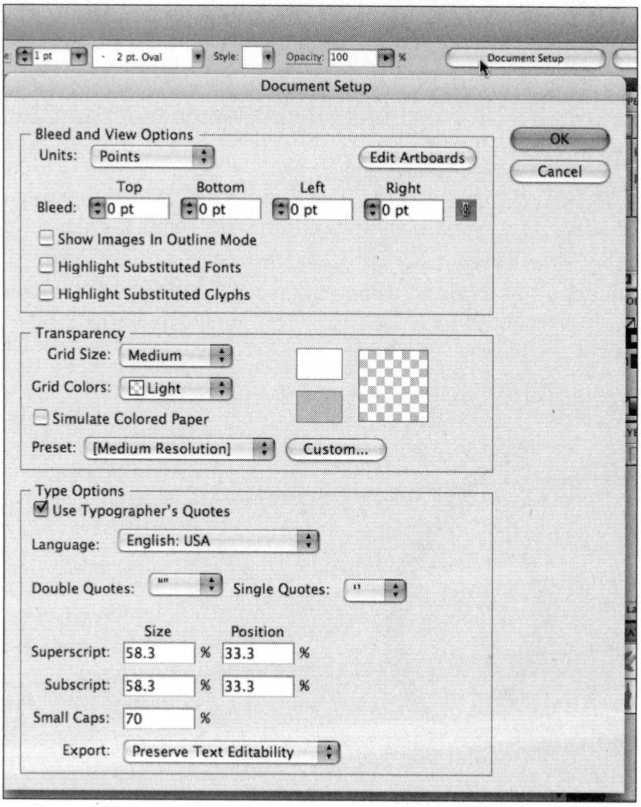

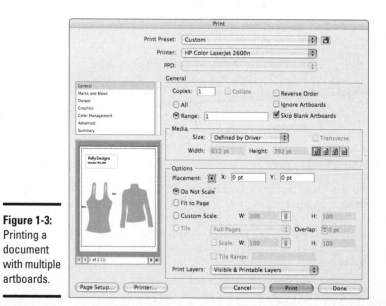

Figure 1-2:
Edit multiple artboards at any time.

Figure 1-3:
Printing a document with multiple artboards.

Fun with the New Blob Brush tool

A brush tool has been in Adobe Illustrator for quite some time, but now you can have the brush control that you have in other applications, such as Photoshop, right in Illustrator.

The Blob Brush is a new tool that's available as shown in Figure 1-4. When you use this tool, notice that it has a radial annotator that shows the size and shape of the current brush. So what's so great about that? Press the right bracket (]) and watch the stroke width of the brush automatically increase; press the left bracket ([) to decrease the width of the stroke.

Figure 1-4: Gain more brush freedom with the new Blob Brush tool.

This new brush tool makes drawing with the brush much more intuitive . . . no more searching for your stroke controls!

Improving Appearances with the Appearance Panel

It's always good to improve your appearance, and Illustrator has done just that with the Appearance panel. The Appearance panel is a huge resource for beginner users as well as power users because it keeps you informed of the attributes that are applied to a selected object.

Notice in Figure 1-5 that you can now choose fills and strokes easily, right in the Appearance panel. You can even duplicate fills and strokes in the Appearance panel, which gives you the ability to create all sorts of interesting combinations. Read more about the Appearance panel in Chapter 12 of this minibook.

Figure 1-5:
Added
controls
in the
Appearance
panel make
it easier
to apply
attributes.

Note that when you have multiple strokes applied to one object, a warning appears in the Control panel notifying you if the topmost stroke isn't selected. This saves you the trouble of applying a new stroke to the wrong stroke.

If you read through the following chapters in this minibook, you discover lots of other incredible additions to Adobe Illustrator CS4. Many of the improvements increase the speed of production and quality of output. Have fun and read on!

Chapter 2: Discovering Illustrator CS4

*A*dobe Illustrator goes hand in hand with the other Adobe products but serves its own unique purpose. Although Adobe Illustrator can create multiple-page artwork (with artboards), it's not meant to create lengthy documents with repeated headers, footers, and page numbers. Those types of files are more appropriate for applications like InDesign. Typically, you wouldn't create artwork from Illustrator that's made from pixels, such as images edited or created in Photoshop. Illustrator is generally used to create vector logos, illustrations, maps, packages, labels, signage, Web art, and more. (See the sidebar, "Vector graphics," for more information.)

This chapter gets you started with Illustrator and helps you understand when Illustrator is the tool that's best suited for creating your art.

Deciding When to Use Illustrator CS4

So how do you draw the line and decide when to create graphics in Illustrator rather than Photoshop? By using Illustrator, you gain the following benefits:

✦ **Illustrator can save and export graphics into most file formats.** By choosing to save or export, you can create a file that can be used in most other applications. For instance, Illustrator files can be saved as .svg, .bmp, .tiff, .pdf, .jpg, and even as a Flash .swf file, to name a few.

✦ **Illustrator files are easily integrated into other Adobe applications.** You can save Illustrator files in their native format and open or place them in other Adobe applications, such as InDesign, Photoshop, Dreamweaver, Fireworks, and Flash. You can also save Illustrator artwork as a .pdf (Portable Document Format). This format allows anyone with the free Acrobat Reader software to open and view the file, but editing capabilities are still maintained when the file is opened later in Illustrator.

✦ **Illustrator is resolution-independent because the resolution of vector artwork isn't determined until output.** In other words, if you print to a 600-dpi (dots per inch) printer, the artwork is printed at 600 dpi; print to a 2,400-dpi printer, and the artwork prints at 2,400 dpi. Illustrator graphics are very different from the bitmap images you create or edit in Photoshop, where resolution is determined upon creation of the artwork.

✦ **Illustrator has limitless scalability.** You can create vector artwork in Illustrator and scale it to the size of your thumb or the size of a barn, and it still looks good. See the "Vector graphics" sidebar in this chapter for more information.

Vector graphics

Vector graphics are made up of lines and curves defined by mathematical objects called *vectors*. Because the *paths* (the lines and curves) are defined mathematically, you can move, resize, or change the color of vector objects without losing quality in the graphic.

Vector graphics are resolution-independent; that is, they can be scaled to any size and printed at any resolution without losing detail. On the other hand, bitmap graphics have a predetermined amount of pixels creating them, so you can't scale (resize) them easily — if you scale them smaller, you throw out pixels; if you scale them larger, you end up with a blocky, jagged picture.

The following figure shows the differences between an enlarged vector graphic on the top (notice the smooth edges) and an enlarged bitmap graphic on the bottom (note the jagged edges). Many companies have their logos created as vectors to avoid problems with scaling: A vector graphic logo maintains its high-quality appearance at any size.

Opening an Existing Document

To familiarize yourself with the basics of Illustrator and what the work area looks like, jump right in by opening an existing document in Illustrator. If you don't have an Illustrator file created already, you can open one of the sample files packaged with the Illustrator application. For example, you can open the `Loyal Order of Wormword` in the Sample Art folder. The path to the file is `C:\Programs\Adobe\Adobe Illustrator CS4\Cool Extras\ Sample Files\Sample Art` **(Windows)** or `Applications\ Adobe Illustrator CS3\Cool Extras\Sample Files\Sample Art` (Mac).

When you launch Illustrator CS4 for the first time, a Welcome screen appears, giving you various options. Click the Open icon and then browse to locate a file to open. (***Note:*** You can select the Don't Show Again check box if you don't want to see the Welcome screen at launch.)

If your preferences have been changed from the original defaults, the Welcome screen may not appear. To open a file in that case, choose File⇨Open and select the file in the Open dialog box. The Open dialog box is used to open existing Adobe Illustrator files or even files from other Adobe applications.

Choose File⇨Open to open PDFs in Illustrator as well as many other file formats.

Creating a New Document

To create a new document in Illustrator, follow these steps:

1. **Choose File⇨New.**

The New Document dialog box appears, as shown in Figure 2-1. This dialog box enables you to determine the new document's profile, size, units of measurement, color mode, and page orientation, as well as how many artboards (pages) you want in the document.

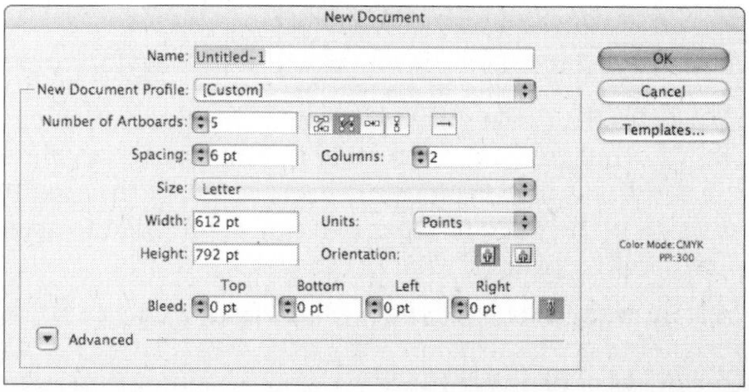

Figure 2-1:
Creating
a new
document in
Illustrator.

2. **Enter a name for your new file in the Name text field.**

You can determine the name of the file now or later when you save the document.

3. **Choose a profile from the New Document Profile drop-down list.**

Selecting the correct profile sets up preferences, such as resolution and colors, correctly. Click the Advanced down arrow (in the lower left of the New Document dialog box) to see what settings are selected for each profile and change them if necessary.

4. **Enter the number of artboards that you want in the document in the Number of Artboards text box.**

If you want a single page document, leave this set at 1.

5. **Enter how much space you want between artboards in the Spacing text box.**

If you want pages butting up to each other, enter **0** (zero) or enter additional values if you want a little space between each artboard. If you're adding artboards, you can enter how many columns of artboards that you want arranged in the document in the Columns text box.

6. **Choose from the Size drop-down list or type measurements in the Width and Height text fields to set the size of the document page.**

The size can be set from several standard sizes available in the Size drop-down list, or you can enter your own measurements in the Width and Height text fields. Note that several Web sizes are listed first, followed by other typical paper sizes.

7. **Choose from the Units drop-down list to select the type of measurement that you're most comfortable with.**

Your selection sets all measurement boxes and rulers to the increments you choose: points, picas, inches, millimeters, centimeters, or pixels.

8. **Pick the orientation for the artboard.**

The *artboard* is your canvas for creating your artwork in Illustrator. You can choose between *Portrait* (the short sides of the artboard at the top and bottom) and *Landscape* (the long sides of the artboard on the top and bottom).

9. **Add values into the Bleed text boxes if necessary.**

A *bleed value* is the amount of image area that extends beyond the artboard. If you want to print from edge to edge, enter a value for the bleed. Keep in mind that most desktop printers need a grip area that forces any image area near the edge of a page to not print. Bleeds are typically used in jobs that will be printed off a press.

10. **When you're finished making your selections, click OK.**

An Illustrator artboard(s) appears.

Don't worry if document size and color mode need to be changed at a later point. You can change them by choosing File⇨Document Setup and by making changes in the Document Setup dialog box.

Taking a Look at the Document Window

To investigate the work area and really get familiar with Illustrator, open a new document and take a look around. In the Illustrator work area, you have a total of 227 inches in width and height to create your artwork (and all artboards) in. That's great, but it also leaves enough space to lose objects, too! The following list explains the areas that you'll work with as you create artwork in Illustrator:

✦ **Imageable area:** The space inside the innermost dotted lines, which marks the printing area on the page. Many printers can't print all the way to the edges of the paper, so the imageable area is determined by the printer that you've selected in the Print dialog box. To turn off or on this dotted border, choose View⇨Hide/Show Page Tiling.

You can move the imageable area around on your page by using the Print Tiling tool. See the nearby sidebar, "The Print Tiling tool," for more on this tool.

✦ **Edge of the page:** The page's edge is marked by the outermost set of dotted lines.

✦ **Nonimageable area:** Choose View⇨Show Page Tiling to see the imageable area based upon the selected print driver. The space on the outside of the dotted lines represents the imageable area and the edge of the page. The nonimageable area is the margin of the page that can't be printed on.

✦ **Artboard:** The area bounded by solid lines that represents the entire region that can contain printable artwork. By default, the artboard is the same size as the page, but it can be enlarged or reduced. The U.S. default artboard is 8.5 x 11 inches, but it can be set as large as 227 x 227 inches. You can hide the artboard boundaries by choosing View⇨Hide Artboard.

✦ **Scratch area:** The area outside the artboard(s) that extends to the edge of the 227-inch square window. The scratch area represents a space on which you can create, edit, and store elements of artwork before moving them onto the artboard. Objects placed onto the scratch area are visible on-screen, but they don't print. However, objects in the scratch area will appear if the document is saved and placed as an image in other applications.

The Print Tiling tool

Use the Print Tiling tool to move the printable area of your page to a different location. For example, if you have a printer that can print only on paper that's 8.5 x 11 inches or less, but you have a page size of 11 x 17, you can use the Print Tiling tool (a hidden tool accessed by holding down the mouse button on the Hand tool) to indicate what part of the page you want to print. Follow these steps to use the Print Tiling tool:

1. **When adjusting page boundaries, choose View⇨Fit in Window so that you can see all your artwork.**

2. **Hold down on the Hand tool to select the hidden Print Tiling tool.**

The pointer becomes a dotted cross when you move it to the active window.

3. **Position the mouse over the artboard and click and drag the page to a new location.**

While you drag, the Print Tiling tool acts as if you're moving the page from its lower-left corner. Two gray rectangles are displayed. The outer rectangle represents the page size, and the inner rectangle represents the printable area of a page. You can move the page anywhere on the artboard; just remember that any part of a page that extends past the printable area boundary won't print.

Basically, the rules regarding the work area are simple: If you're printing directly from Illustrator, make sure that you choose the proper paper size and printer in the Print dialog box. Open the Print dialog box by choosing File⇨Print.

Becoming Familiar with the Tools

As you begin using Illustrator, you'll find it helpful to be familiar with its tools. Tools are used to create, select, and manipulate objects in Illustrator. The tools should be visible as a default, but if not, you can access them by choosing Window⇨Tools.

Table 2-1 lists the tools that we show you how to use throughout this mini-book. Hover the cursor over the tool in the toolbox to see the name of the tool appear in a ToolTip. In parentheses on the ToolTip (and noted in the second column of Table 2-1) is the keyboard command that you can use to access that tool. When you see a small triangle at the lower-right corner of the tool icon, it contains additional hidden tools. Select the tool and hold the mouse button to see any hidden tools.

Table 2-1		**Illustrator CS4 Tools**	
Icon	*Tool/Keyboard Command*	*What It Does*	*Chapter It's Covered in This Minibook*
	Selection (V)	Activates objects	Chapter 3
	Direct Selection (A)	Activates individual points or paths	Chapter 3
	Group Selection (A)	Selects grouped items	Chapter 3
	Magic Wand (Y)	Selects based upon similarity	Chapter 3
	Lasso (Q)	Selects freehand	Chapter 3
	Pen (P)	Creates paths	Chapter 5
	Type (T)	Creates text	Chapter 6
	Line Segment (/)	Draws line segments	Chapter 5
	Shape (M)	Creates shape objects	Chapter 4
	Paint Brush (B)	Creates paths	Chapter 5
	Pencil (N)	Creates paths	Chapter 5
	Blob Brush (Shift+B)	Creates freeform brush paths	Chapter 5
	Eraser (Shift+E)	Erases vector paths	Chapter 2

(continued)

**Book III
Chapter 2**

**Discovering
Illustrator CS4**

Table 2-1 *(continued)*

Icon	Tool/Keyboard Command	What It Does	Chapter It's Covered in This Minibook
	Rotate (R)	Rotates objects	Chapter 10
	Scale (S)	Enlarges or reduces objects	Chapter 10
	Warp (Shift+R)	Warps objects	Chapter 10
	Free Transform (E)	Transforms objects	Chapter 10
	Symbol Sprayer (Shift+S)	Applies symbol instances	Chapter 11
	Graph (J)	Creates graphs	Chapter 11
	Mesh (U)	Creates a gradient mesh	Chapter 11
	Gradient (G)	Modifies gradients	Chapter 11
	Eyedropper (I)	Copies and applies attributes	Chapter 9
	Blend (W)	Creates transitional blends	Chapter 11
	Live Paint Bucket (K)	Applies color to strokes and fills	Chapter 9
	Live Paint Selection (Shift+L)	Selects Live Paint area	Chapter 9
	Crop Area (Shift+O)	Crops multiple areas	Chapter 2
	Slice (Shift K)	Creates HTML slices	Chapter 2

Icon	Tool/Keyboard Command	What It Does	Chapter It's Covered in This Minibook
	Hand (H)	Navigates on the page	Chapter 2
	Zoom (Z)	Increases and decreases the on-screen view	Chapter 2

Checking Out the Panels

The standardized interface is a great boost for users as Illustrator's panel system is similar to all the other products in the Adobe Creative Suite. This consistency makes working and finding tools and features easier.

When you first open Illustrator, notice that some of the panels that have been reduced to icons on the right. To select a panel, click the appropriate icon and the panel appears.

If all that you see is an icon, how do you know which icon brings up which panel? Good question. If you're hunting around for the appropriate panels, you can do one of three things.

✦ **Choose Window⇨*Name of Your Panel*.**

✦ **Position your mouse on the left side of the icons and when you see the double-arrow icon, click and drag to the left.** The panel names appear.

✦ **Click the Expand Panels button in the gray bar at the top of the icons, as shown in Figure 2-2.** The panels expand so that you can see their contents and names.

Book III Chapter 2

Discovering Illustrator CS4

Figure 2-2: Expand the panels to see more options.

The panels that you see as a default are docked together. To *dock* a panel means that, for organizational purposes, the panel is attached in the docking area.

You can arrange panels to make them more helpful for production. You may choose to have only certain panels visible while working. Here's the low-down on using Illustrator's panels:

✦ **To see additional options for each panel (because some of these options are hidden), click the panel menu on the upper right of the panel (see Figure 2-3).**

Figure 2-3:
Some panels have additional options in the panel menu.

✦ **To move a panel group, click and drag above the tabbed panel name.**

✦ **To rearrange or separate a panel from its group, drag the panel's tab.** Dragging a tab outside the docking area creates a new separate panel.

✦ **To move a tab to another panel, drag the tab to that panel.**

Look out for those panels — they can take over your screen! Some panels, but not all, can be resized. Panels that you can resize have an active lower-right corner (denoted by three small lines in the corner). To change the size of a panel, drag the lower-right corner of the panel (Windows) or drag the size box at the lower-right corner of the panel (Mac).

As you become more efficient, you may find it helpful to reduce the clutter on your screen by hiding all panels except those that are necessary for your work. You can save your own panel configuration by choosing Window⇨Workspace⇨Save Workspace. Choose Window⇨Workspace⇨Essentials to return to the default workspace.

Changing Views

When you're working in Illustrator, precision is important, but you also want to see how the artwork really looks. Whether for the Web or print, Illustrator offers several ways in which to view your artwork:

✦ **Preview and Outline views:** By default, Illustrator shows the Preview view, where you see colors, stroke widths, images, and patterns as they should appear when printed or completed for on-screen presentation. Sometimes this view can become a nuisance, especially if you have two thick lines and you're trying to create a corner point by connecting them. At times like this, or whenever you want the strokes and fills reduced to the underlying structure, choose View➪Outline. You now see the outline of the illustration, as shown in Figure 2-4.

Figure 2-4:
Preview
mode (left)
and Outline
mode (right).

✦ **Pixel view:** If you don't want to be surprised when your artwork appears in your Web browser, use the Pixel view. This view, as shown in Figure 2-5, maintains the vectors of your artwork but gives you a view showing how the pixels will appear when the image is viewed on-screen, as if on the Web.

Pixel view is great for previewing what your text will look like on-screen — some fonts just don't look good as pixels, especially if the text is small. With Pixel view, you can go through several different fonts until you find one that is easily readable as pixels.

✦ **Overprint view:** For people in print production, the Overprint preview can be a real timesaver. Choose Window➪Attributes to bring up the Attributes panel, which you can use to set the fill and stroke colors to overprint. This view creates additional colors when printing and aids printers when trapping abutting colors.

Trapping is the slight overprint of a lighter color into a darker color to correct for press *misregistration*. When several colors are printed on one piece, the likelihood that they'll be perfectly aligned is pretty slim! Setting a stroke to Overprint on the Window➪Attributes panel is one solution. With Overprint selected, the stroke is overprinted on the touching colors. This mixing of color produces an additional color, but is less obvious to the viewer than a white space created by misregistration. Select Overprint to see the result of overprinting in Overprint view, as shown in Figure 2-6.

Figure 2-5:
See how your artwork translates into pixels in the Pixel view.

Figure 2-6:
Overprint view.

Navigating the Work Area with Zoom Controls

You can navigate the work area efficiently by using the Hand tool and the various zoom controls. You can change the magnification of the artboard in several ways, including using menu items, the Zoom tool, and keyboard commands. Choose the method you feel most comfortable with:

✦ **Hand tool:** Scroll around the Document window by using the scrollbars or the Hand tool. The Hand tool gives you the ability to scroll by dragging. You can imagine you're pushing a piece of paper around on your desk when you use the Hand tool.

Hold down the spacebar to temporarily access the Hand tool while any tool (except the Type tool) is selected. Holding down the spacebar while the Type tool is selected only gives you spaces!

✦ **View menu:** With the View menu, you can easily select the magnification that you want by using Zoom In, Zoom Out, Fit in Window (especially useful when you get lost in the scratch area), and Actual Size (gives you a 100-percent view of your artwork).

 ✦ **Crop Area tool:** With the new Crop Area tool, you can define crop areas interactively for print or export. You can choose preset formats and define multiple crop areas.

 ✦ **Zoom tool:** With the Zoom tool, you can click the Document window to zoom in; to zoom out, Alt+click (Windows) or Option+click (Mac). Double-click with the Zoom tool to quickly resize the Document window to 100 percent. Control what is visible when using the Zoom tool by clicking and dragging over the area that you want zoomed into.

✦ **Keyboard shortcuts:** If you're not the type of person who likes to use keyboard shortcuts, you may change your mind about using them for magnification. They make sense and are easy to use and remember. Table 2-2 lists the most popular keyboard shortcuts to change magnification.

 The shortcuts in Table 2-2 require a little coordination to use, but they give you more control in your zoom. While holding down the keys, drag from the upper-left to the bottom-right corner of the area you want to zoom to. A marquee appears while you're dragging; when you release the mouse button, the selected area zooms up to the size of your window! The Zoom Out command doesn't give you that much control; it simply zooms back out, much like the commands in Table 2-3.

Book III Chapter 2

Discovering Illustrator CS4

Table 2-2	Magnification Keyboard Shortcuts	
Command	*Windows Shortcut*	*Mac Shortcut*
Actual Size	Ctrl+1	⌘+1
Fit in Window	Ctrl+0 (zero)	⌘+0 (zero)
Zoom In	Ctrl++ (plus)	⌘++ (plus)
Zoom Out	Ctrl+− (minus)	⌘+− (minus)
Hand tool	Spacebar	Spacebar

Table 2-3	Zoom Keyboard Shortcuts	
Command	*Windows Shortcut*	*Mac Shortcut*
Zoom in to Selected Area	Ctrl+spacebar+drag	⌘+spacebar+drag
Zoom Out	Ctrl+Alt+spacebar	⌘+Option+spacebar

Chapter 3: Using the Selection Tools

In This Chapter

✔ Knowing the anchor points, bounding boxes, and selection tools

✔ Working with a selection

✔ Grouping and ungrouping selections

✔ Constraining movement and cloning objects

*I*f someone's been coaching you in using Adobe Illustrator, you may have heard the old line, "You have to select it to affect it." This is because if you want to apply a change to an object in Illustrator, you must have that object selected, or Illustrator won't know what to change. You'll sit there clicking a color swatch over and over again, and nothing will happen. Although making selections may sound simple, it can become tricky when you're working on complicated artwork.

Getting to Know the Selection Tools

Before delving into the world of selecting objects in Illustrator, you must know what the selection tools are. In this section, we take you through a quick tour of the anchor points (integral to the world of selections), the bounding box, and, of course, the selection tools (yes, there are several selection tools).

Anchor points

To understand selections, you must first understand how Illustrator works with anchor points. *Anchor points* act like handles and can be individually selected and moved to other locations. Essentially, the anchor points are what you use to drag objects or parts of objects around the workspace. After you place anchor points on an object, you can create strokes or paths from the anchor points.

You can select several anchor points at the same time (as shown in Figure 3-1) or only one (as shown in Figure 3-2). Selecting all anchor points in an object lets you move the entire object without changing the anchor points in relationship to one another. You can tell which anchor points are selected and active because they appear as solid boxes.

Figure 3-1:
Multiple
anchor
points are
selected.

Figure 3-2:
One anchor
point is
selected.

Bounding boxes

As a default, Illustrator shows a bounding box when an object is selected with the Selection tool (a bounding box is shown in Figure 3-1). This feature can be helpful if you understand its function, but confusing if you don't know how to use it.

By dragging on the handles, you can use the bounding box for quick transforms, such as scaling and rotating. To rotate, you pass the mouse cursor (without clicking) outside a handle until you see a rotate symbol and then drag.

If the bounding box bothers you, you can turn off the feature by choosing View➪Hide Bounding Box.

Selection tools

Illustrator CS4 offers five selection tools:

✦ **Selection:** Selects entire objects or groups. This tool activates all anchor points in an object or group at the same time, allowing you to move an object without changing its shape.

✦ **Direct Selection:** Selects individual points.

✦ **Group Selection:** Hidden in the Direct Selection tool in the toolbox, you use this tool to select items within a group. This tool adds grouped items as you click an object in the order in which objects were grouped. This selection tool will become more useful to you as you find out about grouping objects in Illustrator.

✦ **Magic Wand:** Use the Magic Wand tool to select objects with like values, such as fill and stroke colors, based upon a tolerance and stroke weight. Change the options of this tool by double-clicking it.

✦ **Lasso:** Use the Lasso tool to click and drag around anchor points that you want to select.

You can select an object with the Selection tool using one of three main methods:

✦ **Click the object's path.**

✦ **Click an anchor point of the object.**

✦ **Drag a marquee around part or all the object's path.** (In the later section, "Using a marquee to select an object," we discuss using the marquee method.)

Working with Selections

After you have an understanding about the basics of selections, you'll probably be anxious to try out some techniques. In this section, you're introduced to the basics: making a selection, working with anchor points and the marquee, making multiple selections, and of course, saving your work.

Smart guides are turned on by default in Illustrator CS4, and can help you to make accurate selections. These guides are visible as you are drawing, they display names like anchor point and path, and they also highlight paths when you are lined up with endpoints or center points. You can come to love these helpful aides, but if you don't want to see them, simply choose View➪Smart Guides, or use the keyboard shortcut Ctrl+U (Windows) or ⌘+U (Mac) to toggle the Smart guides off and on.

Creating a selection

To work with selections, you need to actually have something on the page in Illustrator. Use the following steps to make a selection:

1. **Create a new page in Adobe Illustrator (any size or profile is okay).**

Alternatively, you can open an existing illustration; see Chapter 2 of this minibook for instructions. Skip to Step 3 if working with an existing illustration.

2. **If you're starting from a new page, create an object to work with.**

   For example, click and hold down on the Rectangle tool to select the Star tool. Then click and drag from the top left to the lower right to create a star shape.

   Exact size doesn't matter, but make it large enough that you can see it. To start over, choose Edit⇔Undo, or press Ctrl+Z (Windows) or ⌘+Z (Mac).

   As a default, all shapes start with a black stroke and a white fill (see Figure 3-3). If yours isn't black and white, press D, which changes the selected object to the default colors.

   You can see the width and height of your object while you click and drag. If you don't want those values to display, choose Edit⇔Preferences⇔Smart Guides (Windows) or Illustrator⇔Preferences⇔Smart Guides (Mac) and deselect the Measurements Labels check box.

Figure 3-3:
Create
a shape
with the
selection
tools.

3. **With the Selection tool, click the object to make sure that it's active.**

   All anchor points are solid, indicating that all anchor points are active, as shown in Figure 3-3. As a default, you see many additional points that you can use to transform your selected object.

4. **Click and drag the shape to another location.**

   All anchor points travel together.

5. **When completed, deactivate your selection.**

   You can use one of these three methods:

   - *Choose Select⇔Deselect.*
   - *Ctrl-click (Windows) or ⌘-click (Mac) anywhere on the page.*
   - *Use the key command Ctrl+Shift+A (Windows) or ⌘+Shift+A (Mac).*

Selecting an anchor point

When you have a selection to work with (see the preceding numbered list), you can deselect all the active anchor points and then make just one anchor point active. Follow these steps:

1. **Choose Select⇨Deselect to make sure the object isn't selected.**

2. **Select the Direct Selection tool (the white arrow) from the toolbox.**

3. **Click one anchor point.**

Only one anchor point (the one you clicked) is solid, and the others are hollow, as shown in Figure 3-4.

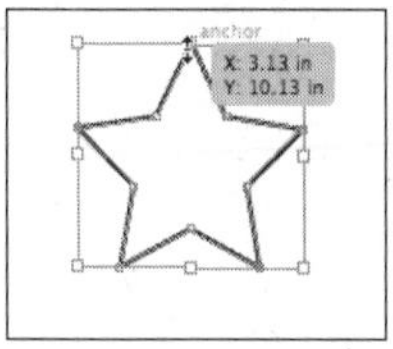

Figure 3-4:
Select only
one anchor
point.

4. **Click and drag that solid anchor point with the Direct Selection tool.**

Only that solid anchor point moves.

Note that an anchor point enlarges when you cross over it with the Direct Selection tool. This enlargement is a big break for those who typically have to squint to see where the anchor points are positioned.

Using a marquee to select an object

Sometimes it's easier to surround what you want selected by dragging the mouse to create a marquee. Follow these steps to select an object by creating a marquee:

1. **Choose the Selection tool.**

2. **Click outside the object and drag over a small part of it, as shown in Figure 3-5.**

The entire object becomes selected.

Figure 3-5:
Select
an entire
object.

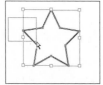

**Book III
Chapter 3**

**Using the Selection
Tools**

You can also select just one anchor point in an object by using the marquee method:

1. **Choose Select⇨Deselect to make sure the object isn't selected and then choose the Direct Selection tool.**

2. **Click outside a corner of the object and drag over just the anchor point that you want to select.**

   Notice that only that anchor point is active, which can be a sight-saver when you're trying to select individual points (see Figure 3-6).

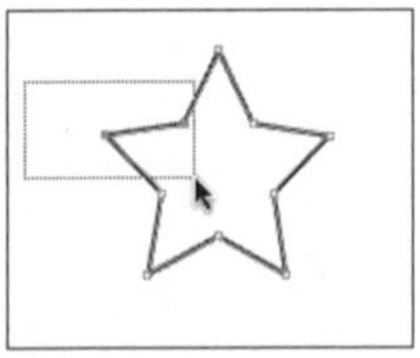

Figure 3-6:
Select individual anchor points.

You can use this method to cross over just the two top points or side anchor points to activate multiple anchor points as well.

Selecting multiple objects

If you have multiple items on your page, you can select them by using one of the following methods:

✦ **Select one object or anchor point and then hold down the Shift key and click another object or anchor point.** Depending on which selection tool you're using, you'll either select all anchor points on an object (Selection tool) or additional anchor points only (Direct Selection tool).

   You can use the Shift key to deactivate an object as well. Shift+click a selected object to deselect it.

✦ **Choose Select⇨All or press Ctrl+A (Windows) or ⌘+A (Mac).**

✦ **Use the marquee selection technique and drag outside and over the objects.** When you use this technique with the Selection tool, all anchor points in the objects are selected; with the Direct Selection tool, only the points that you drag over are selected.

Saving a selection

Spending way too much time trying to make your selections? Illustrator comes to the rescue with the Save Selection feature. After you have a selection that you may need again, choose Select⇨Save Selection and name the selection. The selection now appears at the bottom of the Select menu.

To change the name or delete the saved selection, choose Select⊅Edit Selection. This selection is saved with the document.

Grouping and Ungrouping

Keep objects together by grouping them. The Group function is handy in a situation when you're creating something from multiple objects, such as a logo. With the Group function, you can make sure all the objects that make up the logo stay together when you move, rotate, scale, or copy it.

Creating a group

Follow these steps to create a group:

1. **If you aren't already working with an illustration that contains a whole bunch of objects, create several objects on a new page — anywhere, any size.**

    For example, select the Rectangle tool and click and drag on the page several times to create additional rectangles.

2. **Select the first object with the Selection tool and then hold down the Shift key and click a second object.**

3. **Choose Object⊅Group or press Ctrl+G (Windows) or ⌘+G (Mac).**

4. **Choose Select⊅Deselect and then click one of the objects with the Selection tool.**

    Both objects become selected.

5. **While the first two objects are still selected, Shift+click a third object.**

6. **With all three objects selected, choose Object⊅Group again.**

    Illustrator remembers the grouping order. To prove it, choose Select⊅ Deselect to deselect the group and switch to the Group Selection tool. (Hold down the mouse button on the Direct Selection tool to access the Group Selection tool.)

7. **With the Group Selection tool, click the first object, and all anchor points become active. Click the first object again, and the second object becomes selected. Click the first object yet again, and the third object becomes selected.**

    This tool activates the objects in the order that you grouped them. After you group the objects together, you can treat them as a single object.

To ungroup objects, choose Object⊅Ungroup or use the key command Ctrl+Shift+G (Windows) or ⌘+Shift+G (Mac). In a situation where you group objects twice (because you added an object to the group, for example), you'd have to choose Ungroup twice.

Book III Chapter 3

Using the Selection Tools

Using the Isolation mode

Now in Illustrator you can take advantage of the *Isolation mode,* which allows you to easily select and edit objects in a group without disturbing other parts of your artwork. Simply double-click a group, and it opens in a separate Isolation mode, where all objects outside the group are dimmed and inactive. Do the work that you need to on the group and exit out of the Isolation mode by clicking the arrow to the left of Group in the upper right of the window, as shown in Figure 3-7.

Figure 3-7: The Isolation mode allows you to edit group contents without disturbing other artwork.

 In Illustrator CS4, you can choose the Isolate Selected Object button in the Control panel to quickly access the Isolation mode.

Manipulating Selected Objects

In the following list, you discover a few other cool things that you can do with selected objects:

✦ **Moving selected objects:** When an object is selected, you can drag it to any location on the page, but what if you only want to nudge it a bit? To nudge an item one pixel at a time, select it with the Selection tool and press the left-, right-, up-, or down-arrow key to reposition the object. Hold down the Shift key as you press an arrow key to move an object by ten pixels at a time.

✦ **Constraining movement:** Want to move an object over to the other side of the page without changing its alignment? Constrain something by selecting an object with the Selection tool and dragging the item and then holding down the Shift key before you release the mouse button. By pressing the Shift key mid-drag, you constrain the movement to 45-, 90-, or 180-degree angles!

✦ **Cloning selected objects:** Use the Selection tool to easily *clone* (duplicate) an item and move it to a new location. To clone an item, simply select it with the Selection tool and then hold down the Alt key (Windows) or Option key (Mac). Look for the cursor to change to two arrows (see Figure 3-8) and then drag the item to another location on the page. Notice that the original object is left intact and that a copy of the object has been created and moved.

Figure 3-8:
Drag the double arrow to clone an object.

✦ **Constraining the clone:** By Alt+dragging (Windows) or Option+dragging (Mac) an item and then pressing Shift, you can clone the item and keep it aligned with the original. ***Remember:*** Don't hold down the Shift key until you're in the process of dragging the item; otherwise, pressing Shift will deselect the original object.

After you clone an object to a new location, try this neat trick where you create multiple objects equally apart from each other with the Transform Again command: Choose Object⇨Transform⇨Transform Again, or press Ctrl+D (Windows) or ⌘+D (Mac) to have another object cloned the exact distance as the first cloned object (see Figure 3-9). We discuss transforms in more detail in Chapter 10 of this minibook.

Figure 3-9:
Using the Transform Again command.

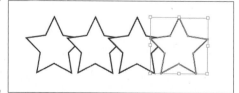

✦ **Using the Select menu:** With the Select menu, you can gain additional selection controls, such as choosing Select⇨Inverse, which allows you to select one object and then turn your selection inside out. Also, choosing the Select⇨Select Same option allows you to select one object and then select additional objects on the page based upon similarities in color, fill, stroke, and other special attributes.

 Take advantage of the new Select Similar button on the Control panel to easily access that feature.

Chapter 4: Creating Basic Shapes

In This Chapter

✔ Introducing rectangles, ellipses, stars, and polygons

✔ Resizing shapes after creation

✔ Creating shapes

Shapes, shapes, shapes . . . they're everywhere in Illustrator. Basic shapes, such as squares, circles, polygons, and stars, are used in all types of illustrations. With the right know-how and the right shape tools, you can easily create these shapes exactly the way you want. In this chapter, we show you how to use these tools to control a shape's outcome, create shapes based on precise measurements, and change the number of points a star has.

The Basic Shape Tools

As a default, the only visible shape tool in the toolbox is the Rectangle tool. Click and hold down that tool, and you have access to the Rounded Rectangle, Ellipse, Polygon, and Star tools, as shown in Figure 4-1. (Although you see the Flare tool, it's not a basic shape.)

Figure 4-1:
The basic shape tools.

You can tear off this tool set so that you don't have to find the hidden shapes in the future. Click and hold on the Rectangle tool and drag to the arrow on the far right. Wait until you see the pop-up hint (Tearoff) and then release the mouse button. These tools are now in a free-floating toolbar that you can drag to another location.

Creating rectangles and ellipses

Rectangles and ellipses are the most fundamental shapes that you can create (see Figure 4-2). To create a rectangle shape freehand, select the Rectangle tool and simply click the page where you want the shape to appear. Then drag diagonally toward the opposite side, drag it the distance that you want the shape to be in size, and release the mouse button. You can drag up or down. You do the same to create an ellipse with the Ellipse tool.

Figure 4-2:
Click and drag diagonally to create a shape.

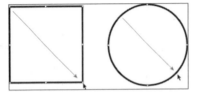

 After you create the shape, adjust its size and position by using the Selection tool. Reposition the shape by clicking the selected object and dragging. Resize the object by grabbing a handle and adjusting in or out. To adjust two sides together, grab a corner handle. To resize your shape proportionally, Shift+drag a corner handle.

Using the Rounded Rectangle tool

You can create a rounded rectangle by using one of two methods:

✦ Clicking and dragging freehand to create the rounded rectangle shape.

✦ Clicking once on the artboard to bring up the Rounded Rectangle dialog box, where you can enter values to define the shape.

The difference between these two methods is that when you open the Rounded Rectangle dialog box (see Figure 4-3), you can enter a value in the Corner Radius text field, which determines how much rounding is applied to the corners of the shape. The smaller the value, the less rounded the corners will be; the higher the value, the more rounded. Be careful; you can actually round a rectangle's corners so much that it becomes an ellipse!

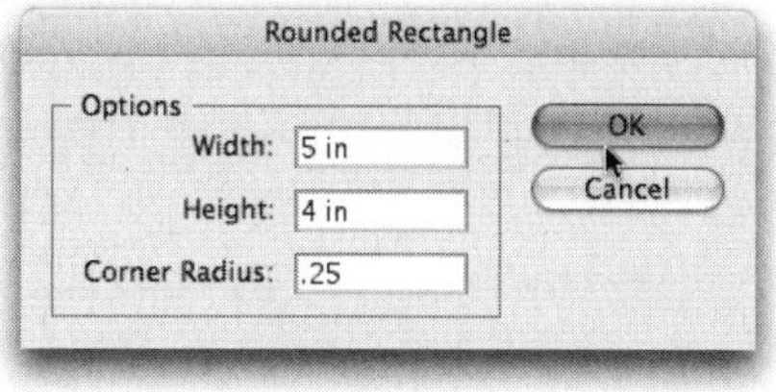

Figure 4-3:
Customize
the size of
a rounded
rectangle.

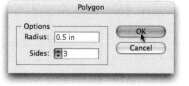

Using the Polygon tool

You create stars and polygons in much the same way as the rectangles
and ellipses. Select the Polygon tool and click and drag from one corner to
another to create the default six-sided polygon shape. You can also select
the Polygon tool and click once on the artboard to change the Polygon tool
options in the Polygon dialog box.

You can change the polygon shape by entering new values in the Radius
and Sides text fields, as shown in Figure 4-4. The radius is determined from
the center to the edge of the polygon. The value for the number of sides can
range from 3 (making triangles a breeze to create) to 1,000. Whoa . . . a polygon with 1,000 sides would look like a circle unless it was the size of Texas!

Figure 4-4:
Creating
a polygon
shape.

Using the Star tool

To create a star shape, select the Star tool from the toolbox. (Remember
that it may be hiding under other shape tools.) If you click once on the artboard to bring up the Star dialog box, you see three text fields in which you
can enter values to customize your star shape:

✦ **Radius 1:** Distance from the outer points to the center of the star.

✦ **Radius 2:** Distance from the inner points to the center of the star.

✦ **Points:** Number of points that make up the star.

The closer together the Radius 1 and Radius 2 values are to each other, the shorter the points on your star. In other words, you can go from a starburst to a seal of approval by entering values that are close in the Radius 1 and Radius 2 text fields, as shown in Figure 4-5.

Figure 4-5:
Radius 1
and Radius
2 are closer
to each
other in the
star on the
bottom.

Resizing Shapes

You often need a shape to be an exact size (for example, 2 x 3 inches). After you create a shape, the best way to resize it to exact measurements is to use the Transform panel, as shown in Figure 4-6. Have your object selected and then choose Window⇨Transform to open the Transform panel. Note that on this panel, you can enter values to place an object in the X and Y fields, as well as enter values in the width (W) and height (H) text fields to determine the exact size of an object.

Figure 4-6:
Precisely
set the size
of a shape.

In many of the Adobe Illustrator panels, you may see measurement increments consisting of points, picas, millimeters, centimeters, or inches, which can be confusing and maybe even intimidating. But you can control which measurement increments to use.

Show rulers by choosing View➪Show Rulers or press Ctrl+R (Windows) or ⌘+R (Mac). Then right-click (Windows) or Control-click (Mac) the ruler to change the measurement increment to an increment you're more familiar with. The contextual menu that appears allows you to change the measurement increment right on the document.

Alternatively, you can simply type the number followed by a measurement extension into the width and height text fields in the Transform panel (refer to Figure 4-6), and the measurement converts properly for you. Table 4-1 lists the extensions that you can use.

Table 4-1	Measurement Extensions
Extension	*Measurement Unit*
" or in	Inches
pt	Points
mm	Millimeters
cm	Centimeters
p	Picas

If you don't want to bother creating a shape freehand and then changing the size, select the shape tool and click the artboard. An Options dialog box specific to the shape you're creating appears, in which you can type values into the width and height text fields.

If you accidentally click and drag, you end up with a very small shape on your page. If this happens, don't fret. Simply get rid of the small shape by selecting it and pressing the Delete key, and then try again.

Tips for Creating Shapes

The following are simple tips to improve your skills at creating basic shapes in Illustrator:

✦ **Press and hold the Shift key while dragging with the Rectangle or Ellipse tool to create a perfect square or circle.** This trick is also helpful when you're using the Polygon and Star tools — holding down the Shift key constrains them so that they're straight (see Figure 4-7).

Figure 4-7:
Use the
Shift key to
constrain
a shape
while you
create it.

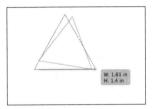

W: 1.61 in
H: 1.4 in

✦ **Create a shape from the center out by holding down the Alt (Windows) or Option (Mac) key while dragging.** Hold down Alt+Shift (Windows) or Option+Shift (Mac) to pull a constrained shape out from the center.

✦ **When creating a star or polygon shape by clicking and dragging, if you keep the mouse button down, you can then press the up- or down-arrow key to interactively add points or sides to your shape.**

Creating advanced shapes

At times, it may be much easier to use advanced tools in Illustrator to create unique shapes. The Pathfinder panel is an incredible tool that allows you to combine, knock out, and even create shapes from other intersected shapes.

You use the Pathfinder panel, as shown in Figure 4-8, to combine objects into new shapes. To use the Pathfinder panel, choose Window➪Pathfinder.

Figure 4-8:
Combine
objects into
new shapes.

Across the top row of the Pathfinder panel are the Shape Modes, which let you control the interaction between selected shapes. You can choose from the shape modes listed in Table 4-2.

Table 4-2	Shape Modes	
Button	*Mode*	*What It Does*
	Add to Shape Area	Essentially unites the selected shape into one.
	Subtract from Shape Area	Cuts out the topmost shape from the underlying shape.
	Intersect Shape Areas	Uses the area of the topmost shape to clip the underlying shape as a mask would.
	Exclude Overlapping Shape Areas	Uses the area of the shape to invert the underlying shape, turning filled regions into holes and vice versa.

If you like the result from using the Exclude Overlapping Shapes mode, you can also get a similar effect by selecting several shapes and choosing Object⇨Compound Path⇨Make. This command takes the topmost shapes and "punches" them out of the bottom shape.

The shapes remain separate so that you can still adjust them, which is great if you like to tweak your artwork (but it drives some people crazy). You can turn the results of using the Shape Mode buttons into one shape by either clicking the Expand button after selecting the shape mode or holding down the Alt key (Windows) or Option key (Mac) when clicking a Shape Mode button.

Using the Pathfinders

The *Pathfinders* are the buttons at the bottom of the Pathfinder panel. They also let you create new shapes out of overlapping objects. Table 4-3 offers a summary of what each Pathfinder does.

**Book III
Chapter 4**

**Creating Basic
Shapes**

Table 4-3		**The Pathfinders**
Button	*Mode*	*What It Does*
	Divide	Divides all the shapes into their own individual shapes. This tool is actually very useful tool when you're trying to create custom shapes.
	Trim	Removes the part of a filled object that's hidden.
	Merge	Removes the part of a filled object that's hidden. Also removes any strokes and merges any adjoining or overlapping objects filled with the same color.
	Crop	Deletes all parts of the artwork that fall outside the boundary of the topmost object. It also removes any strokes. If you want your strokes to remain when using this feature, select them and choose Object⇔Path⇔Outline Stroke.
	Outline	Divides an object into its shape's line segments, or edges. Useful for preparing artwork that needs a trap for overprinting objects.
	Minus Back	Deletes object that is in the back from frontmost object.

Chapter 5: Using the Pen Tool and Placing Images

In This Chapter

✔ Familiarizing yourself with the Pen tool

✔ Creating paths, closed shapes, and curves

✔ Using the hidden Pen tools

✔ Tracing some artwork

✔ Placing images in Illustrator CS4

✔ Working with Layer Comps

You've seen illustrations that you know are made from paths, but how do you make your own? In this chapter, we show you how to use the Pen tool to create paths and closed shapes.

The Pen tool requires a little more coordination than other Illustrator tools. Fortunately, Adobe Illustrator CS4 includes new features to help make using the Pen tool a little easier. After you master the Pen tool, the possibilities for creating illustrations are unlimited. Read this chapter to build your skills with the most popular feature in graphic software, the Bézier curve.

Pen Tool Fundamentals

You can use the Pen tool to create all sorts of things, such as straight lines, curves, and closed shapes, which you can then incorporate into illustrations:

+ **Bézier curve:** Originally developed by Pierre Bézier in the 1970s for CAD/CAM operations, the Bézier curve (as shown in Figure 5-1) became the underpinnings of the entire Adobe PostScript drawing model. A *Bézier curve* is one that you can control the depth and size of by using direction lines.

+ **Anchor points:** You can use anchor points to control the shape of a path or object. Anchor points are created automatically when using shape tools. You can manually create anchor points by clicking from point to point with the Pen tool.

Figure 5-1:
Bézier
curves are
controlled
by direction
lines.

+ **Direction lines:** These lines are essentially the handles that you use on curved points to adjust the depth and angle of curved paths.

+ **Closed shape:** When a path is created, it becomes a closed shape when the start point joins the endpoint.

+ **Simple path:** A *path* consists of one or more straight or curved segments. Anchor points mark the endpoints of the path segments.

In the next section, we show you how to control the anchor points.

Creating a straight line

A basic function of the Pen tool is to create a simple path. You can create a simple, straight line with the Pen tool by following these steps:

1. **Press D or click the small black-and-white color swatches at the bottom of the toolbox.**

You revert back to the default colors of a black stroke and a white fill. With black as a stroke, you can see your path clearly.

The trick of pressing D to change the foreground and background colors to the default of black and white also works in Photoshop and InDesign.

2. **Click the Fill swatch, located at the bottom of the toolbox, to make sure that the Fill swatch is in front of the Stroke swatch and then press the forward slash (/) key to change the fill to None.**

3. **Open a new blank page and select the Pen tool.**

Notice that when you move the mouse over the artboard, the Pen cursor appears with an X beside it, indicating that you're creating the first anchor point of a path.

4. **Click the artboard to create the first anchor point of a line.**

The X disappears.

Don't drag the mouse, or you'll end up creating a curve instead of a straight segment.

5. **Click anywhere else on the document to create the ending anchor point of the line.**

   Illustrator creates a path between the two anchor points. Essentially, the path looks like a line segment with an anchor point at each end (see Figure 5-2).

Figure 5-2:
A path connected by two anchor points.

To make a correction to a line you created with the Pen tool (as described in the preceding steps), follow these steps:

1. **Choose Select⬄Deselect to make sure that no objects are selected currently.**

2. **Select the Direct Selection tool from the toolbox.**

   Notice the helpful feature that enlarges the anchor point when you pass over it with the Direct Selection tool.

3. **Click an anchor to select one point on the line.**

   Notice that the selected anchor point is solid and the other is hollow. *Solid* indicates that the anchor point you clicked is active whereas *hollow* is inactive.

4. **Click and drag the anchor point with the Direct Selection tool.**

   The selected anchor point moves, changing the direction of the path while not affecting the other anchor point. And that's it.

Use the Direct Selection tool (press A to use the keyboard shortcut to select the Direct Selection tool) to make corrections to paths.

Make sure that only the anchor point you want to change is active. If the entire path is selected, all anchor points are solid. If only one anchor point is selected, all but that one point will be hollow.

Creating a constrained straight line

In this section, we show you how to create a real straight line, meaning one that is on multiples of a 45-degree angle. Illustrator makes it easy; just follow these steps:

1. **Select the Pen tool and click anywhere on the artboard to place an anchor point.**

2. **Hold down the Shift key and click another location to place the ending anchor point.**

   Notice that when you're holding the Shift key, the line snaps to a multiple of 45 degrees.

Release the mouse button before you release the Shift key or else the line pops out of alignment.

Creating a curve

In this section, you discover how to use the Bézier path to create a curved segment. We won't guarantee that you'll love it — not at first anyway. But after you know how to use a Bézier path, you'll likely find it useful. To create a Bézier path, follow these steps:

1. **Starting with a blank artboard, select the Pen tool and click anywhere on the artboard to place the first anchor point.**

2. **Click someplace else to place your ending anchor point but don't let go of the mouse button and then drag the cursor until a direction line appears.**

   If you look really close, you see that anchor points are square and the direction lines have circles at the end, as shown in Figure 5-3.

Figure 5-3:
Click and drag with the Pen tool to create a curved path.

3. **Drag the direction line closer to the anchor point to flatten the curve; drag farther away from the anchor point to increase the curve, as shown in Figure 5-4.**

4. **Release the mouse button when you're happy with the curve.**

Figure 5-4:
The
directional
lines
determine
how the
curve
appears.

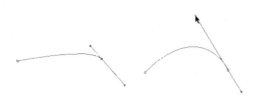

You've created an *open path,* or a path that doesn't form a closed shape. We show you how to reconnect to the starting point of the path to make a closed shape in the next section.

To alter a curved segment after you create it, follow these steps:

1. **Choose Select⇨Deselect to make sure that no objects are currently selected.**

2. **Choose the Direct Selection tool and click the last anchor point created.**

If they're not already visible, the direction lines appear.

If you have a hard time selecting the anchor point, drag a marquee around it with the Direct Selection tool.

3. **Click precisely at the end of one of the direction lines; drag the direction line to change the curve.**

Reconnecting to an existing path

Creating one segment is fine if you just want a line or an arch. But if you want to create a shape, you need to add more anchor points to the original segment. If you want to fill your shape with a color or a gradient, you need to close it, meaning that you need to eventually come back to the starting anchor point.

To add segments to your path and create a closed shape, follow these steps:

1. **Create a segment (straight or curved).**

We show you how in the preceding sections of this chapter.

You can continue from this point, clicking and adding anchor points until you eventually close the shape. For this example, you deselect the path so that you can discover how to continue adding to paths that have already been created. Knowing how to edit existing paths is extremely helpful when you need to make adjustments to artwork.

2. **With the Pen tool selected, move the cursor over an end anchor point on the deselected path.**

3. **Click when you see the Pen icon with a forward slash to connect your next segment.**

   The forward slash indicates that you're connecting to this path.

4. **Click someplace else to create the next anchor point in the path; drag the mouse if you want to create a curved segment.**

5. **Click to place additional anchor points, dragging as needed to curve those segments.**

   Remember that you want to close this shape, so place your anchor points so that you can eventually come back to the first anchor point.

   Figure 5-5 shows a shape that's a result of several linked anchor points.

6. **When you get back to the first anchor point, move the cursor over it and click when the close icon (a small hollow circle) appears, as shown in Figure 5-6.**

   The shape now has no end points.

Figure 5-5:
Adding
more
anchor
points to
create a
shape.

Figure 5-6:
Click when
the close
path icon
appears.

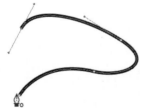

Controlling the curves

After you feel comfortable creating curves and paths, take control of those curves so that you can create them with a greater degree of precision. The following steps walk you through the manual method for changing direction of anchor points, as well as reveal helpful keyboard commands to make controlling paths a little more fluid. At the end of this section, we introduce you to new tools that you may also want to take advantage of to help you get control of the Pen tool.

To control a curve, follow these steps:

1. **Create a new document and then choose View⊅Show Grid to show a series of horizontal and vertical rules that act as guides.**

If it helps, use the Zoom tool to zoom in to the document.

2. **With the Pen tool, click an intersection of any of these lines in the middle area of the page to place your initial anchor point and drag upward.**

Let go, but don't click when the direction line has extended up to the horizontal grid line above it, as shown in Figure 5-7a.

3. **Click to place the second anchor point on the intersection of the grid directly to the right of your initial point; drag the direction line down to the grid line directly below it, as shown in Figure 5-7b.**

If you have a hard time keeping the direction line straight, hold down the Shift key to constrain it.

4. **Choose Select⊅Deselect to deselect your curve.**

Congratulations! You've created a controlled curve. In these steps, we created an arch that's going up, so we first clicked and dragged up. Likewise, to create a downward arch, you must click and drag down. With the grid, try to create a downward arch like the one shown in Figure 5-7c.

Book III
Chapter 5

Using the Pen Tool
and Placing Images

 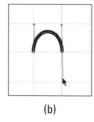 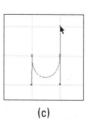

Figure 5-7: Creating a controlled Bézier curve.

(a)   (b)   (c)

Creating a corner point

To change directions of a path from being a curve to a corner, you have to create a *corner point,* as shown on the right in Figure 5-8. A corner point has no direction lines and allows for a sharp direction change in a path.

You can switch from the Pen tool to the Convert Anchor Point tool to change a smooth anchor point into a corner point, but that process is a bit time-consuming. An easier way is to press the Alt (Windows) or Option (Mac) key (the Pen tool temporarily changes into the Convert Anchor Point tool) while clicking the anchor point.

Figure 5-8:
Smooth
versus
corner
points.

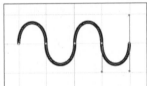 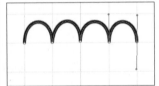

To change a smooth anchor point into a corner point with the shortcut method, follow these steps:

1. **Create an upward arch.**

   We show you how in the preceding section, "Controlling the curves" (refer to Figure 5-7b).

2. **Hold down the Alt (Windows) or Option (Mac) key and position the cursor over the last anchor point (the last point that you created with the Pen tool).**

3. **When the cursor changes to a caret (that's the Convert Anchor Point tool), click and drag until the direction line is up to the grid line above, as shown on the left in Figure 5-9.**

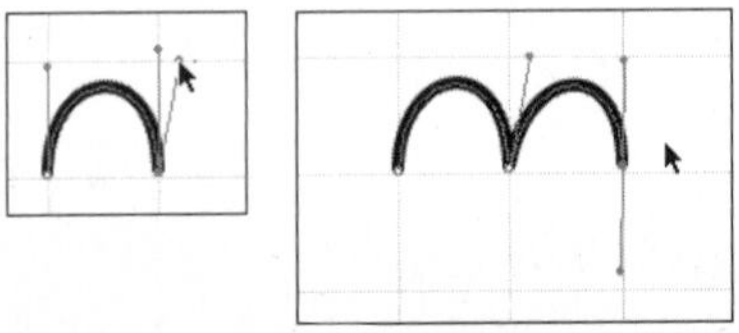

Figure 5-9:
Converting
a smooth
anchor point
to a corner
point.

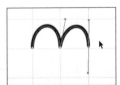

4. **Release the Alt (Windows) or Option (Mac) key and the mouse button, move the cursor to the grid line to the right, and click and drag down.**

The Hidden Pen Tools

Hold down on the Pen tool icon in the toolbox to access additional tools: the Add Anchor Point, Delete Anchor Point, and Convert Anchor Point tools, shown in Table 5-1. In the preceding section, we show you how to create a corner point with the shortcut method, by pressing the Alt (Windows) or Option (Mac) key to access the Convert Anchor Point tool. You may feel more comfortable switching to that tool when you need to convert a point, but switching tools can be more time-consuming.

Table 5-1	The Hidden Pen Tools
Icon	*Tool*
⬥	Pen
⬥+	Add Anchor Point
⬥−	Delete Anchor Point
◤	Convert Anchor Point

Even though you can use a hidden tool to delete and add anchor points, Illustrator automatically does this as a default when you're using the Pen tool. When you move the cursor over an anchor point with the Pen tool, a minus icon appears. To delete that anchor point, simply click. Likewise, when you move the cursor over a part of the path that doesn't contain anchor points, a plus icon appears. Simply click to add an anchor point.

If you prefer to use the tools dedicated to adding and deleting anchor points, choose Edit⇨Preferences⇨General (Windows) or Illustrator⇨Preferences⇨General (Mac); in the Preferences dialog box that appears, select the Disable Auto Add/Delete check box. Then, when you want to add or delete an anchor point, select the appropriate tool and click the path.

Additional tools to help you make paths

Some Pen tool modifiers are available in the Control panel in Illustrator CS4. You can take advantage of them to do many of the Pen tool functions, but using keyboard shortcuts to switch your Pen tool to its various options is probably still faster. Those who may be resistant to contorting your fingers while trying to create a path may appreciate these tools.

In order to see the Control panel tools, select the Pen tool and start creating a path. Notice that the Control panel has a series of buttons available, as shown in Figure 5-10.

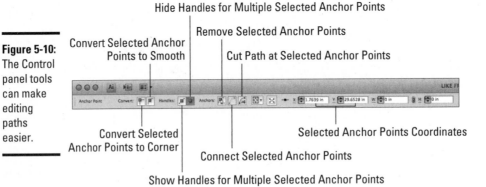

Figure 5-10:
The Control panel tools can make editing paths easier.

Hide Handles for Multiple Selected Anchor Points

Remove Selected Anchor Points

Convert Selected Anchor Points to Smooth

Cut Path at Selected Anchor Points

Selected Anchor Points Coordinates

Convert Selected Anchor Points to Corner

Connect Selected Anchor Points

Show Handles for Multiple Selected Anchor Points

Using the Eraser tool

The Eraser tool is a tool all users will love! The Eraser tool allows you to quickly remove areas of artwork as easily as you erase pixels in Photoshop by stroking with your mouse over any shape or set of shapes.

New paths are automatically created along the edges of your erasure, even preserving the smoothness of your erasure as you see in Figure 5-11.

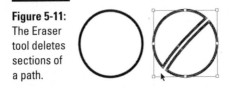

Figure 5-11:
The Eraser tool deletes sections of a path.

By double-clicking the Eraser tool, you can define the diameter, angle, and roundness of your eraser (see Figure 5-12). If you're using a drawing tablet, you can even set Wacom tablet interaction parameters, such as Pressure and Tilt.

If you want to erase more than a single selected object, use Isolation Mode to segregate grouped objects for editing. Remember that to enter Isolation mode, you simply double-click a group of items. You can then use the eraser on all objects in that group at once without disturbing the rest of your design.

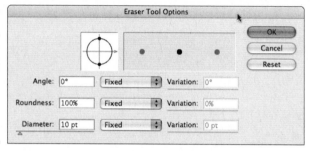

Figure 5-12:
Double-click the Eraser tool to set various tool options.

Tracing Artwork

You can use a template layer to trace an image manually. A *template layer* is a locked, dimmed layer that you can use to draw over placed images with the Pen tool, much like you'd do with a piece of onion skin paper over the top of an image.

Creating a template layer

Just follow these steps to create a template layer:

1. **Take a scanned image or logo and save it in a format that Illustrator can import from your image-editing program, such as Photoshop.**

   Typically, you save the image as an `.eps`, `.tif`, or native `.psd` (Photoshop file).

2. **Choose File➪Place to open the Place dialog box.**

3. **In the Place dialog box, locate the saved image; then select the Template check box and click Place.**

   Note that the Template check box may be in a different location depending upon your platform, but it's always located at the bottom of the dialog box.

   Selecting the Template check box tells Illustrator to lock down the scanned image on a layer. Essentially, you can't reposition or edit your image.

   After you click Place, a template layer is automatically created for you, and another layer is waiting for you to create your path. The newly created top layer is like a piece of tracing paper that's been placed on top of the scanned image.

4. **Re-create the image by tracing over it with the Pen tool.**

5. **When you're done, turn the visibility off the placed image by clicking the Visibility icon to the left of the template layer.**

   You now have a path that you can use in place of the image, which is useful if you're creating an illustration of an image or are digitally re-creating a logo.

For more about layers, check out Chapter 8 of this minibook.

Keep practicing to get more comfortable with clicking and dragging, flowing with the direction line pointing the way that you want the path to be created; everything will fall into place.

Using Live Trace

Use the Live Trace feature, introduced in Illustrator CS2, to automatically trace raster images into vector paths. This does work great in many instances, but is definitely not a "magic pill" for getting your images re-created as vectors. For example, a logo with many precise curves and straight lines isn't a good candidate for this feature, but a hand-drawn illustration, clip art, or other drawing works well.

Here are the steps that you take to use Live Trace:

1. **Choose File⇨Place and place a scan or raster illustration that you want to convert to vector paths.**

2. **Immediately after placing, you see that the Control panel now has some additional buttons available, as shown in Figure 5-13.**

Figure 5-13:
The Live
Trace
Control
panel
features.

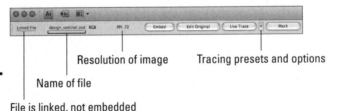

Resolution of image   Tracing presets and options

Name of file

File is linked, not embedded

3. **You can either click the Live Trace button to automatically trace based upon default settings or, better yet, click and hold on the Tracing Options arrow and choose a more appropriate setting.**

Choose Tracing Options from the very bottom of the Tracing Options drop-down list to customize settings.

4. **After you select the settings you're happy with, you can either use the Live Paint features to color in the work or click the Expand button in the Control panel to expand the trace object to vector paths that can be edited.**

   See Chapter 9 of this minibook for more information on painting fills and strokes.

Other Things You Should Know about Placing Images

In the preceding section, you discover how to place an image as a template. But what if you want to place an image to be utilized in your illustration file? Simply choose File⟶Place.

Click once on an image to see the Link check box. If you keep the check box selected, the image is linked to the original file. This is good if you plan on referencing the file several times in the illustration (it saves file space) or if you want to edit the original and have it update the placed image in Illustrator. This option is usually checked by those in the prepress industry who want to have access to the original image file. Just remember to send the image with the Illustrator file if it's to be outputted or used someplace other than on your computer.

If you deselect the Link check box, the image is embedded into the Illustrator file. This option does keep the filing system cleaner but doesn't leave much room to edit the original image at a later point. There are certain instances, such as when you want an image to become a symbol (see Chapter 11 of this minibook), that the image will have to be embedded, but most functions work with linked and unlinked files.

Using Photoshop Layer Comps

Layer Comps are a feature in Photoshop that allow you to set the visibility, appearance, and position of layers. It's a great organizational tool that you can now take advantage of in other Adobe products. Read more about Photoshop in Book II.

You can place a `.psd` (Photoshop) image that's saved Layer Comps from Photoshop and choose which layer comp set you want visible while placing in Adobe Illustrator CS4.

Chapter 6: Using Type in Illustrator

In This Chapter

✔ Introducing the Type tools

✔ Getting to know text areas

✔ Manipulating text along paths and within shapes

✔ Assigning font styles

✔ Discovering the Character, Control, and Paragraph panels

✔ Saving time with text utilities

*O*ne of Illustrator's strongest areas is manipulating text. Whether you're using Illustrator to create logos, business cards, or type to be used on the Web, you have everything you need to create professional text.

In this chapter, you meet the Type tools and discover a few basic (and more advanced) text-editing tricks that you can take advantage of. You then find out about other text tools, such as the Character and Paragraph panels. At the end of this chapter, you get a quick-and-dirty lowdown on the Illustrator text utilities. These utilities can save you loads of time, so don't skip this section.

Working with Type

You can do all sorts of cool things with type, from the simplest tasks of creating a line of text and dealing with text overflow to more complicated tricks, such as placing text along paths and wrapping text around objects.

Figure 6-1 shows the Type tools with an example of what you can do with each one. Click and hold the Type tool to see the hidden tools. The different tools give you the ability to be creative and also accommodate foreign languages.

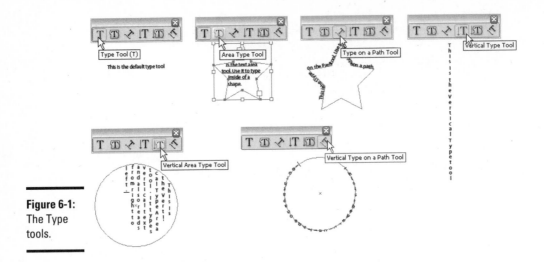

Figure 6-1:
The Type
tools.

Creating text areas

A *text area* is a region that you define. Text, when inserted in this region, is constrained within the shape. To create a text area, click and drag with the Type tool.

As you create and finish typing in a text area, you may want to quickly click and drag a new text area elsewhere on your artboard. Unfortunately, if you're on the Type tool, Illustrator doesn't allow you to do so. You have two options to address this problem:

✦ Choose Select➪Deselect and then create another area.

✦ Hold down the Ctrl (Windows) or ⌘ (Mac) key to temporarily access the Selection tool, and click. When you release the Ctrl (Windows) or ⌘ (Mac) key, you'll still be on the Type tool, and you can then create a new text area.

Creating a line of text

To create a simple line of text, select the Type tool and click the artboard. A blinking insertion point appears. You can now start typing. With this method, the line of type goes on forever and ever (even beyond the end of the Scratch area) until you press Enter (Windows) or Return (Mac) to start a new line of text. This excess length is fine if you just need short lines of text, say for callouts or captions, but it doesn't work well if you're creating a label or anything else that has large amounts of copy.

Many new users click and drag an ever-so-small text area that doesn't allow room for even one letter. If you accidentally do this, switch to the Selection tool, delete the active type area, and then click to create a new text insertion point.

Flowing text into an area

Select the Type tool and then drag on the artboard to create a text area. The cursor appears in the text area; text you type automatically flows to the next line when it reaches the edge of the text area. You can also switch to the Selection tool and adjust the width and height of the text area with the handles.

Need an exact size for a text area? With the Type tool selected, drag to create a text area of any size. Then choose Window➪Transform to view the Transform panel. Type an exact width in the W text field and exact height in the H text field.

Dealing with text overflow

Watch out for excess text! If you create a text area that's too small to hold all the text you want to put into it, a red plus sign appears in the lower-right corner, as shown in Figure 6-2.

When Illustrator indicates to you that you have too much text for the text area, you have several options:

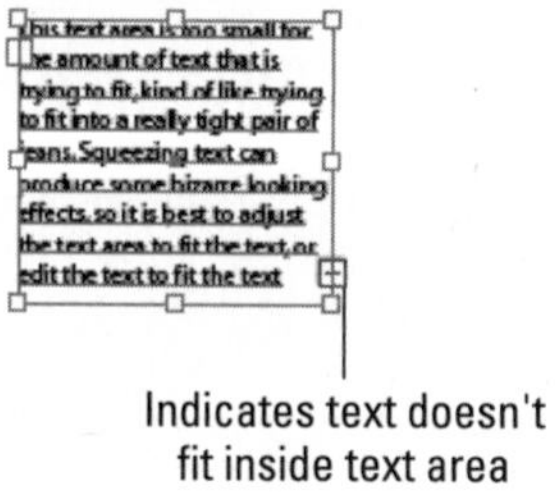

Figure 6-2:
The plus icon notes that text is overflowing.

> This text area is too small for the amount of text that is trying to fit, kind of like trying to fit into a really tight pair of jeans. Squeezing text can produce some bizarre looking effects, so it is best to adjust the text area to fit the text, or edit the text to fit the text

Indicates text doesn't
fit inside text area

✦ Make the text area larger by switching to the Selection tool and dragging the handles.

✦ Make the text smaller until you don't see the overflow indicated.

✦ Link this text area to another, which is *threading* and is covered later in this chapter in the "Threading text into shapes" section.

Creating columns of text with the Area Type tool

The easiest and most practical way to create rows and columns of text is to use the area type options in Adobe Illustrator. This feature lets you create rows and columns from any text area. You can just have rows, or you can just have columns (much like columns of text in a newspaper), or even both.

1. **Select the Type tool and drag on the artboard to create a text area.**

2. **Choose Type⇨Area Type Options.**

   The Area Type Options dialog box appears, as shown in Figure 6-3. At the end of this section, a list explains all the options in the Area Type Options dialog box.

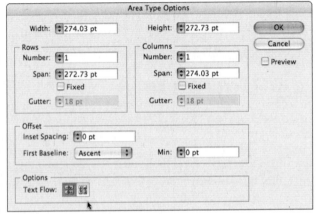

Figure 6-3: The Area Type Options dialog box lets you create columns of text.

3. **In the Area Type Options dialog box, enter the desired width and height in the Width and Height text fields.**

   The Width and Height text fields contain the height and width of your entire text area. In Figure 6-3, 274.03 pt is in the Width text field and 272.73 pt is in the Height text field.

4. **In the Columns area, enter the number of columns you want to create in the Number text field, the span distance in the Span text field, and the gutter space in the Gutter text field.**

   The *span* specifies the height of individual rows and the width of individual columns. The *gutter* is the space between the columns and is automatically set for you, but you can change it to any value you like.

5. **Click OK.**

   When you create two or more columns of text with the Area Type Options dialog box, text flows to the next column when you reach the end of the previous column, as shown in Figure 6-4.

The following is a breakdown of the other options available in the Area Type Options dialog box (refer to Figure 6-3):

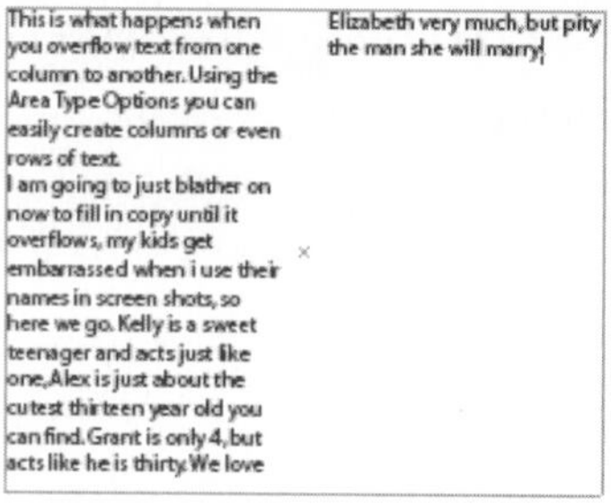

Figure 6-4:
One column of text flows into the next.

✦ **Width and Height:** The present width and height of the entire text area.

✦ **Number:** The number of rows and/or columns that you want the text area to contain.

✦ **Span:** The height of individual rows and the width of individual columns.

✦ **Fixed:** Determines what happens to the span of rows and columns if you resize the type area. When this check box is selected, resizing the area can change the number of rows and columns but not their width. Leave this option deselected if you want to resize the entire text area and have the columns automatically resize with it.

✦ **Gutter:** The empty space between rows or columns.

✦ **Inset Spacing:** The distance from the edges of the text area.

✦ **First Baseline:** Where you want the first line of text to appear. The Ascent option is the default and starts your text normally at the top. If you want to put a fixed size in, such as 50 pts from the top, select Fixed from the drop-down list and enter 50 pt in the Min text field.

✦ **Text Flow:** The direction in which you read the text as it flows to another row or column. You can choose to have the text flow horizontally (across rows) or vertically (down columns).

Threading text into shapes

Create custom columns of text that are in different shapes and sizes by threading closed shapes together. This technique works with rectangles, circles, stars, or any closed shape and can lead to some creative text areas.

1. **Create any shape, any size.**

   For this example, we've created a circle.

2. **Create another shape (it can be any shape) someplace else on the page.**

3. **With the Selection tool, select one shape and Shift-click the other to make just those two shapes active.**

4. **Choose Type⊏⊐Threaded Text⊏⊐Create.**

   A threading line appears, as shown in Figure 6-5, indicating the direction of the threaded text.

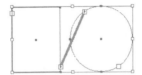

Figure 6-5:
Threaded
text areas
flow from
one area to
another.

5. **Select the Type tool, click the top of the first shape to start the threading, and start typing.**

   Continue typing until the text flows over into the other shape.

   If you don't want the text to be threaded anymore, choose Type⊏⊐Threaded Text⊏⊐Remove Threading, which eliminates all threading from the text shapes. To remove one or more shapes from the threading but not all the shapes, select the shape you want to remove from the threading and choose Type⊏⊐Threaded Text⊏⊐Release Selection.

Wrapping text

Wrapping text isn't quite the same as wrapping a present — it's easier! A *text wrap* forces text to wrap around a graphic, as shown in Figure 6-6. This feature can add a bit of creativity to any piece.

Figure 6-6:
The graphic
is forcing
the text
to wrap
around it.

Kelly thought she was pretty cool, getting her nose pierced and all, thank gosh, as her Mother, I did not have to be the one to tell her to unscrew that thing and look respectable. Her new boss at the coffee shop took care of that. If I could personally thank him I would, he must be a parent too.

Follow these steps to wrap text around another object or group of objects:

1. **Select the wrap object.**

   This is the object that you want the text to wrap around.

2. **Make sure that the wrap object is on top of the text you want to wrap around it by choosing Object➪Arrange➪Bring to Front.**

   If you're working in layers (which we discuss in Chapter 8 of this minibook), make sure that the wrap object is on the top layer.

3. **Choose Object➪Text Wrap➪Make.**

   An outline of the wrap area is visible.

4. **Adjust the wrap area by choosing Object➪Text Wrap➪Text Wrap Options.**

   The Text Wrap Options dialog box appears, as shown in Figure 6-7, giving you the following options:

   - *Offset:* Specifies the amount of space between the text and the wrap object. You can enter a positive or negative value.

   - *Invert Wrap:* Wraps the text on the inside of the wrap object instead of around it.

5. **When you finish making your selections, click OK.**

Figure 6-7:
Adjust the
distance
of the text
wrap from
the object.

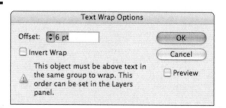

If you want to change the text wrap at a later point, select the object and choose Object➪Text Wrap➪Text Wrap Options. Make your changes and click OK.

If you want to unwrap text from an object, select the wrap object and choose Object➪Text Wrap➪Release.

Outlining text

Illustrator gives you the opportunity to change text into outlines or artwork. Basically, you change the text into an object, so you can no longer edit that text by typing. The plus side is that it saves you the trouble of sending fonts to everyone who wants to use the file. Turning text into outlines makes it appear as though your text was created with the Pen tool. You want to use this tool when creating logos that will be used frequently by other people or artwork that you may not have control over.

To turn text into an outline, follow these steps:

1. **Type some text on your page.**

   For this example, just type a word (say, your name) and make sure that the font size is at least 36 points. You want to have it large enough to see the effect of outlining it.

2. **Switch to the Selection tool and choose Type➪Create Outlines.**

   You can also use the keyboard command Ctrl+Shift+O (Windows) or ⌘+Shift+O (Mac).

   The text is now grouped together in outline form.

3. **If you're being creative, or just particular, and want to move individual letters, use the Group Select tool or choose Object➪Ungroup to separate the letters, as shown in Figure 6-8.**

Figure 6-8:
Letters
converted to
outlines.

When you convert type to outlines, the type loses its hints. *Hints* are the instructions built into fonts to adjust their shape so that your system displays or prints them in the best way based on the size. Without hints, letters like lowercase *e* or *a* might fill in as the letter forms are reduced in size. Make sure that the text is the approximate size that it might be used at before creating outlines. Because the text loses the hints, try not to create outlines on text smaller than 10 pts.

Putting text on a path, in a closed shape, or on the path of a shape

Wow — that's some heading, huh? You've probably seen text following a swirly path or inside some shape. Maybe you think accomplishing such a task is too intimidating to even attempt. In this section, we show you just how easy these things are! There are Type tools dedicated to putting type on a path or a shape (refer to Figure 6-1), but we think you'll find that the key modifiers we show you in this section are easier to use.

Creating text on a path

Follow these steps to put type on a path:

1. **Create a path with the Pen, Line, or Pencil tool.**

   Don't worry if it has a stroke or fill applied.

2. **Select the Type tool and simply cross over the start of the path.**

3. **Look for an I-bar with a squiggle (which indicates that the text will run along the path) to appear and click.**

   The stroke and fill of the path immediately change to None.

4. **Start typing, and the text runs on the path.**

5. **Choose Window⇨Type⇨Paragraph and change the alignment in the Paragraph panel to reposition where the text falls on the path.**

   Alternatively, switch to the Selection tool and drag the I-bar that appears, as shown in Figure 6-9, to move the text freehand. The path in Figure 6-9 was created with the Spiral tool, which is hidden in the Line Segment tool on the toolbar.

Flip the text to the other side of a path by clicking and dragging the I-bar under or over the path.

Book III
Chapter 6

Using Type in Illustrator

Figure 6-9:
With the Selection tool, you can drag the I-bar to adjust the text.

Creating text in a closed shape

Putting text inside a shape can add spunk to a layout. This feature allows you to custom-create a closed shape with the shape tools or the Pen tool and flow text into it. Follow these steps to add text inside a shape:

1. **Create a closed shape — a circle or oval, for example.**

2. **Select the Type tool and cross over the closed shape.**

3. **When you see the I-bar swell or become rounded, click inside the shape.**

4. **Start typing, and the text is contained inside the shape.**

Text on the path of a closed shape

Perhaps you want text to run around the edge of a shape instead of inside it. Follow these steps to have text created on the path of a closed shape:

1. **Create a closed shape, such as a circle.**

2. **Select the Type tool and cross over the path of the circle.**

3. **Don't click when you see the I-bar swell up; hold down the Alt (Windows) or Option (Mac) key instead.**

   The icon now changes into the squiggle I-bar that you see when creating text on a path.

4. **When the squiggle line appears, click.**

5. **Start typing, and the text flows around the path of the shape, as shown in Figure 6-10.**

Figure 6-10: By holding down the Alt or Option key, you can flow text around a closed shape.

To change the origin of the text or move it around, use the alignment options in the Paragraph panel or switch to the Selection tool and drag the I-bar to a new location on the path.

You can drag the I-bar in and out of the shape to flip the text so that it appears on the outside or inside of the path.

Assigning Font Styles

After you have text on your page, you'll often want to change it to be more interesting than the typical 12-pt Times font. Formatting text in Illustrator isn't only simple, but you can do it multiple ways. In the following list, we name and define some basic type components (see Figure 6-11):

Figure 6-11: Components of type.

+ **Font:** A complete set of characters, letters, and symbols of a particular typeface design.

+ **X height:** The height of type, based on the height of the small x in that type family.

+ **Kerning:** The space between two letters. Often used for letters in larger type that need to be pulled closer together, like "W i." Kern a little to get the i to slide in a little closer to the W, maybe even going into the space that the W takes, as shown in Figure 6-12. Kerning doesn't distort the text; it only increases or decreases the space between two letters.

+ **Leading:** Space between the lines of text.

Figure 6-12: The letters before kerning (left) and after (right).

Wi Wi

+ **Tracking:** The space between multiple letters. Designers like to use this technique to spread out words by increasing the space between letters. Adjusting the tracking doesn't distort text; it increases or decreases the space between the letters, as shown in Figure 6-13.

Figure 6-13:
Tracking set at 0 (top) and 300 (bottom).

AGI TRAINING

A G I   T R A I N I N G

Pretty good tracking and kerning has already been determined in most fonts. You don't need to bother with these settings unless you're tweaking the text for a more customized look.

✦ **Baseline:** The line that type sits on. The baseline doesn't include *descenders,* type that extends down, like lowercase *y* and *g.* You adjust the baseline for trademark signs or mathematical formulas, as shown in Figure 6-14.

Figure 6-14:
Adjust the baseline for superscript.

A G I   T R A I N I N G ™

$E = M C^2$

The keyboard shortcuts for type shown in Table 6-1 work with Adobe Illustrator, Photoshop, and InDesign.

Table 6-1	Keyboard Shortcuts for Type	
Command	*Windows*	*Mac*
Align left, right, or center	Shift+Ctrl+L, R, or C	Shift+⌘+L, R, or C
Justify	Shift+Ctrl+J	Shift+⌘+J
Insert soft return	Shift+Enter	Shift+Return
Reset horizontal scale to 100 percent	Shift+Ctrl+X	Shift+⌘+X
Increase/decrease point size	Shift+Ctrl+> or <	Shift+⌘+> or <
Increase/decrease leading	Alt+↑ or ↓	Option+↑ or ↓

Command	Windows	Mac
Set leading to the font size	Double-click the leading icon in the Character panel	Double-click the leading icon in the Character panel
Reset tracking/kerning to 0	Alt+Ctrl+Q	Option+⌘+Q
Add or remove space *(kerning)* between two characters	Alt+→ or ←	Option+→ or ←
Add or remove space *(kerning)* between characters by 5 times the increment value	Alt+Ctrl+→ or ←	Option+⌘+→ or ←
Add or remove space *(kerning)* between selected words	Alt+Ctrl+\ or Backspace	Option+⌘+\ or Backspace
Add or remove space *(kerning)* between words by 5 times the increment value	Shift+Alt+Ctrl+\ or Backspace	Shift+Option+⌘+\ or Backspace
Increase/decrease baseline shift	Alt+Shift+↑ or ↓	Option+Shift+↑ or ↓

Book III
Chapter 6

Using Type in
Illustrator

Using the Character Panel

To visualize changes that you're making to text and to see characteristics that are already selected, choose Window⇨Type⇨Character or press Ctrl+T (Windows) or ⌘+T (Mac), which brings up the Character panel. Click the triangle in the upper-right corner to see a panel menu of additional options. Choose Show Options, and additional type attributes appear, such as baseline shift, underline, and strikethrough.

Pressing Ctrl+T (Windows) or ⌘+T (Mac) is a toggle switch to either show or hide the Character panel. If you don't see the Character panel appear at first, you may have hidden it by pressing the keyboard shortcut. Just try it again.

The following list explains the options in the Character panel (see Figure 6-15):

✦ **Font:** Pick the font that you want to use from this drop-down list.

In the Windows version, you can click and drag across the font name in the Character panel or Control panel, and press the up- or down-arrow key to automatically switch to the next font above or below on the font list. Do this while you have text selected to see the text change live!

✦ **Set font style:** Pick the style (for example, Bold, Italic, or Bold Italic) from this drop-down list. The choices here are limited by the fonts that you have loaded. In other words, if you have only Times regular loaded in your system, you won't have the choice to bold or italicize it.

✦ **Type size:** Choose the size of the type in this combo box. Average readable type is 12 pt; headlines can vary from 18 pts and up.

✦ **Leading:** Select how much space you want between the lines of text in this combo box. Illustrator uses the professional typesetting method of including the type size in the total leading. In other words, if you have 12 pt and want it double-spaced, set the leading at 24 pts.

✦ **Kerning:** Use this combo box by placing the cursor between two letters. Increase the amount by clicking the up arrow or by typing a value to push the letters farther apart from each other; decrease the spacing between the letters by typing a lower value, even negative numbers, or by clicking the down arrow.

✦ **Tracking:** Use the Tracking combo box by selecting multiple letters and increasing or decreasing the space between them all at once by clicking the up or down arrows or by typing a positive or negative value.

✦ **Horizontal scale:** Distorts the selected text by stretching it horizontally. Enter a positive number to increase the size of the letters; enter a negative number to decrease the size.

✦ **Vertical scale:** Distorts the selected text vertically. Enter a positive number to increase the size of the letters; enter a negative number to decrease the size.

Using horizontal or vertical scaling to make text look like condensed type often doesn't give good results. When you distort text, the nice thick and thin characteristics of the typeface also become distorted and can produce weird effects.

✦ **Baseline shift:** Use baseline shift for trademark signs and mathematical formulas that require selected characters to be moved above or below the baseline.

✦ **Character rotation:** Rotate just the selected text by entering an angle in this text field or by clicking the up or down arrows.

✦ **Rotate:** Choose to rotate your selected text on any angle.

✦ **Underline and strikethrough:** These simple text attributes underline and strikethrough selected text.

✦ **Language:** Choose a language from this drop-down list. *Note:* The language you specify here is used by Illustrator's spell checker and hyphenation feature. We discuss these features in the later section, "Text Utilities: Your Key to Efficiency."

Figure 6-15:
The Character panel with additional options showing.

Using the Control Panel

Use the Control panel to quickly access your Type tools and Type panels. Note in Figure 6-16 that, when you have active text, hyperlinked text buttons allow you to quickly access panels, such as the Character and Paragraph panels. You can also use this Control panel as a quick and easy way to select fonts, size, alignment, color, and transparency.

Figure 6-16:
The Control panel type functions.

Using the Paragraph Panel

Access the Paragraph panel quickly by clicking the Paragraph hyperlink in the Control panel or by choosing Window➪Type➪Paragraph. This panel has all the attributes that apply to an entire paragraph (such as alignment and indents, which we discuss in the next two sections, and hyphenation, which we discuss later in this chapter). For example, you can't flush left one word in a paragraph — when you click the Flush Left button, the entire paragraph flushes left. To see additional options in the Paragraph panel, click the triangle in the upper right of the panel (the panel menu) and choose Show Options.

Alignment

You can choose any of the following alignment methods by clicking the appropriate button on the Paragraph panel:

✦ **Flush Left:** All text is flush to the left with a ragged edge on the right. This is the most common way to align text.

✦ **Center:** All text is centered.

✦ **Flush Right:** All text is flush to the right and ragged on the left.

✦ **Justify with the Last Line Aligned Left:** Right and left edges are both straight, with the last line left-aligned.

✦ **Justify with the Last Line Aligned Center:** Right and left edges are both straight, with the last line centered.

✦ **Justify with the Last Line Aligned Right:** Right and left edges are both straight, with the last line right-aligned.

✦ **Justify All Lines:** This method is *forced justification,* where the last line is stretched the entire column width, no matter how short it is. This alignment is used in many publications, but it can create some awful results.

Indents

You can choose from the following methods of indentation:

✦ **First Line Indent:** Indents the first line of every paragraph. In other words, every time you press the Enter (Windows) or Return (Mac) key, this spacing is created.

To avoid first-line indents and space after from occurring, say if you just want to break a line in a specific place, create a line break or a soft return by pressing Shift+Enter (Windows) or Shift+Return (Mac).

✦ **Right Indent:** Indents from the right side of the column of text.

✦ **Left Indent:** Indents from the left side of the column of text.

 Use the Eyedropper tool to copy the character, paragraph, fill, and stroke attributes. Select the text that you want to, select the Eyedropper tool, and click once on the text with the attributes you want to apply to the selected text.

By default, the Eyedropper affects all attributes of a type selection, including appearance attributes. To customize the attributes affected by these tools, double-click the Eyedropper tool to open the Eyedropper dialog box.

Text Utilities: Your Key to Efficiency

After you have text in an Illustrator document, you may need to perform various tasks within that text, such as searching for a word to replace with another word, checking your spelling and grammar, saving and creating your own styles, or changing the case of a block of text. You're in luck because Illustrator provides various text utilities that enable you to easily and efficiently perform all these otherwise tedious tasks. In the following sections, we give you a quick tour of these utilities.

Find and Replace

Generally, artwork created in Illustrator isn't text heavy, but the fact that Illustrator has a Find and Replace feature can be a huge help. Use the Find and Replace dialog box (choose Edit⇨Find and Replace) to search for words that need to be changed, such as changing Smyth to Smith, or to locate items that may be difficult to find otherwise. This feature works pretty much like all other search and replace methods.

Spell checker

Can you believe there was a time when Illustrator didn't have a spell checker? Thankfully, it does now — and its simple design makes it easy to use.

To use the spell checker, choose Edit⇨Check Spelling and then click the Start button in the dialog box that appears. The spell checker works much like the spell checker in Microsoft Word or other popular applications: When a misspelled word is found, you're offered a list of replacements. You can either choose to fix that instance, all instances, ignore the misspelling, or add your word to the dictionary.

If you click the arrow to the left of Options, you can set other specifications, such as whether you want to look for letter case issues or have the spell checker note repeated words.

Note: The spell checker uses whatever language you specify in the Character panel. We discuss this panel in the earlier section, "Using the Character Panel."

If you work in a specialized industry that uses loads of custom words, save yourself time by choosing Edit⇨Edit Custom Dictionary and then add your own words. We recommend that you do so before you're ready to spell check a document so that the spell checker doesn't flag the custom words later (which slows you down).

The Hyphenation feature

Nothing is worse than severely hyphenated copy. Most designers either use hyphenation as little as possible or avoid it altogether by turning off the Hyphenation feature.

Here are a few things that you should know about customizing your hyphenation settings if you decide to use this feature:

✦ **Turning on/off the Hyphenation feature:** Activate or deactivate the feature in the Hyphenation dialog box (see Figure 6-17); access this dialog box by choosing Window➪Type➪Paragraph, clicking the arrow in the upper right of the Paragraph panel to access the panel menu, and then choosing Hyphenation from the list of options that appears. If you won't use the Hyphenation feature, turn it off by deselecting the Hyphenation check box at the top of the Hyphenation dialog box.

You can also simply click the Paragraph hyperlink in the Control panel to access the Paragraph panel.

✦ **Setting specifications in the Hyphenation dialog box:** Set specifications in the dialog box that determine the length of words to hyphenate, how many hyphens should be used in a single document, whether to hyphenate capitalized words, and how words should be hyphenated. The Before Last setting is useful, for example, if you don't want to have a word, such as *liquidated* hyphenated as *liquidat-ed.* Type **3** in the Before Last text field, and Illustrator won't hyphenate words if it leaves only two letters on the next line.

✦ **Setting the Hyphenation Limit and Hyphenation Zone:** They're not diets or worlds in another dimension. The Hyphenation Limit setting enables you to limit the number of hyphens in a row. So, for example, type **2** in the Hyphenation Limit text field so that there are never more than two hyphenated words in a row. The Hyphenation Zone text field enables you to set up an area of hyphenation based upon a measurement. For example, you can specify 1 inch to allow for only one hyphenation every inch. You can also use the slider to determine whether you want better spacing or fewer hyphens. This slider works only with the Single-Line Composer (the default).

The Find Font feature

If you work in production, you'll love the Find Font feature, which enables you to list all the fonts in a file that contains text and then search for and replace fonts (including the font's type style) by name. You do so from the Find Font dialog box (see Figure 6-18), accessed by choosing Type➪Find

Font. Select the font that you want to replace from the Fonts in Document list. Next, select a font from the Replace with Font From list. Note that the font must already appear in the document. Click the Change button to replace the font (or click the Change All button to replace all instances of the font) and then click OK. That's it!

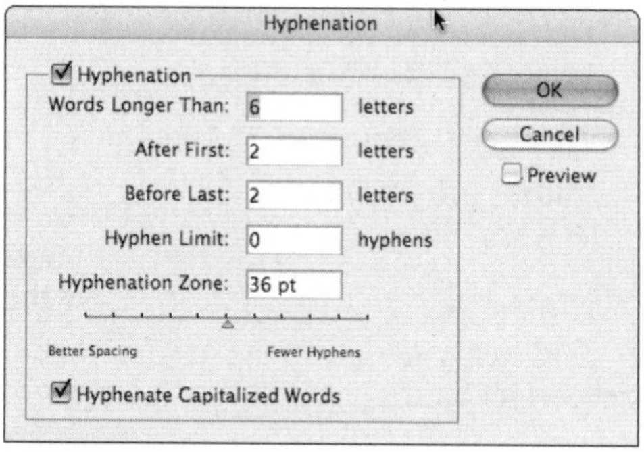

Figure 6-17:
Customizing
hyphenation
settings.

This cool feature enables you to replace fonts with fonts from the current working document or from your entire system. Select System from the Replace with Font From drop-down list to choose from all the fonts loaded in your system.

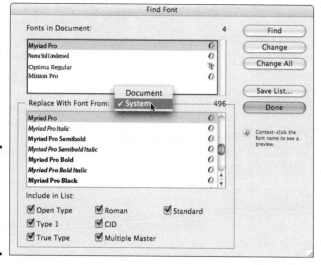

Figure 6-18:
Use the Find
Font dialog
box to find
and replace
typefaces.

The Change Case feature

Doesn't it drive you crazy when you type an entire paragraph before discovering that you somehow pressed the Caps Lock key? Fix it fast by selecting the text, choosing Type➪Change Case, and then choosing one of the following:

✦ **Uppercase:** Makes the selected text all uppercase.

✦ **Lowercase:** Makes the selected text all lowercase.

✦ **Title Case:** Capitalizes the first letter in each word.

✦ **Sentence Case:** Capitalizes just the first letter in the selected sentence(s).

In Illustrator CS4, you use the same type engine used by InDesign for high-quality text control. As a default, you're working in what is referred to as Single-Line Composer. Select Single or Every Line composer from the Paragraph panel menu.

The different options include

✦ **Single-Line Composer:** Useful if you prefer to have manual control over how lines break. In fact, this method had been in place in the past. The Single-Line Composer option doesn't take the entire paragraph into consideration when expanding letter space and word spacing, so justified text can sometimes look odd in its entire form (see Figure 6-19).

✦ **Every-Line Composer:** The Every-Line Composer option is a very professional way of setting text; many factors are taken into account as far as spacing is concerned, and spacing is based on the entire paragraph. With this method, you see few spacing issues that create strange effects, such as the ones on the left of Figure 6-19.

Figure 6-19: Single-Line Composer (left) and Every-Line Composer (right).

AGI was founded as a training provider and maintains a presence as a resource for companies and individuals looking to become more productive with electronic publishing software. AGI maintains a strong relationship with electronic publishing software companies including Adobe Systems and Quark as a member of their authorized training provider network. AGI is also a private, licensed school in the Commonwealth of Pennsylvania.

AGI was founded as a training provider and maintains a presence as a resource for companies and individuals looking to become more productive with electronic publishing software. AGI maintains a strong relationship with electronic publishing software companies including Adobe Systems and Quark as a member of their authorized training provider network. AGI is also a private, licensed school in the Commonwealth of Pennsylvania.

Text styles

A *text style* is a saved set of text attributes, such as font, size, and so on. Creating text styles keeps you consistent and saves you time by enabling you to efficiently implement changes in one step instead of having to select the text attributes for each instance of that style of text (say a heading or caption). So when you're finally happy with the way your headlines appear and how the body copy looks or when your boss asks whether the body copy can be a smidgen smaller (okay . . . how much is a smidgen?), you can confidently answer, "Sure!"

If you've created styles, changing a text attribute is simple. What's more, the change is applied at once to all text that uses that style. Otherwise, you'd have to make the attribute change to every occurrence of body text, which could take a long time if your text is spread out.

Illustrator offers two types of text styles:

✦ **Character styles:** Saves attributes for individual selected text. If you want just the word "New" in a line of text to be red 20 pt Arial, you can save it as a character style. Then, when you apply it, the attributes apply only to the selected text (and not the entire line or paragraph).

✦ **Paragraph styles:** Saves attributes for an entire paragraph. A span of text is considered a paragraph until it reaches a hard return or paragraph break. Note that pressing Shift+Enter (Windows) or Shift+Return (Mac) is considered a soft return, and paragraph styles will continue to apply beyond the soft return.

You can create character and paragraph styles in many ways, but we show you the easiest and most direct methods in the following subsections.

Creating character styles

Create a character style when you want individual sections of text to be treated differently from other text in the paragraph. So instead of manually applying a style over and over again, you create and implement a character style. To do so, open a document containing text and follow these steps:

1. **Set up text with the text attributes you want included in the character style in the Character and Paragraph panels and then choose Window⇨Type⇨Character Styles.**

   The Character Styles panel opens.

 2. **Select the text from Step 1 and Alt-click (Windows) or Option-click (Mac) the New Style button (the dog-eared page icon) at the bottom of the Character Styles panel.**

3. **In the Character Styles Options dialog box that appears, name your style and click OK.**

   Illustrator records what attributes have been applied already to the selected text and builds a style from them.

4. **Create another text area by choosing Select⇨Deselect and using the Type tool to drag out a new text area.**

   We discuss using the Type tool in the earlier section, "Creating text areas."

5. **Change the font and size to something dramatically different from your saved style and type some text.**

6. **Select some (not all) of the new text and then Alt-click (Windows) or Option-click (Mac) the style name in the Character Styles panel.**

   Alt-click (Windows) or Option-click (Mac) to eliminate any attributes that weren't part of the saved style. The attributes of the saved character style are applied to the selected text.

When creating a new panel item (any panel) in Adobe Illustrator, InDesign, or Photoshop, we recommend that you get in the habit of Alt-clicking (Windows) or Option-clicking (Mac) the New Style button. This habit allows you to name the item (style, layer, swatch, and so on) while adding it to the panel.

Creating a paragraph style

Paragraph styles include attributes that are applied to an entire paragraph. What constitutes a paragraph is all text that falls before a hard return (you create a hard return when you press Enter [Windows] or Return [Mac]), so this could be one line of text for a headline or ten lines in a body text paragraph.

To create a paragraph style, open a document that contains text or open a new document and add text to it; then follow these steps:

1. **Choose Window⇨Type⇨Paragraph Styles to open the Paragraph Styles panel.**

2. **Find a paragraph of text that has the same text attributes throughout it and put your cursor anywhere in that paragraph.**

   You don't even have to select the whole paragraph!

3. **Alt-click (Windows) or Option-click (Mac) the Create New Style button (the dog-eared icon at the bottom of the Paragraph panel) to create a new paragraph style; give your new style a name.**

   Your new style now appears in the Paragraph Styles panel list of styles.

4. **Create a paragraph of text elsewhere in your document and make its attributes different from the text in Step 2.**

5. **Put your cursor anywhere in the new paragraph and Alt-click (Windows) or Option-click (Mac) your named style in the Paragraph Styles panel.**

   The attributes from the style are applied to the entire paragraph.

Updating styles

When you use existing text to build styles, reselect the text and assign the style. In other words, if you put the cursor in the original text whose attributes were saved as a style, it doesn't have a style assigned to it in the Styles panel. Assign the style by selecting the text or paragraph and clicking the appropriate style listed in the Styles panel. By doing so, you ensure that any future updates to that style will apply to that original text, as well as to all other instances.

To update a style, simply select its name in either the Character or Paragraph Styles panel. Choose Options from the panel menu, which you access by clicking the arrow in the upper-right corner of the panel. In the resulting dialog box (see Figure 6-20), make changes by clicking the main attribute on the left and then updating the choices on the right. After you do so, all tagged styles are updated.

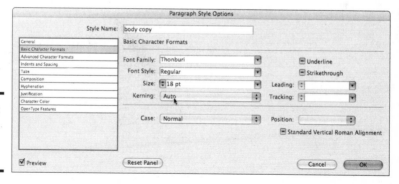

Figure 6-20:
Updating a
paragraph
style.

Documents created in older versions of Adobe Illustrator (Version 10 or earlier) contain *legacy text,* which is text using the older text engine. When these files are opened, you see a warning dialog box, such as the one you see in Figure 6-21.

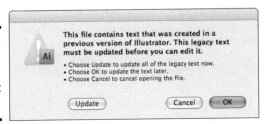

Figure 6-21:
Legacy text
warning;
click OK, not
Update!

This file contains text that was created in a previous version of Illustrator. This legacy text must be updated before you can edit it.

• Choose Update to update all of the legacy text now.
• Choose OK to update the text later.
• Choose Cancel to cancel opening the file.

[Update]   [Cancel]   [OK]

If you click the Update button, any text on the document will most likely reflow, causing line breaks, leading, and other spacing to change.

Click the OK button to update the file after it's opened to lock down the text. If necessary, you can use the Type tool to click a selected text area to update only the contained text. Another Warning dialog box appears that gives you the opportunity to update the selected text, copy the text object, or cancel the text tool selection. This method is the best way to see what changes are occurring so that you can catch any spacing issues right off the bat. See Figure 6-22 for samples of the three options in the warning dialog box.

If you click Copy the Text Object, you can use the underlying locked copy to adjust the new text flow to match the old. Throw away the legacy text layer by clicking and dragging it to the trash icon in the Layers panel, or click the visibility eye icon to the left of the Legacy Text layer to hide it when you're finished.

Figure 6-22:
Original
text (left),
updated text
(middle),
and text
object
copied
(right).

tia della minestrone, i ravioli, e la farinata.
    La città all'ovest della Liguria é San
Remo, che é accanto al Monaco. San
Remo é famosa per il museo di pasta e la festa di musica. La città
all'est della Liguria é La
Spezia, che é conosciu-
ta per una base
navale. La Spezia é
vicino à Carrara, il
posto   dové
Michelangelo prese
la sua marma.
    Da Genova si
andrà in barca alle
Cinque Terre, una zona
che non é possibile rag-

noce, e il pesce. E anche la regione nattia
della minestrone, i ravioli, e la farinata.
    La città all'ovest della Liguria é San
Remo, che é accanto al Monaco. San
Remo é famosa per il museo di pasta e la
festa di musica. La città all'est della Liguria é La Spezia, che é conosciuta
per una base navale. La
Spezia é vicino à Carrara, il
posto dové Michelan-
gelo prese la sua
marma.
    Da Genova si andrà
in barca alle Cinque
Terre, una zona che non
é possibile raggiungere in
machina; si deve andare o in
barca o in treno. Le Cinque Terre

noce, e il pesce. E anche la regione nattia
della minestrone, i ravioli, e la farinata.
    La città all'ovest della Liguria é San
Remo, che é accanto al Monaco. San
Remo é famosa per il museo di pasta e la
festa di musica. La città all'est della Liguria é La Spezia, che é conosciuta
per una base navale. La
Spezia é vicino à Carrara, il
posto. dové Michelan-
gelo prese la sua
marma. dové
Mi Da Genova si andrà
in s barca alle Cinque
Terre, una zona che non
é possibile raggiungere in
machina; si deve andare o in
barca o in treno. Le Cinque Terre

Chapter 7: Organizing Your Illustrations

In This Chapter

✔ Using your rulers

✔ Using ruler and custom guides

✔ Working with the Transform panel for placement

✔ Changing ruler origin

✔ Rearranging, hiding, and locking objects

✔ Masking objects

You can know all the neat special effects in Illustrator, but if you don't have strong organization skills, you can become exasperated when things just don't work as you expect them to. In this chapter, we focus on a few organizational tricks of the trade.

Setting Ruler Increments

Using rulers to help you accurately place objects in your illustration sounds pretty simple (and it is), but not knowing how to effectively use the rulers in Illustrator can drive you over the edge.

To view rulers in Illustrator, choose View➪Show Rulers or press Ctrl+R (Windows) or ⌘+R (Mac). When the rulers appear, they're in the default setting of points (or whatever measurement increment was last set up in the preferences).

You can change the rulers' increments to the measurement system that you prefer in the following ways:

✦ Create a new document and select your preferred measurement units in the New Document dialog box.

✦ Right-click (Windows) or Control-click (Mac) the horizontal or vertical ruler and pick a measurement increment.

✦ Choose Edit➪Preferences➪Units and Display Performance (Windows) or Illustrator➪Preferences➪Units and Display Performance (Mac) to bring up the Preferences dialog box.

Be *very* careful with the Preferences dialog box. Change ruler units only by using the General tab of the Preferences dialog box. If you change the units of measurement in the Stroke and Type tabs, you can end up with 12-*inch* type instead of that dainty 12-*point* type you were expecting! *Remember:* Setting the General Preferences changes the preferences for all future documents.

✦ Choose File➪Document Setup to change measurement units for only the document that you're working on.

Using Guides

Guides can make producing accurate illustrations much easier, and they can even go away when you're done with them. You can use two kinds of guides in Illustrator:

✦ **Ruler guides:** Straight-line guides that are created by clicking the ruler and dragging out to the artboard.

✦ **Custom guides:** Guides created from Illustrator objects, such as shapes or paths. Great for copying the exact angle of a path and replicating it, as shown in Figure 7-1.

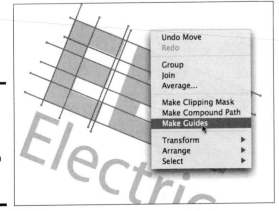

Figure 7-1:
Turn your selected paths and shapes into custom guides.

Creating a ruler guide

A ruler guide is the easiest guide to create. Click anywhere on the vertical or horizontal ruler and drag it to the artboard to create a ruler guide, as shown in Figure 7-2. By default, the horizontal ruler creates horizontal guides (no kidding), and the vertical ruler creates vertical guides. You can Alt+drag (Windows) or Option+drag (Mac) to change the orientation of the guide. The vertical ruler then creates a horizontal guide, and the horizontal ruler then creates a vertical guide.

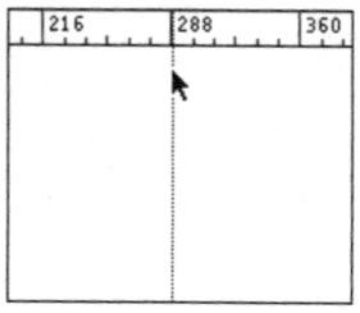

Figure 7-2: Click the ruler and drag out a guide.

Creating a custom guide

Create a custom guide by selecting a path or a shape and choosing View⇨Guides⇨Make Guides. Whatever is selected turns into a non-printing guide. Changing a path into a guide isn't permanent. Choose View⇨Guides⇨Release Guides to turn guides back into paths.

Using the Transform Panel for Placement

Placing shapes and paths precisely where you want them can be difficult for those with even the steadiest of hands. Save yourself aggravation by using the Transform panel to perform such tasks as scaling and rotating objects. On a more practical note, however, the Transform panel also enables you to type in *x, y* coordinates. This way, you can position your objects exactly where you want them.

In Adobe Illustrator and InDesign, the Reference Point Indicator icon is on the left side of the Transform panel. Click the handle of the Reference Point Indicator icon to change the point of reference. If you want to measure from the upper-left corner, click the indicator on the handle in the upper left. Want to know exactly where the center of an object is? Click the center point in the indicator. The point of reference is the spot on the object that falls at the *x, y* coordinates:

✦ **X coordinate:** Sets the placement of the selected object from left to right.

✦ **Y coordinate:** Sets the placement of the selected object from top to bottom.

Did you ever notice that Adobe Illustrator, which is based on PostScript, considers the lower-left corner the zero point? This can be confusing at first. You can change the ruler origin if it really drives you crazy by following the steps in the next section.

Changing the Ruler Origin

In Adobe Illustrator, InDesign, and Photoshop, you can change your *ruler origin*. This action helps define your measuring starting point and defines the part of the page that will print if you use manual tiling.

To change the ruler origin, follow these steps:

1. **Move the pointer to the upper-left corner of the rulers where the rulers intersect, as shown in Figure 7-3.**

Figure 7-3:
Drag where rulers intersect to change the ruler's origin.

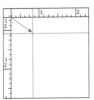

2. **Drag the pointer to where you want the new ruler origin.**

While you drag, a cross hair in the window and in the rulers indicates where the new ruler origin will be placed.

You can put the original ruler origin back in place by double-clicking the ruler intersection.

Thinking about Object Arrangement

Just like stacking paper on your desk, new objects in Illustrator are placed on top of the existing objects. Change this order by choosing the Object⇨Arrange choices.

The easiest choices are to bring an object to the front or send it to the back. The results of sending forward or backward can be a little unnerving if you don't know exactly in what order objects were created. Figure 7-4 shows an illustration that we rearranged with four of the available choices. Figure 7-5 shows the result of each choice.

Figure 7-4:
The objects in their original positions.

To change the stacking order, select the object(s) whose placement you want to change and then choose one of the following:

✦ **Object⇨Arrange⇨Bring to Front:** Brings the selected object(s) to the top of the painting order. In Figure 7-5a, the square is brought in front by using the Bring to Front command.

✦ **Object⇨Arrange⇨Bring Forward:** Brings the selected object(s) in front of the object created just before it, or one level closer to the front. In Figure 7-5b, the circle is pulled up in front of the square with the Bring Forward command.

✦ **Object⇨Arrange⇨Send Backward:** Moves the selected object(s) so that it falls under the object created just before it, or one level further to the back. In Figure 7-5c, the triangle is sent backward so that it's just under the circle.

✦ **Object⇨Arrange⇨Send to Back:** Pushes the selected object(s) to the bottom of the painting order. In Figure 7-5d, the triangle is placed on the bottom with the Send to Back command.

**Book III
Chapter 7**

**Organizing Your
Illustrations**

Figure 7-5:
Rearranging objects.

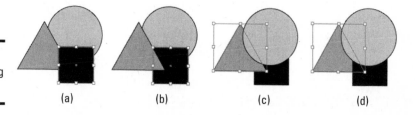

(a)　　　　(b)　　　　(c)　　　　(d)

Hiding Objects

Seasoned Illustrator users love the Hide command. Use it when the object that you want to select is stuck behind something else, or when you need to select one object and another keeps activating instead.

A good opportunity to use the Hide command is when you're creating text inside a shape. In Chapter 6 of this minibook, we show you that as soon as you turn a shape into a text area, the fill and stroke attributes turn into None. Follow these steps to hide a shape:

1. **Create a shape.**

    For this example, we created an ellipse.

2. **Click the Fill color box at the bottom of the Illustrator toolbox and then choose Window⇨Swatches.**

    The Swatches panel appears.

3. **In the Swatches panel, choose a color for the fill.**

    In this example, yellow is selected. The stroke doesn't matter; this one is set it to None.

    When you click a shape with the Type tool, it converts your shape into a text area, and the fill and stroke convert to None. To have a colored shape remain, you must hide a copy.

4. **With your colored shape selected, choose Edit⇨Copy; alternatively, you can press Ctrl+C (Windows) or ⌘+C (Mac).**

    This makes a copy of your shape.

5. **Choose Edit⇨Paste in Back or press Ctrl+B (Windows) or ⌘+B (Mac).**

    This step puts a copy of your shape exactly in back of the original.

6. **Choose Object⇨Hide or press Ctrl+3 (Windows) or ⌘+3 (Mac).**

    The copy of the shape is now hidden; what you see is your original shape.

7. **Switch to the Type tool by selecting the tool in the toolbox or pressing T.**

8. **With the cursor, cross over the edge of the shape to change it to the Area Type tool.**

    The Area Type tool enables you to type into a shape.

9. **When you see the type insertion cursor swell up (as shown in Figure 7-6), click the edge of the shape.**

    The insertion point is now blinking inside the shape, and the fill and stroke attributes of the shape have been changed to None.

Figure 7-6:
The type
insertion
cursor on
the edge of
a shape.

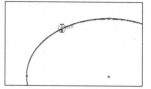

10. **Type some text (see Figure 7-7).**

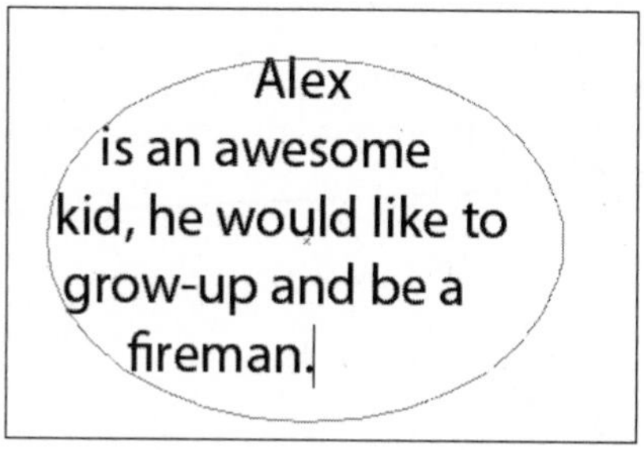

Figure 7-7:
Type
directly into
the shape.

> Alex
> is an awesome
> kid, he would like to
> grow-up and be a
> fireman.

11. **When you're finished entering text, choose Object⇨Show All, or press Ctrl+Alt+3 (Windows) or ⌘+Option+3 (Mac).**

Your colored shape reappears with the text in the middle of it (see Figure 7-8).

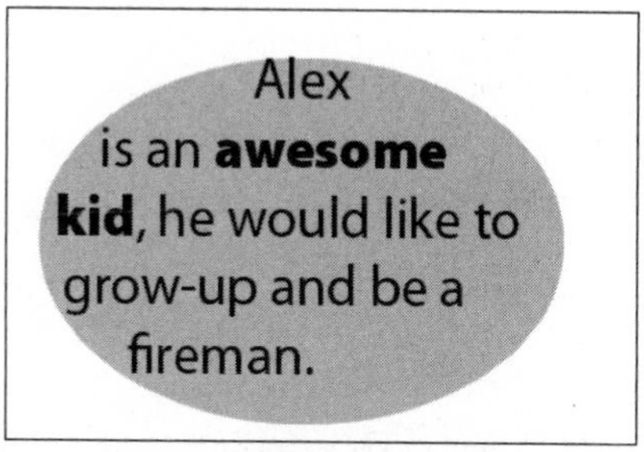

Figure 7-8:
The hidden
shape
reappears
behind the
text.

> Alex
> is an **awesome**
> **kid**, he would like to
> grow-up and be a
> fireman.

Use the Hide command anytime you want to tuck away something for later use. We promise that anything hidden in Illustrator won't be lost. Just use the Show All command, and any hidden objects are revealed, exactly where you left them. Too bad the Show All command can't reveal where you left your car keys!

Locking Objects

Locking items is handy when you're building an illustration. Not only does the Lock command lock down objects that you don't want to make changes to, but it also drives anyone who tries to edit your files crazy! In fact, we mention locking mainly to help preserve your sanity. There will be many times you need to make simple adjustments to another designer's artwork and you just can't, unless the objects are first unlocked. You can lock and unlock objects as follows:

✦ **Lock an object:** Choose Object⇨Lock or press Ctrl+2 (Windows) or ⌘+2 (Mac) to lock an object so that you can't select it, move it, or change its attributes.

✦ **Unlock an object:** Choose Object⇨Unlock All or press Ctrl+Alt+2 (Windows) or ⌘+Option+2 (Mac). Then you can make changes to it.

You can also lock and hide objects with layers. See Chapter 8 in this minibook for more information about using layers.

Creating a Clipping Mask

Creating a clipping mask may sound complex, but it's actually easy and brings together some of the items that we talk about in this chapter, such as arranging objects. A *clipping mask* allows a topmost object to define the selected shapes underneath it. It's similar to you cutting a hole in a piece of paper and peering through it to the objects below, except that with a clipping mask, the area around the defining shape is transparent (see Figure 7-9).

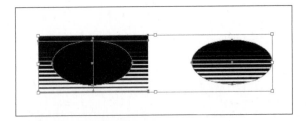

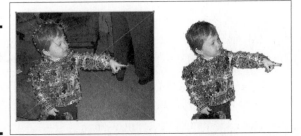

Figure 7-9: Examples of items with the clipping mask feature.

You may remember what a film mask looks like — it's black to block out the picture and clear where you want to view an image, as shown in Figure 7-10.

Figure 7-10: An illustration of a conventional film mask.

The clipping mask feature uses the same principal as the conventional film mask, but the clipping mask is a whole lot easier to create and modify. To create a clipping mask, follow these steps:

1. **Choose File⇨Place to place an image.**

Masks work with objects created in Illustrator, as well as those placed (scanned or otherwise imported into Illustrator), but an example using a single placed image is less complicated.

2. **Create the item that you want to use as a mask by creating a shape or a closed path with the Pen tool.**

For example, in Figure 7-11, the circle is the mask. (The photo underneath it is the placed image from Step 1.) The circle is placed where the mask will be created. It doesn't matter what the shape's color, fill, and stroke are because these automatically change to None when you create a mask.

Note: When creating a clipping mask, make sure that the object to be used as a mask is a closed shape and is at the top of the stacking order.

Figure 7-11: Position the mask shape over the object.

3. **With the Selection tool, select the placed image and the shape.**

Shift-click to add an object to the selection.

4. **Choose Object➪Clipping Mask➪Make.**

Alternatively, you can use the keyboard shortcut Ctrl+7 (Windows) or ⌘+7 (Mac) to create the clipping mask.

Ta-da! The clipping mask is created. The masked items are grouped together, but you can use the Direct Selection tool to move around the image or the mask individually.

5. **To turn off the clipping mask, choose Object➪Clipping Mask➪Release.**

You can also use text as a clipping mask. Just type a word, make sure that it's positioned over an image or other Illustrator object(s), select both the text and the object, and then choose Object➪Clipping Mask➪Make.

Chapter 8: Using Layers

In This Chapter

- ✔ Working with layers
- ✔ Using layers for a selection
- ✔ Changing the stacking order of your layer
- ✔ Moving and cloning objects to another layer
- ✔ Hiding and locking layers

*T*his chapter shows you just how simple it is to use layers and how help-ful layers can be when you're producing complex artwork. Layers are similar to clear pages stacked on top of your artwork: You can place content (text, shapes, and so on) on a layer, lift up a layer, remove a layer, hide and show layers, or lock a layer so that you can't edit the content on it. Layers are an incredible feature that can help you

- ✦ **Organize the painting (stacking) order of objects.**

- ✦ **Activate objects that would otherwise be difficult to select with the Selection or Direct Selection tool.**

- ✦ **Lock items that you don't want to reposition or change.**

- ✦ **Hide items until you need them.**

- ✦ **Repurpose objects for artwork variations.** For example, business cards use the same logo and company address, but the name and contact information change for each person. In this case, placing the logo and company address on one layer and the person's name and contact infor-mation on another layer makes it easy to create a new business card by just changing the name of the person.

Many Illustrator users don't take advantage of layers. Maybe these users don't understand the basic functions of layers, or maybe they think that layers are much more complicated than they really are. By reading this chapter, you'll be able to take advantage of layers in Illustrator.

Unlike in Photoshop, layers in Illustrator don't add an incredible amount of size to the file.

Creating New Layers

When you create a new Illustrator document, you automatically have one layer to start with. To understand how layers work, create a new file and then follow these steps to create new layers and put objects on them:

1. **If the Layers panel isn't already visible, choose Window➪Layers.**

The Layers panel appears. In Illustrator CS4, you see layer color bars to help identify selected objects and the layer they're on, as shown in Figure 8-1.

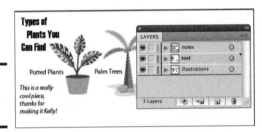

Figure 8-1:
The Layers panel.

In Figure 8-1, the Notes layer name is in italic. This is because the creator double-clicked that layer (to open the Layer Options dialog box) and deselected the Print check box.

2. **Create a shape anywhere on the artboard.**

The size of the shape doesn't matter, but make sure that it has a colored fill so that you can see it easily. For example, create a rectangle.

3. **Click the Fill button in the Control panel and select any color for the shape from the Color Picker that appears, as shown in Figure 8-2.**

The Fill button is the swatch with an arrow on the left side of the Control panel.

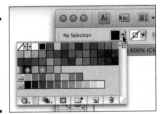

Figure 8-2:
Select any color from the Fill Color Picker.

The blue handle color that appears on the active shape matches the blue-color bar you see in the Layers panel on the left side of the layer name and the small selection square to the right of the radio button. The small selection square on the right disappears if you choose Select➪Deselect. You use that square to see what layer a selected object is on.

Also, notice now that you've added a shape to this layer, and an arrow appears to the left of the layer name. This arrow indicates that you now have a *sublayer,* which is essentially a layer within a layer. Click the arrow to expand the layer and show any sublayers nested under it; sublayers are automatically created when you add objects, which helps when you're making difficult selections.

4. Alt-click (Windows) or Option-click (Mac) the Create New Layer button at the bottom of the Layers panel to create a new layer.

The Layer Options dialog box appears (see Figure 8-3), and you can use it to name a layer and change the selection color. You don't have to hold down the Alt or Option key when making a new layer, but if you don't, you won't have the opportunity to name the layer when you create it.

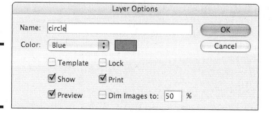

Figure 8-3:
Creating a
new layer.

5. Enter a name for the new layer in the Name text box and click OK.

In Figure 8-3, we entered **circle** because it's the shape that we add in the next step.

A new layer is added to the top of the stack in the Layers panel.

6. Make a shape on the new layer and overlap the shape you created in Step 2 (see Figure 8-4).

We created a circle, as shown in Figure 8-4.

7. Change the fill color for your new shape.

Check out the selection handles: They change to a different color, indicating that you're on a different layer. The different colors of the handles are for organizational purposes only and don't print.

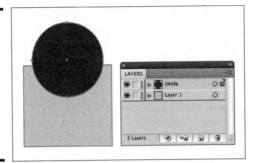

Figure 8-4:
A circle on the new layer overlaps the square on the underlying layer.

8. **Just to be different, this time choose New Layer from the panel menu.**

   The Layer Options dialog box appears.

9. **(Optional) In the Layer Options dialog box, change the color of the selection handles by selecting an option from the Color drop-down list.**

   You can also hide or lock the contents of the layer.

10. **Enter a name for this new layer in the Name text field, click OK, and then create a shape on it.**

   For example, we entered **star** in the Name text box and used the Star tool to create a star on the new layer.

11. **Again, change the fill color of your newest shape so that it's different from the other shapes.**

12. **Use the Selection tool to move the new shape so that it overlaps the others slightly.**

13. **Rename the original layer (Layer 1) by double-clicking the layer's name in the Layers panel, typing a new name, and then pressing Enter (Windows) or Return (Mac).**

   Because we had a rectangle on Layer 1, we typed **rectangle** (that's nice and descriptive) to rename the layer.

You can open up the Options dialog box for any existing layer by choosing Options for Layer (Named Layer) from the panel menu in the Layers panel.

You've created new layers and now have a file that you can use to practice working with layers.

Using Layers for Selections

When you have a selected object on a layer, a color selection square appears to the right of the named layer. If you click the radio button directly to the right of the layer's name in the Layers panel, all objects are selected on that layer.

Sublayers each have their own radio button as well. If you have sublayers visible, you can use this same technique to select objects that may be buried behind others.

If you think that you'll be selecting sublayers frequently, double-click the default name and type a more descriptive name for that layer.

Changing the Layer Stacking Order

In Chapter 7 of this minibook, we tell you about the Object⇨Arrange feature in Illustrator; with layers, this process gets just a little more complicated. Each layer has its own *painting order,* the order in which you see the layers. To move a layer (and thereby change the stacking order of the layers), click and drag that layer until you see the black insertion line where you want the layer to be moved.

As you add shapes to a layer, a sublayer is created, and it has its own little stacking order that's separate from other layers. In other words, if you choose to send an object to the back and it's on the top layer, it will only go to the back of that layer, and still be in front of any objects on layers beneath.

Understanding how the stacking order affects the illustration is probably the most confusing part about layers. Just remember that for an object to appear behind everything else, it has to be on the bottom layer (and at the bottom of all the objects in that bottom layer); for an object to appear in front of everything else, it has to be on the topmost layer.

Moving and Cloning Objects

To move a selected object from one layer to another, click the small color selection square to the right of the layer's radio button in the Layers panel, drag it to the target layer, and release. That's all there is to moving an object from one layer to another.

You can also *clone* an item — that is, make a copy of it while you move the copy to another layer. Clone an object by Alt+dragging (Windows) or Option+dragging (Mac) the color selection square to another layer. A plus sign appears while you drag (so you know that you're making a clone of the object). Release when you get to the cloned object's target layer.

Choose Paste Remembers Layers from the Layers panel to have Illustrator automatically remember which layer you copied an object from. No matter which layer is active, Illustrator will always paste the object back on the original layer that it was copied from.

Hiding Layers

To the left of each layer in the Layers panel is an eye icon. This is a visibility toggle button. Simply clicking the eye icon hides the layer (the eye disappears, denoting that this layer is hidden). Click the empty square (where the eye icon was) to show the layer again.

Alt-click (Windows) or Option-click (Mac) an eye icon to hide all layers except the one you click; Alt-click (Windows) or Option-click (Mac) on the eye icon to show all the layers again.

Ctrl-click (Windows) or ⌘-click (Mac) the eye icon to turn just the selected layer into Outline view mode. In Outline view, all you see are the outlines of the artwork with no stroke widths or fill colors. The rest of your artwork remains in Preview mode, with strokes and fills visible. This technique is pretty tricky and helpful when you're looking for stray points or need to close paths. Ctrl-click (Windows) or ⌘-click (Mac) back on the eye icon to return the layer to Preview mode.

Locking Layers

Lock layers by clicking the empty square to the right of the Visibility (eye) icon. A padlock icon appears so that you know the layer is now locked. Locking a layer prevents you from making changes to the objects on that layer. Click the padlock to unlock the layer.

Chapter 9: Livening Up Illustrations with Color

In This Chapter

✔ Choosing your color mode

✔ Using the Swatches and Color panels

✔ Working with strokes and fills

✔ Changing the width and type of your strokes

✔ Saving and editing colors

✔ Discovering patterns

✔ Employing gradients and copying color attributes

✔ Exploring the Live Trace and Live Paint features

*T*his chapter is all about making your brilliant illustrations come alive with color. Here, we show you how to create new and edit existing colors, save custom colors that you create, create and use patterns and gradients, and even apply color attributes to many different shapes.

Choosing a Color Mode

Every time that you create a new file, you choose a profile. This profile determines, among other things, which color mode your document will be created in. Typically, anything related to Web, mobile, and video is in RGB mode, and the print profile is in CMYK. You can also simply choose Basic CMYK or Basic RGB. Here are the differences between the color modes:

✦ **Basic CMYK (Cyan, Magenta, Yellow, and Black):** This mode is used if you're taking your illustration to a professional printer and the files will be separated into cyan, magenta, yellow, and black plates for printing.

✦ **Basic RGB (Red, Green, Blue):** Use this mode if your final destination is the Web, mobile device, video, color copier or desktop printer, or screen presentation.

The decision that you make affects the premade swatches, brushes, styles, and a slew of other choices in Adobe Illustrator. This all helps you to avoid sending an RGB color to a print shop. Ever see how that turns out? If your prepress person doesn't catch that the file isn't CMYK and sends an RGB file as separations (cyan, magenta, yellow, and black) to a printer, you can end up with a black blob instead of your beautiful illustration.

You can change the color mode at any time without losing information by choosing File➪Document Color Mode.

Using the Swatches Panel

Accessing color from the Control panel is probably the easiest way to make color choices, as using the Fill and Stroke drop-down lists allow you to quickly access the Swatches panel, as shown in Figure 9-1, and at the same time, make sure that the color is actually applying to either the fill or stroke. How many times have you mixed up colors and assigned the stroke color to the fill or vice versa?

You can also access the Swatches panel, which you open by choosing Window➪Swatches. Although limited in choice, its basic colors, patterns, and gradients are ready to go. You can use the buttons at the bottom of the Swatches panel (as shown in Figure 9-1) to quickly open color libraries, select what kinds of colors to view, access swatch options, create color groups, add new swatches, and delete selected swatches.

You may notice some odd color swatches — for example, the cross hair and the diagonal line.

Figure 9-1:
Use these
buttons
to quickly
access
color
options.

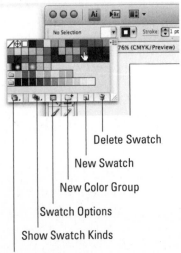

Delete Swatch

New Swatch

New Color Group

Swatch Options

Show Swatch Kinds

Swatch Libraries menu

The cross hair represents the Registration color. Only use this swatch when creating custom crop marks or printer marks. The Registration color looks black, but it's actually created from 100 percent of all colors. This way, when artwork is separated, the crop mark appears on all color separations.

 The diagonal line represents None. Use this option if you want no fill or stroke.

Applying Color to the Fill and Stroke

Illustrator objects are created from *fills* (the inside) and *strokes* (border or path). Look at the bottom of the toolbox for the Fill and Stroke color boxes. If you're applying color to the fill, the Fill color box must be forward in the toolbox. If you're applying color to the stroke, the Stroke color box must be forward.

Table 9-1 lists keyboard shortcuts that can be a tremendous help to you when applying colors to fills and strokes.

Table 9-1	Color Keyboard Shortcuts
Function	*Keyboard Shortcut*
Switch the Fill or Stroke color box position	X
Inverse the Fill and the Stroke color boxes	Shift+X
Default (black stroke, white fill)	D
None	/
Last color used	<
Last gradient used	>
Color Picker	Double-click the Fill or Stroke color box

**Book III
Chapter 9**

**Livening Up
Illustrations with
Color**

 Try this trick: Drag a color from the Swatches panel to the Fill or Stroke color box. This action applies the color to the color box that you dragged to. It doesn't matter which is forward!

To apply a fill color to an existing shape, drag the swatch directly to the shape. Select a swatch, hold down Alt+Shift+Ctrl (Windows) or Option+Shift+⌘ (Mac), and drag a color to a shape to apply that color to the stroke.

Changing the Width and Type of a Stroke

Access the Stroke panel by clicking the Stroke hyperlink in the Control panel. In the Stroke panel, you can choose *caps* (the end of a line), *joins* (the end points of a path or dash), and the *miter limit* (the length of a point). The Stroke panel also enables you to turn a path into a dashed line.

As you can see in Figure 9-2, you can choose, in the Stroke panel options, to align the stroke on the center (default) of a path, the inside of a path, and the outside of a path. Figure 9-3 shows the results.

Figure 9-2:
The Align Stroke options.

This feature is especially helpful when stroking outlined text. See Figure 9-3 to compare text with the traditional centered stroke, as compared to the new option for aligning the stroke outside of a path.

Figure 9-3:
The Align Stroke options affect the placement of the stroke.

Align Stroke to Center

Align Stroke to Outside

Align Stroke to Inside

You can't adjust the alignment of a stroke on text unless you change the text to outlines first. Select the Selection tool and choose Type➪Create Outlines to enable the Align Stroke options.

You can also customize the following aspects of a stroke in the Stroke panel:

✦ **Cap Options:** The endpoints of a path or dash.
- *Butt Cap:* Click this button to make the ends of stroked lines square.
- *Round Cap:* Click this button to make the ends of stroked lines semicircular.
- *Projecting Cap:* Click this button to make the ends of stroked lines square and extend half the line width beyond the end of the line.

✦ **Join Options:** How corner points appear.
- *Miter Join:* Click this button to make stroked lines with pointed corners.
- *Round Join:* Click this button to make stroked lines with rounded corners.
- *Bevel Join:* Click this button to make stroked lines with squared corners.

✦ **Dashed Lines:** Regularly spaced lines, based upon values you set.

To create a dashed line, specify a dash sequence by entering the lengths of dashes and the gaps between them in the Dash Pattern text fields (see Figure 9-4). The numbers entered are repeated in sequence so that after you set up the pattern, you don't need to fill in all the text fields. In other words, if you want an evenly-spaced dashed stroke, just type the same number in the first and second text fields, and all dashes and spaces will be the same length (say, 12 pts). Change that to 12 in the first text field and 24 in the next, and now you have a larger space between the dashes.

**Book III
Chapter 9**

Livening Up
Illustrations with
Color

Figure 9-4:
Setting up
a dashed
stroke.

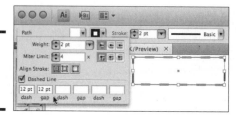

Using the Color Panel

The Color panel (access it by choosing Window⇔Color) offers another method for choosing color. It requires you to custom pick a color using values on the color ramp. As a default, you see only the *color ramp* — the large color well spanning the panel. If you don't see all the color options, choose Show Options from the Color panel's panel menu (click the triangle in the upper-right corner to access the panel menu).

Ever want to create tints of a CMYK color but aren't quite sure how to adjust the individual color sliders? Hold down the Shift key while adjusting the color slider of any color and watch how all colors move to a relative position at the same time!

As shown in Figure 9-5, the panel menu offers many other choices. Even though you may be in the RGB or CMYK color mode, you can still choose to build colors in Grayscale, RGB, HSB (Hue Saturation Brightness), CMYK, or Web Safe RGB. Choosing Invert or Complement from the panel menu takes the selected object and inverses the color or changes it to a complementary color, respectively. You can also choose the Fill and Stroke color boxes in the upper-left corner of the Color panel.

Figure 9-5:
Different color models are available in the Color panel.

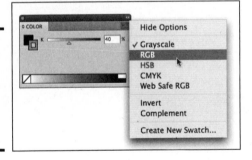

You see the infamous cube and exclamation point in the Color panels in most of Adobe's software. The cube warns you that the color you've selected isn't one of the 216 nondithering, Web-safe colors, and the exclamation point warns you that your color isn't within the CMYK print gamut. In other words, if you see the exclamation point in the Color panel, don't expect that really cool electric blue you see on-screen to print correctly — it may print as dark purple!

Click the cube or exclamation point symbols when you see them to select the closet color in the Web safe or CMYK color gamut.

Saving Colors

Saving colors not only keeps you consistent, but it makes edits and changes to colors easier in the future. Any time you build a color, drag it from the Color panel to the Swatches panel to save it as a color swatch for future use. You can also select an object that uses the color and click the New Swatch button at the bottom of the Swatches panel (refer to Figure 9-1 to see this button). To save a color and name it at the same time, Alt-click (Windows) or Option-click (Mac) the New Swatch icon. The New Swatch dialog box opens, where you can name and edit the color if you want. By double-clicking a swatch in the Swatches panel, you can open the options at any time.

A color in the Swatches panel is available only in the document in which it was created. Read the next section on custom libraries to see how to import swatches from saved documents.

Building and using custom libraries

When you save a color in the Swatches panel, you're essentially saving it to your own custom library. You import the Swatches panel from one document into another by using the Libraries feature.

Retrieve colors saved in a document's Swatches panel by selecting the Swatch Libraries menu button at the bottom of the Swatches panel and dragging down to Other Library. You can also access swatch libraries, including those in other documents, by choosing Window➪Swatch Libraries➪Other Library. Locate the saved document and click Open. A panel appears with the document name, as shown in Figure 9-6. You can't edit the colors in this panel, but you can use the colors in this panel by double-clicking a swatch or dragging a swatch to your current document's Swatches panel.

**Book III
Chapter 9**

**Livening Up
Illustrations with
Color**

Figure 9-6:
An imported
custom
swatch
library.

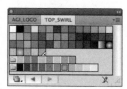

You can also click the Swatch Libraries button to access color libraries for Pantone colors, Web colors, and some neat creative colors, such as jewel tones and metals.

Using the Color Guide and color groups

Perhaps you failed at color in art class or just don't feel that you're one of those people who picks colors that look good together. In Illustrator CS4, you can use the Color Guide to find colors and save them to organized color groups in your Swatches panel. You can create color schemes based on 23 classic color-harmony rules, such as the Complementary, Analogous, Monochromatic, and Triad options, or you can create custom harmony rules.

Sounds complicated, doesn't it? Fortunately, all you have to do is choose a base color and then see what variations you come up with according to rules you choose. Give it a try:

1. **Choose Window⇨Color Guide.**

   The Color Guide appears, as shown in Figure 9-7.

Figure 9-7:
The Color Guide panel identifies related colors.

2. **Select a color from your Swatches panel. If your Swatches panel is not visible choose Window⇨Swatches.**

   Immediately, the Color Guide panel kicks in to provide you with colors that are related to your original swatch.

3. **Change the Harmony Rules by clicking the Edit Colors button at the bottom of the Color Guide panel.**

   The Edit Colors dialog box, as shown in Figure 9-8, appears.

   You could spend days experimenting in the Edit Colors dialog box, but for the scope of this book, you dive into changing simple harmony rules. To do this, click the Harmony Rules arrow to the right of the color bar. A drop-down list appears with many choices as to how you want colors selected, as shown in Figure 9-9. Choose a color harmony.

4. **Save your color selection as a color group by clicking the New Color Group icon.**

   If you like, you can rename the color group by double-clicking the group name in the Color Group section of the Live Color window.

5. **Click OK.**

   The color group is added to the Swatches panel.

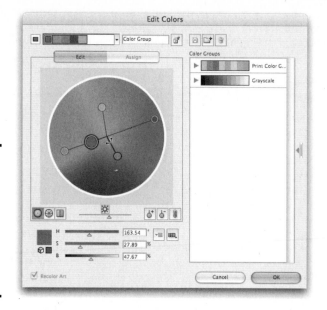

Figure 9-8:
The Edit
Colors
dialog box
allows you
to choose
and save
color
groups.

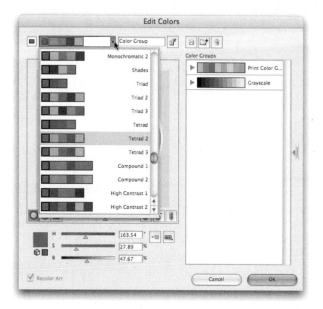

Figure 9-9:
Make a
selection
from the
Harmony
Rule drop-
down list.

You don't have to go through the Edit Colors dialog box in order to save a group of colors. You can Ctrl-click (Windows) or ⌘-click (Mac) to select multiple colors and then click the New Color Group button at the bottom of the Swatches panel.

Adding Pantone colors

If you're looking for the typical Pantone Matching System-numbered swatches, click the Swatch Libraries menu button at the bottom of the Swatches panel. From the drop-down list, choose Color Books and then Pantone solid coated, or whatever Pantone library you want to access.

Colors for the Pantone numbering system are often referred to as PMS 485, or PMS 201, or whatever number the color has been designated. You can locate the numbered swatch by typing the number into the Find text field of the Pantone panel, as shown in Figure 9-10. When that number's corresponding color is highlighted in the panel, click it to add it to your Swatches panel. Many users find it easier to see colored swatches by using the List View. Choose Small List View or Large List View from the panel menu.

Figure 9-10:
Use the Find
text box
to locate
Pantone
colors.

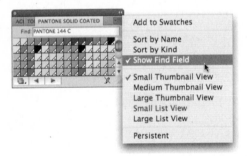

Editing Colors

Edit colors in the Swatches panel by using the Swatch Options dialog box (as shown in Figure 9-11), which you access by double-clicking the color or by choosing Swatch Options from the Swatches panel menu.

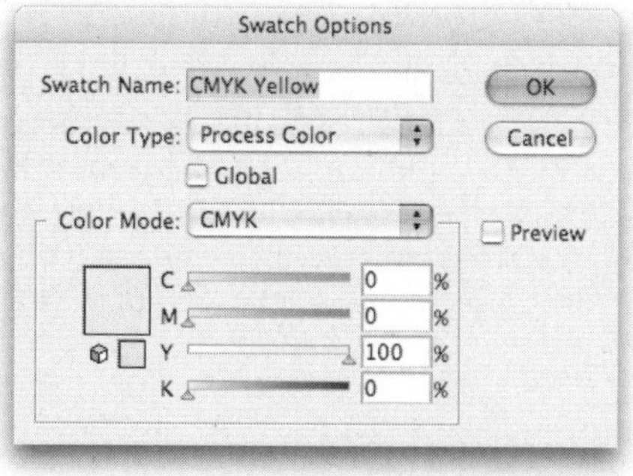

Figure 9-11:
Edit a color
swatch in
the Swatch
Options
dialog box.

Use the Swatch Options dialog box to

✦ **Change the color values:** Change the values in a color by using the sliders or by typing values into the color text fields. Having the ability to enter exact color values is especially helpful if you're given a color build to match. Select the Preview check box to see results as you make the changes.

✦ **Use global colors:** If you plan on using a color frequently, select the Global check box. If the Global check box is selected and you use the swatch throughout the artwork, you only have to change the swatch options one time and all instances of that color are updated.

One important option to note in the Swatch Options dialog box is the Color Type drop-down list. You have two choices here: spot color and process color. What's the difference?

✦ **Spot color:** A color that isn't broken down into the CMYK values. Spot colors are used for 1–2 color print runs or when precise color matching is important.

Suppose that you're printing 20,000 catalogs and decide to run only 2 colors, red and black. If you pick spot colors, the catalogs have to go through the press only two times: once for black and once for red. If red were a process color, however, it'd be created out of a combination of cyan, magenta, yellow, and black inks, and the catalogs would need to go through the press four times in order to build that color. Plus, if you went to a print service and asked for red, what color would you get? Fire-engine red, maroon, or a light and delicate pinkish-red? But if the red you pick is PMS 485, your printer in Lancaster, Pennsylvania can now print the same color of red on your brochure as the printer doing your business cards in Woburn, Massachusetts.

**Book III
Chapter 9**

Livening Up
Illustrations with
Color

✦ **Process color:** A color that's built from four colors (cyan, magenta, yellow, and black). Process colors are used for multicolor jobs.

For example, you'd want to use process colors if you're sending an ad to a four-color magazine. The magazine printers certainly want to use the same inks they're already running, and using a spot color would require another run through the presses in addition to the runs for the cyan, magenta, yellow, and black plates. In this case, you'd take any spot colors created in corporate logos and such and convert them to process colors.

Choose the Spot Colors option from the Swatches panel menu to choose whether you want spot colors changed to Lab or CMYK values:

✦ Choose Lab to get the best possible CMYK conversion for the actual spot color when using a color-calibrated workflow.

✦ Choose CMYK (default) to get the manufacturer's standard recommended conversion of spot colors to process. Results can vary depending upon printing conditions.

Building and Editing Patterns

Using patterns can be as simple or as complicated as you want. If you become familiar with the basics, you can take off in all sorts of creative directions. To build a simple pattern, start by creating the artwork that you want to use as a pattern on your artboard — polka dots, smiley faces, wavy lines, whatever. Then select all the components of the pattern and drag them to the Swatches panel. That's it, you made a pattern! Use the pattern by selecting it as the fill or stroke of an object.

You can't use patterns in artwork that will then be saved as a pattern. If you have a pattern in your artwork and try to drag it into the Swatches panel, Illustrator kicks it back out with no error message. On a good note, you can drag text right into the Swatches panel to become a pattern.

You can update patterns that you created or patterns that already reside in the Swatches panel. To edit an existing pattern, follow these steps:

1. **Click the pattern swatch in the Swatches panel and drag it to the artboard.**

2. **Deselect the pattern and use the Direct Selection tool to change its colors or shapes or whatever.**

Keep making changes until you're happy with the result.

3. **To update the pattern with your new edited version, use the Selection tool to select all pattern elements and Alt+drag (Windows) or Option+drag (Mac) the new pattern over the existing pattern swatch in the Swatches panel.**

4. **When a black border appears around the existing pattern, release the mouse button.**

   All instances of the pattern in your illustration are updated.

If you want to add some space between tiles, as shown in Figure 9-12, create a bounding box using a rectangle shape with no fill or stroke (representing the repeat that you want to create). Send it behind the other objects in the pattern and drag all objects, including the bounding box, to the Swatches panel.

Figure 9-12:
A pattern with a transparent bounding box.

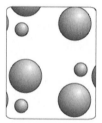

We cover transformations in detail in Chapter 10 of this minibook, but some specific transform features apply to patterns. To scale a pattern, but not the object that it's filling, double-click the Scale tool. In the Scale dialog box that appears, type the value that you want to scale but deselect all options except for Patterns, as shown in Figure 9-13. This works for the Rotate tool as well!

Figure 9-13:
Choose to scale or rotate only the pattern, not the object.

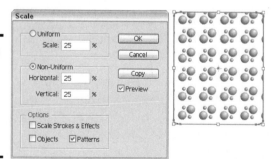

Working with Gradients

Create gradients for nice smooth metallic effects or just to add dimension to illustrations. If you're not sure which swatches are considered gradients, choose Gradient from the Show Swatch Kinds button at the bottom of the Swatches panel.

Once applied, you can access the Gradient panel (as shown in Figure 9-14) by choosing Window⇨Gradient. Choose Show Options from the Gradient panel menu to see more options.

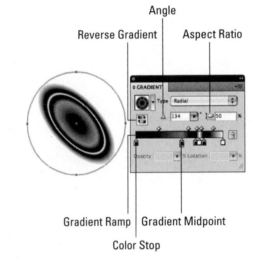

Angle

Reverse Gradient   Aspect Ratio

Figure 9-14:
The
Gradient
panel.

Gradient Ramp   Gradient Midpoint

Color Stop

On the Gradient panel, use the Type drop-down list to choose a *Radial* gradient (one that radiates from the center point) or a *Linear* gradient (one that follows a linear path).

Use the Gradient tool to change the direction and distance of a gradient blend as follows:

1. **Select an object and apply any existing gradient from the Swatches panel to its fill.**

2. **Choose the Gradient tool (press G) and drag in the direction that you want the gradient to go.**

   Drag a long path for a smooth, long gradient. Drag a short path for a short, more defined gradient.

To create a new gradient, click on the basic B & W Linear Gradient swatch in the Swatches panel (this puts you at a good base point), and then follow these steps:

1. With the Gradient panel options visible, click the gradient box at the bottom of the panel.

Two color stops appear, one on each end.

2. Activate a color stop by clicking it.

When a color stop is active, the triangle on the top turns solid.

3. Choose Window⇨Color to access the Color panel and then click the triangle in the upper-right corner to open the panel menu; choose RGB or CMYK colors.

4. Click the gradient ramp (across the bottom) in the Color panel to pick a random color (or enter values in the text fields to select a specific color) for the active color stop in the Gradient panel.

Repeat this step to select colors for other color stops.

To add additional color stops, click beneath the gradient ramp and then choose a color from the Color panel. You can also drag a swatch from the Swatches panel to add a new color to the gradient. To remove a color stop, drag it off the Gradient panel.

In CS4, you can click the gradient ramp to add additional colors and also change the opacity of that location of the ramp by entering values in the Opacity text box. This is a great way to create stripes and other reflective gradients.

Copying Color Attributes

Wouldn't it be great if you had tools that could record all the fill and stroke attributes and apply them to other shapes? You're in luck — the Eyedropper tool can do just that! Copy the fill and stroke of an object and apply it to another object with the Eyedropper tool as follows:

1. Create several shapes with different fill and stroke attributes, or open an existing file that contains several different objects.

2. Select the Eyedropper tool and click a shape that has attributes you want to copy.

3. Alt-click (Windows) or Option-click (Mac) another object to apply those attributes.

Book III
Chapter 9

Livening Up
Illustrations with
Color

Not only is this technique simple, but you can change the attributes that the Eyedropper applies. Do so by double-clicking the Eyedropper tool; in the dialog box that appears, select only the attributes that you want to copy.

The Live Trace Feature

If you're looking for good source art to use to experiment with color, look no further than your own sketches and scanned images. You can automatically trace bitmap images by using a variety of settings that range from black-and-white line art to vector art with multitudes of color that can be extracted from your image.

To use the Live Trace feature, follow these steps:

1. **Choose File⇨Place and select an image that you want to trace.**

   The file you place can be a logo, a sketch, or even a photo. Notice that after you place the image, the Control panel offers additional options.

2. **Click the arrow to the right of the Live Trace button.**

   This drop-down list provides Live Trace presets that may help you better trace your image.

3. **Scroll to the bottom and choose Tracing Options.**

   The Tracing Options dialog box appears.

4. **Select the Preview check box and experiment with the various settings, as shown in Figure 9-15.**

5. **When you find the setting that works best for your image, click the Trace button.**

You can return to the Tracing Options dialog box and change settings over and over again until you find the best one.

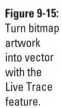

Figure 9-15:
Turn bitmap artwork into vector with the Live Trace feature.

The Live Paint Feature

 Painting made easy! Don't worry about filling closed shapes or letting fills escape out of objects with gaps into unwanted areas. With the Live Paint feature, you can create the image you want and fill in regions with color. The Live Paint bucket automatically detects regions composed of independent intersecting paths and fills them accordingly. The paint within a given region remains live and flows automatically if any of the paths are moved.

If you want to give it a try, follow these steps to put together an example to experiment with:

1. **With the Ellipse tool, create a circle on your page.**

   Make it large enough to accommodate two or three inner circles.

2. **Press D (just D, nothing else).**

   As long as you're not on the Type tool, you revert to the default colors of a black stroke and a white fill.

3. **Double-click the Scale tool and enter 75% in the Uniform Scale text box.**

4. **Press the Copy button and then click OK.**

   You see a smaller circle inside the original.

5. **Press Ctrl+D (Windows) or ⌘+D (Mac) to duplicate the transformation and create another circle inside the last one.**

6. **Choose Select⇨All or press Ctrl+A (Windows) or ⌘+A (Mac) to activate the circles you just created.**

7. **Make sure that the Fill swatch is forward.**

   The Fill swatch is at the bottom of the toolbox.

8. **Use the Swatches or Color panel and choose any fill color.**

9. **Select the Live Paint Bucket tool and move the cursor over the various regions of the circles.**

   See how the different regions become highlighted?

10. **Click when you have the region activated that you want to fill.**

    Now try it with other fill colors in different regions, as shown in Figure 9-16.

Figure 9-16:
Painting
objects
with the
Live Paint
feature.

A companion feature to the Live Paint bucket is support for gap detection. With this feature, Illustrator automatically and dynamically detects and closes small to large gaps that may be part of the artwork. You can determine whether you want paint to flow across region gap boundaries by using the Gap Options dialog box, accessibly by choosing Object⊅Live Paint⊅ Gap Options. The Gap Options dialog box is shown in Figure 9-17.

Before you save a file for an older version of Illustrator that uses the Live Paint feature, it's best to first select the occurrences of Live Paint and choose Object⊅Expand. When the Expand dialog box appears, leave the options at their default and click OK. This setting breaks down the Live Paint objects to individual shapes, which older versions of Illustrator can understand.

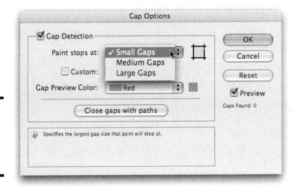

Figure 9-17:
The Gap
Options
dialog box.

Chapter 10: Using the Transform and Distortions Tools

Transformations that you can give to objects in Illustrator include scaling, rotating, skewing, and distorting. In this chapter, we show you how to use the general transform tools as well as some of the neat Liquify and Envelope Distort features available in Illustrator.

Working with Transformations

With just the Selection tool, you can scale and rotate a selected object. Drag the bounding box handles to resize the object (as shown in Figure 10-1) or get outside a handle, and then, when the cursor changes to a flippy arrow (a curved arrow with arrowheads on both ends), drag to rotate the object.

Figure 10-1: Use the bounding box to resize or rotate a selected object.

If you want to scale proportionally, hold down the Shift key while you drag to resize. To rotate an object at 45-degree increments, hold down the Shift key while you're rotating.

When you use the bounding box to rotate a selection, the bounding box rotates with the object, but its handles show the object's original orientation, as shown in Figure 10-2. This can help you to keep track of the original placement but can also interfere when you're building additional artwork. To reset the bounding box so that it's straight at the new orientation, choose Object⇨Transform⇨Reset Bounding Box.

Figure 10-2:
The bounding box shows the original placement.

When you scale, rotate, or use any other type of transformation in Illustrator, the final location becomes the *zero point*. In other applications, such as InDesign, you can rotate an object by any number of degrees (45 degrees, for example) and later enter 0 for the rotation angle in the Transform panel or in the Rotate dialog box to return the object to its original position. With Illustrator, if you enter **0** for the rotation angle to return a rotated object to its original position, the object won't change its position. To return the object to the previous position in Illustrator, you have to enter the negative of the number you originally entered to rotate the object, so you would enter –45 for the degree of rotation in this example.

Transforming an object

The Rotate, Reflect, Scale, and Shear tools all use the same basic steps to perform transformations. Read on for those basic steps, and then follow through some individual examples of the most often used transform tools. The following sections show five ways to transform an object: one for an arbitrary transformation and four others for exact transformations based on a numeric amount that you enter.

Arbitrary transformation method

This method is arbitrary, meaning that you're eyeballing the transformation of an object — in other words, you don't have an exact percentage or angle in mind, and you want to freely transform the object until it looks right. Just follow these steps:

1. **Select an object and then choose a transform tool (the Rotate, Reflect, Scale, or Shear tool).**

2. **Click once on the artboard.**

   Be careful where you click because the click determines the point of reference, or *axis point,* for the transformation, as shown in Figure 10-3.

Figure 10-3:
The first mouse click creates the axis point for the transformation.

Point of reference

3. **Drag in one smooth movement.**

   Just drag until you get the transformation that you want.

Hold down the Alt (Windows) or Option (Mac) key when dragging to clone a newly transformed item while keeping the original object intact. This is especially helpful when you're using the Reflect tool.

Exact transformation methods

In the following methods, we show you how to perform transformations with specific numeric information:

✦ **Exact transformation method 1:** Using the tool's dialog box

   1. *Select an object and then choose the Rotate, Reflect, Scale, or Shear tool.*

   2. *Double-click the transform tool in the toolbox.*

      A dialog box specific to your chosen tool appears. For this example, we selected and then double-clicked the Rotate tool to bring up the Rotate dialog box.

   3. *Type an angle, scaled amount, or percentage in the appropriate text field.*

   4. *Select the Preview check box to see the effect of the transformation before you click OK; click the Copy button instead of OK to keep the original object intact and transform a copy.*

✦ **Exact transformation method 2:** Using the reference point

   1. *Select an object and then choose the Rotate, Reflect, Scale, or Shear tool.*

   2. *Alt-click (Windows) or Option-click (Mac) where you want the reference point to be.*

   3. *In the appropriate transform tool dialog box that appears, enter your values and click OK or click the Copy button to apply your transformation.*

      This is the best method to use if you need to rotate an object an exact amount on a defined axis.

✦ **Exact transformation method 3:** Using the Transform menu

   1. *Select an object and then choose a transform option from the Object⇨Transform menu.*

      The appropriate transform dialog box appears.

   2. *Enter your values and click OK or the Copy button.*

✦ **Exact transformation method 4:** Using the Transform panel

Select an object and choose Window➪Transform to access the Transform panel, as shown in Figure 10-4.

Figure 10-4:
The Transform panel allows you to enter values.

While using the Transform panel is probably the easiest way to go, it doesn't give you the option of specifying an exact reference point (by a click with your mouse) or some other options that apply to the individual transform tools.

Using the Transform tools

In this section, we show you how to use some of the most popular Transform tools to create transformations.

The Reflect tool

Nothing is symmetrical, right? Maybe not, but objects that aren't created symmetrically in Illustrator can look pretty off kilter. With the Reflect tool, you can reflect an object to create an exact mirrored shape of it; just follow these steps:

1. **Open a new document in Illustrator and type some text or create an object.**

If you want to reflect text, make sure that you use at least 60-point type so that you can easily see what you're working with.

2. **Select the Reflect tool (hidden under the Rotate tool) and click the object; if you're using text, click in the middle of the text's baseline.**

This step sets the reference point for the reflection.

3. **Alt+Shift+drag (Windows) or Option+Shift+drag (Mac) and release when the object or text is reflecting itself, as shown in Figure 10-5.**

This step not only clones the reflected object or text, but also snaps it to 45-degree angles.

The Scale tool

With the Scale tool, you can scale an object proportionally or non-uniformly. Most people like to be scaled non-uniformly, maybe a little taller, a little thinner, but on with the topic. Follow these steps to see the Scale tool in action:

1. **Create a shape and give it no fill and a 5-point black stroke.**

   For this example, we created a circle. See Chapter 4 of this minibook if you need a reminder on how to do this.

2. **Select your shape and double-click the Scale tool.**

   The Scale dialog box appears.

3. **Type a number in the Scale text field (in the Uniform section) and click the Copy button.**

   We entered 125 in the Scale text field to increase the size of the object by 125 percent.

4. **Press Ctrl+D (Windows) or ⌘+D (Mac) to repeat the transformation as many times as you want.**

   Each time you press Ctrl+D (Windows) or ⌘+D (Mac), the shape is copied and sized by the percent you entered in the Scale text field. This is especially handy with circles and creates an instant bull's-eye!

To experiment with the Scale tool, create different shapes in Step 1 and enter different values in Step 3. Remember that if you type 50% in the Scale text field, the object is made smaller; go over 100% — say to 150% — to make the object larger. Leaving the Scale text field at 100% has no effect on the object.

The Shear tool

The Shear tool enables you to shear an object by selecting an axis and dragging to set a shear angle, as shown in Figure 10-6.

Figure 10-6:
Create
perspective
with the
Shear tool.

The axis will always be the center of the object unless you use method 1 or method 2 from the earlier section, "Exact transformation methods." Use the Shear tool in combination with the Rotate tool to give an object perspective.

The Reshape tool

The Reshape tool enables you to select anchor points and sections of paths and adjust them in one direction. You determine that direction by dragging an anchor point with the Reshape tool selected.

The Reshape tool works differently from the other transform tools. To use it, follow these steps:

1. **Select just the anchor points on the paths that you want to reshape. Deselect any points that you want to remain in place.**

2. **Select the Reshape tool (hidden under the Scale tool) and position the cursor over the anchor point that you want to modify; click the anchor point.**

If you click a path segment, a highlighted anchor point with a square around it is added to the path.

3. **Shift-click more anchor points or path segments to act as selection points.**

You can highlight an unlimited number of anchor points or path segments.

4. **Drag the highlighted anchor points to adjust the path.**

The Free Transform tool

You use the Free Transform tool pretty much like you use the bounding box. (See the earlier section, "Working with Transformations.") This tool is necessary only if you choose View➪Hide Bounding Box but want free transform capabilities.

Creating Distortions

Bend objects, make them wavy, gooey, or spiky — you can do all these things by creating simple to complex distortions with the Liquify tools and the Envelope Distort features.

The Liquify tools

The Liquify tools can accomplish all sorts of creative or wacky (depending on how you look at it) distortions to your objects. You can choose from seven Liquify tools. Even though we define these for you in Table 10-1, you really need to experiment with these tools to understand their full capabilities. Here are some tips:

✦ A variety of Liquify tools are available by holding down the mouse button on the default selection, the Warp tool. If you use them frequently, drag to the arrow at the end of the tools and release when you see the ToolTip for Tearoff. You can then position the tools anywhere in your work area.

✦ Double-click any of the Liquify tools to bring up a dialog box specific to the selected tool.

✦ When a Liquify tool is selected, the brush size appears. Adjust the diameter and shape of the Liquify tool by holding down the Alt (Windows) or Option (Mac) key while dragging the brush shape smaller or larger. Press the Shift key to constrain the shape to a circle.

Table 10-1		The Liquify Tools
Icon	*Tool Name*	*What It Does*
	Warp tool	Molds objects with the movement of the cursor. Pretend that you're pushing through dough with this tool.
	Twirl tool	Creates swirling distortions within an object.
	Pucker tool	Deflates an object.
	Bloat tool	Inflates an object.
	Scallop tool	Adds curved details to the outline of an object. Think of a seashell with scalloped edges.

Icon	Tool Name	What It Does
	Crystallize tool	Adds many spiked details to the outline of an object, such as crystals on a rock.
	Wrinkle tool	Adds wrinkle-like details to the outline of an object.

Using the Envelope Distort command

Use the Envelope Distort command to arch text and apply other creative distortions to an Illustrator object. To use the Envelope Distort command, you can use a preset warp (the easiest method), a grid, or a top object to determine the amount and type of distortion. In this section, we discuss all three methods.

Using the preset warps

Experimenting is a little more interesting if you have a word or object selected before trying the different warp presets. To warp an object or text to a preset style, follow these steps:

1. **Select the text or object that you want to distort and then choose Object⇨Envelope Distort⇨Make with Warp.**

The Warp Options dialog box appears.

2. **Choose a warp style from the Style drop-down list and then specify any other options you want.**

3. **Click OK to apply your distortion.**

Note: If you want to experiment with warping but also want to revert to the original at any time, choose Effect⇨Warp. You later change or delete the Warp Effect by double-clicking it in the Appearance panel or by dragging the effect to the trash can in the Appearance panel. Find out more about exciting effects that you can apply to objects in Chapter 12 of this minibook.

Reshaping with a mesh grid

You can also assign a grid to the objects to give you the ability to drag different points and create your own custom distortion, as shown in Figure 10-7.

Figure 10-7:
Create a
custom
distortion
with a mesh
grid.

Follow these steps to apply a mesh grid:

1. **Using the Select tool, select the text or object that you want to distort and then choose Object➪Envelope Distort➪Make with Mesh.**

   The Envelope Mesh dialog box appears.

2. **Specify the number of rows and columns that you want the mesh to contain and then click OK.**

3. **Drag any anchor point on the mesh grid with the Direct Selection tool to reshape the object.**

To delete anchor points on the mesh grid, select an anchor point with the Direct Selection tool and press the Delete key.

You can also use the Mesh tool to edit and delete points when using a mesh grid on objects.

Reshaping an object with a different object

To form letters into the shape of an oval or distort selected objects into another object, use this technique:

1. **Create text that you want to distort.**

2. **Create the object that you want to use as the *envelope* (the object to be used to define the distortion).**

3. **Choose Object➪Arrange to make sure that the envelope object is on top, as shown in Figure 10-8.**

Figure 10-8:
Position the
shape over
the text.

4. **Select the text and Shift-click to select the envelope object.**

5. **Choose Object⇨Envelope Distort⇨Make with Top Object.**

The underlying object is distorted to fit the shape of the top (envelope) object.

Choose Effect⇨Distort and Transform⇨Free Distort to take advantage of the Free Distort dialog box, as shown in Figure 10-9. Effects can be edited or undone at any time by clicking or deleting the Free Distort effect from the Appearance menu.

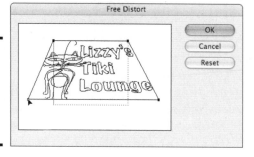

Figure 10-9: Distort an object with the Free Distort dialog box.

Chapter 11: Working with Transparency and Special Effects Tools

In This Chapter

✔ Finding out about the Mesh tool

✔ Getting to know the Blend tool

✔ Using the Symbol Sprayer tool

✔ Discovering transparency, blend modes, and opacity masks

This chapter is full of neat things that you can do using some of the more advanced features in Adobe Illustrator. These special effects tools can help you create art that really makes an impact: Discover how to make your art look like a painting with the Gradient Mesh tool, create morph-like blends with the Blend tool, become a pseudo-graffiti artist by trying out the Symbol Sprayer tool, and see what's underneath objects by using transparency!

The Mesh Tool

If you're creating art in Illustrator that requires solid colors or continuous patterns, you can achieve those results quite easily. But what if you're working on something that requires continuous tones, like a person's face? In that case, you'd turn to the very handy Mesh tool, which enables you to create the impression that you used paint and paintbrushes to create your illustration. Choose to blend one color into another and then use the Mesh tool to adjust where the blends occur and how dramatic the blends should be.

The Mesh tool can be as complex or simple as you want. Create intense illustrations that look like they were created with an airbrush, or just use it to give an object dimension, like the objects shown in Figure 11-1.

We show you how to create a gradient mesh two different ways: First by clicking (which gives you a little more freedom to put mesh points where you want them) and then by manually setting the number of rows and columns in the mesh (which is a more precise method).

Figure 11-1:
Illustrations can be complex or simple with the Mesh tool.

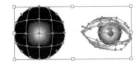

You can change the color in mesh points by choosing the Direct Selection tool and either clicking a mesh point and picking a fill color, or by clicking in the center of a mesh area and choosing a fill. Whether you select the mesh point (see the left side of Figure 11-2) or area in between the mesh points (see the right side of Figure 11-2) changes the painting result. To add a mesh point without changing to the current fill color, Shift-click anywhere in a filled vector object.

Figure 11-2:
The mesh point changes the painting result.

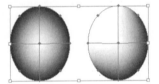

To create a gradient mesh by clicking, follow these steps:

1. **Create any shape using the shape tools and then deselect all objects by choosing Select➪Deselect.**

2. **Select a fill color that you want to apply as a mesh point to an object.**

   For example, if you have a red circle and you want a shaded white spot, choose white for your fill color.

3. **Select the Mesh tool (keyboard shortcut is U) and click anywhere in a filled vector object.**

   The object is converted to a mesh object.

4. **Click the object as many times as you want to add additional mesh points.**

To create a gradient mesh by setting the number of rows and columns, follow these steps:

1. **Select an object.**

2. **Choose Object⇨Create Gradient Mesh.**

The Create Gradient Mesh dialog box appears.

3. **Set the number of rows and columns of mesh lines to create on the object by entering numbers in the Rows and Columns text fields.**

4. **Choose the direction of the highlight from the Appearance drop-down list.**

The direction of the highlight determines in what way the gradient flows (see Figure 11-3); you have the following choices:

- *Flat:* Applies the object's original color evenly across the surface, resulting in no highlight.

- *To Center:* Creates a highlight in the center of the object.

- *To Edge:* Creates a highlight on the edges of the object.

Figure 11-3:
Choose a
highlight
direction.

5. **Enter a percentage of white highlight to apply to the mesh object in the Highlight text field.**

6. **Click OK to apply the gradient mesh to the object.**

The Blend Tool

 Use the Blend tool (located in the main Illustrator toolbox) to transform one object to another to create interesting morphed artwork or to create shaded objects. With the Blend tool, you can give illustrations a rendered look by blending from one color to another, or you can create an even amount of shapes from one point to another. Figure 11-4 shows examples of what you can do with this tool.

Creating a blend isn't difficult, and as you get used to it, you can take it farther and farther, creating incredibly realistic effects with it. Follow these steps to create a simple blend from one sized rectangle to another, creating an algorithmic stripe pattern (a rectangle of one height blended to a rectangle of another height):

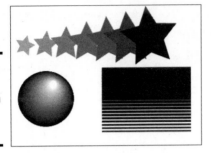

Figure 11-4:
Samples of
objects with
the Blend
tool.

1. **Create a rectangle.**

   Size doesn't really matter for this example; you just want to make sure that you can see a difference in shapes when you blend. We're using a rectangle that's roughly 4 x 1 inches.

2. **Give your shape a fill and assign None to the stroke.**

   You can use other settings here, but we recommend keeping it simple if you're still new to working with blends.

3. **With the Selection tool, click the rectangle and Alt+drag (Windows) or Option+drag (Mac) toward the bottom of the artboard to clone your shape; press the Shift key before you release the mouse button to make sure that the cloned shape stays perfectly aligned with the original shape.**

4. **Reduce the cloned shape to about half its original height by using the Transform panel (if the Transform panel isn't visible, choose Window➪Transform).**

   Alternatively, you can hold down the Shift key and drag the bottom-middle bounding box handle, as shown in Figure 11-5.

5. **In the Swatches panel (choose Window➪Swatches), change the cloned shape's fill to a different color but keep the stroke at None.**

   Changing the color just helps you see the blend effect a little better.

Figure 11-5:
Reduce
the size of
the cloned
shape.

6. **With the Blend tool, click the original shape and then click the cloned shape.**

As a default, the Blend tool creates a smooth blend that transitions from one color to another, as shown in Figure 11-6. To change the blend effect, experiment with the Blend Options dialog box.

Figure 11-6:
A smooth transition is created from one rectangle to the other.

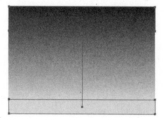

You can change the way that a blend appears by using the Blend Options dialog box, which you access by choosing Object➪Blend➪Blend Options. From the Spacing drop-down list, change the blend to one of the following options:

✦ **Smooth Color:** The blend steps are calculated to provide the optimum number of steps for a smooth transition.

✦ **Specified Steps:** You can determine the number of steps in a blend by typing a number in the text field to the right of the drop-down list.

✦ **Specified Distance:** You control the distance between the steps in the blend by typing a number in the text field to the right of the drop-down list.

You can also choose between two orientation options: *Align to Page* (orients the blend perpendicular to the X-axis of the page) or *Align to Path* (orients the blend perpendicular to the path). You probably won't see a difference when changing orientation unless you've edited the blend path.

You can easily access the Blend tool options by selecting a blended object and double-clicking the Blend tool in the toolbox.

If you're feeling adventurous, try changing a smooth blend (such as the one you create in the preceding steps) into a logarithmic blend. In the Blend Options dialog box, choose Specified Steps from the Spacing drop-down list and change the value to 5. This change creates the blend in 5 steps instead of the 200 plus steps that may have been necessary to create the smooth blend.

Here are a few more tips to help you become more comfortable with blends:

✦ You can blend between an unlimited number of objects, colors, opacities, or gradients.

✦ Blends can be edited directly with tools, such as the Selection tools, the Rotate tool, or the Scale tool.

✦ A straight path is created between blended objects when the blend is first applied. You can switch to the Direct Selection tool and edit the blend path by dragging anchor points.

✦ You can edit blends that you created by moving, resizing, deleting, or adding objects. After you make editing changes, the artwork is re-blended automatically.

The Symbol Sprayer Tool

The Symbol Sprayer tool is a super tool that you must experiment with to understand its full potential. In a nutshell, however, what it does is work like a can of spray paint that, instead of spraying paint, sprays *symbols* — objects that, in Illustrator, can be either vector- or pixel-based. Each symbol is an *instance.*

Illustrator comes with a library of symbols ready for use in the Symbols panel (if the Symbols panel isn't visible, choose Window⇨Symbols). Use this panel as a storage bin or library to save repeatedly used artwork or to create your own symbols to apply as instances in your artwork, like blades of grass or stars in the sky. You can then use the symbolism tools, described in Table 11-1, to adjust and change the appearance of the symbol instances.

Table 11-1		**The Symbol Tools**
Icon	*Tool Name*	*What It Does*
	Symbol Sprayer	Creates a set of symbol instances.
	Symbol Shifter	Moves symbol instances around. It can also change the relative paint order of symbol instances.
	Symbol Scruncher	Pulls symbol instances together or apart.
	Symbol Sizer	Increases or decreases the size of symbol instances.

Icon	Tool Name	What It Does
	Symbol Spinner	Orients the symbol instances in a set. Symbol instances located near the cursor spin in the direction you move the cursor.
	Symbol Stainer	Colorizes symbol instances.
	Symbol Screener	Increases or decreases the transparency of the symbol instances in a set.
	Symbol Styler	Enables you to apply or remove a graphic style from a symbol instance.

Press the Alt (Windows) or Option (Mac) key to reduce the effect of the symbolism tools. In other words, if you're using the Symbol Sizer tool, you click and hold to make the symbol instances larger; hold down the Alt (Windows) or Option (Mac) key to make the symbol instances smaller.

You can also selectively choose the symbols that you want to effect with the Symbolism tools by activating them in the Symbols panel. Ctrl-click (Windows) or ⌘-click (Mac) multiple symbols to change them at the same time.

Just about anything can be a symbol, including placed objects and objects with patterns and gradients. If you're going to use placed images as symbols, however, choose File➪Place and deselect the Linked check box in the Place dialog box.

To create a symbol, select the object and drag it into the Symbols panel or click the New Symbol button at the bottom of the Symbols panel. Yes, it's that easy. Then use the Symbol Sprayer tool to apply the symbol instance on the artboard by following these steps:

1. **Select the symbol instance in the Symbols panel.**

   Either create your own symbol or use one of the default symbols supplied in the panel.

2. **Drag with the Symbol Sprayer tool, spraying the symbol on the artboard (see Figure 11-7).**

   And that's it. You can increase or reduce the area affected by the Symbol Sprayer tool by pressing the bracket keys. Press] repeatedly to enlarge the application area for the symbol or press [to make it smaller.

Figure 11-7:
Using the
Symbol
Sprayer
tool.

Note that you can access all sorts of symbol libraries from the Symbols panel menu. Find 3D, nature, maps, flowers, and even hair and fur symbol collections by selecting Open Symbol Library.

Want to store artwork that you frequently need to access? Simply drag the selected object(s) into the Symbols panel, or Alt-click (Windows) or Option-click (Mac) the New Symbol button to name and store the artwork. Retrieve the artwork later by dragging it from the Symbols panel to the artboard. In fact, you can drag any symbol out to your artboard to change or use it in your own artwork. To release the symbol back into its basic elements, choose Object⇨Expand. In the Expand dialog box, click OK to restore the defaults.

Transparency

Using transparency can add a new level to your illustrations. The transparency feature does exactly what its name implies: It changes an object to make it transparent so that what's underneath that object is visible to varying degrees. You can use the Transparency panel for simple applications of transparency to show through to underlying objects, or you can use transparency for more complex artwork using *opacity masks,* masks that can control the visibility of selected objects.

Choosing Window⇨Transparency brings up the Transparency panel where you can apply different levels of transparency to objects. To do so, create an arrangement of objects that intersect, select the topmost object, and then change the transparency level of the object in the Transparency panel, either by moving the Opacity slider or by entering a value of less than 100 in the Opacity text field.

Blend modes

A *blending mode* determines how the resulting transparency will look. So to achieve different blending effects, you choose different blend modes from the Blend Mode drop-down list in the Transparency panel.

Truly, the best way to find out what all these modes do is to create two shapes that are overlapping and start experimenting. Give the shapes differently colored fills (but note that many of the blending modes don't work with black and white fills). Then select the topmost object and change the blending mode by selecting an option from the Blend Mode drop-down list in the Transparency panel. You'll see all sorts of neat effects and probably end up picking a few favorites.

We define each blend mode in the following list (but we'll say it again, the best way to see what each one does is to apply them — so start experimenting!):

✦ **Normal:** Creates no interaction with underlying colors.

✦ **Darken:** Replaces only the areas that are lighter than the blend color. Areas darker than the blend color don't change.

✦ **Multiply:** Creates an effect similar to drawing on the page with magic markers. Also looks like the colored film you see on theater lights.

✦ **Color Burn:** Darkens the base color to reflect the blend color. If you're using white, no change occurs.

✦ **Lighten:** Replaces only the areas darker than the blend color. Areas lighter than the blend color don't change.

✦ **Screen:** Multiplies the inverse of the underlying colors. The resulting color is always a lighter color.

✦ **Color Dodge:** Brightens the underlying color to reflect the blend color. If you're using black, there's no change.

✦ **Overlay:** Multiplies or screens the colors, depending on the base color.

✦ **Soft Light:** Darkens or lightens the colors, depending on the blend color. The effect is similar to shining a diffused spotlight on the artwork.

✦ **Hard Light:** Multiplies or screens the colors, depending on the blend color. The effect is similar to shining a harsh spotlight on the artwork.

✦ **Difference:** Subtracts either the blend color from the base color or the base color from the blend color, depending on which has the greater brightness value. The effect is similar to a color negative.

✦ **Exclusion:** Creates an effect similar to, but with less contrast than, the Difference mode.

✦ **Hue:** Applies the *hue* (color) of the blend object onto the underlying objects, but keeps the underlying shading, or luminosity.

✦ **Saturation:** Applies the saturation of the blend color, but uses the luminance and hue of the base color.

✦ **Color:** Applies the blend object's color to the underlying objects but preserves the gray levels in the artwork. This is great for tinting objects or changing their color.

✦ **Luminosity:** Creates a resulting color with the hue and saturation of the base color and the luminance of the blend color. This is essentially the opposite of the Color mode.

Opacity masks

Just like in Photoshop, you can use masks to make more interesting artwork in Illustrator. Create an opacity mask from the topmost object in a selection of objects or by drawing a mask on a single object. The mask uses the grayscale of the object selected to be the opacity mask. Black areas are totally transparent; shades of gray are semi-transparent, depending on the amount of gray; and white areas are totally opaque. Figure 11-8 shows the effect of an opacity mask.

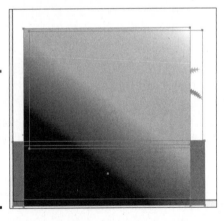

Figure 11-8: An opacity mask takes the topmost object and masks underlying objects.

To create an opacity mask, follow these steps:

1. **Open the Transparency panel menu (click the arrow in the upper-right corner to access this menu) and choose Hide Thumbnails.**

Also, be sure that the Blend Mode drop-down list is set to Normal.

2. **Create a shape anywhere on the artboard or open a document that has artwork on it.**

   We're using a circle, but the shape doesn't matter. Make sure that the artwork has a fill. A solid color will help you see the effect.

3. **Open the Symbols panel (choose Window⇨Symbols Panel) and drag a symbol to the artboard.**

   For this example, we're using the drums symbol.

4. **With the Selection tool, enlarge your symbol so that it fills your shape (see image on the left in Figure 11-9).**

 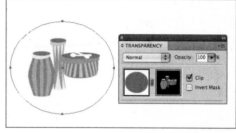

Figure 11-9: Creating an opacity mask.

5. **Select both the symbol and the shape and then choose Make Opacity Mask from the Transparency panel menu (see image on the right in Figure 11-9).**

   The symbol turns into a mask, showing varying levels of the underlying box through, depending on the original color value. To delete an opacity mask, choose Release Opacity Mask from the Transparency panel menu.

Click the right thumbnail (this is the mask) in the Transparency panel, and a black border appears around it, indicating that it's active. You can move the items on the mask or even create items to be added to the mask. The mask works just like the regular artboard, except that anything done on the mask side will only be used as an opacity mask. To work on the regular artboard, click the left thumbnail.

Chapter 12: Using Filters and Effects

In This Chapter

✔ Applying effects

✔ Getting to know the Appearance panel

✔ Discovering graphic styles

✔ Making artwork 3D

✔ Playing with additional fills and strokes

*E*ffects give you the opportunity to do jazzy things to your Illustrator objects, such as adding drop shadows and squiggling artwork. You can even use Photoshop filters right in Illustrator. In this chapter, you find out how to apply, save, and edit effects; this chapter also gives you a quick tour of the Appearance panel (your trusty sidekick when performing these tasks).

Working with Effects

If you're an Adobe Illustrator user from any version before CS4, you might be wondering . . . where's the Filter menu? (If you're just starting to use Illustrator, you really don't need to know about, or even care about, this major change.) All the items that appeared in the Filter menu are now in the Effects menu.

Filters applied permanent changes to artwork, referred to as *destructive changes,* because after you save and close the file, you couldn't undo the results for the filter. On the other hand, an effect is connected dynamically to the object. *Effects* are very different in that you can apply, change, and even remove effects at any time with the Appearance panel (Window⇨Appearance).

Understanding the Appearance panel

You can apply multiple effects to one object and even copy the effects to multiple objects. This is when a good working knowledge of the Appearance panel is necessary. If it isn't visible, choose Window⇨Appearance to show the Appearance panel, as shown in Figure 12-1, alongside an object with several effects applied to it.

Figure 12-1:
Discover
how
useful the
Appearance
panel
can be.

As a default, if you have no effects applied, you see only a fill and a stroke listed in the Appearance panel. As you add effects, they're added to this list. You can even add more strokes and fills to the list. Why would you do that? Because you can do incredible things with additional fills and strokes (which we show you in the upcoming section "Applying an effect"). See Figure 12-2 for a breakdown of the features on the Appearance panel.

Figure 12-2:
Use the
icons in
Appearance
panel for
effects.

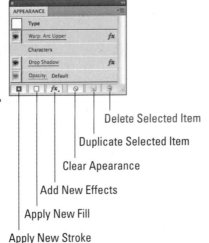

Delete Selected Item

Duplicate Selected Item

Clear Apearance

Add New Effects

Apply New Fill

Apply New Stroke

Applying an effect

In this section, you apply an effect. You can choose from many effects, and they're all applied in much the same manner. In this example, we apply the Arrowhead effect.

Follow these steps to apply an effect:

1. **Create a new document, choose any color mode, and draw a path in your document.**

If you haven't mastered the Pen tool yet (see Chapter 5 of this mini-book), use the Pencil tool.

2. **In the Control panel at the top of the Illustrator document, change the stroke to 3-pt and make sure that fill is set to None.**

Using a 3-point stroke enables you to see the stroke a little better.

3. **Choose Effect⇨Stylize⇨Add Arrowheads.**

Make sure that you choose the top Stylize menu item.

The Add Arrowheads dialog box appears (see Figure 12-3).

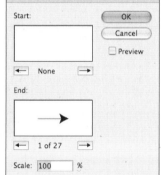

Figure 12-3:
Use the Add Arrowheads dialog box to create arrows.

4. **Add an arrowhead to both the start and the end of the path by using the arrow keys to scroll through the selections.**

Note that the Start arrowhead (top of the Add Arrowhead dialog box) will be placed on the first point you created; the End arrowhead (bottom of the dialog box) will be placed on the last point you created.

5. **Choose the size of the arrowhead by typing a number in the Scale text field.**

You can go anywhere from 1 to 1,000 percent, but typically an arrowhead is set at 50 percent. This scales the arrowhead relative to the selected line stroke weight.

Effects are linked dynamically to the object that they're applied to. They can be scaled, modified, and even deleted with no harm done to the original object.

Adding a Drop Shadow effect

Creating a drop shadow is a quick and easy way of adding dimension and a bit of sophistication to your artwork. The interaction between the object with the drop shadow and the underlying objects can create an interesting look. To add the Drop Shadow effect to an illustration, follow these steps:

1. **Select the object(s) that's to have the drop shadow applied.**

2. **Choose Effect⇨Stylize⇨Drop Shadow.**

3. **In the Drop Shadow dialog box that appears, select the Preview check box in the upper-right corner.**

   You now see the drop shadow applied as you make changes.

4. **Choose from the following options (see Figure 12-4):**

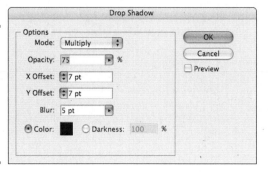

Figure 12-4: The Drop Shadow dialog box gives the effect's options and preview.

- *Mode:* Select a blending mode from this drop-down list to choose how you want your selected object to interact with the objects underneath. The default is *Multiply,* which works well — the effect is similar to coloring with a magic marker.

- *Opacity:* Enter a value or use the drop-down list to determine how opaque or transparent the drop shadow should be. If it's too strong, choose a lower amount.

- *Offset:* Enter a value to determine how close the shadow is to the object. If you're working with text or small artwork, smaller values (and shorter shadow) look best. Otherwise, the drop shadow may look like one big indefinable glob.

  The X Offset shifts the shadow from left to right, and the Y Offset shifts it up or down. You can enter negative or positive numbers.

- *Blur:* Use Blur to control how fuzzy the edges of the shadow are. A lower value makes the edge of the shadow more defined.

- *Color and Darkness:* Select the Color radio button to choose a custom color for the drop shadow. Select the Darkness radio button to add more black to the drop shadow. Zero percent is the lowest amount of black, and 100 percent is the highest.

  As a default, the color of the shadow is based upon the color of your object, sort of . . . the Darkness option has a play in this, also. As a default, the shadow is made up of the color in the object if it's solid. Multicolored objects have a gray shadow.

Saving Graphic Styles

A *graphic style* is a combination of all the settings you choose for a particular filter or effect in the Appearance panel. By saving this information in a graphic style, you store these attributes so that you can quickly and easily apply them to other objects later.

Choose Window⇨Graphics Styles; in the panel that appears are thumbnails of many different styles that Adobe provides to you as a default. Create a new shape, such as a simple rectangle or ellipse, and click any of these graphic styles to apply the style to an active object. Look at the Appearance panel while you click different styles to see that you're applying combinations of attributes, including effects, fills, and strokes (see Figure 12-5).

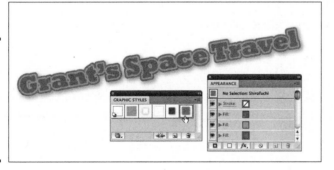

Figure 12-5:
The Graphic Styles panel stores effects and other attributes.

Find more styles by choosing the Graphic Styles panel menu (click the arrow in the upper-right corner of the panel) and selecting Open Graphic Style Library.

You can store attributes as a graphic style in several ways; we show you two easy methods. If you have a combination of attributes already applied to an object, store them by doing one of the following:

✦ With the object selected, Alt+click (Windows) or Option+click (Mac) the New Graphic Style button at the bottom of the Graphic Styles panel. Alt+clicking (Windows) or Option+clicking (Mac) allows you to name the style when it's added.

✦ Drag the selected object right into the Graphic Styles panel. The panel stores its attributes, but you have to double-click the new style to name it.

After you store a graphic style, simply select the object that you want to apply the style to and then click the saved style in the Graphic Styles panel.

Creating 3D Artwork

All the effects in Illustrator are great, but this feature is really swell. Not only can you add dimension by using the 3D effect, you can also *map artwork* (that is, wrap artwork around a 3D object) and apply lighting to the 3D object. This means that you can design a label for a jelly jar and actually adhere it to the jar to show the client!

Here are the three choices for the 3D effect:

✦ **Extrude & Bevel:** This uses the z-axis to extrude an object. For example, a square becomes a cube.

✦ **Revolve:** Uses the z-axis and revolves a shape around it. You can use this to change an arc into a ball.

✦ **Rotate:** Rotates a 3D object created with the Extrude & Bevel or Revolve effects, or you can rotate a 2D object in 3D space. You can also adjust a 3D or 2D object's perspective.

To apply a 3D effect, you need to create an object appropriate for the 3D effect. The Extrude & Bevel feature works great with shapes and text. If you want to edit an object that already has a 3D effect applied to it, double-click the 3D effect in the Appearance panel.

To apply a 3D effect, follow these steps:

1. **Select the object that you want to apply the 3D effect to.**

2. **Choose Effect➪3D➪Extrude & Bevel.**

Options for your chosen 3D effect appear. The Extrude & Bevel Options dialog box is shown in Figure 12-6.

3. **Select the Preview check box so that you can see results as you experiment with these settings.**

4. **Click the Preview pane (which shows a cube in Figure 12-6) and drag to rotate your object in space.**

   It makes selecting the right angle fun, or you can choose the angle from the Position drop-down list above the preview. This is called *positioning the object in space.*

   You should never rotate a 3D object with the Rotate tool, unless you want some very funky results; use the Preview pane in the Extrude & Bevel Options dialog box instead.

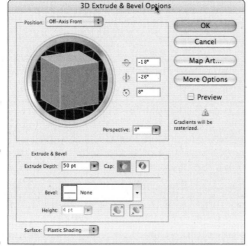

Figure 12-6:
The Extrude
& Bevel
Options
dialog box.

5. **(Optional) Use the Perspective drop-down list to add additional perspective to your object.**

6. **In the Extrude & Bevel section of the dialog box, choose a depth for your object and a cap.**

   The cap determines whether your shape has a solid cap on it or whether it's hollow, as shown in Figure 12-7.

Figure 12-7:
Cap on (left)
and cap off
(right).

7. **Choose a bevel (edge shape) from the Bevel drop-down list and set the height using the Height drop-down list.**

   You have a choice of two ways to apply the bevel:

   - *Bevel Extent Out:* The bevel is added to the object.
   - *Bevel Extent In:* The bevel is subtracted from the object.

8. **Choose a rendering style from the Surface drop-down list or click the More Options button for in-depth lighting options, such as changing the direction or adding additional lighting.**

9. **Click the Map Art button.**

   The Map Art dialog box opens. Use this dialog box to apply artwork to a 3D object.

10. **With the Surface arrow buttons, select which surface you want the artwork applied to and then choose a symbol from the Symbol drop-down list, as shown in Figure 12-8.**

    The result is shown on the bottom in Figure 12-8.

Keep the following points in mind when mapping artwork:

✦ **An object must be a symbol to be used as mapped artwork.** You'd simply need to select and drag the artwork that you want mapped to the Symbols panel to make it a selectable item in the Map Art dialog box.

✦ **The light gray areas in the Preview pane are the visible areas based upon the object's present position.** Drag and scale the artwork in this pane to get the artwork where you want it.

✦ **Shaded artwork (enabled by selecting the Shaded Artwork check box at the bottom of the Map Art dialog box) looks good but can take a long time to render.**

Note: All 3D effects are rendered at 72 dpi (dots per inch; low resolution) so as not to slow down processing speed. You can determine the resolution by choosing Effect⇨Document Raster Effects Settings, or when you save or export the file. You can also select the object and choose Object⇨Rasterize. After the object is rasterized, it can no longer be used as an Illustrator 3D object, so save the original!

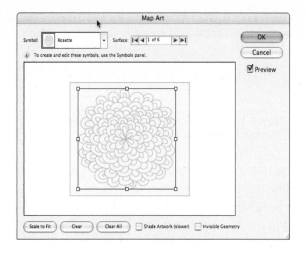

Figure 12-8:
In the Map Art dialog box, you can select a surface and apply a symbol to it.

Adding Multiple Fills and Strokes

With the panel menu in the Appearance panel, you can add more fills and strokes. With this feature, you can put different colored fills on top of each other and individually apply effects to each one, creating really interesting and creative results.

Just for fun, follow along to see what you can do to a single object with the Appearance panel:

1. **Create a star shape.**

   It doesn't matter how many points it has, or how large it is, just make it large enough to work with.

2. **Use the Swatches panel (choose Window⇨Swatches) to fill it with yellow and give it a black stroke.**

3. **Choose Window⇨Stroke to use the Stroke panel to make the stroke 1 pt; alternatively, choose 1 from the Stroke drop-down list in the Control panel.**

   Notice that in the Appearance panel, the present fill and stroke are listed. Even in the simplest form, the Appearance panel helps track basic attributes. You can easily take advantage of the tracking to apply effects to just a fill or a stroke.

4. **Click Stroke in the Appearance panel.**

   If the Appearance panel isn't visible, choose Window⇨Appearance.

5. **Choose Effect⇨Path⇨Offset Path.**

6. **In the Offset Path dialog box that appears, enter –5pt in the Offset text box and select the Preview check box.**

   Notice that the stroke moves into the fill instead of on the edge.

7. **Change the offset to something that works with your star shape and click OK.**

   Depending on the size of your star, you may want to adjust the amount of offset up or down.

8. **From the panel menu of the Appearance panel, add an additional fill to the star shape.**

   This may sound ridiculous, but you can create some super effects with multiple fills.

9. **Click Fill in the Appearance panel (the top one) and choose Effect⇨Distort and Transform⇨Twist.**

10. **In the Twist dialog box that appears, type 45 into the Angle text field and select the Preview check box.**

    Notice how only the second fill is twisted? Pretty neat, right?

11. **Click OK to exit the Twist dialog box.**

12. **Select the top fill from the Appearance panel again.**

You always have to be sure that you select the fill or stroke you want before doing anything that's meant to change just that specific fill or stroke.

13. **In the Transparency panel (choose Window⇨Transparency), choose 50% from the Opacity slider or simply type 50% in the Opacity text field.**

Now you can see your original shape through the new fill!

14. **With that top fill still selected, change the color or choose a pattern in the Swatches panel for a really different appearance.**

You could go on for hours playing around with combinations of fills and strokes. Hopefully, this clicks, and you can take it further on your own.

Book III
Chapter 12

Using Filters
and Effects

Chapter 13: Using Your Illustrator Images

In This Chapter

✔ Saving Illustrator files

✔ Exporting files for use in other applications

✔ Preparing art for the Web

✔ Exporting to Flash

✔ Flattening your transparency

✔ Printing in Illustrator

So you have beautiful artwork, but you aren't sure how to get it off your screen. You could have a party and invite all interested clients to stand around your monitor and ooh and ah, or you could actually share or sell your artwork by putting it on the Internet or printing it.

In this chapter, we show you how to use your illustrations in a variety of workflows, from using Illustrator files in page layout programs, to exporting files for Photoshop (and other programs) and the Web. This chapter can help you really use your artwork and understand the saving and flattening choices available in Adobe Illustrator.

Saving and Exporting Illustrator Files

In this section, we show you how the general choices in the Save As dialog box (choose File➪Save As) differ and the benefits of each.

When you choose File➪Save or File➪Save As, you have the choice of saving in the Adobe Illustrator, EPS, Template, PDF, FXG (a vector-based file format that describes graphical elements.), SVG Compressed, or SVG. We discuss all these formats throughout this chapter.

If you need a file format that isn't listed in the regular Save As dialog box, choose File➪Export to see additional choices. With the File Export command, you can choose to save your files in any of the formats in Table 13-1.

Table 13-1	Available File Formats
File Format	*Extension*
AutoCAD Drawing	.dwg
AutoCAD Interchange File	.dxf
BMP	.bmp
Enhanced Metafile	.emf
Flash	.swf
JPEG	.jpg
Macintosh PICT	.pct
Photoshop	.psd
PNG	.png
Targa	.tga
Text Format	.txt
TIFF	.tif
Windows Metafile	.wmf

Many of these formats *rasterize* your artwork, meaning that they'll no longer maintain vector paths and the benefits of being vector. Scalability isn't limited, for example. If you think that you may want to edit your image again later, be sure to save a copy of the file and keep the original in the .ai format.

The native Adobe Illustrator file format

If you're working with the programs in the Creative Suite, the best way to save your file is as a native Illustrator .ai file. For instance, the .ai format works with Adobe applications such as Adobe InDesign for page layout, Adobe Dreamweaver for Web page creation, Adobe Photoshop for photo-retouching, and Adobe Acrobat for cross-platform documents.

Understanding when it's best to use the .ai format is important. Saving your illustration as an .ai file ensures that your file is editable; it also ensures that any transparency is retained, even if you use the file in another application.

To save and use a file in the native Illustrator format, follow these steps:

1. **Make an illustration with transparency (50 percent transparent, for example) in Adobe Illustrator and choose File➪Save As.**

2. **Select Adobe Illustrator Document (.ai) from the Save as Type drop-down list, give the file a name, and click Save.**

3. **Leave the Illustrator Native Options at the defaults and click OK.**

After you follow the preceding steps to prepare your Illustrator file, you can use the illustration in other Adobe applications:

✦ **Adobe Acrobat:** Open the Acrobat application and choose File➪Open. Locate the .ai file. The native Illustrator file opens within the Acrobat application.

✦ **Adobe InDesign:** Choose File➪Place. This method supports transparency created in Adobe Illustrator. (However, copying and pasting from Illustrator to InDesign does *not* support transparency.) See Figure 13-1.

Figure 13-1: InDesign supports transparency, even over text.

✦ **Adobe Photoshop:** Choose File➪Place. By placing an Illustrator file into Adobe Photoshop, you automatically create a Photoshop Smart Object. You can scale, rotate, and even apply effects to the Illustrator file and return to the original illustration at any time. Read more about Smart Objects in Photoshop in Book II, Chapter 9.

If you really want to go crazy with an Illustrator file in Photoshop, when you save the file in Illustrator, choose File➪Export and select the Photoshop (.psd) format from the Save as Type drop-down list. Choose a resolution from the options window. If you used layers, leave the Write Layers option selected.

In Photoshop, choose File➪Open, select the file that you just saved in Illustrator as a .psd, and click Open. The file opens in Photoshop with the layers intact.

✦ **Adobe Flash:** New integration features built into Adobe Illustrator CS4 allow you to cut and paste directly into Adobe Flash CS4. If you Choose Edit➪Copy from Adobe Illustrator, you can then switch to Adobe Flash CS4 and choose Edit➪Paste. The Paste dialog box appears.

You can also choose File➪Import in Flash for additional import choices. As shown in Figure 13-2, when a native Illustrator file was selected to Import to Stage, the Import to Stage dialog box appears (right in Flash!)

and gives you the opportunity to import only certain layers or sublayers, as well as provides warning messages about incompatible objects.

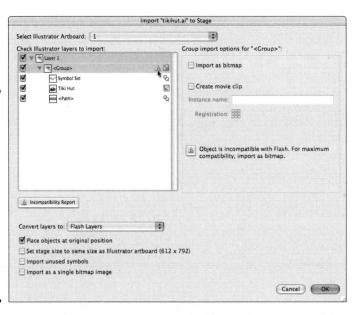

Figure 13-2: Flash CS4 offers the opportunity to select individual layers and sublayers when you import native Illustrator files.

✦ **Adobe Dreamweaver:** By choosing File⇨Save for Web & Devices, you can choose to save your Illustrator document in the `.gif`, `.jpg`, `.png`, `.swf`, `.svg`, or `.wbmp` format. You can then insert images in those file formats into Dreamweaver by choosing Insert⇨Image in Adobe Dreamweaver.

Click the Image button in the Insert panel in Dreamweaver. When the Select Image Source dialog box appears, navigate to the location where you saved your optimized file. Select it and click OK (Windows) or Choose (Mac). If your file is located out of the root folder for the site you're working on, an alert window appears, offering the opportunity to save the file with your other site assets. See Book IV, Chapter 4 for more information about importing images in Dreamweaver.

Saving Illustrator files back to previous versions

When saving an `.ai` or `.eps` file, you can choose File⇨Save As, choose an Illustrator format, and then click OK.

When the Illustrator Options dialog box appears, choose a version from the Version drop-down list. Keep in mind that any features specific to newer versions of Illustrator will not be supported in older file formats, so make sure that you save a copy and keep the original file intact. Adobe helps you understand the risk of saving back to older versions by putting a warning sign next to the Version drop-down list and showing you specific issues with the version you've selected in the Warnings window.

The EPS file format

Encapsulated PostScript File (EPS) is the file format that most text editing and page layout applications accept; EPS supports vector data and is completely scalable. The Illustrator .eps format is based on PostScript, which means that you can reopen an EPS file and edit it in Illustrator at any time.

To save a file in Illustrator as an EPS, follow these steps:

1. **Choose File⇨Save As and select EPS from the Save as Type drop-down list.**

2. **From the Version drop-down list, choose the Illustrator version you're saving to.**

3. **In the EPS Options dialog box that appears (as shown in Figure 13-3), choose the preview from the Format drop-down list:**

   - *(8-Bit Color):* A color preview for either Mac or PC.

   - *(Black & White):* A low-resolution black-and-white preview.

4. **Select either the Transparent or Opaque radio button, depending on whether you want the non-image areas in your artwork to be transparent or opaque.**

5. **Set your Transparency settings.**

   These settings are grayed out if you haven't used transparency in the file. (See the "Flattening Transparency" section, later in this chapter, for more about this setting.)

6. **Leave the Embed Fonts (for Other Applications) check box selected to leave fonts you used embedded in the EPS file format.**

7. **In the Options section, leave the Include CMYK PostScript in RGB Files check box selected.**

   If you don't know which Adobe Postscript level you want to save to, leave it at the default.

8. **Click OK to save your file as an EPS.**

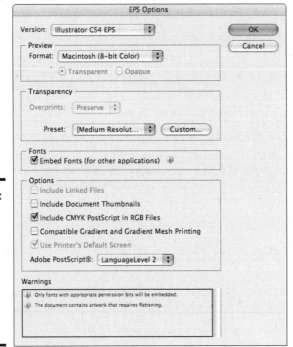

Figure 13-3:
The EPS
Options
dialog box
allows you
to choose
a preview
and other
important
settings.

The PDF file format

If you want to save your file in a format that supports over a dozen platforms
and requires only the Acrobat Reader, available as a free download at www.
adobe.com, choose to save as a PDF (Portable Document Format).

If you can open an Illustrator file in Acrobat, why would you need to save a
file as a PDF? Well, for one thing, you can compress a PDF down to a smaller
size; also, the receiver can double-click the file, and Acrobat or Acrobat
Reader launches automatically.

Depending on how you save the PDF, you can allow some level of editability
in Adobe Illustrator. To save a file as a PDF, follow these steps:

1. **Choose File⇨Save As, choose Illustrator PDF (.pdf) from the Save as
Type drop-down list, and then click Save.**

2. **In the Adobe PDF Options dialog box that appears, choose one of the
following options from the Preset drop-down list:**

• *Illustrator Default:* Creates a PDF file in which all Illustrator data is
preserved. PDF files created with this preset can be reopened in
Illustrator without any loss of data.

- *High Quality Print:* Creates PDFs for desktop printers and proofers.

- *PDF/X-1a:2001:* This method is the least flexible delivery of PDF content data, but it can be very powerful. It requires that the color of all objects be in CMYK (Cyan, Magenta, Yellow, Black) or spot colors. Elements in RGB (Red, Green, Blue) or Lab color spaces or tagged with International Color Consortium (ICC) profiles are prohibited. It also requires that all fonts used in the job be embedded in the supplied PDF file.

- *PDF/X-3:2002:* This method of creating a PDF has slightly more flexibility than the X-1a:2001 method in that color managed workflows are supported elements in Lab, and attached ICC source profiles may also be used.

- *PDF/X-4:2008:* This preset is based on PDF 1.4, which includes support for live transparency. PDF/X-4 has the same color management and ICC color specifications as PDF/X-3. You can open PDF files created with PDF/X-4 compliance in Acrobat 7.0 and Reader 7.0 and later.

- *Press Quality:* Creates a PDF file that can be printed to a high-resolution output device. The file will be large, but it will maintain all the information that a commercial printer or service provider needs to print your file correctly. This option automatically converts the color mode to CMYK, embeds all fonts used in the file, prints at a higher resolution, and uses other settings to preserve the maximum amount of information contained in the original document.

Before creating an Adobe PDF file with the Press Quality preset, check with your commercial printer to find out what the output resolution and other settings should be.

- *Smallest File Size:* Creates a low-resolution PDF suitable for posting on the Internet or sending via e-mail.

- *Standard:* Don't pick a PDF/X standard unless you have a specific need or have been requested to. Through the Standard drop-down list, you can select the type of PDF/X file you want to create.

- *Compatibility:* Different features are available for different versions, such as the ability to support layers in Version 6 or higher. If you want the most compatible file type, choose Acrobat 5 (PDF 1.4). But if you want to take advantage of layers or need to preserve spot colors, you must choose Acrobat 6 or higher.

3. Click Save PDF to save your file as a PDF.

If you want to be able to reopen the PDF file and edit it in Illustrator, make sure that you leave the Preserve Illustrator Editing Capabilities check box selected in the Adobe PDF Options dialog box.

In the Adobe PDF Options dialog box, to the left of the preset choices are options that you can change to customize your settings. Scan through them to see how you can change resolution settings and even add printer's marks. Take a look at Book VIII on Acrobat to find out more about the additional PDF options.

 Want a Press Quality PDF but don't want to convert all your colors to CMYK? Choose the Press setting and then click the Output options. In the Color Conversion drop-down list, select No Conversion.

Saving Your Artwork for the Web

If you need to save artwork for the Web, there's no better feature than Save for Web & Devices. The Save for Web & Devices dialog box gives you a preview pane where you can test different file formats before you actually save the file.

To save an Illustrator file that you intend to use in a Web page, just follow these steps:

1. **Choose File⇨Save for Web & Devices.**

The Save for Web & Devices dialog box appears, showing your artwork on the Optimized tab.

2. **Choose a tabbed view: Original, Optimized, 2-Up, or 4-Up.**

As a default, you see the artwork in the Optimized view, which previews the artwork as it will appear based upon the settings on the right. The 2-Up view is probably the best choice because it shows your original image versus the optimized version.

3. **Choose a setting for your file from the options on the right.**

If you want to make it easy on yourself, choose a preset from the Preset drop-down list. Keep in mind these points:

• *Graphics Interchange Format (GIF) is generally used for artwork with spans of solid color.* GIF isn't a lossy format. You can make your artwork smaller by reducing the number of colors in the image — hence the choices, such as GIF 64 No Dither (64 colors). The lower the number of colors, the smaller the file size. You can also increase or decrease the number of colors in the file by changing the preset values in the Color text field or by using the arrows to the left of the Color text field.

- *Dithering tries to make your artwork look like it has more colors by creating a pattern in the colors.* It looks like a checkerboard pattern up close and even far away, as shown in Figure 13-4. It also makes a larger file size, so why use it? Most designers don't like the effect and choose the No Dither option.

- *Joint Photographic Experts Group (JPEG) is used for artwork that has subtle gradations from one shade to another.* Photographs are often saved in this format. If you have drop shadows or blends in your artwork, select this format. JPEG is a *lossy* file format — it will reduce your image to a lesser quality and can create odd artifacts in your artwork. You have choices, such as High, Medium, and Low in the Settings drop-down list. Make sure that you choose wisely. You can also use the Quality slider to tweak the compression.

Figure 13-4:
An example
of dithering.

- *PNG-8 is very similar to a GIF file format.* Unless you have a certain reason for saving as PNG-8, stick with the GIF file format.

- *PNG-24 supports the best of two formats (GIF and JPEG).* Not only does the Portable Network Graphics (PNG) format support the nice gradients from one tonal value to another (like JPEGs), but it also supports transparency (like GIFs). Not just any old transparency; if you make an object 50 percent transparent in Adobe Illustrator and then save it with Save for Web & Devices as a PNG-24 file with the Transparency check box selected, the image shows through to any other objects underneath it on its destination page.

- *The Shockwave Flash (SWF) graphic file format is a version of the Adobe Flash Player vector-based graphics format.* Because a SWF file is vector-based, its graphics are scalable and play back smoothly on any screen size and across multiple platforms. With the Save for Web & Devices dialog box, you can save your image directly to SWF from Adobe Illustrator. With the SWF choice, you can preview and make decisions as to how you want to export to the file as well as make decisions about how layers should be exported.

**Book III
Chapter 13**

**Using Your
Illustrator Images**

- *Scalable Vector Graphics (SVG) is an emerging Web standard for two-dimensional graphics.* SVG is written in plain text and rendered by the browser, except that in this case, it's not just text that's rendered but also shapes and images, which can be animated and made interactive. SVG is written in XML (Extensible Markup Language). You can choose to save Scalable Vector Graphics out of Adobe Illustrator with the Save for Web & Devices dialog box.

- *Use the Wireless Application Protocol Bitmap Format (WBMP) format for bitmap images for mobile devices.*

4. **When you're satisfied with your chosen settings, save your file by clicking Save.**

When saving illustrations for the Web, keep the following points in mind, which make the whole process much easier for you and anyone who uses your illustrations:

✦ **Keep the file size small.** Don't forget that if you're saving illustrations for a Web page, many other elements will be on that page. Try to conserve on file size to make downloading the page quicker for viewers with dial-up connections. Most visitors won't wait more than ten seconds for a page to download before giving up and moving on to another Web site.

When you make your choices, keep an eye on the file size and the optimized artwork in the lower-left corner of the preview window. On average, a GIF should be around 10K and a JPEG around 15K. These rules aren't written in stone, but please don't try to put a 100K JPEG on a Web page!

You can change the download time by selecting the panel menu in the upper-right corner of the Save for Web & Devices dialog box and choosing Optimize to File Size to input a final file size and have Illustrator create your settings in the Save for Web & Devices dialog box.

✦ **Preview the file before saving it.** If you want to see the artwork in a Web browser before saving it, click the Preview in Default Browser button at the bottom of the Save for Web & Devices dialog box. The browser of choice appears with your artwork in the quality and size in which it will appear. If you have no browser selected, click and hold down the Preview in Default Browser button to choose Other and then browse to locate a browser that you want to use for previewing. Close the browser to return to the Save for Web & Devices dialog box.

✦ **Change the size.** Many misconceptions abound about size when it comes to Web artwork. Generally, most people view their browser windows in an area approximately 700 x 500 pixels. Depending on the screen resolution, this may cover the entire screen on a 14-inch monitor, but even viewers with a 21-inch monitor with a high resolution often don't want to have their entire screen covered with a browser's window, so they still have a browser window area of around 700 x 500 pixels. When choosing a size for your artwork, use proportions of this amount to help you. For example, if you want an illustration to take up about a quarter of the browser window's width, make your image about 175 pixels wide (700÷4 = 175). If you notice that the height of your image is over 500 pixels, whittle the height down in size as well, or your viewers will have to scroll to see the whole image (and it will probably take too long to download!).

Use the Image Size tab to input new sizes. As long as the Constrain Proportions check box is selected, both the height and width of the image will be changed proportionally. Click the Apply button to change the size but don't close the Save for Web & Devices dialog box.

✦ **Finish the save.** If you aren't finished with the artwork but want to save the settings, hold down the Alt (Windows) or Option (Mac) key and click the Remember button. (When you're not holding down the Alt or Option key, the Remember button is the Done button.) If you're finished, click the Save button and save your file in the appropriate location.

Flattening Transparency

You may find that all those cool effects that you put into your illustration don't print correctly. When you print a file that has effects, such as drop shadows, cool gradient blends, and feathering, Illustrator turns transparent areas that overlap other objects into pixels and leaves what it can as vectors — this process is *flattening*.

So what actually is flattening? Look at Figure 13-5 to see the difference between the original artwork (on the left) and the flattened artwork (on the right). Notice that in Figure 13-5, when the artwork was flattened, some of the areas turned into pixels. But at what resolution? This is why you want to know about flattening so that you can determine the quality of art — before getting an unpleasant surprise at the outcome.

Figure 13-5:
Artwork
before
and after
flattening is
applied.

Flattening a file

If you've taken advantage of transparency or effects using transparency (which we discuss in Chapter 11 of this minibook), follow these steps to get the highest quality artwork from your file:

1. **Make sure that you've created the artwork in the CMYK mode.**

   You can change the document's color mode by choosing File⇨Document Color Mode.

2. **Choose Effects⇨Document Raster Effects Settings.**

   The Document Raster Effects Settings dialog box appears, as shown in Figure 13-6.

3. **Choose the resolution that you want to use by selecting an option in the Resolution area.**

   Select Screen (72 ppi) option, for web graphics,. Medium (150 ppi) for desktop printers and copiers, and High (300 ppi) for graphics that will be printed on a press.

4. **Choose whether you want a white or transparent background.**

   If you select the Transparent option, you create an alpha channel. The alpha channel is retained if the artwork is exported into Photoshop.

5. **You can generally leave the items in the Options section deselected:**

   - *The Anti-Alias check box* applies anti-aliasing to reduce the appearance of jagged edges in the rasterized image. Deselect this option to maintain the crispness of fine lines and small text.

   - *The Create Clipping Mask check box* creates a mask that makes the background of the rasterized image appear transparent. You don't need to create a clipping mask if you select the Transparent option for your background.

   - *The Add around Object text field* adds the specified number of pixels around the rasterized image.

6. **Click OK.**

   The next step is to set the transparency options in the Document Setup dialog box.

7. **Choose File⇨Document Setup.**

   From the Transparency section in the middle of the dialog box, click the Preset drop-down list and select the Low, Medium, High, or Custom option. Select the Low option for on-screen viewing, the Medium option for printers and copiers, or the High option for press. Click the Custom button to the right of the drop-down list if you want to control more of the settings.

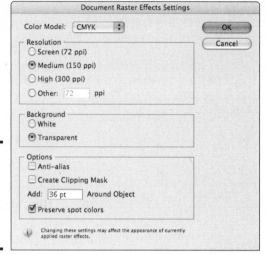

Figure 13-6:
Choosing
the quality
of your
rasterized
artwork.

8. **Click OK.**

If you find yourself customizing the settings on a regular basis, choose
Edit⇨Transparency Flattener Presets to create and store your own presets.

You can apply the flattening in several ways. Here are three simple methods:

✦ Select the object(s) that requires flattening and choose Object⇨Flatten
Transparency. Choose one of the default settings or a custom preset
that you created from the Preset drop-down list and click OK.

✦ Choose File⇨Print and select Advanced from the list of print options
on the left. Choose a preset from the Overprint and Transparency
Flattener options. If you used the Attributes panel to create overprints
(for trapping used in high-end printing), make sure that you preserve
the overprints.

Note: Overprints aren't preserved in areas that use transparency.

✦ Choose File⇨Save As and choose Illustrator EPS. In the Transparency
section of the EPS Options dialog box, choose a flattening setting from
the Preset drop-down list. If your Transparency options are grayed out,
you have no transparency in your file.

Using the Flattener Preview panel

Want to preview your flattening? Use the Flattener Preview panel by choosing Window⇨Flattener Preview.

The Flattener Preview panel doesn't apply the flattening, but it gives you a preview based upon your settings. Click the Refresh button and choose Show Options from the panel menu. Test various settings without actually flattening the file. Experiment with different settings and then save your presets by selecting Save Transparency Flattener Preset from the panel menu. The saved settings can be accessed in the Preset drop-down list in the Options dialog boxes that appear when you save a file as an EPS or in the Document Setup dialog box.

Click the Refresh button after making changes to update the preview.

Zoom in on the artwork by clicking in the preview pane. Scroll the artwork in the preview pane by holding down the spacebar and dragging. Zoom out by Alt+clicking (Windows) or Option+clicking (Mac).

Printing from Illustrator

Printing from Illustrator gives you lots of capabilities, such as printing composites to separations and adding printer's marks.

To print your illustration, follow these steps:

1. **Choose File⇨Print.**

2. **In the Print dialog box that appears, select a printer if one isn't already selected.**

3. **If the PPD isn't selected, choose one from the PPD drop-down list.**

   A *PPD* is a printer description file. Illustrator needs this to determine the specifics of the PostScript printer you're sending your file to. This setting lets Illustrator know whether the printer can print in color, the paper size it can handle, and the resolution, as well as many other important details.

4. **Choose from other options as follows:**

   Use the General options area to pick what pages to print. In the Media area, select the size of media that you're printing to. In the Options area, choose whether you want layers to print and any options specific to printing layers.

5. **Click the Print button to print your illustration.**

And that's it. Printing your illustration can be really simple, but the following list highlights some basic things to keep in mind as you prepare your illustration for printing:

✦ **Printing a composite:** A *composite* is the full-color image, where all the inks are applied to the page (and not separated out onto individual pages — one for cyan, one for magenta, one for yellow, and one for black). To make sure that your settings are correct, click Output in the print options pane on the left side of the Print dialog box and select Composite from the Mode drop-down list.

✦ **Printing separations:** To separate colors, click Output in the print options pane on the left side of the Print dialog box; from the Mode drop-down list, choose the Separations (Host-Based) option. Select the In-RIP Separations option only if your service provider or printer asks you to. Other options to select from are as follows:

   • The resolution is determined by your PPD, based upon the dots per inch (dpi) in the printer description. You may have only one option available in the Printer Resolution drop-down list.

   • Select the Convert Spot Colors to Process check box to make your file 4-color.

   • Click the printer icons to the left of the listed colors to turn off or on the colors that you want to print.

✦ **Printer's marks and bleeds:** Click Marks and Bleeds in the print options pane on the left side of the Print dialog box to turn on all printer's marks, or just select the ones that you want to appear.

   Specify a bleed area if you're extending images beyond the trim area of a page. If you don't specify a bleed, the artwork stops at the edge of the page and doesn't leave a trim area for the printer.

After you create a good set of options specific to your needs, click the Save Preset. Name your preset appropriately; when you want to use that preset, select it from the Print Preset drop-down list at the top of the Print dialog box for future print jobs.

**Book III
Chapter 13**

**Using Your
Illustrator Images**

Book IV

Dreamweaver CS4

Contents at a Glance

Chapter 1: Getting Familiar with New Features in Dreamweaver

In This Chapter

✔ Looking at the new interface

✔ Discovering the improved Property inspector panel

✔ Looking at Photoshop support

✔ Understanding the Browser Compatibility Check and CSS Advisor

✔ Using Live View, Code Navigator, and Spry widgets

✔ Jumping to related documents

✔ Finding out about the improved CSS capabilities

Dreamweaver CS4 lets you create and manage single pages, such as e-mail newsletters or groups of pages that are linked to each other, referred to as a *site*. Users can create basic Web sites with simple links from one page to another or advanced Web sites that include custom coding and interaction with those viewing the pages.

Since being included as part of the Adobe Creative Suite, Dreamweaver CS4 has been made to work better than ever with other Adobe applications, such as Photoshop CS4, Illustrator CS4, Bridge, and Device Central. Even if you've never used Dreamweaver, you'll be impressed with the many tools, panels, and powerful features that make Web-page building easy and intuitive.

If you're a GoLive user, moving to Dreamweaver is actually a smooth transition. Dreamweaver CS4 is an industry-standard Web site creation and management tool, with the tools needed to do advanced coding or create data-driven Web sites.

All New CS4 Interface

New and previous Dreamweaver users alike will be excited to see the new interface that's been put into place in Dreamweaver CS4, as shown in Figure 1-1. A more streamlined, easy-to-organize interface and improved relocation and redesign of some key panels mean a better workflow. You'll even find some new workspace presets that are suited for different types of Dreamweaver users, including those geared for designers and hardcore coders.

The panels are tabbed, and you can separate them by dragging the tab to another location, just as in other Adobe applications. If you choose View➪Toolbars➪Standard, you can even use the Go to Bridge button to navigate and use Adobe Bridge. Using Adobe Bridge with Dreamweaver CS4 is a big improvement, as you can search and navigate your assets, such as text, Flash, and images files. You can then drag and drop them right on to your page. (Read more about adding imagery to your Web page in Chapter 4 of this minibook.)

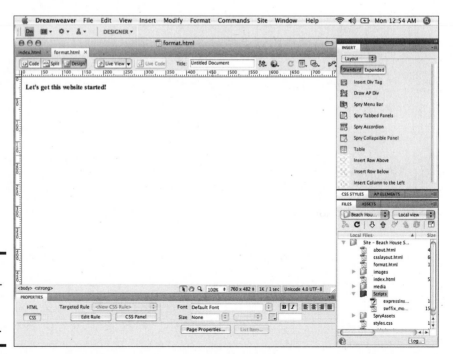

Figure 1-1:
The Dream-weaver Designer workspace.

Improved Property Inspector Panel

The Dreamweaver Property inspector is now split into two views! The Property inspector is your all-purpose detail view for anything you select on the page. It's been improved to include specific views for HTML and CSS tasks: On the HTML tab, you can work specifically on tag and structural elements, or switch to the CSS tab to apply, create, and edit CSS formatting for a selected element (see Figure 1-2).

The HTML view lets you work specifically with HTML elements and apply basic formatting with HTML as well as create bullet-point lists and set text alignment.

The CSS view lets you create, edit, and apply CSS selectors (styles) to text and other page elements. This view provides more control than previous versions for modifying and naming styles, and lets you create any type of selector you need, when you need it.

Figure 1-2:
The Property inspector now includes HTML and CSS tabs.

Photoshop Smart Objects

The addition of Photoshop support in Dreamweaver CS3 was a huge work-flow improvement for designers, and now version CS4 takes it further with full support for *Photoshop Smart Objects,* which allow you to maintain a link to the original PSD file so that edits are easily recorded and applied to the optimized image in your page.

Images placed from PSD files display a handy icon (as shown in Figure 1-3), which lets you know if its original file has changed, and the Update from Original button (located on the Property inspector) automatically regenerates and updates your image from the original Photoshop file.

**Book IV
Chapter 1**

**Getting Familiar
with New Features
in Dreamweaver**

In addition, Dreamweaver CS4 continues to support direct placement of Photoshop (.psd) files, allowing full optimization and creation of Web-friendly formats on the fly! This speeds up your workflow by letting you do more in Dreamweaver without jumping between different applications.

Figure 1-3:
The new Photoshop Smart Objects feature places an icon in the corner of an image to let you know when the image needs to be updated from the original.

Browser Compatibility Check and the CSS Advisor

The *Browser Compatibility Check (BCC)* was introduced in Dreamweaver CS3 and allows you to check if CSS rules used within your page will work and appear consistently in most modern browsers on both Mac and Windows platforms.

If the Browser Compatibility Check finds any compatibility issues, you'll see them in the Results panel with an explanation of the problem (and browser version, if applicable). BCC also provides a direct link to Adobe's new CSS resource site, the CSS Advisor, for possible solutions or workarounds to your specific issue.

Adobe's *CSS Advisor* is an online resource portal that helps find and address common solutions to many CSS-related issues and questions. Best of all, it's just a click away from the Browser Compatibility Check!

You can visit Adobe's CSS Advisor Web site directly at www.adobe.com/ cfusion/communityengine/indexcfm?event=homepage&productId=1.

To use this feature, select the Check Page button on the Document toolbar. (If you don't see your Document toolbar, choose View➪Toolbars➪Document.) From the Check Page drop-down list, choose Check Browser Compatibility. The Browser Compatibility tab appears, as shown in Figure 1-4.

Very often, solutions to your problem can be addressed in the CSS Styles panel, or in some cases, may involve editing some code by hand. (Read about the basics of coding and HTML in Chapter 3 of this minibook.)

Figure 1-4: Feel confident that your page will work in most browsers after checking the Browser Compatibility tab.

Live View

Dreamweaver adds a new Document view — the Live View — making it possible to see your page in a browser-simulated environment without leaving the application. Live View displays your page just as it would in a Web browser, as shown in Figure 1-5, allowing you to get a more accurate view of your work.

Figure 1-5:
The new
Live View
displays
your page
as you
would see
it in a Web
browser.

Code Navigator

 The new Code Navigator, as shown in Figure 1-6, helps you easily target and edit code included on or applied to elements on your page. Page content controlled by or with external code appears with a steering wheel icon, and a small window displays any external code, such as CSS rules or parent library item files so that you can jump to them for quick editing in Split view.

This is a huge help when working with lots of CSS rules and JavaScript code, as locating these manually to make changes can be a very tedious process.

Figure 1-6:
The Code Navigator gives you convenient view-and-click power over any code that controls elements on your page.

New Spry Widgets

The Spry Framework isn't covered in detail in this book, but you should at least be familiar with what it allows you to create. The Spry Framework helps users, beginner to advanced, take advantage of interactive page elements and cool widgets commonly used within rich-internet applications built in AJAX (Asynchronous JavaScript and XML).

AJAX is a Web-development technique for creating interactive Web applications. The intention is to make Web pages feel more responsive by exchanging small amounts of data with the server behind the scenes so that the entire Web page doesn't have to reload each time the user requests a change. By not reloading the entire page, you can increase the Web page's interactivity, speed, and usability. Still confused? Check out the samples on Adobe Labs at `http://labs.adobe.com/technologies/spry`.

Dreamweaver CS4 includes a collection of objects (a *library*) that contains ready-to-use Spry elements, such as cool drop-down lists, tabbed panels, and page elements that automatically update from XML files. When one of these elements is placed on a page, it creates an area that can change without the entire page reloading. For example, a user can create a photo gallery in which a person can click a smaller image and see a larger image with a Spry Framework library item.

This feature is really worth investigating, especially if you're leaning toward including more sophisticated interactivity on your page. The Spry Framework contains *Spry widgets and data objects,* which are commonly used elements that you can easily add to pages without complex code. Widgets include form elements, database tables, and menu bars.

The Spry widgets, including some cool new validating form objects and data elements can be found under the Insert panel's Spry category, and some widgets are also available from the Insert panel's Layout category.

You can also use Spry *effects* to apply fun transition effects, such as grow and shrink, appear and fade, and shake, to objects on the page. Because these effects are based on the Spry Framework, when the transition is applied, only the object is affected.

Related Documents

Very often, your pages rely on several other files, such as attached style sheets and JavaScript files. The Document toolbar now includes a Related Documents section, where you can see and jump to other documents utilized by and attached to your page. Selecting a document in the Related Documents toolbar displays a special Split view where you can edit the selected file in Code view while continuing to work with the original page in Design view below, as shown in Figure 1-7.

The best part is you don't have to jump between multiple Document windows; just edit while you watch the changes applied to your document!

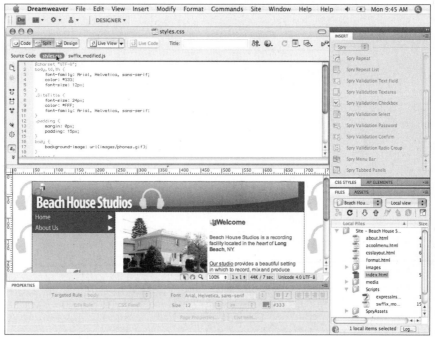

Figure 1-7:
The Related
Documents
toolbar
lets you
view and
edit other
files that
your page
depends
on, such as
style sheets,
JavaScript
files,
and more.

Improved CSS Capabilities

Cascading Style Sheets (CSS) is a language that gives Web-site developers and users more control over how text is formatted and pages are displayed. With CSS, designers and users can create style sheets that define how different elements, such as headers and links, appear and then apply these style sheets to any Web page. If you're familiar with paragraph and character styles in InDesign and Illustrator, you'll understand the concept of CSS. In addition, CSS provides a powerful way of creating full Web-page layouts, a method that's been adopted by most Web designers and developers as the new standard.

In addition, CSS provides a wealth of additional attributes that you can apply to a page's format and text and the ability to make changes across an entire Web site quickly. Although Dreamweaver has provided full support for CSS for some time now, CS4 offers some great new convenience features that make it even easier to manage and create CSS styles directly from the Property inspector (available by choosing Window➪Properties).

**Book IV
Chapter 1**

**Getting Familiar
with New Features
in Dreamweaver**

Direct formatting and CSS styling from the Property inspector provide three new key improvements:

✦ You name CSS rules at creation time (which avoids lots of vaguely named rules) and have the ability to set the type of CSS selector you want to create.

✦ You can add a new CSS rule to either an internal (in-page) or external (outside file) style sheet. Previously, the Property inspector could create styles only within the page itself (internal), even when an external style sheet existed.

✦ You have more control — you can determine whether modifications to an existing style generate a new rule or modify the existing one (the default).

The words *rule* and *style* are used interchangeably here and in other chapters throughout this minibook. The proper term, however, for a new set of CSS attributes in CSS-speak is *rule*.

Chapter 2: Introducing Dreamweaver CS4

In This Chapter

✔ **Familiarizing yourself with the workspace**

✔ **Finding out about panels**

✔ **Creating a new Web site**

✔ **Discovering the Property inspector**

✔ **Using Live View to preview your page**

✔ **Understanding the Dreamweaver preferences**

Dreamweaver CS4 lets you create and manage Web pages and complete Web sites. In this chapter, you find out how to start a Web site and build pages within it. Basically, a *Web site* is simply a group of linked pages that contain text and images and can also contain media, such as Flash movies, sound, and video.

Getting to Know the New Workspace Setup

As a default, most workspace options are available to you in the form of panels, toolbars, or inspectors. This workspace can take some getting used to because it isn't totally consistent with the other Adobe applications in the suite.

When Dreamweaver is first launched, you see a Welcome screen. This screen provides the option to open any recent items (if you've created pages already), but also allows you to create new HTML, CSS, XML, sites, and many other files. You can also choose a selection from the Create from Samples column.

Dreamweaver provides you with all the tools you need in the initial workspace (see Figure 2-1).

Document bar   Insert panel

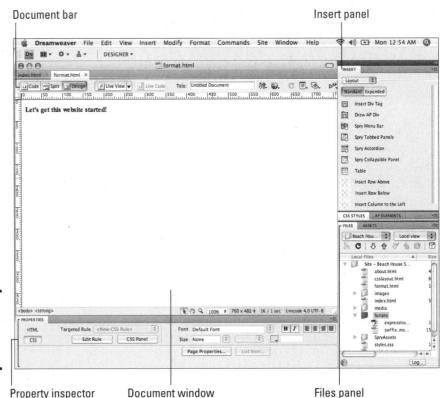

Figure 2-1:
The Dream-
weaver
workspace.

Property inspector   Document window   Files panel

The Insert panel

The Dreamweaver CS4 Insert panel provides you with tools to insert common page elements, such as hyperlinks, e-mail links, tables, and images to your page, as well as more advanced coding related to CSS (Cascading Style Sheets) and AJAX (Spry elements).

The Insert panel is divided into eight categories that provide you with different elements to add to your page. You can switch between these categories by using the drop-down list at the top of the panel.

- ✦ **Common:** Contains the most commonly used objects, such as images and tables.

- ✦ **Layout:** Contains layout elements, such as tables and CSS elements like the DIV tag, that help you create a Web page layout.

- ✦ **Forms:** Contains the elements necessary to create a form in your Dreamweaver page.

✦ **Data:** Contains elements related to dynamic content and some Spry data objects.

✦ **Spry:** Contains the new Spry Framework objects, used to create pages and widgets, such as Spry tables and accordion menus.

✦ **Text:** Provides you with text formatting tags.

✦ **Favorites:** Allows you to group and organize the Insert panel buttons you use the most within one common location.

✦ **Extensions:** Here you'll find some more obscure properties, such as forced page breaks, filters, and cursor effects.

To bring up the Customize Favorite Objects dialog box, simply right-click (Windows) or Control-click (Mac) within the Insert panel and choose Customize Favorites from the contextual menu. The Customize Favorite Objects dialog box, as shown in Figure 2-2, appears. Click an object in the Available Objects window and then click the double arrow to add the object to your Favorites category.

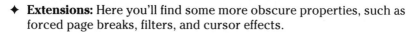

Figure 2-2: Customizing your Favorites category in the Insert panel.

The Document toolbar

The Document toolbar, as shown in Figure 2-3, contains helpful tools to help you view your document in different modes, such as Code and Design views, as well as address such items as the document title and browser compatibility.

✦ **Show Code View:** Show the code and only the code using this view. Dreamweaver helps you to decipher code by color coding tags, attributes, CSS, and other elements.

✦ **Show Code and Design Views:** Selecting this option splits the Document window between the Code and Design views. If you understand a little about code, this view can be extremely helpful because you see both the design and code simultaneously.

✦ **Show Design View:** This option displays your page in the Design view in the Document window.

✦ **Live View:** The new Live View renders your page as you'd see it in an actual browser, free of borders, guides, and other visual aids. In Live View, you can't edit the previewed content — however, you can still jump to Code, Split, or Design views and modify your page content.

✦ **Live Code:** When Live View is enabled, you can view the source code of your document as a user would see it in a browser (via the View Source or Page Source menu options in most browsers). You can't edit your page code in this view.

✦ **Related Documents:** Documents utilized by and attached to your page, such as external CSS and JavaScript files, are listed below (Mac) or above (Windows) the view selection (Code/Split/Design) buttons. You can click any listed document to edit the attached file in Split view without having to switch documents.

Note: XML, JavaScript, CSS, or other code-based file types are visible only in Code view; the Design and Split buttons appear dimmed out.

✦ **Document Title:** Enter the name of your document in this field.

✦ **File Management:** Click this button to display the File Management pop-up list. Use this menu to check in and out of your document.

✦ **Preview/Debug in Browser:** Clicking this button allows you to preview or debug your document in a browser that you select from a drop-down list.

✦ **Refresh Design View:** Click this button to refresh the document's Design view after you make changes in Code view. Changes you make in Code view don't appear automatically in Design view until you perform certain actions, such as saving the file or clicking this button.

Note: Refreshing also updates code features that are Document Object Model (DOM) dependent, such as the ability to select a code block's opening or closing tags.

✦ **View Options:** Click and select options from the View Options drop-down list. This button allows you to set options for Code view and Design view, including which view should appear above the other. Options in the menu are for the current view: Design view, Code view, or both.

✦ **Visual Aids:** Click this button to select different visual aids to help you see various elements and make designing your pages easier.

✦ **Validate Markup:** Click this button to validate the current document or a selected tag.

✦ **Check Page:** This menu shows options that let you check page integrity, such as accessibility or whether your CSS rules are compatible across different browsers.

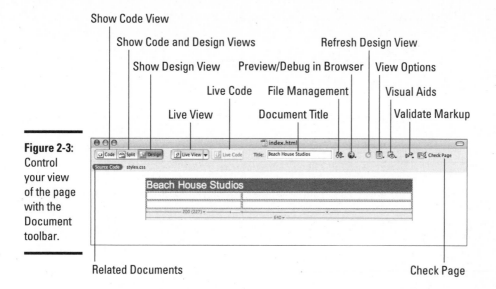

Show Code View

Show Code and Design Views

Show Design View   Preview/Debug in Browser

Live Code   File Management

Live View   Document Title

Refresh Design View

View Options

Visual Aids

Validate Markup

Figure 2-3:
Control
your view
of the page
with the
Document
toolbar.

Related Documents   Check Page

Using the panel groups

Dreamweaver provides you with a panel docking area off to the right of your workspace. The panels in Dreamweaver appear grouped and tabbed, and can easily access the appropriate panel for the job by either clicking the tab of the panel to bring it forward or by selecting the named panel from the Window menu.

Close a panel by either selecting the name of the panel from the Window menu or by tearing the panel out of the group and clicking the close icon.

Saving your workspace

Just like the other Creative Suite 4 applications, you can organize your workspace by turning on the visibility of the panels and toolbars that you use on a regular basis and closing the others. You can also save your workspace so you can recall it at any time:

1. **Choose Window⇨Workspace Layout⇨New Workspace.**

    The New Workspace Layout dialog box appears.

2. **Type an appropriate name in the name text box.**

3. **Click OK to create the new workspace.**

**Book IV
Chapter 2**

**Introducing
Dreamweaver CS4**

To recall a workspace you've previously saved, you can either:

✦ Select the workspace from the Workspace menu in the upper-right corner of the screen (above the panel group).

Or

✦ Open your workspace by choosing Window➪Workspace Layout➪*[Your workspace name]*.

Dreamweaver CS4 features several new workspaces geared toward different types of users as well as different tasks. You can recall any of these workspaces using either of the ways described in the previous list or by selecting a workspace from the application bar, which appears at the top of your screen, as shown in Figure 2-4.

You can hide the application toolbar by choosing View➪Application Bar.

Figure 2-4:
The
Workspace
toolbar
allows
you easy
access to
your saved
workspaces.

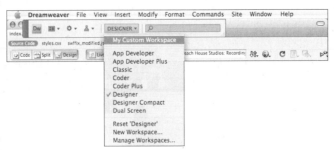

Creating a Site

Sites are very important to maintain links, consistency, and general organization of your Web pages. (See Chapter 3 of this minibook for more on sites.)

To create a site, follow these steps:

1. **Choose Site➪New Site.**

The Site Definition dialog box appears; make sure the Basic tab is selected at the top.

This dialog box takes you through the steps to create a new site. In this chapter, you breeze through the steps, but you can find more details about them in Chapter 3 of this minibook.

2. **In the text field below What Would You Like to Name Your Site?, type a name for your new site and click Next.**

For this example, we entered **chap2** for the site's name.

3. **Make sure the No radio button is selected on the Server Technology page and click Next.**

4. **Make sure the Edit Local Copies on My Machine radio button is selected on the Files page and click Next.**

5. **Type a location where you want the site to be stored in the Site Location text box or click the Browse button to locate a folder to put site assets into; click Next.**

6. **Choose None from the How Do You Want to Connect to Your Remote Server drop-down list and click Next.**

7. **Click Done in the Summary page.**

   The site appears in the Files panel.

Checking Out the Property Inspector

After you have a site created, you can begin to add new pages as well as assets, such as images, to that site. The Property inspector becomes one of your most useful panels because it provides you with information about any element that you've selected. This contextual panel, as shown in Figure 2-5, displays text attributes when text is selected or image attributes when images are selected, and so on.

Figure 2-5:
The Property inspector with text selected (top) and with an image selected (bottom).

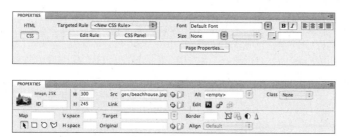

To see this panel in action, open a page with various elements on it. (If you don't have any of your own pages yet, you can use one of the sample pages that loaded with your Dreamweaver CS4 installation.) Then follow these steps:

1. **Choose File⇨New to open a sample page in Dreamweaver.**

   The New Document dialog box appears.

2. **Select the page you want to open and click Create.**

   If you want to open a sample page, click the Page from Sample icon on the left side of the New Document dialog box. Choose Starter Page (Theme) from the Sample Folder column, Lodging — Home from the Starter page column (or any page that you think looks interesting), and click Create.

   Make sure that the page you select has text and images on it.

   The Save As dialog box appears. Dreamweaver wants to make sure that the page is saved immediately.

3. **Type a name in the Save As text box.**

   The location is routed automatically to the site folder that you created. See the "Creating a Site" section in this chapter to see how to create a site.

4. **Click Save.**

   The Copy Dependent Files dialog box appears. Dreamweaver even provides you with the image files.

5. **Click Copy.**

   Dreamweaver places the image files into your site folder, and the sample page appears.

6. **After you have a document with text and images open, select various elements, such as an image, text, table, or hyperlink (linked text).**

   With each selection, your Property inspector provides you with specific information about that element (refer to Figure 2-5).

The Property inspector is analogous to the Option bar, which appears at the top of the Photoshop, Illustrator, and InDesign workspaces, and the Property inspector in Flash. If you're a former GoLive user, the concept of using the Property inspector is also very familiar to you because this same feature existed in that application as well.

Previewing Your Page in a Browser or with Live View

Perhaps you've completed your page and want to investigate how it looks on a browser. You can quickly preview your file by simply clicking the Preview/ Debug in Browser button on the Document toolbar and selecting the browser you want to preview your page in, as shown in Figure 2-6. You can also preview your page in Adobe's Device Central, which simulates several different mobile and PDA devices.

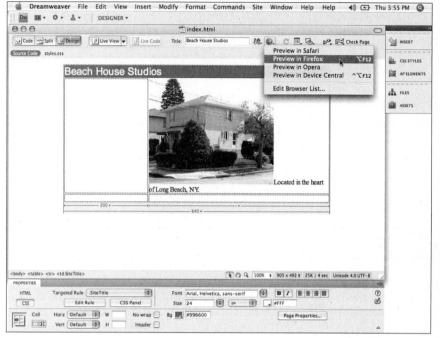

Figure 2-6:
The
Preview/
Debug in
Browser
button
lets you
select from
browsers
installed on
your system.

You can always add browsers through the Preferences panel by
choosing Dreamweaver⇨Preferences⇨Preview in Browser (Mac), or
Edit⇨Preferences⇨Preview in Browser (Windows).

Previewing your page using Live View

Dreamweaver CS4's new Live View displays your page as you would see it
in a browser. This is a nice alternative to the Preview in Browser command
because you don't ever need to exit Dreamweaver.

To view your page in Live View, follow these steps:

1. **With a page open in the Document window, click the Live View button
on the Document toolbar.**

2. **To see the resulting source code of your page, click the Live Code
button that appears next to the Live View button.**

   This is equivalent to the View Page Source or View Source options available in most every browser. In this mode, you can only view the code,
   not edit it.

3. **To edit your page code, switch to Split or Code view in the Document
toolbar.**

Understanding Dreamweaver Preferences

You can change many preferences in Dreamweaver CS4 (see Figure 2-7 for Mac OS X preferences). You see categories, such as General, Accessibility, and AP Elements, in the panel on the left, along with subcategories that appear in the panel to the right.

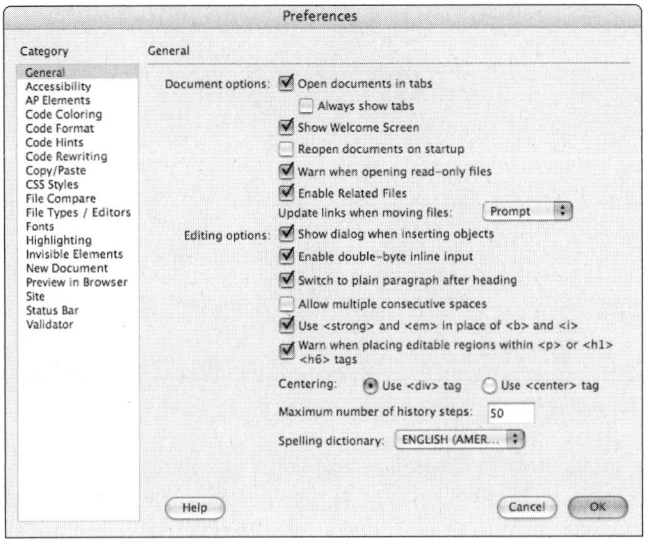

Figure 2-7: You can change numerous preferences to help you work better in Dreamweaver CS4.

To access general preferences, choose Edit➪Preferences (Windows) or Dreamweaver➪Preferences (Mac). The general rule for changing preferences is that if you don't know what it means, don't touch it. But if you want to tweak certain things, this is the place to go.

Preferences are especially helpful to those who hand-code and want to enter their own code hints, highlight colors, or change the font that appears in the Code view.

Chapter 3: Creating a Web Site

In This Chapter

✔ Creating a site

✔ Creating a page for your site

✔ Adding images to your pages

✔ Keeping track of your Web site files

✔ Discovering HTML

*I*n this chapter, you discover the basics of putting a Web site together, from creating that first new, blank site, to adding files to Web sites, to playing (just a little bit) with HTML.

Web Site Basics

A *Web site* is a collection of related pages linked to one another, preferably in an organized manner. With the proper planning and an end goal in sight, you can easily accomplish the task of creating a great Web site. Figure 3-1 shows the general structure of a Web site. Web sites start with a main page (or the *home page*), the central link to other pages in the site. The main page is also the page viewers see first when they type your URL in a browser. The main page is typically named `index.html`, but it may also be `index.htm` or even `default.htm`. Check with your provider to find the correct name.

Pages are linked together with *hyperlinks,* references that take viewers from one point in an HTML document to another or from one document to another. (Read more about hyperlinks and how to create them in Chapter 6 of this minibook.)

The following are terms that you should understand when you forge through the steps to create a Web site:

✦ **TCP/IP (Transmission Control Protocol/Internet Protocol):** Underlying protocols that make communication between computers on the Internet possible. TCP/IP ensures that information being exchanged goes to the right place, in a form that can be used, and gets there intact.

- ✦ **URL (Universal Resource Locator):** A standard for specifying the location of an object on the Internet, such as a file. The URL is what you type into a Web browser to visit a Web page, such as `www.dummies.com`. URLs are also used in HTML documents (Web pages) to specify the target of a link, which is often another Web page.

- ✦ **FTP (File Transfer Protocol):** Allows a user on one computer to transfer files to and from another computer over a TCP/IP network. FTP is also the client program the user executes to transfer files. You may use FTP to transfer Web pages, images, and other files to a host Web server when you publish your site.

- ✦ **HTTP (Hypertext Transfer Protocol):** The client-server TCP/IP protocol used on the Internet for the exchange of HTML documents.

Figure 3-1:
A diagram
of the
structure of
a Web site.

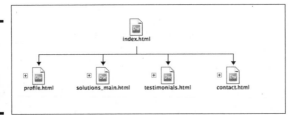

How Web sites are organized is important. Typically, the purpose of a Web site is to sell something — a product, a service, or a thought, such as "Vote for me!" Without sound organization, a Web site may fail to sell to its visitors. Read these words slowly: *Plan your site.* Seriously, you'll save an extraordinary amount of time if you just think ahead and plan your site's organization. Think about the topics you want to cover and then organize your site as you would a high school essay project, planning the topic sentence, subtopics, and so on. This plan can be a tremendous aid when you start mapping which pages should be linked to others.

Starting a New Site

Even if you're creating only one page, it's best to create a site. A site gives you an organized method for keeping images and other assets together and offers additional options for management of those files.

To create a new site, follow these steps:

1. **In Dreamweaver CS4, choose Site⇨New Site.**

You could also choose Dreamweaver Site from the Create New column of the Welcome screen. The Site Definition dialog box appears. Make sure the Basic tab is selected.

2. **In the Site Name text box, enter a name for the site, and click Next.**

For example, if your site's focus is on bikes, you might name the site **biking.**

Because you're creating a new page but not immediately uploading it, leave the HTTP address blank.

3. **Select the No, I Do Not Want to Use Server Technology radio button and click Next.**

This step allows you to design a Web site on your computer and test it in various browsers without setting up complicated server information. If you're actually using ASP, ColdFusion, and JSP, you can choose your server technology, but that path isn't covered in this example.

4. **Because you haven't yet defined a server (where your pages will be accessible on the Internet), select the Edit Local Copies radio button.**

It's best to leave this option selected, even if you do have a server set up, because you can keep originals intact on your computer until they're ready to be uploaded.

5. **Click the Browse Folder icon to the right of the File Path text box. As shown in Figure 3-2, browse to the location where you want to create the site folder that you'll use to store all the site's assets and click Next.**

If you already have a folder where you've saved your assets (such as images, .doc files, and media), choose this folder. Otherwise, Dreamweaver creates a new, empty one.

The Sharing Files Site Definition dialog box appears.

6. **Choose None from the Remote Server drop-down list and click Next.**

You can set up the server information later.

The Summary window appears.

7. **Review the information and, if you want to make changes, click the Back button; otherwise, click Done.**

You've created a local folder on your computer.

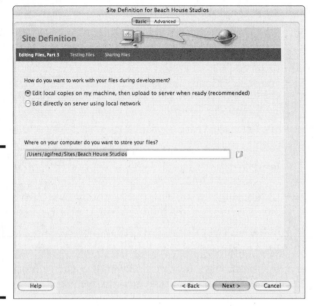

As soon as you create a site, your site folder is waiting in the Files panel, as shown in Figure 3-3. Think of the Files panel as the central control center for all your files, folders, and other assets, such as images, sound, and video, that you'll use to create your Web site.

Figure 3-3:
The Files
panel acts
as a file
browser and
manager.

The Files panel allows you to view files and folders, whether they're related to your Dreamweaver site or not. You can use the Files panel to do typical file operations, such as opening and moving your files.

Creating a New Page for Your Site

After you create a site, you typically build your main page, the `index.html` or `index.htm` page. `index.html` and `index.htm` are reserved filenames that are recognized by most every Web server as the starting page for a Web site. In addition, `default.html` and `default.htm` are also commonly recognized as starting pages. Check with your Web site hosting company or Internet service provider because in some instances, your server may require a different name or may prefer one naming convention over another.

The following steps walk you through creating a new page and placing an image on it:

1. **Choose File⇨New.**

The New Page dialog box appears.

You can create many types of new files, from blank pages to more advanced pages that include layouts already created in CSS.

2. **To create a blank page, choose Blank Page⇨HTML⇨<none> and then click Create.**

A blank untitled HTML page appears.

3. **Choose File⇨Save.**

The Save As dialog box appears.

4. **In the File Name text box, type** index.html.

Note that the file is already mapped to your site folder. If you don't see the site's *root* directory (the main folder where all the pages and assets are stored), click the Site Root button in the Save As dialog box to locate it.

5. **Click Save.**

Note that when you save a file, it appears in your Files panel.

Adding an Image to Your Page

After you have a blank page, you can add an image to it, including native Photoshop (PSD) files and Fireworks (PNG) images. You can find out more about images in Chapter 4 of this minibook, but in this section, you can take a look at how placing images affects your Files panel.

To place an image on a page, follow these steps:

1. **Choose Insert⇨Image.**

Alternatively, click the Common tab of the Insert panel and click the Images button.

The Select Image Source dialog box appears.

2. **Navigate to the location of your image and click Choose.**

If you choose a native Photoshop (PSD) or Fireworks (PNG) file, an Image Preview dialog box appears, allowing you to optimize your image right in Dreamweaver.

If you select a Web-ready image, such as JPG, GIF, or PNG, and the image is outside your site folder, you see a warning. Dreamweaver alerts you that your image is outside the root folder, which causes issues when you copy your pages to a Web server. Click Yes to copy the file to your site's root directory. Assign a new name here or just click Save to keep the same name and duplicate the image file into your site folder.

The Image Tag Accessibility Attributes dialog box appears.

All images should have *Alt (alternate) text* — text that appears before the image has downloaded or that appears if the viewer has turned off the option to see images.

3. **Add an appropriate description of the image in the Alternate Text text box.**

If the image is a logo, the description should include the company name as the Alt text, or if it's a photo or illustration, describe the image in a few words.

From an accessibility standpoint, Alt text aids screen readers (such as those used by the visually impaired) in identifying image content to users. In addition, Alt text is a valuable tool in providing search engines a way of indexing image content included on your site.

4. **Click OK.**

The image is added to the page and to the Files panel, as shown in Figure 3-4.

You can edit your image by double-clicking it in the Files panel. You can also use the Property inspector to see info about your image, including dimensions and file size. From here, you can modify image properties, including border, hyperlink, and vertical/horizontal padding.

When you create a larger site with multiple pages linked to each other, you may want to change the view of the Files panel. By clicking the drop-down list (on the left side of the Files panel) where your site is located, you can locate folders and other sites that you've used recently. By clicking the View drop-down list to the right, you can change the appearance of the Files panel. See Figure 3-4 for an example of how a site appears in Local view.

Open your files from the Files panel by double-clicking them.

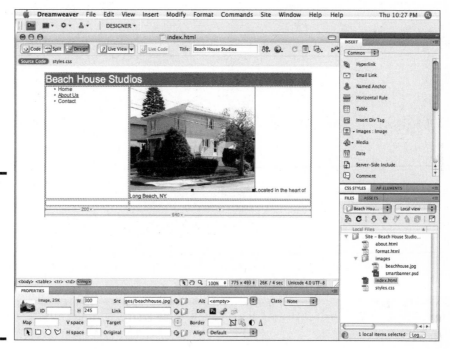

Figure 3-4: Use the Property inspector to see info about your image and modify image properties.

Naming Files

Get in the habit right away of naming your files and folders correctly. Follow these rules to make sure that links and pages appear when they're supposed to:

✦ **Use lowercase for all filenames.** Using all lowercase letters in filenames is an easy way to ensure that you don't have broken links because you couldn't remember whether you initial-capped a filename. Some Web servers (such as those based on UNIX or Mac OS X) are very case-sensitive. Although a Windows server may be more forgiving of case, you don't want to count on that in the event that your files are moved to a different type of server.

✦ **Don't use spaces in filenames.** If you need to separate words in a filename, use the underscore character instead of a space. For example, instead of `file new.html`, use `file_new.html` or even `filenew.html`.

✦ **Use only one dot, followed by the extension.** Macintosh users are used to having no naming restrictions, so this rule can be the toughest to adhere to. Don't name your files something like `finally.done.feb.9.jpg`. That is B-A-D for the Internet. Examples of dot-extensions are as follows: `.jpg`, `.gif`, `.png`, `.htm`, `.html`, `.cgi`, `.swf`, and so on.

✦ **Avoid odd characters.** Characters to avoid include dashes (-) or forward slashes (/) at the beginning of the filename. These characters can mean other things to the Web server and will create errors on the site.

Managing Your Web Site Files

You can find out more about uploading your site in Chapter 9 of this minibook, but for now, understand that you can go back into your Site Definition dialog box at any time by choosing Site➪Manage Sites. The Manage Sites dialog box that appears offers options for editing, duplicating, removing, exporting, and importing sites. Click Edit to add an FTP server or change the name of your site, as well as change any of your original site definition settings.

Delving into HTML Basics

The Web page itself is a collection of text, images, links, and possibly media and scripts. The Web page can be as complex or simple as you want, both being equally effective if created properly. In this section, we show you how to create a page in Dreamweaver and then investigate the HTML that creates it.

To create a blank page, choose File➪New➪Blank Page➪HTML➪<none> and then click Create. A blank untitled HTML page appears. This blank page has no formatting until you add tables or layers (see Chapter 7 of this minibook). When you type on the page in the document, text appears on the Web page. But there's much more to it than that; type some text (say, your name) on the page and click the Code button on the Document toolbar.

Dreamweaver's working in the background to make sure that your page works in most all recent versions of common Web browsers, such as Internet Explorer, Firefox, and Safari. Lots of code is created to help the Web browser recognize that this is HTML and which version of HTML it uses.

By default, Dreamweaver uses the XHTML 1.0 Transitional standard each time you create a new HTML page. XHTML combines the strictness of XML (Extensible Markup Language) with HTML tags to create a language that works dependably and consistently across Web browsers and new devices (such as cellphones and PDAs) alike.

Select the Split view by clicking the Split button on the Document toolbar; this displays both the Design and Code view simultaneously so you can see how your changes affect HTML behind the scenes. Select the text, click the Text tab in the Insert panel, and select B (for bold). The text turns bold. Click the Code button to switch back to the Split view, and you see that the `<strong>` tag was added before the text and the `</strong>` tag was added after the text, as shown in Figure 3-5.

HTML code, though easy, is just like any other language, in that you must figure out the *syntax* (the proper sequence and formation of the code) and vocabulary (memorize lots of tags). You don't have to have gobs of tape on your glasses to build good, clean Web pages, but you do have to review the following HTML basics.

If you're an experienced user, you know that by copying and pasting code, you can figure out a lot about HTML code. If you're a new user, copying and pasting code can help you understand what others have implemented on their pages and perhaps give you some ideas. Working in Split view also helps you understand how the items you add from the toolbars and panels translate into code.

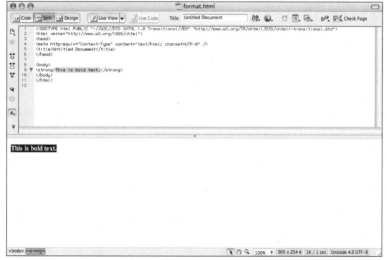

Figure 3-5:
Working in Split view helps you see how elements are formatted with HTML tags.

**Book IV
Chapter 3**

Creating a Web Site

In general, HTML tags are composed of three parts:

✦ **Tag:** The main part of the HTML information — for example, <strong> for strong or bold, <font> for the font tag, <table> for an HTML table, and so on. Tags always are constructed of a keyword enclosed in a set of brackets, such as <p>, or <blockquote>.

Most tags come in pairs, meaning that you must enter an opening tag (<p>) and a closing tag (</p>). In XHTML 1.0 Transitional (the standard used for all new pages created in Dreamweaver), all tags must be closed. You can either close a tag or create a self-closing tag by including the slash before the closing bracket like so: <br/>.

For example, if you make text bold by adding the tag <b>, tell the text where to stop applying boldface by inserting a closing tag </b>. Otherwise, the text continues to appear bold throughout the remainder of the page.

✦ **Attribute:** An attribute gives you a way of further fine-tuning the appearance of a specific HTML tag. Attributes are always added to an opening tag and can take different values to control color, size, the destination of a link, and so on. For example, bgcolor is an attribute of the <body> tag that specifies what color the background of the Web page should be. You'll also see that many HTML tags share the same attributes: For instance, both the <body> and <table> tags can accept a bgcolor attribute.

An example of a paragraph (<p>) tag with an attribute added:

```
<p align="center">This is centered text</p>
```

✦ **Value:** The actual color, size, destination of a link, and so on, specified in an attribute. For example, you can specify a hexadecimal number as the value for a color attribute. An example of a value for the bgcolor attribute of the <body> tag (which controls overall page appearance) could be "red" or "#CC0000".

One last thing: *Nesting* is the order in which your tags appear. If a <strong> tag is applied, it looks like this: <strong>This text is bold</strong>. Add an italic tag, and you have <strong><em>This text is bold and italic.</em></strong>. Notice the in-to-out placement of the tags; you work your way from the inside to the outside when closing tags.

Chapter 4: Working with Images

In This Chapter

✔ Making images work for the Web

✔ Inserting Photoshop files and working with Smart Objects

✔ Touring the Property inspector

✔ Aligning images and adding space around them

✔ Creating backgrounds from images

✔ Creating a rollover

✔ Inserting a Flash movie on your page

*P*lacing images that are interesting and informative is one of the most exciting parts of building a Web page. In this chapter, you discover how to insert and optimize native Photoshop (PSD) files directly in Dreamweaver, as well take care of basic needs, such as resizing, cropping, and positioning the image. You also find out how to create interesting backgrounds and create easy rollovers.

If you plan on following along with some of the steps in this chapter, create a site or have a practice site open. Images are much-needed linked assets on your page. You don't want to lose track of them in your filing system. If you don't know how to create a site, read Chapter 3 of this minibook.

Creating Images for the Web

Placing images isn't difficult, but you must consider which format images are saved in and how large the files are. (See Book II, Chapter 10 for details on selecting the correct format and using the Save for Web & Devices feature in Photoshop.)

Putting images on a Web page requires planning to make sure that sizes are exactly what you want them to be. You also need to make sure that you don't have too many images to keep the page loading quickly.

If you look in the lower right of your Document window, you see the page file size and its approximate download time. In Figure 4-1, the page file size is 26K, and the download time is 4 seconds. This download time is based upon the preference of 56K per second. You can change the download speed by choosing Edit➪Preferences (Windows) or Dreamweaver➪Preferences (Mac), selecting the Status Bar category, and clicking the Connection Speed drop-down list.

The jury is always out as to how fast a page should download, but less than 15 seconds is a good target. Unless you have some really compelling content, you'll probably lose viewers after that.

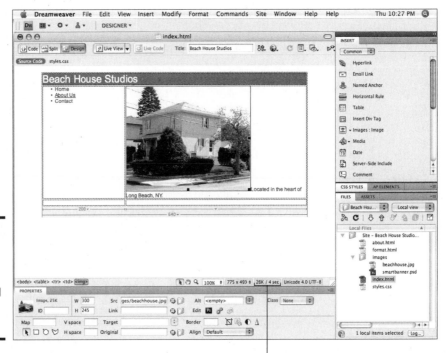

Figure 4-1: Check your Document window for file size and download time.

File size and download time

Putting Images on a Page

Putting your images on a Web page in Dreamweaver is easier than ever, mostly because of the integration with other Adobe products. You can use menu items, copy and paste, and even drag and drop images on to your Dreamweaver page. In the following sections, you not only find out how to place your images, but you also discover some general helpful tips that relate to putting graphics on the Web.

Inserting an image

If you're preparing images ahead of time, save or move the optimized images into your site folder. It's not that you can't select an image from anywhere in your directory; it just adds another step, copying the image into your site folder.

After you have a page open, you can insert an image as follows:

1. **Click to put your insertion point on the page where you want the image placed.**

2. **Locate the Common tab on the Insert panel and click the Insert Image button or choose Insert⇨Image.**

   If image isn't the default for your Insert Image button, click and hold the arrow to the right of the button and choose Image from the drop-down list.

   The Select Image Source dialog box appears.

3. **Navigate to where your image is located and click OK (Windows) or Choose (Mac) to place the selected image.**

   If your images are located in your site folder, you can click the Site Root button shown on the Select Image Source dialog box to navigate there quickly. If your image isn't in your site folder, you see an alert dialog box, asking whether you want to copy the file there now.

4. **If you're prompted to copy the image to your site's root folder, click Yes, and in the Copy File As dialog box that appears, verify that the name is correct and click Save.**

   You now see the Image Tag Accessibility Attributes dialog box, requesting that you enter Alt text. (For more on Alt text, see the sidebar "Gotta have that Alt text.")

5. **Type a word or two that best describes your image (such as** Our Family Photo**) in the Alternate Text text box and click OK.**

   The image is placed.

Dragging and dropping an image

In addition to the Image object found in the Insert panel, if your Files panel is visible within the workspace, you can click and drag images directly to the page from the Files panel onto the page. If you're dragging an image, the cursor follows you while you move around the document until you release the mouse button and drop the image.

If you're taking advantage of the Adobe Bridge workflow, you can leave Bridge running and drag images as you need them right from the Bridge window into your Dreamweaver page. You can access Bridge by choosing File⇨Browse in Bridge.

**Book IV
Chapter 4**

Working with Images

Gotta have that Alt text

You've probably seen *Alt text* a gazillion times; it's the text that appears before an image when a Web page is loading. Alt text also appears as a ToolTip when you hover your mouse cursor over an image in a Web page.

Alt text is helpful because it tells viewers something about the image before the image appears, but Alt text also is necessary for viewers who turn off their preference for viewing graphics (such as in certain e-mail applications), or for folks using a Web-reading program like those for the visually impaired. U.S. federal regulations also require Alt tags for any work completed for federal agencies. These tags are also helpful for people with slow Internet connections.

In addition, Alt text is a valuable tool for indexing image content for search engines: Search engines, such as Google, Yahoo!, and MSN, all utilize Alt text as a key method of indexing images for their respective image search listings.

To assign or change Alt text to an image that's been placed already, type your descriptive copy in the Alt text box located in the Property inspector.

If the image is a native Photoshop (PSD) or Fireworks (PNG) file, the Image Preview dialog box appears, giving you the opportunity to optimize the image before placing it.

You can also drag and drop an optimized image from your desktop or other folders right into a Dreamweaver page. If they're not in your site folder, you get the opportunity to copy the image to your site folder.

Getting to Know the Property Inspector

Many of the tools you use when working with images are located on the Property inspector (see Figure 4-2).

Figure 4-2:
The Property inspector's image-editing options.

You can choose from these properties when an image is selected:

✦ **Editing the original:** If you want to make a quick change, it shouldn't have to involve a lot of navigating through the directories on your operating system. To edit your original image file, select it and click the Edit in Photoshop button on the Property inspector. The image is launched in Photoshop, where you can make changes and re-save the image.

You can select the default image editing application for different image file types with the Preferences⇨Files Types/Editors. By default, Photoshop CS4 and Fireworks CS4 are the primary or secondary editors for most any image type.

✦ **Optimizing an image:** You do have the opportunity to optimize images right off your Dreamweaver page, but this method doesn't provide quite the same capabilities that you have when placing a native Photoshop or Fireworks file because the image you're selecting has already been optimized. It may already be a JPEG or GIF — and yes, you can reduce the number of colors in the GIF or change a JPEG to a GIF, but you really can't increase color levels or quality on these images, as they're not linked to the original image file.

✦ **Cropping an image:** This feature is sure to become a favorite because you can make cropping decisions right on your Dreamweaver page. Simply click the Crop tool, acknowledge the warning message telling you that you're editing the image, and then click and drag the handles to the desired size. Press the Enter key, and you're done!

✦ **Resampling an image:** You may have heard that you shouldn't resize an image placed on a Dreamweaver page because, if you were making the image larger, it would become pixilated, and if you were making the image smaller, you were wasting lots of bandwidth downloading the file. Fortunately, you can now use the Resample button on the Property inspector after you resize the image. Just keep in mind that making the image larger still causes some quality issues, so it's best to reduce the file size before choosing the Resample button. If you need to make an image considerably larger, find the original and optimize it to the proper size.

To resize an image, you can either click and drag out the lower-right corner handle of the image or type a pixel value in the W (Width) and H (Height) text boxes in the Property inspector.

✦ **Brightness and contrast:** If high quality is important to you, open your original image in Photoshop and make tonal corrections with professional digital imaging tools. If volume and quickly getting lots of images and pages posted is important, take advantage of the Brightness and Contrast controls built right into Adobe Dreamweaver. Simply click the Brightness and Contrast button in the Property inspector, acknowledge the Dreamweaver dialog box, and adjust the sliders to create the best image.

Book IV Chapter 4

Working with Images

✦ **Sharpen:** Add crispness to your image by applying the Sharpness controls available in Dreamweaver. Just like some of the other image-editing features in Dreamweaver, you're better off using the Unsharp mask filter in Photoshop, but in a pinch, this feature is a great quick tool to take advantage of. To use the Sharpening feature, click the Sharpen button, acknowledge the warning that you're changing the image, and use the slider to sharpen the image.

Placing Photoshop Files

If you've created artwork or prepared images in Photoshop, you can place your original PSD files directly into your pages. The Image Preview window lets you save your Photoshop files into Web-ready image formats, such as PNG, GIF, and JPEG, as well as scale and crop your artwork before it's placed on the page.

Photoshop Smart Objects

The ability to work with Photoshop files is great for most designers who depend on Photoshop as part of their workflow. Now, when you place Photoshop files on a page, Dreamweaver creates a *Smart Object* — an image that maintains a connection to the original Photoshop file from which it was created.

The image now displays an icon that lets you know if the original file was updated, and you can apply the changes in the original file to the image in one click.

To place a Photoshop file in your page:

1. **Click where you want to place the new image and then click the Image object in the Insert panel's Common category.**

2. **When the Select Image Source dialog box appears, browse and select a Photoshop PSD file and then click Choose/Select to select the image.**

3. **The Image Preview dialog box appears, where you can optimize, crop, scale, and save your image in the Web-friendly JPEG, GIF, or PNG formats, as shown in Figure 4-3.**

4. **In the Options tab, select the file format you want to save your image in from the Format drop-down list, and choose the quality settings that best suit your image from the Quality drop-down list.**

You can use the Saved Settings drop-down list at the top of the dialog box to choose one of the image quality presets.

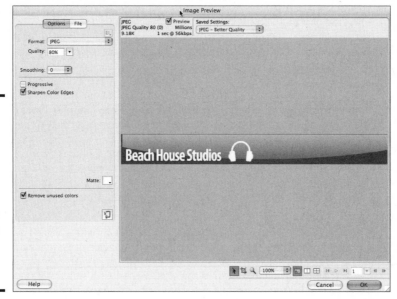

Figure 4-3:
The Image
Preview
dialog box
lets you
optimize
and save a
Web-ready
image from
a selected
Photoshop
file.

5. **(Optional) Click the File tab to switch to the File options and then enter settings to scale your image or use the Crop tool at the bottom of the preview window to crop your image.**

6. **Click OK to save the image.**

7. **When the Save Web image dialog box appears, navigate to your site's root folder and click OK to save the image into the appropriate folder (for instance, your default images folder).**

   If the Image Tab Accessibility Attributes dialog box appears, type a short description of your image in the Alternate text field and click OK to place the image.

   The new image is placed, and a small icon appears in the upper-right corner of the image. This Smart Object indicator shows two green arrows, indicating that your image is up to date.

Select the image you just placed in the preceding steps list and locate the Original text field on the Property inspector — this displays the location of the original Photoshop file. To edit the image, you can simply click the Edit in Photoshop button on the right side of the Property inspector to open the source file in Photoshop.

Updating Photoshop Smart Objects

If you make any changes to the original Photoshop file, the image you placed in your page displays a red and green arrow icon to let you know that it's not up to date.

 To update a Smart Object when you see the green and red circular arrows indicator, select the image and click the Update from Original button on the Property inspector to apply the new changes to the placed image.

 Moving the original PSD file connected to a page image displays an alert icon on the image and disables the link between the two. Keep your original PSD files in a set location and make sure to revise the location of your source file by selecting the image and updating the original in the Property inspector.

Aligning an Image

As a default, images and any adjacent text sit on the same baseline, forcing text to run in one line off to the right of the image. To control the wrapping/runaround of the text, change the alignment of the image by selecting the image and then choosing an option from the Align drop-down list in the Property inspector.

The Align drop-down list provides the following options:

✦ **Default:** Uses Baseline alignment (described next).

✦ **Baseline (Default):** Aligns the bottom of the image with the baseline of the current line of text.

✦ **Top:** Image aligns itself with the top of the tallest item in the line of text.

✦ **Middle:** Image aligns the baseline of the current line of text with the middle of the image.

✦ **Bottom:** Baseline aligns the bottom of the image with the baseline of the current line of text.

✦ **Text Top:** Image aligns itself with the top of the tallest text in the line. This is usually (but not always) the same as `ALIGN=top`.

✦ **Absolute Middle:** Aligns the middle of the current line with the middle of the image.

✦ **Absolute Bottom:** Aligns the bottom of the image with the bottom of the current line of text.

✦ **Left:** Aligns the image to the left, text flushes to the right of the image.

✦ **Right:** Aligns image to the right, text flushes to the left of the image.

Adding Space around the Image

You may want some space around the image to keep the text from butting right up to the image. To create a space around the image, enter values into the H Space and V Space text fields in the Property inspector.

If you want space added only to one side of the image, CSS (Cascading Style Sheets) provides the ability to add margins to one side of an image only. See Chapter 5 of this minibook for more on using CSS to format text and page elements.

In addition, you can open the image in Photoshop and choose Image⇨ Canvas Size. In the Canvas Size dialog box that appears, click the middle-left square in the Anchor section and add a value in pixels to your total image size. Click the right-middle square to add the size to the left side of the image.

Using an Image as a Background

Creating backgrounds for Web pages is fun and can be pursued in more ways than most people think. You can create a repeating pattern with a single small image, create a watermark, or use a large image to fill an entire background. As a default, HTML backgrounds repeat the selected image until the entire screen is filled. In conjunction with CSS properties, you can control or eliminate repeating behavior, and even set precise positioning for a single background image.

If you're filling your background with a pattern, make sure that you create a pattern image that has no discernable edges. (In Photoshop, choose Filter⇨Texture⇨Texturizer to see some good choices in the Texturizer dialog box.)

To utilize the default, repeated tiling for a background image to your advantage, follow these steps:

1. **In Photoshop, choose File⇨New to create a new image.**

2. **In the New dialog box that appears, create an image that's much wider than it is high, choose RGB, choose 72 dpi, and then click OK.**

   For example, enter **1000** in the Height text field and **20** in the Width text field.

3. **Select a foreground and background color to create a blend; then with the Gradient tool, Shift+drag from the top to bottom of the image area to create a gradient fill.**

4. **Choose File⇨Save for Web and save the image as a JPEG into your site's Web content folder and then close the image.**

   See Book II, Chapter 10 for more about the Save for Web & Devices feature.

5. **In Dreamweaver, choose Modify⇨Page Properties or click the Page Properties button on the Property inspector to place the image as a background image in your Web page.**

   If the Page Properties button isn't visible, click the page, making sure that you don't select another element, such as an image.

6. **In the Page Properties dialog box that appears, click the Browse button to the right of the background image, navigate to the location of your saved background image, and then click Choose; click OK in the Page Properties dialog box.**

   The image appears in the background, repeating and creating a cool background gradient across the page!

Depending on the size and resolution of a user's monitor, your background image may be forced to repeat. This can be used in many creative ways as demonstrated in the text earlier.

In certain cases, you may not see your background until you click the Preview/Debug in Browser button and preview the page in your default browser.

Creating Rollovers

With Dreamweaver, you can insert image objects. These image objects include image placeholders, *rollover images* (images that change when a viewer crosses over the image), navigation bars, and Fireworks HTML. Access these image objects by choosing Image⇨Image Objects.

To create a rollover image, follow these steps:

1. **Create the images that'll be used as the rollover.**

   You can generate these images with Illustrator, Photoshop, Fireworks, or any application capable of saving images optimized for the Web.

2. **Put your cursor on the page where you want the rollover to appear and choose Insert⇨Image Objects⇨Rollover Image, or click the Rollover Image button in the Insert panel.**

   The Insert Rollover Image dialog box, as shown in Figure 4-4, appears.

3. **Type an image name without spaces in the Image name text box.**

   This name is used in the script creating the rollover.

Figure 4-4:
Rollovers are made easy in Dream-weaver.

Insert Rollover Image

Image name:	Home Button
Original image:	images/home_on.gif
Rollover image:	imaoes/home_off.aif
	☑ Preload rollover image
Alternate text:	Click here to go home
When clicked, Go to URL:	index.html

OK
Cancel
Help

4. **Click the Browse buttons to the right of Original Image and Rollover Image text boxes to locate the image that you want to appear as a default on the page and the image that will appear only when someone mouses over the image.**

5. **Leave the Preload Rollover Image check box selected.**

   This option downloads the rollover image when the page is downloaded to avoid delays in rollovers.

6. **Type the appropriate descriptive Alt text in the Alternate text text box.**

7. **In the When Clicked, Go to URL text box, instruct Dreamweaver as to where viewers are directed when they click your rollover image.**

   You can either click the Browse button to locate another page in your site or enter a URL.

8. **Click OK.**

   The rollover image is created on your page.

9. **To preview your new rollover image, choose File⇨Preview in Browser or select the Live View button on the Document toolbar.**

If you don't have a real link to use for a button or hyperlink just yet, you can enter a pound sign (#) to create a dead link. The link or button appears clickable but won't go anywhere when clicked. This is a better option than creating a white space for a link, as that generates a Page Not Found error when clicked.

Inserting Media Content

Make your pages more interactive and interesting by adding Flash and Shockwave content. Dreamweaver makes it simple by providing you with the tools that you need to add Flash animation, FlashPaper, Flash Text, Flash Button, and Flash video (. flv) files.

Follow these steps to place a Flash file on to your Dreamweaver page:

1. **Put the cursor on your page where you want to insert the Flash file.**

2. **Choose Insert⇨Media⇨SWF.**

The Select File dialog box appears.

3. **Navigate to the SWF file that you want to place and click OK (Windows) or Choose (Mac) to select the file.**

4. **In the Object Tag Accessibility Attributes dialog box, type a descriptive title for the movie in the Title field and click OK.**

The Flash file is placed on the page.

5. **On the Property inspector, click the Play button to preview your new Flash movie.**

You can also adjust settings for your movie, as shown in Figure 4-5.

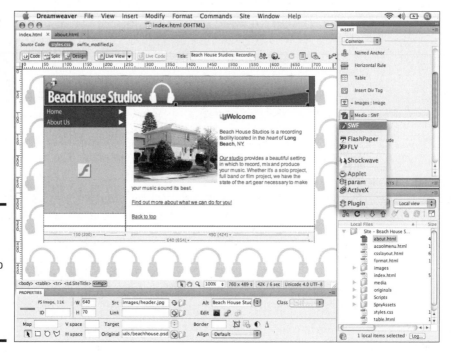

Figure 4-5:
Use the
Property
inspector to
adjust and
preview
Flash
movies.

Chapter 5: Putting Text on the Page

In This Chapter

- ✔ Adding text to your page
- ✔ Choosing and editing fonts
- ✔ Understanding CSS
- ✔ Creating an external style sheet

*A*dding text to your Web page requires more than just typing on a page. You must carefully plan your Web pages so that search engines (and viewers) can easily find relevant content on your Web site. In this chapter, you discover fundamentals of text formatting for your Web pages, from the basics of font size and font family, to spell checking your text, to implementing Cascading Style Sheets (CSS).

Because you can assign type properties quickly and update several instances in a few easy steps with CSS, CSS is viewed as the most efficient and preferred method of applying text attributes on a Web page. When you create text for the body of your page, include keywords that provide descriptions of your site's content. This makes your page more relevant to the search engine and the viewer.

 As a default, Dreamweaver formats all text on your page with CSS, which is the standard for formatting a styling text. In previous versions of Dreamweaver, you still had the option to enable and use archaic `<font>` tags to format text if you so chose; this option has been removed from the CS4 preferences. Now, formatting with font tags can only be done by manually inserting `<font>` tags by choosing Insert➪Tag or by hand-coding methods. By default, when you format text directly from the Property inspector, CSS styles are always created to save and apply the formatting you choose.

Adding Text

To add text to your Web page, simply click the page wherever you want the text to appear; an insertion point appears where you can start typing. You can add text right to the page, in a CSS layer, or in the cell of a table.

Formatting text

Formatting text in Dreamweaver can be as simple as formatting text in any a word-processing application or applications such as InDesign or Illustrator. By using the Property inspector, you can easily apply basic font attributes, such as color, typeface, size, and alignment options. Clicking the Text category of the Insert panel gives you several different HTML text tags to apply to your selected text (see Figure 5-1).

Figure 5-1: You can use the Text category of the Insert panel to do basic text formatting.

Most of the options in the Text category are apparent, but here's a breakdown of some text tags that may be unfamiliar to you. To use these tags, simply select the text that you want the tag to be applied to and then click the tag on the Insert panel:

✦ **Bold:** Bolds text

✦ **Italic:** Italicizes text

✦ **Strong:** Bolds text

✦ **Emphasis:** Indicates emphasis, looks like italic

Dreamweaver favors the accessibility friendly `<strong>` and `<em>` tags over `<b>` and `<i>`, although both bold and italicize text, respectively, `<strong>` and `<em>`, are used in almost all cases, even when you click the B and I buttons.

When you press the Enter or Return key, a `<p>` tag is created automatically in the HTML source code. This tag may create more space than you like between lines and create new list items. Pressing Shift+Enter (Windows) or Shift+Return (Mac) creates a `<br>` tag, which is essentially a line break or soft return. See Figure 5-2.

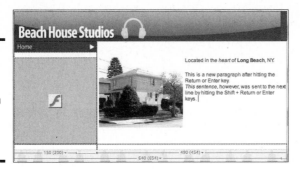

Figure 5-2:
A new paragraph break and a soft return or line break.

Using the Property inspector to style text

Use the Property inspector, as shown in Figure 5-3, to apply HTML tags and build CSS classes to format text color, face, size, and more. The Property inspector is divided into two views: HTML and CSS. You can toggle between these two different views with the buttons on the left side of the panel.

Figure 5-3:
Change text attributes.

Click to toggle between HTML and CSS properties.

Here's what all the buttons on the Property inspector mean:

✦ **Format (HTML):** Use the Format drop-down list to apply HTML tags that format an entire paragraph. This includes heading tags (Heading 1–Heading 6) that are generally applied to headers and titles, the paragraph tag, and the preformatted text tag. You can easily fine-tune each of these tags' attributes (color, size, font family, and so on) later by using CSS.

Note that Heading 1 is the largest format size (on average, about equivalent to 24-point text), and Heading 6 is the smallest. This makes sense if you think about how these tags were originally used to create technical documents and outlines on the Internet, where text contained in Heading 1 should be treated as more important than text in Headings 2 or 3.

The last choice in the Format drop-down list is Preformatted. Sometimes, you want the browser to display text exactly the way you composed it — with indents, line breaks, and extra spaces. You can line up text this way if you choose Preformatted; it's not pretty, but for down and dirty lists and columns, it can work well.

✦ **ID (HTML):** This applies a CSS ID style to an element. IDs are a specific type of CSS rule (or *selector*) that are used to store formatting information that's unique to a single item on the page (for instance, positioning information for a container).

✦ **Class (HTML):** This drop-down list applies an existing class style to a selection on the page. Class styles can be created with the Property inspector (discussed later in this chapter) or directly from the CSS styles panel. *Note:* This drop-down list was labeled Style in previous versions of Dreamweaver.

✦ **Link (HTML):** Type a hyperlink (such as www.wiley.com) or click the folder icon to browse and link to another page within your Web site. The selected text becomes linked (preview your page in a browser or enable Live View to see this work).

✦ **Target (HTML):** Choose where the linked target will appear. (Read about targets in Chapter 6 of this minibook.)

✦ **Bold (HTML/CSS):** Bolds your selected text.

✦ **Italic (HTML/CSS):** Italicizes your text.

✦ **Alignment (CSS):** You can click the alignment buttons on the toolbar to apply left, center, and right alignment. To revert to the default left alignment, click the currently selected alignment button again.

✦ **Unordered List (HTML):** Automatically puts bullets in front of the listed items. As you advance in the use of Cascading Style Sheets, you can apply many more attributes to lists, including customizing the bullets.

✦ **Ordered List (HTML):** Automatically numbers each additional line of text every time you press the Enter (Windows) or Return (Mac) key. To force the text to another line without adding the automatic numbering, press Shift+Enter (Windows) or Shift+Return (Mac).

✦ **Text Outdent (HTML):** Undo an Indent with the Text Outdent button. This removes the <blockquote> tag that the Text Indent button creates.

✦ **Text Indent (HTML):** Use to indent your text. Simply put your cursor in the paragraph of text that you want to indent and press the Text Indent button. A <blockquote> tag is applied. You can apply this tag multiple times to a paragraph to indent it further and further.

✦ **Targeted Rule (CSS):** This allows you to modify an existing CSS rule or create a new one; in previous versions of Dreamweaver, this was vague as to whether changes made to an existing CSS class would modify it or create a new one. This drop-down list lets you be very clear as to what your actions on the Property inspector will actually do.

✦ **Edit Rule / CSS Panel buttons (CSS):** For the rule shown in the Targeted Rule drop-down list, you can either edit the properties and values for that rule in the CSS Rule Definition dialog box or view it in the CSS Styles panel on the right, respectively.

✦ **Font (CSS):** Use this drop-down list to select a font family. The *font* is the typeface that you choose to display your text in. The lack of typeface selection isn't a restriction in Dreamweaver, but rather in Web design as a whole. Keep in mind that what font the viewer sees on your Web page is based upon the availability of the fonts on that user's computer. For this reason, font sets are limited to basic system fonts that are installed on most every computer, regardless of operating system.

The viewer may not have fonts that you load in your font sets, so try to stick to common typefaces like the ones already included in Dreamweaver's existing font sets.

✦ **Size (CSS):** With the Font Size drop-down list, you can apply a fixed font size from 9–36 (pixels) or enter a value by typing it directly in. You can use the relative sizes shown (x-small, small, and so on), which resize the font relatively larger or smaller according to the user's browser preferences for font size. If you don't change the font size, it defaults to 12 pixels (px). By default, the unit of measurement is set to pixels, but you can use the neighboring drop-down list to set other units of measurement including points, picas, ems, and more.

Keep in mind that the user can set his browser preferences to override the size settings you've chosen.

✦ **Color (CSS):** Assign a color to your selection by clicking the swatch icon and selecting a swatch from the panel that appears. Colors are represented in HTML and CSS by *hexadecimal codes,* 6-character codes that represent the RGB (Red, Green, Blue) values that form that color. This code is shown at the top of the Swatches panel whenever you select a color.

Spell checking your text

You can spell check just the file that you have open or multiple files by choosing Commands⇨Check Spelling. With the Check Spelling dialog box, as shown in Figure 5-4, you can choose to add words to your personal dictionary, ignore words, or change the spelling of words.

Figure 5-4:
Make sure
that your
spelling is
correct.

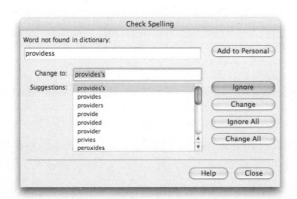

Assigning and editing fonts

When a viewer opens a page referencing a font set, the text is displayed using the first available font in the font family. If the first font face on the list isn't available, the next font face is referenced, continuing down the list in the font family until a font in the font set is found on the viewer's computer. If you choose Edit Font List from the Font drop-down list, the Edit Font List dialog box appears (see figure).

Click the existing font lists to see which fonts are included in each set. You can add new fonts to the sets by clicking the double arrow pointing from the Available Fonts panel into the Chosen Fonts panel. Delete a font from an existing font list by clicking the font in the Chosen Fonts panel and clicking the double arrow pointing toward the Available Fonts panel. You can even create an entirely new list yourself by clicking the + (plus sign) in the upper left of the Edit Font List dialog box.

Understanding Cascading Style Sheets

Using *Cascading Style Sheets* (CSS) is definitely the cleanest and most effi-cient method for stylizing text on your Web pages, and is the method that Dreamweaver uses. Style sheets are a powerful design tool that allows you to assign properties to type and other page elements quickly and update all instances in a few easy steps. The reason for the name Cascading Style Sheets is because certain *cascading rules* apply when several styles (and style sheets) are used at once.

If you apply many different styles to a page, whether they're internally built on the page or linked to external style sheets, you may have conflicts. Conflicts occur when two (or more) styles assign different properties to the same element. For example, if you specify in an internal style sheet that anything bolded is blue but an external style sheet instructs the browser to display anything bolded as red, which style wins? The blue instruction from the internal style sheet wins. If conflicts occur in external style sheets, you can set the order of importance by using the up and down arrows. By default, the Web page's style sheet overrides the browser's default values.

Keep in mind that style sheets are compatible with most all modern browser versions, but some older browsers may not provide consistent (if any) support for CSS. Always preview your pages in multiple browsers or use the Check Browser Compatibility button (located under the Check Page list on the Document toolbar) to test CSS properties you've used against a variety of browsers and versions.

We definitely offer the quick-and-dirty course on CSS here. If you're interested in finding out more about this topic, check out *CSS Web Design For Dummies* by Richard Mansfield (Wiley Publishing, Inc.).

Dreamweaver CS4 uses Cascading Styles Sheets (CSS) exclusively to format text and no longer provides direct support for `<font>` tags. You can still add `<font>` tags if you absolutely need to by choosing Insert➪Tag.

Dreamweaver offers CSS starter pages that have CSS layouts available and that include CSS hints visible only in the Code view (see Figure 5-5). Find the CSS starter pages by choosing File➪New➪Blank Page➪HTML Template.

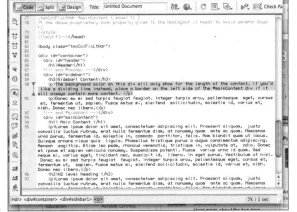

Figure 5-5: Helpful CSS tips are built into the CSS starter pages.

Using CSS for text

Using Cascading Style Sheets in Dreamweaver is very intuitive; simply create a blank HTML page, add and select some text, and begin styling your selection directly in the Property inspector CSS view by selecting properties for color, size, typeface, and more.

Assigning formatting to a selection opens the New CSS Rule Dialog box, allowing you to save the choices you've made into a new CSS rule (or *style*). You can choose a name, selector type, and a location for the new rule.

Several types of selectors determine what style properties should be applied and where. When Dreamweaver finds a selector, it applies the properties and values you've chosen. This means you make formatting choices once and reapply them over and over in a single click!

(You can find out how to take advantage of advanced properties for creating layouts in Chapter 8 of this minibook.)

Creating a new tag style

Creating a tag (or an *element*) selector is a simple and safe route for new users to understand CSS because you can work with existing HTML tags, such as H1, H2, and so on. With existing element tags on your page, you can choose to apply automatic formatting wherever existing HTML tags are used. For instance, you can make anything inside a `<strong>` tag automatically italic, 20 px, and red.

To create a tag style with the Property inspector, follow these steps:

1. **Open an HTML page that contains text.**

2. **On the Property inspector, click the CSS button on the left of the panel to display the Property inspector in CSS view.**

3. **Locate the Targeted Rule drop-down list and make sure it's set to <New CSS Rule>.**

4. **Select some text on the page and assign the `<strong>` tag by clicking the B button.**

   The New CSS Rule dialog box appears, as shown in Figure 5-6.

5. **Use the color selector on the right side of the panel (located below the B and I buttons) to select a new color for any text appearing inside the `<strong>` tag (bold text).**

6. **From the Selector Type drop-down list, choose Tag (Redefines an HTML Element); choose Strong from the Selector Name drop-down list; choose (This Document Only) from the Rule Definition drop-down list.**

   See Figure 5-7. The selector type determines how the formatting will be applied to elements on the page. Tag styles change the appearance of any element formatted with a specific HTML tag.

7. **Click OK to create the new tag style and exit the panel.**

By choosing to define the style in this document only, it inserts the CSS rule in the head section of this page only. The `<strong>` tag would be adjusted to your definition only on this page. This can be beneficial if you have one page in your site that's black, for example, and you want the `<strong>` tag to be white for that one page only.

Figure 5-6:
The New
CSS Rule
dialog box.

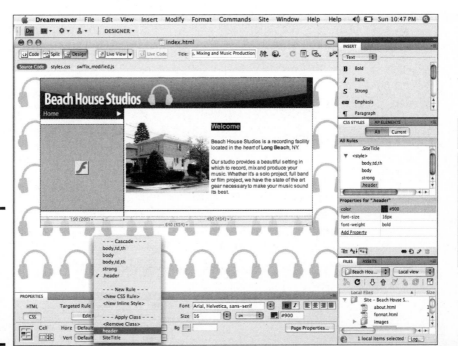

Figure 5-7:
Choose the
attributes
that you
want
assigned
to the CSS
selector.

**Book IV
Chapter 5**

**Putting Text on
the Page**

Here are a few things to keep in mind as you choose your attributes:

- *Font family:* Notice that you can apply a font family with the Font drop-down list. This is the preferred method of assigning a font family.

- *Font size:* Enter a text size and then, with the Unit drop-down list to the right of the size, enter it as pixels, points, inches, centimeters, and other units of measurement. By specifying a size and unit of measurement here — 12 px, for example — you can be assured that the text appears as relatively the same size on both the Windows and Macintosh platforms.

- *Line height:* By assigning a size in any unit, you can define the space between lines of text. For example, if the type size is 12, the line height of 24 px is essentially the same as double-spacing. If you come from the typesetting or design world, it works much like leading.

- *Font decoration:* Hmm, if you want it, get it here! Blinking isn't a good idea, as it is just plain B-A-D and also not compatible on all browsers. Try and use underlines to make key text stand out, or use underlines to create a line underneath paragraph or page headers.

Don't like underlines under your links? Create a tag style for the `<a>` tag (this is the HTML tag used to create a link) and select None in the Decoration drop-down list.

- *Font-Weight:* Make your text lighter or heavier with this drop-down list. Just so you know, a value of 700 is the typical boldness of bold text; any heavier is bolder than bold.

- *Font-Variant:* Use this drop-down list to choose small caps.

You may be wondering why Normal is a choice in the Style drop-down list. Normal is choice because you may have defined small caps, for example, as the variant for all instances of the `<strong>` tag, but then decided that on one page you wanted to override that attribute. By creating a style defined in the document only with Normal selected in variant, you can override the style (small caps) definition on the external style sheet.

- *Font transform:* Choose from Capitalize, Uppercase, Lowercase, or None.

- *Color:* Assign a color to your selector by clicking the arrow in the lower-right corner of the Color definition swatch or type a number in the Color text box.

8. Click Apply.

Block level versus inline

You may find that when you assign certain properties, you see varying results because some properties that you select affect only block level elements as compared to inline elements. *Block level elements* apply to elements that take up their own horizontal space on a page, such as an entire paragraph or an ordered/unordered list. If you create a P element style and change the line spacing, the space takes effect within the block-level element.

An *inline element* is one that applies formatting to tags or items that fall within the flow with text, such as the `<strong>` tag. If you choose to apply line spacing to the b element, the leading in paragraphs that contain the `<strong>` tag aren't affected.

You'll eventually figure out which properties work with which tags. Just keep this point in mind so that you're not dumbfounded when some properties don't work as expected!

Creating a new class style

For more styling control over your page, you can create *class selectors,* which are named styles for body, text, headlines, subheads, and so on. Unlike tag selectors, you can choose just about any name for a class and apply its style selectively to items if and when you want.

If you choose properties that work on a variety of elements, you can get a lot of mileage from a single class style in many places throughout your page. Essentially, class styles are like creating your own character or paragraph styles, if you're familiar with that feature from common page-layout applications, such as InDesign.

This time, you can also make your new rule available to more than one page in your site by defining a new external style sheet. This saves your rules in an external file which can be attached to several pages at once.

Follow these steps to create a class style from the CSS Styles panel:

1. **Locate your CSS panel, off to the right, and click the New CSS Rule button at the bottom or choose Format⇨CSS Styles⇨New.**

   The New CSS Rule dialog box appears (refer to Figure 5-6).

2. **From the Selector Type drop-down list, choose Class (Can Apply to Any HTML Element).**

3. **In the Selector Name text box, enter a name to your new class.**

   You can enter any name that you want but make sure that it has no spaces and is descriptive of how you'll use it. Reallycoolstyle is a bad name; headlinestyle is a better name. Dreamweaver inserts the period at the front of the style name as it's a necessary naming convention.

4. **From the Rule Definition drop-down list at the bottom, choose (New Stylesheet File).**

5. **Click OK.**

   The Save Style Sheet File As dialog box appears. Locate your site folder (or if you haven't defined a site, a folder where you'll keep all relevant information, such as image files and pages for your site).

6. **Enter a name for your style sheet.**

   Enter something appropriate, such as **main.css** or **basic.css** if it's the main set of styles you're creating for your Web site. (Make sure to include the .css extension at the end of the name.)

7. **Leave the URL as is and the Relative To drop-down list set to Document.**

8. **Click Save.**

   You've now created a new .css file, or external stylesheet. The CSS Rule Definition dialog box appears.

   In this dialog box, you can create the set of attributes that you want included in the CSS definition for the style you're creating. As you might notice, this dialog box is the same definition that you work with when you create a tag style (see the previous section). The difference with the tag and class styles is really only in the application of the style.

9. **Apply a font, size, style, line height (leading), and any other attributes that you couldn't apply to text using straight HTML coding.**

10. **After you select attributes for your class style, click OK to exit the dialog box and return to your page.**

Now you can apply the CSS class style to some text. When applying a class style, you can choose to apply it to only some text or to an entire paragraph of text. Follow these steps to apply a class style to an entire paragraph:

1. **Place your cursor into a paragraph of text or click and drag to select a line of text.**

2. **If the Property inspector isn't visible, choose Window⇨Properties. Click the HTML button on the left side of the Property inspector to toggle to HTML view.**

3. **From the Class drop-down list shown in the Property inspector HTML view, select your new style to apply it to the selection, as shown in Figure 5-8.**

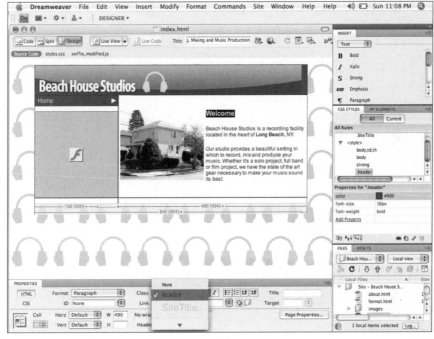

Figure 5-8:
Apply a class style to a selected piece of text with the Class drop-down list.

Chapter 6: Linking It Together

In This Chapter

✔ **Using internal links**

✔ **Discovering how to use anchors**

✔ **Linking to external documents, e-mail, and PDFs**

✔ **Making sure that your links work**

*L*inks are a major and necessary component of any Web site. You must incorporate links on your Web site; this way your viewers can easily navigate throughout your site to get the information they're seeking. In this chapter, we show you how to add links easily and effectively with Dreamweaver.

The Basics of Linking

Links (also referred to as *hyperlinks*) are navigational aids; viewers click links to go to other Web pages, a downloadable resource file, an e-mail address, or a specific spot on a Web page (known as an *anchor*). As you create the first link from one of your Web pages to another, you've essentially created a Web site — it may be a small site, but it's a start. While you're still in the small site stage, here are a couple of things we recommend that you keep in mind as you add more pages and create more links, making your site ever bigger:

✦ Essentially, there are two kinds of links: internal and external. *Internal links* connect viewers to other parts of your Web site; *external links* connect viewers to other pages or content outside your site. We show you how to create each kind of link in this chapter.

✦ Before you start working with any pages that are to be linked, make sure that you've created a Dreamweaver site; this helps you locate local files to link to, and later you'll have the ability to check and validate links between pages in your site.

Implementing Internal Links

Internal links, an essential part of any user-friendly site, help your viewers easily and quickly navigate to other parts of your Web site.

If you need to change names of files after they've been linked anywhere, do so *only* within the Files panel in Dreamweaver. Otherwise, you'll end up with broken links. Take a look at the "Resolving Link Errors" section, later in this chapter, to find out how to change the names of linked files without breaking the links.

You can create a link out of text or an image (such as a button graphic). The following sections outline several methods that you can use for creating links.

Using the Hyperlink dialog box to create a link

To create a hyperlink with text as the link, you can use the Hyperlink command:

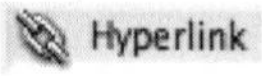

1. **Select some text, make sure that the Common category of the Insert panel is forward, and click the Hyperlink button.**

   The Hyperlink dialog box appears with your selected text already entered in the Text field, as shown in Figure 6-1. (You can also choose Insert⇨Hyperlink.)

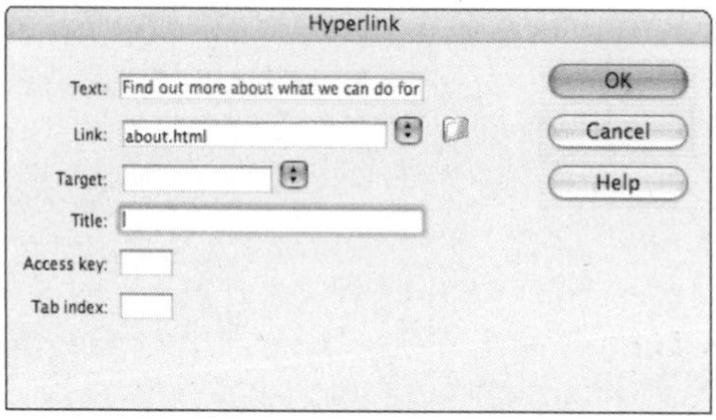

Figure 6-1:
Create a
link from
selected
text with the
Hyperlink
button.

	Hyperlink	
Text: Find out more about what we can do for		OK
Link: about.html		Cancel
Target:		Help
Title:		
Access key:		
Tab index:		

2. **You can either enter a URL (or location of a file) or click the Browse folder icon to the right of the Link drop-down list and browse to the file you want to link to.**

   You can also enter an external link here; see how to link to external locations a little later in the "Linking to Pages and Files Outside Your Web Site" section.

3a. If you want the page to appear in the same Document window, essentially replacing the existing page, leave the Target drop-down list blank or choose _self.

3b. If you want to force the link to create its own Document window, choose _blank.

4. Click OK to create your link.

Using the Property inspector to create a link

You can link text and images with the Property inspector HTML view.

1. Select the element on your page that you want to link up.

2. With your text or image selected, select the HTML button on the left of the Property inspector to switch to HTML view and then type the link location into the Link text box.

3. To locate the destination file, click the Browse folder icon to the right of the Point to File button.

The Select File dialog box opens.

4. Navigate to the folder containing the file you want to link to, select it, and click OK (Windows) or Choose (Mac).

Creating hyperlinks with Point to File

In a hurry and want a more visual way of linking up your pages? You'll love this quick method for creating hyperlinks:

1. Select the text you want to use as a link on your page.

2. On the Property inspector, find the Point to File icon located next to the Link field; click and drag it and pull toward the Files panel — an arrow follows you.

3. Move the arrow pointer over the file in the Files panel that you want to link to and release the mouse button (see Figure 6-2).

Voilá! The connection is made, the filename appears in the Hyperlink text box, and the selection is now hyperlinked to your selected file.

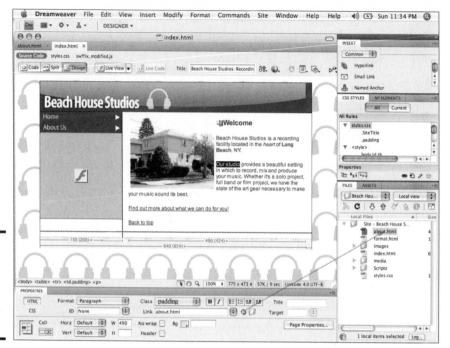

Figure 6-2:
Creating a
hyperlink
with the
Property
inspector.

Creating Anchors

Anchors are a link to a specific section of a page, either on the same page as the link or on another page entirely. Anchors are especially handy for long pages that have a lot of text. You've probably seen and used anchors, for example, when clicking a Back to Top button or when navigating within a page using a Table of Contents. Anchors are extremely helpful to the viewer and should be implemented whenever possible.

To create an anchor in Dreamweaver, follow these steps:

1. **Insert your cursor where you want the destination to be for your link.**

The anchor may be placed before a line of text or on its own line.

2. **Click the Named Anchor button in the Common category of the Insert panel.**

The Named Anchor dialog box, as shown in Figure 6-3, appears.

You can avoid clicking the Anchor button by using the keyboard short-cut Ctrl+Alt+A (Windows) or ⌘+Option+A (Mac).

3. **Type a short name that's relevant to what the link is connected to.**

   In Figure 6-3, you see that **top** was entered because this anchor returns the viewer back to the top of the page. Keep the name all lowercase, as anchors are case sensitive.

4. **Click OK.**

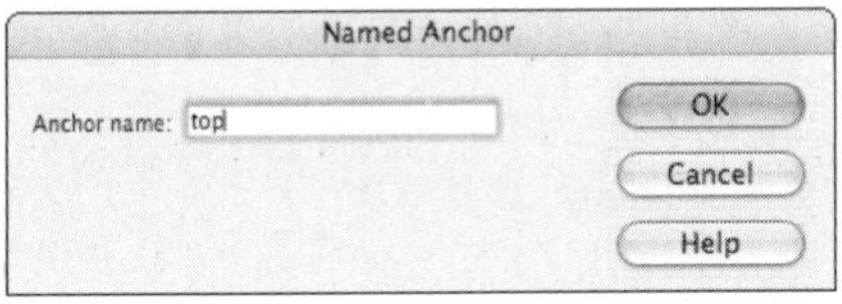

Figure 6-3:
Create
a simple
anchor
name.

You've now created the anchor but have no links directed to it yet. You can define an anchor as a link manually or by using the Point to File tool, as described in the following two sections.

Linking to an anchor manually

Here's one reason why a short, appropriate name is useful for anchors: You may end up having to type it! By manually linking to an anchor, you can link within the page you're working on or direct the link to an anchor on a completely different page.

You can manually define an anchor as a link by following these steps:

1. **Select the text that's to be the link.**

2. **If the Property inspector isn't open, choose Window⟳Properties.**

3. **Select the text you want to link to your new named anchor and click the Hyperlink button located on the Insert panel.**

4. **In the Hyperlink dialog box, locate the Link field and click the drop-down list directly next to it.**

   Your named anchor appears as a selection, as shown in Figure 6-4.

5. **Select your anchor to apply it and then click OK.**

You can also link to a page and add an anchor reference to it with the Property inspector. For example, if you wanted to link to this spot from another page, you'd select an element on that page and in the Link text box (in HTML view), type the name of the page, a pound sign (#), and the name of the anchor — for example, type **birds.html#canary**. This directs the browser to the birds page and then to the canary anchor within that page.

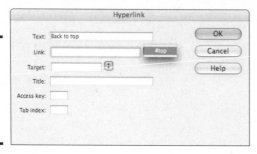

Figure 6-4:
Select the
anchor
name in the
Hyperlink
dialog box.

Frequently, you see anchors separated by the pipe sign (|). You can create this type character by pressing Shift+\. The backslash key is directly above the Enter (Windows) or the Return (Mac) key.

Linking to anchors with Point to File

You can use the same cool Point to File icon you used earlier to create hyperlinks for creating anchors. The Point to File icon on the Property inspector can also target anchors you've created on your page.

1. **Select the text you want to use as a link on your page.**

2. **On the Property inspector, find the Point to File icon located next to the Link field, click and drag over it, and release the arrow directly over an anchor icon on your page.**

   The text is now linked to the anchor, and the anchor's name appears in the Property inspector's Link text field preceded by a pound sign (such as `#canary`).

Linking to Pages and Files Outside Your Web Site

You can link to pages anywhere, in your site or out. An *internal link* (sometimes referred to as a relative URL) is one within your site. The link to another page in your site may appear as `contact.html` in your Link text box in the Property inspector. But if you're directing people to a contact page posted on another site, you'd have a link that looks more like `http://www.aquent.com/contact`. By typing the `http://` and the address of the external link (sometimes referred to as an absolute URL) in the Property inspector, you're essentially directing the browser to a site out on the Internet and away from your site.

It's essential to include the `http://` prefix before a Web address — omitting this results in a Page Not Found error in your browser. This is because the browser may interpret `www.aquent.com` as a local filename rather than an outside Web address.

Linking to E-Mail

Linking to an e-mail address opens a new mail message on the viewer's computer that's already addressed to the e-mail address you specify in the link. (This, of course, requires that the viewer has set up an e-mail program on his or her machine.)

Linking to an e-mail address is easy and extremely helpful if you want to give your users an easy way to contact someone through your Web site. To create an e-mail link, follow these steps:

1. **Select the element that will be the link to an e-mail.**

   It can be text or an image.

2. **In the Property inspector, locate the Link text box and type** `mailto:`*(address)*, **and then press Enter/Return.**

   For example, type **mailto:info@agitraining.com** and press the Enter or Return key. The `mailto:` directive tells the browser that the link is to an e-mail address so that the default e-mail application on the user's computer opens with a new, pre-addressed message.

Linking to a PDF File

To link to a PDF file instead of a Web page, you link to the name and location of the PDF file. If you link to a PDF file and the Acrobat PDF plug-in is loaded in the viewer's browser, the PDF is opened in the browser window. If the viewer doesn't have the Acrobat plug-in (free from `www.adobe.com`), the Save dialog box appears, and the viewer can browse to save the file to open with Acrobat Reader at another time.

Resolving Link Errors

Page names can change and pages can be deleted (intentionally or not), so periodically checking for broken links is a good idea. You can check to make sure that links are working correctly in several ways. The most cumbersome is previewing your page and clicking each and every link. This method would take you a long time and wouldn't be much fun. To check your local links more efficiently and quickly, try the following:

1. **Choose Site⇨Check Links Sitewide.**

   The Results panel appears, with the Link Checker tab active.

   Any links appear, including page, scripts, images, and so on, as shown in Figure 6-5.

2. **Use the Show drop-down list in the top-left corner to sort the link results by Broken Links, External Links, or Orphaned Files.**

   To focus only on broken links, leave Broken Links selected.

Figure 6-5: Check to make sure that your links aren't broken.

If you don't have broken links . . . congratulations! If you do, you can fix them right in the Results panel. The page that has the broken link is listed in the Files column on the left. The broken link appears under the Broken Link column on the right.

3. **Click the name of the broken link and correct the filename, if it's a problem, or click the Browse folder icon to locate the correct location or file.**

4. **Click OK (Windows) or Choose (Mac).**

   The broken link is repaired.

Orphaned files are pages, images, or any other assets that aren't linked to anything else within your site. Although these aren't necessarily a problem, take a glance at any orphaned files by selecting Orphaned Files from the Link Checker tab Show menu. Make sure no pages are unlinked that shouldn't be.

Chapter 7: Creating Tables

In This Chapter

✔ **Creating tables**

✔ **Manipulating rows, columns, and cells**

✔ **Selecting tables and cells**

✔ **Changing colors of a table or cells**

✔ **Adding and importing your content**

*T*ables are great for presenting data, such as schedules and pricing, and can be helpful in instances where you're trying to arrange elements in a tabular format.

In this chapter, you find out how to create a table and make changes that alter the look of the table. Tables are also used as an alternate method for creating page layouts.

Working with Tables

When you think of a *table,* think of a grid that has multiple cells in it, much like a spreadsheet. Tables are used in HTML pages so that elements can be contained and positioned within specific cells. You can change the colors of cells in tables, divide or *span* the cells (that is, combine them with other cells), and apply borders to them.

In some cases, you don't actually see the table itself because you can place content into row and column form without showing the table itself; in this case, the table is just a formatting tool. When you create a table, you can determine how many rows and columns it contains. You can also choose to span rows and columns to create unique tables, as shown in Figure 7-1.

To create a table in Dreamweaver, follow these steps:

1. **Put your cursor where you want the table to appear, make sure that the Common tab of the Insert panel is visible, and then click the Table button.**

Alternatively, you can choose Insert⇨Table. Whatever method you use, the Table dialog box appears, as shown in Figure 7-2.

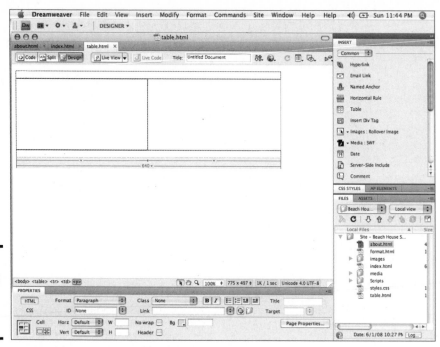

Figure 7-1:
A table with rows and columns merged.

Figure 7-2:
Set table specifications in the Table dialog box.

2. **Enter or select the attributes of the table that you want to create:**

   • *Rows:* Enter how many rows you want in your table in the Rows text box. Rows stack vertically and can be added or deleted after you create the table.

- *Columns:* Enter how many columns you want in your table in the Columns text box. Columns are created horizontally across your table and can be added or deleted after you create the table.

- *Table width:* Enter the desired width in the Table Width text box and then select a measurement (Pixels or Percent) from the drop-down list to the right. Table width is an important attribute because it sets the default size for the table. If you leave this set to 100 percent, the table will take up 100 percent of your Web page, dynamically expanding and reducing in size when the page is resized. You can change the width to a different percentage, such as 50 percent, to have the table take up half the width of your Web page, or enter a pixel value to assure that the table always stays the same size.

- *Border thickness:* Enter the thickness you want for the width of the border (in pixels) surrounding the cells and outside the table. If you don't want to see the table formatting, type **0** in the Border Thickness text box. *Note:* In Design view, you still see dashed table borders — this is only a visual aid. You see the actual borders when you view the page in a browser or in Live View.

- *Cell padding:* Enter a number in the Cell Padding text box if you want to use padding to create a margin around all contents inside the cell.

- *Cell spacing:* Enter a number in the Cell Spacing text box if you want to change the spacing to push cells apart.

- *Header:* Select the type of header you want to include in your table (or select None if you don't want any headers). Including headers is important, especially if you're creating a table containing data to assist viewers in associating the header with the data. Screen readers rely on headers to help visually-impaired users navigate through the table without getting lost.

- *Accessibility:* You can provide some additional information to help visually-impaired users understand the contents of your table. Add a caption that's relevant to your table in the Caption text box. In the Summary area, include several lines of text to provide more information about the purpose of the table.

3. **Click OK.**

   Your table's created.

When working with tables, it may help to take advantage of the Expanded table feature in Dreamweaver. (Find the Expanded button on the Layout category of the Insert panel.) The Expanded view adds cell padding and spacing in a table, as well as increases the size of the border to make selection easier. It's important to return to the Standard view (click the Standard button in the Layout category of the Insert panel) after you're finished editing for the most accurate preview.

Editing your table's attributes

Even if you've already created your table, you can go back and edit the table's attributes by selecting the table and entering changes in the Property inspector, as shown in Figure 7-3.

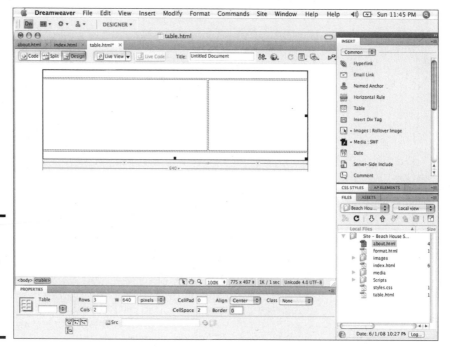

Figure 7-3:
Make changes to your table with the Property inspector.

If your Property inspector isn't expanded, as in Figure 7-3, click the arrow in the lower right of the inspector. The inspector then expands, offering additional options.

When a table is selected, you can use the handles that appear in the lower-right corner as well as the bottom and left sides to resize the table manually.

Adding and deleting rows and columns

You can add rows and columns as well as delete them as fast as your client's (or boss's) needs require with the Property inspector, but the Modify menu gives you a little more control as to which rows and columns are deleted and where new ones are added.

To add a row, follow these steps:

1. **Insert your cursor in a cell in the row that you want a new row added above or below.**

2. **Choose Insert⇨Table Objects⇨Insert Row Above or Insert Row Below.**

    Alternatively, press Shift+M.

    The new row appears.

If you want to add more rows to the bottom of the table, place your cursor in the last current row and press the Tab key to add rows.

Follow these steps to delete a row:

1. **Insert your cursor in a cell of the row you want to delete.**

2. **Choose Modify⇨Table⇨Delete Row.**

    Alternatively, press Shift+Ctrl+M (Windows) or Shift+⌘+M (Mac).

    The row is deleted.

To add a column, follow these steps:

1. **Insert your cursor in a cell.**

    Insert your cursor in the cell in the column that you want a new column added to the left or right of.

2. **Choose Insert⇨Table Objects⇨Insert Column to the Left or Insert Column to the Right.**

    The new column appears.

Follow these steps to delete a column:

1. **Insert your cursor in a cell of the column you want to delete.**

2. **Choose Modify⇨Table⇨Delete Column.**

    Alternatively, press Shift+Ctrl+– (minus) (Windows) or Shift+⌘+– (minus) (Mac).

    The column is deleted.

Spanning or merging cells

Often, you need to span or merge cells. You can combine cells with other cells horizontally or vertically. By merging cells, you can create more interesting and useful tables. Figure 7-4 contains a table with one large merged cell across the top.

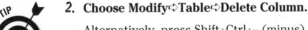

**Book IV
Chapter 7**

Creating Tables

Figure 7-4:
The top
row's
columns
have been
merged.

Follow these steps to merge cells in a row or column:

1. **Double-click a cell to select it, and then drag across to select contiguous cells in the row or drag down to select contiguous cells in the column.**

2. **Choose Modify⇨Table⇨Merge Cells.**

The cells are merged.

If you want to split a merged cell back to into separate cells, follow these steps:

1. **Put your cursor in the merged cell or column.**

2. **Choose Modify⇨Table⇨Split Cell.**

The Split Cell dialog box appears, as shown in Figure 7-5.

Figure 7-5:
Split cells
as easily as
you merge
them.

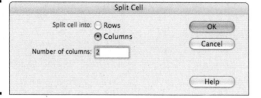

3. **Choose whether you want to split into rows or columns by selecting either the Rows or Columns radio button.**

4. **Enter how many rows or columns you want to create by splitting the cell in the Number of Rows/Columns text box.**

5. **Click OK.**

The merged cell is now split into the number of cells you specified.

Selecting a Table and a Cell

You can use several methods to select a cell or the whole table. After a cell or table is selected, you can change all sorts of attributes for the selected cell or table, including color, size, and format of its contents.

To select a table or cell, follow these steps:

1. **In Design view, select the Layout category from the Insert panel and select Expanded to put your table in the Expanded view.**

It's easier to select and make changes in this view. (Remember to click the Standard button to get a more realistic preview of what your table will look like.)

2. **Select a cell by Ctrl-clicking (Windows) or ⌘-clicking (Mac) it.**

Another option is to use the tag selector in the lower-left corner of your Document window, as shown in Figure 7-6. The tag selector is an incredible tool to use to select any tag element, but it's especially helpful when selecting individual components of a table or a nested table.

To use the tag selector, just put your cursor inside a cell. The tag selector shows the tags that apply to where the insertion point is. Then select `<td>` to select the cell that the cursor is in, `<tr>` to select the entire row, or `<table>` to select the entire table.

The tag for table is `<table>` (a difficult one to remember, right?), and each row is in a `<tr>` tag, which stands for *Table Row.* Each cell is in a `<td>` *(Table Data)* tag. Tables created with a header also make use of the `<th>` *(Table Header)* tag.

Figure 7-6:
Use the tag selector to select cells and tables.

**Book IV
Chapter 7**

Creating Tables

Changing the Color of Table Cells

You can change colors of a single cell, multiple cells, or an entire row in Dreamweaver. You can use either standard HTML attributes or use CSS rules to apply color to any portion of a table, but the easiest way is to use the Property inspector to assign a background color.

To change the color of cell or multiple cells in a table:

1. **Ctrl-click (Windows) or ⌘-click (Mac) anywhere within a cell to select that cell.**

   You can continue to add cells to your selection by keeping the key pressed and clicking more cells.

2. **In the Property inspector, make sure the HTML view is selected (click the HTML tab on the left edge of the panel), and locate the Bg Color Picker.**

3. **Assign color to a cell(s) using one of the following methods.**

   - Click the swatch to the right of Bg and select a color from the Color Picker that appears. Remember that you can choose from additional color models by clicking the palette menu in the upper right of the Color Picker.

   - If you know the hexadecimal number for your color, you can type it in the text field next to the Bg color swatch.

   - Select a color from any element that you can see on the screen by clicking and holding the color fill box to the right of Bg and then moving the Eyedropper tool over any color on your screen that you want the cell color to pick up. Click when the color appears in the Color Picker preview window.

4. **The color is applied as a background to the selected cell(s).**

In addition to using the Property inspector, you can include background color settings in a new CSS rule and apply them to an entire table, cell, or row with the Property inspector.

You can add a color to a cell or table using CSS by following these steps:

1. **Create a CSS rule from either the Property inspector or the CSS styles panel (as discussed in Chapter 5 of this minibook).**

2. **Under the Background category in the CSS Rule Definition dialog box, assign a color to the Background color property.**

3. **Apply the style by selecting the table or cell you want to modify.**

4. **Assign a class by using the Class drop-down list on the Property inspector.**

Adding and Importing Content

Adding content to a table is easy — insert your cursor into the cell and type directly into a cell for text or click Image in the Common category of the Insert panel to insert an image in a cell. You can also cut, copy, and paste content from documents and other Web pages directly into table cells.

Importing CSV and tab-delimited files

If you already have spreadsheet style data in text form it's not necessary to retype it into a Dreamweaver table. Dreamweaver has an incredibly easy feature that you can use to bring in tabular data as a formatted table: Import Tabular Data.

CSV (comma separated values) and tab-delimited files are plain text files that can be generated from a number of popular programs, such as Microsoft Excel. This allows you to save spreadsheet data in a way that can be exchanged with other applications such as Dreamweaver.

In CSV files, columns are noted by commas between values, and each line return indicates a new row. In tab-delimited files, a tab between values indicates a new column, and a line return forces a new row. To import tabular data, follow these steps:

1. **Put your cursor on the page where you want the table created.**

2. **Choose File⇨Import⇨Tabular Data.**

   The Import Tabular Data dialog box appears.

3. **Browse to the location of a comma separated values (`.csv`) file or a tab-delimited (`.txt`) plain text file with the Browse button.**

4. **Verify or select the delimiter that your file uses.**

   Typically, the *delimiter* (where a new column will be created) is a comma or tab; however, you can also instruct Dreamweaver to create a new column from other delimiters, such as Comma, Semicolon, Colon, or other options, by using the Delimited drop-down list.

5. **Determine the table width.**

   You can choose to have the table automatically sized to fit the data by leaving the Fit to Data radio button selected, or you can enter a number in the Set To text box to set a percent or pixel value.

6. **Enter numbers in the Padding, Spacing, and Border text boxes and specify top row formatting with the Format Top Row drop-down list at the bottom of the dialog box.**

7. **When you're finished with these settings, click OK.**

   Your table's created!

You can export table data from Dreamweaver just as easily by selecting a table and choosing File⇨Export⇨Table. When the Export Table dialog box appears, choose what you want the delimiter to be and the type of line break. Click Export, determine where you want to save the file, and click Save.

Setting alignment for table cells

As a default, all elements center vertically inside a cell and are flush left. Change this on a cell-by-cell basis by selecting the cell(s) and then changing the Horz (horizontal) and Vert (vertical) alignment in the Property inspector.

Make sure the Property inspector is fully expanded to see the Horz and Vert drop-down lists.

If you select every cell in a row, you also have the opportunity to change the alignment of an entire row. In the Property inspector, you'll find a horizontal alignment drop-down list that changes the alignment for an entire row or selected cell. Choose from Left (default), Center, or Right. Note that any changes you make in the individual cell alignment override the row alignment.

You can also change the vertical alignment in the Property inspector when you have a row selected. Click the Vert drop-down list and choose Default, Top, Middle Bottom, or Baseline.

To select an entire row at once, position your cursor on the left side of the row you want to select. When the black arrow appears, simply click. You can also use this method for selecting an entire column by positioning your cursor on the top of the column you want to select until the black arrow appears.

Chapter 8: Creating CSS Layouts

In This Chapter

✓ **Getting started with CSS pages**

✓ **Modifying layouts**

✓ **Positioning content with the new AP Div tool**

✓ **Using behaviors with DIV tags**

Creating a page layout sometimes requires more precision than what tables or standard HTML tags are capable of. More designers are moving to the flexible and preferred method of Cascading Style Sheets (CSS) positioning to create innovative layouts without boundaries. Dreamweaver provides you with an extensive gallery of CSS-based layouts to get started, or you can build your own using the Insert panel's Layout tools, including the Insert DIV and AP Div objects.

Using CSS Starter Pages

Dreamweaver provides you with a library of sample pages with CSS-based layouts as an alternative to starting from scratch. These CSS sample pages feature useful and common layout ideas, and because they're created with CSS positioning, they're highly flexible. You can modify them directly from the CSS Styles panel or the Property inspector. Just add your content and go!

Follow these steps to create a new document from a CSS sample page:

1. **Choose File➪New.**

   The New Document panel appears.

2. **Choose Blank Page from the left, select a layout from the Layout column on the right (for example, the 2 Column Elastic, Left Sidebar, Header and Footer layout), and click Create.**

   A new untitled page opens based on the layout you chose.

3. **Choose File➪Save to name and save the document.**

4. **Replace the placeholder text in each column with your own content.**

Modifying a New Layout

As the name indicates, CSS layouts are controlled completely by style sheet rules, so you can modify the look and feel of the page directly from the CSS Styles panel and the Property inspector. Each column, box, and space on your new page is positioned and sized using CSS rules and properties, all of which you can adjust from either the Property inspector (on the CSS Styles panel) or the CSS Rule Definition panel.

You can modify the layout by following these steps:

1. **If not already open, choose Window⇨CSS Styles to open the CSS Styles panel.**

2. **Select the All tab to display the style sheet and its rules.**

   The internal style sheet is shown as `<style>` at the top. Click the arrow to its left to expand it and show all the rules it contains. ***Note:*** Layouts using an attached (external) style sheet will display the style sheet name (such as `styles.css`) instead of the `<style>` tag.

3. **Select the** `body` **rule.**

   This tag-based style controls the general formatting of the entire page (everything inside the `<body>` tag).

4. **Click the field next to the background rule to edit it; instead of #666666 (medium gray), type a hexadecimal color (such as #CC0000 for red) to change your page's background color.**

5. **Click the swatch next to the color rule to open the Swatches panel; pick a new default type color for the text on your page.**

6. **At the top of the CSS Styles panel, select another style (for example, the** `.twoColElstHdr #container` **style) to view its properties.**

   The `.twoColHybLtHdr #container` style is an ID style that controls the size and appearance of the main layout container on your page.

7. **In the Property inspector, edit the properties to change the appearance of the style.**

   For example, you can change the width of the rule by entering a new number in the Width Rule text box. If you enter **95%**, for example, you make the entire layout wider.

Each column and section that composes your layout is controlled by one of the ID styles listed in the CSS Styles panel. Most every ID style features a width property that you can use to change the size of different areas on the page.

Continue to modify different styles listed in the CSS Styles panel and see how they affect different elements on your page. Try changing type color, font family, and other properties, such as padding and background color.

To figure out exactly which ID controls which column or section, click within the page area and look at the tag selector at the bottom of the Document window. The last `<div>` tag at the end of the chain shows you which container you're currently in and its corresponding ID in the CSS Styles panel (for example, `<div#mainBox>`).

Creating AP Divs

Dreamweaver uses CSS-positioned virtual containers, or *boxes,* created by the DIV tag to freely position content on a page. *DIV* tags are a basic tag used to create areas for content on your page. You can create DIV tags from several places in Dreamweaver, including the Layout category of the Insert panel. Each DIV tag can have a unique ID style assigned to it to control its position, appearance, and size. The process of placing content often requires two steps: creating the DIV tag and then creating its corresponding style.

Dreamweaver makes this task easy with the AP Div tool, which enables you to draw boxes freely on the page and place your content inside.

AP Div is short for *absolute-positioned* DIV; an item with an *absolute* position means that it's fixed at a specific location on the page. When you draw an AP Div, its position is commonly set using the *top* and *left* CSS properties, with the top-left corner of the page as its reference point.

For those of you who have used much earlier versions of Dreamweaver, you may remember Dreamweaver layers. The AP Div object replaced the Layer object as of version CS3, and the AP Elements panel now replaces the Layers panel.

CSS treats every element on a page as a box that holds content; this approach is referred to as the CSS Box model. Although CSS can consider most any containing element on a page (such as a table or a list) a box, DIV tags are most commonly used to create virtual boxes that you can use to position text, images, and even other boxes.

Each box can have its own width, height, position (via the top and left properties), border, margins, and padding; each one is set using CSS rules.

To create AP Divs, follow these steps:

1. **On the Insert panel, select the Layout category.**

2. **Click the Draw AP Div object.**

Your cursor appears as a cross hair when you move it back over the page.

3. **Click anywhere on the page and drag to draw a new AP Div, as shown in Figure 8-1; release the mouse button.**

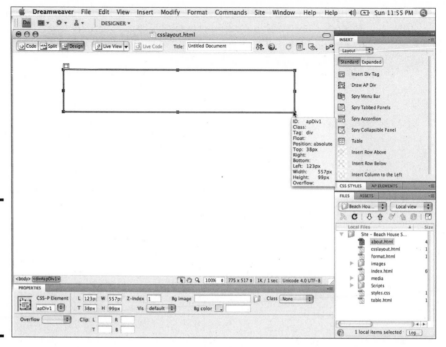

Figure 8-1:
Click and
drag on the
page with
the Draw
AP Div tool
to create
a box.

4. **Move the mouse pointer over the edge of the box until it changes to a hand; click once and handles appear on all sides.**

5. **Click and drag any of these handles to resize the box vertically or horizontally.**

6. **To move the box, click and drag it by the tab that sits on its top-left edge and place the box where you want it on the page.**

    Take a look at the Property inspector, and you see the name as well as many of the DIV's properties listed.

7. **If the CSS Styles panel isn't open, choose Window⇔CSS Styles to open it; under the All panel, click to the left of the style sheet (<style>) to expand it.**

    You see a new #apDiv1 ID style that's attached to the new AP Div you created. For each new DIV created, Dreamweaver assigns apDiv with a corresponding number in order of creation.

8. **Click inside the new box to type, paste, or insert new content.**

    When you draw an AP Div on the page, two things occur: Dreamweaver inserts a tag to create the box and creates an ID selector that stores the DIV's position, width, height, and other properties. After you create an AP Div, you can type, paste, or insert content directly inside it. You can also assign a class rule to any DIV from the Property inspector — this is most often for handling content formatting, leaving the ID selector to control positioning and dimensions.

Each AP Div that you draw is listed automatically in the AP Elements panel (choose Window⇨AP Elements to display it). The AP Elements panel can help you select, hide, and show any AP Divs on the page. This panel is handy when you have lots of AP Divs on the page and want to navigate among them accurately. Most of all, because you can modify the properties for any AP Div from its corresponding ID style, the panel helps you figure out which ID style belongs to an AP Div.

The AP Elements panel is often grouped with the CSS Styles panel, just in case you're looking for it!

To modify a box (AP Div), follow these steps:

1. **Choose Window⇨AP Elements to open the AP Elements panel.**

2. **In the panel, locate and select** `apDiv1` **to highlight it on the page, as shown in Figure 8-2.**

   The Property inspector displays its size and position in addition to other properties.

3. **With the text boxes on the Property inspector, change the box's width by entering a number into the W field and change its height by entering a number in the H field.**

4. **Click the swatch next to Bg Color and choose a color from the pop-up Swatches panel to set a background color for the box.**

   For additional properties, such as border or padding, add them in the CSS Styles panel.

5. **If the CSS Styles panel isn't already visible, open it by choosing Window⇨CSS Styles.**

6. **Double-click the** `#apDiv1 ID` **style that controls the box.**

   The CSS Rule Definition dialog box appears, as shown in Figure 8-3.

7. **Select the Border category from the left to change the border.**

8. **In the Style column, use the Top drop-down list to set a border style (such as Solid) to all four sides.**

   Use the Top drop-down list under the Width category to select a border thickness (for example, medium) for all four sides. Use the topmost Color Picker under the Color column to assign a border color to all four sides.

   To assign different values to any or all sides for style, width, or color, deselect the Same for All check box under their respective columns.

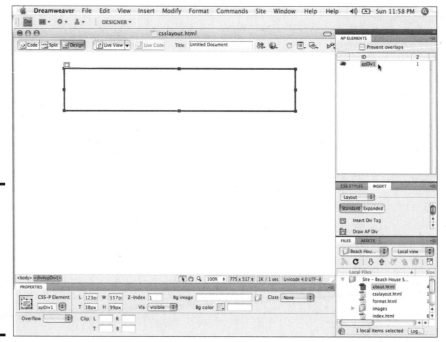

Figure 8-2:
Use the AP Elements panel to select, hide, and rearrange AP Divs in your page.

Figure 8-3:
Add CSS properties across a variety of categories to build rules.

9. **In the Box category on the left, under Padding, set the padding for all four sides of the box to the desired thickness (for example, enter** 10 px **in the text boxes).**

10. **Click OK to exit the panel and apply the changes.**

    You see how the CSS properties you applied affect the apDiv1 box on the page.

To hide a box shown under the AP Elements panel, click the column to the left of its name (under the Eye icon) until a closed Eye icon appears. To make the box re-appear, click the Eye icon until the box opens again.

You may notice the Prevent Overlaps check box at the top of the AP Elements panel. Because AP Divs can easily overlap each other, selecting this check box overrides that behavior by forcing boxes next to each other and preventing the creation of new boxes on top of each other. Because this is usually a desired effect, the check box is deselected by default.

Creating Relatively Positioned DIVs

The precision and to-the-pixel positioning of AP Divs can be very liberating for designers, especially those who desire the flexibility of print-based layouts. However, on certain occasions, you may want boxes to flow inline with other content on the page. AP Divs literally float above other elements, so shifting other page content has no effect on their position.

For more traditional inline behavior, you can create DIVs that use *relative positioning*. Relative positioning allows an element to be shifted along with content surrounding it, making for a more liquid layout. This is important for nested content or any situation where you need items to fall in line with other page content. For this task, use the Insert Div Tag tool, which can be found within the Insert panel's Common and Layout categories.

Follow these steps to create a relatively positioned DIV:

1. **Click within the body of your page to position your cursor and then click the Insert Div Tag tool under the Insert panel's Common and Layout categories.**

2. **When the Insert Div Tag dialog box appears, fine-tune the location of your new DIV by selecting a location from the Insert drop-down list, as shown in Figure 8-4.**

   (For example, choose After Start of Tag to place it after a specific tag in your page.)

   You can also place the DIV before, after, or inside existing elements on the page using this menu. Leave the Insert drop-down list set to At Insertion Point to leave the box where you drew it or choose another location where you want the DIV created.

3. **If you have an existing class selector you want to apply, choose it from the Class drop-down list; otherwise, leave it blank.**

4. **Assign an ID selector to the DIV to control its appearance by selecting from the ID drop-down list.**

**Book IV
Chapter 8**

**Creating CSS
Layouts**

If one isn't available, enter a new name and click the New CSS Rule button to create one. When the New CSS Rule dialog box appears, make sure your new selector is set to ID and that the name has a pound sign (#) in front of it. Click OK.

5. **When the CSS Rule Definition dialog box appears, click and select Positioning from the Category list on the left to view CSS positioning properties.**

6. **Under Positioning, select Relative from the Position menu, enter a width and height value in the Width and Height text boxes, and then click OK.**

7. **Click OK to exit the Insert Div Tag dialog box.**

A new relatively positioned DIV appears with placeholder text, as shown in Figure 8-5.

Figure 8-4:
Choose a specific location to create the new DIV.

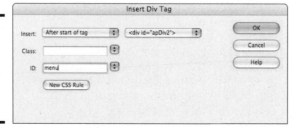

Figure 8-5:
You can create a new DIV box on top of another box.

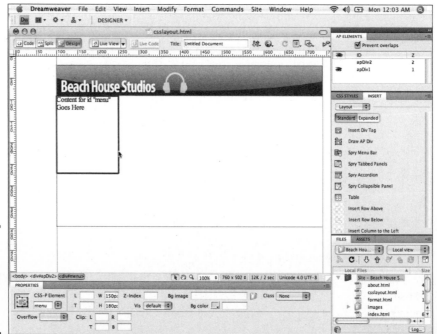

Using Behaviors with Boxes

To add cool effects and serious interactivity, you can use Dreamweaver's built-in *behaviors,* a collection of ready-to-use scripts that you can apply to boxes, form elements, text, and images on your page. When used with boxes (AP Divs), behaviors can enhance them with special effects or mouse interaction (such as clicks and rollovers) to make your page more exciting.

The Behaviors panel features a whole new set of effects, such as Fade/ Appear, Shrink, Highlight, Slide, and more — all of which you can apply to the AP Divs that you create.

You can add behaviors by following these steps:

1. **Choose Window⇨Behaviors to open the Behaviors panel.**

2. **Select a box using the AP Elements panel or select it directly on the stage.**

3. **In the Behaviors panel, click the plus sign.**

    The menu of available behaviors appears.

4. **From the menu, choose the behavior you want to apply.**

    For example, to apply a fade effect, choose Effects⇨Appear/Fade, as shown in Figure 8-6.

    The Appear/Fade dialog box appears.

5. **Make sure the effect is set to Fade and click the Toggle Effect check box to make sure that the box reappears when it's clicked a second time.**

    The behavior is added to the list. The phrase onClick to its left indicates this action occurs when the box is clicked.

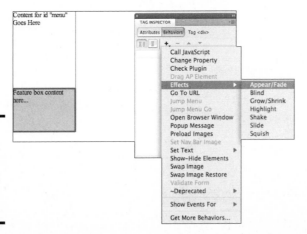

Figure 8-6: Add a cool Appear/ Fade effect to a DIV on your page.

6. **Choose File⇨Save to save the page.**

   To see the effect in action, preview the page in a browser.

7. **Choose File⇨Preview in Browser and pick a browser to launch the page in.**

When you test the page, clicking the box makes it disappear or reappear — lots of fun for you and highly interactive for your user!

If your browser is restricting the Web page from running scripts or ActiveX controls, click the message at the top of your browser window and select Allow Blocked Content to properly test the new behaviors.

When effects behaviors are used, Dreamweaver needs to copy several files to your local site that make the effects possible.

Chapter 9: Publishing Your Web Site

In This Chapter

✓ Checking for broken links and missing files

✓ Running your site reports

✓ Checking browser compatibility

✓ Publishing to a Web server

✓ Making site improvements

*W*hen you're ready to launch your Web site, you can take lots of steps to ensure that your site looks and works great. Dreamweaver's tools and reports streamline the process of testing and fixing any problems so that you can present your visitors with a great first impression.

Clean Up after Yourself!

The first step toward getting your Web site ready for the world is making sure everything works and all your files are in order. Dreamweaver is packed full of tools that let you know exactly what's broken, what can be done better, and how your site will perform across a spectrum of different browsers.

One of the key benefits of a Dreamweaver site is its ability to see relationships between your various pages and files and detect any broken links or missing images before you copy the site up for public viewing. Choose Files➪Check Links Sitewide to comb your entire site to find broken links, missing, or *orphaned* (unlinked) files.

To use the Check Links Sitewide feature, follow these steps:

1. **Choose Window➪Files to open the Files panel.**

   You can also use the F8 shortcut key (Windows or Mac).

2. **Open the Files panel menu (it's in the upper-right corner) and choose Site➪Check Links Sitewide.**

   The Link Checker panel appears and displays the results (if any). Each listing shows the broken link and the name of the page that contains it to the left, as shown in Figure 9-1.

Figure 9-1:
The Link
Checker
lists the
filename
and the
broken link.

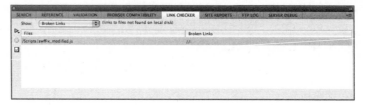

3. **To open and edit the page to correct the link, double-click the filename shown.**

   You can then edit the broken link directly from the Link Checker panel without opening the file. Click the broken link displayed, and a folder icon appears next to it on the right.

4. **Double-click the folder to open the Select File dialog box and choose an available file to correct the link or re-link it to a different file.**

5. **Click OK (Windows) or Choose (Mac).**

If you want to change a link that appears across several pages, open the Files panel menu and choose Site➪Change Links Sitewide. When the panel appears, you're asked what file the original link points to and you can specify a new file to link to instead. *Warning:* This answer changes all links to that file sitewide, so don't use it if you want to change that link only on certain pages.

Running Site Reports

Dreamweaver's site reports provide a detailed look at potential issues lurking within your site, as well as assistance in cleaning out redundant or empty tags from your pages.

Reports are broken down into two categories:

✦ **Workflow reports** show you where your files have been, and when, and are useful if you're using functions, such as the Check In/Check Out feature to share your work with others.

✦ **HTML reports** point out design and accessibility issues, such as missing ALT tags for images, improperly nested tags, or empty tags that you can clean up.

You can run a site report by following these steps:

1. **Choose Site➪Reports.**

   The Reports dialog box appears, as shown in Figure 9-2.

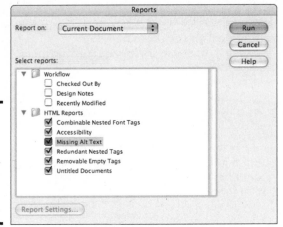

Figure 9-2:
Use the
Reports
dialog box
to choose
reports you
want to run.

2. **Choose each report that you want to see by selecting the check box next to the report name.**

   As shown in Figure 9-2, we chose all the reports under the HTML Reports category.

3. **Click the Run button to run the selected reports.**

   The Results panel appears to display the results of each report.

   Each report result displays the file, line number, and a description of the problem.

4. **To address a problem shown, double-click the filename to open the page.**

   The page opens for editing, and the section in which the problem occurs appears highlighted in Split view.

Checking CSS Compatibility

If you're using CSS for formatting and layout throughout your site, make sure that your page appears properly across all popular browsers, such as Internet Explorer, Firefox, Netscape, and Safari. Over the years, different browsers adopted CSS at different levels and paces, requiring designers to test pages in a variety of browsers and versions.

To eliminate this time-consuming task, Dreamweaver introduces the new Browser Compatibility Check, which works hand-in-hand with the CSS Advisor to discover and report any CSS-related display issues that may occur in selected browsers and versions. By default, the Browser Compatibility Check checks CSS compatibility in the following browsers: Firefox 1–3; Internet Explorer (Windows) 6.0–8.0b1; Internet Explorer (Macintosh) 5.2; Netscape Navigator 7.0–8.0; Opera 7.0–9.0; and Safari 1.0–3.0.

**Book IV
Chapter 9**

**Publishing Your
Web Site**

For any problem that the Browser Compatibility Check discovers, the Results panel displays a description of the problem along with a direct link to the Adobe CSS Advisor Web site. The CSS Advisor reports on known browser display issues and possible solutions for fixing them.

Follow these steps to test a page with the Browser Compatibility Check:

1. **Open a page for editing by choosing File⇨Open or by selecting it from the Files panel.**

2. **At the top-right corner of the Document window, click and hold the Check Page button and then choose Check Browser Compatibility from the menu that appears, as shown in Figure 9-3.**

Figure 9-3:
Use the Check Page button to check the CSS in your page.

The Results panel appears, with the Browser Compatibility tab forward. Any results are displayed in this tab.

3. **To view details and possible solutions for any results that may appear, select the result (see Figure 9-4).**

The description, as well as a link to the Adobe CSS Advisor, appears on the right side of the panel.

Possible compatibility issues are listed along with the filename, line number, and a description of the problem.

4. **Click the link below the detail panel to jump to Adobe's CSS Advisor Web site for solutions.**

Figure 9-4:
Browser Compatibility displays any problems.

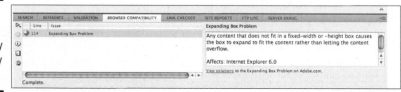

Getting Connected

When you're ready to publish your site for the world to see, set up a remote server in your site definition so that you can connect and copy files to your Web-hosting account or dedicated server.

Typical remote server information consists of an ID and password, an FTP (File Transfer Protocol) or network address, and the name of the specific directory where your files need to go. This information is available from the company whom your hosting service was purchased from or from your network administrator.

To set up your remote connection, follow these steps:

1. **Choose Site⇨Manage Sites.**

   The Manage Sites panel appears.

2. **Select your site from the list and click the Edit button.**

3. **When the Site Definition dialog box appears, select the Advanced tab at the top and select the Remote Info category that appears on the left.**

4. **Select the method that you use to connect to your Web site from the Access drop-down list.**

   For most hosting accounts, choose the FTP from Access drop-down list. If you're unsure of how to connect to your remote server, contact your hosting company or network administrator.

5. **If you're using an FTP host, enter the address in the FTP Host text box.**

   The address is typically a numerical IP or FTP address, such as `192.1.1.1` or `ftp.mywebsite.com`.

6. **If necessary, type the name of the host directory in the Host Directory text field.**

   The *host directory* is the path to the specific folder where your site files are kept on the server. Some FTP addresses are set up to bring you directly to the right directory.

7. **Enter the your login name and password for your account in the Login and Password text boxes, respectively; to avoid being prompted for your password in the future, select the Save check box next to the Password text box.**

8. **To make sure that all your information is correct and the connection is set up properly, click the Test button.**

   A dialog box lets you know that Dreamweaver connected to your site successfully. If it doesn't, double-check the information you entered and try again.

9. **Click OK to update the site definition.**

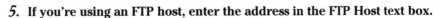

**Book IV
Chapter 9**

**Publishing Your
Web Site**

If you experience difficulty connecting to your remote server or the connection is taking unusually long, check the Use Passive FTP option found by choosing Site⇨Manage Sites⇨*[Your Site]*⇨Advanced⇨Remote Info. Passive FTP can be a workaround if you're trying to connect from behind a firewall.

Your Web site — live!

After your connection is up and running, you're ready to upload your files and present your Web site to the world. Files can be transferred to and from your remote Web server using the built-in FTP functionality of the Files panel. The Files panel displays files in your local directory and the remote server, and between them, you can put, get, or synchronize site files.

Follow these steps to upload your Web site to a remote Web server:

1. **Choose Window⇨Files to open the Files panel.**

2. **Click the Expand to Show Local and Remote Sites icon.**

   The panel expands so that you see both the local site and the remote site in which you want to copy (upload) the files to.

3. **Make sure that the correct site definition is selected in the Show drop-down list at the top-left corner of the panel.**

   Your local files appear on the right.

4. **To connect to and display files on the remote Web server, click the Connect button at the top of the panel.**

   When the connection is made, all the files (if any) are displayed on the left side of the panel.

5. **To copy files, select and drag them from the local files on the right to the remote files on the left.**

   Alternatively, select the files you want to copy on the right and click the Put button at the top of the Files panel.

   You can put an entire site at once by selecting the root folder at the top of your local files panel and clicking the Put button.

6. **After you copy all the files to the remote Web server, test your site by opening a browser and typing the Web site's URL.**

   The URL is a full address, such as www.mywebsite.com, or an IP address, such as http://192.1.1.1.

   If you notice broken images or files, return to Dreamweaver and double-check that all files were copied to the server and run the Link Checker by choosing Site⇨Check Links Sitewide.

To retrieve files from a remote Web server, follow these steps:

1. **Select the file(s) you want to retrieve from the remote files on the left side of the Files panel.**

2. **Click the Get button at the top of the panel or drag the files to the local root folder on the right.**

To return your Files panel back to its original position on the right side of the workspace, click the Expand button in the top-right corner of the panel to deselect it. The Files panel minimizes and docks back with the panel group on the right.

Synchronizing your site

Dreamweaver's handy site synchronization feature compares files between your local and remote sites to ensure that both are using the same and the most recent versions of your site files. This check is essential if there's a chance that files on the remote server may be more up-to-date or if you're unsure which files have been updated since the last time you worked on a Web site.

Follow these steps to synchronize your local and remote directories:

1. **If the Files panel isn't already visible, choose Window⇨Files to open the Files panel.**

2. **Select the site you want to synchronize in the Show drop-down list at the top-left corner of the panel.**

   Your local files appear on the right.

3. **Click the Connect button at the top of the panel to connect to the remote server.**

   If you're not viewing your Files panel in Expanded view, choose Remote View from the drop-down list at the top to display your remote files.

4. **Click the Synchronize button at the top of the Files panel.**

   The Synchronize Files dialog box appears.

5. **From the Synchronize drop-down list, choose whether you want to synchronize the whole local site or only files selected in the Files panel (if any).**

6. **From the Direction drop-down list, choose whether you want newer files put to the remote server, retrieved from the remote sever, or both.**

7. **To clean up unused or old files on your remote server, select the Delete Remote Files Not on Local Drive check box.**

8. **Click the Preview button to begin the process.**

This step may take a while depending on the number of files in your site.

The Synchronize Files dialog box appears and displays all changes that will be made between the local and remote folders, as shown in Figure 9-5.

9. **Select, change, or delete any actions as necessary.**

10. **Click OK to have Dreamweaver complete the synchronization process.**

Be careful when using the Delete Remote Files Not on Local Drive option; some files on the remote server are installed by the Web-hosting company and are necessary for the operation of your site.

Figure 9-5:
Choose the
actions to
take place.

Improving Your Site

Remember that a site is like a living organism; it continues to grow and will still need care after it's live. As you add to your site, find new and innovative ways to present information to site visitors; after all, it's all about giving your visitors what they came looking for.

To improve your site and keep visitors coming back, try the following tips:

✦ **Solicit feedback from focus groups or colleagues in different fields on best and worst features of the site.** Use this feedback to assist in design, layout, and content decisions.

✦ **Use Web statistics (often provided free by Web-hosting companies) to see where your users are spending the most time and where they exit the site.**

✦ **Provide a feedback form to allow site visitors to comment on service and information they received, with the opportunity to provide comments and suggestions.**

✦ **Always keep your content fresh.** Stale information and features can deter return visits and ruin first impressions.

✦ **Don't ignore problems that surface.** Address broken links, images, or misspellings right away.

Book V
Fireworks CS4

The 5th Wave   By Rich Tennant

"Maybe it would help our Web site if we showed our products in action."

Contents at a Glance

Chapter 1: Introducing Fireworks CS4

In This Chapter

✔ Understanding when you should use Fireworks

✔ Discovering the workspace

✔ Finding out about the tools

✔ Looking into the views

✔ Using the basic selection tools

*A*dobe Fireworks is an incredible application with specific solutions to meet online designers' needs. With Fireworks, you have the freedom to create test Web sites, experiment with advanced scripting features, and come up with compelling graphics that look good and work well on Web pages.

In this chapter, you encounter the software and its workspace. You also discover how to use selection tools so that you can start to manipulate graphics in Fireworks right away.

Why Use Fireworks?

With all the applications included in the Creative Suite, why do you need one more? The reason is mostly because after CS2 (and the removal of ImageReady), the Creative Suite provided no easy way to create interesting Web graphics. Sure, you can save images for online use in Photoshop and Illustrator using the Save for Web & Devices feature, but what about rollovers, easy image maps, and interactive wireframes? (A *wireframe* is a low-fidelity mock-up, page-schematic rough draft. In Web design, wireframes are basic visual guides used to suggest the layout and placement of fundamental design elements.)

With Fireworks, you can work intuitively by taking advantage of the logical interface. This interface provides panels and features that relate to the Web and that offer you the easiest way to *optimize* (make Web-ready) your graphics.

Jumping Right into the Interface

So what's the big deal about Fireworks being built specifically for Web graphics? Well, first of all, you are working strictly with pixels — no messy *dpi* (dots per inch) or *lpi* (lines per inch), which are typical printing terms.

Figure 1-1 shows the dialog box that appears when you choose File⇨Open to open a vector graphic from Illustrator. The dialog box offers conversion choices but emphasizes pixel dimensions.

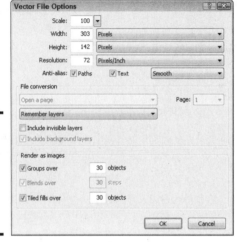

Figure 1-1: Pixel dimensions play an important role in Fireworks.

When you're working with Web images, it's a good idea to know the approximate width, in pixels, of your final page. Typical Web pages range all the way from 650 to 1,000 pixels wide, but most designers stick with a page built to span approximately 800 pixels. When you create images, you must think about how they will fit within the context of your total page. An image 600 pixels wide would take up most of your page, whereas one that's 1,200 pixels wide would force the viewer to scroll to see the entire image.

Touring the workspace

Upon launching Fireworks CS4, you notice right away that its workspace is similar to the workspaces in the other CS4 applications. Adobe has done a good job of organizing each application so that the learning curve is quick and integration is easy.

You shouldn't be surprised to find a toolbox to the left of the workspace and panels to the right. The tools even look very much like the tools you may already be familiar with from working in other CS4 applications.

Using the tools

The Tools panel is broken into six categories: Select, Bitmap, Vector, Web, Colors, and View. Table 1-1 lists the tools by category and the keys you can press to access them easily.

Table 1-1		Fireworks Tools	
Icon	*Tool*	*Purpose*	*Keyboard Shortcut*
Selection tools			
	Pointer	Selects paths and objects	V+0
	Subselection	Adjusts paths, much like the Direct Select tool in Illustrator and Photoshop.	A+1
	Scale	Scales objects or selections	Q
	Crop	Crops images	C
Bitmap tools			
	Marquee	Makes rectangular selections	M
	Lasso	Makes freeform selections	L
	Magic Wand	Selects similar colors	W
	Brush	Paints on image	B (toggles with Pencil)
	Pencil	Draws bitmap paths	B (toggles with Brush)
	Eraser	Erases bitmap data	E

(continued)

Table 1-1 *(continued)*

Icon	Tool	Purpose	Keyboard Shortcut
Bitmap tools			
	Blur	Blurs image	R
	Rubber Stamp	Clones image data	S
Vector tools			
	Line	Creates vector lines	N
	Pen	Creates Bezier paths	P
	Rectangle	Creates vector shapes	U
	Type	Creates text	T
	Freeform	Creates freeform paths	O
	Knife	Cuts paths	Y
Web tools			
	Rectangle Hotspot	Creates image map hotspots	J
	Slice	Creates slices for tables or CSS	K
	Hide Slices and Hotspots	Hides slices and image map hotspots	2
	Show Slices and Hotspots	Displays slices and image map hotspots	2

Icon	*Tool*	*Purpose*	*Keyboard Shortcut*
Color tools			
	Eyedropper	Samples color	I
	Paint Bucket	Fills color	G
View tools			
	Hand	Pans the artboard	
	Zoom	Zooms in and out of artboard	x

As you select each tool, notice that the Properties panel displays additional options. (If your Properties panel isn't visible, choose Window⇨Properties.)

Understanding the views

The tabs at the top of an image give you the opportunity to view it in four ways:

✦ **Original** displays your image as it appears before being optimized for the Web.

✦ **Preview** displays the image as it will appear when it's saved for the Web, based on your current settings. (You find out more about those settings in Chapter 5 of this minibook.)

✦ **2-Up** offers the opportunity to see your image in two windows, with different settings applied in each window. Most users tend to compare the original and optimized images in this view (see Figure 1-2).

✦ **4-Up** is for those who are never quite sure which is the best way to optimize an image. You don't necessarily need to compare different formats when you use this view; you can experiment with different options for one format, such as pushing the limit with the amount of colors you want to keep in a GIF, as shown in Figure 1-3.

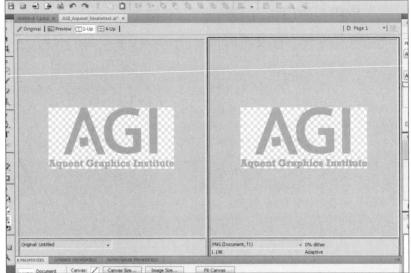

Figure 1-2:
Compare
original
(left) and
optimized
image (right)
in 2-Up
view.

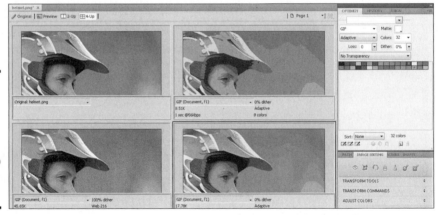

Figure 1-3:
In 4-Up
view,
you can
experiment
with ways to
optimize an
image.

Investigating the panels

Not unlike the other CS4 applications, Fireworks lets you detach panels from the docking area on the right side of the workspace. Because this procedure is so similar to the methods you use to dock and undock panels in other CS4 applications, we won't bore you with the details here.

If you can't locate a panel, choose its name from the Window menu.

Working with basic selection tools

You can work in Fireworks using the same selection tools for both vector and bitmap images.

Making a selection with the Marquee and Lasso tools

If you are familiar with Photoshop selection techniques, you will have no problem using the same tools in Fireworks.

To make a selection with the Marquee tool, simply select the tool from the Tools panel, and then click and drag to surround the area that you want to select.

You can add to the selection by holding down the Shift key and dragging another marquee region, or deselect some of the active selection by holding down the Alt (Windows) or Option (Mac) key while dragging with the Marquee tool.

To use the Lasso tool, select the Lasso tool from the Tools panel and click and drag to create a path that will then become your selection. As mentioned in the Marquee tool, you can add to the selection by holding down the Shift key and creating another selection region, or subtract from the selection by holding down the Alt (Windows) or Option (Mac) key while dragging a selection region with the Lasso tool.

You can use both the Marquee and Lasso tools interchangeably when making a selection.

By making a selection with the Marquee or Lasso tool and then clicking and dragging with the Pointer tool, you can move one part of an image to another, as shown in Figure 1-4. If you make no selection before you drag, everything on the existing layer is moved.

Figure 1-4:
Drag a
selection
move it.

Switch to the Subselection tool, and notice that if you have an existing selection, the pointer changes to a double arrow. This double arrow indicates that you will *clone* (copy) the selection when you click and drag it.

Making a selection in a vector image

With the same tools you use to select bitmap images, you can adjust vector paths. Use the Pointer tool to move an entire vector shape, as shown in Figure 1-5.

Figure 1-5:
The Pointer tool lets you move a vector shape.

Use the Subselection tool to move the individual points on the path.

Chapter 2: Free to Create

In This Chapter

✓ Understanding layers in Fireworks

✓ Finding the difference between vector and bitmap images

✓ Using the bitmap and vector drawing tools

✓ Discovering masking

You can easily import graphics into Fireworks from the other Creative Suite 4 applications or create your own graphics. Fireworks comes with a full set of tools for creating both bitmap and vector images. This chapter briefly discusses bitmap and vector graphics; you can find out more by reading Book I, Chapter 6.

Knowing What Happens in Layers

Create a new document by choosing File⇨New. If the Layers panel is not visible, choose Window⇨Layers. By default, the Layers panel contains two layers: Web Layer and Layer 1.

Web Layer is reserved for Web objects, such as hotspots, slices, and other interactive objects. You can't delete, duplicate, or rename objects in this layer. You find out more about the Web Layer in Chapter 6 of this minibook.

You also have Layer 1 as a default layer. Everything that you create or import, whether it's a bitmap or a vector graphic, lands here, essentially becoming a sublayer of Layer 1.

You can rename both main layers and sublayers. You can also reposition, delete, and duplicate them by using the tools at the bottom of the Layers panel (see Figure 2-1).

Figure 2-1:
The Layers panel always includes Web Layer and Layer 1.

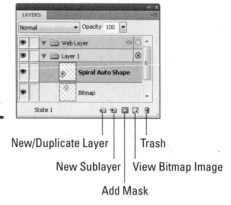

New/Duplicate Layer | Trash

New Sublayer | View Bitmap Image

Add Mask

Understanding this layer organization and how it relates to drawing in Fireworks is important. When you use bitmap tools to paint and create pixels, everything falls onto one layer, much as you would expect. But when you start creating vector shapes, every new shape lands on a new layer. This arrangement makes it easier for you to move the shapes independently but can be confusing to new Fireworks users at first.

Choosing Vector or Bitmap Graphics

If you haven't read enough about vector versus bitmap graphics before this minibook, you get even more information in this section.

Fireworks lets you work in a painterly fashion with the bitmap tools. These tools work like the brush and retouching tools in Photoshop, in that they are pixel based. You can use the bitmap tools to create smoother transitions and more realistic contours and shapes.

So why not use bitmap images for all your artwork? One drawback is that bitmap images tend to be a little larger in file size than vector images. Also, bitmap images aren't scalable, as vector graphics are. Sometimes, it's fairly clear when to use a bitmap instead of a vector image; see Figure 2-2 for an example.

Most designers use bitmap images for more realistic artwork, such as photo-realistic renderings, and vector images for more graphical artwork, such as stylized buttons and logos.

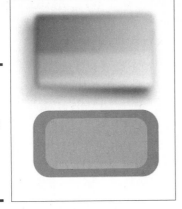

Figure 2-2:
You can draw both bitmap (top) and vector (bottom) graphics in Fireworks.

No matter whether you use bitmap or vector drawing tools to create a graphic, it will be a bitmap image when it's optimized (saved for the Web). Even if you use vector drawing tools in Fireworks, you see the graphic broken into pixels in the preview windows.

Creating with Bitmap Tools

The first set of tools that we investigate in this chapter are the bitmap tools: Marquee, Lasso, Magic Wand, Brush, Pencil, Eraser, Blur, and Rubber Stamp. We cover these tools briefly, focusing on the differences between using them in Fireworks and in other bitmap applications, such as Photoshop. If you don't see the Tools panel, choose Window⇨Tools.

The selection tools let you grab hold of pixels. You use the Marquee tool, for example, to select a section of pixels that you want to move, clone, or change in some way. To experiment with the Marquee tool, follow these steps:

1. **Choose File⇨New to create a new Fireworks document.**

    The New dialog box appears.

2. **Type 500 in both the Width and Height text boxes; leave Canvas set to White; then click OK.**

    A new blank document opens.

3. With the Marquee tool, click and drag in the workspace from top left to bottom right to create a rectangular marquee.

4. Choose File⇨Swatches to open the Swatches panel.

5. Click any color you want to use for the fill of your selection.

6. Click the Paint Bucket tool (in the Colors section of the Tools panel) and then click inside your selection marquee to fill it with your selected color.

You've successfully created a bitmap graphic in Fireworks. In the next section, you use other bitmap tools to make changes in this artwork.

Moving pixels

In this section, you use the Marquee tool to move the pixels to another location. If you're a Photoshop user, notice that the Marquee tool works just like the selection tools in Photoshop.

To move the graphic you just selected, follow these steps:

1. With the Marquee tool, click and drag over the bottom of your bitmap rectangle.

2. Select the Pointer tool and then drag the marquee down, as shown in Figure 2-3.

Figure 2-3:
Move a
selection
with the
Pointer tool.

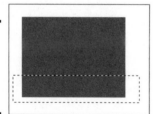

Changing the way pixels appear

If you've followed along, you know how to select and move pixels and you're ready to change the way selected pixels appear. To do that, follow these steps:

1. Choose Select⇨Deselect, or use the keyboard shortcut Ctrl+D (Windows) or ⌘+D (Mac), to make sure that there are no active selections.

2. Hold down the Marquee tool to select the hidden Oval tool.

3. **Holding down the Alt (Windows) or Option (Mac) key, click and drag from the center of the rectangle that you created (see the top of Figure 2-4).**

Many of the shortcuts you use in Illustrator and Photoshop also work in Fireworks . . . but not all. Finding compatible shortcuts is sort of hit-or-miss when you're in the beginning stage with Fireworks. You can choose Help⇨ Fireworks Help and select Preferences and Keyboard Shortcuts in the list of topics on the left side of the Help window for details.

4. **To *feather* (soften) the edges of the selection, choose Feather from the Edge drop-down list in the Properties panel and set a feathering value (10 pixels is the default) in the combo box to the right of the Edge drop-down list, as shown in the middle of Figure 2-4.**

The bottom of Figure 2-4 shows the result.

Figure 2-4:
Making a feathered, oval selection.

Using additional bitmap tools

You'll also use some additional bitmap tools:

✦ **Brush:** The Brush tool lets you paint just like you would in Photoshop, and you can mix it up with the selection tools to create interesting artwork.

Options for the Brush tool — such as size, softness, and transparency — are located in the Properties panel at the bottom of the workspace. Unfortunately, not all the great brush shortcuts in Photoshop work in Fireworks, so you may have to access the Properties panel in Fireworks more often than you may be used to.

✦ **Editing tools:** Because you are working with pixels, you can edit those pixels rather easily.

- *Pencil:* Use the Pencil tool to add detail.

- *Blur:* The Blur tool softens edges.

- *Eraser:* The Eraser tool eliminates pixels.

✦ **Rubber Stamp:** The Rubber Stamp tool is similar to the one in Photoshop, and you use it the same way. Simply Alt-click (Windows) or Option-click (Mac) a bitmap source that you want to clone; then release the Alt/Option key and start painting somewhere else in the image area. The source is re-created or cloned as you paint with the Rubber Stamp tool.

If you make a mistake, you can undo multiple steps in Fireworks by pressing Ctrl+Z (Windows) or ⌘+Z (Mac) repeatedly. If you want to redo a step (essentially undoing an undo), press Ctrl+Y (Windows) or ⌘+Y (Mac).

Creating with Vector Tools

The Vector tools in Fireworks are similar to the ones you may be used to in Illustrator or Photoshop. What you should notice right off the bat in Fireworks is that every time you create a new vector shape with one of the vector tools (such as Line, Pen, Shape, or Type), Fireworks creates a new sublayer automatically. This arrangement lets you move the shapes freely and independently.

Before repositioning or making other transformations in your vector images, confirm which sublayer is active by looking for the highlighted sublayer in the Layers panel. Otherwise, you may unexpectedly move the wrong image.

Using shape tools

To use a shape tool, simply click it and drag in the workspace. A shape is created, and a new sublayer is added automatically in the Layers panel.

In addition to the basic shape tools, Fireworks has more shapes that are useful for designing buttons, icons, and other Web graphics. To find these shapes, click and hold the Rectangle tool in the Tools panel. Hidden shape tools appear such as stars, arrows, and beveled rectangles, to name a few.

After you create a shape using a shape tool, you can edit it by using the Pointer and Subselection tools as follows:

✦ **Pointer:** If you need to reposition the shape, select the Pointer tool, and click and drag it to a new location. You can also grab the highlighted anchor points to resize the shape.

✦ **Subselection:** If you need to make more defined shape changes (such as changing the corner radius, bevel, or overall shape of the vector graphic), you want to switch to the Subselection tool. This tool works very much like the Select and Direct Select tools in Illustrator and Photoshop.

Creating a path

The most popular vector tool in most applications is the Pen tool. Using this tool in a freeform manner, you can create any shape you want (including the type you need to make a button look like it has a reflection, for example) or create your own custom graphics.

Fireworks offers three types of path tools, as shown in Figure 2-5:

✦ **The Pen tool** works much like other Pen tools. You create a path by clicking from one location to another (creating anchor points) or by clicking and dragging to create curved sections of paths.

✦ **The Vector Path tool** lets you click and drag in a painterly fashion to create a path.

✦ **The Redraw Path tool** lets you reshape a path (by dragging it over an existing path) while maintaining the original stroke information.

Figure 2-5:
Create
paths in
Fireworks
with three
tools.

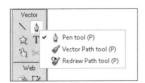

Changing an existing path

If you have a hard time using the Pen tool or want to make freeform adjustments, you can get really great results by using the Freeform tool.

When you use the Freeform tool or some of the other hidden path tools (refer to the "Using shape tools" section, earlier in this chapter), you may get a warning message, essentially indicating that you could get unexpected results, as shown in Figure 2-6. Click OK and cross your fingers.

Figure 2-6:
You may
get an error
when you
use the
Freeform
tool.

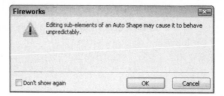

To use the Freeform tool with an existing path active (select it with the Pointer tool), follow these steps:

1. **Click the Freeform tool to select it; then click and drag in the workspace to change the way the path looks.**

You can bend the path in different smooth directions.

2. **In the Properties panel, set options to specify the width of the change.**

Another tool hidden in the Freeform tool is the Reshape Area tool, which is handy for reshaping existing paths (see Figure 2-7). This tool lets you set a reshape size area in the Properties panel and then edit selected paths by clicking and dragging over them.

Figure 2-7:
Change
existing
paths with
the Reshape
Area tool.

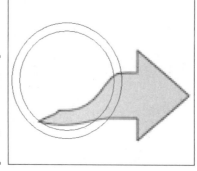

The additional path-scrubber tools let you edit paths that have pressure-sensitive strokes. In fact if you did not have paths created using a pressure-sensitive device, you cannot use these tools.

Working with type

Feel free to scale your text to your heart's delight; text is vector! To create text in your image area, simply select the Text tool, click to set your insertion point, and then start typing. Use the Properties panel to change the font and size, as well as other text attributes. Chapter 4 in this minibook discusses text and its formatting capabilities.

Masking: Going Beyond Tape

You can mask in Fireworks, but you don't use quite the same method that you'd use in Photoshop, Illustrator, or InDesign. The result is essentially the same, however.

A *mask* lets you choose which part of a graphic is exposed and which part is covered (by the mask). See Figure 2-8 for an example of two vector graphics that have been masked with a gradient fill to fade the transparency from 100 percent to none.

Figure 2-8:
An example
of two
vector
shapes
with masks
applied
to them.

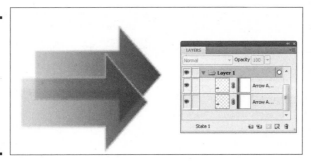

To apply a gradient mask, follow these steps:

1. **Create a vector shape (such as an arrow).**

2. **In the Layers panel, choose Add Mask from the panel menu.**

   A blank mask appears to the right of the vector shape's sublayer, as shown in Figure 2-9.

3. **With the new mask active, click and hold the Paint Bucket tool to select the hidden Gradient tool.**

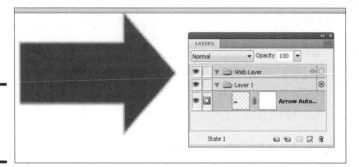

Figure 2-9:
Adding a mask to a sublayer.

4. **With the Gradient tool, click and drag across the shape to make the gradient on the mask and create the transparency effect on the vector shape.**

   Notice that where the gradient is darker, the image is less visible, and where the gradient is lighter, the vector shape is more visible, as shown in Figure 2-10.

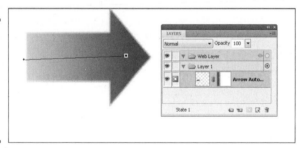

Figure 2-10:
The arrow shows through more where the gradient is lighter.

You can experiment with this effect on other shapes. Also, you can try clicking and dragging the gradient until you get the depth and direction you want.

A gradient tends to work better as a mask if you use its default colors: black and white.

Chapter 3: Livening Up Your Artwork with Color

In This Chapter

✔ Defining colors for the Web

✔ Finding and applying colors to graphics

✔ Creating your own colors in Fireworks

✔ Using gradient fills

*L*ike most other Creative Suite applications, Fireworks lets you define an object's fill and stroke. You can use some unique tools for that selection, as well as some hidden features that work slightly differently from what you may be used to.

In this chapter, you find out how to get the fill or stroke color you want applied to your artwork, and you discover the basics of working with gradient fills.

Choosing Web Colors

Colors appear different on a monitor from the way they do when you view them off-screen, but this issue isn't as serious now as it was in the past. Years ago, you had to base your color selections on the lowest common denominator. Today, most viewers have monitors that can display thousands, if not millions, of colors.

When you're choosing a color for the Web, it's best not to fret over the exactness of a color when viewed on different monitors unless precision is critical. Critical color could apply to your company logo or to fabrics that viewers might be comparing onscreen.

In Fireworks, you can choose color from several panels, with each panel offering a different model from which to create your colors. Even though you are working in RGB (Red, Green, Blue), you can still enter CMYK (Cyan, Magenta, Yellow, Key or Black) or HSB (Hue, Saturation, Brightness) values.

Finding Colors in Fireworks

Perhaps you want to create a simple shape with a fill, which seems easy, but if you are unfamiliar with Fireworks, you may need a little direction to get this task done.

You can find most of Fireworks's color functions in the Colors section of the Tools panel. This section features an Eyedropper tool for sampling color, as well as color boxes that make it easy for you to stroke and fill both bitmap and vector graphics.

You can set additional attributes for color in the Properties panel, including textures that you can apply from the Texture drop-down list.

Applying Colors to Objects

To create and color an object, follow these steps:

1. **Choose File⇨New to create a new blank document.**

2. **Create a path or a shape with the bitmap or vector drawing tools and leave that object selected.**

3. **To apply a fill color, click the Fill Color box located at the Colors section of the Tools panel and then click the color you want to apply from the pop-up Swatches panel (see Figure 3-1).**

4. **To apply a stroke color, click the Stroke Color box in the Tools panel and then click the color you want to apply from the pop-up Swatches panel.**

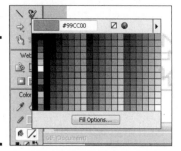

Figure 3-1:
Take
advantage
of the
Fill Color
options.

Adding Colors to Fireworks

Assigning a fill or stroke color to graphics is relatively simple. But what if the color you want to use isn't in the default Swatches panel? In that case, you need to create a color and add it to the panel. You can accomplish this task in several ways. In the following sections, we cover using the Eyedropper tool and the color palette.

Adding a color with the Eyedropper tool

The Eyedropper tool is useful when you have a color to sample. Just select the tool, click any color (in your working document or in any other open Fireworks document), and then choose Window⇨Swatches. When the Swatches panel pops up, click an empty area, and your sample color is added.

To remove a color from the Swatches panel, position your mouse pointer over the color that you want to delete, and press Ctrl+Alt (Windows) or ⌘+Option (Mac). When the scissors pointer appears, click the mouse; the color is deleted.

Adding a color with the color palette

The color palette is a dynamic and fun way to set color. It consists of three tabs, each tab offering the opportunity to choose a stroke or fill color and a different method of selecting that color.

You can open the Color palette by choosing Windows⇨Others⇨Color Palette.

The three color palette tabs are

✦ **Selector:** The Selector tab (see Figure 3-2) lets you pick a color in any of four color models: HLS (hue, lightness, saturation), HSV, CMYK, and RGB. Click the large color panel and then enter color values by using the sliders or text boxes at the bottom. To adjust the tonal value, use the slider to the right of the large color panel.

✦ **Mixers:** The Mixers tab (see Figure 3-3) lets you assign multiple colors by using the color wheel. You can also create a tint build at the bottom of the window so that you can build combinations of colors. In addition, you can export the colors as a bitmap or a table using the Export buttons on the left side of the Mixer tab, which makes it easy to reference them later.

✦ **Blender:** The Blender tab (see Figure 3-4) lets you select two colors and then view and choose combinations of those colors.

Figure 3-2:
The color palette's Selector tab gives you a choice of four color models.

Figure 3-3:
In the Mixers tab, create colors with the color wheel or the tint builder.

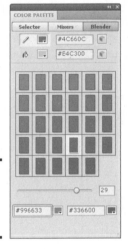

Figure 3-4:
Blend two
colors in
this tab.

Creating Gradients

You can add some dimension to a graphic by filling it with a gradient. To
create a gradient in Fireworks, follow these steps:

1. **Create a shape that you want to fill with a gradient.**

2. **With the shape selected, click and hold the Paint Bucket tool in the
Colors section of the Tools panel and then select the hidden Gradient
tool (see Figure 3-5).**

Figure 3-5:
Select the
Gradient
tool.

3. **Click the Fill Color box in the Tools panel to assign colors to the
gradient.**

The Fill Options window appears (see Figure 3-6).

4. **To assign colors to the gradient, simply click the existing color stops,
and choose a color from the pop-up palette.**

5. **Click anywhere on the gradient ramp to add a stop, and edit the color.**

6. **If you don't want to create your own gradient, click the Preset drop-
down list to choose among existing gradients (see Figure 3-7).**

Figure 3-6:
Assign the
gradient
colors.

Figure 3-7:
Pick a
preset
gradient
from this
drop-down
list.

Chapter 4: Creating Text in Fireworks

In This Chapter

- ✔ Creating and formatting text
- ✔ Setting a text attribute
- ✔ Working on spacing, alignment, and orientation
- ✔ Applying your effects
- ✔ Styling your text
- ✔ Checking your spelling
- ✔ Setting text on a path
- ✔ Outlining your text

You definitely don't want to attempt to create a brochure in Fireworks, but you can take advantage of its excellent capabilities to format your on-screen text. Whether you're working with paragraphs or single lines of text, you have lots of options for fonts, styles, and interesting effects. In this chapter, you find out where to find the features you need to get the words looking just the way you like them.

Creating Text

You can create text in either of two ways:

- ✦ Select the Type tool, click in the image area, and begin typing.
- ✦ Copy (or cut) text from another application, select the Type tool, and paste it on the artboard.

In a hurry? You can select text from one application and then click and drag it into the Fireworks workspace.

Setting Text Attributes

Text can create mood and feeling, so you want to make sure you have the right font and style for your message. You can apply text attributes via two main methods: the Type menu or the Properties panel. In this chapter, you use the Properties panel (see Figure 4-1), as it provides an easier method for locating text attributes. If your Properties panel isn't visible at the bottom of the Fireworks workspace, choose Window⇨Properties.

Whether you use the Type menu or Properties panel, you can set your text attributes with the Properties panel either before or after you enter text.

Figure 4-1:
Choose
font, size,
and other
attributes.

The same rule applies in Fireworks as in all other applications: You have to select it to affect it. Before you apply any attributes, use the Pointer tool to select the text you want to format.

To set text attributes with the Properties panel, follow these steps:

1. **Select the text that you want to format.**

2. **Choose a font from the Font drop-down list and then choose a style from the Style drop-down list.**

If you don't see your favorite font in bold, you can take advantage of the Bold button to create faux bold text (not really the bold font, but kind of close). The same trick works with the Italic button.

3. **To assign color, click the color selector box to the right of the Size drop-down list and then choose a color from the pop-up Swatches panel.**

Fine-Tuning Spacing, Alignment, and Orientation

Unfortunately, Fireworks's text controls leave much to be desired compared with the other Creative Suite applications. But if you want to fine-tune your text, you might consider adjusting the spacing between characters or lines.

Sliders are available in the Properties panel for adjusting the *kerning* (spacing between two characters), *tracking* (spacing between multiple letters), and *leading* (spacing between lines of text). Select the text you want to format, adjust the slider as shown in Figure 4-2, and then click off the slider to confirm the change.

Kerning and tracking are controlled using the same Kerning tool. To kern between two letters, insert the cursor between the two letters before making a change. To adjust tracking, select multiple letters before making a change.

Figure 4-2:
Adjust
kerning,
tracking,
and leading.

Kerning and Tracking   Leading Units

Leading

To align selected text, click the Left, Center, Right, or Justified alignment button in the Properties panel.

You can also change the orientation of selected text by clicking the Set Text Orientation button, shown in Figure 4-3.

Figure 4-3:
Change text
orientation.

Set Text Orientation button

Adding Effects

Spunk up your text by adding Live Effects from Photoshop. You can add drop shadows or 3D effects, or even make your text look like wood!

To add effects to your text, follow these steps:

1. **With the Pointer tool, select your text and then click the Add Filters button in the Properties panel.**

2. **Select Photoshop Live Effects from the pop-up window that appears.**

   The Photoshop Live Effects dialog box appears (see Figure 4-4).

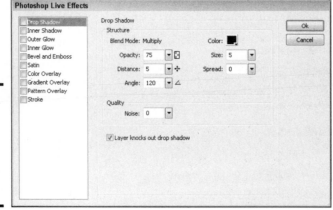

Figure 4-4:
Set text effects in the Photoshop Live Effects dialog box.

3. **In the list on the left side of the dialog box, check the effect that you want to apply.**

4. **Set the related options on the right side of the dialog box and click OK.**

   The effects are applied to your text, as shown in Figure 4-5.

Figure 4-5:
Create interesting text effects.

GREENBEANS

You've heard it before, but we have to say it again: Just because you *can* do something doesn't mean that you always *should*. Translation: Don't apply all these effects to your text at the same time.

Giving Your Text Some Style

You can choose among an array of interesting default styles to apply to both objects and text. You can also create your own styles — an extremely helpful capability when text needs to be consistent throughout an entire Web site.

Styles are applied to the entire text area.

Applying an existing style

To apply an existing text style, follow these steps:

1. **Create your text by typing, cutting/copying and pasting, or dragging the text on the artboard.**

2. **With the Pointer tool, select the text that you want to affect.**

3. **Choose Window⇨Style.**

   The Styles panel appears (see Figure 4-6).

4. **From the drop-down list, choose a category of style that you want to apply.**

   In Figure 4-6 the Chrome Styles category was selected.

5. **Click the style preview that you wish to apply to your selected text.**

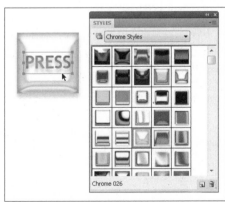

Figure 4-6:
Click a style
to apply
interesting
attributes
to your
selection.

Creating your own style

Save yourself time by applying all the text attributes you need to get your text looking just right.

To create a custom style, follow these steps:

1. **Select your text and apply all the formatting and effects that you want to use, following the procedures described earlier in this chapter.**

2. **Choose Window➪Styles to display the Styles panel.**

3. **With the Style Category drop-down list, choose the category that you want the style to be saved in.**

4. **Click the New Style button in the bottom-right corner.**

   The New Style dialog box appears.

5. **Type an appropriate name for the style in the Name text box.**

6. **Check the attributes that you want to save and click OK.**

   You have a saved style that you can apply to selected text at any time.

Spell-Checking Your Text

Checking your spelling is simple, right? It certainly is simple in Fireworks, so you have no excuse for typographical errors.

To check the spelling of your text in Fireworks, follow these steps:

1. **Choose Text➪Spelling Setup.**

   The Spelling Setup dialog box appears.

2. **Choose the language that you want to use for the spelling check.**

3. **Set any other options you want to use and click OK.**

4. **Choose Text➪Check Spelling.**

   The Check Spelling dialog box appears with the first questionable spelling highlighted.

If you want to add any unique words in your document to the spell-checking dictionary, click the Add to Personal button in the top-right corner of the Check Spelling dialog box.

Attaching Text to a Path

Add some excitement by attaching text to a path. In Figure 4-7, the text is attached to a curvy path, but you could just as easily create angled text or text that follows a circle.

Figure 4-7:
You can
make text
curve by
attaching
the text
to a path.

Follow these steps to attach text to a path:

1. **Select the text that you want to attach to the path.**

2. **Create a path with the Pen, Line, or Shape tool.**

See Chapter 2 in this minibook for details on creating a path.

3. **With the Pointer tool, select the text area and then Shift-click the path.**

Both the text and the path are selected.

4. **Choose Text➪Attach to Path.**

If you want the text to run inside a shape, such as a circle, choose Text➪Attach in Path.

To change the orientation of the attached text on the path, choose Text➪ Orientation and then choose an orientation option from the submenu. In Figure 4-8, the orientation has been changed to Skew Vertical.

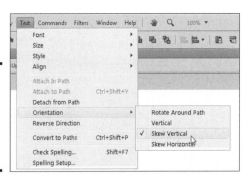

Figure 4-8:
You can
change
the text
orientation
on the path.

Outlining Text

Creating interesting text with unique fonts can be fun. But what if you need to send the text to someone who perhaps doesn't have your funky Giddyup font? No problem — Fireworks lets you *outline* text, which means essentially turning it into a vector path.

The content of your text isn't editable after it's been outlined.

To outline your text, follow these steps:

1. **Create your text with the desired attributes, including font.**

   The size doesn't have to be exact, however; you can rescale even after outlining the text.

2. **With the Pointer tool, select the text area.**

   Note: You can't outline individual letters or words within a text area.

3. **Choose Text⇨Convert Text to Paths.**

   The text is outlined.

To edit the new vector path, switch to the Subselection tool and click an individual letter, as shown in Figure 4-9.

Figure 4-9:
Turn your
text into
vector
paths.

KellyKakes

Chapter 5: Getting Images In and Out of Fireworks

In This Chapter

✔ Importing images

✔ Editing your images

✔ Optimizing and exporting images

Creating images for your Web site is most likely what you'll use Fireworks for most often. In this chapter, you find out how to work with images from various sources, discover the importance of optimizing, and see how to export your images.

Getting Images into Fireworks

Besides making your own graphics and illustrations, you can use four main methods for getting images into Fireworks:

✦ **Open:** Fireworks isn't too picky. As long as you open images (vector or raster) by choosing File➪Open, you can open pretty much anything in Fireworks.

In some cases, depending on the file format and color mode, choosing this command opens the Photoshop File Open Options dialog box (see Figure 5-1). This dialog box forces you to make some decisions about how the image will be rasterized in Fireworks before proceeding any further.

✦ **Import:** By choosing File➪Import, you can place an image directly in an existing image. The imported image is placed as a sublayer in the selected layer.

✦ **Drag and drop:** You can drag and drop an image from other applications, such as Adobe Illustrator and Adobe Photoshop, right into the Fireworks workspace.

To drag and drop between Adobe applications on the Windows platform, you must drag your selection down to the application's tab in the taskbar and wait for the application to come forward. Then you can drag into the work area.

✦ **Browse:** Just as you can in the rest of the Creative Suite applications, you can take advantage of Adobe Bridge to preview, search, and organize your images before opening them in Fireworks. Because images typically open in Photoshop by default, you need to right-click the image and choose Open with Adobe Fireworks CS4 from the contextual menu.

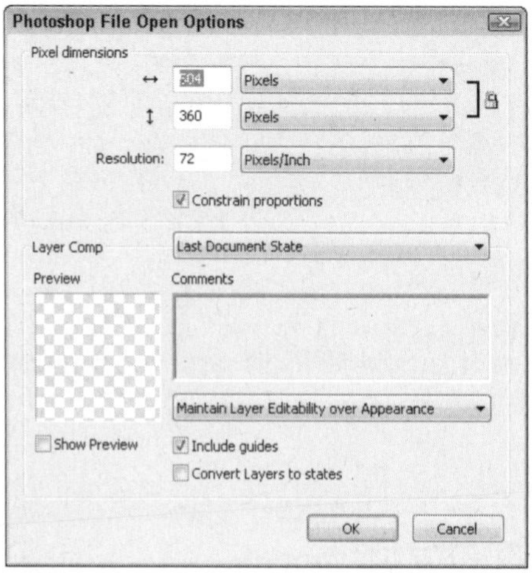

Figure 5-1:
Some images require you to make conversion decisions before opening them in Fireworks.

Editing Images

After you have an image, you can start editing it. The editing features in Fireworks are similar to those in Photoshop but not quite as extensive. You can do many of the basic tasks in Fireworks — cropping, painting, and even curve adjustments — but we suggest that you perform most in-depth retouching in Photoshop.

This section introduces five basic image-editing tasks that you typically perform when creating Web graphics. We also discuss the Image Editing panel, which lets you choose among multiple editing tools.

Scaling

Making images the right size is important. If an image is too large, you waste valuable download time; if it's too small, the image will look pixelized and out of focus. We cover three scaling methods in the following sections.

Proportional scaling

To scale an image in Fireworks proportionally (keeping the same width and height ratio), follow these steps:

1. **Select the layer(s) that you want to scale.**

If you have multiple layers, you can hold down the Ctrl (Windows) or ⌘ (Mac) key and click the layers in the Layers panel to add them to the selection.

2. **Select the Scale tool in the Select section of the Tools panel.**

Anchor points surround your selection.

3. **To make an image smaller, Shift-click a corner anchor point and drag in toward the center; to make an image larger, Shift-click a corner anchor point and drag outward.**

Typically, you don't want to scale an image up, as it may become pixelized.

Nonproportional scaling

If you *don't* want to scale proportionally, follow these steps:

1. **Select the layer(s) that you want to scale.**

2. **Select the Scale tool in the Select section of the Tools panel.**

3. **To resize an image, click and drag a corner anchor point without using the Shift key.**

Numeric scaling

If you need to constrain scaling to an exact amount, you are better off using the Image Editing panel. Follow these steps to perform numeric scaling:

1. **Select the layer(s) that you want to scale.**

2. **Choose Window⇨Others⇨Image Editing.**

The Image Editing panel appears.

3. **Click Transform Commands and choose Numeric Transform from the drop-down list, as shown in Figure 5-2.**

4. **In the Width and Height text boxes, type the percentage by which you want to scale and click OK.**

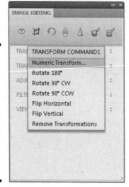

Figure 5-2:
You can scale numerically by using the Image Editing panel.

Cropping

If you don't need part of an image, get rid of it. Unwanted image data is a bad thing for Web graphics as it takes up valuable time when downloading. Follow these steps to eliminate unwanted image areas:

1. **Select the Crop tool from the Select area of the Tools panel or from the Image Editing panel.**

   Refer to the "Numeric scaling" section, earlier in this chapter, to see how to open the Image Editing panel.

2. **Click and drag to select the area that you want to keep when the crop is complete.**

3. **Press the Enter/Return key.**

   The image is cropped to the selected area, and the Crop tool is deselected.

If you're working with a wireframe of a larger Web page design you may want to export only a small portion. For example, perhaps you want to export just the navigational tools, but not the rest of the page. To crop only when exporting, follow these steps:

1. **Click and hold the Crop tool to select the Export Area tool.**

2. **Click and drag to select the area that you want to keep when the image is exported.**

3. **Double-click in the middle of the cropped area.**

   The Image Preview window appears, offering you the opportunity to set export settings for this section of your image.

4. **Choose your export settings.**

   You can choose preset GIF and JPEG settings from the Saved Settings drop-down list in the upper right of the Image Preview dialog box, or use the Options, File, and Animation tabs on the left to set up custom export options.

5. **Click Export.**

   The selected area is exported to a location that you choose, and you are returned to your image, which is still intact.

Painting

Fireworks has many of the same painting capabilities as Photoshop, but the method in which you use them can be very different at times.

When you select the Brush tool from the Bitmap section of the Tools panel, for example, you make decisions about the size of the brush, paint color, and blending mode in the Properties panel (see Figure 5-3) rather than the Options panel, as in Photoshop.

Tip Size

Brush Color | Stroke Category

Figure 5-3:
Change your
Brush tool
settings.

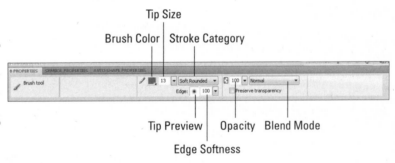

Tip Preview | Opacity   Blend Mode

Edge Softness

Cloning

The Rubber Stamp tool works much like the Clone Stamp tool in Photoshop. Follow these steps to clone (copy) pixels in Fireworks:

1. **Select the Rubber Stamp tool in the Bitmap section of the Tools panel.**

2. **Hold down the Alt (Windows) or Option (Mac) key, and click the part of the image you want to clone.**

   On the left side of Figure 5-4, the head is selected as the source for cloning.

Figure 5-4:
Selecting
pixels for
cloning
and start
painting.

3. **Position the mouse pointer over the area where you want the cloned pixels to appear, and start painting.**

    The cloned pixels appear in the image area (see the right side of Figure 5-4).

As you paint, follow the marker for the source; it moves simultaneously with the mouse pointer. You can use the Properties panel to change brush attributes.

Filtering

Filters offer you many opportunities to edit your images. You can choose to blur your image or adjust the colors by using the Curves or Hue Adjustment layer. To access your filters, you can choose them from the Filters menu, or choose Window⇨Others⇨Image Editing.

If you want to apply additional filters that you can change later or even delete, click the Add Filters button in the Properties panel and choose Photoshop Live Effects from the drop-down list. The Photoshop Live Effects dialog box appears (see Figure 5-5).

Figure 5-5:
Use
Photoshop
Live Effects
to create
non-
destructive
changes
to your
artwork.

Photoshop Live Effects

Drop Shadow	
☑ Inner Shadow	
Outer Glow	
Inner Glow	
☑ Bevel and Emboss	
Satin	
Color Overlay	
Gradient Overlay	
Pattern Overlay	
Stroke	

Bevel and Emboss
Structure

Style: Inner Bevel   Depth: 100
Technique: Smooth   Size: 5
Direction: Up   Soften: 5

Shading

Angle: 120
Highlight: Screen   75
Shadow: Multiply   75

Ok
Cancel

Red eye be gone!

Red eye is a typical result of using a camera with a built-in flash, but you can fix this problem easily. Click and hold the Rubber Stamp tool to select the Red Eye tool; then simply click and drag a marquee around each red-eye occurrence.

In the following example, you use the Hue/Saturation filter to add a color tint to an image. Follow these steps:

1. **Open an image and select it with the Pointer tool.**

2. **Click the Add Filter button in the Properties panel.**

3. **Choose Adjust Color and then Hue/Saturation.**

The Hue/Saturation dialog box appears (see Figure 5-6).

Figure 5-6:
Applying
a color
tint with
the Hue/
Saturation
filter.

4. **Check the Colorize check box to apply a color tint.**

5. **Adjust the Hue slider until you find a color that you want and click OK.**

The Add Filter button in the Properties panel now reads Edit Filter.

6. **Click the Edit Filter button at any time to open the Filters panel and double-click the Hue/Saturation filter.**

The Hue/Saturation Filter panel opens, where you can make changes to the filter.

7. **Delete a filter by selecting it from the filter list and clicking the minus icon (–) located in the top-left section of the Filter panel.**

Optimizing Images for the Web

Now that you have created and edited your image, you're ready to prepare it for the Web. You must consider two major factors in Web graphics: speed of download and appearance. Having the best of both worlds is difficult, however; usually, you opt to give up some appearance for better speed. This process is *optimization*.

Previewing Web settings

Fireworks helps you with the optimization process right from the beginning. By using the 2-Up preview in the top-left section of the image window, you can easily compare your optimized image with the original, based on your settings in the Optimize panel.

You can even use the preview windows to compare two to four Web formats and see which one looks best but has the most reasonable file size. Each preview window includes important information such as file size.

If you want to go really crazy, you can compare four settings by clicking 4-Up (see Figure 5-7). With the preview windows, you can quickly change various settings — such as format, number of colors, and quality — and see the effect immediately, without previewing the image on the Web.

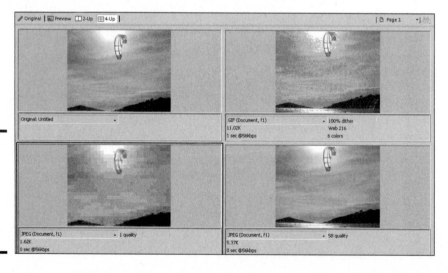

Figure 5-7:
Compare four Web image formats by choosing 4-Up view.

Working with the Optimize panel

Now that you know how to compare images, where do you make the necessary optimization changes? In the Optimize panel, of course (see Figure 5-8). For a thorough description of each file format, including its benefits and drawbacks, see Book II, Chapter 10, which covers Web optimization in Photoshop CS4.

When you understand the Web-format settings, you can click the preview image that you want to optimize; choose Window⇨Optimize to open the Optimize panel; and apply settings that provide the best, most size-efficient image. Then you can export the image, as the following section explains.

Figure 5-8:
Use the Optimize panel to find the best quality at the smallest file size.

Exporting for the Web

You can export individual images or entire Web pages by using the Export feature of Fireworks. The Export dialog box offers many of the same options as the Save for Web & Devices dialog box, which is described in depth in Book II, Chapter 10.

To export a Fireworks document, follow these steps:

1. **Choose File⇨Export.**

The Export dialog box opens, as shown in Figure 5-9.

2. **Navigate to an appropriate location to save your file.**

If you intend to use this image on a Web site, the best practice is to save it in the folder that you typically use for Web images.

3. **Type a name in the File Name text box.**

4. **Choose Images Only from the Export drop-down list and click Save.**

In Chapter 6 in this minibook, you discover how to export entire pages with sliced images.

Figure 5-9:
After it's optimized, you can export your document for Web use.

Chapter 6: Hotspots, Slices, and CSS Layouts

In This Chapter

✔ Getting familiar with Fireworks layers

✔ Hyperlinking with hotspots and image maps

✔ Creating slices

✔ Exporting images and HTML as tables or CSS

A simple method for organizing content and making a Web site dynamic is the faithful hyperlink. You can link to another location from a button, text, or even a move of the mouse pointer. By using layers in Fireworks, you can make those links dynamic and visually interesting.

In this chapter, you find out how Fireworks uses layers and then create navigational links by using the slice feature.

Understanding Layers

Even though you may be an Adobe Photoshop or Illustrator user, the Layers panel in Fireworks may be somewhat of a mystery, as it works a little differently than you might expect. (Read on to find out how to take advantage of Fireworks layers.) To see the Layers panel, choose Window⇨Layers.

Navigating the Layers panel

Figure 6-1 shows the two main components of the Layers panel:

✦ **The Web Layer,** which serves as a repository for anything code related, such as links and slices

✦ **The default Layer 1,** which includes sublayers that are created automatically for every object you add to the Fireworks canvas

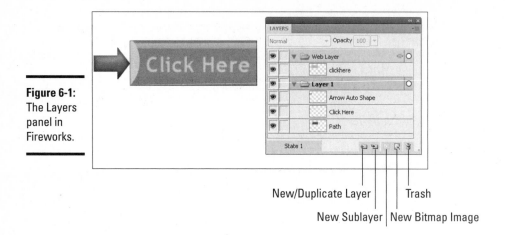

Figure 6-1:
The Layers
panel in
Fireworks.

New/Duplicate Layer — Trash

New Sublayer — New Bitmap Image

Working with the Layers panel

Here are just some of the things you can do in the Layers panel to organize your artwork better:

✦ **Hide and show layers:** Click the Visibility (Eye) icon to hide or show a layer or sublayer.

✦ **Send objects forward and backward:** Drag individual layers and sublayers to arrange objects on those layers in front of or behind each other.

✦ **Rename layers:** By double-clicking the layer or sublayer name, you can rename the layer, which can be a huge help later when you're trying to find a specific object.

✦ **Organize layers:** Create appropriately named layers to house related sublayers, thereby gaining the ability to move, copy, or delete multiple layers at the same time.

✦ **Keep Web components separate:** Use the Web Layer to keep track of hotspots and slices, as well as control the visibility of those items.

Creating Hotspots

Fireworks gives you lots of ways to take advantage of hyperlinks. In this section, you see how to create a *hotspot* — essentially, a simple link from text or a graphic to a URL (Universal Resource Locator) on the Web. In Chapter 7 of this minibook, you find out how to create buttons that interact with the user.

Defining a hotspot

To link text or a graphic to a Web URL, you must first define it as a hotspot. You can define a hotspot by using either of two methods:

+ Select the Hotspot tool in the Web section of the Tools panel, and click and drag over the part of the image that you want to create as the linked part of the image.

+ Select the item (text or graphics) and then right-click (Windows) or Control-click (Mac) the selected item, and choose Insert Hotspot from the contextual menu.

Linking a hotspot

After you define a hotspot, you can define the location (typically, a Web page) that you want the hotspot to link to. Follow these steps:

1. **Choose Window⇨URL.**

The URL panel appears (see Figure 6-2).

2. **Type a URL address that you wish the viewer to go to after selecting this region.**

In Figure 6-2, a link to an external Web site (`http://www.adobe.com`) is referenced.

When you reference pages beyond your Web site *(external links),* you must start the link with `http://`.

Figure 6-2:
Assign a link
to a hotspot.

3. **Choose Window⇨Layers to display the Layers panel, if it isn't already open.**

The hotspot you created appears as a separate sublayer of the Web Layer.

4. **Double-click the name of this sublayer and give it a more appropriate name, as shown in Figure 6-3.**

In the next section, you discover options for working with multiple hotspots.

Figure 6-3:
A new
hotspot
layer
appears
under the
Web layer.

Working with Image Maps

When you create a graphic and add multiple hotspots to it, the graphic becomes an *image map.* In Figure 6-4, the image map was created from a polygon.

Figure 6-4:
An image
map allows
you to
define
clickable
regions in
an image.

Creating an image map

To create an image map of your own, follow these steps:

1. **Open a graphic file that you want to assign multiple hotspots to.**

2. **Click and hold the Rectangle Hot Spot tool in the Web section of the Tools panel and choose one of the three hidden hotspot tools: Rectangle, Circle, or Polygon.**

3. **If you choose the Rectangle or Circle tool in Step 2, simply click and drag to define the hotspot.**

Alternatively, to create a region with the Polygon tool, simply click and release from point to point to create a custom region.

If you didn't get the shapes just right, don't fret. You can use the Pointer and Subselection tools to move and resize images.

Linking an image map

After you create an image map, you can define hotspots on it and link those hotspots to URLs. For directions on both procedures, refer to the "Creating Hotspots" section, earlier in this chapter.

Here are some types of links other than URLs that you can use:

✦ **E-mail address:** Type **mailto:***youremail address* in the URL text box to create a link that opens a message window, with your address already entered and ready to go!

✦ **Non-HTML files on the server:** You can type **2008/catalog.pdf**, for example, to instruct the browser to open a PDF file named `catalog` that is inside the `2008` folder.

Repeat the process of defining hotspots and assigning URLs as many times as you like.

Testing and exporting an image map

After you've created and linked your image map, you're ready to test and export it for use on your Web page. Follow these steps:

1. **Test your image map by choosing File⇨Preview in Browser.**

2. **If you're happy with the results, close the browser window and return to Fireworks to export your file.**

3. **Choose File⇨Export.**

   The Export dialog box appears.

4. **Type a name in the Name text box.**

5. **Choose HTML and Images from the Export drop-down list.**

6. **Select Export HTML File from the HTML drop-down list.**

7. **Choose None from the Slices drop-down list and click Save.**

That's it! Now you can choose File⇨Open in your browser and locate the HTML file to test your actual finished project, or choose File⇨Open in a Web-editing program (such as Adobe Dreamweaver) to modify the HTML file.

In Figure 6-5, you see the completed file in a Web browser, along with the associated code that was created in Fireworks.

Figure 6-5:
The finished image map, as viewed in a Web browser (top), and the HTML code created for the image map (bottom).

```
File  Edit  View  Help

<!DOCTYPE html PUBLIC "-//W3C//DTD XHTML 1.0 Transitional//EN"
"http://www.w3.org/TR/xhtml1/DTD/xhtml1-transitional.dtd">
<!-- saved from url=(0014)about:internet -->
<html xmlns="http://www.w3.org/1999/xhtml">
<head>
<title>puzzle.gif</title>
<meta http-equiv="Content-Type" content="text/html; charset=utf-8" />
<!--Fireworks CS3 Dreamweaver CS3 target.  Created Thu Jul 31 00:03:56
GMT-0400 (Eastern Daylight Time) 2008-->
</head>
<body bgcolor="#ffffff">
<img name="puzzle" src="puzzle.gif" width="300" height="200" border="0"
id="puzzle" usemap="#m_puzzle" alt="" /><map name="m_puzzle"
id="m_puzzle">
<area shape="poly"
coords="121,100,125,69,142,73,145,60,158,62,154,77,174,86,171,108,185,113
href="http://www.agitraining.com" alt="" />
</map>
</body>
```

Slicing Up Your Art

Slicing is a technique for breaking large files into smaller packets so that they download faster on the Web. It's also a method for attaching URLs to different regions of an image, like image maps. Unlike image maps, however, slices are created in a grid pattern.

You can even use slices to optimize different parts of an image with separate settings. Perhaps you can get away with having one section of an image be of lower quality than another section.

A perfect candidate for sliced artwork is a navigation bar, such as the one you see in Figure 6-6. Each tab is an individual slice that, when clicked in a Web browser, takes the viewer to a different location.

Figure 6-6:
Use slices for navbars.

| Home | About | Contact | Downloads |

Creating the basic image

First, you create the basic image — a rectangle, for this example. Follow these steps:

1. **Choose File➪New to open the New Document dialog box.**

2. **Type** 500 **in the Width text box and** 200 **in the Height text box; then click OK.**

   The new blank document opens. (Notice that the document is larger than the image you're creating; you see how to modify it later in these steps.)

3. **Select the Rectangle tool in the Vector section of the Tools panel, and click and drag to create a rectangle.**

   For this exercise, any size is fine.

4. **With the rectangle selected, click Fill Color in the Colors section of the Tools panel, and choose a color.**

   For this exercise, we chose a light color (yellow).

5. **Choose Window➪Info to open the Info panel.**

6. **Enter** 300 **in the W (Width) text box and** 50 **in the H (Height) text box.**

   The rectangle is resized.

7. **With the Pointer tool, click anywhere in the canvas outside the rectangle to deselect the rectangle.**

8. **Right-click (Windows) or Control-click (Mac), and choose Modify Canvas➪Fit Canvas from the contextual menu (see Figure 6-7).**

   The canvas adjusts to the size of the rectangle (see Figure 6-8).

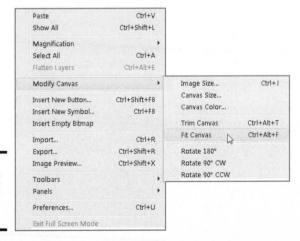

Figure 6-7: Choose the Fit Canvas command.

Figure 6-8:
The canvas
adjusts to fit
your object.

Figure 6-8:
The canvas
adjusts to fit
your object.

Adding text

Now you add some text areas to the navbar. Follow these steps:

1. **Select the Text tool in the Vector section of the Tools panel.**

2. **Click Fill Color in the Colors section of the Tools panel, and choose a color.**

For this exercise, we chose a dark color (black).

3. **Set the font and font size in the Properties panel.**

For this exercise, we changed the font to Myriad Pro, and used the Font Size slider to change the size to 25.

4. **Click the left half of the rectangle to position the insertion point where you want the text to begin, and type the text.**

For this exercise, we typed **Home**, as shown in Figure 6-9.

Figure 6-9:
Adding
text to the
navbar.

5. **Click twice to the right of the text area to deselect the active text area and create a new one.**

6. **Type a word or two for your next navigation tab.**

For example, we typed **About**.

7. **Use the Pointer tool to reposition the text.**

Doing the actual slicing and dicing

Now that you've prepared your simple but efficient navbar, use the Slice tool to create a couple of slices and then export them. Follow these steps:

1. **Select the Slice tool in the Web section of the Tools panel; then click and drag from the top-left corner of the Home section of the rectangle toward the bottom-right corner, as shown in Figure 6-10.**

Your drag doesn't have to be exact.

If you're going for perfection, choose View⇨Rulers to display the rulers. When the rulers are visible, you can click and drag guides out of them.

When you have an active slice, the Properties panel changes to offer you various slice options.

Figure 6-10:
Creating
a slice.

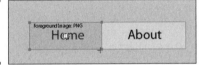

2. **Change the format by making a choice from the Slice Export Settings drop-down list.**

Choose the GIF format if the artwork has lots of solid color, or choose JPEG for images with lots of gradation of color.

3. **Enter a link in the Link text box.**

4. **Enter a brief description of the link in the Alt text box.**

Alt text is the text that appears while a page is downloading. It also appears in place of the graphic if a viewer has turned graphics display off in his Web browser.

5. **To test the link feature, type** http://www.agitraining.com.

6. **Type** Training **in the Alt text box, as shown in Figure 6-11.**

Figure 6-11:
Enter the
URL and
Alt text.

7. **With the Slice tool, click and drag to surround the second half of the navbar.**

8. **Type** http://www.adobe.com **into the Link text box and type** Adobe, Inc. **into the Alt text box.**

That is slicing in simple form. You can make the process as complicated as you want by creating entire sliced pages (because search engines like to search for text content) to navbars with many links and destinations.

In the next section, you find out how to get your navbar out of Fireworks and on a Web page.

Exporting Slices

You can export finished slices for use on a Web page.

Exporting slices as tables

To export sliced artwork as tables (for these steps, your test navbar), follow these steps:

1. **Choose File⇨Export.**

   The Export dialog box appears.

2. **Browse to the folder where you store your Web files and make sure that you pick a file connected with the Web site that you're creating your images for.**

3. **In the File Name text box, enter a name.**

   For this exercise, we typed **navbar.htm**.

4. **Choose Export HTML and Images from the Export drop-down list.**

5. **Choose Export Slices from the Slices drop-down list and click Save.**

Now that you've exported the HTML code and the image, you can open the image in a Web-editing program like Dreamweaver and add elements or simply copy and paste it into an existing page or template. Find out more about Dreamweaver in Book IV.

Changing the export format from table to CSS

If you want more control of your slices, you can change the code that Fireworks creates upon output.

In Figure 6-12, the selection for CSS and Images creates CSS (Cascading Style Sheets) rather than an HTML table when exported.

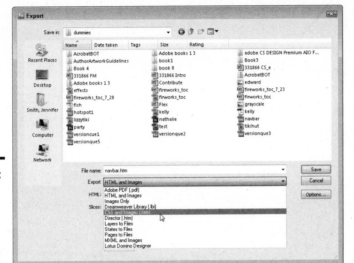

Figure 6-12:
You can
choose
to export
slices
as CSS.

Typically, creating a layout of a page using CSS code is beneficial because
the information is more accessible and flexible for the user.

Chapter 7: Using Buttons and Symbols

In This Chapter

✔ Understanding states

✔ Creating rollover buttons

✔ Converting graphics to symbols

*B*efore you jump into creating buttons and animations, you need to understand states and how they work in Fireworks. States let you organize layers in such a way that you can create several versions of your artwork; these states could be used for rollovers or animations.

Using States in Fireworks

You may want to use states for two reasons:

✦ **States for animation:** You can build and edit animated GIFs with states like the one you see in Figure 7-1. One step of the animation goes into each frame. The states (sometimes referred to as *frames*) are played one after another to create the appearance of motion — an effect a little like those cool flip books you may have found in caramel-corn boxes. By using layers, you can specify which items are animated and which items remain static.

✦ **States for rollovers:** You can also use states to produce rollovers. By slicing an image (discussed in Chapter 6 of this minibook), you can trigger the different versions (or states) that appear when the user's mouse pointer crosses over the artwork.

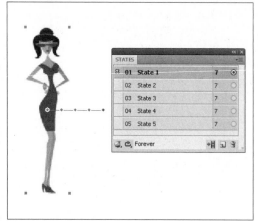

Figure 7-1:
In this
example,
the woman
moves
from left to
right in five
separate
states.

Making a Rollover Button

You can create interactive buttons in Fireworks to make rollovers, swap images, and react to other interactions with viewers. For all these effects, use the States panel.

In this section, you find out how to use states to create a *rollover* button — a button that changes when a mouse pointer passes over it.

Creating the basic art

First, you need to create the basic art for the button. (For this exercise, the button is a rounded rectangle, but you can substitute another shape.) Follow these steps:

1. **Click and hold the Rectangle tool in the Vector section of the Tools panel and then select Rounded Rectangle from the list of hidden tools.**

2. **Click and drag in the workspace to create a shape.**

   Any size is fine for this exercise.

3. **Choose Window⇨Styles to open the Styles panel.**

4. **Choose a style from the drop-down list (see Figure 7-2).**

   This basic button is what the viewer will initially see on your Web page.

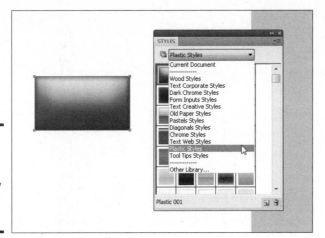

Figure 7-2:
Using the
Styles
panel, apply
any style to
the shape.

Adding rollover behavior

In this section, you add rollover behavior to the button and create the version of the button artwork that the viewers will see when their mouse pointers pass over it. Follow these steps:

1. **Select the Slice tool from the Web section of the Tools panel and then click and drag around the shape you created in the preceding section to create a slice.**

2. **Right-click (Windows) or Control-click (Mac) the center of the slice and choose Add Simple Rollover Behavior from the contextual menu (see Figure 7-3).**

3. **Choose Window⇨States to open the States panel.**

Figure 7-3:
Choose
Add Simple
Rollover
Behavior to
make your
button a
rollover.

Foreground Image: PNG

Export Selected Slice...
Arrange ▶

Add Simple Rollover Behavior
Add Swap Image Behavior...
Add Status Bar Message...
Add Nav Bar...
Add Pop-up Menu...
Edit Pop-up Menu...

Delete All Behaviors

Exit Full Screen Mode

4. **From the States panel menu, choose Duplicate State.**

   The Duplicate State dialog box appears. Keep the settings at the default of state 1 being inserted after the current state.

5. **Click OK.**

   A state 2 row appears in the States panel.

6. **Click the Hide Slices and Hotspots tool in the Web section of the Tools panel to hide your slice.**

7. **With the Pointer tool, select the original shape that you created.**

8. **Choose Window⇨Styles to open the Styles panel.**

9. **Choose a new style from the drop-down list.**

   This step creates the version of the button that will appear when viewers pass their mouse pointers over the button.

10. **Save the file.**

Testing and exporting the button

Now you're ready to test and export your new rollover button. Follow these steps:

1. **Choose File⇨Preview in Browser to test your button.**

2. **If you're happy with the effect and want to use the button on a Web page, choose File⇨Export to open the Export dialog box.**

3. **Name the file.**

   Remember that you need to follow standard Web-based naming conventions.

4. **Choose HTML and Images from the Export drop-down list.**

5. **Make sure that Export HTML File is selected in the HTML drop-down list and that Export Slices is selected in the Slices drop-down list and then click Export.**

Discovering Fireworks Symbols

When you make Web graphics, you may discover that you create the same button or the same background image over and over. To stay consistent and save lots of time, you can turn artwork into a symbol or use some of the pre-created symbols in the Common Library panel.

Symbols are simply elements that you can store in the Common Library or Document Library panel. Use the Common Library to store symbols that you can access across Fireworks; the Document Library is for symbols to be accessed only within the associated document.

Fireworks has three types of symbols: graphic, animation, and button. In this section, you find out how to use and modify symbols.

Symbol instances are the actual placement of the symbols on the artboard. Symbol instances are dynamically linked back to the original symbol used to create it.

If you convert artwork to a symbol, the new symbol object is linked dynamically to all the instances of that symbol on the artboard. If you change the symbol object, all instances are updated automatically.

Working with a precreated symbol

To use a precreated symbol in Fireworks, follow these steps:

1. **Choose Window⇨Common Library to open the Common Library panel.**

The precreated symbols in this library are organized in categories, such as Animations, Buttons, and Flex Components.

2. **Double-click the category you want to use.**

3. **Select a symbol to see a preview in the preview pane at the top of the Common Library panel.**

4. **When you find a symbol that you want to use, drag it out to the artboard.**

The symbol instance is placed on the artboard (see Figure 7-4).

If you're creating a navigation bar with four buttons, for example, repeat Step 4 three more times.

Figure 7-4:
Creating
a symbol
instance.

Converting artwork to a symbol

If you find yourself in the position of repeatedly creating the same button, animation, or graphic, follow these steps to convert that artwork to a symbol:

1. **With the Pointer tool, select the artwork that you want to convert.**

2. **Choose Modify⇨Symbol⇨Convert to Symbol.**

   The Convert to Symbol dialog box opens.

3. **Type a name for the symbol in the Name text box.**

4. **Select the symbol type: Graphic, Animation, or Button.**

5. **To scale the symbol without distorting it, check the Enable 9-Slice Scaling Guides check box (see Figure 7-5).**

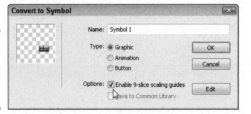

Figure 7-5: Setting symbol options.

6. **To store the symbol so that it can be used in multiple documents, check the Save to Common Library check box.**

7. **Click OK to save the symbol.**

   The saved symbol can now be found by selecting Window⇨Common Library. Double-click the Custom Symbols folder to locate any symbols created and saved to the Common Library.

Adobe Illustrator has many symbols you can borrow from its symbol libraries. Simply drag a symbol from the Illustrator Symbols panel onto the artboard and then copy and paste it into Fireworks. All components, such as vector shapes, are maintained. Find out more about Illustrator symbols in Book III, Chapter 11.

Editing a symbol

You can edit a symbol object or just one instance of it. You might want to edit the symbol object if you decide to change the color of all your buttons to orange at the same time, but you'd edit each symbol instance individually if you want each button to have a different word on it.

To edit a symbol object or instance, double-click it. Then use your tools to reposition, recolor, retype, and make any other modifications that you'd make to any other graphic in Fireworks.

If you no longer want an object to be a symbol, choose Modify⇨Symbol⇨ Break Apart.

Editing a symbol without breaking the link

At times, you may want to change an instance but maintain its link to the symbol object. Perhaps you are creating a cool graphic effect of butterflies and want to change one butterfly's position and opacity, as shown in Figure 7-6.

Figure 7-6:
Edit
properties
of symbol
instances
without
breaking
the link to
the original
symbol.

You can use the Properties panel to modify the following instance properties without affecting the symbol object or other symbol instances:

+ Blending mode
+ Opacity
+ Filters
+ Width and height
+ X and y coordinates

Editing a symbol component

At times, you need to break a symbol apart so that you can edit its components, perhaps to change their colors. To edit individual components of a symbol, follow these steps:

1. **Select the symbol instance that you want to modify.**

2. **Choose Modify⇨Symbol⇨Break Apart.**

   The symbol instance is no longer linked to the symbol object.

3. **With the Subselection tool, select the components of the artwork that you want to edit.**

   They're now ready for you to make any changes that you would make to regular (non-symbol) objects on your artboard.

   When you modify the original symbol object, this instance is longer be affected.

Scaling with 9-slice

A helpful feature of Fireworks is *9-slice scaling,* which lets you determine what part of a symbol will be scaled. This feature can be extremely helpful when you are working with buttons that have rounded corners or other elements that you don't want to scale. To use this feature, simply check the Enable 9-Slice Scaling Guides check box in the Convert to Symbol dialog box.

Chapter 8: Don't Just Sit There — Animate!

In This Chapter

✓ Creating and editing animations

✓ Adjusting your playback

✓ Working with tweening

✓ Animating with masks

✓ Exporting animations for the Web

A nimations, used in moderation, can liven up a page. You can make simple animations to create effects of light and movement — or go to the max with dancing babies. The subtle approach probably is better, as most folks are more intrigued by interesting content than by distracting animations. Still, you find animations being used every day, especially in rotating banner ads.

The animations that you produce in Fireworks aren't quite the same those in Flash. Fireworks animations typically are smaller and are saved in the GIF format, which doesn't require a plug-in to view. You create them by using the States panel, which we cover in detail in Chapter 7 of this book.

In this chapter, you use the States panel to create multiple versions of your artwork that play one after another to create an animation

The terms *states* and *frames* can be used interchangeably (though we generally prefer the term *states*).

As you create images for animation, experiment to find out how many colors you can include without increasing the file size dramatically. If you're working with size restrictions (as many advertising sites require), you may have to make the image files smaller by deleting states or adjusting color. Creating animations is a give-and-take process, in which you're trying to get the best effects from the smallest files.

Getting Started with Animation

Creating images is a simple process in Fireworks. Creating images for animations is also simple but slightly different, in that the images are created from several states that play one after another to create the illusion of movement. In the first two sections of this chapter, you create a simple manual animation of a bouncing ball. Later in the chapter, you find out how to automate the process.

Creating an animation

To create an image for animation, follow these steps:

1. **Create or open the object that you want to animate.**

For this example, create a circle with the Ellipse tool.

2. **With the Pointer tool, select the circle.**

3. **Choose Window⇨States.**

The States panel appears, listing one state (see Figure 8-1).

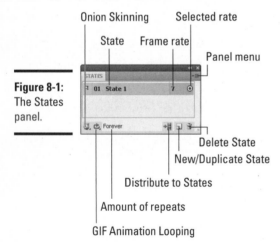

Onion Skinning   Selected rate

State   Frame rate

Panel menu

Figure 8-1:
The States
panel.

Delete State

New/Duplicate State

Distribute to States

Amount of repeats

GIF Animation Looping

4. **From the panel menu in the top-right corner, choose Duplicate State.**

The Duplicate State dialog box appears (see Figure 8-2).

5. **Use the Number slider to add three new states.**

6. **In the Insert New States section, select the After Current State radio button and then click OK.**

Because all the states are identical, you see no change. The objects are positioned on top of one another.

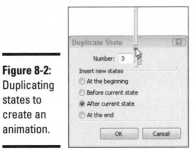

Figure 8-2:
Duplicating
states to
create an
animation.

Onion skinning

Onion skinning can be a huge help when you're trying to create a good
flow for an animation. Onion skinning gives you the opportunity to edit the
selected state but view (in a dimmed view) the states that come before and
after the selected state, as shown in Figure 8-3.

Figure 8-3:
Keep track
of the states
with onion
skinning.

To use onion skinning in your animation, follow these steps:

1. **Select the State 2 row in the States panel.**

2. **Click the Onion Skinning button in the bottom-left corner of the panel
(refer to Figure 8-1).**

   A drop-down list appears.

3. **Select Show All States to show one state before and one after the
selected state.**

Making the animation move

Creating the actual animation certainly isn't rocket science, but you need to pay attention to the state you select before making your move.

To put your animation in motion, follow these steps:

1. **Select State 2 in the States panel to view the state 2 circle.**

2. **With the Pointer tool, drag the circle slightly up and to the right.**

3. **Select State 3 to view the state 3 circle.**

4. **Drag the circle below and to the right of the state 2 circle.**

5. **Select State 4 to view the state 4 circle.**

6. **Drag the circle above and to the right of the state 3 circle.**

   You should see a flow that — in a very primitive way — represents a bouncing ball (see Figure 8-4).

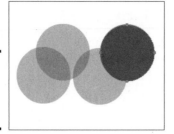

Figure 8-4:
Creating an animation manually.

Testing the animation

You can test an animation right in the Fireworks artboard or on the Web.

Testing in Fireworks

Fireworks provides several playback controls on the right side of the artboard window, as shown in Figure 8-5.

To use these controls to test an animation in Fireworks, follow these steps:

1. **Click the Play button to start the animation.**

   Notice that the Play button changes to the Stop button.

2. **After playing the animation, click the Stop button to stop the animation.**

Figure 8-5:
Test the
animation
in Fireworks
with the
playback
controls.

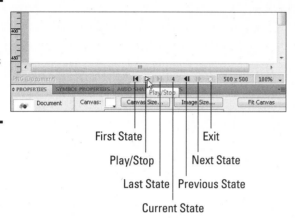

First State

Play/Stop

Last State

Current State

Exit

Next State

Previous State

In the "Adjusting Playback" section, later in this chapter, you find out how to control the speed of each state (or frame) and discover where to turn *looping* (repeat) off and on.

Adding an object to multiple states

Perhaps you created the perfect animation but then discovered that you forgot to include an element. You can copy or create the missing object in one state and then add it to all the other states. Follow these steps:

1. **Select the state in which you want the new object to appear.**

2. **Copy and paste the artwork for the new object to the selected state, or create the new object in that state.**

3. **Make sure that the new artwork is selected, right-click (Windows) or Control-click (Mac) the selected state in the States panel, and choose Copy to States from the contextual menu.**

   The Copy to States dialog box appears.

4. **Select the All States radio button (see the following figure), and click OK.**

   The selected object is included in all the states.

Testing on the Web

The Preview in Browser feature gives you a more accurate idea of how your animation will appear to the viewer. This procedure is so easy that no steps are necessary: Choose File➪Preview in Browser and select the browser in which you want to preview the animation.

Adjusting Playback

You can speed or slow an entire animation, or control the speed of each slide individually. Controlling the timing of individual states can be helpful in an advertising animation, for example, if you want to keep one state visible longer than the others. You can also loop an animation. This section describes both types of changes.

Changing the frame rate

The *frame rate* is the speed at which your animation will play. To change the frame rate, follow these steps:

1. **Select the states(s) for which you want to set the frame rate.**

2. **Choose Properties from the panel menu in the top-right corner of the States panel.**

The State Delay pop-up appears, as shown in Figure 8-6.

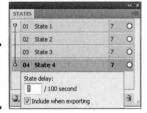

Figure 8-6:
Change the
frame rate.

3. **In the text box, enter a value (in 100ths of a second) to make the animation go faster or slower.**

The lower the value you enter, the faster the animation plays. Make sure the Include when Exporting check box is selected. Click anywhere on the artboard to close the window.

4. **(Optional) To test the results of you frame rate change, press the Play button in the lower-right side of the artboard window.**

Want to display one state longer than the others? Select only that particular state and then change its frame rate to be slower than the other states' frame rates.

Playing it again: Looping

You can choose to loop an animation into eternity or just a certain number of times. To do this, follow these steps:

1. **Click the GIF Animation Looping button in the bottom-left corner of the States panel (refer to Figure 8-1).**

   A menu drops down.

2. **Choose the number of times you want the animation to loop (see Figure 8-7).**

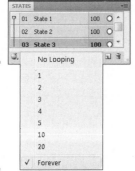

Figure 8-7:
Set the
loop for the
animation in
the States
panel.

3. **Save and close the animation.**

You've completed a manual animation. In the next section, you find out how to create an animation in which Fireworks creates the states for you automatically.

Tweening in Fireworks

Tweening is the process of creating a state between two others, usually as a start or stop point for the animation. Use tweening to simulate an object moving, like a ball bouncing, or fading an image in or out of an animation.

Creating a symbol

To use the tweening feature in Fireworks, you must have a symbol — for this example, an arrow. To create this symbol, follow these steps:

1. **Choose File⇨New and create a new document large enough to contain your animation.**

For this exercise, create a document 500 pixels by 500 pixels.

2. **Click and hold the Rectangle tool, and select the Arrow tool from the Vector section of the Tools panel.**

3. **In the top-left corner of the canvas, click and drag to create a small arrow.**

4. **Choose Modify⇨Symbol⇨Convert to Symbol.**

The Convert to Symbol dialog box appears.

5. **Type an appropriate name for the symbol in the Name text box (such as** Arrow**), select the Graphic radio button, and click OK.**

Fireworks converts your arrow graphic to a symbol.

Cloning the symbol

After you create a symbol, you need to clone the symbol to create start and end points for the animation. Follow these steps:

1. **Select the arrow symbol on the canvas.**

2. **Holding down the Alt (Windows) or Option (Mac) key, drag the arrow to the bottom-right corner of the canvas.**

As shown in Figure 8-8, by holding down the Alt/Option key while you drag, you're cloning the arrow.

3. **Choose the Scale tool in the Select section of the Tools panel, and make the cloned arrow (in the bottom-right corner) larger than the original.**

4. **With the Pointer tool, position both arrow symbols on the canvas the way you want them.**

These symbols are the start and end points for your animation, so place them where you want the animation to begin and end.

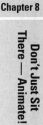

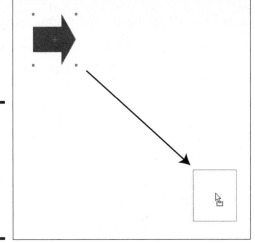

Figure 8-8:
Create a
start and
end point
for the
animation
by cloning
the symbol.

Tweening the symbols

When you have two instances of the symbol on the artboard, you're ready to tween the symbols to create an animation. Follow these steps:

1. **With the Pointer tool, select one of the arrow symbols and then Shift-click the other to select both at the same time.**

2. **Choose Modify⇨Symbol⇨Tween Instances.**

   The Tween Instances dialog box appears.

3. **Enter a value in the Steps text box.**

   For this example, enter **5** (see Figure 8-9) to create 5 new states (or frames) for transforming the small arrow into the large arrow.

Figure 8-9:
Set the
number of
states.

4. (Optional) If you want the symbols to appear one at a time, you want those states to be distributed to separate states in the States panel, so check the Distribute to States check box.

5. Click OK.

6. Test your animation by clicking the Play button in the bottom-right section of the Fireworks workspace and then save the file.

Animating with Masks

If you're a Photoshop user, you're probably familiar with masks. Masks let you choose the viewable area of an image. The process is much like cutting a hole in a piece of paper and then placing an image under it. The hole in the paper shows only the area of the image below that you want to expose; the rest of the paper masks (covers) the parts of the image that you don't want to expose.

You can take this masking feature a step further in Fireworks by animating a mask. In this section, you create a simple object and mask, and then animate the mask.

Creating an image and mask

To create the image and mask for your animation, follow these steps:

1. Create a new document that's 500 pixels by 500 pixels in size.

2. With the Star tool (hidden in the Rectangle tool), create lots of stars close together.

   Use any colors and sizes you want for the stars. This step creates multiple layers.

3. Choose Window➪Layers to open the Layers panel.

4. Click the top layer listed in the Layers panel and then Shift-click the bottom layer to select all the layers that you created.

5. From the panel menu in the Layers panel, choose Flatten Selection.

   The layers are flattened into one bitmap layer.

6. Select the Marquee tool in the Bitmap section of the Tools panel, make a narrow rectangular selection through the middle of the stars, and then click the Add Mask button at the bottom of the Layers panel (see Figure 8-10).

   Fireworks creates a mask based on the image area you selected.

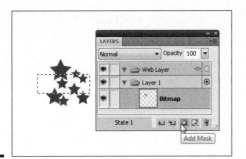

Figure 8-10:
Select an
area for
masking
(top) and the
mask based
on the
selection
(bottom).

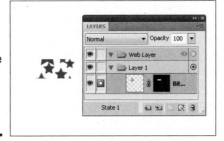

Animating the mask

In this section, you animate the mask but not the stars. Follow these steps:

1. **In the Layers panel, click the chain that appears between the stars layer and the mask.**

   This chain lets you move the layer and mask independently.

2. **In the Layers panel, click the mask to select it.**

3. **From the panel menu in the States panel, choose Duplicate State.**

   The Duplicate State dialog box appears.

4. **Select the After Current State radio button, and click OK.**

   State 2 appears.

5. **With the Pointer tool, drag the mask down slightly on the canvas.**

   The stars stay in place; only the mask moves.

6. **Repeat Step 5 at least once.**

7. **Test your animation by clicking the Play button in the bottom-right section of the Fireworks workspace.**

You can come up with some creative animations by using this technique, perhaps using a logo or other text as a mask.

Exporting an Animation

You created it, you tested it, you previewed it, and now you want to use it. To make an animation work, all you have to do is choose the GIF format in the Optimize panel. (GIF is the Web format that supports animation.) No HTML is needed.

To export an animation, follow these steps:

1. **Choose File➪Export.**

The Export dialog box appears.

2. **Choose Images Only from the Export drop-down list.**

3. **Name the file.**

4. **Put the file in your site location by navigating to the correct folder and clicking Export.**

Book VI
Soundbooth

Contents at a Glance

Chapter 1: Getting Started with Soundbooth CS4

In This Chapter

✔ **Knowing the lifecycle of Soundbooth projects**

✔ **Discovering digital audio basics**

✔ **Figuring out the Soundbooth workspace**

✔ **Creating a Soundbooth project**

✔ **Saving files into ASND format**

*I*n modern interactive projects, you find a convergence of ideas, technologies, and media — which means you need to use more tools than ever. These days it's not unusual for a simple ad banner to include animation, sound effects, and even video clips.

Audio has become a major part of any interactive project. Whether it's a Web site, an ad banner, a podcast, or a rich media presentation, you'll find that sound effects, narrative, and music are the icing on the cake; they make for a truly immersive experience for your end user.

The role of the interactive content producer has also extended to stand-alone audio/video production in the form of podcasts. A *podcast* is a downloadable audio or video file (often produced in radio- or TV-style format) that is typically downloaded from a Web site or syndicated through applications, such as iTunes.

Given all these audio possibilities, it's no surprise that Adobe's comprehensive Web Premium Creative Suite edition includes a comprehensive, full-featured audio-editing and production tool: Soundbooth CS4.

Soundbooth is a powerful, yet simple audio-editing application, geared toward media professionals who need to create high-quality audio for video, interactive applications (such as Flash movies), and Web delivery. The goal of Soundbooth is to provide the essential tools you need to create professional-quality audio even if you have no background in sound editing or production.

Soundbooth is often considered the "little brother" of *Adobe Audition,* which offers a more complete feature set dedicated to audio professionals, such as recording engineers and sound designers.

In this chapter, you find an introduction to what Soundbooth can do and to a few digital audio basics that are helpful to know as you work with Soundbooth. You also find a quick tour of the Soundbooth interface and steps that walk you through setting up a new audio project and saving it for editing later.

Discovering the Lifecycle of a Soundbooth Audio Project

Chances are you've worked on a project (or many) where music or sound effects would've added a special extra dimension to the finished product. Whether it's background music in a Flash movie, an audio narrative, or sound effects on a button, sound can create a more immersive and in turn, better overall user experience.

The trick of course is, "Where do I get that sound and how do I make it usable in my projects?" This often requires the following overall steps:

1. **Create or otherwise acquire a sound file.**

You might capture music from a CD or sound with a microphone. (See Chapter 2 of this minibook.) Alternatively, you might buy or download a free sound file from the Web. Make sure that you have permission to use this file in your project; just because you can grab the file from the Web doesn't mean it isn't under copyright.

2. **Set up your audio project in Soundbooth.**

To do so, create an empty audio file in Soundbooth and then import your sound file. See "Setting Up a Soundbooth Project" later in this chapter

3. **Edit your sound clips to the correct length and time.**

After you add audio clips to a single or multi-track project, you can cut, splice, trim, and extract audio to the length you need.

4. **Correct volume and noise issues.**

For example, if you want to post an interview on your Web site, deleting repetitious use of "um" or any popping sounds in the audio is a good idea.

5. **Export the sound to a common and useable format, such as WAV, AIFF, or MP3.**

We introduce these formats later in this chapter. You find out details of how to export in Chapter 4 of this minibook.

The good news is that Soundbooth gives you the tools to easily accomplish all these steps, so you can capture, edit, and produce audio that you can import and use in your projects. You can even take it a step farther by

✦ **Layering multiple sounds** with Soundbooth's multi-tracking capabilities (see "Creating a multi-track file" later in this chapter and in Chapter 2 of this minibook).

   Multi-track audio refers to the technique of layering sound clips one on top of another to create a combined program, musical composition, or score. This technique is used in all major music, broadcast, and podcast productions.

✦ **Adding special or creative effects,** such as echoes and pitch shifting (see Chapter 3 of this minibook).

✦ **Creating more complex soundscapes,** such as layered backgrounds for video or Flash movies.

Understanding Digital Audio Basics

Before you get deeper into working with digital audio, it makes sense to understand a little bit more about how it works. You find an introduction to converters in the sections that follow. Also, as with digital photography, there are unique ways of measuring the quality and depth of digital recorded sound, and a variety of formats that you can produce and use. Read on for details.

Capturing sounds as bytes

Sound, as we hear it in nature, is produced by a series of mechanical vibrations conducted through air, liquid, and any type of solid physical matter. Historically, these sounds have been captured into one of many analog formats, such as vinyl records, reel-to-reel tape, and audiocassettes. In these formats, some physical aspect of the medium captures and then reproduces the audio.

In the world of digital audio, sound is translated into zeroes and ones (sequences of binary numbers), which represent import aspects of that sound, such as volume and dynamics. Sound is captured from natural or analog sources and converted into digital audio by the use of *converters*.

Your computer's input jack contains a basic analog-to-digital converter that lets you capture audio from an attached microphone and then converts it into the digital realm on your computer. Along the same lines, your PC's headphone jack contains a basic digital-to-analog converter that lets you hear digital audio from your computer back through the electro-magnetic mechanism in your headphones.

In most cases, these converters you find in your computer work just fine. However many companies manufacture professional-grade digital audio converters (often called *audio interfaces*) that allow for finer capture resolution, multiple inputs, and other features.

Soundbooth supports a good deal of third-party audio hardware. If you're already using an audio interface, you can enable it in Soundbooth's Preferences panel.

Introducing sample rate and bit depth

In the world of digital photography, quality is measured by resolution and bit depth. The combinations of these two aspects determine clarity, color depth, and more. When working with digital audio, sample rate and bit depth are key in determining the quality of a sound file.

✦ **Sample rate** stands for how many samples per second represent a sound wave. The more samples per second you have, the higher the audio quality but also the larger the sound file (and the longer the download time). Sample rate is represented in khz (kilohertz), and depending on the application, you can capture and export audio at several different sample rates. Common sample rates include 22 khz (low quality audio), 44.1 khz (CD-quality audio), and 48 khz (often used for high-quality audio and video applications).

✦ **Bit depth** represents how much information each sample contains. Bit depth is crucial to the clarity and dynamics of digitally recorded sound, and as such, is often kept at 8 bits and higher. For reference, commercial CDs use a bit depth of 16 bits to accurately capture the nuances of speech, ambient sound, and of course, recorded voice and instruments.

A commercial CD stores audio at 44.1 khz/16 bits.

In Soundbooth, you can choose the sample rate and bit depth for a project as well as for any files you export from a project, as we discuss later in this chapter.

Audio can be recorded at one sample rate and bit depth and then exported at another; however, I recommend avoiding up-sampling (increasing sample rate) or converting lower-quality audio to higher-quality audio simply by changing sample rate and bit depth. As with forcibly increasing pixel resolution of a digital photo, this creates unwanted artifacts and doesn't actually increase the resulting quality of the audio.

Choosing mono versus stereo

Most audio you hear, such as music coming from your car stereo, your favorite CDs, or songs in your MP3 collection are represented in *stereo,* or two independent left and right audio channels. *Mono* (or *monaural*) sound reproduces sound through a single channel.

✦ **Stereo:** The left and right audio channels are what create the illusion of space or the placement of sounds, and is close to what you hear in real life. Stereo allows you to hear the spatial relationships among multiple instruments, voices, or ambient sounds and is best heard through a properly configured set of stereo speakers or headphones.

✦ **Mono:** With only one channel, mono sound lacks the spatial effects of stereo sound. However, mono sound still plays an important role in audio production because many sounds (such as a single voice or a bass guitar) are typically captured as a mono sound. Very often, several mono channels are mixed together and arranged spatially to create stereo sound files.

The choice of recording in mono or stereo varies for each project and application. It's safe to say, however, that many sound sources, such as a single voice or one instrument, are often captured as mono and mixed and arranged with other sounds into a final stereo image. Live music, however, is typically captured (with a proper stereo microphone) in stereo because a natural spatial arrangement already exists. If you want to record music and add a singer or a speech track, check out *Home Recording For Musicians For Dummies,* 3rd Edition, by Jeff Strong (Wiley).

When recording digital audio, a stereo sound occupies twice as much space on your hard drive as a mono sound. Recording in stereo doesn't necessarily increase sound quality and often is unnecessary unless the source has some spatial properties to it already.

Checking out common audio file formats

The specific file format you choose isn't quite as crucial as the recorded quality and production; however, Soundbooth supports several different formats and depending on your final project, some applications favor a single format.

Soundbooth supports the import and export of many common formats, including

+ **AIFF (Audio Interchange File Format)** is an uncompressed audio format commonly used on Mac-based systems and can be imported by other applications, such as Flash and iTunes.

+ **WAV (Windows Waveform Audio Format)** is an uncompressed audio format most commonly utilized by Windows-based computer systems, although like AIFF, is widely supported in a variety of applications on both platforms.

+ **MP3 (MPEG 1 Audio Layer 3)** compresses audio files to a small size, using *lossy* compression, which substantially reduces the amount of data in an audio file while faithfully reproducing the original audio. For this reason, MP3, even at higher bit rates, is often considered sub-CD quality. Unlike WAV or AIFF, MP3 uses bit rate (rather than sample rate or bit depth) to determine quality.

MP3 is typically used for Web delivery of audio and as the standard file format for digital audio players, such as iPods and Zunes.

+ **MOV (Apple QuickTime)** is often recognized as a video format but can also exclusively contain audio. QuickTime is Apple's versatile media format and can be generated from Soundbooth as well as many other applications, such as QuickTime Pro, Final Cut Pro, and Adobe Premiere.

All the above listed formats can be exported at different sample rates and bit depths, or in some cases (such as MP3), have quality settings that are unique to that format alone. See Chapter 4 in this minibook for details about exporting.

Getting to Know the Soundbooth Workspace

Soundbooth has a simple, yet powerful set of tools and panels that put most every audio task at your fingertips. You can manage your audio resources, record, edit, and sequence complex multi-track files, and apply effects. As shown in Figure 1-1, the toolbar and Files panel are always handy:

+ **Toolbar:** These tools allow you to make selections and move clips in the editing window. You also have additional tools to view your clip and make selections in the Spectral Frequency Display.

+ **Files panel:** Displays any currently open project files and files you've recorded or imported into the current active project. Multi-track projects appear with their respective source files listed and indented below them.

Spectral Frequency Display

Time Selection

Move

Hand

Zoom

Lasso

Frequency Selector

Rectangular Marquee

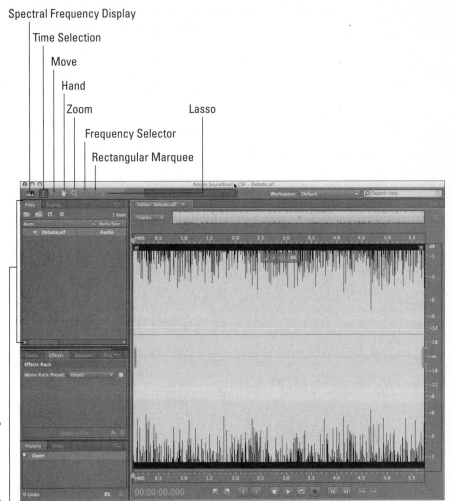

Figure 1-1:
The
Soundbooth
workspace.

Files panel

Setting Up a Soundbooth Project

The first steps to getting up and running are to make sure that you understand how to create and work with new files and import audio. You can create simple projects for quick work on a single audio file or more elaborate ones that combine multiple tracks of audio with complex effects and edits. Before you get started, remember to set up an empty audio file in Soundbooth and then import audio files you want to use as source material into that Soundbooth file.

If you plan to use Soundbooth to record live audio input from your computer's built-in microphone, an attached mic, or an audio device, flip to Chapter 2 in this minibook.

Creating a new empty audio file

If you're planning on working with a single audio file, you can create a single track project, which allows you to compose and edit one file to be saved in the file format of your choice. Files can also be saved to the ASND (Adobe Soundbooth) file format if you want to keep certain project settings and resume editing later.

To create a new empty audio file:

1. **Choose File⇨New⇨Empty Audio File, as shown in Figure 1-2.**

   The New Audio File dialog box appears, where you can choose sample rate and channel settings for your project.

2. **Select a sample rate from the Sample Rate drop-down list.**

   This varies based on your source files and your project needs.

   A sample rate of 44,100 is equal to 44.1 khz (CD-quality audio), as we discuss earlier in this chapter. Sample rate is equal to cycles divided by 1,000 (48,000 = 48 khz).

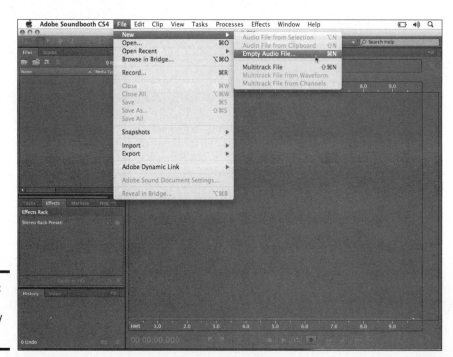

Figure 1-2:
Create a new empty audio file.

3. **Choose your channel configuration by selecting the Mono or Stereo radio button, as shown in Figure 1-3.**

   If you plan on editing music or combined audio material (voice, music, and sound effects), you most likely want to select the Stereo radio button for your channel configuration.

4. **Click OK to exit the dialog box.**

   A new empty editor window appears in the workspace. You can now import a source file into your project, as we explain in the upcoming section, "Importing audio files."

Figure 1-3:
Choose
a sample
rate and
a channel
config-
uration.

Creating a multi-track file

You can create a single piece of audio from multiple source files if necessary by creating a multi-track file. *Multi-track files* allow you to layer several pieces of audio on top of each other to create complex audio files that include music, narration, sound effects, and more. This approach is especially useful when you're creating backgrounds and soundscapes for interactive or video projects but can also be used to weave several files together into one. Almost every album you enjoy in your music collection was recorded this way!

To create a new multi-track file, choose File⇨New⇨Multi-Track File. Select a sample rate and bit depth for your project and click OK. A new, empty multi-track editing window appears in the workspace. You can now import a source file into your project, as we explain in the following section, "Importing audio files."

Importing audio files

Every one of your single or multi-track files begins with some type of source audio. Source audio can come from a file that already exists on your hard drive or that you downloaded from the Internet. Source audio can be music or audio content captured from a CD or audio you recorded directly into Soundbooth with a microphone or a line attached to your computer's mic input.

Most commonly, you take audio from a variety of sources to compose one single audio track or layer them together in a multi-track audio file. Before you can save a file, import some source audio content into your project. Audio can be imported from one of the common audio file formats you already read about (if you've followed along in this chapter) or from a source video file, such as a DV (digital video format taken by most cameras) or QuickTime movie.

To import audio into a project:

1. **Create a new empty audio file or multi-track project, which we discuss earlier in this chapter.**

2. **Choose File⇨Import⇨Files.**

The Import Files dialog box appears.

3. **Locate and select one or more audio or video files that you want to import.**

Select multiple files by clicking while holding down the Shift key.

4. **Click Open to import the files.**

Note: Source audio files will be converted to the sample rate you selected for your project. The audio files you selected will appear in the Files panel in the upper-left corner of the workspace, as shown in Figure 1-4.

Figure 1-4: Imported files will appear in your Files panel.

Saving Files from Soundbooth

If you're ready to save a final file or if you want to save your current project and work on it later, you can save your single or multi-track file into a number of different formats, including WAV, AIFF, MP3, or the QuickTime and Soundbooth ASND format. You can read about many of these common formats earlier in this chapter.

Adobe Soundbooth can save files in the handy and portable ASND file format, which allows you to save edits, source clips, and settings so you can continue editing a single or multi-track project later. The ASND file format packages together all your current work and source audio clips so the file can be easily moved without the need to locate your original source clips later.

Because ASND packages all your source audio in one file, ASND files can be rather large. Make sure that you have a sufficient amount of hard drive space available to accommodate any ASND files you create.

To save a single audio file:

1. **Choose File⇨Save As.**

The Save As dialog box appears.

2. **Choose a location on your hard drive to save the file in, and type a name for your file in the File Name/Save As field.**

3. **Click the Save as Type/Format drop-down list to choose a format and click Save.**

Note: If you choose any file format other than ASND, you're presented with the one of a few different dialog boxes that allow you to choose save options for your new file. These dialog boxes and their settings are discussed in detail in Chapter 4 of this minibook.

Chapter 2: Recording and Editing Audio

In This Chapter

✔ Recording audio in Soundbooth

✔ Sequencing, editing, and mixing audio

✔ Working in multi-track files

✔ Balancing clip levels

✔ Sequencing audio in a multi-track file

✔ Using the History panel and snapshots

Soundbooth makes it possible for you to also record audio from a built-in or attached microphone on your computer, allowing you to create your own narration and to record sound effects, live music, or even audio from devices, such as CD and tape players.

After you have some audio (either imported or recorded) in your file, you're ready to perform edits, such as fades, transitions, trims, and full-on splicing among different files to create composites. When working with multi-track files, you can even perform complex edits across several tracks and layer and sequence lots of different source files together! This chapter shows you how.

To work with the steps in this chapter, you need to know how to create new files and import audio into those files from various sources. For an introduction to these tasks, flip to Chapter 1 of this minibook.

Recording Audio with Soundbooth

Soundbooth can easily work with the built-in microphone on your computer or an attached microphone to capture live audio from whatever source you choose. You can add narration to an existing music track, capture ambient sounds, or even make some noise to create a useful sound effect for your project. Audio recording is a world of its own, but you don't need to be an engineer to get some great results from Soundbooth.

The following sections explain how to choose a microphone and record your own audio. You also find tips for previewing and playing back your recorded file.

Choosing a microphone

The right microphone can make a huge difference when trying to faithfully capture a sound as it's heard. The built-in microphone on most computers is suitable for very basic audio needs, but if your computer has an audio input jack or a USB (Universal Serial Bus) port, you have a few more options in terms of microphone type and quality.

✦ **Computer microphones** are usually built specifically for basic media applications or meant to be a slight upgrade to a built-in computer mic. Companies, such as Logitech, Plantronics, and Sony make a variety of multimedia microphones that range in price and style. Most computer mics connect via the computer's ⅛ inch stereo audio jack, USB port, or both.

✦ **Hand-held and pro audio microphones** are typically built for more intensive audio needs and deliver higher quality and sensitivity across a variety of price ranges. Companies, such as Audio-Technica, Electro-Voice, Sennheiser, and Samson make a variety of dynamic (magnet-based) or condenser (electro-static) microphones that plug in via a USB, a standard XLR (a 3-pin standard microphone cable) or a ¼ inch connector.

Choosing a microphone comes down to two important factors: price and performance. After you select a price range, choose a microphone based on the type of source audio it's best suited for. If you're recording music, you may choose a stereo microphone, such as the Sony ECM series microphones. For narration, dialog, or sound effects, the Samson C03U USB is a good example of a mid-priced condenser microphone that captures a substantial amount of detail.

Note: I mention these specific manufacturer's and models for example purposes only, not to endorse a specific product or a manufacturer. You'll find a lot of mics on the market, and it pays to shop around, try them out, and find one you're comfortable with.

If you're new to recording but plan to invest in music recording equipment for the long term, check out *Home Recording for Musicians For Dummies,* 3rd Edition, by Jeff Strong.

Recording audio into a Soundbooth file

To record new audio into your file:

1. **Create a new empty audio file or a multi-track file, as we explain in Chapter 1 of this minibook.**

2. **Choose File⇨Record.**

   The Record dialog box appears.

3. **Under the Input section at the top of the dialog box, select your recording device from the Device drop-down list.**

This can be the built-in audio input of your computer, your audio card name, or an external audio interface if you have one.

4. **Select a sample rate for the new file from the Sample Rate drop-down list.**

   For best results, select the rate that matches your current file. We explain sample rate in Chapter 1 of this minibook.

5. **From the Port drop-down list, select the port where your input device (microphone) is connected.**

   This will likely be your internal mic, the computer's audio jack, or a USB port.

6. **Under the Save section, enter a name for your new recording in the File Name field.**

7. **Directly to the right of the File Name field, choose how you want Soundbooth to uniquely name several audio files recorded in the same session.**

   For instance, you can have each file have a unique numerical ID, as shown in Figure 2-1, or time stamp.

8. **Click the Browse button and select a new folder or disc to choose where you want to save your recorded audio file.**

9. **Do a brief level test by speaking into the mic or playing the audio that you want to record.**

   If you've chosen a valid device and port, you see the meter on the right side of the Record dialog box moving up and down as the microphone picks up sound.

   The levels should send the meter no more than about ³/₄ of the way up (in yellow), as shown in Figure 2-2. If you see red bars at the top, your level is too high and should be adjusted.

Figure 2-1: The Record dialog box lets you check levels and choose settings for any newly recorded audio files.

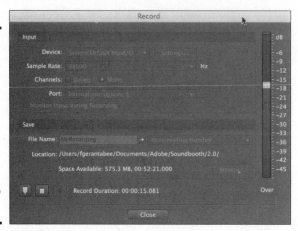

10. (Optional) **Adjust audio levels** by moving the microphone farther away from the source audio (such as your mouth or an instrument), or by clicking the Settings button on the Record dialog box and adjusting input levels for your device.

11. **Click the Record button** at the bottom of the dialog box to begin recording; click the Stop button when you're done recording.

12. (Optional) **Repeat Steps 6–11** to record several clips.

13. **Click the Close button** when you're done recording to exit the dialog box.

    The clip(s) you recorded appear in the Files panel of your current project, as shown in Figure 2-3.

Previewing and playing back audio

At any time, you can listen to an active clip in the editing window, an entire sequence in a multi-track file, or a selected piece of audio. When recording your own audio, playing back your recording is especially important because you want to ensure that the quality and clarity of the recording meets your needs.

You may want to do a test run to ensure that your recording is free from extraneous noise (such as machine noise or chair squeaks), is at a useable volume, and that mic placement isn't causing too many pops or clicks. Although some of these can be fixed in editing, it's best to make sure that you create the cleanest quality original recording possible.

✦ **To listen to an active clip, multi-track sequence, or a selection** in the editing window, press the spacebar. To stop playing the clip, press the spacebar again.

✦ **To move the playhead slowly through an audio clip or a sequence (referred to as *scrubbing*),** grab the playhead from its handle on the time ruler at the top of the editing window and drag it back and forth along the ruler. This allows you to move slowly through an audio clip to review a specific section.

✦ **Use the transport controls** located at the bottom of the editing window, to play, stop, or skip to the beginning or end of an audio clip or selection. See Figure 2-4.

Your recorded clip appears in the Files panel

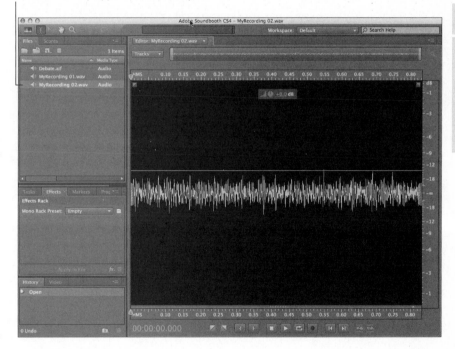

Figure 2-3:
Your newly recorded files appear in the Files panel with the naming convention and increment you chose.

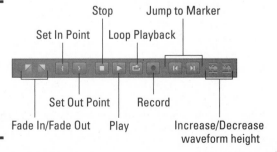

Figure 2-4:
The transport bar lets you play back, rewind, and loop your clip.

Stop

Jump to Marker

Set In Point

Loop Playback

Set Out Point

Play

Record

Fade In/Fade Out

Increase/Decrease
waveform height

The following explains each button on the transport bar from left to right:

✦ **Fade In/Fade Out:** Creates a fade in from the beginning of the clip to the position of the playhead or a fade out from the position of the playhead to the end of the clip, respectively.

✦ **Set In/Out Point:** Sets the in point of the clip at the playhead position or sets the out point of the clip at the playhead position, respectively.

✦ **Stop:** Stops playback.

✦ **Play:** Plays clip from current playhead position.

✦ **Loop Playback:** Repeats playback of the current selection in the window.

✦ **Record:** Activates recording with an attached line device or a microphone.

✦ **Jump to Marker:** Jumps to the previous or next marker along the timeline.

✦ **Increase/Decrease Waveform Height:** Increases the size of audio waveforms to make editing and viewing easier.

Editing and Sequencing Audio

The power and purpose of Soundbooth lies in its simple, yet effective, editing abilities. For each and every project, whether a Web site, an interactive presentation, a video project, or a podcast, you'll have a reason and a need to edit audio for length, content, and quality.

You can perform lots of editing tasks directly in the editing window, all while viewing a graphical waveform representation of your audio. Cut and splice between different audio files, trim start or end times, or create cool fade ins and outs. The following sections outline the steps you need to take to polish your recorded audio.

Placing audio files in the editing window

After you import or record audio and have files sitting in the Files panel, you can place them in the editing window so you can begin to work with them right away.

To place an audio file in a multi-track file:

1. **Choose File⇨Open, locate a Soundbooth multi-track ASND project file, and choose Open to open the project.**

2. **With a multi-track project open, locate the Files panel in the upper-left corner of your workspace.**

3. **If you haven't already, import some files into your project so they appear in the Files panel.**

   See Chapter 1 of this minibook for a refresher on importing files.

4. **Click and drag a file from the Files panel into the editing window on the right.**

   The clip appears as a waveform on a track in the editing window.

Trimming, cutting, and pasting

Very often, you need to trim down your source audio files or cut and paste between several audio files to get the single result you need. Soundbooth lets you use many of the keyboard shortcuts you may be familiar with in other applications as well as several visual tools to get your audio looking and sounding exactly the way you want it!

To trim an audio file:

1. **In a new single or multi-track file, place an audio file from your Files panel into the editing window.**

   Note: To trim a clip in a multi-track file, you must first double-click the clip you want to edit; it then appears in a new editing window.

   When you are done editing a clip in a multi-track project, use the Back button that sits in the top left corner of the editing window to return back to the multi-track view.

2. **Move your pointer over the trim handle that sits at the beginning of the active clip so that your cursor displays a bracketed arrow.**

   The trim handle appears as a small grey bar on the left and right sides of a selected clip in the editing window.

3. **Click and drag toward the right to move the handle and adjust the beginning point of your audio. Release the mouse to set the new start point.**

   To undo the trim point you just set, choose Edit⇨Undo to undo the last trim operation.

4. **Move your pointer over the trim handle at the end of the audio clip until your cursor displays a bracketed arrow; click and drag to the left to move the handle and trim the ending point of your file, as shown in Figure 2-5.**

Time Selection tool   Click and drag a handle

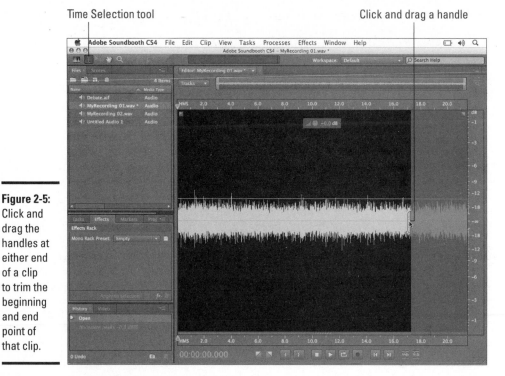

Figure 2-5:
Click and
drag the
handles at
either end
of a clip
to trim the
beginning
and end
point of
that clip.

To crop or cut an audio file:

1. **From the toolbar in the top-left corner of the workspace, select the
Time Selection tool.**

2. **Click and drag your cursor over an audio clip in the editing window
to highlight a portion of the clip.**

The selection appears in white.

3. **To adjust the beginning of your selection, move your pointer over
the left edge of the selected area on the clip until a bracketed arrow
appears; click and drag to adjust the beginning point of the selection.**

4. **Do one of the following:**

- *To cut and remove the selection from the clip,* choose Edit⇨Cut or
Ctrl+X (Windows)/⌘+X (Mac).

- *To crop the clip and leave behind only the selected audio,* choose
Edit⇨Crop.

- *To copy a selected portion of a clip to paste in another clip or track,*
choose Edit⇨Copy or Ctrl+C (Windows)/⌘+C (Mac).

- *To paste a clip or selected audio to a new location on a single audio file or to another track,* reposition the playhead by dragging it or clicking in the editing window and choosing Edit➪Paste or Ctrl+V (Windows)/⌘+V (Mac).

Creating fade ins and fade outs

One of the most common and effective ways of introducing, ending, or switching among audio clips is a *fade* — a gradual rise or drop in volume. This provides a smooth intro to a piece of music, a transition between two pieces of audio, or just a good way to clean up an edit performed on a clip.

Soundbooth makes it easy to create fades with a special set of Fade In and Fade Out handles that appear on each clip in a single or multi-track file.

To create a fade in or a fade out:

1. **Select a clip on a specific track in a multi-track file or place a single file from the Files panel into the editing window in a new empty audio file.**

 2. **Locate and move your mouse pointer over the Fade In handle in the top-left corner of the clip's waveform view in the editing window.**

The 4-way arrow cursor appears.

3. **Click and drag toward the right.**

A diagonal line appears from the bottom to the top of the waveform, representing the gradual rise in volume from the beginning of the clip.

4. **For a longer fade in, pull the handle to the right; for a shorter fade, pull it toward the left. Release the mouse button to set the fade.**

5. **Locate and move your pointer over the Fade Out handle in the upper-right corner of the waveform until the 4-way arrow cursor appears.**

6. **Click and drag toward the left to set a fade out.**

As with the fade in, a diagonal line is drawn to indicate the gradual drop in volume to the end of the clip, as shown in Figure 2-6.

 7. **Release the mouse when you've created a fade out of the desired length.**

The farther the handle is from the end of the clip, the longer the fade out effect.

 8. **Press the spacebar to preview the clip.**

You can easily readjust your fade ins and fade outs by repeating Steps 2–7.

To create smooth transition between two overlapping audio clips, you can create a cross fade. A cross fade is a fade out on one clip that occurs at the same time as a fade in on another, creating a smooth dissolve between the two clips.

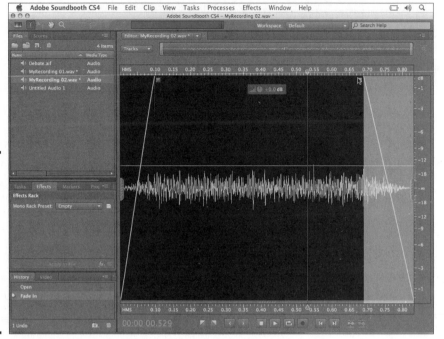

Figure 2-6:
Create fade ins and fade outs by dragging the fade handles in the upper corners of the waveform.

To create a cross fade between two clips in a multi-track file:

1. **Locate two overlapping clips on two separate tracks in your multi-track file.**

2. **Select the first (the first clip that will play) of the two clips.**

   Fade In and Fade Out handles appear on the top-left and top-right corners of the clip.

3. **Use the techniques shown in the preceding exercise (about how to create a fade in or a fade out) to create a fade out at the end of the selected clip, as shown in Figure 2-7.**

4. **Select the second clip that plays after the first.**

5. **Use the techniques shown in the preceding exercise (about how to create a fade in or a fade out) to create a fade in at the beginning of the selected clip.**

6. **Preview the new transition by pressing the spacebar to play back the sequence.**

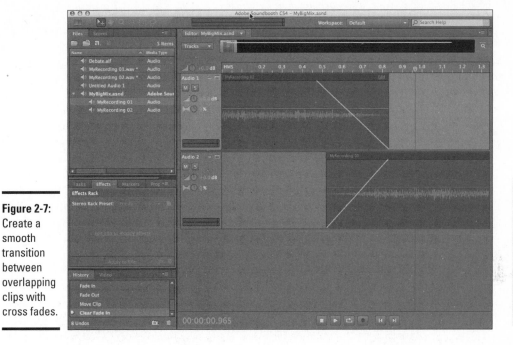

**Book VI
Chapter 2**

Recording and
Editing Audio

Figure 2-7:
Create a
smooth
transition
between
overlapping
clips with
cross fades.

Adjusting clip volume

One task that you may need to perform often is to change the volume level of a clip or several clips in a project. You can raise or lower the overall volume of a clip or a selected portion of a clip as necessary. This is especially useful if you're trying to balance the levels of two overlapping clips in a multi-track file or even out multiple audio events within a single clip.

Soundbooth provides control over the volume envelope in a very visual and tactile way directly in the editing window. You can also automatically match volumes between different clips in your project with the Match Volume menu command and panel.

Changing the volume for part of clip

To edit the volume envelope for a specific portion of a clip:

1. **In a single or multi-track file, select a clip in the editing window.**

You see a pale blue line running horizontally across the waveform — this represents the volume level of your clip.

2. **Move your pointer over the blue line at the point where you want to change the clip's volume and click. See Figure 2-8.**

   A handle is created on the line at that point.

3. **Click and drag the handle up or down.**

   While you drag, a small flag displays the current level at that point (such as +2.0). *Note:* You may have to create more than one handle to properly adjust the volume for a specific portion of a clip.

4. **(Optional) You can always return to any handles you've created and adjust them, using the same techniques as in Step 3.**

By default, the level for a clip is set to 0 dB, which represents the actual recorded volume of the clip. Raising the level above 0 dB increases *gain,* or boosting levels above the clip's original volume. Lowering the level below 0 dB is referred to as *attenuation* because you're actually decreasing the clip's original volume. Values range from –30 dB to +30 dB.

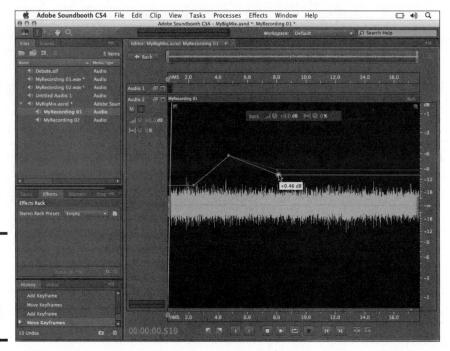

Figure 2-8:
Modify the volume of your clip at different points.

Changing the volume of an entire clip or selection

To raise or lower volume for an entire clip or selection:

1. **In a single or multi-track file, select a clip in the editing window or use the Time Selection tool to select a portion of an active clip.**

   A volume pop-up bubble appears over the selected clip or section, which features a rotary knob style control and a slider that displays the current volume.

2. **Click and drag over the knob or the value to the left or right to decrease or increase the volume, respectively.**

   The height of the waveform increases vertically as volume increases.

Waveforms are a graphic representation of *amplitude,* or the level of audio throughout a clip. The *spikes* (peaks) and *dips* (valleys) reflect the overall dynamics of a clip. Use these as a visual aid when balancing levels between different portions of a single clip.

Matching volume among clips

Soundbooth has a very handy feature that allows you to match the volume between several clips in your Files panel. This is especially crucial when your source audio comes from many different places. Depending on how the audio was recorded, the content of the clip, and the treatment applied afterward, each clip will likely have a different overall perceived level.

The Match Volume menu command and panel allow you to apply a standard level across several of your source audio files and even to match them by using an existing file in your Files panel as a reference.

To match volume between clips:

1. **Choose Tasks⇨Match Volume.**

   The Match Volume panel expands on the left side of your workspace (within the Tasks panel group).

2. **In your Files panel, select any and all clips whose volume you want to match.**

3. **Drag the selected files from the Files panel to the Files to Match panel, as shown in Figure 2-9.**

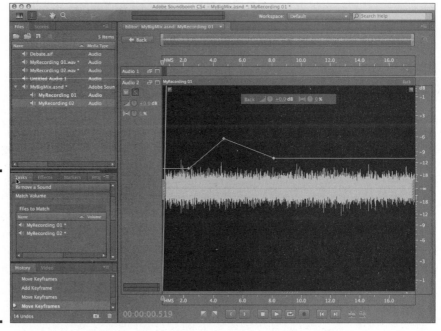

Figure 2-9:
Drag
several
clips to
match their
volume to a
reference
clip or a set
value.

4. **Choose from one of two ways to balance the clips:**

   - *To match the volume by using a manually-specified average for all clips,* select the Match to Volume radio button below the Files to Match panel. Directly to the right of the radio button, click and drag left or right over the volume value to set an average level for all clips.

   - *To match clips to the volume of an existing clip,* select the Match to File radio button. From the drop-down list shown, select a file from your Files panel to use as the reference point.

5. **Click the Match Volume button below the Files to Match panel to complete the operation.**

Match Volume permanently alters the overall level of files in your Files panel. To do basic level adjustments or balancing among tracks, use the techniques shown earlier in this chapter in the "Adjusting clip volume" section.

Working with Multi-Track Files

A new and welcome addition to Soundbooth's extensive feature set is the ability to create multi-track files, allowing you to sequence and layer together several clips simultaneously. This opens the door to complex arrangements of music, sound effects, narration, and more that are usually possible only with more expensive audio software.

Creating a new multi-track file is discussed in Chapter 1 of this minibook. In that chapter, you read how to add to that file and sequence and stack several clips across different tracks.

What are tracks and how do they help?

Think of a track as an audio *layer,* much like you'd layer artwork in a graphics application, such as Photoshop or Illustrator. However, instead of two overlapping clips obscuring one another, they actually blend and play simultaneously. This is actually how most of your favorite albums are recorded, with each of many instruments being recorded to a separate track and composed together into one, complete song.

By using a multi-track file, you can isolate, sequence, mix, and spatially spread out several clips at once. These tracks can later be exported to a single mono or stereo audio file to be used in your project.

Adding tracks

To add tracks to a multi-track file:

1. **Choose File⇨New⇨Multi-Track File to create a new, empty multi-track file.**

2. **Import two or more audio clips, which we discuss in Chapter 1 of this minibook, so that you have several individual clips to work with in the Files panel.**

3. **To add more tracks, do one of the following:**

   • Choose Edit⇨Track⇨Add Audio Track.

   • Right-click on the track title or track controls on the left side of the editing window and choose Insert Audio Track from the context menu that appears, as shown in Figure 2-10.

4. **To add a clip to the empty track, click and drag a clip from the Files panel directly onto the track in the editing window.**

   Your clip is now ready to sequence or mix, as we explain later in this chapter.

You can create several tracks at once by dragging several clips from the Files panel. Hold down the Shift key and click to select more than one track in the Files panel.

Tracks appear from top to bottom in the order they were created. If you're creating tracks by dragging clips to the editing window, drag them one by one in the order that you want them to appear.

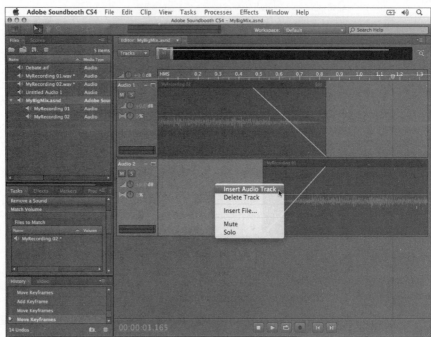

Figure 2-10:
You can
add tracks
by right-
clicking
near the
track
title and
controls and
choosing
Insert Audio
Track.

Renaming tracks

New tracks will appear generically named (Audio 1, Audio 2, and so on) until
you rename them. We always recommend naming your tracks with a descriptive name (such as Narration) to make it easy to navigate clips in your project. To rename a track, double-click the track title on its far left. Type in a
new name and hit Enter/Return.

Controlling multi-track views

After you begin a multi-track project and build several tracks, take some time
to modify the appearance of those tracks in the editing window. This includes
zooming in or out of the waveform display, collapsing tracks and more:

✦ **To collapse or expand a track,** use the collapse or expand icons in the
  upper-left corner of the track itself (directly to the right of the track title).

✦ **To view more tracks,** use the horizontal scroll bar on the right side of
  the editing window to go up or down in the track display.

✦ **To zoom in/out and see more or less of the waveform display,** use the
  + or – keys (respectively), or grab and drag the right edge of the track
  navigator at the top of the editing window.

✦ **To view audio outside the immediate view of the editing window,** grab the ridged icon in the middle of the track navigator at the top of the editing window and drag it back and forth.

✦ **To resize the track display or track controls,** move your mouse pointer over the divider between the track display and the track controls on the left. When your cursor turns into a double arrow, click and drag the divider to resize the track controls and track display.

✦ **To fit the entire sequence (horizontally) in the editing window,** choose View➪Zoom Out Full or click the Zoom Out Full button in the top-right corner of the editing window.

Sequencing and Mixing Audio

If you've followed along so far, you've built a multi-track file and placed several audio clips, time to begin moving things around, balancing levels, and positioning audio spatially in the stereo spectrum.

The following steps outline a typical workflow:

1. A good mix starts when each clip has a proper volume relative to other clips within the sequence. See the "Adjusting clip volume" section earlier in this chapter.

2. Pan (position between the left and right speakers) each clip so that it has a place within the stereo spectrum.

3. Arrange clips along the timeline to sequence audio in the order you want it to play back.

4. Perform some clean edits and smooth transitions (such as cross fades) and you're on your way to a great finished product.

Sequencing tracks

To move a clip along a track to a specific point in time:

1. **Open or create a multi-track file with several clips placed across two or more tracks in the editing window.**

2. **Move your pointer over a clip in the editing window; click and drag back and forth to move the clip farther down or up, respectively, in the sequence.**

This controls the point in time that the audio clip plays relative to the others in your project.

3. **To trim the beginning or end of a clip without moving it, move your cursor over the beginning or end of a clip until you see the bracketed arrow appear; click and drag to the left or right to trim or expand, respectively, the clip.**

   Editing the in and out time of a clip further controls when and what portion of that sound plays back in your sequence.

   See the "Trimming, cutting, and pasting" section earlier in this chapter for a more detailed explanation of trimming.

4. **To move a clip from one track to another, click and drag on a clip and drag it up or down to a different track.**

   This is useful if you want to sequence two clips back to back on the same track, or *stagger* audio clips to easily perform cross fades and transitions.

   Note: Moving a clip from its original track doesn't remove that track, even if it's empty.

Working with mute, solo, and pan

Each track has a set of controls that allows you to alter several aspects of all audio on that track at once:

✦ **Mute:** You can *mute,* or silence, a track when you don't want to hear it in the mix either temporarily or permanently.

✦ **Solo:** This is handy when you want to hear the audio on a specific track without the other tracks.

✦ **Pan:** To change a track's position between the right and left speakers, use the Pan control.

Each of these settings contributes to a track's place in the mix and can all be accomplished from the track controls on the far-left side of the track.

To mute or solo a track:

1. **Click the Mute button on a specific track.**

   This silences the track when the sequence plays back.

2. **Press the spacebar or the Play button at the bottom of the editing window to listen to your sequence.**

   The muted track no longer plays back.

3. **Choose a track and click the Solo button.**

4. **Press the spacebar or the Play button at the bottom of the editing window to listen to your sequence.**

   Only the track with solo activated will be heard.

The track controls feature a pan knob that allows you to change the perceived position of a sound in the stereo image. This is how a sound can appear to be coming from the left, right, center, or moving around within the soundstage.

Panning is also an effective way of spreading out several tracks and giving each their own *space* within the stereo image. This reproduces how your ears may hear several sounds in an enclosed space or outdoors.

To pan a track:

1. **Choose a track that you want to pan and locate the pan knob on the left side of the track.**

   The knob appears in the middle position with a value of zero (center).

2. **Click and drag over the knob to the left or right, as shown in Figure 2-11.**

   The value changes and is preceded by an L (Left) or an R (Right), depending on the direction you move it.

   Turning the Pan control to R100 or L100 removes it completely from the opposite channel.

3. **Press the spacebar or the Play button at the bottom of the editing window to listen to your sequence.**

   The track you panned is now stronger on the left or right channel depending on your chosen setting.

   Note: For an accurate listening experience, use a pair of stereo headphones or speakers.

Figure 2-11:
The track
controls for
a Narration
audio track
in solo with
a slight right-
side pan.

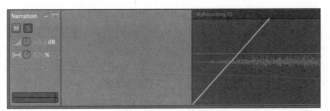

Undoing with the History Panel and Snapshots

Soundbooth, like some applications you may already use, has a History panel that lets you step back in time to return to tasks you've done previously. This is useful when you want to undo several commands at once or start over from a certain point in your workflow.

In addition, you can save snapshots of your work at different points in time in the event that you want to revert to a previous point and state in your project.

Working with the History panel

To open and work with the History panel, click its tab in the lower-left corner of your workspace. If the History panel isn't visible, choose Window➪History to open it. Each time you carry out a task, such as performing an edit or a fade or adding a track, you see a new history state listed in the History panel. You may see several already from your work up until this point.

The following are two of the most useful tasks in the History panel:

+ **To jump to a previous state in your work,** click and select that state in the History panel. Each state contains a description that helps you understand what occurred (such as Move Clip or Cut Selection).

+ **To delete a state,** click to select it and then click the Trash can icon located at the bottom of the History panel. *Note:* Deleting states can save valuable hard drive space when working with large files.

Changing settings, such as pan, doesn't reflect in the History panel; however, these settings are captured as part of snapshots (see the next section, "Creating and recalling snapshots").

Creating and recalling snapshots

A *snapshot* saves the overall state of your project at a specific point in time and lets you revert your file back to that state at any point during your work. This is useful if you're making major changes and decide later that you may want to go back and start over.

Snapshots save valuable information such as files, track control settings (volume and pan), and effects settings.

To create a snapshot:

1. **Locate the History panel and click its tab to bring it forward.**

   Note: If the History panel isn't visible, choose Window➪History to open it.

2. **Click the Snapshot icon at the bottom of the History panel to open the Snapshot menu.**

3. **Select New Snapshot from the menu.**

   The New Snapshot dialog box appears.

4. **Type a name for your snapshot in the Name field and click OK to create your new snapshot.**

To recall a snapshot:

1. **Click the Snapshot icon at the bottom of the History panel to open the Snapshot menu.**

All your snapshots are listed at the top of the menu.

2. **Select the Snapshot you want to recall, as shown in Figure 2-12.**

Your project reloads to the exact settings and appearance that you saved with your snapshot.

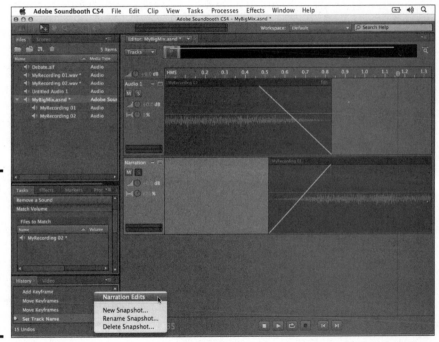

Figure 2-12: You can recall your saved snapshots or create new ones from the Snapshot menu.

Chapter 3: Applying EQ, Effects, and Dynamics

In This Chapter

✔ Sweetening audio with EQ

✔ Adding equalizer settings

✔ Controlling dynamics with compression

✔ Working with effects

✔ Saving effects presets

*P*utting the finishing touches on a sound file sometimes requires more than basic editing and sequencing. Depending on how your source audio was recorded or what type of overall sound you're looking for, you may want to make use of Soundbooth's extensive set of sonic shaping tools, such as equalizers (EQ) and effects. Whether you're looking for a way to clean or enhance recorded audio, to blend sounds more fluidly, or to create artistic soundscapes, you can leverage and combine the many included effects in the Effect panel for a polished result.

Working with Equalizers (EQ)

You may not realize it but you've very likely worked with equalizers before. Each time you adjust the bass or treble in your car stereo, choose an EQ preset from your iPod, or play with the equalizer settings (such as bass and treble) in your home stereo, you're increasing or decreasing certain frequencies in a recorded piece of audio. Ultimately, this makes that music or audio sound better to your ears.

In professional audio recording, EQ is part art, part science. Audio engineers use equalizers to sculpt sound in ways that make it sound natural, yet brilliant, to the consumer.

What is equalization?

Equalization is a method of decreasing or increasing certain frequencies in a recorded piece of audio in order to fix deficiencies (such as tinny sound or too much bass) and make the audio cleaner and more natural. Most would say that the purpose of equalization is to restore the original qualities of a sound that may have been lost in the recording process. Others may use EQ in a more artistic fashion, manipulating sounds in a way that is creative and at times, unnatural.

The frequency spectrum of an audio file is broken down commonly into lows (bass), low mids, mids, high mids, and highs (treble). Most consumer stereos restrict equalization to bass, mid, and treble, but Soundbooth gives you very fine control over each position of the spectrum for the most surgical of equalization tasks.

Applying an equalizer preset

Soundbooth lets you add effects to any selected audio clip in a single or multi-track audio file — including equalizer presets. You can combine several effects in the Effects Rack for a single clip, giving you lots of practical and creative freedom.

The Effects panel is located on the left side of your workspace (docked in a group with the Properties, Tasks, and Markers panels).To add and use an equalizer preset on a selected clip:

1. **Choose File⇨Open and locate a single audio clip or multi-track file (ASND) for editing.**

   The clip appears in the editing window.

   Note: To open a clip for editing in a multi-track file, double-click it in the editing window.

2. **Locate the Effects panel on the left side of the workspace and click its tab to bring it forward.**

   If it's not visible, choose Window⇨Effects to open it.

3. **Under the Effects Rack, click the Stereo Rack Preset drop-down list to view the available effects presets.**

   This includes preconfigured settings for one or a combination of Soundbooths's included equalizers and spatial effects, such as reverbs.

4. **For this example, select the EQ: Classic V preset, which adds a single, preconfigured graphic equalizer to the Effects Rack.**

5. **Take a closer look at the effect and its settings and then click Settings above the effect name in the Effects Rack.**

   You can also edit an effect's settings by double-clicking it in the Effects Rack.

   The Graphic Equalizer dialog box opens.

6. **(Optional) With the graphic equalizer sliders, boost or decrease a particular frequency in the spectrum.**

Although each slider affects a very specific frequency, remember that at its most basic, the sliders are affecting bass, mids, and treble from left to right. See Figure 3-1.

The preset shown here raises bass and treble while decreasing mids, producing a *deep* sound.

7. **Click the top-left corner of the Graphic Equalizer dialog box to close it and then press the spacebar to listen to your sound with the new equalizer applied to it.**

8. **(Optional) Click the Power Effect Off button in the upper-left corner of that effect in the Effects Rack to turn off the effect.**

You can temporarily deactivate the effect, without deleting it, to make a comparison.

Book VI
Chapter 3

Applying EQ,
Effects, and
Dynamics

Creating your own equalizer settings

Soundbooth includes many useful EQ presets that can handle most any common task. As your needs change and your ears become more trained, you may decide to manually set up an equalizer and dial in the exact frequency settings you need.

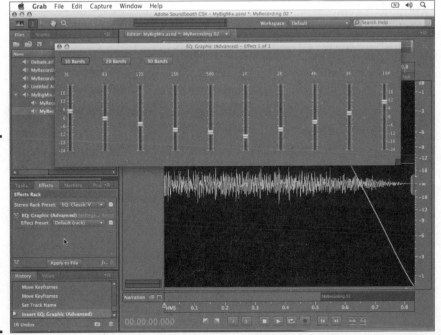

Figure 3-1:
The EQ you added to the Effects Rack; the graphic equalizer lets you control different frequencies with sliders.

You can experiment with different EQ settings across different frequencies to fix problems, such as tinny or harsh sound, muddiness, and noise issues. You can also apply equalization in more artistic ways that sculpt sound in unusual ways.

To add and manually set up an equalizer:

1. **In a single or multi-track audio file, open a clip in the editing window.**

   Note: To open a clip for editing in a multi-track file, double-click it in the editing window.

2. **Locate the Effects panel on the left side of the workspace and click its tab to bring it forward.**

   If it's not visible, choose Window➪Effects to open it.

3. **In the lower-right corner of the Effects panel, click the *fx* button to reveal Soundbooth's included effects modules.**

4. **Choose Advanced➪EQ: Graphic (Advanced) from the menu to add a new, unconfigured graphic equalizer effect to the Effects Rack.**

   See Figure 3-2.

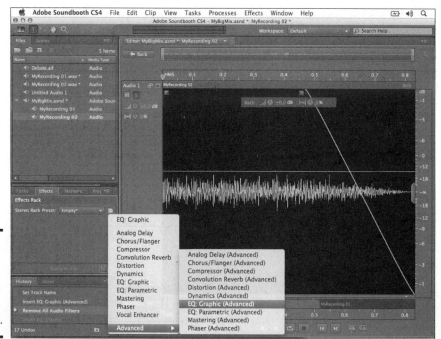

Figure 3-2:
Add a new
EQ: Graphic
(Advanced)
to the
Effects Rack.

5. **Double-click the newly added effect to open the Graphic Equalizer dialog box and then click and drag each slider up or down to boost or decrease that frequency.**

   If you're not sure what you're doing, don't worry — have fun! You'll discover the most by experimenting and listening.

6. **Press the spacebar to listen to your clip with the applied EQ. While the clip plays, move the sliders to see how the sound changes.**

Adding Compression to Control Dynamics

The *compressor* is one of the most important effects for controlling volume and overall dynamics for a clip. Compressors act to both increase and limit the volume of a clip, making it a powerful way to raise overall levels while preventing unpleasant sudden jumps in volume.

Compressors are used religiously in professional recording, mixing, and mastering to automatically control levels for erratic audio sources. Think of a compressor as a helpful hand on the volume knob that knows when to turn up the volume (quiet moments) and when to turn down volume (loud moments or volume spikes).

Although most professionally recorded audio (such as music from a CD) has already gone through a good deal of compression, you can use compressors to help along audio that's been recorded at low levels or tame audio that has some unwanted volume surges.

Adding compression to a clip

Add a compressor to a clip as follows:

1. **Select a clip for editing in either a single or multi-track file and bring forward the Effects panel.**

   See "Applying an equalizer preset" earlier in this chapter for details on this step.

2. **Click the *fx* button in the lower-right corner of the Effects panel and then choose Advanced⇨Compressor (Advanced).**

   A new compressor is added to the Effects Rack.

3. **Double-click the new compressor to edit its settings.**

   The Compressor dialog box appears, featuring five sliders: Threshold, Ratio, Attack, Release, and Output Gain. See Figure 3-3.

Figure 3-3:
Adjust
the newly
added
compressor
to increase
volume and
tame erratic
audio levels.

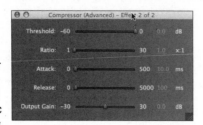

4. **(Optional) For low volume audio files, increase the overall level by clicking and dragging the Output Gain slider to the right; press the spacebar to listen to the clip while adjusting the Output Gain.**

5. **(Optional) For files with lots of erratic volume spikes, click and drag the Threshold slider to the left (start with a setting of about –20 dB [decibels]). Click and drag the Ratio slider to the right to a value of about 5.**

6. **(Optional) Continue to adjust settings as necessary until the levels of your file sound more consistent across lower and higher volume sections.**

Avoid *over-compressing,* which makes a clip sound artificial. Good compression should be fairly transparent, allowing the natural dynamics of the clip to come through with just enough to limit passages that are uncharacteristically too soft or too loud.

Understanding the compression settings

The compressor is a powerful tool, and understanding what each setting and slider on the compressor can do gives you lots of control and makes your work with the compressor even more effective.

✦ **Threshold:** Controls the point at which the compressor begins to work. A Threshold setting of –20 dB, for example, which means the compressor goes into affect only when a portion of audio reaches levels above –20 dB.

✦ **Ratio:** Determines how much the volume should be *attenuated* (reduced) if audio reaches levels above the set threshold level. A Ratio setting of 5 (5:1) means that every 5 decibels above the threshold level will be reduced to 1 dB.

For example, an audio clip with a volume of –10 dB audio with a threshold of –20 dB and ratio of 5 applied will result in a final volume of –18 dB.

+ **Attack:** Determines (in milliseconds) how quickly the compressor goes into effect when the threshold is reached.

+ **Release:** Determines (in milliseconds) how quickly the compressor shuts off after audio is below threshold levels.

+ **Output Gain:** Sets or decreases the overall *gain* (volume) for the audio. Output Gain is in effect at all times, even when audio is below the set threshold level.

Creating Space with Reverb and Delay Effects

To create depth and the illusion of space, you can make use of Reverb and Delay effects included with Soundbooth. Reverb and Delay are used to simulate reflections that occur in spaces of different sizes. You can simulate anything as basic as a small, uncarpeted room or as complex as a large cathedral to add interesting spatial effects to your clip or project.

+ **Reverb:** Represents a series of short, controlled reflections, or repeats that simulate the acoustics of a space, such as a room or a cathedral. The short duration and repetition of the repeats makes them indistinguishable from one another but creates the impression of space.

+ **Delay:** Uses a series of timed, obvious repeats to simulate an echo. In addition to simulating natural echoes, delays can be applied to a sound to create the impression of large space or time duration.

Applying effects

To apply Reverb and Delay effects:

1. **Select a clip for editing in either a single or multi-track file and bring forward the Effects panel.**

   See the earlier steps lists in this chapter if you don't remember how to do this.

2. **Click the *fx* button in the lower-right corner of the Effects panel and select Convolution Reverb.**

   A new Convolution Reverb is added to the Effects Rack, as shown in Figure 3-4.

3. **Locate the Effect Preset drop-down list and choose the Clean Room — Moderate preset.**

   This is one of several presets that simulates different acoustic environments, such as rooms, halls, and more.

Figure 3-4:
Add a
Reverb
effect and
choose a
preset to
add the
illusion of
space and
distance.

4. **Press the spacebar or the Play button to listen to your clip with the new effect applied.**

5. **Click the *fx* button in the lower-right corner of the Effects panel and select Analog Delay.**

   A new Analog Delay is added to the Effects Rack.

6. **Locate the Analog Delay's Effect Preset drop-down list and select the 50's Slapback — Moderate preset.**

7. **Press the spacebar or the Play button to listen to your clip with the new effect applied.**

Most all of Soundbooth's included effects can be run in Standard or Advanced mode. Standard effects (such as the ones chosen from the first level of the *fx* menu) don't provide access to their settings and can be modified only with presets. Advanced effects (such as the ones chosen from the Advanced category of the *fx* menu) provide access to all the effect's controls so you can dial in your own settings.

Saving rack and effects presets

If you're happy with the effects you've applied to a specific clip and want to save the entire Effects Rack, you can create a new rack preset that captures the current effects you've added and their exact settings.

In addition, for saving the specific settings of a single effect, such as an equalizer or a compressor, you can create individual effects presets that can be recalled from any instance of that effect at any time.

In both cases, you can recall your settings in any project or for any clip because rack and effects presets are saved in the application itself.

To save your effect's current settings as a new effect preset, follow these steps:

1. **Add an effect to the rack, and edit its settings, which we discuss earlier in this chapter.**

2. **In the Effects Rack next to the effect's settings you want to save, click the Save Effect Preset button.**

The Save Rack Preset dialog box appears.

3. **Enter a name for your new preset (such as** Big Announcer Voice**) in the Rack Preset Name field and click OK to create the new preset.**

The new preset appears as the effect's current Effect Preset and is available in the Effect Preset drop-down list for the selected effect.

To save the entire Effects Rack in a new preset, follow these steps:

1. **Add one or more effect(s) to your Effects Rack and adjust each individual effect or assign a preset to it as necessary.**

2. **Directly to the right of the Stereo Rack Preset drop-down list, click the Save Rack Preset button.**

The Save Rack Preset dialog box appears.

3. **Enter a name for your new preset (such as** Big Sound Effects Rack**) in the Rack Preset Name field and click OK to create the new preset.**

The new preset appears as the rack's current Stereo Rack Preset and is available in the Stereo Rack Preset drop-down list in the Effects Rack, as shown in Figure 3-5.

**Book VI
Chapter 3**

**Applying EQ,
Effects, and
Dynamics**

Figure 3-5:
Top: Assign a name to the new Effects Rack preset. Bottom: The preset is added to the Stereo Rack Preset drop-down list.

Chapter 4: Finalizing and Exporting Audio

In This Chapter

🗸 **Reducing glitches and noise**

🗸 **Finalizing and mastering audio with the Effects Rack**

🗸 **Exporting your final mix**

*I*t's time to prepare your final audio for use in an interactive project or a video, and you can use Soundbooth's effective noise reduction and repair tools before final export to guarantee a great result. You can export your entire single or multi-track file to a variety of popular formats, save specific selections and clips, or move a clip you've worked on into another project if you want.

Reducing Noise and Glitches

Recording audio under certain conditions can produce unwanted artifacts that you'll want to clean up before finalizing your file. Clicks, pops, rumbles, and noises, such as hums or buzzes, can occur as part of the recording process. This is especially true if you're using a highly sensitive microphone or are recording under less than prime conditions (such as in a noisy or echo-prone room).

The good news is that most of these unwanted artifacts can be tamed or removed by using Soundbooth's included noise reduction tools. You can even *train* Soundbooth to recognize a certain type of noise, look for it, and remove it throughout your file by using a noise print.

Reducing noise with a noise print

Think of a *noise print* as a way of telling Soundbooth to look for a certain type of unwanted noise throughout your file. You can select a portion of a clip that contains that noise, and Soundbooth analyzes it to form a noise print. From there, Soundbooth can effectively remove similar noise throughout your file and give it a good cleanup.

To capture a noise print and reduce noise:

1. **Choose File⇨Open and select a single audio file or multi-track project to open.**

In a single clip file, a clip appears in the editing window. In a multi-track file, double-click a clip in the editing window to open that clip for editing.

2. **Choose the Time Selection tool from the tools at the top of the workspace.**

3. **Click and drag over a portion of the waveform in the editing window to select a portion of your clip that contains the noise you want to remove.**

For best results, select a "quiet" point in your clip where other content (such as music or narration) isn't playing, but background or ambient noise is still audible.

4. **Choose Processes⇨Capture Noise Print, as shown in Figure 4-1.**

Soundbooth detects noise from the section of audio you've selected.

5. **Adjust your waveform selection if needed.**

• *If you want to apply noise reduction to only the selected audio,* leave the selection active in the editing window.

• *If you want to apply it to the entire file,* double-click the waveform to select the entire clip.

6. **Choose Processes⇨Reduce Noise.**

The Noise dialog box appears, as shown in Figure 4-2.

7. **Make sure that the Use Captured Noise Print check box is selected.**

8. **Click the Preview button to listen to what Soundbooth will do based on the settings and noise print you've selected; adjust the settings as needed.**

To apply more noise reduction, move the Reduction and Reduce By sliders farther right. Continue to listen to the preview to adjust your settings.

A little bit of residual noise is sometimes okay and can make the recording sound more natural depending on the nature of the audio. Avoid over-reduction, as this may make your clip sound choppy and artificial.

9. **Click OK to apply the noise reduction.**

The waveform is redrawn to reflect the changes you've made.

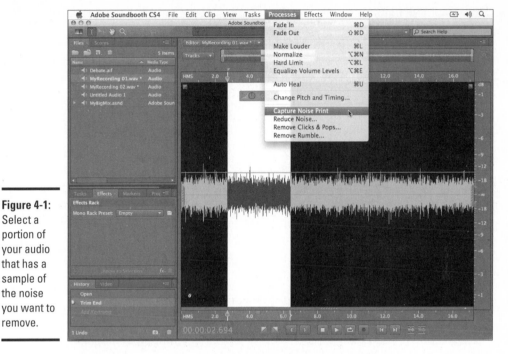

Figure 4-1:
Select a portion of your audio that has a sample of the noise you want to remove.

Figure 4-2:
After you capture a noise print, you can remove noise for an entire clip or a specific selection in the Noise dialog box.

Removing clicks and pops

Clicks and pops can occur in recorded clips for a variety of reasons: A narrator may move too close to the mic, a mic stand may be moved mid-recording, or levels may be too high during initial recording. Another danger of digital recording is *clipping,* or unpleasant glitches caused by audio levels exceeding the maximum allowable recording level.

Soundbooth can detect and remove these different types of unwanted artifacts for a specific selection or an entire clip, allowing you to fine-tune the amount to suit your needs. To remove clicks and pops:

1. **Choose the Time Selection tool from the tools at the top of the workspace.**

2. **Click and drag a waveform in your editing window to select a piece of audio to remove clicks and pops from.**

To select the entire clip, double-click the waveform with the Time Selection tool.

3. **Choose Processes⇨Remove Clicks and Pops.**

The Clicks & Pops dialog box appears, as shown in Figure 4-3.

4. **Click the Preview button to listen to your clip with the process applied.**

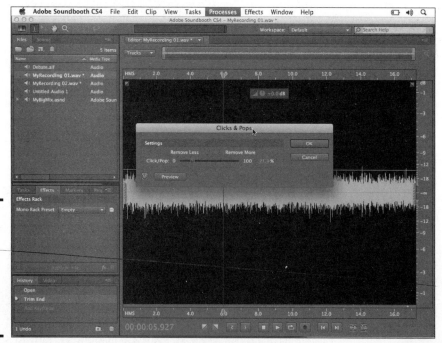

Figure 4-3: Remove unwanted clicks and pops in the Clicks & Pops dialog box.

5. **Adjust the amount and intensity of the removal process with the Click/Pop slider, moving it right to remove more or left to remove less.**

6. **Click OK to apply the process to the selected audio.**

Silencing a rumble

Rumble usually occurs in the low end of the frequency spectrum (or what most consumers know as bass or sub-bass levels). The Rumble dialog box reduces the amount of low end in a specific portion of the frequency spectrum (80 hertz and lower) to attempt to remove unwanted rumble.

To remove rumble:

1. **Choose the Time Selection tool from the tools at the top of the workspace.**

2. **Click and drag a waveform in your editing window to select a piece of audio to remove rumble from or double-click the waveform to select the entire clip.**

3. **Choose Processes⇨Remove Rumble.**

    The Rumble dialog box appears.

4. **Press the Preview button to listen to your clip with the process applied.**

5. **Adjust the amount and intensity of the removal process with the Rumble slider, moving it right to remove more or left to remove less.**

6. **Click OK to apply the process to the selected audio.**

Finalizing and Mastering Audio

A big part of the professional audio world centers around the art of *mastering* — the process of applying final equalization, compression, and enhancement to audio before it's released for final use. Generally the idea of mastering is to

✦ Increase the perceived levels of a mix.

   Perceived levels often describe the impression of loudness even when the overall average volume of a clip hasn't been exceeded. Compressors and limiters achieve this by pushing lower volume passages up to the highest possible limits while keeping overall clip volume at a set and manageable level. This can also be achieved with equalizers by raising certain frequency levels to help elements of a mix *cut through*.

✦ Do any last minute corrections (such as removing excess bass).

✦ Enhance the stereo image so everything sounds arranged well in stereo headphones and speakers.

Whether you're working with a single or multi-track file, you can export your entire mix to a single, new clip and apply mastering presets from the Effects Rack to enhance your file.

This is a multi-step process that involves the following:

1. Exporting a clip or multiple tracks to a single file in a new project

2. Applying mastering presets from the Effects Rack

3. Exporting the final version to a file format of your choice for use in your project

The following sections explain each of these overall steps in more detail.

Exporting mixes, clips, and selections

The first step in finalizing audio is to open a file and select the audio that you want to export. You can export a selected portion of a clip, an entire clip in a single file project, or an entire mix from a multi-track file.

After you export audio, you can use it as-is, add it to a new project for mastering, or import it to the Files panel of another project for use later.

Exporting clips and selections

You can save a new file from an existing single file project to add to your Files panel and use in other projects. This is useful if you're using a dedicated file (such as an ASND file) to perform edits on a single clip that will be added to a larger project or mastered in a separate file later.

To export a clip or selection from a single file project:

1. **Open a single file project and select the Time Selection tool from the tools at the top of the workspace.**

2. **Click and drag the waveform in the editing window to make a selection or double-click the waveform to select the entire clip.**

3. **Choose File⇨Save As.**

If you have effects active in the Effects Rack, a dialog box prompts you to apply effects to the entire file or selection. Choose Apply to Entire File or Apply to Selection.

The Save As dialog box appears.

4. **From the Save as Type/Format drop-down list, choose the file format that you want to save the audio as.**

You can choose from most common file formats, such as WAV, AIFF, MP3, or QuickTime.

5. **Enter a name for your file and click Save.**

   Saving a file into any format other than ASND results in your history and snapshots being discarded. If you're saving this file from an existing ASND file, you can always reopen your original ASND file to make changes later.

6. **In the Save as Options dialog box that appears (see Figure 4-4), select final settings for your file, such as sample rate, channels, and sample type.**

   In this example, the Save as Options dialog box appears, but depending upon what file type you chose, a different dialog box might appear.

   This varies based on your project, but for reference, CD quality audio is stereo with a sample rate of 44100 and a sample type of 16 bit.

7. **Click OK to save the new file in your default save location.**

   If you're saving from an ASND file, the file is added to the Files panel of that project.

Exporting a final mixdown

A *mixdown* describes a complete audio file that's been edited, balanced, and sequenced. This could be a single audio file or the combination of several tracks in a multi-track file.

To export a final mix from a single or multi-track file:

1. **Open a single or multi-track project.**

2. **For a multi-track project, choose File⇨Export⇨Multitrack Mixdown, as shown in Figure 4-5; for a single track project, choose File⇨Export⇨ Single Track Mixdown.**

   The Save As dialog box appears.

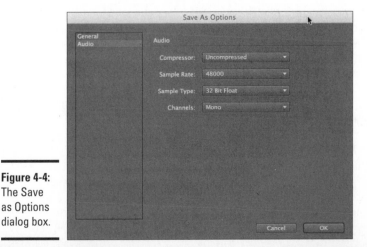

Figure 4-4:
The Save
as Options
dialog box.

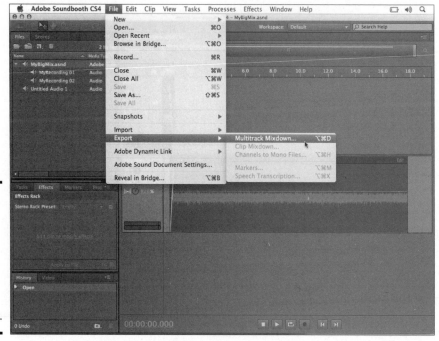

Figure 4-5:
You can
export a
multi-track
mixdown
to a single
file for final
delivery of
your project.

3. **Choose a file format from the Save as Type/Format drop-down list, enter a name for your new mixdown file, and click Save.**

   The Save as Options dialog box appears.

4. **Select final settings for your file, such as sample rate, channels, and sample type and then click OK when you're done.**

   The new file is created in your chosen save location.

Mastering a final mixdown or saved clip

After you export a multi-track mixdown to a single file or save a clip and its effects to a new file, you can add it to a new project for mastering and enhancement. This is usually the last step before sending a file to a Flash project, a video file, or for use in a podcast or other audio content.

To master and finalize a clip:

1. **Save a new stereo or mono audio file or mixdown.**

   See the previous section, "Exporting mixes, clips, and selections."

2. **Choose File⇨New Empty Audio File.**

   The New Audio File dialog box appears.

3. **Choose the sample rate and channel configuration for your file.**

   For final mixes, this generally matches the sample rate of your saved clip or exported mixdown and is typically stereo.

4. **Click OK to create the file.**

5. **Choose File⇨Import⇨Files to locate and import a mixdown or a saved clip into the new project.**

6. **Click and drag the clip from the Files panel to the editing window so its waveform is visible and you can apply effects.**

7. **Locate the Effects panel and bring it forward by clicking its tab in the panel group on the left side of your workspace.**

   From here you'll apply one of the precreated Effects Rack presets that are meant especially for mastering. Chapter 3 in this minibook offers an introduction to the Effects panel.

8. **Click the Stereo Rack Preset (or Mono Rack Preset) drop-down list and locate the Mastering presets in the middle of the list.**

9. **Select a preset, such as Mastering: Mix 1, to apply that preset to the Effects Rack. See Figure 4-6.**

   This adds several preconfigured effects modules that enhance the loudness, dynamics, and overall sound of your file.

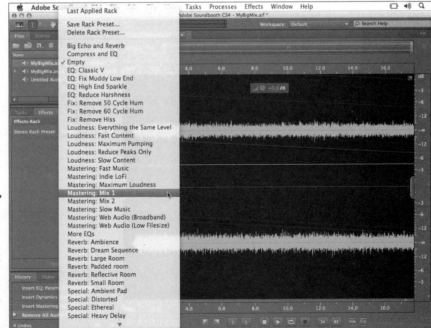

Figure 4-6: Select the Mastering: Mix 1 preset from the Stereo Rack Preset drop-down list.

10. Press the spacebar to listen to your mix with the new mastering effects applied (see Figure 4-7).

11. Choose File⇨Save As.

12. In the Save As dialog box that appears, choose a file format from the Save as Type/Format drop-down list, enter a name for your new mastered mixdown file, and click Save.

    The Save as Options dialog box appears.

13. Select the final settings for your file, such as sample rate, channel, and sample type, and then click OK.

    The new file is created in your chosen save location.

You will almost always want to make sure you are leaving the channels for any selected file format to Stereo, especially if your original clip is stereo. On occasion, however, you may need to create a Mono version of a stereo mixdown or clip for specific cases (such as delivery to AM radio).

Figure 4-7:
The
Mastering:
Mix 1
preset adds
several
effects to
increase
loudness
and
clarity and
enhance
dynamics.

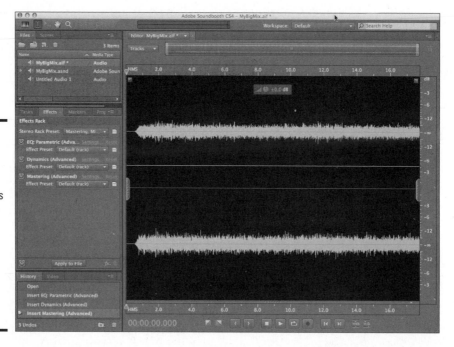

Book VII
Flash CS4

Contents at a Glance

Chapter 1: Getting Started in Flash CS4

In This Chapter

✓ Creating, saving, and opening documents

✓ Getting familiar with the workspace and tools

✓ Creating and saving your workspaces

✓ Introducing Flash Player 10

✓ Understanding layers

✓ Importing and exporting files

✓ Understanding the publishing process

*W*elcome to the world of Flash, one of today's hottest applications for creating eye-catching motion graphics featuring sound, video, and visual effects. In this minibook, you explore the whole process, from basic graphics creation and animation to complex effects and user interaction.

Creating Your First Flash Document

To get started, create a new blank Flash document and set up your workspace. You can create a new document in two ways:

✦ From the Start page, choose Flash File (ActionScript 3.0) under the Create New column.

✦ Choose File⇨New⇨Flash File (ActionScript 3.0).

Your new document is created, and the workspace appears. Before you get to work, specify some important settings, such as width and height, for your file by using the Document Properties dialog box.

To open the Document Properties dialog box, choose Modify⇨Document and set the following options:

✦ **Frames Rate:** Because Flash files behave like movies, the Frame Rate is an important setting that impacts the performance and playback speed of your movie. The default setting of 24 fps (frames per second) should do fine.

✦ **Dimensions:** The width and height set here determine the size of your stage and in turn, the visible area of your final movie. For now, leave the default setting of 550 pixels wide by 400 pixels in height.

✦ **Background Color:** Click the swatch to pick a background color for your stage from the Web-safe color palette. This also sets the background color of any Web pages created by Flash when you publish your movie to the Web.

✦ **Ruler Units:** This drop-down list lets you select the unit of measurement used for all measurement values in your document, including document size, width and height values, and ruler increments when rules are visible in the workspace.

When you're done fine-tuning your document's properties, click OK.

Getting Familiar with the Workspace

The Flash workspace, as shown in Figure 1-1, is where you create your Flash movies. The most prominent item you'll notice is at the top of your screen: the stage. The *stage* is where the action happens — where you draw, build, or import graphics, create text, and construct layouts.

The gray area surrounding the stage is your *pasteboard.* Items placed here aren't visible in your final movie because they're outside the bounds of the stage. However, it helps to think of this area as *backstage* — where text, artwork, and images can make their entrance or exit or be placed until they're ready to appear in your movie.

The Tools panel

What CS4 application would be complete without a fancy toolbar? Flash has a comprehensive set of tools for just about any drawing task you'll need to wrap your hands around. Table 1-1 gives you a rundown and description of the tools you'll find. The Tools panel, as shown in Figure 1-2, has been redesigned to make your work area flow better. A double arrow at the top lets you toggle between expanded and icon views to maximize your work area.

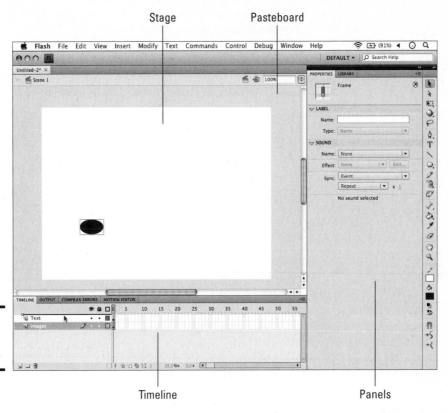

Stage   Pasteboard

Figure 1-1:
The Flash
workspace.

Timeline   Panels

Table 1-1	The Tools Panel
Tool	*Description*
Selection tool	Selects and moves objects on the stage and work area
Subselection tool	Selects and moves specific points on a path or a shape
Free Transform tool	Changes the dimensions, rotation, or proportions of an object
Gradient Transform tool	Changes the size, intensity, and direction of a gradient fill
3D Rotation tool	Translates 2D artwork into the 3D plane and lets you rotate it around an x,y and z axis
3D Translation tool	Click and drag artwork along the x,y or z axis to illustrate depth and distance
Lasso tool	Creates freehand selections around one or more points
Pen tool	Creates accurate , point-by-point straight and curved paths

(continued)

Table 1-1 *(continued)*

Tool	Description
Delete Anchor Point	Removes anchor points from an existing path
Convert Anchor Point	Changes the curve orientation of an existing point
Text tool	Creates text on the stage
Line tool	Draws straight lines
Shape tools	Creates rectangular, oval, or multisided shapes on the stage
Primitive tools	Creates rounded rectangles and multi-radiused ovals that can be modified
Pencil tool	Draws freehand paths
Brush tool	Draws broad, freehand fill areas
Spray Brush tool	Creates a spattered, airbrush-like painting with symbols from the library
Deco tool	Creates animated or non-animated "flower and leaf" style fills or symmetrical artwork with symbols
Bone tool	Joins together shapes or symbols with virtual "bones" for creating posable IK (inverse kinematics) objects
Bind tool	Edits connections between objects created with the Bone tool
Paint Bucket	Applies or modifies the fill color of an area
Ink Bottle	Applies or modifies the stroke color and style of a shape or path
Eyedropper	Samples the color property from an object
Eraser	Erases parts of a fill or path
Hand	Repositions the stage and work area within the workspace
Zoom	Zooms in or out of a selected area of the stage

The Timeline

Below the stage sits the *Timeline,* where you bring your artwork to life through animation. The Timeline is composed of frames, each one representing a point in time moving left to right. The Timeline is further broken out into *layers;* new documents automatically contain one new layer labeled *Layer 1.* Each layer on the Timeline is composed of frames that span horizontally from left to right, each one representing a point in time, just like frames in a movie reel (see Figure 1-3).

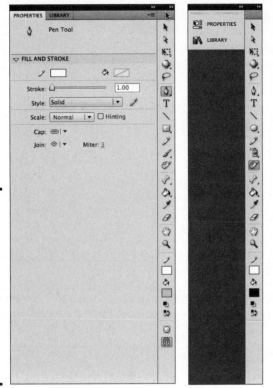

Figure 1-2:
Use the double arrows on top of the panel group on the right to switch between expanded and icon views.

Figure 1-3:
The Timeline contains frames and layers.

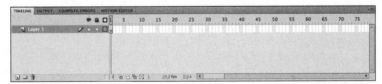

The Motion Editor

The all-new Motion Editor allows you to see and modify all properties of an animation in a graph-style format. All properties that can be animated are displayed in rows, each of which contains a value line that can be manipulated to change the behavior of a selected tween. You can also add complex forces, such as gravity and inertia, and even add to or subtract from your tween without using the Timeline or stage.

The Property inspector

Sitting at the right side of your workspace, the Property inspector allows you to get (and set) attributes (such as height and width) for a selected item on the stage or work area (see Figure 1-4). When nothing is selected, the Property inspector displays your document properties.

You can modify your document's properties at any time with the Property inspector when no items on the stage are selected or by choosing Modify➪Document.

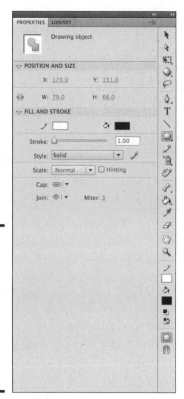

Figure 1-4: The Property inspector shows options for selected graphics, frames, or tools.

Panels (right side)

The many panels included in Flash give you total control over most aspects of your movie, from creating and managing colors to exploring the structure of your project.

The default workspace launches with the Property inspector and Library panel.

Get familiar with panel behaviors and features so that you can manage their appearance and make organizing your workspace a snap.

The panel group

The panel group sits on the right of the workspace and features multiple panels grouped together. Panels can be added to or removed from the panel group on the right.

The panel group can't be freely repositioned in the workspace. However, it can be resized or collapsed down to icon view with the double arrows found in its upper-right corner.

You can remove and float panels from the panel group. Simply click and drag a panel away from the group by its title tab. To add a panel into the group, drag it into the panel group on the right.

Managing individual panels

You can position each panel individually anywhere in the workspace by dragging it by its title tab. You can find additional appearance options under each panel's menu, accessible from the icon in its upper-right (see Figure 1-5). Each panel's panel menu also provides another way of getting to that panel's primary tasks.

Expand/Collapse

Panel menu

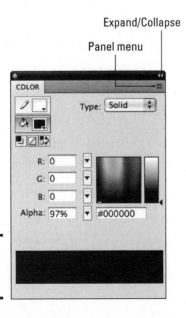

Figure 1-5:
Anatomy of
a panel.

To group panels together, simply drag one on top of the other; after they are grouped together, you can move and minimize several panels as one unit. This is handy for keeping commonly used or related panels together.

You can save panel groups and panel positions as part of custom workspaces. (See the following section "Creating and Saving Workspaces.")

Panels can always be toggled on or off from the Window menu. If you don't see a panel you need or have accidentally closed one, look for it in the Window menu. Many panels have shortcut keys; if you use a panel often, use its shortcut key combination for easy access.

Creating and Saving Workspaces

One of the most useful additions in recent versions of Flash is the ability to save your *workspaces* (the appearance and layout of workspace items, such as the toolbar, Timeline, Property inspector, and panels).

Saving workspaces is essential if you're sharing a computer workstation with others and want to recall your favorite panels and setup instantly. However, it can also be useful for maintaining different workspaces for different projects, even if you're the only person working on your computer.

To create and save your workspace layout, follow these steps:

1. **Open and position any panels you want available, including the Tools panel, Timeline, Motion Editor, and Property inspector.**

   You can toggle panels on or off from the Window menu.

2. **Choose Window⇨Workspace⇨New Workspace.**

3. **Enter a new name for your workspace and click OK.**

To recall a workspace, choose Window⇨Workspace⇨*Your Workspace Name* or select your workspace from the Workspace selector at the top-right corner of your screen. The current workspace rebuilds and appears exactly as you saved it.

You can view all your saved workspaces at any point by choosing Window⇨Workspace⇨Manage Workspaces. From this panel, you can choose to delete or rename existing workspaces at any point.

The default workspaces, such as Default, Classic, and Designer, can't be modified, deleted, or renamed.

Saving and Opening Documents

It's always recommended that you save your document after you make any significant changes or additions, and although not necessary, it's also a good idea to save a new document immediately after creating it. To save a document, choose File➪Save. Enter a name for your file and choose a location on your hard drive to save it to.

To open an existing document, choose File➪Open and locate the Flash file on your hard drive. Flash files are saved with a `.fla` extension, and published Flash movies are saved with `.swf` extensions.

You may need at some point to save a copy of your document under a new name, either to create an alternate version or perhaps to make it compatible with an older version of Flash.

To save a copy of your document under a new name, choose File➪Save As. Choose a location on your hard drive and enter a new filename. The drop-down list at the bottom of the Save As dialog box lets you choose what version of Flash you want to save the file in. For example, you can save files one version backward into Flash CS3 format.

Saving a document for an older version of Flash may make some newer features unavailable. Avoid saving your file in an older file format unless you absolutely need to make it available to an older version of Flash.

Getting to Know Flash Player 10

The Flash Player is at the heart of Flash technology. The player, which you can find as a plug-in to Web browsers or as a standalone application, runs and plays completed Flash movies, known as SWF (ShockWave Flash) files.

Beyond simple playback, the Flash Player is also responsible for deciphering and carrying out instructions written in *ActionScript,* Flash's powerful built-in scripting language. ActionScript, which is discussed in Chapter 7 in this minibook, gives your Flash movies many more abilities, including playback control, real-time user interaction, and complex effects.

Your end user needs the Flash Player in order to view your movies. Fortunately, at the time of this writing, the Flash Player is in use by 96 percent of Internet-enabled PCs worldwide. If a user doesn't have the Flash Player installed, it's available as a free download from the Adobe Web site at `www.adobe.com`.

Book VII Chapter 1

Getting Started in Flash CS4

Talking about Layers

If you've worked with other programs that utilize layers (such as Photoshop or Illustrator), the concept is very much the same. If you're new to *layers,* think of them as clear pieces of film stacked on top of each other. Each layer can contain its own artwork and animations.

In Flash, you use layers to stack artwork and animations on the stage, allowing them to exist together visually but to be edited or moved independently from one another. You can reorder layers to position artwork in front of or behind artwork on other layers.

 To create a new layer, click the New Layer icon at the bottom of the Timeline. The layer is automatically assigned a name; you can rename any layer by double-clicking its name and typing a new name.

To delete a layer, follow these steps:

1. **In the Timeline window below the stage, select the layer you want to delete.**

   Hold down the Shift key to select multiple layers. You can then click the Trash icon to delete all the selected layers at once.

 2. **Click the Delete Layer icon below the Timeline.**

The beauty of working with layers is that you can easily change the stacking order and appearance of artwork and animations distributed across those layers. To reorder layers, simply select a layer by clicking its label on the Timeline and then click and drag the layer up or down in the stacking order and release it to its new position (see Figure 1-6). Layers at the top of the list will appear in front of other objects in lower layers; in contrast, layers at the bottom of the list will appear below or behind items on higher layers.

Two additional aspects of managing layers include toggling a layer and its contents visible or invisible, and locking layers to prevent their contents from being accidentally moved or modified.

 To toggle a layer's visibility on or off, click any layer in the column below the Eye icon. To toggle all layers on or off, click the Eye icon at the top of the column.

 To prevent layer contents from being modified, click any layer in the column below the Padlock icon. To unlock it, click the Padlock icon again. To lock or unlock all layers, click the Padlock icon at the top of the column.

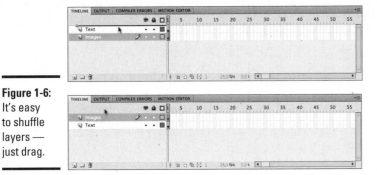

Figure 1-6:
It's easy
to shuffle
layers —
just drag.

Locking layers ensures that you won't accidentally move or delete the art-work it contains. Make a habit of locking layers whenever you're not working with them.

WARNING!

Layer visibility only affects what you see inside the authoring environment and has no effect on the finished SWF file. Layers whose visibility is toggled off in your document will still appear when published.

Importing Files

There will be times when you need to bring resources — such as artwork or photo files created in Adobe Photoshop or Illustrator, MP3 sound files, and even video files — that weren't created in Flash. You can import the follow-ing file formats into Flash:

+ **JPEG, GIF, PNG, TIFF, EPS files**

+ **Flash SWF files**

+ **Native Adobe Illustrator (.ai) and Photoshop (.psd) files**

+ **AIFF, WAV, and MP3 audio files**

+ **MPEG, MOV, DV, QuickTime, and FLV video files**

You can import these files directly to the stage for immediate use or to your document's library (which you find out more about in Chapter 3 of this mini-book) for storage until you're ready to place them on the stage.

Follow these steps to import files to the stage:

1. **Choose File➪Import➪Import to Stage.**

2. **Select the file(s) from your hard drive that you want to import.**

   Imported items are placed on the stage on the currently selected layer and frame.

To import files directly to the library:

1. **Choose File⇨Import⇨Import to Library.**

2. **Select the files from your hard drive that you want to import and click the Open button.**

   Imported files don't appear on the stage but are available in the Library panel for use later on.

To select multiple files for import, hold down the Shift key when prompted to select files from your hard drive. You'll be able to bring several files to the stage or library in one step.

Exporting Files from Flash

In contrast to the Import menu, the Export menu is used to generate files from your current document *out* of Flash, most often to create a compressed SWF file (movie) for final delivery. Additionally, it can be used to generate static images (such as JPEGs or GIFs) from specific frames in your movie.

FLA and SWF files

The life of a Flash project involves at least two different types of files: your authoring file (FLA) in which all your work is created; and the final product, your compressed movie or SWF file.

FLA files work only within the Flash CS4 application (the authoring environment). When you're ready to distribute your finished movie, publish an SWF file that can be displayed by the Flash Player.

These SWF files can be created from the Publish or Export menu options and are compressed movie files (typically smaller than their FLA counterparts) that contain all the graphics and information necessary to display your movie.

The Flash Player can't read FLA files, and SWF files can't be deconstructed into usable FLA files. Changes to your Flash movie are always done in the original FLA file and must be re-exported to a new SWF file if you want to view them in the Flash Player.

Publishing Your Final Movie

The final step in getting your movie ready to be posted on the Web, distributed on a CD-ROM, or sent through e-mail is the *publishing* process. The publishing process handles two important tasks: exporting the final SWF file playable by the Flash Player and creating any additional files (such as Web pages) necessary to display your movie. The File menu's Publish Settings and Publish options handle the setup and publishing of your movie so that you can show the world your new creation.

Flash can create any and all the following file types at publish time:

- ✦ **SWF files**
- ✦ **JPG, GIF, or PNG bitmap files**
- ✦ **Projector files**

    If you want to distribute your movie as a standalone file, you can create a Mac or PC compatible *projector* that includes the Flash Player.

- ✦ **HTML files**

    To display your movies on the Web, you'll need to contain them within a Web page, or HTML file. Flash takes care of creating this page for you.

- ✦ **QuickTime movies**

Chapter 9 of this minibook explores publishing in more detail.

Chapter 2: Drawing in Flash CS4

In This Chapter

✔ **Creating shapes and lines**

✔ **Editing and selecting shapes**

✔ **Tweaking and splicing shapes and lines**

✔ **Transforming shapes and artwork**

✔ **Creating and modifying text**

✔ **Working with colors and gradients**

✔ **Using the Paintbrush tool**

*M*any great creations start with the most basic of shapes and build from there. In this chapter, you discover the secrets of drawing shapes and lines and working with colors in Flash.

Drawing Shapes and Lines

To get your creation started, become familiar with the Shape and Line tools on the Tools panel and use them as the starting point for everything from basic buttons to complex illustrations.

When you're ready to create more complex artwork beyond what the Shape and Line tools offer, the Pen and Pencil tools are standing by. These tools work very differently, and for that reason, should be chosen based on the kind of artwork you want to create.

The following sections show you how to get started creating basic shapes and lines.

Drawing basic shapes with the shape tools

 On the Tools panel, locate the Rectangle tool; also notice a small arrow at the lower-right corner of the icon, which means that more tools are hidden underneath. Click and hold the Rectangle tool to reveal the Oval and Polystar tools; select the shape tool you want to use.

Before you draw the shape, set some colors for your shape with the two swatches located at the bottom of the Tools panel. The Fill color swatch (indicated by the paint bucket icon) lets you set what color your shape will be filled with. The Stroke Color swatch (indicated by the ink bottle icon) controls the outline color.

Flash lets you choose colors from the Swatches panel. You can add your own colors to this panel, but for now, choose one of the available colors for your shape's fill and stroke.

Click and drag on the stage to create a shape. Notice that by default, shapes are drawn from the left corner outward. You can draw shapes from the center (which is sometimes easier) by holding down the Option (Mac) or Alt (Windows) key while drawing the shape.

To constrain a shape proportionally, hold down the Shift key while drawing or resizing.

Merging shapes

If you overlap two or more shapes in Flash, they automatically *merge,* or become one complete shape. You can take advantage of this behavior by using an overlapping shape to knock out another, or you can make more complex shapes by combining simpler ones.

You may also find that overlapping strokes results in divided fill areas, which can be a desirable effect. Experiment by drawing and overlapping shapes and using the Selection tool to select parts of the resulting object.

Creating perfect lines with the Line tool

The Line tool makes constructing perfect, straight lines quick and easy. To create a straight line, choose the Line tool from the Tools panel, click and drag on your stage where you want the line to start, and release the mouse button where you want the line to end.

To modify your line's color or appearance, select it with the Selection tool and use the Property inspector to change the stroke color and size. You also find a Style drop-down list, which lets you choose among straight, dotted, dashed, and artistic stroke styles.

To create perfectly vertical or horizontal lines, hold down the Shift key while using the Line tool. You can also create diagonal lines in 45-degree increments with this same method.

Creating lines and curves with the Pen tool

Using the Pen tool may be a bit different than you're used to, unless of course, you've used the Pen tool in applications like Illustrator or Photoshop. The Pen tool isn't a freehand drawing tool; rather, it allows you to create *paths,* or outlines, composed by connecting anchor points. When you click and create new points, lines are automatically drawn connecting those points together. You can then either bend those lines into precise curves or leave them straight.

The best way to understand the Pen tool is to practice working with it. Visualize a shape you want to draw (for example, a leaf), and try to create it with the Pen tool.

To get started, follow these steps:

1. **Select the Pen tool from the Tools panel.**

2. **Use the Color swatch on the bottom of the Tools panel to set a stroke color.**

3. **Click to set the first point on the stage and then construct a line by clicking again to set a second point where you want the line to end.**

4. **Click to set a new point and before releasing the mouse button, drag to the left or right to bend the new line into a curve.**

   The more you drag in a particular direction, the more extreme the curve will be.

5. **Continue creating new points and experimenting with different curves.**

6. **Move your mouse pointer over the first point you created (a loop appears above the icon) and click to close the path and complete the shape.**

The Pen tool attempts to continue a curve in the same direction even after a new point is set. To reset the last point drawn back to a straight line, hold down the Option (Mac) or Alt (Windows) key and click the last point created before setting a new one.

Drawing freehand with the Pencil tool

The precise nature of the Pen tool is great for certain situations, but if you prefer the intuitive feel of freehand drawing or want to create more natural or rough artwork, consider using the Pencil tool.

An attractive feature of the Pencil tool is that it has three different modes to choose from. Each mode provides a different level of *smoothing,* so even if your hand isn't the steadiest, the Pencil tool compensates by automatically smoothing out lines or curves while you create them.

Select the Pencil tool and choose the appropriate smoothing mode using the selector at the bottom-right corner of the Tools panel:

✦ **Straighten:** Forces lines to the nearest straight line; perfect for drawing or tracing straight edges or boxy outlines.

✦ **Smooth:** Smoothes out lines or curves to the next closest perfect curve.

✦ **Ink:** Provides less smoothing and keeps lines and curves as natural as possible.

The mode you select depends completely on what type of shapes and lines you're trying to draw. If your shape is more diverse than one mode can handle, you can switch modes from line to line as needed.

Selecting and Editing Shapes

After you create a shape, you can select and move it by using the Selection tool at the top of the Tools panel. Flash shapes are easy to edit because you can select the stroke and fill independently to separate one from the other.

To select and move the stroke or fill only, follow these steps:

1. **Select the Selection tool from the Tools panel.**

2. **Click once on either your shape's stroke or fill to activate it.**

To select the entire shape, double-click the fill of your shape or use the Selection tool to drag around it on the stage (see Figure 2-1).

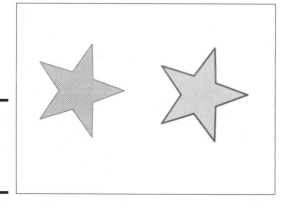

Figure 2-1:
Select the
fill (left) or
the stroke
(right).

3. **Click and drag the selected stroke or fill or use the arrow keys to separate it from the rest of the shape.**

Modifying fill and stroke colors

You can choose your fill and stroke colors ahead of time before you start drawing, but if you change your mind, modifying colors is easy to do.

You can modify either the fill or stroke colors of a pre-existing shape in the three ways:

✦ Select the entire shape and change its fill and/or stroke colors from the swatches on the Property inspector (see Figure 2-2).

✦ Select the entire shape and change your fill and/or stroke colors with the Fill and Stroke swatches on the Tools panel.

✦ Set your colors on the Tools panel and use the Ink Bottle tool by clicking the stroke or use the Paint Bucket tool by clicking the fill.

To apply a fill color to your shape, select it on the stage and choose a color from the Fill swatch at the bottom of the Tools panel. Grab the Paint Bucket tool and click inside of your shape. To apply a stroke color, select a color from the Stroke swatch at the bottom of the Tools panel, and select the Ink Bottle tool. Click once on the edge of your shape to set a stroke with the selected color.

You can also set Fill or Stroke colors from the Fill and Stroke section of the Property inspector when the Ink Bottle or Paint Bucket tools are selected.

To remove a fill or stroke completely, select a shape, and select None from either the Fill or Stroke color swatch.

Figure 2-2:
Use the
Property
inspector on
a selected
shape on
your stage
to change
the fill or
stroke color,
as well as
the stroke
width and
style.

Merge versus Object Drawing mode

The ability to freely tear apart shapes can be very flexible and useful, but some prefer to work with shapes as single objects (similar to how Illustrator CS4 does). For this reason, *Object Drawing mode* was created; this optional mode automatically combines the stroke and fill of a shape into a single object, which you can move and resize as a whole. Shapes drawn in Object Drawing mode have a bounding box around them; the stroke and fill are moved together as one object.

 You can enable Object Drawing mode when any drawing or shape tool is selected, as shown in Figure 2-3, by selecting the Object Drawing mode button at the bottom of the Tools panel. Try drawing a shape on the stage with this enabled; you'll notice that the shape appears with a bounding box around it, and the stroke and fill can no longer be individually selected and separated.

To convert a shape drawn with Object Drawing mode to its raw form, select the shape and choose Modify➪Break Apart, or double-click the shape to edit it within the Drawing Object itself.

Figure 2-3:
A shape drawn in Object Drawing mode.

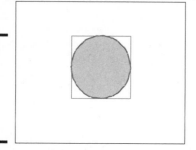

 Unlike shapes drawn in standard mode, Drawing Objects can't be merged together; break any Drawing Objects apart first, or choose Modify➪ Combine Objects➪Union to merge them together.

Splicing and Tweaking Shapes and Lines

You can easily dissect mergeable shapes (not Drawing Objects) by selecting only certain portions with the Selection or Lasso tools, as shown in Figure 2-4. Try drawing a marquee around only half the shape with the Selection or Subselection arrow; notice that only half the shape or line becomes selected, and you can then separate it.

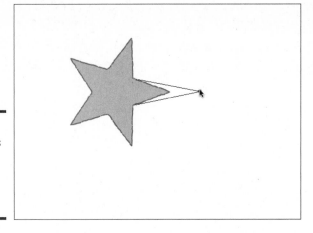

Figure 2-4:
Grab edges
or corners
to reshape
your
artwork.

Tweaking a shape with the Selection and Subselection tools

If you need to tweak the shape beyond its original form, you can use
Selection or Subselection tools to tweak, distort, and reshape. To tweak
or reshape with the Selection tool, move it outside and close to an edge or
corner of your shape; notice a small curved or angled line icon appears next
to your pointer. Click and drag to bend, reshape, and distort the outline of
your shape, as shown in Figure 2-5.

Figure 2-5:
Modify
curves
with the
Selection
tool by
dragging an
edge.

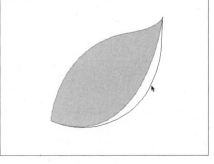

You can use the Selection tool to bend straight edges into curves. Try it on a
line or straight edge from a rectangle, and you'll see that you can easily pull
the line into a curve!

To tweak or reshape with the Subselection tool, click the outside edge or stroke of a shape to activate its path. Each point is represented by a hollow box. Click any point to activate it; click and drag it or move it using the arrow keys to reshape (see Figure 2-6).

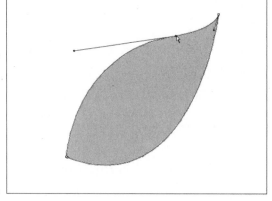

Figure 2-6:
Use the Sub-selection tool to modify specific points.

Editing a shape with the Lasso tool

When you need to create a selection with more precision than the Selection tool allows (for example, around an odd shape or a tricky area), use the Lasso tool. The Lasso tool draws freehand selections around specific areas of your artwork. To draw a selection with the Lasso tool, select it from the Tools panel and click and drag to draw a selection around the target area, as shown in Figure 2-7. Make sure to close the selection by overlapping the starting and ending points.

Figure 2-7:
Select areas with the Lasso tool; close the path for best results.

You can perform partial selections only with *raw* (broken apart) shapes and lines. Artwork drawn in Object Drawing mode needs to be broken apart first (choose Modify➪Break Apart) or modified in edit mode. To enter a Drawing Object's edit mode, double-click it with the Selection tool.

Modifying artwork created with the Pen and Pencil tools

Interestingly enough, although the Pen and Pencil tools behave in completely different ways, both ultimately create the same thing: paths. These paths can be filled (if closed) or modified on a point-by-point basis, or you can apply a stroke to them.

To fine-tune a path, choose the Subselection tool (white arrow) from the Tools panel. Click the path; it becomes highlighted, and the points show up as hollow boxes. You can now select any individual point and selectively drag it or move it with the arrow keys to reshape the path.

To adjust a curve with the Subselection tool, highlight the point adjacent to the curve you want to modify. A handle appears; you can grab and move this handle to adjust the curve.

To add or subtract points, click and hold down on the Pen tool to select the Add Anchor Point or Subtract Anchor Point tools. Click exactly on the path where you want to add an anchor point or click directly on a point to remove it.

Transforming Artwork and Shapes

After you have some drawing done, you may want to adjust the width, height, or rotation of your artwork. Depending on the level of precision you're looking for, you can do this in two ways: manually with the Transform tool or by dialing in exact values on the Transform panel.

Using the Transform tool

 Select a shape or artwork on your stage and then choose the Transform tool from the Tools panel. A bounding box with handles at all four sides and corners appears, as shown in Figure 2-8. You can drag any of the side handles to resize the width and height.

To rotate your artwork, hover over any corner handle until you see the rotation icon (a circular arrow) and then click and drag to rotate your artwork freely.

**Book VII
Chapter 2**

**Drawing
in Flash CS4**

To resize your art proportionally, hold down the Shift key while dragging a handle. If you hold down the Shift key while in rotation mode, it limits your movements to precise 45-degree increments.

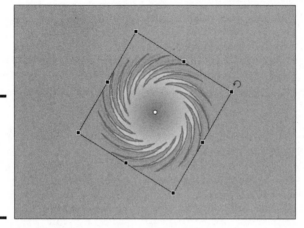

Figure 2-8:
Use the Transform tool on a drawing to rotate and resize.

Using the Transform panel

For those times when you need to dial in exact transformation values, you can use the Transform panel, which you can open by choosing Window⇨Transform (see Figure 2-9). The Transform panel uses text boxes where you can enter exact transformation values for width and height or a specific rotation angle in degrees.

Follow these steps to transform artwork with the Transform panel:

1. **Select the object you want to transform on the stage and open the Transform panel by choosing Window⇨Transform.**

2. **To increase the size of the artwork, enter width and height percentage values above 100 percent; to decrease the size, enter values below 100 percent. To keep the sizes proportional, select the Constrain Values check box.**

3. **To rotate your artwork, select the Rotate radio button, click the number to activate the text box, type a value above 0 degrees, and press Enter.**

Rotation is performed clockwise; to rotate counter-clockwise, enter a negative number.

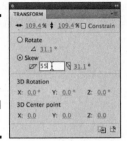

Figure 2-9:
Enter precise amounts of scaling, rotation, and skewing.

Skewing your artwork

Skewing transforms your artwork on a 3D plane and can add interesting perspective to your shape. You can perform skewing with the Transform panel by selecting the Skew option button and entering values for horizontal and vertical skew amounts.

Give it a try: Select your shape, type in some Skew values, and press Enter to see the transformation applied. If you're not happy, don't fret; simply click the Remove Transform button in the lower-right corner of the Transform panel to set everything back to normal.

Working with Type

If you're looking to display important information in your Flash movie or simply want to add creative text elements to your design, Flash's flexible Text tool can create attractive type for design elements, buttons, titles, and informational text areas.

To create a line of type, select the Text tool from the Tools panel, click a location on the stage, and begin typing. With the Property inspector, fine-tune your text's size, typeface, alignment, and color, as shown in Figure 2-10. Additional options in the Property inspector, such as paragraph formatting and alignment, can help with larger blocks of text.

To edit type, choose the Text tool and click the text you want to edit. When the blinking cursor appears, you can select, add, or modify the text. While the text is selected, you can also change colors, typeface, and size with the Property inspector.

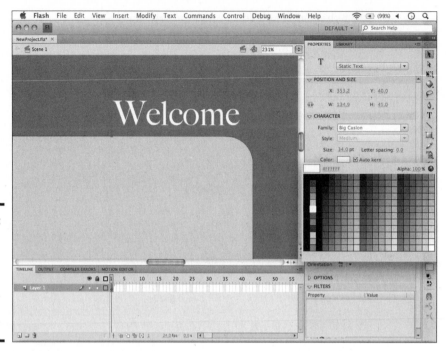

Figure 2-10:
Use the
Property
inspector
to modify
typeface,
style, size,
and colors.

Transforming type

You can transform type just like shapes and artwork by using either the Transform tool or the Transform panel. Regardless of any transformations you put your type through, it remains editable.

To transform a line of type, make sure that it's active by first selecting it with the Selection or Text tools. To transform, choose the Transform tool or open the Transform panel.

Distorting and modifying character shapes

You can distort and modify type outlines just like any other shape or path. However, type is created on a special type path so that it can be edited at any point. You'll need to break your type characters off a path first in order to tweak any of their outlines.

To modify or distort type outlines, follow these steps:

1. **Select the type you want to modify and choose Modify⇨Break Apart.**

2. **If your type is longer than a single character, repeat Step 1.**

3. **Use the Selection or Subselection tool to modify the outlines (as demonstrated with shapes earlier in the chapter).**

4. **(Optional) Use the Ink Bottle tool to apply a stroke to your type.**

Creating Colors and Gradients

You've undoubtedly seen and made use of the built-in color swatches in Flash, but suppose that you want to use colors that are *not* included in the Swatches panel. Here's where the Color panel comes into play. From this panel, you can mix and create your own color swatches, make gradients, and even apply transparency effects to existing colors on the stage.

You've already seen the Swatches panel in action — you used it to select fill and stroke colors from the Tools panel and Property inspector. The Swatches panel exists on its own free-floating panel as well, which you can open by choosing Window⇨Swatches.

The 256 colors on this panel represent the Web-safe color spectrum, which is optimized to make sure that any user, even those with monitors using lower color depth settings, can enjoy your creations.

You can add colors to the Swatches panel from the Color panel, which means that you have access to your own custom colors from anywhere the Swatches panel appears.

Creating and adding colors from the Color panel

The Color panel features two ways to select a precise color: the color wheel on the right or the sliders on the left. You can combine the two methods to hone in on just the right shade. After you choose the color you want, you can easily add it as a swatch to the Swatches panel by choosing Add Swatch from the panel menu, as shown in Figure 2-11.

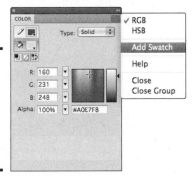

Figure 2-11:
Select a custom color with the sliders or color wheel.

To apply a color choice automatically to the stroke or fill swatches, click either the Fill or Stroke color swatch on the top-left corner of the Color panel. Any changes made using the color wheel or sliders are applied automatically to the selected swatch.

To select a color on the color wheel, click and drag the cross hair inside the color wheel until you find the right hue (for example, greens). Use the slider to the right to select the exact shade of that color.

To select a color with the sliders, first select either the RGB (Red, Green, Blue) or HSB (Hue, Saturation, Brightness) sliders from the Color panel's panel menu. Move the sliders to find the exact color you want. You can fine-tune this color further with the color wheel and slider.

To save your new color as a swatch, find your desired color and choose Add Swatch from the panel menu. Your new color appears as a new swatch on the Swatches panel, and you can select it anywhere the Swatches panel appears.

Creating gradients

Gradients are blends between two or more colors that you can use to fill any area or shape, just like a solid color. If you look at the Swatches panel, you see some gradient presets that you can use right away. You can also use the Color panel to create your own gradients and add them to the Swatches panel.

Follow these steps to create a gradient:

1. **Open the Color panel by choosing Window➪Color and choose Linear from the Type drop-down list.**

   Linear is one of two gradient types that you can create.

2. **Double-click one of the horizontal sliders that appears above the gradient ramp at the bottom to see the Swatches panel; pick a color to apply to that slider.**

   To add more colors to your gradient, click anywhere on the gradient ramp to add a slider. You can then double-click this slider to set the color.

3. **Adjust the color blends of the gradient by moving the sliders closer together or farther apart.**

   To remove colors or sliders, click the slider you want to remove and drag it off the panel to the left or right.

4. **Choose Add Swatch from the panel menu to save your new gradient.**

   The gradient swatch is added to your Swatches panel alongside the existing gradients.

In addition to *linear gradients,* which blend colors evenly in a straight line, you can create radial gradients. *Radial gradients* are a special type of gradient shape where colors blend from the center outward in a circular motion. To set a gradient as a radial gradient, choose Radial from the Type drop-down list on the Color panel. To set a gradient as a linear gradient, choose Linear from the Type drop-down list.

Both gradient types are created and added to the Swatches panel in the exact same manner, as described in the preceding step list.

Applying and transforming gradients

After you create a gradient, you can use it to fill a shape the same way you'd set a solid fill color. After you apply a gradient to a shape on the stage, you can use the Gradient tool to modify the gradient's direction, size, and intensity.

To modify a gradient fill, follow these steps:

1. **Click and hold down your mouse pointer on the Free Transform tool to select the Gradient Transform tool. Select a shape with a gradient fill.**

   A bounding box appears.

2. **Use the bounding box's center point to move the transition point of the gradient.**

3. **Use the handle on the right side to modify the intensity of the gradient.**

4. **Change the direction of the gradient by using the rotating arrow icon at the upper-right corner of the selection area.**

If you're working with a radial gradient, you'll notice the Gradient Transform tool behaves slightly differently. An extra round handle appears to let you scale the gradient, and the rotating arrow icon (which rotates the gradient area) is located on the bottom right. Experiment with both linear and radial gradients to see the differences.

Working with the Paintbrush Tool

Tools, such as the Pen and Pencil, offer you different ways of creating stroked paths. In contrast, the Paintbrush tool paints with fills. A lot like a good old-fashioned paintbrush, this tool can create thick, broad strokes with solid colors or gradients for excellent artistic effects.

The Paintbrush tool features several different brush sizes and tips, as well as five modes for controlling how (and where) the Paintbrush tool does its magic.

**Book VII
Chapter 2**

**Drawing
in Flash CS4**

Follow these steps to use the Paintbrush tool:

1. **With the Paintbrush tool selected, choose a brush size and tip shape from the very bottom of the Tools panel.**

2. **Choose a fill color from the Fill color swatch on the Tools panel, Property inspector, or Color panel.**

3. **Freely paint on the stage to see the Paintbrush tool in action.**

The different Paintbrush modes change where and how the tool works against different objects on the stage. A good way to see these modes in action is to draw a shape on the stage and make sure that the shape has both a stroke and fill set. Experiment by changing between the different modes and trying to paint over the shape (see Figure 2-12). In Figure 2-12, the selected object was painted over with the Paintbrush tool in Paint Selection mode. This mode affects only the area of the selected shape.

Figure 2-12:
Painting with Paint Selection mode affects only the selected shape.

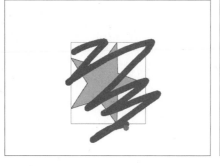 

Because the strokes left behind by the Paintbrush tool are simply filled shapes, you can apply a stroke to it, change its fill color, or use it to create interesting shapes that you can tweak by using the same methods demonstrated in the "Transforming Artwork and Shapes" section, earlier in this chapter.

To apply an outline to a painted area, set a color by using the Stroke color swatch on the Tools panel, select the Ink Bottle tool, and click the outer edge of the fill. You can now use the Property inspector to change the width, color, and style of the stroke as well.

Chapter 3: Now You're in Motion

*A*fter you're familiar with Flash's drawing tools, explore what Flash is best known for: animation. In this chapter, you bring your creations to life with movement, interactivity, and sounds. Flash CS4 introduces some significant new changes to the way animation is created on the Timeline, which will be exciting for new and experienced users alike.

First, you'll explore some central concepts in Flash: symbols and the library. Because symbols are an essential part of creating animation in Flash, you'll discover how to create and modify symbols before diving into your first animation tasks.

Visiting the Library

Each Flash document contains a *library*, a repository of reusable graphics, animations, buttons, sounds, video, and even fonts. As you build your Flash movie, you can add any piece of artwork you've created on the stage to your library, where the artwork's stored as a *symbol* (as shown in Figure 3-1).

What makes symbols so powerful is that you can reuse them as many times as necessary. Simply drag and drop a copy (referred to as an *instance*) from the Library panel onto the stage anywhere in your movie. Most importantly, each instance remains linked to the original in your library. Any changes made to the original (or *master*) automatically update any instances of that same symbol used throughout the movie.

Symbols are broken down into three main categories: graphics, buttons, and movie clips. You can find out more about button and movie clip symbols in Chapters 6 and 7 of this minibook.

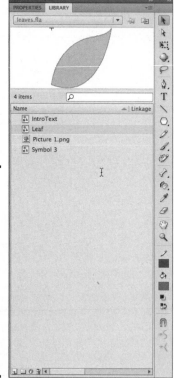

Figure 3-1:
The Library panel stores symbols that you create from graphics and animations, as well as sounds, images, and fonts.

Creating and Modifying Graphic Symbols

Certain types of animation in Flash require the use of symbols, so it's a good time to become familiar with the most basic of symbol types: *graphics*. You can convert any object on the stage into a graphic symbol, allowing you to take advantage of additional features unique to symbols. You can also create empty graphic symbols from the Library panel or by choosing Insert⇨ New Symbol and adding content to them afterward.

Follow these steps to create a graphic symbol:

1. **Choose Insert⇨New Symbol or choose New Symbol from the panel menu located in the top-right corner of the Library panel.**

The Create New Symbol dialog box appears.

2. **Assign a name to the symbol, choose Graphic from the Type drop-down list, and click OK.**

You see a blank slate on the stage where you can add to your symbol.

3. **Choose Scene 1 from the navigation bar above the stage to exit the symbol and return to the main Timeline.**

   You now see your new symbol listed in the Library panel.

Follow these steps to create a graphic symbol from existing artwork on the stage:

1. **With the Selection tool, select the object(s) on the stage that you want to convert to a symbol.**

2. **Choose Modify⇨Convert to Symbol.**

   The Convert to Symbol dialog box appears.

3. **Enter a name for the symbol, choose Graphic from the Type drop-down list, and click OK.**

   Your new symbol now appears listed in the Library panel.

 Whenever you convert existing graphics to a symbol, the graphics remain on the stage, enclosed inside a blue bounding box (see Figure 3-2). Your Property inspector confirms that the selection is now a graphic symbol (indicated by the icon).

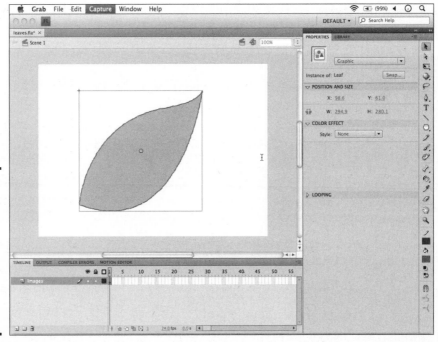

Figure 3-2: A symbol is enclosed in a bounding box, and the Property inspector shows the symbol's name.

Don't confuse symbols with Drawing Objects — both display artwork inside a bounding box, but Drawing Objects don't have the same abilities that symbols have, nor are they stored automatically in your library. Use the Property inspector to determine whether an object is a symbol or a Drawing Object if you're unsure — a distinctive icon and description appear for each one at the top of the Property inspector.

Adding symbols to the stage

After you add graphic symbols to your library, if you need to reuse one, you can simply drag a copy from the Library panel and drop it on to the stage (see Figure 3-3). Each copy of a symbol is referred to as an *instance* in Flash. Although all these instances remain linked to the original, you have the flexibility to scale, transform, and rotate each instance individually.

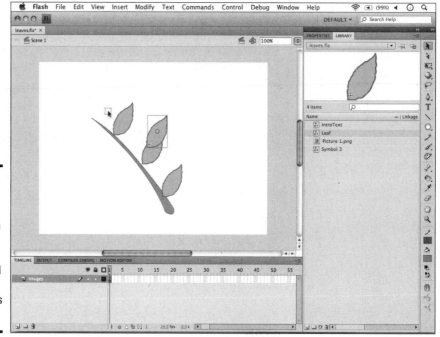

Figure 3-3: Drag and drop a symbol from your library onto the stage to add as many instances as you want.

Follow these steps to add symbols to the stage:

1. **Locate a symbol in your library that you want to add to the stage.**

2. **Drag a copy from the Library panel to the stage; repeat this a few times so that you have several instances on the stage.**

3. **Select each instance individually and experiment with different scaling, transforming, and rotating for each one.**

Modifying symbols

After you create symbols, you can modify them from within the library or directly on the stage. Changes made to a symbol are applied to all instances of that symbol throughout the movie.

To edit a symbol from within the library, follow these steps:

1. **Select a symbol in your Library panel and choose Edit from the panel menu, or double-click any symbol in the Library panel.**

   To really see the effect of editing the master symbol, use a symbol you dragged previously to the stage.

   The symbol appears on the stage in edit mode.

2. **Make some changes in color, shape, or size.**

3. **Exit the symbol by selecting Scene 1 from the navigation bar above the stage to return to the main Timeline.**

   Instances of this symbol on the stage reflect the changes you've made to the symbol in the library.

Editing a symbol in place on the stage can be more intuitive, as you may want to modify it to work better with other artwork on the stage. You can directly edit a symbol from any of its instances on the stage (as shown in Figure 3-4), but keep in mind that regardless of which instance you edit, all instances will be affected.

To edit a symbol in place, follow these steps:

1. **Select and double-click any symbol instance on the stage.**

   You're now in the symbol's edit mode, but you can still see the other objects on the stage in the background. Flash dims objects in the background so that you can see your changes in context.

2. **Make your changes and exit the symbol's edit mode by selecting Scene 1 on the navigation bar above the stage.**

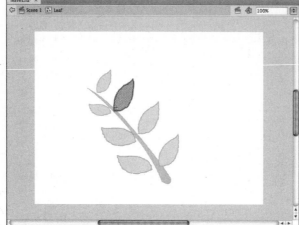

Figure 3-4:
Double-click
a symbol
instance
to edit the
symbol in
place on the
stage.

A closer look at the Library panel

Your Library panel is the main storage location for all your symbols, and very much like any library, it has essential organizational tools that make managing your symbols easy.

The most basic and common functions are made easy through several icons found along the bottom of the panel (see figure):

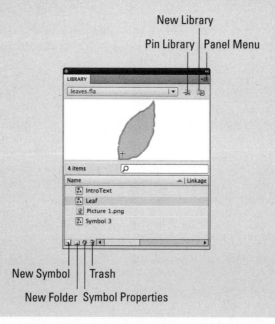

✔ **Panel menu:** All panels have panel menus, which offer additional options or modify the view of the panel itself. The Library panel's panel menu carries out additional symbol and library-related tasks.

✔ **Pin Library:** Clicking this icon makes sure that the current library stays active even when you switch between other open documents. Normal behavior *(unpinned)* is for library views to switch automatically when moving between open documents.

✔ **New Library:** Creates a duplicate Library panel in case you want multiple, distinctive views of your current library. You can also open a new Library panel to view libraries from other currently open documents.

✔ **Search:** The text box and magnifying glass under the preview panel allow you to search for symbols by name in the library, which is especially helpful for large libraries. Simply type a full or partial name and the panel will display matches (if any exist).

✔ **New Symbol:** Create a new symbol, identical to the command found by choosing Insert⇨New Symbol.

✔ **New Folder:** Create folders that you can sort your symbols into for easy categorization. You can create folders within folders for even finer sorting capabilities.

✔ **Properties:** If a symbol is highlighted in your library, clicking the Properties icon opens the Symbol Properties window. From here, you can redefine the symbol's name, type, or registration point.

✔ **Trash Can:** Yes, you guessed it — this symbol deletes *(trashes)* the currently highlighted symbol in the library. *Be careful with this:* No warning is given before the deed is done. However, you can choose Edit⇨Undo to reverse this action, if necessary.

Sorting symbols

Symbols in your library can be sorted using any of the column headers at the top of the symbol list. You may only be able to see Name and Linkage at first glance, but if you use the horizontal scroll bar at the bottom of the panel, you can see additional columns for Use Count, Date Modified, and Type.

To sort by any column, click the column name. If the arrow next to the column name is pointing up, the sort is descending, with the highest value up; if the arrow is pointing down, the sort is ascending, with the lowest value up top.

Duplicating symbols

You may want to create a variation of one of your symbols that goes beyond what you can do on an instance-by-instance basis. A good example is two birds that are similar in appearance, but one has different shaped wings or a different base color. This instance would be a good case for duplicating an existing symbol so that any changes can be made to the copy and treated as a new symbol.

To duplicate a symbol, select the symbol in the library you want to copy and choose Duplicate from the panel menu in the top-right corner of the panel. You're given a chance to name the new version of the symbol when the Duplicate Symbol dialog box appears.

You can rename any symbol directly from the Library panel. Select the symbol and choose Rename from the panel menu.

Painting with Symbols

Flash CS4 introduces two new tools that enable you to get truly creative with symbols: the Spray Brush and Deco tools. These tools rely on symbols from your library, allowing you to paint random textures or fill areas with complex patterns. You can even easily draw symmetrical artwork with the Deco tool's included Symmetry Brush mode.

The Spray Brush tool

The Spray Brush tool paints with instances of a single symbol from your library. You can use the Property inspector to dial in settings for scaling, randomness, and brush size.

Follow these steps to paint with the Spray Brush tool:

1. **Click the New Layer button (found below the Timeline) to create a new, empty layer to paint on.**

2. **Select the Spray Brush tool from the Tools panel (click and hold down on the Brush tool to find the Spray Brush tool).**

    The Property inspector displays options for the Spray Brush tool.

3. **In the Property inspector, click the Edit button in the Symbol options area.**

    The Swap Symbol dialog box appears, prompting you to select a symbol from your library.

4. **Choose a symbol and click OK to exit the dialog box.**

5. **In the Symbol options area, use the Scale Width and Scale Height sliders to reduce or increase the scaling for each instance painted on the stage.**

6. **In the Brush options area, enter values for the Width and Height of the brush, and if desired, Brush Angle.**

7. **Click and drag on the stage to begin painting.**

The Spray Brush paints with the symbol you selected using the settings you chose in the Property inspector, as shown in Figure 3-5.

The Spray Brush tool creates groups from all the paint droplets it leaves behind. You can break apart these groups by choosing Modify➪Break Apart, or edit its contents by double-clicking the group on the stage.

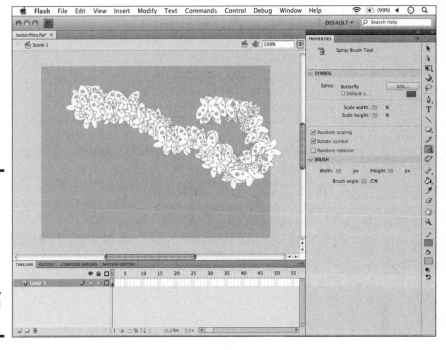

Figure 3-5: The Spray Brush paints with symbols from your library. You control size, scatter, and scaling.

The Deco tool

The new Deco tool features three different modes: Vine Fill, Grid Fill, and the Symmetry Brush for creating interesting textures, patterns, and symmetrical drawings. Like the Spray Brush tool, the Deco tool uses symbols from your library.

In the following steps, we show you how to experiment with the Deco tool's three different drawing effects using symbols from your library. First, we show you how to use the Vine Fill:

1. **Open or create a new Flash document, and add at least two graphic symbols to your library with the methods described earlier in this chapter.**

2. **Select the Deco tool from the Tools panel.**

   The Property inspector changes to reflect that the current drawing effect is set to Vine Fill.

   Vine Fill mode creates a vine-style pattern between two symbols, using one as the *leaf* (that decorates the vine path) and one as the *flower* (that appears at the end of each *vine*).

3. **In the Leaf section of the Property inspector, click the Edit button to select a symbol from your library to serve as the leaf.**

4. **From the dialog box that appears, choose a symbol from your library and click OK to set that symbol.**

5. **In the Flower section of the Property inspector, click the Edit button to select a symbol from your library to serve as the flower.**

6. **From the dialog box that appears, select a symbol from your library and click OK to set that symbol.**

7. **In the Advanced Options section of the Property inspector, click the color swatch and choose a color for the vine that will interconnect the two symbols you've chosen when the pattern is created.**

8. **Click the New Layer button below the Timeline to create a new, empty layer to paint on.**

9. **Click the stage, and the Deco tool begins to draw a new vine pattern using the symbols you've chosen.**

   The Deco tool draws a vine and caps the vine with the flower symbol you chose. Continue to click and release to draw new vines.

To give the Grid Fill drawing effect a try, follow these steps:

1. **Click the New Layer button below the Timeline to create a new empty layer to use with the Grid Fill.**

2. **If the Deco tool isn't active, select Deco tool from the Tools panel.**

3. **Change the drawing effect from Vine Fill to Grid Fill with the drop-down list at the top of the Property inspector.**

   Grid Fill creates a uniform grid-style pattern within a selected area. You can use Grid Fill to fill a specific shape on the stage, or the entire stage itself.

4. **Click the Edit button to select the fill symbol.**

5. **When the Swap Symbol dialog box appears, choose a symbol from your library to use as a pattern and click OK.**

6. In the Property inspector, click and drag over the Horizontal Spacing and Vertical Spacing values to set the desired distance (in pixels) between each row and column.

7. (Optional) Use the Pattern Scale slider to reduce or increase the size of the symbol used to create the pattern.

8. Click the stage with the Deco tool, and the stage fills up with a grid pattern using the symbol and settings you chose, as shown in Figure 3-6.

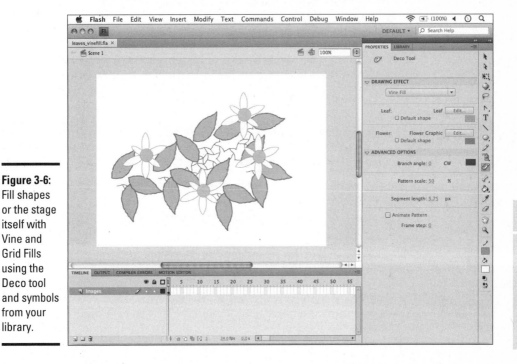

Figure 3-6: Fill shapes or the stage itself with Vine and Grid Fills using the Deco tool and symbols from your library.

The last drawing effect we show you how to use is the *Symmetry Brush,* which lets you draw cool symmetrical artwork with symbols. Follow these steps to use the Symmetry Brush:

1. Click the New Layer button to insert a new layer on the Timeline.

2. If the Deco tool isn't active, select the Deco tool from the Tools panel.

3. On the Property inspector, select Symmetry Brush from the Drawing Effect drop-down list.

4. To the right of Module, click the Edit button.

5. From the Swap Symbol dialog box that appears, select a symbol from your library to use with the Symmetry Brush and then click OK.

6. On the stage, click and drag to begin drawing with the Symmetry Brush.

The symbol you chose is duplicated in a rotating pattern around your brush point. Release the mouse button to stop drawing.

The new pattern displays two handles — one to adjust pattern size, and one to adjust the distance between each symbol.

7. Move your cursor over the top of the vertical handle until you see a black arrow; click and drag to readjust the size of the pattern.

8. Move your cursor over the end of the horizontal handle until you see a black arrow; click and drag clockwise or counter-clockwise to reduce or increase the distance between symbol instances, respectively.

If you look at the Advanced Options for the Symmetry Brush (on the bottom of the Property inspector), you'll see quite a few other interesting modes that let you reflect symbols or reconfigure them into a grid. Experiment with these and try different symbols from your library for contrast.

Understanding Frames and Keyframes

The *Timeline,* located above the stage, is where your animation is created. It's important to take a detailed look at the components that make the Timeline tick: frames, keyframes, and the playhead.

The Timeline is composed of a series of consecutive *frames* (see Figure 3-7), each of which represents a point in time (much like a historical timeline). When the Flash Player plays your movie, the playhead moves from left to right across the Timeline. The *playhead* is represented by a red vertical line in your Timeline window. The numbers above the Timeline represent specific frame numbers.

Keyframe   Frame number

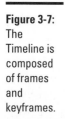

Figure 3-7:
The Timeline is composed of frames and keyframes.

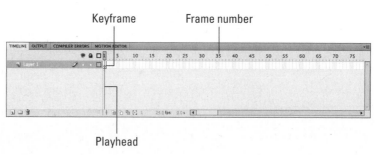

Playhead

Think of historical milestones represented at specific points on a Timeline with prominent markers. On a Flash Timeline, significant events (such as the beginning and end of an animation sequence) are represented as *keyframes*.

Every time you want to place a graphic, animation, or sound, first create a keyframe at the specific point on the Timeline where you want it to occur. When you create a new document, a single keyframe is automatically created on frame 1. Keyframes look like standard frames, except with a hollow or black circle inside.

Add more keyframes as necessary to create animations or have graphics appear and disappear at specific points along the Timeline.

Creating Animation with Motion and Shape Tweens

When you understand the basics of the Timeline (see preceding section), you're ready to create your first animation. The good news is that Flash does a lot of the hard work for you!

Flash can automatically create animation sequences from nothing more than a starting point and an ending point, figuring out everything in between. This type of animation is a *tween*. Motion and shape are the two types of tweens.

Creating a motion tween

A *motion* tween is a type of Flash-generated animation that requires the use of symbols and is best for creating movement, size, and rotation changes, fades, and color effects. All you need to do is tell Flash where to change the appearance of a symbol instance, and it fills in the blanks in between to create an animation sequence.

Only one object can be tweened on one layer at a time. If you want to tween several objects simultaneously, each object needs to occupy its own layer and have its own tween applied.

To create a motion tween, follow these steps:

1. **Drag a symbol from your library to the stage to a new layer.**

The symbol is added to frame 1. For example, we positioned the symbol on the left edge of the stage, which is where the motion will begin.

2. **Right-click the first frame of the layer that your symbol is on and choose Create Motion Tween from the contextual menu that appears.**

A shaded span of frames appears on the Timeline, called a *tween span,* and the layer is converted to a *tween layer.*

To create animation, you can now move the playhead to different points along the tween span and make changes to your object's appearance or position.

3. **Drag the playhead to a new frame and then reposition your symbol.**

   For this example, we dragged to frame 15 and repositioned the symbol in the middle of the stage.

   A new keyframe (which appears as a bullet point) has been created automatically at this frame to mark the change.

4. **Drag the playhead to another frame and move the symbol instance to another location on the stage, as shown in Figure 3-8.**

   For this example, we dragged to frame 24 and repositioned the symbol on the left side of the stage.

   In addition to another keyframe, a motion path is created on the stage to show the path of animation that the symbol will take.

5. **Press Enter/Return to play the Timeline and preview your animation.**

   For the motion tween we created, the symbol moves from left to right.

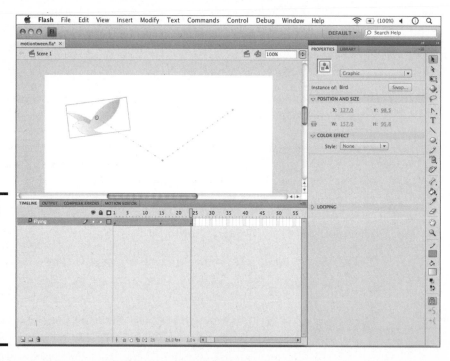

Figure 3-8:
A motion path is created to show the trajectory of your tweened object.

To see all frames of your animation at once, select the Onion Skin option underneath the Timeline. This option lets you select and show several frames at once so that you see the frames that the Flash tween has created for you.

You're just scratching the surface of what Flash can do; feel free to experiment further with different symbols and positions, and alter the length of your animations by placing starting and ending keyframes closer together or farther apart.

Resizing tween spans

If you want a tween to play out longer or shorter, or have more time for additional keyframes and motion, you can expand the number of frames in a tween span. By default, the length of each new tween span is based on your frame rate. A frame rate of 24 fps (frames per second) creates a 24-frame tween span each time, a frame rate of 30 fps creates a 30-frame tween span, and so on.

To expand or trim a tween span, follow these steps:

1. **Locate and select a tween span on the Timeline and select the last frame in the span.**
2. **Move your cursor over the last frame of the span until a double-arrow icon appears.**
3. **Click and drag left or right to trim or lengthen the span, respectively.**

 If you resize a tween span after animation already has been created, existing keyframes will shift from their original positions on the Timeline. This will cause certain animations to begin or end at different times than you originally intended.

Using the new Motion Editor panel

Flash CS4 features a brand new Motion Editor panel, which gives you precise control over each aspect of a motion tween. The Motion Editor displays the various properties of a motion tween (such as motion, scale, and transparency) in a graph-style format that you can use to edit or add to your animations. You can use the Motion Editor only on motion tween spans; it can't be used to modify shape tweens or *classic* tweens (motion tweens created in Flash CS3 or earlier).

The Motion Editor can be found behind the Timeline panel at the bottom of your default workspace.

**Book VII
Chapter 3**

**Now You're
in Motion**

Follow these steps to modify a motion tween with the Motion Editor:

1. **Clicking the Motion Editor tab (you can find it behind the Timeline panel) to bring the Motion Editor panel forward.**

2. **Select a tweened object on the stage; you can click either the object or the motion path to select the tween.**

    The Motion Editor displays each property as a row with a graph line running through it, as shown in Figure 3-9. The graph line represents the changes in a property value (such as scaling percentage) throughout the course of a tween span.

3. **Locate a property that your tween is using, such as Alpha, X, or Y, and click the row's title to expand it.**

    Along each line you'll find points, or *keyframes,* that mark changes in the value of that property at different points in time.

4. **Select a keyframe and drag it up or down to change the value of the current property.**

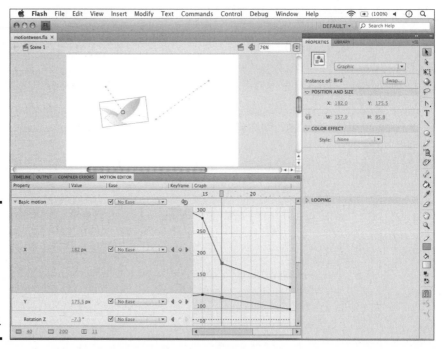

Figure 3-9:
Edit each property of a selected tween with precision in the Motion Editor panel.

5. **Move your pointer over a different portion of the line. While holding down the Ctrl key (Windows) or the ⌘ key (Mac), click directly on the line to create a new point (or keyframe).**

   Drag this point up or down to change the property's value at this position.

6. **Press the Enter/Return key to play back your Timeline and see how your modifications have affected the current tween.**

Creating a shape tween

It's easy to see how Flash can open up new worlds for creating quick, sleek animation without too much effort. After experimenting with motion tweens (see the preceding sections), you may find working with symbols a bit limiting, especially if your goal is to modify the shape of an object from start to finish, such as morphing a star into a circle. In this case, you'd want to take advantage of *shape tweens.*

For the most part, shape tweens are created in a very similar manner to motion tweens. However, unlike motion tweens, shape tweens must use raw shapes instead of symbols.

In addition to morphing between distinctively different shapes, shape tweens can morph color. Like motion tweens, you can tween only one shape at a time on a single layer. If you want to create multiple shape tweens simultaneously, isolate each one on its own layer.

Follow these steps to create a shape tween:

1. **Create a new Flash document. At the bottom of the workspace, click the Timeline panel's tab to bring it forward.**

2. **On an empty layer, draw a shape (for example, a star or polygon with the Polystar tool) on frame 1.**

   You can include a stroke and a fill, as the shape tween can handle both.

3. **Create a blank keyframe on frame 30 by choosing Insert⇨Timeline⇨Blank Keyframe.**

   As opposed to the motion tween, we choose a blank keyframe here because we don't want a copy of the shape drawn on frame 1 to be carried over to the new keyframe.

4. **Draw a distinctively different shape on the new blank keyframe on frame 30.**

5. **Select frame 1 and choose Insert⇨Shape Tween.**

   You see an arrow and green shaded area appear between the starting and ending keyframes, indicating that you've successfully created a shape tween.

6. **Turn on the Onion Skin Outlines option below the Timeline (see Figure 3-10) to see the frames that Flash has created for you.**

7. **Press Enter/Return to play back your animation.**

   You now see the original shape transform into the final shape.

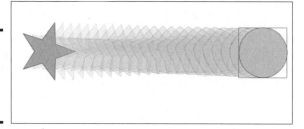

Figure 3-10:
A shape tween with Onion Skin Outlines on.

Try creating a tween between two type characters with the preceding steps. Create the letters using the Text tool. Break the characters into their raw forms before creating a shape tween by choosing Modify⇨Break Apart.

Tweened versus Frame-by-Frame Animation

If you come from a traditional animation background, you may want to create animation the old-fashioned way: frame-by-frame. Flash easily supports this method, but it's best to decide which method you want to use based on what type of animation you want to create.

There are advantages to both methods: Although motion and shape tweens give you the power to create sleek animations quickly and easily, you may find they're limited. Frame-by-frame animation is significantly more time-consuming and complex to create but can afford some detail and flexibility that you can't otherwise achieve.

To create a frame-by-frame animation, follow these steps:

1. **Create a blank keyframe for each frame you want to include in your animation.**

   Frames don't have to be consecutive; you can leave space between keyframes to control the time that elapses between each.

2. **Draw (or insert) a graphic for each state of your animation on the appropriate keyframes.**

3. **Play back your animation by pressing the Enter/Return key.**

In Chapter 4 of this minibook, you explore advanced animation techniques using Flash's new IK and Armature features, which allow you to create sophisticated animation with the ease of tweens, but the complexity of frame-by-frame animation.

If your goal is to simply move an object from one location to another, create fades, or transform size and rotation, it makes sense to use motion tweens and let Flash do the thinking for you. If you're trying to create highly complex animations that tweens can't handle (for example, a person running), you may want to try the more traditional frame-by-frame approach.

In some cases, you can break your artwork into individual moving parts (like wheels on a bicycle) across several layers to achieve similar affects to frame-by-frame by using motion tweens. You can explore these further in the next chapter.

Understanding Frame Rate

Frame rate plays an important part in the performance and appearance of your Flash movie. It dictates how many frames are played back per second by the Flash Player, in turn affecting the speed and smoothness of your animations.

You can modify frame rate in three ways:

+ **Choose Modify⇨Document.**
+ **With nothing on the stage selected, use the Property inspector.** You'll see your document properties.
+ **Click and drag over the frame rate value displayed at the bottom of the Timeline panel.**

Frame rate is completely based upon the result you're trying to achieve. Although the default frame rate in Flash is 24 fps (frames per second), you may also want to consider something around 30 fps, which is consistent with broadcast/digital video frame rates and should provide a good starting point for smooth, consistent animation. To keep things in perspective, keep in mind that a film projector (like the one at your local movie theater) runs at 24 fps.

If you want to increase the overall speed and smoothness of your animation, you can try increasing the frame rate gradually until you find the one that's right for you. Flash can support frame rates of up to 120 fps.

Changing frame rate affects the playback of your entire movie. If you're trying to adjust the speed of one specific animation, consider modifying the tween itself.

Chapter 4: Applying More Advanced Animation

In This Chapter

✔ Creating zoom and fade effects

✔ Creating a custom motion path

✔ Creating fade outs and fade ins

✔ Copying and pasting motion

✔ Creating gravity and inertia effects with easing

✔ Morphing graphics with shape tweens

✔ Animating poses with the IK and Armature tools

✔ Masking artwork and animation

✔ Previewing a movie

*W*ith motion and shape tweens, creative animation possibilities are limited only by your imagination. You'll no doubt want to explore what's possible, and in this chapter, you get started with some popular animation effects, such as fades and transformations. In addition, we show you how to use new features, such as Inverse Kinematics (IK), which give you new and unprecedented abilities to create sophisticated animation with less effort.

Creating Transformations

Some of the most common effects, such as zooms, flips, leans, and spins, are all different types of *transformations*, or changes to a symbol's dimensions, rotation, or skew. You can perform transformations on a symbol from the Tools panel, Transform panel, or Modify menu, and combine transformations for many animation possibilities.

Follow these steps to create a zoom-in effect:

1. **On the first frame of a new layer, create an interesting shape on the stage with one of the Shape tools.**

2. **With the shape selected, choose Modify⇨Convert to Symbol.**

   The Convert to Symbol dialog box appears.

3. **Enter a name for the symbol in the Name text box, (for example, type Zoom Shape), choose Graphic from the Type drop-down list, and click OK.**

   The symbol is added to your library and is ready to be used as part of a motion tween.

4. **Select the first keyframe; right-click and choose Create Motion Tween from the contextual menu that appears.**

   A new tween span is created on the layer. If you're working with the default frame rate of 24 fps, the tween span should be exactly 24 frames long, as shown in Figure 4-1.

5. **Click the frame ruler above the Timeline at frame 24 to reposition the playhead at this point.**

6. **Choose Window⇨Transform to open the Transform panel. With the Transform panel, enter 300% in the Scale Width and Scale Height text boxes.**

Figure 4-1:
Create a motion tween span for your new symbol.

Logo and illustration courtesy of Jambone Creative (www.jambonecreative.com).

A new keyframe is created automatically at frame 24 within the tween span — this marks the change in scaling you've just made.

7. **Press Enter/Return to play your movie.**

    The smaller instance slowly tweens into the larger one, creating the illusion that you're zooming in closer to the object.

The zoom-out effect is identical to the animation you just created, but in reverse. Rather than starting with the smaller symbol instance, you start with the larger one and gradually pull away by tweening into the smaller one. Instead of creating a new animation, you can copy and reverse the existing one using a few handy shortcuts from the Timeline menu, which appears when you right-click (Windows) or Control-click (Mac) a frame.

To duplicate and reverse the existing tween, follow these steps:

1. **Right-click your tween span directly on the Timeline and choose Copy Frames from the contextual menu that appears.**

2. **Select the next empty frame on the same layer.**

    If your tween span is 24 frames long, this will be frame 25.

3. **Right-click and choose Paste Frames from the contextual menu that appears.**

    A copy of your tween span is pasted back-to-back with the existing one.

4. **Right-click the new tween span, and choose Reverse Keyframes from the contextual menu that appears.**

5. **Click frame 1 and then press Enter/Return to play back your animation.**

    The zoom-in effect will play, followed immediately by the exact reverse (zoom-out).

Joining Motion

The beauty of the new tween engine is that you no longer need to create several tweens or keyframes to have lots of different motion changes. You can create several different movements, transformations, and color effects sequentially within a single tween span.

On occasion, you may end up with two or more tween spans back-to-back. This is true if you copy and paste tween spans, as described in the previous section. You can, however, easily join tweens together into a single span for easier editing and tweaking.

Follow these steps to join multiple tween spans together:

1. **While holding down the Shift key, click and select two or more consecutive tween spans on a single layer.**

2. **Right-click (Windows) or Control-click (Mac) any of the selected tweens and then choose Join Motions from the contextual menu that appears.**

   The tween spans are now joined together as one. You can now edit the tween span as a whole directly on the Timeline or with the Motion Editor.

 You can undo joined motion by choosing Split Motion from the Timeline's contextual menu.

Creating Fade Ins and Fade Outs

Fade effects are very popular because they can add a cinematic feel to images, text, and graphics. You can see fades used in familiar media, such as photo slideshows or film, where images or scenes fade from one to another.

In Flash, fades are a type of basic color transformation that you can apply to any symbol by modifying its transparency, or *alpha.*

To create a fade in, follow these steps:

1. **Click the New Layer icon at the bottom of the Timeline to create a new layer; select the Type tool and create some text on the new layer.**

   Use no more than two words with a font size of 24 points. You can set the type size and style from the Property inspector's Character options when the Type tool is active, so make sure that the panel is visible by choosing Window⇨Properties.

2. **Select the type with the Selection tool and convert it to a graphic symbol by choosing Modify⇨Convert to Symbol.**

   This step adds the type to the library as a symbol and makes it available for tweening.

3. **Right–click (Windows) or Control-click (Mac) the first keyframe of the current layer and choose Create Motion Tween from the contextual menu that appears.**

   A new tween span is created, and the playhead moves ahead to the end of the tween span.

4. **Grab the playhead and drag it back to frame 1. With the Selection tool, click the new symbol once to select it.**

5. **In the Property inspector's Color Effects section, choose Alpha from the Style drop-down list.**

6. **Use the slider or text box to set the alpha of the symbol instance to 0 percent.**

   The symbol becomes fully transparent and seems to disappear. (Don't worry; it's still there!)

7. **Click frame 24 in the Timeline; with the Selection tool, select the symbol.**

8. **In the Property inspector, choose Alpha from the Style drop-down list and then use the slider or text box to set the alpha to 100 percent.**

9. **Press Enter/Return to play the movie.**

   The text appears to fade in from nowhere onto the stage!

Very much like your zoom-out effect, the fade out is simply a reverse of a fade in. You can use the Timeline menu's Reverse Frames command to turn your fade in into a fade out as follows:

1. **Select the tween span that contains your fade in.**

2. **Right-click (Windows) or Control-click (Mac) anywhere on the selected frames to open the contextual menu and choose Reverse Keyframes.**

   The action reverses the animation so that the symbol starts out fully opaque.

3. **Press Enter/Return to play the movie.**

   The text you created now fades out on the stage.

Try duplicating and then reversing the fade-in tween to have the text fade in and then out.

Copying and Pasting Motion

A recent addition to Flash is the ability to copy the behavior of a motion tween and then paste it to a completely different symbol instance. This technique is handy if you need to have multiple objects follow the same exact animation behavior, such as birds of different colors and sizes all following the same flight pattern.

To copy and paste motion, you need an existing tween to copy *from* and then a symbol instance on a different layer to copy *to.* The following steps show you how to copy animation behavior from one tween that you can paste and apply to a different symbol afterwards:

1. **Select an existing tween span on your Timeline, right-click (Windows) or Control-click (Mac), and then choose Copy Motion from the contextual menu that appears.**

2. **On a new layer, place an instance of a symbol from your library.**

   It can be the same symbol you've already tweened or a completely different symbol.

3. **Right-click (Windows) or Control-click (Mac) the first keyframe of the new layer, and choose Paste Motion from the contextual menu that appears.**

   A new tween span is created.

4. **Press Enter/Return to play your movie.**

   The new symbol instance animates in the same way as the original object from which its motion was copied.

 You can work with two instances of the same symbol, but the beauty of this feature is that you can copy and paste animation between completely nonrelated symbol instances. You can also paste motion between symbol instances that have drastically different size, color, and rotation properties.

Animating along a Path with Motion Guides

The motion tweens described earlier in the chapter have involved simple animation from one location to another. For some tweens, you'll want to have your symbol follow a more elaborate path of motion, such as a race car following a track. For these cases, you can give your tween a specific path to follow by creating a custom motion path.

Experienced Flash users may notice the absence of the Add Motion Guide button below the Timeline. Because the animation engine has been completely revised, the process of creating motion guides no longer requires a separate layer. You can now modify or replace the motion paths that are created automatically with each new tween span.

Motion guides are especially useful when you work with a shape that has an obvious orientation (or direction, such as the nose of a car or an airplane). For this reason, make sure you use a symbol with an obvious orientation as your tweened object in the following steps:

1. **Create a new layer on the Timeline and place or create a new graphic symbol on the layer.**

2. **With the Selection tool, select the entire graphic and press the F8 shortcut key to convert it to a symbol.**

3. **When the Convert to Symbol dialog box appears, choose Graphic from the Type drop-down list and enter a name for the symbol in the Name text box.**

4. **Create another new layer on the Timeline, select the Pencil tool in the Tools panel, and select a stroke color from the Property inspector on the right.**

   Note: Make sure that Object Drawing mode is OFF. This button can be found on the bottom of the Tools panel when the Pencil tool is selected.

5. **Draw a path on the stage with the Pencil tool, as shown in Figure 4-2.**

Figure 4-2:
Use the Pencil tool to create a unique path for your symbol to follow.

Logo and illustration courtesy of Jambone Creative (www.jambonecreative.com).

6. **Switch to the Selection tool and double-click the path you just created.**

7. **Choose Edit⇨Cut to remove it from the stage temporarily.**

8. **Right-click (Windows) or Control-click (Mac) frame 1 of the layer which contains your symbol and choose Create Motion Tween from the contextual menu that appears.**

   A new tween span is created for your triangle symbol.

9. **Choose Edit⇨Paste in Place to paste the path you created earlier.**

   Flash automatically converts it to a motion path, and your symbol snaps to the path, as shown in Figure 4-3.

Figure 4-3:
Pasting a complete path to a tween layer converts it to a motion path.

Logo and illustration courtesy of Jambone Creative (www.jambonecreative.com).

10. **Press Enter/Return to play your movie.**

The symbol follows the path you created. Next, you can tweak the tween so that the symbol follows the exact orientation of the path.

11. **Select frame 1 of your tween span; on the Property inspector, locate and select the Orient to Path check box (it's located under the Rotation options).**

12. **Press Enter/Return again to play your movie and you'll see that the symbol now changes rotation to match the direction of the path.**

Snap to it: The importance of snapping

Snapping is an essential part of your workflow and can very often make positioning items on the stage much easier and more accurate. Snapping is like turning on a magnet; when you drag an object, it jumps to the closest guide, path, or object that it finds on the stage, depending on what type of snapping you've enabled. Snapping is great for lining up objects with each other, for positioning artwork on a ruler guide, and especially for positioning a symbol on the beginning or end of a motion guide path.

By default, snapping is enabled for alignment, guides, and objects. Additionally, you can choose View➪Snapping➪Snap to Grid (when working with a grid) or View➪Snapping➪ Snap to Pixels, which makes sure that objects are positioned on the stage to the nearest whole pixel.

You can find snapping options by choosing View➪Snapping, and you can also fine-tune snapping behavior by choosing View➪Snapping➪Edit Snapping.

Starting your symbol off on the right foot often helps get better results when using Orient to Path. If the symbol orientation isn't what you expect, try rotating the symbol in the right direction at both the beginning and ending frames of the tween span.

Be cautious of paths that overlap themselves; the results may not be what you expect!

Creating Inertia and Gravity with Easing

When objects take motion in real life, several factors affect their speed as they move. Take the example of a ball bouncing up and down on a sidewalk: When the ball hits the ground and bounces, it loses speed as it moves upward because gravity pulls it back toward the ground. When the ball changes direction and moves back downward, increased gravity makes it pick up speed as it nears the ground again.

You can reproduce the two most recognizable forces, inertia and gravity, by using a special tween option — *Ease.* The new animation engine makes lots of easing behaviors available, including Bounce, Spring, Ease In (speed up), Ease Out (slow down), and more. You can assign easing to any tween span with the Motion Editor.

To create an easing behavior, follow these steps:

1. **Select the Oval tool and on a new layer, create a perfect circle at the bottom of the stage.**

   Hold down the Shift key to constrain the circle while you draw it.

2. **With the new circle selected, press the F8 keyboard shortcut; when the Convert to Symbol dialog box appears, choose Graphic from the Type drop-down list and enter a name for the symbol in the Name text box.**

   In this example, we named the circle Ball.

3. **Right-click (Windows) or Control-click (Mac) the first frame of the layer and choose Create Motion Tween from the contextual menu that appears.**

   A new tween span is created, and the playhead advances to the last frame of the tween span.

4. **With the Selection tool, select and move the symbol straight up to the top of the stage while leaving its horizontal position the same (see Figure 4-4).**

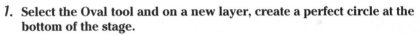

Book VII
Chapter 4

Applying
More Advanced
Animation

TIP

Drag the symbol slowly toward the top of the stage to keep it from shifting left or right. The Snap to Objects behavior keeps the symbol aligned with its original horizontal position until you release it.

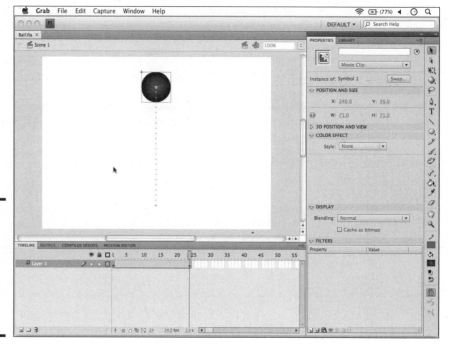

Figure 4-4:
Move the
Ball on
frame 24
straight
up while
holding the
Shift key.

5. **Press Enter/Return to preview the animation.**

   The Ball should now move from the bottom to the top of the stage.

6. **Click directly on the tween span on the Timeline to select it and then click the Motion Editor's panel tab to bring it forward.**

   You see the various properties of your tween represented on the Motion Editor panel.

7. **Scroll to the bottom of the Motion Editor, locate the Eases row, and change the Simple (slow) value from 0 to 100.**

   You can click and drag over the value to change it, or double-click and enter the value by hand.

   You see the default Simple (slow) ease is already listed. You can add other types of eases to use later on, but for now, the default will do fine.

   Changing the value creates an *Ease Out,* which slows the animation as it comes to completion.

8. **Scroll up to the top of your Motion Editor and locate the Basic Motion row; directly to the right, choose Simple (slow) from the drop-down list.**

   This applies the ease to the motion properties of your tween.

9. **Press Enter/Return to play back and preview your animation.**

   The animation slows down gradually as it reaches completion.

You can see how easing affects the speed of the tween as it progresses, and now a simple animation becomes much more lifelike. However, what goes up must come down, so the following steps walk you through making the Ball return to the ground:

1. **Click the Timeline tab and then click directly on the layer anywhere within the tween span to select the entire motion tween.**

2. **Right-click (Windows) or Control-click (Mac) the selected frames to open the contextual menu and choose Copy Frames.**

3. **On the same layer, select the next empty frame right after the tween span ends.**

4. **With the frame selected, right-click (Windows) or Control-click (Mac) and choose Paste Frames from the contextual menu that appears to paste the tween you copied in Step 2.**

5. **Click the newly pasted tween span to select it.**

6. **Right click (Windows) or Control-click (Mac) the selected frames and choose Reverse Keyframes from the contextual menu that appears to flip the tween backward.**

7. **Press Enter/Return to preview your animation.**

   The Ball now goes up and then down, and conveniently the animation is not only reversed, but so is easing.

Fine-Tuning Shape Tweens with Shape Hinting

Chapter 3 of this minibook explores the possibilities of morphing shape and color with shape tweens. Flash does a great job of recalculating shapes during a tween, but sometimes you need to give it a little help, especially when you have two shapes that have common features. Flash may overthink things and perform more shape morphing than it has to. For these cases, you can use *shape hints* — sets of matched markers that can tell Flash that two points on two different shapes are related. You can attach shape hints to the outlines of shapes on the starting and ending frames of a shape tween to let Flash know what common points exist between the two.

A good example of related shapes are the letters F and T. The two letters have many common angles. A shape tween between the two is a great way to make use of shape hints.

Before you get started, create a new document. Select the Type tool and, with the Property inspector, set the font style to Arial Black (or equivalent) and set the font size to 200. Then follow these steps:

1. **On the first frame of a new layer, type F in the middle of the stage.**

2. **Select the letter with the Selection tool and choose Modify⇨ Break Apart to break the type down to its raw outlines.**

3. **On frame 20 of the same layer, create a new blank keyframe with the F7 keyboard shortcut.**

4. **Type T on the new keyframe and position it in the same place as the F on the first frame.**

   You can use the Property inspector to match the X and Y positions, if necessary.

5. **Break the T apart by choosing Modify⇨Break Apart.**

6. **Create a shape tween by right-clicking (Windows) or Control-clicking (Mac) the first frame and choosing Create Shape Tween from the contextual menu that appears.**

   An arrow and green shaded area appear, indicating that the tween was created successfully.

7. **Press Enter/Return to preview your movie.**

   The F morphs into the T.

Even though the shape tween was successful, the outcome may not have been what you expected. Chances are the F seems to get mashed up (instead of a smooth transition) before being completely reconstructed into the T because Flash can't see the common angles between the two shapes (even though you can). That's where shape hints come in. You can add shape hints to suggest common points to Flash and smooth out the tween.

Before you get started, make sure that Snap to Objects is enabled by choosing View⇨Snapping⇨Snap to Objects. Then follow these steps:

1. **Select frame 1 of your shape tween and choose View⇨Show Shape Hints to turn on shape hinting.**

2. **Choose Modify⇨Shape⇨Add Shape Hint to create a new shape hint on the stage.**

   A red button, labeled with the letter *a,* appears.

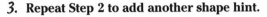

3. Repeat Step 2 to add another shape hint.

This time, the shape hint appears labeled with the letter *b*.

Sometimes shape hints stack on top of each other; move one to reveal the others underneath if only one is visible.

4. Position the two shape hints on the outline of the F.

To do so, move shape hint (b) over just a bit so that you can see shape hint (a). Then move (a) and snap it to the lower-left corner of the F. Position the second shape hint (b) in the upper-left corner of the F.

5. Select frame 20.

You see the companions to the shape hints you created, waiting to be positioned.

6. Position shape hints (a) and (b).

This step matches the bottom-left and top-left corners of the T to the ones in F, and the buttons turn green to indicate a successful match.

7. Press Enter/Return to preview your animation.

If you watch carefully, you see that the shape hints are keeping those two corners anchored while the rest of the shape transforms, creating a smoother transition.

Note: Like motion guides, shape hints don't appear in your final, published movie.

Add Shape Hints with the shortcut key combination: Shift+Ctrl+H (Windows) or Shift+⌘+H (Mac).

You can also add some remaining hints to finalize your tween by following these steps:

1. Select frame 1 of your shape tween and make sure that shape hints are still visible by choosing View➪Show Shape Hints.

If they're already enabled, you see a check mark.

2. Create one new shape hint with the keyboard shortcut Shift+Ctrl+H (Windows) or Shift+⌘+H (Mac).

The shape hint is automatically labeled with the letter *c*.

3. Position the (c) shape hint on the F (see Figure 4-5) on the top-right corner.

4. Select frame 20 and you see the companion to the new shape hint waiting to be placed.

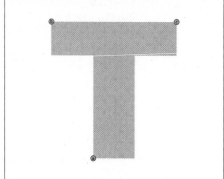

Figure 4-5:
Position the new shape hint as shown on both the F (left) and T (right).

5. **Position the shape hint on the T to match the angle you marked on the F.**

6. **Press Enter/Return to play your animation.**

   You see that the shape hints have provided a much smoother transition from what you initially started with.

Shape hints have their own contextual menu that appears when you right-click (Windows) or Control-click (Mac) on any shape hint on the first frame of a shape tween. To clear a selected shape hint, choose Remove Shape Hint or choose Remove All Hints to clear all hints on the stage and start over.

While it's often not necessary to add more than a handful of shape hints, you may be wondering: What is the maximum number of shape hints allowed? The answer is 26 — the exact amount of letters in the alphabet. Once Flash runs out of letters to label shape hints, it won't allow you to create any additional ones.

Creating Inverse Kinematics Poses and Animation

A significant new addition for designers and animators is Flash's support for *Inverse Kinematics (IK),* a principle relied upon in 3D and computer animation and modeling. Inverse Kinematics determines how jointed or connected objects position themselves relative to one another when moved.

For example, when animating a human arm, if the forearm changes position, it ultimately affects the position of the connected hand and upper arm. It's these principles that help create life-like animation and interaction.

Flash adds two new tools, the Bone tool and the Bind tool, that you'll use to connect objects together and edit those connections. Connected objects can be posed, and changes between those poses can ultimately be animated. You can create IK relationships between symbol instances or shapes.

To create and connect IK container objects, follow these steps:

1. **Create a new Flash document, and place two symbol instances on a new layer.**

   These can be instances of the same symbol or of two different symbols.

2. **Select the Bone tool from the Tools panel, move your pointer over the first object until a plus sign appears, drag until the cursor is over the second object, and release the mouse button, as shown in Figure 4-6.**

   This draws a virtual bone between the two shapes, connecting them together.

Figure 4-6: Drag the Bone tool to draw virtual *bones* that connect two shapes or symbols.

Book VII Chapter 4

Applying More Advanced Animation

You've now converted the two symbol instances to IK container objects, and the layer's been converted to an Armature layer.

3. **Choose the Selection tool and drag either of the connected symbols to see how the connected objects will behave.**

   The second symbol changes its position based on the position of the first.

You can add more objects to the chain. Although you can't add objects randomly to an Armature layer, you can connect existing IK container objects to artwork on other layers to add them to the chain.

Follow these steps to add objects to an existing Armature layer:

1. **Create a new layer on the Timeline and drag a symbol instance to it from the Library panel.**

   Position the symbol where you want it relative to the existing IK container objects on the stage.

2. **Choose the Selection tool and select the object in the existing Armature layer that you want to connect the new symbol to.**

3. **Choose the Bone tool, locate the *joint* (or connection point) on the selected IK container object, and click and drag from that point to the new symbol.**

   A new bone is drawn to connect the two objects together, and the symbol is removed from its original layer and added to the Armature layer.

4. **Choose the Selection tool and drag the new symbol around to see how its motion affects the other objects in the chain.**

Creating animation with poses

After you create a series of connected IK objects, you can put them into motion with poses. *Poses* capture different positions of your IK objects, and Flash can animate from pose-to-pose to create sophisticated animation sequences.

After an Armature layer is created, poses can be inserted (much like keyframes) to note different points along the Timeline where a new pose will be created.

To create and animate poses, follow these steps:

1. **Click and select an empty frame on an existing Armature layer (for example, frame 15).**

2. **Right-click (Windows) or Control-click (Mac) the selected frame and choose Insert Pose from the contextual menu that appears, as shown in Figure 4-7.**

   A new keyframe is created here, where you can re-pose the IK objects.

   Very much like a keyframe, a pose lets you change the position of IK objects at a specific point on the Timeline.

3. **Choose the Selection tool and reposition the connected objects on your Armature layer to create a unique pose, as shown in Figure 4-8.**

4. **Press Enter/Return to play back the Timeline.**

   Flash creates an animation to transition from one pose to the next!

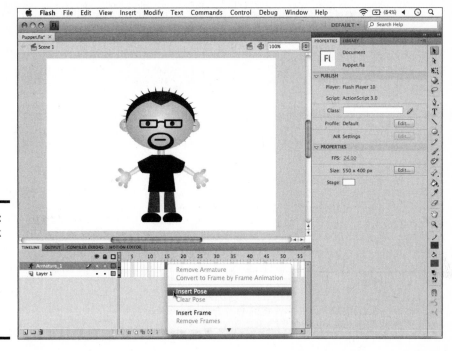

Figure 4-7:
Right-click any frame on an Armature layer to insert a pose.

Figure 4-8:
Change the position of any of your IK objects when you insert a pose.

Adding easing to Armature layers

Just as with motion tweens, you can mimic the forces of gravity and inertia using easing with IK animations. Although the Motion Editor isn't available for posed animation, you can easily add easing behavior from the Property inspector to give your IK animation a more realistic look and feel.

Follow these steps to add easing to an Armature layer:

1. **Click and select the first frame of an existing IK Armature layer on the Timeline.**

2. **Locate the Ease options on the Property inspector on the right — the default value is set to zero (no ease) — and then click and drag to change the value to 100 (Ease Out).**

3. **(Optional) Select another type of ease from the Type drop-down list.**

4. **Press Enter/Return to view the animation.**

   You see the easing change the behavior of your animation.

Using Mask Layers

The concept of masking involves using a shape (or shapes) to hide or reveal portions of a piece of artwork — working very much like a small window in your house. You can see only what the window allows you to see when you're inside. Flash features a special type of layer, known as a *mask,* and its contents are used to selectively reveal (or hide) artwork or animation on another layer.

You can convert any layer into a mask by using the Layer contextual menu, which is launched by right-clicking (Windows) or Control-clicking (Mac) the layer's name area. Artwork on a mask layer isn't visible; the content of a mask layer always represents the *visible* area of the layer underneath.

Animated text is a great candidate for masking. The following steps take you through creating a tween to which you add a mask layer for added effect. Before you get started, create a new document and select the Type tool. Choose a stroke and fill color and then use your Property inspector to set the type face to Arial Black (or something similar) and the font size to 40. Then follow these steps:

1. **On a new layer, select the Text tool and type a few words on the layer.**

   For this example, we typed **FLASH ROCKS** in capital letters.

2. **Switch to the Selection tool, and select the text. Choose Modify⇨ Convert to Symbol or press the F8 keyboard shortcut to convert the text to a new graphic symbol.**

3. **In the Convert to Symbol dialog box, choose Graphic from the Type drop-down list and enter a name for the symbol in the Name text box.**

4. **Place the text off the stage to the left so that it's sitting in the paste-board area.**

   You animate the text to bring it across the stage, entering from one side and exiting on the other.

5. **Right-click (Windows) or Control-click (Mac) the layer that contains your text, and choose Create Motion Tween from the contextual menu that appears to create a new tween span.**

   An instance of the text is created there as well.

6. **Move your pointer over the last frame of the new tween span until you see the double arrows. Click and drag to extend the tween span to frame 40.**

7. **On frame 40, select the text and drag it all the way to the right side of the stage.**

   A keyframe is created at frame 40, and this creates a tween that moves the text from left to right across the stage.

8. **Insert a new layer above the tween layer and name it Mask; create a shape to use as your mask on this layer. Make sure that the shape is at least as tall as the text symbol you created.**

   For example, we used the Polystar tool to create a star in the center of the stage. The Star option for the Polystar tool is available on the Property inspector under Options.

9. **Right-click (Windows) or Control-click (Mac) the new layer name and choose Mask from the contextual menu that appears.**

   The new layer is converted to a mask layer, and the tween layer appears indented underneath, as shown in Figure 4-9. Both layers are locked automatically.

10. **Press Enter/Return to play your movie.**

    The text animates, appearing through the shape (a star, in this example), much like you're viewing the animation through a window.

Book VII
Chapter 4

Applying
More Advanced
Animation

For the masking layer to take effect, both the mask layer and the layer being masked must be locked. To edit the contents of either layer, unlock the layers by clicking and removing the padlock icons on each layer.

Mask layers can contain just about anything a standard layer can, including tweens. Try creating a motion tween on your mask layer and see what happens!

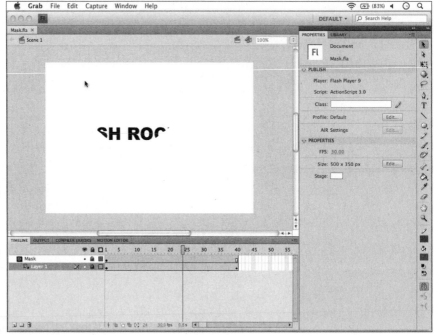

Figure 4-9:
Your text
animation
reveals itself
partially
behind the
star shape
you created.

Previewing Your Movie

Previewing your movie in the Flash Player to check its speed and size is a good idea. To view your movie in Preview mode, choose File➪Publish Preview➪Flash or use the keyboard shortcut Ctrl+Enter (Windows) or ⌘+Return (Mac).

This step creates an .swf file from your current authoring file and displays it immediately in the Flash Player. Previewing is a great way to see how your movie will actually appear to your users and can highlight any potential snags.

Ultimately, the final viewing environment for most Flash movies is on the Web in a browser, such as Internet Explorer, Safari, or Firefox. Part of what Flash creates for you at publish time isn't only a finished .swf but also an HTML (HyperText Markup Language) page to contain your movie. To see how your movie looks as viewed in a browser, choose File➪Publish Preview➪Default (HTML). Your default system browser launches and presents your movie in a Web page, just as your user will see it.

Chapter 5: Importing Graphics and Sounds

---

*Y*ou may decide to enhance your Flash movies with the addition of photos or graphics created in other applications, such as Photoshop CS4 and Illustrator CS4. Flash natively supports Photoshop and Illustrator file format imports, as well as many popular image formats. Combine this feature with the ability to import and utilize `.mp3` and other popular sound formats, and you can truly make your Flash movies an immersive multimedia experience.

Bitmap versus Vector Artwork

In computer-based design, you need to be aware of two graphic types: bitmap and vector. The drawing environment in Flash natively creates vector graphics, but you can use both bitmap and vector graphics in a Flash movie.

Vector graphics refer to scalable artwork consisting of points, paths, and fills that the computer creates based on mathematical formulas. While you may see a plain red rectangle, Flash sees an equation that creates the points, paths, and fill color necessary to re-create the graphic. Changing the rectangle's size, position, or color is a matter of simply recalculating the formula and redrawing the shape. As a result, vector graphics maintain crisp quality even when scaled far beyond their original size. Flash (like its cousin Illustrator CS4) can natively create detailed vector illustrations and typography that you can easily scale or modify.

Bitmap graphics are created very much like the picture on your TV set. If you ever looked closely at a tube television, you'll see the picture is created from lots of multicolored, tightly arranged dots. The same is true of bitmap graphics, which are created from many pixels of varying colors on your computer screen. The detail of the image can vary based on how many *pixels,* or dots, are used per inch to create the image. This amount is referred to as *dpi,* or dots per inch. Due to the immense range of colors and detail that bitmap images can re-create, they're the format of choice for digital photographs and photo art. Flash doesn't natively create bitmap graphics, but easily imports a variety of popular image formats and natively supports Photoshop (.psd) files.

Bitmap images are created with a certain amount of pixel data; rescaling the image means either eliminating that data or trying to create information where it didn't exist before. For this reason, bitmaps are far more limited than vectors in terms of scalability and can lose quality quickly if scaled too far beyond their original size, as shown in Figure 5-1. In Figure 5-1, both stars are zoomed at 400 percent. The bitmap image begins to pixelate as you zoom in, revealing the pixels that create it.

Figure 5-1:
Left: A star created with vector graphics. Right: The same star as a bitmap.

Importing Other File Formats

Your choice of file formats will be based on what applications you commonly work with. Flash supports many popular file formats, as well as industry-standard Photoshop and Illustrator file formats, giving you lots of flexibility. Flash doesn't generate bitmap artwork, though, so you may ask yourself what format you should use to save photos, graphics, and type created in other applications before you import them into Flash.

Flash supports and imports the following file formats:

- Illustrator (`.ai`)
- Photoshop (`.psd`)
- Encapsulated PostScript (`.eps`)
- Flash SWF (`.swf`)
- JPEG
- GIF
- PNG

Flash, like many Web-centric applications, works at screen resolution: 72 dpi. Images at higher (or lower) resolutions are conformed to screen resolution upon import, and their sizes on the Flash stage may be different than what you expect.

Vector graphics, such as illustrations and typography, can be created in applications like Adobe Illustrator CS4. Artwork that contains layers should be saved natively as Illustrator (`.ai`) format because Flash can import and re-create those layers exactly as they were in the original document without loss of quality. You work with the Adobe Illustrator Import panel to view and distribute imported layers in the "Importing Photoshop and Illustrator Files" section in this chapter.

Bitmap graphics, such as photos, can be saved and imported in a variety of formats. If you're working with a layered Photoshop document, you can import the document (`.psd`) directly into Flash with the new Photoshop Import panel. Like the Illustrator Import panel, you can view and choose how to distribute layers into Flash. Layer effects, such as drop shadows, are maintained, and where possible, they're converted into their Flash equivalents.

Other popular formats include JPEG, GIF, and PNG:

- **JPEG** (Joint Photographic Experts Group) can reproduce the wide range of color and detail necessary to reproduce photographs while keeping file size reasonable, and as such, are the best choice for photo-centric documents (see Figure 5-2).

- **GIF** (Graphics Interchange Format; see Figure 5-3) is a lightweight format with a limited color gamut (range) of 256 colors and is a good choice for reproducing crisp type, logos, and titling. GIF also supports transparency, so it's a good choice when the graphics you need to import need to be placed discretely against varying backgrounds.

- **PNG** (Portable Network Graphics) format has capabilities that cross over between those of JPEGs and GIFs. PNG also supports transparency and opacity. Between the two PNG types (PNG-8 or PNG-24), you can reproduce both simple graphics and photos with depth and accuracy.

Figure 5-2:
JPEGs have the color depth necessary to reproduce detailed photos.

Figure 5-3:
GIFs are great for logos and type.

Ultimately, your choice of format depends on what type of graphics you're working with and how they work in context with the rest of your Flash movie.

Importing Bitmap Images

When you need to make use of a photo or graphic file, such as JPEG, GIF, or PNG, import it into Flash by choosing File⇨Import.

Imported bitmaps are added to your library as *assets*. Assets aren't to be mistaken for symbols, which you can duplicate and manage from the library. Assets are simply non-Flash items that you import, store, and use throughout your movie. Although bitmap assets can be converted to symbols, they're not automatically converted upon import; you still need to add them as symbols (see Chapter 3 of this minibook).

To import a bitmap image, follow these steps:

1. **In a new Flash document, choose File⇨Import⇨Import to Stage.**

   The Import dialog box appears, asking you to find a file on your local computer.

To import an image (or images) to the library for later use, such as a series of photos that will be used in a photo gallery, choose File⇨ Import⇨Import to Library. This command places the chosen images directly in the library so that you can use them when you're ready.

2. **Locate a bitmap file (such as a JPEG or a GIF) from your hard drive, select it, and click Open (Windows) or Import (Mac).**

   The file is imported and placed on your stage on the currently active layer.

3. **Locate and open your Library panel (choose Window⇨Library), and you see that the bitmap has also been placed in your library.**

If you try to import an image to the stage and the currently active layer is locked, the Import to Stage option will be unavailable (grayed out). In that case, choose a different, unlocked layer or unlock the currently active layer.

Converting Bitmap Images to Symbols

When the bitmap is on the stage or in the library, the image can be converted to a symbol just like any other graphic on your stage. The process is the same, and the image inherits the same abilities that graphic symbols do, including tween ability, tint, transparency, and management from a master symbol in the library.

Follow these steps to convert a bitmap image to a symbol:

1. **Choose an imported bitmap image from the library and drag it to the stage.**

   If you already have a bitmap on the stage, select it with the Selection tool.

2. **Choose Modify⇨Convert to Symbol.**

   The Convert to Symbol dialog box appears.

3. **Enter a name in the Name text box, choose Graphic from the Type drop-down list, and set the registration point using the grid.**

   You can also convert bitmaps to buttons or movie clips by choosing Button or Movie Clip from the Type drop-down list.

4. **Click OK to complete the conversion.**

   Your bitmap image appears as a new graphic symbol in your library. You can now drag several instances to the stage and then tween and transform it.

Symbols created from imported bitmaps create dependencies and continue to reference the original raw bitmaps in the library. Deleting raw bitmap assets from the library causes them to disappear from any symbols that use them.

Modifying tint and transparency

After you convert a bitmap image to a symbol, you can apply the same transparency and color effects available to graphic symbols. To create these effects, use the Color drop-down list on the Property inspector, so make sure that your Property inspector is visible (choose Window⇨Properties) before you get started.

Follow these steps to apply a color tint:

1. **Drag a symbol from the Library panel onto the stage that uses an imported image.**

2. **Locate the Color Effect section of the Property inspector on the right; from the Style drop-down list, select Tint.**

   A percentage slider and color swatch appear.

3. **Click the swatch to choose a color from the Swatches panel and then adjust the amount of color applied using the percentage slider (see Figure 5-4).**

Figure 5-4:
A 50-percent color tint applied creates an interesting color overlay effect.

Note: Flash remembers color settings, such as Tint and Alpha percentages between uses (see Figure 5-4). If you set an object to 50 percent alpha, the next time you select Alpha for a symbol, Flash automatically applies the same 50 percent setting again (which you can easily change with the slider).

Applying motion tweens

Any bitmap that's been converted to a symbol can have motion tweens applied in the exact same way as you would with any other symbol.

When you're working with symbols created from images, you open up creative options, such as cinematic fades, moving slideshows, and unique presentation ideas.

To create a motion tween with a bitmap image, follow these steps:

1. **Drag an instance of a bitmap-based symbol to your stage from the Library panel onto a new, empty layer. Position it on the one side of the stage.**

   For this example, we placed a symbol on the left side of the stage. The instance should be on frame 1 of the new layer.

2. **Right-click (Windows) or Control-click (Mac) the first keyframe of the new layer and select Create Motion Tween from the contextual menu that appears.**

   The playhead advances to the end of a new tween span (at the default frame rate, this is frame 24).

3. **Position the symbol on the other side of the stage. Select the symbol once more and drag the playhead back to the beginning of the tween span at frame 1.**

   We moved the symbol to the right side of the stage for this example.

4. **With the Selection tool, click the symbol once to select it.**

5. **Locate the Style drop-down list in the Color Effect section on the Property inspector, choose Alpha, and set the percentage to 0%.**

   The symbol is set to full transparency and disappears.

6. **To make sure the symbol returns to full opacity later on, drag the playhead back to frame 24, and use the Alpha slider on the Property inspector to return the symbol's opacity to 100%.**

7. **Press Enter/Return to play the animation.**

   The image (symbol) appears to slide and fade in from the left side of the stage, as shown in Onion Skin view in Figure 5-5.

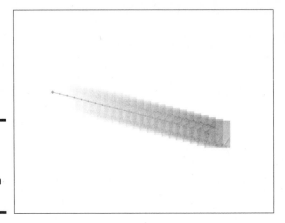

Figure 5-5:
The image
fades and
flies in from
the left.

Creating Bitmap Fills

As an alternative to solid colors or gradients, bitmap images can be used as fills for shapes, illustrations, and even type. Bitmap fills can create very cool effects and let you add interesting photographic textures to enhance your artwork.

You can create bitmap fills from existing bitmaps that have already been imported into your library, or you can use the Color panel to import a bitmap whenever you need to create a new bitmap fill.

Follow these steps to create a bitmap fill:

1. **Create a shape on the stage, as shown in Figure 5-6; set a fill and stroke color with the swatches at the bottom of the Tools panel.**

To use a bitmap fill on type, you first have to break the type apart by choosing Modify➪Break Apart. Type is created and edited on a type path, so you need to break it off the path and down to its raw form (points and paths).

2. **Select the shape with the Selection tool and choose Window➪Color to launch the Color panel.**

3. **Make the fill color active by clicking the Paint Bucket icon on the Color panel.**

4. **Locate the Type drop-down list and choose Bitmap.**

If you have no bitmaps in your library, choose a bitmap file from the Import to Library dialog box that appears.

Or, if you have bitmaps already in your library, a thumbnail preview of each appears at the bottom of the Color panel. Click the one you want to fill the shape with.

The shape is now filled with the bitmap you chose (see Figure 5-7).

Figure 5-6: Create an interesting shape with the shape or drawing tools.

Figure 5-7: The imported bitmap image fills the shape like a picture frame.

After you apply a bitmap fill, you may want to adjust the positioning and size of the bitmap within the fill area. Use the Gradient Transform tool (located underneath the Transform tool). Gradients and bitmap fills, although very different, both have a visible orientation point that you can adjust.

To position a bitmap fill, select the Gradient Transform tool and select a shape that uses a bitmap fill. Drag the center point of the circular bounding box that appears to reposition the bitmap, or use the outside handles to rotate, scale, and skew the bitmap.

Importing Photoshop and Illustrator Files

Flash offers seamless import of Photoshop and Illustrator files with the all-new Illustrator and Photoshop Import panels. Graphics created in these applications can be imported with ease and the highest quality possible, which is great news if Photoshop and Illustrator are already essential parts of your creative workflow.

With the Import panels, you can view, select, and convert Photoshop layers to symbols or keyframes or distribute them to Flash layers while maintaining common layer effects, such as drop shadows and blurs. The ability to select individual layers means that you can use specific elements from .psd and .ai files without the need to bring in lots of unnecessary art from complex files.

Importing Photoshop (.psd) files

Whether you need a simple photograph or complex compiled artwork, the Photoshop Import options make it easy to import any .psd file while keeping individual layers editable, even with type and layer styles. You can distribute Photoshop layers to Flash layers, sequence them as keyframes, or individually convert layer contents to symbols that are added to the library.

Flash even supports Photoshop Layer Comps, so you can choose from and import any Layer Comp in your .psd file.

Before you begin, locate a Photoshop file that you want to import into Flash. A great example would be a file that combines layers, type, and basic use of Photoshop layer styles (such as drop shadows).

To import a Photoshop file, follow these steps:

1. **Choose File⇨Import⇨Import to Stage.**

2. **When the Import dialog box appears, as shown in Figure 5-8, choose a Photoshop file from your hard drive and click Open (Windows) or Choose (Mac).**

Figure 5-8: You can choose which layers to import and even convert individual layers into symbols.

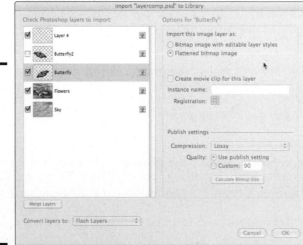

The Import to Library dialog box appears with full Photoshop file import options and a full view of all layers in your file.

3. **With the check boxes next to each layer, select the layers you want to import into Flash.**

Now, you can set options for how to import the contents of each layer.

4. **Highlight one of the layers you've chosen to import.**

You can choose from several options that appear on the right side of the panel. (See the sidebar "The Photoshop Import Options panel," for a detailed explanation of each option.)

5. **Click OK to import the file.**

The artwork you selected appears on your stage.

Because you can selectively import layers and merge layers together directly from the Import panel, consider using `.psd` files instead of importing flattened artwork (such as JPEGs or GIFs). This new panel allows you to extract specific elements and maintain transparency from Photoshop layers.

The Photoshop Import Options panel

The Photoshop Import Options panel gives you a detailed choice of what is imported and how from `.psd` files. You can send bitmap artwork directly to the library as assets or movie clips; type and vector layers can be converted or kept as editable paths or type layers.

Here's a detailed look at what you see in this new panel:

✔ **Select Photoshop Layer Comp:** If your document contains Layer Comps, you can select one from this drop-down list. The layers and positioning that makes up the selected comp become active in the Layer view.

✔ **Layers view:** All layers in your `.psd` appear listed on the left side of the Import to Library panel, and you can choose which layers to import by selecting the check boxes to the left. Highlighting a layer displays its import options on the right.

✔ **Merge Layers button:** When more than one layer is highlighted, you can choose to merge the layers on import into a single layer, which has no effect on the original `.psd`.

✔ **Convert Layers to Flash Layers or Convert Layers to Keyframes:** Selecting the Flash Layers option keeps layer structure (as well as layer groups) and distributes layer contents exactly as they are in your `.psd` file. Selecting the Keyframes option distributes layer contents across a sequence of keyframes on the Timeline.

✔ **Place Layers at Original Position:** This check box (selected by default) positions layer contents exactly as they are in the original `.psd`.

✔ **Set Stage to Same Size as Photoshop Canvas:** Selecting this option resizes your movie to match the original size of the `.psd` file.

(continued)

(continued)

✓ **Import This Image As:** Selecting this option converts the layer contents to either a bitmap image with editable Flash filter effects (converted from Photoshop layer styles or a flattened bitmap image, which merges any applied layer styles along with the bitmap image).

✓ **Editable Paths and Layer Styles (Shape Layers Only):** You can keep shape layers and vector artwork editable in Flash by selecting this option, which places artwork on the stage as drawing objects.

✓ **Editable Text (Type Layers Only):** Selecting this option keeps imported text layers editable, re-creating Photoshop type layers as Flash type layers.

✓ **Vector Outlines (Type Layers Only):** Selecting this option converts type layers into raw vector graphics (drawing objects).

Type is no longer editable, but its outline can be manipulated with tools, such as the Subselection tool and Pen tool.

✓ **Create Movie Clip for This Layer:** Selecting this option converts the layer contents to a new movie clip symbol that's also added to the library. You have the option of setting a registration point as well as an instance name. (See Chapter 7 of this minibook for more on instance names.)

✓ **Publish settings:** For each layer, you can set individual compression and quality settings or choose to use the document's publish settings instead. A handy Calculate Bitmap Size button lets you see how your selected compression and quality settings affect the resulting file size of the imported content.

Importing Illustrator (.ai) files

Because Illustrator and Flash both natively create vector artwork, you can import graphics created in Illustrator into Flash for placement or editing with tools, such as the Pen tool and Subselection tool.

Importing .ai files is nearly identical to importing .psd files, with a full layer view and lots of options for converting and distributing artwork and type from Illustrator layers. In addition to the new import options, the quality of imported Illustrator artwork is superior to past versions of Flash.

Before you begin, select an Illustrator file that you want to use. The flexibility of the Illustrator Import panel can best be explored with files that make use of type and graphics.

To import an Illustrator file, follow these steps:

1. **In a new Flash document, choose File⇨Import⇨Import to Stage; choose an Illustrator file from your hard drive and choose Open (Windows) or Import (Mac).**

The Import to Stage dialog box appears with a full view of all layers in your Illustrator document.

2. **With the check boxes, select the layers you want to import into your document.**

3. **Highlight each layer you've chosen for import to set options for each one, as shown in Figure 5-9.**

   You can import each layer and individual path as either a bitmap or an editable path. You can import groups as bitmaps or movie clips.

4. **Click OK to import the artwork to the Flash stage.**

   Check out the stage and the Library panel to see how your artwork was placed in Flash (see Figure 5-10).

Look for the Incompatibility Report button at the bottom of the layer view in your Import panel. This button can indicate potential problems that can prevent the artwork from importing properly into Flash. If you see the Incompatibility Report button, click it and read the warnings to address any pending issues before import.

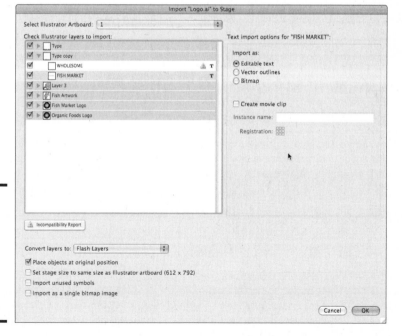

Figure 5-9:
You can bring Illustrator type paths into Flash as editable text.

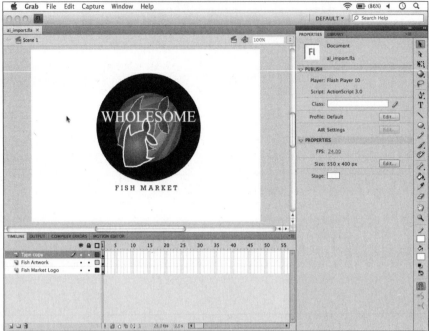

Figure 5-10:
A finished import, with all the Illustrator layers converted to Flash layers.

A view of the Illustrator Import Options panel

The Illustrator Import Options panel gives you a detailed choice of what gets imported from .ai files. You can convert grouped artwork, compound paths, and type layers to movie clips or bitmaps or keep them as editable paths or type layers.

Layer view: All layers in your .ai appear in this panel, and you can choose which layers to import by selecting the check boxes to the left. Highlighting a layer displays its import options on the right.

Incompatibility Report button: When this button is active, potential issues exist in your Illustrator file that may need to be resolved for a clean, successful import. Click this button and review the report to resolve any problems before completing the import.

Convert Layers to Flash Layers or Convert Layers to Keyframes: Selecting the Flash Layers option keeps layer structure (as well as layer groups) and distributes layer contents exactly as they are in your .ai file. Selecting the Keyframes option distributes layer contents across a sequence of keyframes on the Timeline.

Place Layers at Original Position: This check box (selected by default) positions layer contents exactly as they appear in the original Illustrator file.

Set Stage to Same Size as Illustrator Canvas: Selecting this option resizes your movie dimensions to match the original size of the .ai file.

Import as

✔ **Bitmap Image:** Selecting this option *rasterizes* (converts vector to bitmap) the selected artwork and imports it to the stage and library as a bitmap. Any vector artwork or type loses its editability.

✔ **Editable Path (Individual Paths Only):** Selecting this option places vector paths in Illustrator as drawing objects that you can further modify on the Flash stage.

✔ **Editable Text (Type Layers Only):** Selecting this option keeps imported text layers editable, re-creating Illustrator type paths as Flash type layers.

Create Movie Clip for This Layer: Selecting this option converts the layer contents to a new movie clip symbol, which is also added to the library. You have the option of setting a registration point as well as an instance name. (See Chapter 6 of this minibook for more on instance names.) This option and Convert to Bitmap are the only available options for entire Illustrator layers and grouped artwork.

Import Unused Symbols: Illustrator CS4 files can contain their own symbol libraries, which work in a similar manner to Flash symbols. Symbols that exist in an imported .ai file but that aren't being used on the canvas are added to the Flash library when you select this check box.

Note: You can choose to import an Illustrator document's entire symbol library without importing any visible artwork from its canvas.

Import as a Single Bitmap Image: Selecting this option flattens and rasterizes the entire Illustrator document and places it as a bitmap image on the stage, as well as a bitmap asset in your Flash document's library.

Importing Sounds

The best multimedia creations not only use visuals and motion, but also sound and music, so your Flash movies should, too! Flash fully supports the import, placement, and control of sounds in lots of different formats, so you can easily bring in loops, sound effect files, and even music from your .mp3 collection.

You can enhance your movie with background music or narrative, and sound effects can make using buttons and menus more intuitive. Flash can stream longer sounds (such as soundtracks or long form narration) to minimize loading time so that your user gets right to the good stuff.

Flash imports the following audio file formats:

✦ MP3

✦ Windows WAV

✦ AIFF

Note: Additional file formats are available with the optional QuickTime plug-in installed.

Follow these steps to import a sound into your library:

1. **Create a new Flash document and choose File➪Import➪Import to Library.**

2. **Browse and choose an** `.mp3`, `.wav`, **or** `.aiff` **file from your hard drive and click Open (Windows) or Choose (Mac).**

3. **Choose Window➪Library to launch the Library panel.**

   The sound appears in the library with a speaker icon, as shown in Figure 5-11.

Figure 5-11: Imported sounds appear next to a speaker icon in your Library panel.

4. **Select the sound and check out the Preview window.**

   A waveform preview of your sound appears, and you can listen to your sound with the Stop and Play buttons in the upper-right corner of the panel.

If you need audio files to work with, many Web sites, such as Flash Kit, and FlashSound, provide low-cost or free sound effects and loops in Flash-friendly formats. Adobe also has a listing of sound effects sites at www. adobe.com/cfusion/knowledgebase/index.cfm?id=tn_14274.

Placing sounds on the Timeline

After you have your favorite sounds into your Flash document, you can place them on keyframes along the Timeline to have them play at specific points in your movie.

You can assign sounds with the Property inspector, which displays the Sound section when a keyframe is selected. Sounds can be combined across different layers and utilized inside buttons to create sound effects for controls and navigation menus.

To place a sound on the Timeline, follow these steps:

1. **On a new layer, create a blank keyframe along the Timeline and launch the Property inspector (if it's not already visible).**

2. **On the right side of the Property inspector, locate the Sound section and select a sound from the Name drop-down list.**

   This drop-down list gives all the sounds currently in your library (see Figure 5-12).

   The sound is now placed on your Timeline.

3. **Press Enter/Return to play your movie.**

   The sound plays when the playhead reaches the keyframe.

Figure 5-12: Place sounds on a keyframe with the Sound section on the Property inspector.

After you place a sound on your Timeline, you can use additional options on the Property inspector to control looping, repeats, and playback performance. The most common options to experiment with are the Repeat and Loop options, which control the number of times (if any) a sound should repeat when it's played.

To repeat the sound, follow these steps:

1. **Select the keyframe where you already have a sound placed and locate the Sound options on the Property inspector.**

2. **Locate the Repeat drop-down list and enter the number of times you want the sound to repeat in the text box to the right.**

   By default, the sound repeats at least once, but if you enter **2** for example, your sound repeats twice.

3. **Press Enter/Return to play your movie.**

   The sound you placed plays and then repeats the number of times you entered in Step 2.

To *loop* (repeat endlessly) the sound, follow these steps:

1. **Select the keyframe and, with the Sound options, click the arrow beside Repeat and choose Loop from the drop-down list.**

   The sound is now set to loop continuously until the movie is shut down or another action turns it off.

2. **Choose File⇨Publish Preview⇨Flash to preview your movie.**

   The sound plays and then continues to repeat until you close the preview.

Editing sounds

One of Flash's hidden treasures is the Edit Envelope dialog box, which performs trims and volume effects and lets you dial in volume and pan settings for each sound placed in your movie. Although nothing quite replaces well-recorded and edited source files, you can do last-minute, nondestructive edits so that your sounds complement the rest of your movie.

To edit a sound, select a keyframe that has a sound placed on it or add a sound to a new keyframe, and then follow these steps:

1. **Select the keyframe on which the sound is placed.**

2. **In the Property inspector, locate and click the Edit button in the Sound section.**

   The Edit Envelope dialog box appears with a waveform preview. The center time ruler has two sliders on the far left and far right.

3. **Move these sliders to edit the in and out points of the sound or to trim unnecessary silence, as shown in Figure 5-13.**

   The lines above each waveform represent the volume envelope.

Figure 5-13:
Eliminate silence by sliding the starting trim point right and the ending trim point left.

4. **Click the lines above each waveform and drag them up or down to adjust the overall volume of the sound or to add handles and vary the volume at different points during the sound.**

   The higher the line or handle, the louder the sound.

5. **Use the Effect drop-down list in the top-left corner to choose from several preset volume and pan effects to enhance your sound.**

6. **When you're done, click OK and then press Return/Enter to play your movie and hear the changes made to your sound.**

Playing it right with Sync options

In the Sound section of the Property inspector, you see the Sync Options drop-down list, which controls how individual sounds load and play in your movie. Because a sound can serve different purposes (background music, narrative, and sound effect), the sync options can tell sounds to stream, stop, start, or fully load before playback so that they keep in step with animation and events in your movie.

(continued)

(continued)

Here are four options in the Sync Options drop-down list, each of which is tailored for a specific sound situation:

- **Event:** Choose Event when sounds need to fully load in your movie before they can play. This option is a good choice for short sounds and effects used on the Timeline, buttons, or navigation elements. Like their namesake, these sounds are best suited for responding to non-synchronized events, such as a button being clicked or the playhead hitting a specific frame.

- **Start:** Choose Start to set a sound in motion, but also keep more than one instance of that sound from playing at a time, preventing overlap. You can use this option for sounds that can potentially be triggered multiple times (such as an introductory narrative on the first frame). A sound with the Start option plays until the end and can be interrupted only by a sound with the Stop option.

- **Stop:** Choose Stop when you don't actually play a chosen sound, but want to stop that sound if it's already playing. A sound with the Stop option can be used to terminate a sound with the Start or Event options of the same name.

- **Stream:** Choose Stream for long form sounds, such as a soundtrack or a narrative that needs to remain in sync with animation on the Timeline. When a sound is set to Stream, it starts immediately, even as the remainder of the sound continues to load in the background. Flash ensures that the sound keeps playing in sync with the Timeline, even if it has to drop frames from the animation.

Chapter 6: Lights, Camera, Movie Clips!

In This Chapter

✔ Exploring movie clip uses and advantages

✔ Creating and updating movie clips

✔ Previewing movie clip animation

✔ Transforming and tweening movie clip instances

✔ Modifying your movie clips

✔ Using the new 3D Translation and 3D Rotation tools

Complicated machines, such as an automobile, are made from many smaller machines and moving parts. To build an automobile any other way is just not possible. Along those lines, you may find that some animations are too elaborate to create on the main Timeline alone. You'll want to break them down into smaller animations that can be brought together as part of a larger animation.

You'll also find that your movie may need to reuse several, identical animations. (Think about the four spinning wheels on a car.) For these cases, you have *movie clips*.

What Are Movie Clips?

The *movie clip* is a powerful and versatile symbol type that can include entire, independent animations, yet be placed and maintained in your movie just as easily as graphic symbols. It's one of three symbol types in Flash, and just like graphic symbols (see Chapter 3 of this minibook), they can be easily duplicated and maintained from a single master symbol in the library.

Movie clips are unique in that each one contains its very own timeline that looks and works just like the main Timeline. This timeline is completely self-contained, so animations in movie clips don't depend on or rely on the length of an animation contained within the main Timeline. Movie clips can almost be thought of as movies within your movie. Movie clips behave just like other symbols, so several instances of the same movie clip can be dragged to the main stage to easily duplicate animations. If you need to change an animation that appears several times throughout your movie, you need to modify only the original movie clip in the library that contains it.

Movie clips have all the same features as graphic symbols: You can easily drag multiple instances to the stage, and each instance can have its own scaling, tint, alpha, and rotation applied.

Because movie clips are capable of containing independent animations, they're a great way to break down complex animations into smaller, more manageable pieces. Trying to coordinate too many animations across the main Timeline may not only be very difficult, but in some cases, impossible, depending on what you're trying to create.

Movie clips can also be nested inside other movie clips, giving you virtually unlimited levels of depth and complexity!

Frame rate is a global setting for your movie and sets the rate for all movie clips as well as the main Timeline. To speed up or slow down individual movie clip animations, consider modifying the length of any included tweens before adjusting the overall frame rate.

In conjunction with Flash Player 10, movie clips provide 3D support, allowing you to take 2D artwork contained in movie clip symbols and rotate and position them in the 3D realm. In addition, all 3D properties can be animated, opening the door for stunning camera, rotation, and depth effects.

Flash CS4 adds two new tools: 3D Rotation and 3D Translation tools, which let you transform movie clip instances along x, y, and z axes. You can animate 3D properties as part of a standard motion tween and modify them with the Motion Editor panel. You explore these in detail later in this chapter.

Creating and Placing Movie Clips

Movie clips are created as new, empty symbols as well as from existing content on the stage. If you create a movie clip from scratch, you can add animation and graphics later by editing the symbol.

Follow these steps to create a movie clip from existing graphics:

1. **Create some interesting graphics on the stage with the drawing tools.**

2. **Select the new artwork and choose Modify⇨Convert to Symbol.**

   The Convert to Symbol dialog box appears (see Figure 6-1).

3. **Enter a name for your new movie clip in the Name text box, choose Movie Clip from the Type drop-down list, select a Folder (if other than the main Library root), and click OK.**

   The artwork now appears as a movie clip on the stage.

4. **Choose Window➪Library to check out your new symbol in the library with a special Movie Clip icon next to it.**

Figure 6-1:
Add artwork
to your
library as a
movie clip
symbol.

Nonanimated graphics converted to movie clips behave the same as graphic symbols, so you can place, tween, and modify instances on the stage. The difference, however, is that you can always add animated content later to the movie clip by editing it and creating tweens on its own Timeline.

In most cases, you'll want to take full advantage of movie clips by adding animation in a new movie clip symbol. To do so, you can start with a new empty movie clip symbol and add the animated content afterward.

To create a new movie clip symbol and add animation, follow these steps:

1. **Choose Insert➪New Symbol.**

   The Create New Symbol dialog box appears.

2. **Enter a name for your movie clip in the Name text box, select Movie Clip from the Type drop-down list, choose a Folder (if other than the Library root) to sort the new symbol into, and click OK to create the new symbol.**

   You see a new Timeline, as shown in Figure 6-2, and you will be inside the symbol ready to add animation. This Timeline works just like the main Timeline: You can add and reorder layers and create tweens. You still need to convert any artwork to graphic symbols before creating motion tweens.

3. **Create a new graphic on frame 1 of the existing layer 1, select the graphic, choose Modify➪Convert to Symbol, and choose Graphic from the Type drop-down list.**

4. **Right-click frame 1 and choose Create Motion Tween to create a new tween span on the layer; click and drag the last frame of the tween span to shorten it to 24 frames (only if the span is greater than 24 frames).**

5. **On frame 24, change the position or rotation of your symbol to set it in motion.**

6. **Press Enter/Return to preview the new Movieclip Timeline and make sure your animation plays back properly.**

7. **Click the Scene 1 link above the stage to return back to the main Timeline.**

8. **Locate your new movie clip symbol in the Library panel and drag two instances of it to the stage, as shown in Figure 6-3.**

If you hit the Enter/Return key to watch your movie clip play on the stage, you'll probably be a little disappointed. Don't worry; to see your movie clip in action, you just need to preview your movie in the Flash Player.

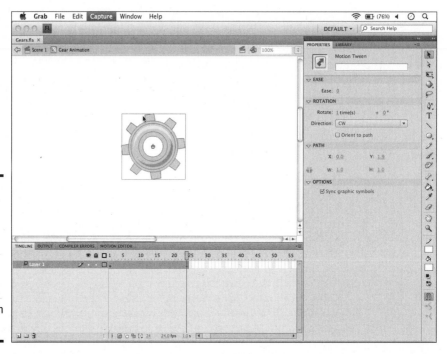

Figure 6-2:
The Timeline of your new movie clip symbol can contain tweens just like the main Timeline.

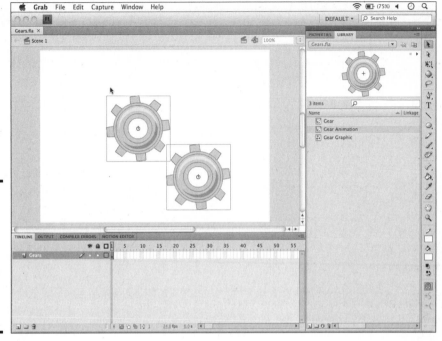

Figure 6-3:
Drag two instances of the new movie clip from your Library panel to the main stage.

Previewing Movie Clip Animation

Movie clips contain their own Timelines, and pressing Enter/Return doesn't start the movie clip's Timeline, but rather the main Timeline instead. To view movie clip animation, preview your movie in the Flash Player using one of two methods:

✦ **Test Movie** mode exports a compressed (.swf) Flash movie and immediately launches it in the Flash Player. Test Movie is used to give you a quick look at how the finished movie will appear to your end user as you build. Test the new movie clip by choosing Control➪Test Movie.

  You can preview your movie in Test Movie mode by using the shortcut key combination Ctrl+Enter (Windows) or ⌘+Return (Mac).

✦ **Publish Preview** works similar to Test Movie but exports the .swf (compressed Flash movie) using the final delivery settings you've already created under File➪Publish Settings. Publish Preview can also display your movie in an HTML (Web) page in your system's default browser. To preview your movie in Publish Preview, choose File➪Publish Preview➪HTML or File➪Publish Preview➪Flash.

Chapter 9 of this minibook covers publish settings for your movie, but it's important to know how these seemingly identical methods differ. Both methods let you accurately preview movie clip animation while you create it in your movie.

Modifying Movie Clip Instances

You can modify each movie clip instance with its own size, transformation, and color settings. This type of flexibility lets you get lots of mileage from a single movie clip symbol before having to create a new version or variation of your symbol in the Library panel. Just like graphic symbols, these transformations don't affect the master symbol or other instances on the stage.

Although all instances of a movie clip share a Timeline with its master symbol in the library, each individual instance can be stopped, started, and controlled individually with ActionScript. For more on how to control movie clip instances with ActionScript, see Chapter 7 of this minibook.

To transform any instance of a movie clip, you can use the Transform tool, the Transform panel, or the Transform submenu located at Modify⇨Transform. Try dragging two more instances of your new movie clip on the stage and applying different transformations to each.

To apply a transformation to a movie clip instance, choose the Transform tool from the Tools panel and select an instance on the stage. Use the handles to resize, distort, and skew the instance or select an instance on the stage with the Selection tool and use the Transform panel (open it by choosing Window⇨Transform) to type exact amounts for horizontal and vertical scale, rotation, and skew.

Use the Style drop-down list in the Color Effect section of the Property inspector with any selected movie clip instance to apply unique tints and alpha (transparency) effects and change brightness. To apply a color effect to a movie clip instance, select an instance on the stage and choose an effect from the Style drop-down list. Use the option controls to dial in the exact amount and type of color effect you need.

Combining Movie Clips

To create a new animation from several smaller ones, you can create a new movie clip from other movie clip instances on the stage. This technique allows you to group together several movie clips and drag them as one instance to the stage. Unlike a group, however, you gain all the advantages of working with symbols, including the ability to duplicate, maintain, and tween the combined movie clips as one unit.

The practice of including one movie clip inside another is sometimes referred to as *nesting*. Although movie clips can include other movie clips, graphic symbols, and buttons, graphic symbols shouldn't include movie clip instances. Movie clips should always be included in other movie clips so that their animation plays back properly.

Follow these steps to create a new movie clip from other movie clips on the stage:

1. **Select two or more movie clip instances on the stage.**

    These can be instances of different movie clips symbols in your library or of the same symbol.

2. **Choose Modify⇨Convert to Symbol.**

    The Convert to Symbol dialog box appears, as shown in Figure 6-4.

3. **Enter a name for your new symbol in the Name text box, choose the movie clip from the Type drop-down list, set the Registration Point by clicking a point on the grid shown to the right. Click OK to create the new symbol.**

    The Registration Point sets the location from which a symbol's position is determined on the stage. This can be any of the four corners, four sides, or the center of the symbol.

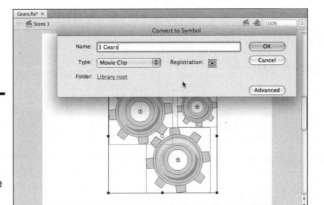

Figure 6-4:
You can combine multiple movie clips into a single movie clip.

    The symbol instances appear on the stage as a single movie clip, and a new movie clip appears in your library.

4. **Convert the selected instances to a new movie clip symbol as you would with a single graphic.**

You can now drag and drop several instances of the new movie clip to the stage. Experiment by adding a few instances to the stage and applying different transformations or color effects to each. Preview your movie by choosing Control➪Test Movie, and you see that the movie clips now are treated as one item, but still animate and behave as they did when they were separate instances on the stage.

When you nest movie clips inside each other, you're creating *dependencies* between those symbols in your library. Movie clips that include other movie clip symbols do so by *reference;* the included movie clip symbols aren't duplicated but are *connected* to the movie clip that includes them.

Movie clips become dependent on any other symbols they're created from. The smaller symbols remain in the library and are referenced by the movie clip that includes them. This means that you can't remove included movie clips without destroying the symbols that they're part of. For this reason, make sure that you don't trash any symbols in your Library panel until you're sure that they're not being used in your movie *or* by another movie clip symbol.

A great way to check what symbols are in use is to choose Select Unused Items from the Library panel's panel menu. This highlights symbols in your Library panel that aren't being used anywhere on the stage or by other symbols in the library. If a movie clip isn't used on the stage but is included in another symbol, it isn't highlighted, indicating that it's "in use."

Rendering and Animating Movie Clips in the 3D Realm

A welcome new addition to Flash's extensive capabilities is 3D rendering via the 3D Translation and 3D Rotation tools. You can use each of these tools to rotate and position 2D content in any movie clip instance around or along x, y, and z axes.

Combined with Flash's powerful animation engine, you can animate these properties as part of a motion tween to add cool depth, camera panning, and rotation effects to your movies.

The 3D Rotation tool

 This new tool can be used on any movie clip instance to rotate and transform the symbol around x, y, and z axes.

To render a movie clip instance in 3D, follow these steps:

1. **Place a movie clip instance on a new layer on the Timeline by dragging it from the Library panel.**

2. **Select the 3D Rotation tool from the Tools panel and click the new movie clip instance to select it.**

   Color-coded circular handles appear, each one corresponding to an axis along which the movie clip can be rotated.

3. **Rotate your movie clip as follows (see Figure 6-5):**

   - Click and drag the green line that crosses horizontally through your movie clip directly on the line to spin your movie clip around the y (vertical) axis.

   - Click and drag the red line that crosses vertically through your movie clip to rotate your movie clip around the x (horizontal) axis.

   - Click and drag on the blue circle that surrounds your movie clip to rotate it around the z axis (depth).

   - Click and drag the outermost red circle in any direction to rotate multiple axes at once.

To reset all transformations performed with the 3D Rotation tool, select the movie clip and hold down Ctrl+Shift+Z (Windows) or ⌘+Shift+Z (Mac).

**Book VII
Chapter 6**

**Lights, Camera,
Movie Clips!**

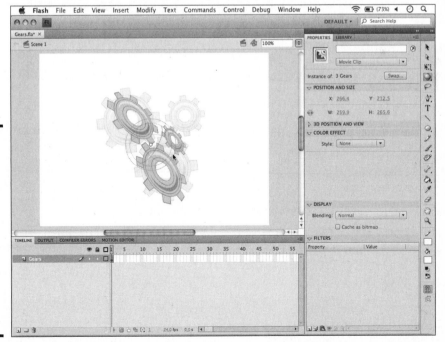

Figure 6-5:
When working with the 3D Rotation tool, use the handles to rotate a movie clip around the x, y, and z axes, or all at once.

Using the 3D Translation tool

In contrast to the 3D Rotation tool, which rotates movie clips *around* an axis, the 3D Translation tool slides a movie clip *along* a specific axis to change its perceived distance and depth relative to other objects on the stage.

Think of it as having three train tracks going left to right, up and down, or forward and backward that your movie clip can ride along.

To use the 3D Translation tool to move your movie clip in three dimensions, follow these steps:

1. **With the Selection tool, place a movie clip from by dragging it from the Library panel, or click to select an existing movie clip instance on the stage.**

2. **Choose the 3D Translation tool from the Tools panel, which you can find under the 3D Rotation tool.**

   Three guides appear corresponding to the x, y, and z axes. You can slide your movie clip along any of these three guides by clicking and dragging the appropriate guide, as shown in Figure 6-6:

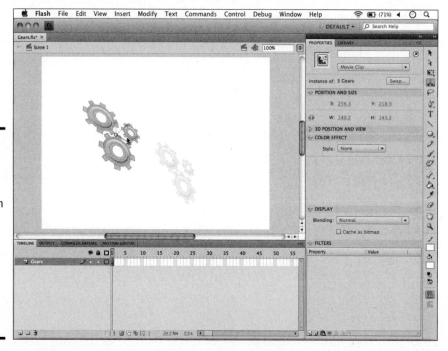

Figure 6-6:
Use the 3D Translation tool to slide and position a movie clip along the x, y, and z axes to change perceived depth and distance.

- *To slide your move clip left to right along the x axis,* click and drag the arrow connected to the red horizontal guide line.

- *To slide your movie clip up or down along the y axis,* click and drag the arrow connected to the green vertical guide line.

- *To change the perceived distance of your movie clip on the stage,* click and drag the blue center point to slide it along the z axis.

3D Translation and 3D Rotation transformations can be combined on the same movie clip for interesting perspective effects.

Tweening 3D properties

After you have a feel for how the 3D Rotation and 3D Translation tools transform your movie clips, you can incorporate these effects into a motion tween just as easily as you would with position and transparency.

Follow these steps to create a tween with 3D properties:

1. **Place a single movie clip instance on a new layer on the Timeline by dragging it from the Library panel.**

2. **Right-click (Windows) or Control-click (Mac) the first frame of the new layer and choose Create Motion Tween from the contextual menu that appears.**

    A new tween span is created, and the playhead jumps to the end of the span.

3. **Select the 3D Rotation tool and click the movie clip to make it active; circular handles appear around the instance.**

4. **Click and drag the axes to rotate your movie clip until you've set an angle and position you want.**

5. **Press the Enter/Return key to play back your Timeline, and your movie clip tweens from its original 2D position to the 3D settings you applied, as shown in Figure 6-7.**

6. **Repeat Steps 3–5 with the 3D Translation tool to see your movie clip slide in three dimensions.**

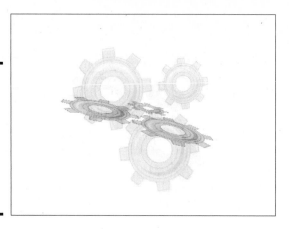

Figure 6-7:
3D rotation and translation can be tweened to create stunning effects.

Chapter 7: Controlling Your Movie with ActionScript

In This Chapter

✓ **Introducing ActionScript**

✓ **Adding actions to the Timeline**

✓ **Creating button controls**

✓ **Working with buttons in ActionScript**

*W*hether you're creating a Web site, presentation, or game, a truly interactive experience is one in which your users can control the action. If you want to take your movies to the next level, ActionScript can help. Flash's built-in scripting language has come a long way and can do anything from controlling movie playback to creating complex games.

This chapter introduces you to ActionScript and shows you how to use it to create interactive elements, such as clickable buttons, in your movies.

Getting to Know ActionScript

ActionScript is a powerful scripting language that you can incorporate into your movies to control playback, navigation, and imported media, such as images, video, and audio. ActionScript is written as a series of commands (or *actions*) that are placed on the Timeline, buttons, movie clip, and external files using the Actions panel. Think of ActionScript as a set of instructions that you can give your movie to tell it how to behave and add abilities.

ActionScript is often used for timeline control so that your animations can be told when and where to stop, loop, play, or jump to other points along a Timeline. You can also make truly interactive movies by adding ActionScript to buttons on the stage so that your users can control the animation, too!

The Actions panel

All ActionScript throughout your movie is placed using the Actions panel (see Figure 7-1), which acts as a wizard, reference book, and script editor all in one. You can add actions from the Actions toolbox using a categorized tray or drop-down list, or you can type them directly into the script editor.

A handy Script Assist mode (see the next section) is available so that you can add and modify actions without typing the code by hand (we highly recommend the Script Assist mode for new users).

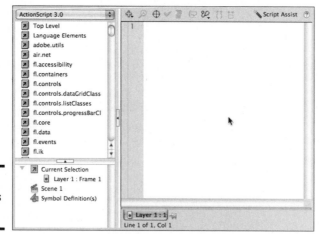

Figure 7-1:
The Actions panel.

To launch the Actions panel, choose Window⇨Actions or use the F9 (Windows) or Option+F9 (Mac) shortcut key combination.

To place an action on a frame, select the frame on the Timeline and launch the Actions panel. To place an action on a button or movie clip (ActionScript 2.0 only), select the button or movie clip instance on the stage and launch the Actions panel.

Script Assist mode

For users who are new to ActionScript, the *Script Assist mode* is a wizard that lets you use a series of menus, buttons, and text boxes to build your scripts without getting into the nuts and bolts of the code itself. Script Assist mode helps prevent time-consuming errors so that you spend more time being creative and less time troubleshooting.

Throughout this chapter, you use Script Assist mode while you become more familiar with ActionScript and how it works.

To enable Script Assist mode, click the Script Assist button in the upper-right corner of the Actions panel.

ActionScript is understood and processed by the Flash Player, so some scripted movies need tested by choosing Control⇨Test Movie. However, you can also enable simple actions in the authoring environment so that you can see your work in progress while still working from the Timeline.

ActionScript 3.0 versus ActionScript 2.0

ActionScript Version 3.0 brings many new major changes and improvements to the way ActionScript performs, as well as how it's created within your movies. ActionScript 3.0 requires the placement of actions on the Timeline or within external files (you can no longer place actions directly on movie clips or buttons) to make the code as modular as possible.

For first-time coders or users who aren't familiar with the principles of Object Oriented Programming (OOP) languages, these concepts may present a significant learning curve.

ActionScript 2.0 doesn't take advantage of the new methods, abilities, and speed improvements of ActionScript 3.0, but it does allow for more flexibility by allowing scripts to be added directly on buttons and movie clips. In addition to a smaller learning curve, ActionScript 2.0 is still utilized in movies created in earlier versions of Flash.

Note: ActionScript 3.0 support is available only in Flash Player versions 9 and 10. However, these later versions continue to support ActionScript 2.0 as well.

This chapter illustrates both versions wherever possible to give you the ability to work with movies published for either version. This is especially true of *legacy* (or older) files that you may need to update.

Specifying the correct publish settings

Depending on whether you choose to use ActionScript 2.0 or 3.0, you'll need to adjust the ActionScript version in your publish settings to match the version you choose to work in. In most cases, you can't publish newer 3.0 scripts in a version 2.0 movie, and vice versa. To choose the appropriate ActionScript version, choose File➪Publish Settings; click the Flash tab and choose ActionScript Version 2.0 or ActionScript Version 3.0 from the Script drop-down list.

You can also open the Publish Settings dialog box from the Property inspector by making sure no objects or frames are selected and then clicking the Edit button in the Publish section.

Adding Scripts to the Timeline

To add actions to a specific point on the Timeline, create a keyframe that you can put your ActionScript in. You can add ActionScript to keyframes with existing content, but it's always a good practice to separate your scripts from visual elements on the stage by creating a dedicated layer for your ActionScript. This layer prevents accidentally selecting the wrong thing when you try to add ActionScript to a keyframe or symbol.

The following sections use basic ActionScript to control a new tween on your Timeline. Before getting started, you need to create a new graphic symbol from artwork or typography on your stage.

Using stop ( )

The stop() action does exactly what it sounds like: stops the Timeline at whatever frames the action's placed on. A common use of stop() is to keep a movie from looping, which is the default behavior for the Flash Player.

Follow these steps to create a stop action in your movie:

1. **On a new layer, create a motion or shape tween from frames 1–24 and press Enter/Return to play back and preview the animation.**

   For more information on creating tweens, see Chapter 3 of this minibook.

2. **Click the New Layer button below the Timeline to create a new layer and name it** Actions. **If necessary, drag the layer upwards so it's the topmost layer in the stack.**

   This dedicated layer is where you add ActionScript to control your new motion tween.

3. **Add a keyframe on frame 24 of the new Actions layer with the F6 shortcut key.**

4. **Select the keyframe and choose Window⇨Actions to launch the Actions panel.**

5. **In the Actions panel, locate the Script Assist button and click it.**

   The top panel expands, and you're now working in Script Assist mode.

6. **Add a** stop **method, which stops the Timeline of a movie clip (including the main Timeline).**

   Here's how:

   - *In ActionScript 3.0:* Click the plus sign at the top of the Actions panel and choose flash.display⇨MovieClip⇨Methods⇨Stop. Specify the name of the object you want to control in the Object text box up top. Because you're stopping the current (main) Timeline, refer to it by entering this in the Object text box, as shown in Figure 7-2. The actions panel reads

     ```
     import flash.display.MovieClip;
     this.stop();
     ```

   - *In ActionScript 2.0:* Click the plus sign at the top of the Actions panel and choose Global Functions⇨Timeline Control⇨Stop. The actions panel should read stop();.

Take a look at your Timeline and you'll notice that a lowercase *a* now appears inside the keyframe, which indicates that ActionScript on the keyframe. These scripts run when the playhead passes that keyframe.

7. **Choose Control⇨Test Movie to preview your movie.**

   The animation plays until frame 24 and then stops.

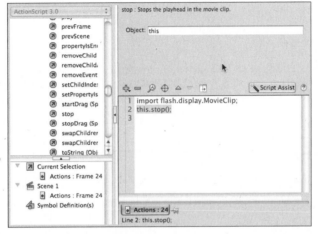

**Book VII
Chapter 7**

**Controlling Your
Movie with
ActionScript**

Figure 7-2:
The Actions panel view, showing a stop() action (top).

Using goto: gotoAndPlay() and gotoAndStop()

To loop a movie or to send the playhead to a different point on the Timeline, you can tell your movie to jump forward or backward to a specific frame with one of two variations of the `goto` action: `gotoAndPlay()` and `gotoAndStop()`. Each of these two actions requires a frame name or number so that the action knows where to send the playhead. When placed on a frame, these actions send the playhead forward or backward to the specified frame and stop, or they resume playback from that point.

To use `gotoAndStop`, follow these steps:

1. **On the Actions layer, select and create a new keyframe at frame 23.**

2. **Choose Window⇨Actions to open the Actions panel.**

3. **Apply a** `gotoAndStop` **action on this frame to send the playhead to a specific frame and have it stop.**

Here's how:

- *In ActionScript 3.0:* Click the plus sign and choose flash.display⇨ MovieClip⇨Methods⇨gotoAndStop. In the Object field, have the Timeline refer to itself by entering **this** in the Object text box. Enter **1** in the Frame text box and make sure the Scene text box is empty. The actions should now read

```
import flash.display.MovieClip;
this.gotoAndStop(1);
```

- *In ActionScript 2.0:* Click the plus sign and choose Global Functions⇨ Timeline Control⇨goto. The action defaults to `gotoAndPlay()` — select the `gotoAndStop()` radio button instead. Leave 1 in the Frame text box. The action should now read

```
gotoAndStop(1);
```

4. **Choose Control⇨Test Movie to preview your movie.**

The tween plays and jumps to the first frame, where it stops.

Follow these steps to use `gotoAndPlay()`:

1. **Select and create a new keyframe at frame 22 on your Actions layer and launch your Actions panel.**

2. **Apply a** `gotoAndPlay` **action at frame 22 to create a loop between this frame and frame 5 of your movie.**

Here's how:

- *In ActionScript 3.0:* Click the plus sign and choose flash.display⇨ MovieClip⇨Methods⇨gotoAndPlay. In the Object text box, have the Timeline refer to itself by typing **this**. Enter **5** in the Frame text box and make sure the Scene text box is empty (see Figure 7-3). The actions should now read

```
import flash.display.MovieClip;
this.gotoAndPlay(5);
```

- *In ActionScript 2.0:* Click the plus sign and choose Global Functions⇨ Timeline Control⇨Goto. The action defaults to `gotoAndPlay()`, so you don't need to change it. Enter **5** in the Frame text box. The actions should now read

```
gotoAndPlay(5);
```

3. **Choose Control⇨Test Movie to preview your movie.**

The animation plays until frame 22 and loops between frames 5 and 22.

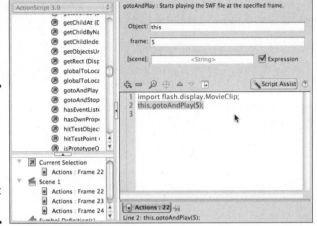

Figure 7-3:
The
gotoAnd
Play()
action,
placed in
ActionScript
3.0.

Creating Button Symbols

In everyday life, buttons give you control over your world, whether it's switching on a light or your TV at home or navigating through Web pages and e-mail messages online. To make your movies better, you can use buttons to give your users control over the action with Timeline control and navigation.

In Flash, *buttons* are special symbol types built to respond to mouse or keyboard interaction, such as clicks, rollovers, and specific key presses. When paired with ActionScript, buttons can be used for just about any navigation or control task. Buttons are created in the same way as other symbol types, and you can easily drag instances to the stage from your library to create more buttons.

Creating a new button

Like graphic symbols, you can create buttons from existing content on the stage or as new empty symbols to which you can add content later.

Follow these steps to create a new button symbol from existing content:

1. **On a new layer in your document, create a new, solid shape on the stage that you want to use as a button and select the shape with the Selection tool.**

2. **Choose Modify⇨Convert to Symbol.**

The Convert to Symbol dialog box appears.

3. **Enter a name for your new button in the Name text box and choose Button from the Type drop-down list.**

4. **Click OK to create the button.**

Choose Window⇨Library to launch the Library panel, and you see the new symbol with the special button icon next to it.

Button states

Take a look inside your button by double-clicking it on the stage or in the Library panel; its unique Timeline contains four specially marked frames: Up, Over, Down, and Hit. Each frame represents a button *state,* or the appearance of a button, as it interacts with a mouse in different ways.

Each frame, or state, can contain unique artwork so that your button can change appearance as it's clicked, pressed, or released. You can even add layers inside your button to stack artwork for more creative flexibility. Here are the states and what they represent:

✦ **Up:** The appearance of your button when it's not pressed or rolled over. This is the state you see most of the time as the button sits on the stage.

✦ **Over:** The appearance of the button when the mouse pointer rolls over it. Adding unique content to this frame creates the rollover effect many people know and love from Web buttons.

✦ **Down:** The appearance of the button when it's clicked and the mouse button is held down.

✦ **Hit:** The contents of this frame aren't actually visible but set the *hot spot,* or clickable area, of your button. If the Hit frame is empty, it uses the shape on the last available state by default. You can create a more specific clickable area if you want to give the user more or less area to work with or simplify usability for odd-shaped buttons.

Use a filled shape in the Hit frame so that the end user has no problem interacting with your button.

Adding content to button states

You can add content to each frame of your button to make it complete as follows:

1. **If it's not already open, edit your new button by double-clicking it on the stage or in the Library panel.**

You should have some content on the Up state from when you created the button. Now you can define content for remaining states as well.

2. **Select the Over frame on the button's Timeline and add a new keyframe with the F6 shortcut key.**

3. **Use the Selection tool, Property inspector, or additional drawing tools to modify the artwork on the Over frame (see Figure 7-4).**

4. **Select the Down frame and insert a new keyframe with the F6 shortcut key.**

5. **Modify or add content to the Down frame.**

    This determines how the button appears when the user clicks and holds down the mouse button.

6. **Select the Hit frame and create a new keyframe by pressing the F6 shortcut key.**

7. **Use the existing artwork that is copied to this keyframe, or one of the shape tools to fill this frame with a large, filled Hit area.**

8. **Exit the button by clicking Scene 1 above the stage.**

9. **Choose Control⇨Test Movie to preview your movie.**

    Rollover and click your new button to see the different states in action.

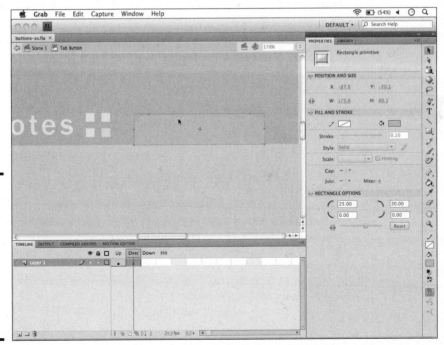

Figure 7-4:
Modified content for the Over frame appears when the user rolls over the button.

Enable simple buttons

Although choosing Control⇨Test Movie to preview your work is always a good idea, you may want to see how certain elements of your movie behave in real time on the stage. To see buttons in action on the stage as you build your movie, you can choose Control⇨Enable Simple Buttons. You then see buttons as they'd appear and respond to your user in the Flash Player.

Keep in mind that buttons can't be selected or modified on the stage in this mode; you need to disable Enable Simple Buttons to apply actions or transformations, or to edit the button in place.

Modifying button instances

Individual button instances can each have unique transformations and color effects applied, just like graphic symbol instances. In addition, each button can have a unique ActionScript applied to it, so you can use several instances of a single button symbol to create an entire menu or control bar.

Here's how you add and modify additional instances of your button on the stage:

1. **Choose Window⇨Library to make sure that your Library panel is visible.**

2. **Drag two more instances of your button symbol onto the same layer as your existing button instance.**

   If necessary, position the buttons so that they're spread apart from each other.

3. **Select one of the button instances and choose Window⇨Properties.**

   The Property inspector opens.

4. **Choose Tint from the Style drop-down list in the Color Effect section.**

5. **Select a color and set the tint percentage to 100 percent.**

   The button becomes tinted with the chosen color.

6. **Select a different button instance, choose the Transform tool from the Tools panel, and use the Transform tool to resize or rotate the selected button.**

Preview your buttons by choosing Control⇨Test Movie or by choosing Control⇨Enable Simple Buttons.

Using Buttons with ActionScript

The real power of buttons is realized when you combine them with ActionScript. In ActionScript 2.0, you can apply actions directly to button instances; in ActionScript 3.0, you define button actions and the events that trigger them on the Timeline or in external ActionScript files.

The tasks described in the following sections take place in ActionScript 3.0. Before you get started, make sure your publish settings are set to ActionScript Version 3.0. Choose File➪Publish Settings; in the dialog box that appears, click the Flash tab and then choose ActionScript 3.0 from the Script drop-down list.

Understanding event handlers

In the following sections, you get a chance to define actions for your button, as well as the event handlers that trigger them. An *event handler* tells your button what actions to perform if and when a certain event occurs, such as clicks, rollovers, and key presses.

Unlike frame-based actions, which always occur at the same time and only respond to the playhead, you can use buttons at any time (or not at all) and respond to several different types of user interaction. For this reason, as you place actions on buttons in Script Assist mode, event handlers are added automatically.

Creating a stop button

To get rolling (or clicking), you can use the button instances you've already placed as controls for the tween on your Timeline. You can add unique scripts to each of these buttons to tell the Timeline to stop, play, or jump to specific points on it.

An important step you need to take before trying to connect actions to a button is assigning that button an instance name. *Instance names* are how ActionScript can identify a specific object on the stage.

Before you get started, make sure that you remove and re-create the Actions layer if you've created one (described in the earlier section, "Using stop()"); the actions on this layer will conflict with your button actions.

To create a stop button, follow these steps:

1. **Create a new Flash document.**

   Add some basic animation to the Timeline by creating a symbol, placing it on a new layer, and creating a Motion tween.

2. **Create a new button and drag it from the library to a new layer on the Timeline.**

3. **Select the button instance on the stage and in the Property inspector, enter a name (such as** stop_btn) **for the button instance in the text box to the right of the button icon (see Figure 7-5).**

   Before you can control this button with ActionScript, assign it an instance name. You use this name from this point in your ActionScript to refer to and to control this specific button instance.

4. **Create a new layer on the Timeline, and name it Actions.**

Figure 7-5:
Assign
a button
instance a
name with
the Property
inspector;
ActionScript
can't control
the button
without it.

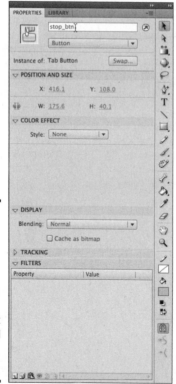

5. **Select the first keyframe of the new Actions layer and choose Window⇨Actions to open the Actions panel if it's not already open.**

   In the upper-right corner, make sure the Script Assist button is turned *off.*

6. **Click in the Script window and enter the following:**

   ```
   function stopAnim(evt:Event):void {
   stop();
   }
   ```

   This code represents the *event handler* — the instructions that respond when the stop button is clicked. Just as described earlier in this chapter, you're using the same basic `stop()` action, but this time, it runs in response to the button click and not at any specific point when the movie plays back.

   Here, the event handler is given the arbitrary `stopAnim` name, but it could be named just about anything. The `function` statement lets ActionScript know that all the code that follows is grouped under `stopAnim`.

   A `function` is a group of related ActionScript statements. Just like how you can physically group together graphics on the stage, a `function` statement virtually groups together multiple lines of ActionScript code that need to run together for a common purpose.

7. **Assign this new block of code to a specific button instance on the stage — in this case, the button you assigned an instance name to in Step 1.**

   Press Enter/Return a few times to move down a few lines under the code you just typed and enter the following line of code:

   ```
   stop_btn.addEventListener(ìclickî,stopAnim);
   ```

   This code assigns an *event listener,* which tells the button to wait for a click, and when clicked, to respond using the new `stopAnim` event handler you created. You'll notice that ActionScript can now refer to your button by its new instance name, `stop_btn`, and assign code directly to it this way.

8. **Save your file.**

9. **Choose Control⇨Test Movie and click your stop button to test it.**

   Any animation in your movie comes to a halt.

If you receive compiler errors in the Compiler Errors window, make sure to check spelling, casing, and look for the presence of any odd characters in your code. ActionScript is extremely sensitive to case and spelling, so this is the first place you look when troubleshooting. Compare your code to the code shown in the preceding steps. Also, make sure that the instance name you gave your button matches exactly with the name you're referring to in ActionScript.

Using goto

Unlike the `stop` or `play` actions, which park or resume playback at the current frame, you can use `goto` to jump forward or backward on the Timeline. You can use one of two variations: `gotoAndPlay()` or `gotoAndStop()` to resume or stop playback from the selected frame, respectively.

To use `goto` in your movie, follow these steps:

1. Place a new button instance on the stage and select it.

Make sure it's selected by verifying that its options are displayed in the Property inspector.

2. At the top of the Property inspector, assign the new button an instance name by typing in the text box to the right of the button icon.

For example, we entered **rewind_btn** for the instance name.

3. Select the first keyframe of the Actions layer you created in the steps in the previous section; choose Window⇨Actions to open the Actions panel.

4. Press the Enter/Return key to make a few lines of room underneath any code already in the Script window.

5. Type the following on a new line in the Script window:

```
function rewindAnim(evt:Event):void {
gotoAndStop(1);
}
```

This new event handler, `rewindAnim`, instructs the Timeline to return to the first frame and stop.

6. Below the new event handler code, make a new line and enter the following:

```
rewind_btn.addEventListener(ìclickî,rewindAnim);
```

An event listener has been assigned to the button instance you named `rewind_btn`, instructing it to run the code in `rewindAnim` when it's clicked.

7. Choose Control⇨Test Movie.

Clicking the rewind button on the stage now forces the playhead to frame 1 and playback stops.

Using frame labels

Many actions often reference exact frame numbers to move backward and forward on the Timeline. If you happen to change the placement of something on your Timeline, however (such as the start or end of an animation), frame numbers may become inaccurate. For cases like these, assign names directly to keyframes on the Timeline that you can call directly from ActionScript.

Frame labels are familiar names that you can assign to any keyframe (such as `start`, `end`, or `big_finale`). You can then tell ActionScript to jump to these frames by name as an alternative to using a frame number. If the location of the named frame changes, scripts still function as long as the label name is the same. When you move a keyframe, the label you assign to it moves with it.

Here's how you can modify a button to use a frame label instead of a frame number:

1. **On an animation layer, select frame 1 of your current Timeline.**

2. **Enter a name for your frame label in the Name text box in the Label area of the Property inspector, as shown in Figure 7-6.**

   For example, we assigned this keyframe the label name of `top`.

3. **Select frame 1 of your Actions layer and choose Window➪Actions to open the Actions panel (if it's not already open).**

   If you haven't already, follow the steps in the previous section, "Using goto," to create the `rewindAnim` function (or event handler).

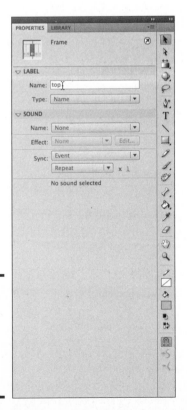

Figure 7-6:
Assign any keyframe a label name with the Property inspector.

4. **Locate the line that reads** `gotoAndStop(1)`. **Replace 1 with the name of your new frame label in double quotes.**

The code now reads

```
function rewindAnim(evt:Event):void {
gotoAndStop(ìtopî);
}
```

5. **Choose Control⇨Test Movie to preview your changes.**

Click the rewind button and you'll see the animation jumps to the beginning just as it did earlier. This time, however, the code uses a frame label instead of an absolute frame number.

Now, no matter where you move the keyframe, the script follows automatically as long as the frame label remains the same.

Naming frame labels and instances

Because ns and instance names both end up utilized within the ActionScript language, you're limited to certain "programming-friendly" naming conventions:

✔ Frame labels and instance names can't contain empty spaces, such as `my label`. You can, however, use underscores if you want to string several words together, such as `my_label`.

✔ Frame labels and instance names can contain numbers but not in the first character position, such as `2ndframe`.

✔ Avoid punctuation of any type, such as `My_label!!!!`

✔ You can use both upper- and lowercase letters but make sure that you reference the frame with the exact case you named it with; ActionScript interprets `myButton` and `mybutton` as completely different items.

Chapter 8: Getting Into the (Work)flow

In This Chapter

✔ Creating and managing workspace layouts

✔ Setting up grids and guides

✔ Using snap options and the Align panel

✔ Using animation helpers

✔ Creating custom keyboard shortcuts

✔ Using the Movie Explorer panel

Sometimes the difference between a good project and a great project is having a seamless workflow. Visual aids, such as guides and grids, alignment aids, and proper placement of tools and panels are essential parts of creating better movies in less time. The Flash workspace is highly customizable so that you can work in the most efficient way possible and spend more time being creative. Flash CS4 includes a new, easy-to-use interface, as well as some great workspace presets for most every type of user.

Using Workspace Layouts

Your Flash workspace consists of all the panels and tools you rely on, so why not take some time to customize it? You can save the position and appearance of these essential components by creating custom workspace layouts.

Workspace layouts take a snapshot of the appearance and position of panels you're using so that you can recall that same configuration at any time. You can save as many workspace layouts as you want for different projects or different designers who may share the same computer with you.

Choose Window⇨Workspace to recall, save, reset, or manage your workspace layouts.

Flash CS4 comes with several layout presets: Default, Classic, Debug, Designer, Developer, and Essentials. You can select and use these layouts as a starting point for a new workspace layout or to reset the workspace. The default layouts *can't* be deleted or overwritten (even by saving a layout under the same name).

Creating new layouts

Before creating a new workspace layout, open any panels you need, close any panels you don't use often, and position and size them exactly how you think is best. All panels can be toggled on or off with the Window menu. Grouping options for each panel are available under their respective panel menus, or you can drag and drop panels on top of one another to group them together.

To create a new workspace layout, follow these steps:

1. **Position all panels and toolbars as you want to see them.**

2. **Group any panels together or resize individual panels and groups.**

    You can also collapse any panels or groups to Icon mode to maximize screen area.

3. **Choose Window⇨Workspace⇨New Workspace.**

    A dialog box appears, prompting you to name the new layout.

4. **Enter a name for the new layout in the Name text box and click OK.**

    The new workspace is created.

5. **Choose Window⇨Workspace.**

    You see the new workspace as an available selection.

Managing layouts

After you create workspace layouts, you can rename, delete, or update them as needed. Deleting layouts you no longer use is good practice so that you can keep the list manageable. Also rename layouts to indicate when they were created (for example, MyLayoutFeb2009). You can manage layouts by using the Manage panel (choose Window⇨Workspace⇨ Manage Workspaces).

To delete a layout, choose Window⇨Workspace⇨Manage Workspaces. Select the layout you want to delete and click the Delete button. Click OK to exit the Manage Workspaces dialog box. *Note:* You can't undo this action, but a dialog box gives you the same warning and a chance to change your mind.

To rename a layout, choose Window⇨Workspace⇨Manage Workspaces. Select the layout you want to rename and click the Rename button. Enter the new name in the Name text box, click OK, and then click OK again to exit the dialog box.

To update (or overwrite) an existing layout, recall the layout by choosing it in the Workspace menu. Make any adjustments to your workspace and choose Window⇨Workspace⇨New Workspace. When prompted, assign it the name of the layout you're trying to update. A warning alerts you that you're about to replace an existing layout by the same name; click OK to overwrite the layout with the new changes.

To condense right-side panels to Icon view, collapse the entire panel group with the double arrows at the top-right corner of the screen. To hide the labels and just view the icons alone, use the ridged handle at the top-left corner of the panel group to resize it as narrow as it will go.

Fine-Tuning with Grids and Guides

Having lots of visual aides right at your fingertips is indispensable when you need to line up, arrange, or measure objects on your stage with absolute accuracy. You'll want some designs to take advantage of the place-it-anywhere flexibility that Flash provides, but other designs demand more precise control over placement and sizing. For these cases, you can take advantage of Flash's large array of visual aides and helpers, many of which you can enable and set in the View menu.

These visual aides don't appear in any way in your final movie; they're strictly for your benefit during the design and building process.

Enabling rulers and guides

Flash's built-in rulers appear on the top and left edges of your stage and are used to position and measure objects on the stage. You also use the rulers to create vertical and horizontal guides by dragging them off the ruler bars. Ruler units are in pixels by default, but you can choose Modify⇨Document to change to other measurement units, such as inches, centimeters, or millimeters.

The top ruler represents the *X*, or horizontal axis, and the left ruler represents the *Y*, or vertical axis. The top-left corner of the stage represents absolute 0 for both X and Y, with X increasing as you move right, and Y increasing as you move down.

To set up and use rulers and guides, follow these steps:

1. In a new document, choose View⇨Rulers.

The rulers appear on the top and left edges of your stage.

2. Click and drag anywhere on the stage.

Markers on both rulers follow to indicate your X and Y positions and the width of your selection area. Now you can create guides that you can use to position artwork on the stage.

3. Click the top ruler bar and drag down.

You're carrying a guide with you while you drag.

4. Watch the ruler on the left and drop the guide where you want it (see Figure 8-1).

Use the left ruler for reference so that you know exactly how far down you're placing the new guide — for example, at 200 pixels.

5. Click the ruler on the left and drag toward the right to place another guide.

Position this one using the top ruler for reference — for example, place it at 250 pixels.

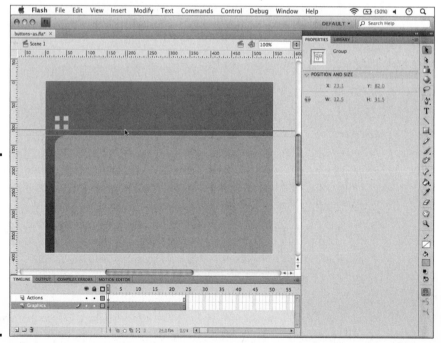

Figure 8-1:
To create a new horizontal guide, click and drag from the top ruler and release a guide on your stage.

6. **Grab your Type tool and create a single line of type on the stage, as shown in Figure 8-2.**

   Use a large enough font so that you can easily see and drag the new text.

7. **Choose your Selection tool; grab the text with the Selection tool and drag it until the bottom and left sides of the text snap in place to the guides you created.**

Your text snaps easily to the new guides because of a built-in mechanism — *snapping*. Think of snapping as turning on a magnetic force that allows objects to adhere to each other or to visual helpers (such as guides) to make positioning easier. By default, Snap Align, Snap to Guides, and Snap to Objects are enabled (choose View➪Snapping). You can also enable Snap to Pixels and Snap to Grid.

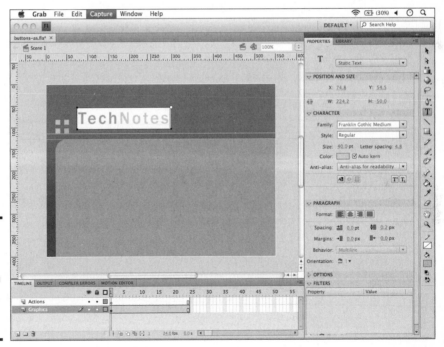

**Book VII
Chapter 8**

Getting Into the
(Work)flow

Figure 8-2: Create a line of type and position it with the help of guides.

Enabling the grid

If you've ever drawn on graph paper, you know how fun it can be to follow the lines and create perfect shapes and drawings. Like good old graph paper, you can enable and use the Flash grid to draw and position objects and create precise layouts by just following the lines. Like guides, you can snap type, drawing objects, and symbols to gridlines. You can also draw along gridlines to easily measure and match shapes.

To enable the grid, choose View⇨Grid⇨Show Grid (see Figure 8-3). To take full advantage of the grid, choose View⇨Snapping⇨Snap to Grid to make it *magnetic.*

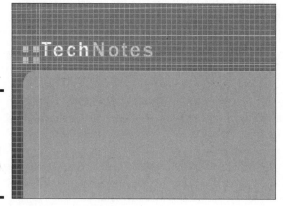

Figure 8-3:
You can position objects and draw on top of the grid.

Follow these steps to draw and position objects with the grid:

1. **Choose View⇨Grid⇨Show Grid to make sure the grid is enabled and choose View⇨Snapping⇨Snap to Grid turn on snapping for the grid.**

2. **Grab your Rectangle tool, choose a stroke color, and set the fill color to None.**

3. **Draw a rectangle with the gridlines as a guide.**

The shape snaps to the nearest gridline while you draw.

4. **Use the Selection tool to click and drag the new shape and snap it into place, as shown in Figure 8-4.**

When you move objects along the grid, they snap by their registration point to the gridlines. Use the gridlines to snap the object to the exact position you want.

To customize the appearance of your grid, choose View⇨Grid⇨Edit Grid. From this dialog box, you can specify the grid's size, color, and how accurate you want the snapping to be.

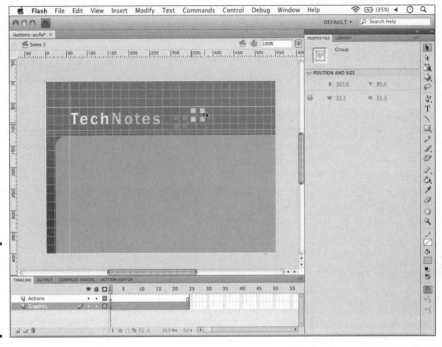

Figure 8-4:
The object
snaps to the
grid while
you move it.

Aligning Artwork

If you need to line up or space out several graphics on the stage, you can use the handy Align panel to assist you. The Align panel lets you line up, distribute, or space two or more objects relative to each other or the stage.

To experiment with the Align options, create a new layer, draw a shape on the stage, and place it on the bottom below any graphics you already have on the stage. Then follow these steps to align and distribute two or more graphics:

1. **Select a graphic on the stage and duplicate it two to three times by choosing Edit⇨Copy and then choosing Edit⇨Paste.**

2. **Loosely position the graphics across the stage from left to right.**

3. **Select all the new copies you created with the Selection tool and launch the Align panel by choosing Window⇨Align.**

   The first row contains all the Align buttons, broken down into two groups: vertical and horizontal.

4. **Click the Align Vertical Center button to align the selected graphics horizontally by their top edge.**

The graphics reposition themselves so that they're all flush by the top edge. Align the selected graphics horizontally with each other with the buttons under the Align row. The second row contains buttons that evenly distribute graphics vertically or horizontally by their center, top, or bottom edges.

5. **Click the middle button of the second group (Distribute Horizontal Center) to distribute your graphics evenly based on their center points, as shown in Figure 8-5.**

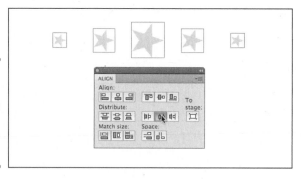

Figure 8-5:
Distribute
the graphics
horizontally
across the
stage.

Distributing to the stage

The To Stage button (located on right side of the Align panel) can be enabled so that any distribution uses the stage as a point of reference. The distribute options are useful if you want to distribute objects across the full width of the stage regardless of their distance from each other.

To distribute objects across the stage, follow these steps:

1. **Select two or more graphics on the stage.**
2. **Locate the To Stage button on the Align panel and click it.**
3. **Click any of the horizontal distribution buttons in the Distribute row.**

The graphics redistribute and spread across the full width of the stage.

Using Match Size options

If you need to resize two or more objects on the stage so that they're all the same width and height, you can take advantage of the Match Size options in the Align panel. Match Size options can conform two objects to the same width, height, or both.

To match two objects in size, follow these steps:

1. **Select two or more different-sized graphics, symbols, or drawing objects on the stage (refer to Figure 8-5).**

2. **Choose Window⇨Align to launch the Align panel (if it's not already open).**

3. **Locate the Match Size button group on the bottom of the panel and click the last button of the three (Match Width and Height).**

   The objects resize to the same width and height, as shown in Figure 8-6.

   Note: You can also match only width or height by clicking either the first or second buttons of the group, respectively.

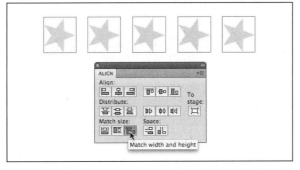

Figure 8-6: Match the width and height of two or more graphics.

With the Stage button enabled, Match Size resizes any selected object(s) to the full width and height of your stage. This is an easy way to create a full-sized background or to stretch a graphic to fit the entire stage.

When using Match Size, the largest of the selected objects always dictates the resize. All other objects are resized to match the largest selected object.

Experimenting with Animation Helpers

Sitting discretely below the Timeline are some highly useful icons that can be a big help while you're developing and fine-tuning your animations. The Onion Skin, Onion Skin Outlines, and Edit Multiple Frames options let you view, move, and manipulate entire animations at once to save time and guarantee better results.

When creating animation, you can enable onion skinning to view several frames at a time. With tweened animation, onion skinning can reveal all frames created in between the starting and ending keyframes to help you make adjustments and see them in action. You can choose between two types of onion skinning, depending on whether you want to view frames as outlines or full-color previews.

Before you get started, create a new motion tween or open a document with an existing tween that you can use for this example.

To enable onion skinning, follow these steps:

1. **Select the Onion Skin icon underneath the Timeline.**

   A set of brackets appears above the Timeline.

2. **Adjust the brackets so that all the frames in your tween are selected.**

   You see a full preview of all the frames generated by your tween.

You can't select the frames shown in between, but you can move the instances on the starting and ending keyframe. Select the symbol instance on the starting keyframe of your tween and move it. The onion skin reveals how the frames in between change when you shift your starting or ending instances.

As an alternative to seeing frames in your tween in full color, you can preview them as outlines by using the Onion Skin Outlines option (see Figure 8-7). This option works exactly like the Onion Skin option but shows selected frames using a wire frame-style outline view. The Onion Skin Outlines option can be a better choice if the full-color preview looks too cluttered.

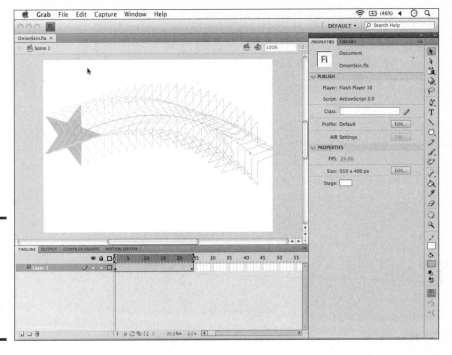

Figure 8-7:
An animation shown in Onion Skin Outlines mode.

Using Keyboard Shortcuts

Part of creating a smooth and fast work environment is having your favorite commands, panels, and tools right at your fingertips. Most Flash menu items and panels are equipped with shortcut key combinations that provide easy access without the combing through several menus. If you need your own custom keyboard shortcuts, Flash lets you create and save keyboard short-cut sets that you can fully customize to speed up your workflow.

To view the default keyboard shortcuts and create your own, choose Edit➪Keyboard Shortcuts (Windows) or Flash➪Keyboard Shortcuts (Mac).

You can map almost any available tool, command, or panel to a keyboard shortcut. You can choose to memorize existing keyboard shortcuts for commonly used items or create custom keyboard shortcuts that are more intuitive for you.

To create a new keyboard shortcut, follow these steps:

1. Choose Edit➪Keyboard Shortcuts (Windows) or Flash➪ Keyboard Shortcuts (Mac).

The Keyboard Shortcuts dialog box launches (see Figure 8-8).

2. Scroll down and click the plus sign (Windows) or triangle (Mac) to the left of where it reads Control.

You see all menu items under the Control menu and any keyboard shortcuts assigned to them.

3. Locate and select the menu command you want to create a shortcut for, as shown in Figure 8-8.

For this example, we selected Control⇨Loop Playback.

The default set can't be modified, so you'll need to duplicate the default set and make changes to the new copy.

Figure 8-8: Drill down through the menus to select the command you want to create a shortcut for.

4. Click the Duplicate Set icon at the top of the dialog box and type My Custom Set **in the Name text box when prompted; click OK to create the new set.**

5. With the current menu item selected, locate and click the plus sign beside Shortcuts to add a new shortcut for the menu item.

The word <empty> appears, ready for you to enter a keyboard shortcut.

6. Hold down Ctrl+Shift (Windows) or ⌘+Shift (Mac) plus the key you want to assign as the keyboard shortcut (for example, Ctrl+Shift+G or ⌘+Shift+G).

Use a letter or a number for a keyboard shortcut. You can also use the Shift, Ctrl, and Alt keys (Windows) or Shift, ⌘, and Option keys (Mac) in combination with a letter or a number to create keyboard shortcuts.

You may receive a warning if the keyboard shortcut you've selected is already in use. Make sure the shortcut is not assigned to a crucial menu command before you decide to overwrite it.

The Shortcuts text box fills in the keyboard shortcut as you hold it. Note that if the keyboard shortcut already exists, a warning appears.

7. **To confirm the shortcut, click the Change button.**

8. **Click OK to exit the dialog box and save the shortcut to your new set.**

At any time, you can return to your custom set in the Keyboard Shortcuts dialog box to add new shortcuts or modify existing ones. If at any point you want to switch sets, return to the Keyboard Shortcuts dialog box and select a different set from the Current Set menu.

Working with the Movie Explorer

As a Flash project grows and becomes more complex, getting around your document can be a bit of a guessing game. As you add movie clips, ActionScript, media files, and more, the inner workings can overwhelm even the most organized of designers.

For these cases, the Movie Explorer panel (see Figure 8-9) offers an at-a-glance view of your movie. From this panel, you see exactly what's being used and where and can navigate directly to any item on the list. You can filter the panel to show only the types of items you want, whether it's ActionScript, movie clips, sounds, or type, by clicking and selecting the icon buttons at the top of the panel. To launch the Movie Explorer, choose Window⇨Movie Explorer.

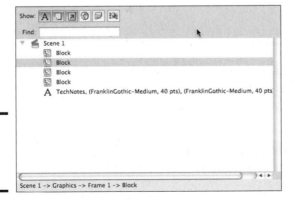

Figure 8-9:
The Movie
Explorer
panel.

Chapter 9: Publishing and Final Delivery

In This Chapter

✓ **Getting ready to publish**

✓ **Choosing a publish format**

✓ **Previewing your work**

✓ **Publishing for the Web and CD-ROM**

✓ **Choosing the right settings for your movie**

✓ **Creating custom publish profiles**

*T*o show your creations to the world, publish the final movie with the Publish command. Before publishing, you can use the Publish Settings option to specify important settings for your final movie, including quality and version settings as well as your choice of file formats. Different options let you publish for the Web, CD-ROM, and even mobile phones. We cover all those options in this chapter.

Getting Familiar with the Publish Process

The `.fla` file you build your movie in is intended for the Flash authoring environment only. When you're ready to deliver a final product, create a final `.swf` (ShockWave Flash; compressed movie) file that the Flash Player can play. The Flash Player is responsible for displaying your movie in Web pages, mobile phones, and on CD-ROM (when packaged as a projector).

The Publish command, activated when you choose File⇨Publish, creates your final `.swf` (often pronounced *swiff*), as well as additional files, such as `.html` (Web) pages that you need to display your movie in different environments. When the Publish process is complete, you can then upload the completed files to the Web, copy them to CD-ROM, or package them for mobile phone delivery.

Before publishing your final movie, use the Publish Settings dialog box to tell Flash exactly what files you want to generate and what settings to use for each file type. You can specify settings for every file format you choose, as well as quality settings for sounds and images used in your movie. The file types you choose depend on your movie's final destination, whether it be the Web, CD-ROM, mobile devices, or standalone, kiosk-style presentation.

Selecting Your Formats

Depending on where and how you plan to distribute your movie, you can have Flash create a variety of different formats at publish time. Although the most common deployment for Flash is a SWF file and a companion HTML (HyperText Markup Language) file for the Web, it's capable of generating files that can be used for CD-ROMs and mobile phones as well.

To choose your file formats, choose File⇨Publish Settings and open the Publish Settings dialog box (see Figure 9-1). In the Formats tab, select the check box next to each format you want to create. Enter the file path in the text box or click the folder icon to browse to the destination (optional) for each file you create. By default, all files use the same name and are published to the same location as the original .fla file.

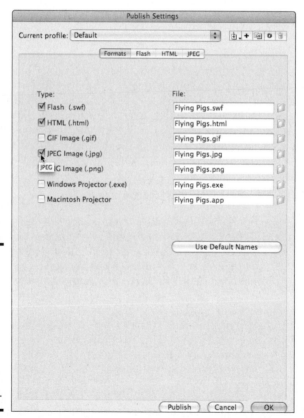

Figure 9-1:
Choose the files that you want to create during the publish process from the Formats tab.

Take a look at the different file formats you can publish and where they're used:

✦ **Flash (.swf):** SWF is the most common file type you'll publish; it's what the Flash Player and plug-in use. Think about the Flash Player as a movie projector and the SWF file as a movie reel that you load onto it. When publishing for the Web, this is the file type you'll choose, most often accompanied by an HTML (Web) page that contains it.

✦ **HTML (.html):** An HTML file, or a Web page, is used as a container for your Flash movie when the target venue is the Web. HTML files also can provide an extra level of abilities, such as checking for the Flash plug-in or enabling additional run-time parameters, such as looping.

✦ **GIF Image (.gif), JPEG Image (.jpg), and PNG Image (.png):** These selections create static images from your movie in the Web-friendly JPEG, GIF, and PNG formats (depending on which check box or check boxes you selected). You can use these images as placeholders (in the event that the user doesn't have the Flash Player or plug-in) or as elements that you can use if you're creating a non-Flash version of your site.

Keep in mind, however, that images are generated only from the first frame of your movie, so exporting an image from your movie may not yield too much if your movie starts out blank or with minimal content.

✦ **Windows Projector (.exe) or Macintosh Projector:** A *projector* is a package that includes your movie and the Flash Player all in one. Projectors are commonly used for delivery on non-Web formats, such as CD-ROM, but you can use them for any situation where you want standalone distribution, such as through e-mail. Because the projector contains the Flash Player, your user doesn't need anything (even the Flash Player installed) to view your movie. Projectors are created as EXE files for Windows or APP files for the Mac. If you're delivering to users on both platforms, publish a projector for each.

Projectors can't be viewed in a Web browser, so they're not a viable choice if you're trying to work around requiring your users to have the Flash Player or plug-in.

Book VII
Chapter 9

Publishing and
Final Delivery

Previewing Your Settings

Before you publish, it's always a good idea to use Publish Preview to test the settings you created in the Publish Settings dialog box. Like the Test Movie command, Publish Preview can immediately create and display a SWF file in the Flash Player for immediate viewing, but that's where the similarity ends.

Publish Preview creates a preview for any of the file formats you choose in the Publish Settings dialog box, including Web pages, images, and projectors. The preview lets you see how these files will look before you do your final publish and gives you a chance to adjust your publish settings for the best results possible.

To preview any of your selected publish formats, choose File⇨Publish Preview and select the format you want to preview. The default is a SWF file with an accompanying HTML page.

Publish Preview shows how the final movie will look in an HTML page. To preview an HTML and an embedded SWF file, choose File⇨Publish Preview⇨HTML.

Press the Publish Preview shortcut key combination Ctrl+F12 (Windows) or ⌘+F12 (Mac) to create a preview from the default selection (HTML page and SWF file) at any time.

If HTML or SWF aren't among your selected publish formats, the Publish Preview defaults to the next format you selected after choosing Publish Settings⇨Format.

When previewing your movie with either the Test Movie or Publish Preview (Flash option only) command, you can use the Bandwidth Profiler. This graph, as shown in Figure 9-2, appears at the top of your preview window and shows the total file size of your movie, as well as where and how data is loaded as the movie plays. This step can be important in gauging whether the file size may be too much to download for the end user or whether you should distribute data-intensive items (such as sound files or images) more effectively across the Timeline.

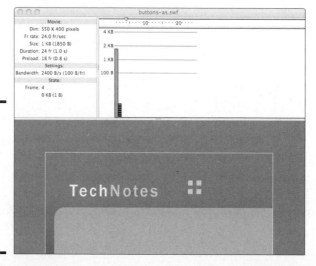

Figure 9-2:
View the file size, download rate, and how data loads as your movie plays.

The bars across the graph appear at frames where data is loaded, and the height of the bar indicates how much data was loaded when the playhead reached that frame.

To view your movie with the Bandwidth Profiler, choose File⇨Publish Preview⇨Flash. When the movie appears in the Flash Player, choose View⇨Bandwidth Profiler.

Publishing for the Web

If your movie's final destination is the Web, select two necessary file formats in the Publish Settings dialog box: Select the HTML (`.html`) and Flash (`.swf`) check boxes. The HTML file (or Web page) acts as a container for your SWF file, displaying it in the browser and placing it against a matching background. This HTML file also contains code that sets additional options in your movie at run time (such as instructions to loop automatically).

Playback of the actual SWF file is handled by the Flash Player, which works as a plug-in for all major Web browsers.

Uploading your files to the Web with FTP

File Transfer Protocol (FTP) is the method used to connect and transfer files between your local computer and a remote Web server and is the most common way of posting your finished files onto the Web for the public to see.

FTP connections occur between your computer and a server that opens the connection to receive the files. Servers often are maintained by a hosting company that provides you an account and a space for your Web site files. You may also be posting your work to a network machine or a dedicated server maintained by your company. Flash doesn't have FTP capabilities, but there are many FTP programs are out there that vary in price and features that you can install on your computer.

Adobe Dreamweaver CS4 includes full FTP functionality and can create and store connections to several different servers or hosting accounts. If you want a more basic (and free) option, you can connect to a Web server via FTP directly from Windows Explorer or choose the Go⇨Connect to Server option in the Finder on Macintosh OS X. Alternately, browsers such as Firefox support cool, free add-ons such as FireFTP. In most applications, copying files to and from the server is as simple as dragging and dropping from one window to another.

Remember: In order to connect to a server, you need to purchase or have access to a Web-hosting account, network computer, or dedicated server. Most FTP connections require a user ID and password; check with your server administrator or hosting company to get information for your specific account.

When you publish your final movie and HTML file, you upload both files to your Web-hosting account, company server, or wherever your movie needs to go to make it available for public viewing.

To publish the necessary files for the Web viewing, choose File⇨Publish Settings and select the HTML (.html) and Flash (.swf) check boxes on the Formats tab. Click the Publish button to create the final files that you'll upload to your Web server of choice.

Publishing for CD-ROM

Flash's ability to include full-featured video, audio, and graphics has made it a very popular choice for creating CD-ROM based presentations, e-brochures, learning materials, and interactive application installers. When packaging for a CD-ROM, consider that a SWF file alone may not be enough, especially because it's possible that users won't have a standalone version of the Flash Player installed on their computers.

For this reason, you can package movies for CD-ROM as projectors. (See the section "Selecting Your Formats," earlier in this chapter, for more on projectors.)

To create standalone projectors for Mac and/or Windows, select the Windows Projector (.exe) and/or Macintosh Projector check boxes on the Formats tab of the Publish Settings dialog box. The projector(s) are created when you publish, along with other formats you've chosen. These projectors can then be copied to and distributed on a CD or a DVD.

Choosing the Right Settings

After you pick the file types you want to publish, you can specify settings for each selected format in the Publish Settings dialog box. Make sure that you take time to familiarize yourself with the available options and experiment with different settings until you get a finished movie that's just right.

Flash stores publish settings as part of your document, so you need to set these settings only once for each Flash movie. Make sure to save your movie after you choose your publish settings so that your settings are available the next time you open the document.

Choosing settings for Flash (.swf) files

SWF files are compressed movies used by the Flash Player for display on the Web or directly on a user's computer. When you choose to publish a SWF file, you have the opportunity to specify settings that determine version, security, and quality.

The Flash settings are available on the Flash tab in the Publish Settings dialog box (see Figure 9-3). (First, make sure you select the Flash [.swf] check box on the Formats tab.) The following list takes a look at some of the settings you'll work with and how each one affects the performance and quality of your Flash movie:

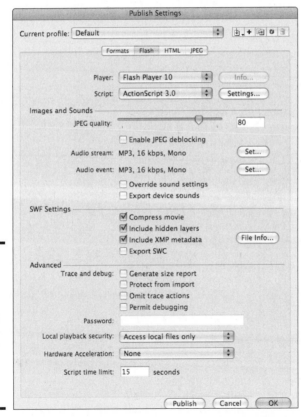

Figure 9-3: The Flash tab is available when Flash (.swf) is one of your selected publish formats.

✦ **Player:** This drop-down list controls which version of the Flash Player your movie is created for. In most cases, you want to select the latest version, Flash Player 10, so that you can take advantage of the player's latest features. In some cases, you may need to publish your movie to be compatible with a previous version of the Flash Player; here, you can specify versions as far back as Flash Player 1. You can also publish your movies for Adobe AIR, as well as *Flash Lite,* a version of the Flash player developed for mobile devices.

✦ **Script:** What you choose in this drop-down list is completely dependent on which version of ActionScript (if any) you're working with. Because each version contains differences in both features and structure (particularly between ActionScript 3.0 and previous versions), publish in the version you've used throughout your movie. If your movie doesn't use any ActionScript, leave the default setting for the Flash Player version you choose.

Chapter 7 of this minibook discusses ActionScript and the differences between Versions 2.0 and 3.0.

✦ **JPEG Quality:** Flash performs a certain amount of compression on bitmap graphics in your movie (such as imported photos) to reduce file size and increase performance. Use this slider to determine the amount of compression applied and, in turn, the resulting file size and quality of your movie. The higher the quality, the less compression applied, and the larger the resulting file size.

✦ **Audio Stream and Audio Event:** If your movie includes sound, you can set the quality of the sound in your final SWF file by clicking the Set button beside either Audio Streams or Audio Events. By default, sound is converted to 16 khz, mono MP3 format, but you can change both compression and quality settings as needed. Keep in mind that, like the JPEG quality settings, higher quality settings for sound likely increases the overall file size of your movie.

Chapter 5 of this minibook discusses stream and event sounds.

✦ **SWF Settings area:** In previous versions of Flash, hidden layers were published by default to your final movie. This behavior can be toggled off by selecting the Include Hidden Layers check box to insure that layers that are turned off in your FLA file won't show in the resulting SWF file.

The Compress Movie check box, which is selected by default, compresses your SWF file to reduce the file size and, in turn, the download time. Leave this check box selected, especially if your file is ActionScript or text intensive.

✦ **Advanced area:** The Flash authoring software can't open or decompile SWF files for editing, but it can import them as frame-by-frame movies into a FLA document. This opens the door for artwork and graphic resources to be extracted, perhaps against your will. Selecting the Protect from Import check box prevents SWF files from being imported into the Flash authoring environment. The Password text box below the check boxes becomes active when the Protect from Import check box is selected so that you can assign a password to allow only certain parties (such as a colleague or client, for example) to import the SWF file if they need to.

Choosing settings for HTML files

For presentation on the Web, publish an HTML file that contains your SWF file. This HTML file not only displays your movie, but also includes all the code necessary to control dimensions, appearance, and run-time options (such as telling your movie to loop). Your HTML file features the same background color as your movie so that it matches seamlessly when viewed in a browser.

Select the HTML (.html) check box in the Formats tab of the Publish Settings dialog box and then click the HTML tab. On the HTML tab, you can choose from the following options for your published HTML file:

✦ **Template:** This setting generates your HTML file based on different possible environments, such as standard browsers, Pocket PCs, or additional options for full-screen support.

For any template selected, an AC_RunActiveContent.js file is created. Copy this file to your Web server with any other files generated. This file is a workaround for recent changes to Internet Explorer's handling of active content.

✦ **Detect Flash Player Version check box:** This option adds code in your HTML file to display alternate content if the end user doesn't have the Flash Player installed. You can customize this content in any HTML editor. The default content provides a link for the user to download and install the latest version of Flash Player.

✦ **Dimensions:** The code in your HTML file specifies a size for your Flash movie, which, by default, matches your movie's actual dimensions. You can override this setting and force your movie to a different size in either pixels or percent by typing values in the Width and Height text boxes.

✦ **Playback:** Check boxes in this area set run-time options for your Flash movie. By default, the Flash Player is directed to loop movies and to make the contextual menu available to the user. You can disable either of these features, as well as force the movie to pause at the start, or use *device fonts* (fonts from the end user's machine instead of embedded fonts).

✦ **Quality:** Controls the overall display quality of your movie by allowing you to select a Low, Medium, or High quality setting from the provided drop-down list.

✦ **Window Mode:** This drop-down list lets you choose how Flash appears in context of your Web page. You can set Flash movies to be opaque or transparent to reveal the background of the page.

✦ **HTML Alignment:** Select a Left, Right, Top, or Bottom alignment of your movie as determined by the HTML code using the provided drop-down list.

✦ **Scale:** This drop-down list lets you choose if the HTML page scales the Flash movie to a size other than its default size.

✦ **Flash alignment:** This option controls the positioning of your Flash movie within the page. Use the drop-down lists to select Vertical and/or Horizontal alignment values.

Creating Publish Profiles

If you want to use the same publish settings across multiple movies, you can capture your settings as a profile that you can recall and use in other documents.

To create a new publish profile, follow these steps:

1. **Choose File⇨Publish Settings to open the Publish Settings dialog box (refer to Figure 9-1).**

2. **Select your formats and choose your settings as described earlier in this chapter.**

3. **Locate the Create New Profile icon in the upper-right corner of the dialog box and click it.**

The Create New Profile dialog box appears, prompting you to assign the new profile a name.

4. **Enter the profile name in the Profile name text box and click OK.**

The profile is created and is an available option under the Current Profile drop-down list at the top of the Publish Settings dialog box.

To make your profile available to other documents, export it:

1. **Choose File⇨Publish Settings to open the Publish Settings dialog box.**

2. **Choose Export from the Import/Export icon at the top of the Publish Settings dialog box.**

   You're prompted to name and save your profile (stored as a separate `.xml` file). Although you can save the file anywhere, it's best to keep it in the Flash application's Publish Profiles folder, which is the default location.

3. **Assign the XML file a name by typing it in the Save As text box, choose a Save location, and click Save.**

To import a profile from another document, follow these steps:

1. **Choose File⇨Publish Settings to open the Publish Settings dialog box.**

2. **Choose Import from the Import/Export icon at the top of the dialog box.**

   The Import Profile dialog box appears, as shown in Figure 9-4.

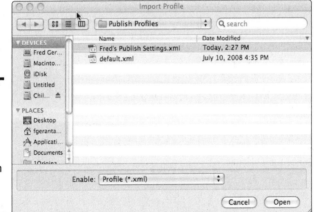

Figure 9-4: Import profiles you've exported to locations on your hard drive.

3. **Locate the XML file you created when you exported the profile and click Open.**

   The profile is now available under the Current Profiles drop-down list at the top of the Publish Settings dialog box.

Additional resources

One of the great things about working with Flash is the community that supports it. Countless Web sites are dedicated to Flash tutorials, training videos, example files, free resources (such as fonts and sounds), and forums to discuss and assist developers of all levels with a variety of Flash help topics.

There are too many to list them all, but here's a short list of established and highly visited sites that can get you started. (***Note:*** This isn't a complete list, nor is it an endorsement of any specific Web site. These Web sites have been shown to be reputable and highly useful resources for Flash developers. You're encouraged to be a part of the Flash community by utilizing and contributing to these and other online resources to further your own knowledge.)

Adobe's Flash Exchange and Support Center:

```
www.adobe.com/cfusion/exchange/
index.cfm
```

Adobe XMP metadata information:

```
www.adobe.com/products/xmp/
overview.html
```

Colin Moock: `www.moock.org`

FFiles.com: `www.ffiles.com`

Kirupa.com: `www.kirupa.com`

ActionScript.org:
`www.actionscript.org`

FlashKit: `www.flashkit.com`

Moluv.com: `www.moluv.com`

Flash Magazine:
`www.flashmagazine.com`

Fonts for Flash:
`www.fontsforflash.com`

Book VIII

Acrobat 9.0

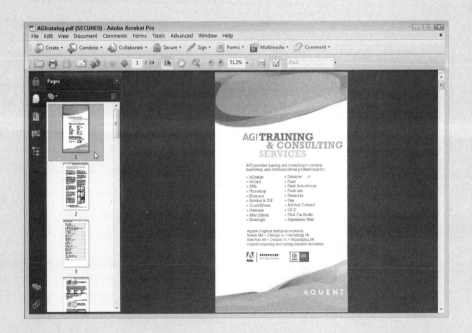

Contents at a Glance

Chapter 1: Discovering Essential Acrobat Information

In This Chapter

✔ Discovering Acrobat and PDF files

✔ Understanding when to use PDF files

✔ Becoming familiar with the Acrobat workspace and tools

*A*dobe Acrobat 9 provides a variety of tools for sharing and reviewing documents. Adobe Creative Suite applications can create Portable Document Format (PDF) files, and you can also use Acrobat to create PDF files from programs that aren't part of the Creative Suite. After you create a PDF file, you can use Acrobat to enhance the files by adding interactivity, merging PDF documents together, adding comments or annotations, or applying security that restricts features, such as printing or editing.

In this chapter, you find out why you may want to create PDF files and acquaint yourself with the Adobe Acrobat tools and workspace. You see how easy it is to navigate through PDF files with the navigational tools, tabs, and viewing options in Acrobat. In the following chapters of this minibook, you explore how to use Acrobat to create PDF files from documents produced in a variety of programs and discover ways to enhance your PDF files with Acrobat.

Working with PDF Files

Adobe Acrobat is used to create, review, and modify PDF files. You can use PDF as a way to share documents created with the Adobe Creative Suite. Because PDF is a common file format, you can use it to share Creative Suite files for review, approval, or final publication. When you use a program in the Creative Suite, such as Illustrator or InDesign, to create a document, others would need the same software to open or edit the files. By converting your documents to PDF, they can easily be shared with others who might not have the same software as you because PDF files can be viewed by users on virtually all types of computers and operating systems.

PDF provides a common file format for viewing files, regardless of what software program was used to create them. Additionally, Acrobat provides extensive tools for reviewing, commenting, and marking files so that you can easily collaborate on a project without modifying the original document, along with tools to make PDF files interactive, merge related documents together, and secure files to restrict viewing or editing.

Because the software to view PDF files is free, you can be assured that those receiving your files don't need to purchase any special software. In fact, the odds are quite good that most users already have some type of free PDF viewing software, such as Adobe Reader.

PDF has become a popular way to share files because it provides a true reproduction of an original document. PDF is used by the Internal Revenue Service to distribute tax forms online. Many financial services firms and insurance companies use PDF because the electronic documents can be secured, and they accurately represent documents that have been approved for distribution. Graphic artists even use PDF files to send books, like the one you're reading now, to the printing plant.

Although PDF files provide a high-quality representation of an original file, they're more than just a picture of a document. PDF files retain the high-quality appearance of text while keeping the text searchable. Logos and illustrations created with Adobe Illustrator retain a high-quality appearance when converted to PDF, and intricate details from bitmap images, such as those edited with Adobe Photoshop, can also be maintained. PDF files allow you to distribute a high-fidelity electronic document. When creating a PDF file, you can choose settings that make the file suitable for high-quality printing or make the file smaller and more suitable for posting to a Web site or sharing as an e-mail attachment.

Although Acrobat is part of the Creative Suite, it's *not* a design tool — rather, it's a tool for distributing documents created in other software programs and enhancing these documents for online distribution. You generally don't use Acrobat to build new documents. Acrobat is a medium for sharing files, not for creating them. With Acrobat, you can

✦ **Share documents with users who don't have the same software or fonts that you use.**

✦ **Review and mark PDF files that others send you.** With Adobe Acrobat, you can enable a PDF file to be reviewed by users with the free Adobe Reader software.

✦ **Combine documents created in other programs.** You can use Acrobat to merge PDF files together into one document, even files that may have been originally created in different programs.

✦ **Create a PDF portfolio.** You can combine various file formats into a single PDF package and yet retain the files in their original file formats.

✦ **Edit Adobe PDF files to make minor changes to text or graphics.**

✦ **Apply security to PDF files when you don't want them changed or you want to restrict viewing to certain individuals.**

✦ **Add interactivity to PDF files by enhancing them with sounds, movies, animations, and buttons.**

✦ **Create interactive forms to collect information electronically, avoiding the need for manual data collection.**

We cover these capabilities throughout the rest of this minibook.

Knowing When to Use Adobe PDF Files

So when does it make sense to use Adobe PDF files? Here are some examples:

✦ **When you want to review a document quickly and efficiently:** When documents need to be reviewed or approved, Acrobat really shines. The reviewers don't need to have the Creative Suite software — or whatever you used to create the document. They only need a program to view PDF files, such as the free Adobe Reader or the Apple Preview application. Recipients can then use commenting, markup, and annotation tools to add suggestions and edits to a file. You can even combine comments from multiple reviewers into a single document and manage the review process online or via e-mail.

✦ **When you've created a document that you don't want others to edit:** Your recipients may have the same software you used to build the document, but you can keep them from editing the original file by distributing it as a PDF file. Whether you want to secure a spreadsheet from editing or an InDesign document from modification, Acrobat includes security options that allow you to protect your original content.

✦ **When you've created a presentation that includes files from different programs:** By converting the documents to PDF, you can combine them into a single file. For example, you can merge PowerPoint, Excel, and InDesign files into a single PDF document. Whether you need to protect your brand and identity by keeping documents from being edited or simply want to ease the process of sharing files, PDF makes it easy to share your ideas.

✦ **When you have a sensitive document:** If you have a document containing information that you don't want unauthorized persons viewing or you don't want printed, you can enhance the file with security with the Adobe Acrobat security tools. With the security options, you can require users to enter a password to view the file, or you can limit other features, such as the ability to print or edit the document.

**Book VIII
Chapter 1**

**Discovering
Essential Acrobat
Information**

Introducing the Adobe Acrobat Workspace and Tools

To take advantage of all that Acrobat has to offer, you'll want to discover the workspace and tools so you can get around within a PDF file. Acrobat opens with a blank workspace, and most tools and capabilities aren't available until you open a document. You can open a document by clicking the folder icon in the upper-left corner of the Document window or choosing File⇨Open.

When you open a document, you see the Acrobat workspace, which is divided into three areas. The largest portion of the workspace is the *Document window,* which displays the document you have opened. Across the top, the tools are stored in the toolbar well. Along the left side of the window, you find the navigation panels that help you find your way through the document. When you open a PDF document with Acrobat, you can use the toolbars and buttons in the toolbar well to navigate a file and you can use the navigation panel to move through a PDF file. For example, a PDF file may contain multiple pages. You can use the navigational buttons or the Pages panel to move between pages and then use a tool to manipulate the file, such as the commenting tools.

In the toolbar, you find useful information for navigating through your document, including

✦ **Current page and total pages:** To move to a specific page, click in the area showing the current page, type a different page number, and press Enter (Windows) or Return (Mac).

✦ **Previous Page and Next Page buttons:** Use these navigational buttons to skip forward or backward one page at a time.

Changing page magnification

Sometimes you want to see the entire page of a document; other times, you may only need to read the text or examine a small portion of a page. Acrobat provides several preset viewing options to help you with this, and you can also customize the magnification to zoom in on the page.

If things are a bit too small for you to see clearly, increase the magnification used for viewing pages with the Zoom drop-down list in the toolbar. Preset magnification choices are available in this drop-down list. You can also use the minus (–) and plus (+) symbols to the left of the current magnification level to zoom out or in.

The Marquee Zoom tool is the magnifying glass icon located to the left of the minus and plus symbols. You can use the Marquee Zoom tool to identify specific portions of a page that you want to magnify. Select this tool and then click and drag around a portion of the page to increase the magnification. You can also click multiple times on an area with this tool to increase the page magnification, but clicking and dragging a box with the Marquee Zoom tool is generally a much faster way to focus on a portion of a page you want to view. You can change the Marquee Zoom from its default attribute of increasing the magnification to decreasing the zoom by selecting the Marquee Zoom tool and Ctrl-clicking (PC) or Option-clicking (Mac) in the Document window. The magnifier's plus (+) sign changes to a minus sign (–) to indicate that you're decreasing the document's magnification. It's usually faster to choose a preset zoom percentage though.

To the right of the magnification percentage box are page buttons that you can use to change the page magnification:

✦ **Scrolling Pages:** Use this button to avoid scrolling from left to right when reading a document. The view is changed to fit the document's width in the available space on your display, making it necessary to only scroll up and down on a page. This also sets the page view to display the top or bottom of adjacent pages. When you scroll and reach the bottom of one page, the top of the next page becomes visible.

✦ **One Full Page:** Use this button to fit the current page within the available screen space on your monitor. For smaller documents, such as a business card, the magnification is increased. For larger documents, the magnification is generally decreased unless you have a large monitor. When viewing pages in the Fit Page mode, only one page is displayed at a time. This mode is good for viewing the entire display of a page layout.

Toolbars

The toolbars in Acrobat 9 are customizable, so you can display different toolbars or change the location of existing toolbars to meet your needs.

Customizing the location of toolbars on your screen can make it easier for you to work with PDF files in Acrobat. For example, you may want all the tools for navigating through your documents in one section of the toolbar well. To achieve this, you can rearrange the location of specific toolbars.

Along the left edge of every group of tools is a dotted double line. By clicking and holding onto this edge with your mouse, you can drag any toolbar to a new location on your screen. This new location can be within the same area holding the other toolbars, or anywhere in the Acrobat work area. If you pull a toolbar out of the docking area, the toolbar becomes independent and floating. You can reposition or drag floating toolbars back into the docking area when you're finished working with them. You can also close a floating toolbar by clicking its Close Window button. You can place toolbars along the left or right side of the Acrobat work area — turning either side of the Acrobat workspace into a docking area for toolbars.

Although the flexibility of placing toolbars anywhere you like is useful, it may lead to a chaotic work environment. Instead of leaving toolbars all over your screen, you can have Acrobat clean up the workspace by choosing View⇨Toolbars⇨Reset Toolbars.

Toolbars contain both tools and buttons. For example, you choose the Marquee Zoom tool to change the magnification by clicking or selecting an area of the page. Buttons perform an immediate task, such as printing, saving, or applying security to a PDF document. In general, most of the task buttons are on the top row of the docking area, immediately below the menu bar, and most of the tools are on the bottom row — but you can move these toolbars.

Some tools and task buttons also include additional options that you can access through drop-down lists within the toolbars. Tools and buttons that contain additional choices are noted by the small triangle immediately to the right of the icon. Click this small triangle, and you see a drop-down list providing the additional choices for that tool or button.

Less than half the toolbars are visible in the default Acrobat display. You can add to the tools that are displayed or limit them by clicking the check box next to those you want to display or hide in the More Tools dialog box. Toolbars that have a check mark next to their names are visible, whereas those without a check mark aren't visible.

To display additional tools, choose View⇨Toolbars⇨More Tools. In the More Tools dialog box that appears, select the tools you want displayed in the toolbar and then click OK. The Selecting and Zoom Toolbar section displays the navigation tool choices that can be displayed.

You can choose to show or hide additional toolbars by right-clicking (Windows) or Control-clicking (Mac) in the toolbar well. After right-clicking/Control-clicking, choose the toolbar you want to show or hide from the contextual menu that appears.

Viewing modes

Acrobat provides several viewing modes that control how the document's displayed. For example, you can choose to display the pages of a book or a magazine side-by-side, or view only one page at a time. You can choose which viewing mode is used by choosing View⇨Page Display and selecting the viewing option you want.

The viewing modes are

✦ **Single Page:** This mode displays only the current document page on-screen and doesn't show any adjoining pages. When you scroll to the top or bottom of the current page, other pages aren't visible at the same time as the current page.

✦ **Single Page Continuous:** With this mode, you can see the current document page, and if you scroll to the top (or bottom) of the current page, the adjoining page is also visible. If you reduce your page viewing magnification, many document pages are visible.

✦ **Two-Up (previously known as Facing):** Use this mode to see pages as a *spread,* where you can view both the left and right sides of adjoining pages at the same time. When you have documents with pictures or text that spans a pair of pages, use this option to see the pages presented side-by-side in Acrobat. As with the Single Page mode, other pages that go before or fall after the spread aren't visible — only the one pair of pages is visible on-screen, regardless of the magnification or scrolling.

✦ **Two-Up Continuous (previously known as Continuous-Facing):** If you have a document with many pages containing text or pictures on their adjoining pages, you can use this mode to scroll from one pair of visible pages to the next. When the Two-Up Continuous view is selected, you can see adjoining page spreads. This option is identical to the Two-Up option, but it also shows pages above or below the spread you're presently viewing.

If you have pages where images or text goes across pages, the Two-Up choice is useful. By default, the pages generally display incorrectly. For example, a magazine will display the cover (page 1) and page 2 together, instead of pages 2 and 3. To correct this, choose View⇨Page Display⇨Show Cover Page during Two-Up. Additionally, the default option is for Acrobat to display a space between pages that are displayed together in the Two-Up mode. You can replace the space with a dotted line to divide the adjoining pages by choosing View⇨Page Display⇨Show Gaps between Pages.

You can add viewing modes as menu buttons by choosing View⇨Toolbars⇨ More Tools, as described earlier in the "Toolbars" section of this chapter.

Additional viewing options

Acrobat has two additional options for changing your document display:

✦ **Full Screen mode (View⇨Full Screen Mode):** You can use the Full Screen mode option to hide all menus, toolbars, and other parts of the Acrobat interface. This option is useful if you want to focus on the document being displayed, not the program being used to view it. Use this mode, for example, when you've a converted PowerPoint file to a PDF document and want to deliver the presentation with Acrobat. If you're viewing a document in the Full Screen mode, press the Esc key to return to the regular viewing mode.

When using the Full Screen mode, you can select Edit⇨Preferences and choose Full Screen to define attributes that change the way the file displays. You can set the display to advance automatically from one page to the next at a certain interval, choose from many different page transition types, and define the background color.

You can set a document to automatically open in Full Screen mode by choosing File⇨Properties and choosing this option from the Initial View panel of the Document Properties dialog box.

✦ **Reading mode (View⇨Reading Mode):** The many toolbars and buttons of Acrobat can get in the way of the document you wish to review. Use Reading mode to temporarily hide all the toolbars and buttons, making it easier to focus on the content of the PDF file.

Navigation panels

Acrobat offers a variety of panels that are helpful when navigating through PDF documents. The navigation panels are displayed along the left side of your Document window as small icons. Click an icon to make its panel visible. For example, click the Pages icon to display thumbnail-size representations of each page, as shown in Figure 1-1.

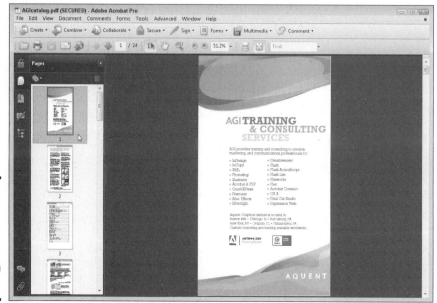

Figure 1-1:
Click the icons to the left to see navigational panels, such as Pages.

In the Pages panel, click a thumbnail page to display that page in the Document window. You can also choose View⇨Navigation Panels to access these same panels. There are 12 panels: Articles, Attachments, Bookmarks, Comments, Content, Destinations, Layers, Model Tree, Order, Pages, Signatures, and Tags.

Many panels have more advanced uses that are covered in later chapters of this minibook. In this chapter, we provide you with a brief understanding of how you can use the Pages panel to more easily navigate through a PDF document. Follow these steps:

1. **Make sure that the Pages panel is visible by clicking its panel icon.**

2. **In the Pages panel, click any page thumbnail to navigate directly to that page.**

   A dark border appears around the selected page and a red box in the Pages panel indicates what portion of the page is being viewed.

   You can click in the corner of the small red box and drag diagonally upward to increase the magnification on the section of the page contained within the box. Alternatively, make the box larger by clicking and dragging down and out to expand the size of the viewing area. Changing the size of the red box displayed on the page in the Pages panel changes the focus of the magnification.

Chapter 2: Creating PDF Files

In This Chapter

- ✔ Creating PDF files from Microsoft Office documents
- ✔ Creating PDF files from Creative Suite applications
- ✔ Creating PDF files from all other electronic formats
- ✔ Creating PDF files from the Web and paper documents

Converting documents to the Portable Document Format (PDF) is a great way to share files when readers don't have the same software as you or when you want to consolidate multiple file types together into a single document. Adobe Acrobat lets you create files from all software programs and scanned documents and even pages from the Web. Although you can also create PDF files from Adobe Creative Suite 4 (CS4) documents, you don't need Acrobat for this because the ability to create PDF files is built into the individual Creative Suite programs, such as Photoshop, Illustrator, and InDesign. In this chapter, you find out how to create Adobe PDF files from a variety of programs.

Creating PDF Files from Microsoft Office

Adobe Acrobat includes tools that make it easy to convert Microsoft Word, Excel, and PowerPoint files to PDF.

These capabilities are much more robust for the Windows versions of these programs, so Macintosh users may discover that not all these options are available.

When you install Acrobat on your computer, it looks for Microsoft Office programs. If Acrobat locates Word, Excel, PowerPoint, or Outlook, it installs an add-in — the PDF Maker — to these programs that helps convert Microsoft Office documents to PDF in a single click.

You can tell whether the PDF Maker add-in has been installed in your Microsoft Office programs by looking for the Acrobat toolbar or the Acrobat tab, depending upon which version of Microsoft Office you use. In Office 2007, the Acrobat tab appears to the right of the View tab. In earlier versions of Microsoft Office, the toolbar appears at the top of the Document window. If the toolbar isn't visible, choose View➪Toolbars to see whether the Acrobat toolbar is available in the Toolbars submenu. If it remains unavailable, you may need to reinstall Adobe Acrobat to gain access to the PDF Maker tools.

When you convert documents to PDF, the original file remains unchanged, so you have both the original file and a separate PDF document. The original document and the PDF file aren't linked, so changes to the original source file aren't reflected in the PDF file. When you edit the PDF document, the changes don't update in the original file.

PDF conversion options

PDF Maker provides a variety of controls over how PDF files are created from Microsoft Office programs, such as Word and Excel. For example, you can have Acrobat create the file without asking you to confirm the location and name of the file each time you click the Create PDF button, and Acrobat will simply save the file in the same location as the original document. Similarly, you can choose to create PDF files that balance your need for quality and file size.

PDF Maker also provides controls over the type of PDF file you create because some PDF files may need to be of a higher quality for printing and others may need to be smaller to allow for fast electronic distribution. For example, you may want to post a PDF document to a Web site, where you want to make the file small so that it can be downloaded quickly.

When working in Microsoft Word, Excel, or PowerPoint, you can access the PDF Maker controls by clicking the Acrobat tab and then clicking the Preferences button (Office 2007) or by choosing Adobe PDF⇨Change Conversion Settings (earlier versions of Microsoft Office). In the Acrobat PDF Maker dialog box that appears, you can then choose from a variety of settings that control how the PDF file is created. In this section, we focus on the most useful options for Microsoft Office users.

From the Conversion Settings drop-down list in the Acrobat PDF Maker dialog box, you can find these useful options that control how the PDF file is generated:

✦ **Standard:** Choose this option to create PDF files that will be printed on an office laser printer or distributed via e-mail. This setting meets the needs of most users — it provides some compression of graphics, but they remain clear on-screen and look reasonably good when printed. In addition, this setting builds the fonts into the PDF file to maintain an exact representation of the document, regardless of where the file is viewed.

✦ **Smallest File Size:** With this setting, you can control the file size of the PDF documents you create. This setting provides significant compression of images and also reduces resolution, which causes graphics within the files to lose some clarity and perhaps appear jagged.

In addition, fonts aren't embedded in PDF files created with this setting. If the fonts used in the document aren't available on a computer where a PDF created with the Smallest File Size setting is viewed, Acrobat uses a font substitution technology to replicate the size and shape of the fonts used in the document. This feature typically provides a similar appearance to the original document, but it's not always an exact match of the original file.

Because this setting is so lossy, use it only if you need to compress a large file to a small enough size to send as an e-mail attachment. Make certain the recipient has the fonts used in the document installed on his or her computer. Otherwise, Adobe uses font substitution.

✦ **Press Quality:** If you need to provide PDF files to your commercial printer or copy shop, use this setting to create a PDF file that's designed for high-quality print reproduction. Along with including fonts in the PDF file, the graphics aren't significantly compressed, and they maintain a much higher resolution. Overall, these files tend to be larger than similar PDF files created with different settings, but the quality of the PDF file is more important than the file size when you're having the PDF professionally printed.

Several other highly technical options might be useful for you if you have a specialized profession. For example, if you archive items with PDF, the PDF/A options are designed for this. Additionally, the PDF/X options are useful for those submitting advertisements to publications that require the PDF advertisements adhere to the PDF/X standard.

PDF conversion options from Microsoft Word and Excel

Although Microsoft Word and Excel are widespread standards on many corporate computers, they aren't always the best choice for distributing documents. Formatting of Microsoft Word documents and Excel spreadsheets changes depending on the fonts available on users' computer or even the printer with which they print, whereas PDF files can keep the file looking consistent on various computer types. In addition, Microsoft Word and Excel files can be easily edited, and users can also copy and extract information from these files with few limitations, whereas PDF files are more difficult to copy from, and they can be secured with robust security options.

Converting a Word or Excel file to a PDF file overcomes these limitations and is quite straightforward. Choose from two methods:

✦ From inside Microsoft Word or Excel, make sure that the document you want to convert to a PDF file is open and then click the Create PDF button in the main toolbar to convert the document.

✦ With Office 2003 or earlier, choose Adobe PDF➪Convert to Adobe PDF.

No matter which method you choose, you must specify the location of the PDF file that's created and name the file unless you have changed the PDF Maker preferences.

In Office 2007, click the Preferences button in the Acrobat tab, or with earlier versions of Office, choose Acrobat⇨Change Conversion Settings. In the Adobe PDF Maker dialog box, deselect the Prompt for PDF Filename option so that PDF files are generated in one step, without inputting the PDF filename.

You can add functionality into the PDF documents you create. Click the Preference tab if you're working in Office 2007 or choose Acrobat⇨Change Conversion Settings in earlier versions of Office. In the dialog box that appears, review the following settings:

✦ **Attach Source File:** Causes the original Office document to become embedded within the PDF file as an attachment. When the PDF file is distributed, the original source file is included within the PDF file.

✦ **Create Bookmarks:** Adds interactive bookmarks that make navigating the PDF file easy. Bookmarks are added based on Microsoft Word styles, such as text that's styled as Heading 1. The bookmarks appear in the Bookmarks panel when viewing the PDF.

✦ **Add Links:** Automatically converts Word links, such as Web addresses, into PDF links that you can use when viewing the file in Acrobat or Adobe Reader. Within the PDF Maker preferences dialog box, click the Word tab to access additional link options that can be built into PDF files created from Word.

Converting PowerPoint files to PDF

You can convert your PowerPoint presentations to Adobe PDF documents with the PDF Maker add-in that installs with Adobe Acrobat. PDF versions of PowerPoint presentations can be distributed to avoid concerns about the file being edited or concerns that the recipient may not have the same fonts that you used, causing the presentation to look different on various computers.

From PowerPoint, click the Create PDF button to save the file as a PDF file. Of course, make sure that the presentation you're converting is open before you click the button. In older versions of Office, you can also choose Acrobat⇨Convert to Adobe PDF from PowerPoint's main menu. If you're working with a new file, you must save it before PDF Maker will convert the file.

As with Word and Excel, you can select options relating to the conversion of your PowerPoint documents to PDF. To access the preferences, click the Preference button in the Acrobat tab or in older versions of Office, choose Acrobat⇨Change Conversion Settings. Along with the conversion settings that impact the quality of the resulting PDF file, select two additional options:

✦ **Preserve Slide Transitions:** With this option, you can have the slide transitions that were created in PowerPoint converted into PDF transitions that will be used when the presentation is delivered using Adobe Acrobat's Full Screen mode option.

✦ **Convert Multimedia:** Because Adobe PDF files can contain integrated sound and movie files, you can choose this option to have sounds and movies used in a PowerPoint file converted into the PDF document.

After you create the PDF, you can use Acrobat as the tool for delivering your presentations that have been created using PowerPoint. After you convert the file to PDF, open it in Acrobat and choose View⇨Full Screen Mode. You can even distribute the document to users with the free Adobe Reader, and they can use the free Adobe Reader software to view and display the PowerPoint presentation file. Press the Esc key to stop viewing a document in the Full Screen mode. To distribute a document so that it always opens in Full Screen mode, open the document, choose File⇨Document Properties, and select the Open in Full Screen Mode check box.

Creating PDF Files from Adobe Creative Suite Applications

You can also convert Photoshop files, Illustrator files, or InDesign documents to the PDF format. In this section, we show you how.

Converting Photoshop and Illustrator files to PDF

Both Adobe Photoshop CS4 and Adobe Illustrator CS4 can save documents directly in the Adobe PDF file format. To do so, simply choose File⇨Save or File⇨Save As. Then, from the File Type drop-down list, choose Adobe PDF (Illustrator) or Photoshop PDF (Photoshop). In these programs, you can create PDF files without Adobe Acrobat or Acrobat Distiller because they've integrated PDF creation capabilities.

You can use Adobe Reader or Acrobat to view PDF files created from Photoshop or Illustrator. You can also open and edit PDF files using the same program in which they were created.

Converting InDesign documents to PDF

Like Photoshop and Illustrator, the ability to convert InDesign documents to PDF is integrated into the application. With Adobe InDesign, you can choose File⇨Export and select Adobe PDF from the File Type drop-down list. InDesign provides a significant number of options for controlling the size and quality of the resulting PDF file. Many of these options are similar to those available for PDF Maker for Microsoft Office.

**Book VIII
Chapter 2**

Creating PDF Files

In the Adobe InDesign Export PDF dialog box, you can choose from the Preset drop-down list at the top of the dialog box. The choices are many, but we list and describe here the most commonly used settings:

✦ **Smallest File Size:** Creates compact Adobe PDF files that are intended for display on the Internet or to be distributed via e-mail. Use this setting to create PDF files that will be viewed primarily on-screen.

✦ **High Quality Print:** Creates Adobe PDF files that are intended for desktop printers and digital copiers.

✦ **Press Quality:** Use this setting to create PDF files that will be delivered to a commercial printer for high-quality, offset print reproduction.

When creating PDF files to be used for high-resolution printing, here are some settings you should use. Select Marks and Bleeds in the list on the left of the Export PDF dialog box, as shown in Figure 2-1, and specify the amount of space items need to extend off the page, referred to as a *bleed*. If you're delivering the file to a printing firm, they can provide you with guidance as to the required value. A good rule to follow is to use at least .125 inches if you have any items in your layout that extend to the edge of your document pages and beyond. Specify the value you want by entering the number in the Bleed and Slug section of the Marks and Bleeds tab. If the amount of bleed needs to be the same on all four sides, type the value in the Top text box and then click the link icon to the right of the Top and Bottom Bleed text boxes.

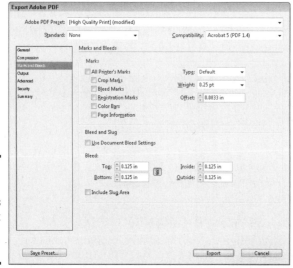

Figure 2-1:
Setting the bleed values in the Export Adobe PDF dialog box.

Converting Other Electronic Documents to PDF

As described earlier in this chapter, creating PDF files from Creative Suite applications and Microsoft Office programs is simple. You can also create PDF files from many other programs. When you installed the Adobe Creative Suite on your computer, you also installed a new printer — the *Adobe PDF printer* — which is used to convert electronic documents to PDF files. The Adobe PDF printer captures all the same information that's normally sent to your printer, and, instead of printing on paper, the information is converted into an Adobe PDF file.

To create a PDF file from any program, choose File➪Print. In the Print dialog box, select Adobe PDF as the printer and click OK (Windows) or Print (Mac).

To change the type of PDF file that's created, such as a smaller file for Internet Web posting or a higher quality file for delivery to a commercial printer, do this:

✦ **Windows:** Click the Properties button in the Print dialog box to open the Adobe PDF Document Properties dialog box, as shown in Figure 2-2. Here, you can choose the settings you want to use to control the quality and size of the resulting PDF file.

✦ **Mac OS:** Choose PDF Options from the Copies and Pages drop-down list in the Print dialog box and then select the PDF settings you want to use.

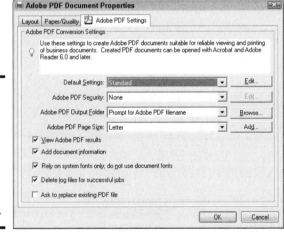

Figure 2-2:
You can change conversion settings when printing to the Adobe PDF printer.

We discuss the PDF conversion settings earlier in this chapter, in the "PDF conversion options" section.

Using the Print menu to control the quality of PDF files created from non-Adobe programs may appear strange, but it's the easiest way for Adobe to capture all the same information that you'd expect to see when you print your files. This provides an easy and standard method for generating PDF files from any program. In fact, you can even use this method for creating PDF files from Adobe Creative Suite programs. It's useful to have this available as an option if you're having difficulty with the Export command. The Print and Export commands use different processes for creating PDF files, so you can use one option if you have difficulty with the other when creating PDF files from Creative Suite programs.

Bookmarks, links, page transitions, and multimedia aren't exported if a PDF is generated with the Print menu option. You must use the Export option to have these items included in PDF files.

Creating PDF Files from Paper Documents and the Web

PDF files don't need to start as electronic publishing files. Adobe Acrobat provides options for converting both paper documents and Internet Web pages into PDF format.

Converting paper documents to PDF

To convert paper documents into PDF, you need a scanner to digitize the information. If you expect to scan a large number of pages into PDF, consider purchasing a scanner with an automatic document feeder. Some scanners can scan both the front and backside of a document at the same time. Scanners, such as the Fujitsu ScanSnap, now fit easily on your desktop and let you convert a large number of paper documents to PDF in a short period of time. Some scanners, such as the ScanSnap, automatically launch Acrobat and convert scanned documents to PDF; others require you to scan the file. If a scanner is already hooked to the computer on which you use Acrobat and doesn't automatically start Acrobat, follow these steps to scan in a paper document and then convert it to PDF format:

1. **From the Acrobat main menu, choose File⊏⟩Create PDF⊏⟩ From Scanner.**

   Then choose the type of PDF document you wish to create. For pages with text, choose one of the Document options: Black and White for line art or text that contains no shades of gray; Grayscale for documents that contain varying shades of gray; or Color for documents that contain color. For photographs, choose the Image option.

2. **Make sure that your scanner is turned on, put the document to be scanned into the scanner, and then click the Scan button.**

If necessary, continue to scan multiple pages into a single document. When you're done scanning, the scanned page appears in Acrobat.

If you have a PDF open and choose Create PDF from Scanner, a window appears, giving you the opportunity to *append* the file (add to the existing file) or create a new PDF file.

The scanned document opens in Acrobat.

If the pages need to be rotated, choose Document⇨Rotate Pages.

3. **Choose File⇨Save to save the finished document as a PDF.**

Scanned text is fully searchable if you use one of the Document preset choices because Acrobat uses Optical Character Recognition (OCR) to convert the image to text. If you open a previously scanned file, you can use Acrobat's OCR capability by choosing Document⇨ OCR Text Recognition⇨Recognize Text using OCR. This command makes previously scanned text searchable.

Converting Web pages to PDFs

By converting online content to Adobe PDF, you can capture contents from an Internet Web site. Because Web content can change rapidly, you can capture something that may not remain online for a long period of time. You can convert things, such as news stories or business information, from a Web site into PDF. Because PDF files can easily be combined together, you can merge a PDF from a Web site with other PDF files, such as spreadsheets, word-processing documents, and brochures.

If you want to convert only a single page and are using Internet Explorer, click the Convert Web Page to PDF button. This step converts the current Web page to a PDF. If you want to convert more than a single page, follow these steps from within Acrobat (not your Web browser):

1. **From the Acrobat main menu, choose File⇨Create PDF⇨From Web Page.**

The Create PDF from Web Page dialog box opens.

2. **In the URL text box, enter the URL for the Web site you're converting to PDF.**

3. **To capture additional pages that are linked from the main page you're capturing, click the Capture Multiple Levels button, and then select one of the following:**

- Select the Stay On Same Path check box if you want only pages from the entered URL converted to PDF.

- Select the Stay On Same Server check box to download only pages that are on the same server as the entered URL.

Be cautious about selecting the Get Entire Site radio button instead of the Get Only radio button. The Get Entire Site option may take an enormous amount of time and not have any relevance to what you need.

4. **Click the Settings button to open the Web Page Conversion Settings dialog box and see accepted file types and change PDF settings (on the General tab).**

5. **On the Page Layout tab of the Web Page Conversion Settings dialog box, make changes to page size, orientation, and margins if the Web page requires a wider or longer layout. See Figure 2-3.**

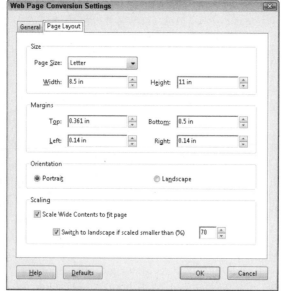

Figure 2-3:
Changing the layout of Web pages converted to PDF.

6. **When you're done making changes in the Web Page Conversion Settings dialog box, click OK.**

7. **In the Create PDF from Web Page dialog box, click the Create button to generate a PDF.**

The Downloading Status window opens, showing the rate of download.

When the download is complete, the Web page (for the entered URL) selected appears as a PDF document, with *hyperlinks* (links to other pages within the site) intact. When links on the converted Web page are selected, you can open the linked page either in Acrobat or the Web browser.

Chapter 3: Adding Interactivity to PDF Files

In This Chapter

✔ Adding interactive bookmarks

✔ Creating and editing links

✔ Using buttons for easy navigation

Because many Adobe PDF documents are viewed online, you need to make the documents easy for readers to navigate. With Acrobat, you can design documents that are easier to navigate than their printed counterparts and that include rich interactive features that simply aren't available with paper documents.

Rather than making readers scroll through a document to find what they want, you can add links within an index or a table of contents, or you can add links to Web sites and e-mail addresses. Acrobat also includes features (known as *bookmarks*) to build your own online table of contents, and you can add buttons that link to specific pages within a PDF document or that cause an action to occur when clicked, such as closing the document. We discuss all these features in this chapter.

Adding Bookmarks to Ease PDF Navigation

One reason for distributing PDF documents is that it's convenient and cost-effective. But if users can't easily find the information they need or they can't effectively understand how the contents of a file are structured, they may become frustrated or they may need to print the document, which defeats the purpose of electronic distribution.

A table of contents in a traditional, printed book doesn't work well with electronic PDF files. It requires you to constantly return to the page containing the table of contents and then navigate to the page containing the data you need. But you can make your documents more user-friendly by adding bookmarks, which are the equivalent of a table of contents that's always available, no matter what page is being viewed in the Document window.

Bookmarks provide a listing of contents that reside within a PDF file or links to relevant external content. Bookmarks sit within a panel, and when you click one, you're taken to a specific destination in the PDF document (or possibly to an external file), much like a hyperlink. You can create bookmarks from existing text, or you can use your own text to describe the content, which is useful if the destination of the bookmark is a figure, chart, or a graphic.

By default, the Bookmarks icon resides along the left side of the Acrobat Document window in the *navigation panel.* Click the Bookmarks icon to make the panel appear; click the Bookmarks icon a second time to hide it. If the icon isn't visible, choose View⇨Navigation Panels⇨Bookmarks to make it appear.

Creating bookmarks that link to a page

By navigating to a page, and to a specific view on a page, you can establish the destination of a bookmark link. With a PDF document open, follow these steps:

1. **If the Bookmark icon isn't visible, choose View⇨Navigation Panels⇨Bookmarks.**

   The Bookmarks panel appears on the left of the Document window.

2. **In the Document window, navigate to the page that you want as the bookmark's destination.**

3. **Set the magnification of the view that you want by using the Marquee Zoom tool to either zoom in or zoom out.**

   The zoom level that you're at when you create the bookmark is the view that viewers see when they click the bookmark.

4. **In the Bookmarks panel, click the Options icon (it shows gears) and from the menu that appears, choose New Bookmark.**

   The new bookmark appears in the Bookmarks panel as Untitled.

5. **Change the name by typing something more descriptive.**

   If you leave the bookmark as Untitled but want to rename it later, you must click the bookmark and then choose Options⇨Rename Bookmark from the menu in the Bookmark panel.

6. **Test your bookmark by scrolling to another page and viewing it in the Document window; then click your saved bookmark in the Bookmark panel.**

   The Document window shows the exact location and zoom that you selected when you created the bookmark.

If you use the Selection tool to highlight text, such as a headline or a caption, that's part of the bookmark destination and then choose Options⇨ New Bookmark, the selected text becomes the title of the new bookmark. You can use this shortcut to avoid entering a new name for new bookmark titles. You can also press Ctrl+B (Windows) or ⌘+B (Mac) to quickly create a bookmark.

Creating bookmarks that link to external files

Although bookmarks are most commonly used to link to content within a PDF file, you can also use bookmarks to create links to other documents. To create a link to an external file, follow these steps:

1. **Choose Options⇨New Bookmark in the Bookmarks panel.**

2. **Replace the Untitled bookmark entry that appears in the Bookmarks panel with an appropriate title for the bookmark.**

3. **Choose Options⇨Properties from the Bookmarks panel menu.**

   The Bookmark Properties dialog box appears. With this dialog box, you can change a bookmark so that it links to any type of file. In this example, we use a PDF document, but the bookmark could be a link to another PDF file, a Photoshop file, or even a Microsoft Excel file. Just remember that this bookmark creates a relative link. The linked file must travel with the PDF document in order for the link to work.

4. **In the Bookmark Properties dialog box, click the Actions tab, choose Open a File from the Select Action drop-down list, and then click the Add button.**

    The Select File to Open dialog box appears.

   You can create links to Web sites as well. Choose Open a Web Link to access an Internet Web address.

5. **Click the Browse button, choose a file to which the bookmark will navigate, and then click the Select button.**

 Note that the other file isn't attached to the current document. If you distribute a PDF file containing the bookmarks to external files, you must distribute any external files that are referenced along with the source file; otherwise, the links won't work. In addition, the linked files need to be in the same relative location as the original documents — so don't change the name of the linked file or the folder in which it's located.

Using bookmarks

Bookmarks are intuitive to use, which make them an attractive option to add to PDF files. After you click a bookmark, the action associated with it is performed, which typically navigates you to a certain page within the PDF file.

Unfortunately, the Bookmarks panel doesn't open automatically with a document, even when bookmarks are present within a file. To display the Bookmarks panel when a file is opened, follow these steps:

1. **Choose File⇨Properties.**

2. **In the Document Properties dialog box that opens, select the Initial View tab, as shown in Figure 3-1.**

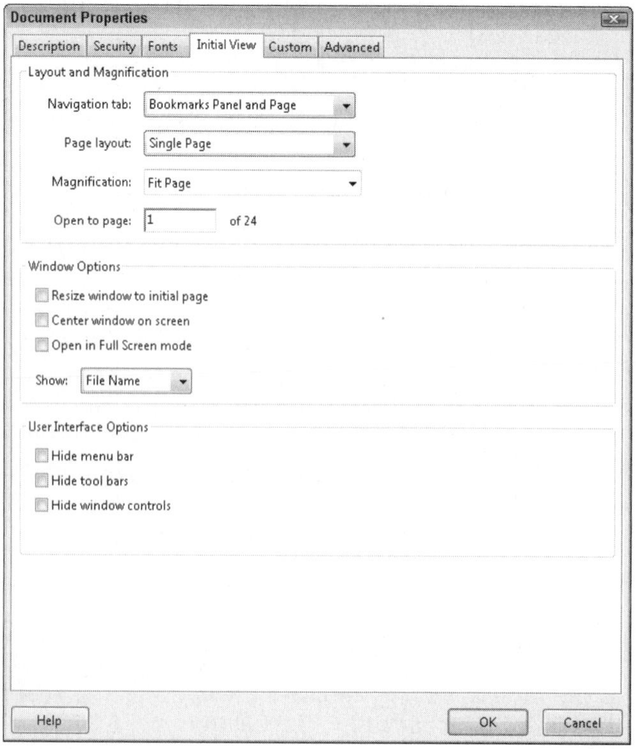

Figure 3-1:
The Document Properties dialog box in Adobe Acrobat.

3. **From the Navigation drop-down list, choose Bookmarks Panel and Page and then click OK.**

After the file is saved and then reopened, the Bookmarks panel is displayed whenever the document is opened.

Editing bookmarks

You can change the attributes of bookmarks so that they link to other locations by clicking to select a bookmark and then choosing Options⇨Properties in the Bookmarks panel. In the Bookmark Properties dialog box, choose the color and font type of the bookmark on the

Appearance tab: To change the bookmark's font style, choose a style from the Style drop-down list; to change the bookmark's color, click the Color box and choose a color from the Color Picker.

On the Actions tab of the Bookmark Properties dialog box, you can delete existing actions (in the Actions section of the Actions tab) by clicking to select an action and then clicking the Delete button. Also, you can add actions by choosing another action from the Add Action section and then clicking the Add button. You can add more than one action to a bookmark.

Adding Interactive Links

When viewing a PDF file electronically, you can add links for e-mail addresses, Web addresses, and references to other pages. Links are attached to a region of a page, which you identify with the Link tool.

To add an interactive link to your PDF document, follow these steps:

1. **Locate an area of a page where you want to add a link and then choose View➪Toolbars➪Advanced Editing to display the Advanced Editing toolbar.**

2. **Select the Link tool and then click and drag to select the region that you want to link to.**

   The Create Link dialog box appears.

3. **Choose an action that the link will perform:**

   - *Go to a Page View:* This option is the default, where you can scroll to the page that is the destination of the link.

   - *Open a File:* Alternatively, you can choose to link to another file; click the Browse button to locate the file.

   - *Open a Web Page:* If you choose this option, you're choosing to link to a Web address. In the Address text box, enter the complete address of the Web site to which the link should direct viewers. To create a link to an e-mail address, type **mailto:** followed by an e-mail address. (Note that mailto: is all one word with no spaces.)

   - *Custom Link:* Use this option to choose from other types of links in the Link Properties dialog box.

4. **Click Next and follow the instructions in the next dialog box before clicking OK.**

The Link tool is relatively simple to use, but you may prefer to create links from text in another way: With the Selection tool, select the text, right-click (Windows) or Control-click (Mac) the selected text, and then choose Create Link from the contextual menu that appears.

You can have links transferred automatically from your original Microsoft Office documents when using PDF Maker.

You can edit links by choosing the Link tool and double-clicking the link to open the Link Properties dialog box. While editing a link, you can change how it's presented in the Appearance tab. Make a link invisible or add a border to the link, such as a blue border that commonly is used to define hyperlinks. On the Actions tab of the Link Properties dialog box, you can add, edit, or delete actions, just as you can with bookmarks (see the preceding section).

Adding Buttons to Simplify Your PDF Files

Along with links and bookmarks, buttons provide another way to make your files more useful when they're viewed online. You can create interactive buttons entirely within Acrobat — designing their appearance and adding text to them. Or you can import buttons created in other Adobe Creative Suite applications, such as Photoshop and Illustrator. For example, you can create buttons that advance the viewer to the next page in a document.

Additional form editing tools are only available on the Windows platform.

 Buttons are added by entering the Form Editing mode. Choose Forms➪Add or Edit Fields to open the Forms Editor. You may have to click OK to have a scan for form fields performed.

To add a button to your PDF document, follow these steps:

1. **Choose View➪Toolbars➪Advanced Editing.**

    The Advanced Editing toolbar appears.

2. **Click the OK Button tool and drag where you want the button to appear in the document.**

3. **Type in an appropriate name for your button in the Field Name dialog box that appears.**

4. **Click the Show All Properties button to see the Button Properties dialog box.**

5. **In the General tab, you can enter a name for the button in the Name text box and provide a ToolTip in the ToolTip text box.**

    A *ToolTip* is the text that appears whenever the mouse cursor is positioned over the button.

6. **In the Appearance tab, establish how your button will look by setting the following options:**

- *Border Color/Fill Color:* Click the square to the right of the appropriate attribute in the Borders and Colors section of the Appearance tab and then choose a color from the Color Picker.

- *Line Thickness and Style:* These options don't appear unless you change the border color from None (red diagonal line) to another selection.

- *Font Size/Font:* Change the size and font of the button text by making a selection from the Font Size and the Font drop-down lists.

- *Text Color:* Change the color of the text by clicking the color square and choosing a color from the Color Picker.

7. **In the Options tab, make these selections:**

   - *Layout:* Use the Layout drop-down list to specify whether you want to use a *label* (text that you enter in Acrobat that appears on the face of the button) or whether you want an *icon* (an imported button graphic that you may have designed in Photoshop or Illustrator).

   - *Behavior:* Choose Push from the Behavior drop-down list to create different appearances for a button so that it changes based upon whether the mouse cursor is positioned over the button. The button appearance can also change when clicked.

   - *State:* To specify the different appearances (see Behavior, discussed in the preceding paragraph), click the State on the left side of the Options tab and then choose the Label or Icon status for each state.

   - *Label:* If you choose to use a label, enter the text for it in the Label text field.

   - *Icon:* If you choose to use an icon, specify the location of the graphic file by clicking the Choose Icon button. You can create button icons in either Photoshop or Illustrator.

8. **In the Actions tab, choose an action from the Select Action drop-down list and then click the Add button.**

   Actions are applied to buttons similar to the way in which they're applied to links and bookmarks:

   - To choose actions that are a part of the menu commands, such as printing a document, closing a file, or navigating to the next or preceding page, choose the Execute Menu Item action and then specify the command to be accessed.

   - You can also choose the activity that causes the action to occur, known as the *trigger.* The default trigger is *Mouse Up,* which causes the action to occur when the mouse button is depressed and then released. You can choose other actions, such as the mouse cursor merely rolling over the button without the need to click it.

9. **After you make all your changes in the Button Properties dialog box, click Close.**

Book VIII Chapter 3

Adding Interactivity to PDF Files

Chapter 4: Editing and Extracting Text and Graphics

In This Chapter

✔ Manipulating text with the TouchUp tools

✔ Modifying graphics with the TouchUp tools

✔ Pulling text and graphics out of PDFs for use in other documents

*Y*ou may assume that PDF files are mere pictures of your documents and can't be edited, but nothing is further from the truth. Adobe Acrobat includes a variety of tools for editing both text and graphics. You can use these tools as long as the file hasn't been secured to prohibit editing. We introduce you to these great tools in this chapter. (We discuss security, which allows you to limit access to these tools, in Chapter 6 of this minibook.)

Editing Text

The tools for editing text and graphics are located on the Advanced Editing toolbar (see Figure 4-1).

Figure 4-1: The Advanced Editing toolbar.

You can add several TouchUp tools to the Advanced Editing toolbar by choosing View➪Toolbars➪More Tools and checking the tools you want to add.

For text tools, you have three choices:

✦ **TouchUp Text tool:** Used to manipulate text.

✦ **TouchUp Object tool:** Used to manipulate objects.

✦ **TouchUp Reading Order tool:** Used to correct the reading order or structure of the document.

The TouchUp Reading Order tool isn't used for changing the appearance of the document, so we don't discuss it in this chapter.

Using the TouchUp Text tool to manipulate text

The TouchUp Text tool is used for *touching up,* or manipulating, text. This touchup can include changing actual text characters or the appearance of text. You can change *cat* to read *dog,* or you can change black text to blue, or you can even change the Helvetica font to the Times font.

When you change a PDF file, the original source document isn't modified.

You have a few ways to accomplish text edits:

✦ Choose the TouchUp Text tool, click within the text that you want to change to obtain an insertion point, and then start typing the new text.

✦ Click with the TouchUp tool in your text and press the Backspace or Delete key to delete text.

✦ With the TouchUp tool, drag to highlight text and enter new text to replace the highlighted text.

When changing text — whether you're adding or deleting — Acrobat tries to use the font that was specified in the original document. Sometimes, this font is built into the PDF file, which means that it's *embedded* in the file. Other times, the font may not be available either because it hasn't been embedded or it's been embedded as a *subset* where only some of the characters from the font are included in the PDF file. In these cases, Acrobat may provide the following warning message:

```
All or part of the selection has no available system font. You cannot
add or delete text using the currently selected font.
```

Fortunately, you can change the font if you need to edit the text. However, when you change the font, the text may not retain the same appearance as the original document. In some instances, you may not have the exact same font on your computer as the font used in the PDF document, but you may have a similar font you can use without causing a noticeable change — most people won't notice the difference between Helvetica and Arial or between Times and Times New Roman. Fonts with the same name but from different font designers often look very similar. For example, Adobe Garamond looks similar to ITC Garamond, even though they're two different fonts.

To change the font that's used for a word or a range of words, follow these steps:

1. **With the TouchUp Text tool, drag over the text you wish to select.**

You may get a `Loading System Fonts` message followed by another `Loading Document Fonts` message. Depending on the number of fonts installed on your system, it may take a while for this message to disappear.

2. **Right-click (Windows) or Control-click (Mac) the highlighted text and choose Properties from the contextual menu.**

The TouchUp Properties dialog box appears, as shown in Figure 4-2.

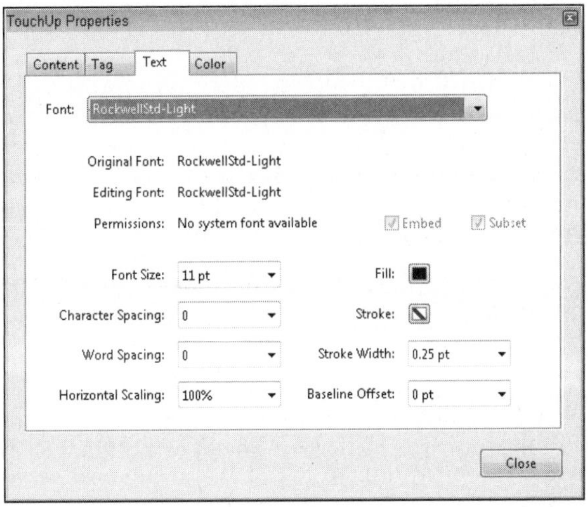

Figure 4-2:
The
TouchUp
Properties
dialog box.

3. **In the Text tab, choose the typeface you want to use from the Font drop-down list and make any other changes you want.**

In this dialog box, you can also change the size by selecting or typing a number into the Font Size drop-down list. In addition, you can modify the color by clicking the Fill color swatch.

4. **When you're satisfied with your changes, click the Close button to apply your changes to the selected text.**

Using the TouchUp Object tool to edit graphics

You can use the TouchUp Object tool to access editing software for modifying graphics. For example, you can use the TouchUp Object tool to select a graphic, bring the graphic into Photoshop, and then save the modified version back into the PDF file. In other words, you can edit the graphics used in PDF documents, even if you don't have access to the original graphic files.

Book VIII
Chapter 4

Editing and
Extracting Text
and Graphics

To edit a photographic file from Acrobat in Photoshop, follow these steps:

1. **Select the image with the TouchUp Object tool, right-click (Windows) or Control-click (Mac) on a photographic image with the TouchUp Object tool, and then choose Edit Image from the contextual menu.**

   The image file opens in Adobe Photoshop.

2. **With the many tools of Photoshop, make the necessary changes to the graphic and then choose File⇨Save.**

   When you return to the PDF file in Acrobat, the graphic is updated automatically in the PDF document.

If you have the original graphic file, it remains untouched — only the version used within the PDF file is modified. It isn't necessary to have the original graphic file to perform these steps.

You can also use Acrobat to edit vector objects from within PDF files, such as those created with Adobe Illustrator. Just follow these steps:

1. **Select a piece of vector artwork with the TouchUp Object tool, right-click (Windows) or Control-click (Mac) the vector artwork, and then choose Edit Object from the contextual menu.**

   Note: Acrobat displays Edit Object in the contextual menu if it detects a vector object, and it displays Edit Image if it detects a bitmap image. Acrobat also displays Edit Objects (note the plural) if you have more than one object selected.

   If you're editing a complex illustration, be sure to select all its components by holding down the Ctrl (Windows) or ⌘ (Mac) key while clicking them with the TouchUp Object tool.

   After choosing Edit Object, the object opens for editing in Adobe Illustrator.

2. **Make the necessary changes in Illustrator, choose File⇨Save.**

   The graphic is updated in the PDF document.

If Acrobat doesn't start Photoshop or Illustrator after choosing the Edit Image or Edit Object command, you may need to access preferences by choosing Edit⇨Preferences⇨Touch Up and then specifying which programs should be used for editing images or objects.

You can also use the TouchUp Object tool to edit the position of text or graphic objects on a page, which includes the ability to relocate individual lines of text or to change the position of a graphic on a page. After you select an object with the TouchUp Object tool, you can simply drag it to a new location on the page.

Typewriter tool

You can use the Typewriter tool to type anywhere on the document. This tool resembles the Text Box tool, though its default properties are different. Access the Typewriter tool by choosing Tools⇨Typewriter⇨Show Typewriter Toolbar. Then select the Typewriter icon, position your cursor where you want to begin typing and type, pressing the Enter or Return key whenever you want to add a line. The Increase and Decrease size buttons will enlarge or diminish your type size.

Likewise, to change the leading, you select the text and click the Increase or Decrease Line Spacing buttons. You can move or resize the Typewriter block by selecting it with the Select tool and either moving or resizing the text box. Your text remains editable. So, if you've made a mistake and want to correct it, or want to add or delete text, you select the Typewriter tool again and double-click in the type box.

Exporting Text and Graphics

Although editing text and graphics is helpful, you may need to take text or images from a PDF document and use them in another file. Fortunately, Acrobat also includes tools to make this a breeze. Of course, you should always make certain that you have the permission of the owner of a document before reusing content that isn't your original work.

You need the Select & Zoom toolbar for extracting text and graphics, so make sure that it's visible. If it isn't, choose View⇨Toolbars⇨Select & Zoom.

You can export text, images, or charts from Acrobat by copying and pasting, by saving as a specific file type, or by using the Snapshot tool. These methods are discussed in detail in the following sections.

Exporting text with Select, Copy, and Paste

Make sure that the Select & Zoom toolbar is visible (choose View⇨Toolbars⇨ Select & Zoom) and then follow these steps to select, copy, and paste text from a PDF file:

1. **With the Select tool, highlight the text you want to export.**

The Select tool is the I-bar/black arrow in the toolbar. When you hold the arrow over a section of your document, it turns into an I-bar cursor, which you can drag to select the text you want to copy.

If the Cut, Copy, and Paste commands are unavailable after you've selected some text, the author of the document may have set the security settings to disallow copying. If you can't select the text, you may be trying to copy text that is part of an image.

2. **Right-click (Windows) or Control-click (Mac) the selected text and choose Copy from the contextual menu.**

   Being able to extract the text out of a PDF document by selecting and copying it is useful if you don't have access to the original source document, but you need to use the text from a PDF file.

3. **Open another text-editing program, such as Adobe InDesign or Microsoft Word.**

   You can paste the copied text into a new document or a preexisting file.

4. **Insert your cursor in the document at the appropriate spot and choose File⇨Paste or Edit⇨Paste.**

   The text is pasted into the document, ready for you to use.

Exporting text with Save As

The File⇨Save As command exports all the text in your PDF file. The Save as Type drop-down list gives you various format options. After choosing an option and any settings, click the OK button to select the settings and click the Save button to save the text. The File⇨Export command gives you the same options.

Here are the formats you can use to export text:

✦ **Microsoft Word Document:** Click the Settings button to choose whether to save the comments or images with your document. If you choose to save the comments or images, you can select additional formatting options.

✦ **Rich Text Format:** Click the Settings button to choose whether to save the comments or images with your document. If you choose to save the comments or images, you can select additional formatting options.

✦ **Text (Accessible):** Use this format to create a file that can be printed to a Braille printer.

✦ **Text (Plain) (Secondary Settings):** This format creates a plain vanilla file with no formatting. You can save some secondary options in various file encodings. Also, you can select to save the images in your PDF in a separate images folder.

✦ **Encapsulated PostScript, PostScript:** These formats are generally used by commercial printers or IT professionals that need PostScript output.

✦ **Various Adobe PDF options, such as PDF/E for engineering or PDF/A for archiving:** These are used to switch to a specific subset of the PDF file format used for a particular industry or line of work.

✦ **Various graphics formats (JPEG, JPEG2000, PNG, TIFF):** If you choose one of these options, your text will no longer be editable as the entire PDF pages are converted to an image.

Text that's copied from a PDF file is no longer linked to the original document. Edits made to the extracted text aren't reflected within the PDF file, and it's extremely difficult to have the extracted text reinserted into the PDF document. Think of the extraction process as a one-way trip for the text, which can be extracted but not reinserted.

You can also copy text within a table to the Clipboard or open it directly in a spreadsheet program, such as Microsoft Excel, and maintain the table's formatting after it's extracted. Just follow these steps:

1. **Click the Select tool and click and drag to select the text in the table.**

   Depending upon how the table was created, you may also be able to position your cursor just outside the edge of the table and then draw a box around a table.

   A border appears around the selected table.

2. **Right-click (Windows) or Control-click (Mac) and choose Open Table in Spreadsheet from the contextual menu.**

   Alternatively, you can save the table directly to a file or copy to the Clipboard to be pasted later: If Acrobat has trouble identifying the text in the table, it may be saved as an image file, which is not editable text.

   - *To save the table directly to a file,* choose Save as Table from the contextual menu.

   - *To copy the table to the Clipboard so that you can paste it into other documents,* choose Copy as Table from the contextual menu.

   The table opens in Excel or whatever spreadsheet program you have installed on your computer.

   And that's it. You can now use that table in another program.

Extracting graphics

You can also extract graphics from PDF files, but extracting graphics is very different from editing them. We discuss editing graphics and vector objects earlier in this chapter. When editing graphics, you open the original graphic file at its highest possible quality. Extracting graphics is different because they're removed at the quality of the screen display resolution, which may be of much lower quality than the original, embedded graphics.

With the Select tool, right-click (Windows) or Control-click (Mac) an image, or drag with the Select tool to select a part of the image. Then you can either drag and drop the selection into an open document or choose Copy Image from the contextual menu. The image is now available to be pasted into other applications. The other option in the contextual menu is to Save Image As and save the selected area as a BMP graphics file.

Book VIII
Chapter 4

Editing and Extracting Text and Graphics

Snapshot tool

You can use the Snapshot tool to select both text and images and create a picture of a certain area within a PDF file. The result is commonly referred to as a *screen grab* of a section within a PDF file. The result is an image, and your text is no longer editable.

To use the Snapshot tool, choose Tools➪Select & Zoom➪Snapshot Tool. You then have two options.

✦ After you select the Snapshot tool, click anywhere in the page. The snapshot tool automatically captures everything displayed on the screen.

✦ After you select the Snapshot tool, click and drag a rectangle around an area of the page.

You can include text and images. The area you've selected will be saved to the Clipboard so that you can paste it into another document. The Snapshot tool remains active so that you can keep selecting areas and saving them to the Clipboard. However, the previous selection in your Clipboard is deleted when you make a new selection. So, make certain you've pasted a selection into your other document before you make a new selection.

You have to select another tool to deactivate the Snapshot tool.

Chapter 5: Using Commenting and Annotation Tools

In This Chapter

✔ Adding comments to PDF files

✔ Working with comments

*O*ne of the fantastic features of Acrobat is the capability to mark up documents electronically with virtual sticky notes, or *comments*. You can mark up text to indicate changes and add annotations and drawing comments to a PDF (Portable Document Format) file. The Acrobat commenting tools don't change the original file, and you can remove the comments at any time, which means you can disable comments for printing or viewing at any time. In this chapter, we describe these great features and show you how to put them to work for you.

Creating Comments with the Comment & Markup Toolbar

You can easily add annotations to PDF files, including stamps, text highlights, callouts, and electronic sticky notes by using the Comment & Markup toolbar, which you can access by clicking the Comment option in the Tasks toolbar. You can then choose Show the Comment & Markup Tools.

You can also access the Comment & Markup toolbar by choosing View⇨Toolbars⇨Comment & Markup.

The Comment & Markup toolbar, as shown in Figure 5-1, provides several tools for adding comments to PDF documents. It also includes a Show menu to help manage comments and the process of adding comments. We discuss these tools in the following sections.

Figure 5-1:
The
Comment
& Markup
toolbar.

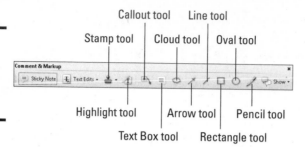

The Sticky Note tool

Use the Sticky Note tool to add electronic sticky notes to your files. You can click the location where you want the note to appear within a PDF document. An icon, representing the note, appears, along with a window where you can enter text. After entering text in the sticky note, close the window so that the document isn't hidden beneath it.

You can change the icon and color used to represent the note by right-clicking (Windows) or Control-clicking (Mac) the note and choosing Properties from the contextual menu. In the Properties dialog box that appears, make the changes to the note icon or color and then click Close.

The Text Edits tool

The Text Edits tool is actually six separate text commenting tools. Use these tools to replace selected text, highlight selected text, add a note to selected text, insert text at cursor, underline selected text, and cross out text for deletion.

To use the Text Edits tool, follow these steps:

1. **Choose the Text Edits tool and drag to select text that requires a change or comment.**

2. **Click the arrow to the right of the Text Edits tool to access the drop-down list containing your six choices.**

3. **Choose an option from the list of available editing choices:**

   • *Replace Selected Text:* Replaces the selected text.

   • *Highlight Selected Text:* Highlights the selected text.

   • *Add a Note to Selected Text:* Allows you to add a note to the selected text.

- *Insert Text at Cursor:* Places a cursor at the end of the selected text.
- *Underline Selected Text:* Underlines the selected text.
- *Cross Out Text for Deletion:* Crosses out the selected text.

Your selected text changes, depending on what you choose from the list.

After selecting the text that requires a comment, you can press the Delete or Backspace key to indicate a text edit to remove the text. Similarly, you can start to type, and Acrobat will create an insertion point. Also, if you right-click (Windows) or Control-click (Mac) after selecting the text, you can select the type of edit or comment you want to insert from the contextual menu.

The Stamp tool

You can use stamps to identify documents or to highlight a certain part of a document. Common stamps include Confidential, Draft, Sign Here, and Approved.

The stamps are grouped into sections. Some stamps automatically add your default username along with the date and time you applied them to the document; these stamps are available under the Dynamic category in the Stamps menu. The more traditional business stamps, such as Confidential, appear under the Standard Business category. You can access each of the different categories by clicking the arrow to the right of the Stamp tool in the Comment & Markup toolbar, as shown in Figure 5-2.

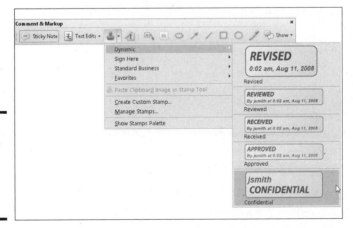

Figure 5-2: Access the different types of stamp groups.

To apply a stamp to your document, follow these steps:

1. **Select the Stamp tool from the Comment & Markup toolbar.**

2. **Click the arrow to the right of the Stamp tool and from the menu, choose the stamp you want to apply to the document.**

3. **Drag within your document at the location where you want the stamp to appear.**

The Highlight Text, Underline Text, and Cross Out Text tools

The Highlight Text, Cross Out Text, and Underline Text tools provide the same functionality and options that are available with the Text Edits tool, but with easier access. If you want to delete the highlighted, crossed-out, or underlined formatting to your text, just click the formatted area and hit the Delete or Backspace key. Your text will remain, but the formatting will disappear.

To highlight text, follow these steps:

1. **Select the Highlight Text tool from the Comment & Markup toolbar.**

2. **Drag over the text that you want highlighted.**

   The text is now highlighted.

To underline text, follow these steps:

1. **Select the Underline Text tool by selecting Tools⇨Comment & Markup Tools⇨Underline Text.**

2. **Drag over the text that you want underlined.**

   The text is now underlined.

To cross out text, follow these steps:

1. **Select the Cross Out Text tool by choosing Tools⇨Comment & Markup Tools⇨Cross Out Text Tool.**

2. **Drag over the text that you want crossed out.**

   The text is now crossed out.

The Attach File tools

With the Attach File tools, you can attach an existing text file, a sound file, or any file copied to the Clipboard from your computer (or computer network) and attach it to the PDF.

Follow these steps for file and sound attachments:

1. **Choose Comments➪Comment & Markup Tools➪Attach a File as a Comment.**

   A pushpin icon appears.

2. **Click where you want the attachment noted.**

   The Add Attachment dialog box appears.

3. **In the Add Attachment dialog box, browse to the file that you want to attach and click the Select button.**

   You can attach text, graphic, or sound files.

4. **Select the type of icon to represent the attached file and then click OK.**

   Several types of icons can represent the attached file. You can select a paperclip, a graph, a pushpin, or a tag. Whatever icon you select appears on your document to denote that another file is attached. When you roll over the icon, a little annotation appears telling you the filename.

   With the Record Audio Comment tool, you can share a verbal comment by using a microphone and a recording a message directly into the PDF. The sound is added as a comment.

The file(s) that you attach with the Attach File tools becomes embedded within the PDF file. The attached file remains in its original file format, even if the attached file isn't a PDF file. For example, you can attach an Excel spreadsheet to a PDF document.

The drawing tools

There are three shape tools, two line tools, and a pencil in the Comment & Markup toolbar. Use the drawing tools to add lines, ovals, rectangles, and other shapes to your PDF file. These shapes can call attention to specific portions of a document.

To use the Cloud Shape tool, follow these steps:

1. **Select the Cloud Shape tool from the Comment & Markup toolbar.**

2. **Click in your document to begin the shape.**

3. **Click again in another position to set the length of the first part of the cloud and then click again to begin shaping your cloud.**

   Click as often as you like to create your shape.

4. **When you're finished with your shape, double-click to close the cloud shape.**

5. **While the Cloud Shape tool is selected, click the shape you created and drag the corner points to resize, if necessary.**

6. **After creating the cloud shape, right-click (Windows) or Control-click (Mac) the shape and choose Properties from the contextual menu to change the color and thickness of the line values; when you're finished, click OK.**

   You can also use the Style drop-down list in the Properties dialog box to change the appearance of a selected comment. Instead of the cloud edges, you can change them to dotted lines, dashed lines, and so on.

To use the rectangle and oval shapes, follow these steps:

1. **Select either the Rectangle or Oval Shape tool from the Comment & Markup toolbar.**

2. **Click and drag in your document to draw the shape.**

3. **While the drawing tool you chose is selected, click the shape you created and drag the corner points to resize, if necessary.**

4. **After creating the shape, right-click (Windows) or Control-click (Mac) the shape and choose Properties from the contextual menu to change the color and thickness of the line values; when you're finished, click OK.**

   You can also use the Style drop-down list in the Properties dialog box to change the appearance of the shape.

The Text Box tool

When creating notes that you want to prominently display on a document, you can use the Text Box tool.

Follow these steps to add a text box to hold your comments:

1. **Select the Text Box tool from the Comment & Markup toolbar.**

   A text field is placed directly on the document.

2. **Drag to add the comment.**

3. **Right-click (Windows) or Control-click (Mac) and choose Properties from the contextual menu to set the color of the text box that contains the note.**

4. **Make your choices to modify the appearance of the text box and then click OK.**

You can select the text box and move it to another position any time you want. You can resize the text box by dragging an anchor point.

The Callout tool

The Callout tool creates a callout text box that points to a section of your document with an arrow. The callout text box is made up of three parts: the text box, the knee line, and the end point line. You can resize each part individually to customize the callout area of your document.

To use the Callout tool, follow these steps:

1. **Select the Callout tool from the Comment & Markup toolbar.**

2. **Click where you want the arrowhead point to be.**

3. **Drag up or down or to the side to position the text box and begin typing.**

You can click the text box and then use the anchor points on the line to resize the box.

4. **Right-click (Windows) or Control-click (Mac) and choose Properties from the contextual menu to set the color of the callout text box.**

You can change the size, color, and font characteristics of the text in the callout **text** box.

5. **Make your choices to modify the appearance of the callout text box and then click OK.**

You can select the callout text box and move it to another position any time you want. You can resize the text box by dragging an anchor point.

The Pencil tool

With the Pencil tool, you can create freeform lines on your documents. These lines can be useful when you're trying to attract attention to a specific portion of a page. Just follow these steps:

1. **Select the Pencil tool from the Comment & Markup toolbar.**

2. **Click and drag to draw on your document.**

3. **Edit the color and thickness of lines created with the Pencil tool by right-clicking (Windows) or Control-clicking (Mac) the line and choosing Properties from the contextual menu.**

Alternatively, you can press Ctrl+E (Windows) or ⌘+E (Mac) to access the Properties toolbar.

4. **Make your choices and click OK.**

By right-clicking (Windows) or Control-clicking (Mac) the Pencil tool, you can choose the Pencil Eraser tool. Use the Pencil Eraser tool to remove portions of lines that had previously been created with the Pencil tool.

Managing Comments

One of the most powerful features of PDF commenting is the ability to easily manage and share comments and annotations among reviewers. For example, you can determine which comments are displayed at any time, and you can filter the comments by author or by the type of commenting tool used to create the comment. In addition, you can indicate a response to a comment and track the changes that may have been made to a document based upon a comment. Also, you can consolidate comments from multiple reviewers into a single document.

Viewing comments

You can use any of several methods to see a document's list of comments:

✦ Click the Comments tab along the bottom left side of the document window in the Navigation panel.

✦ Choose Comment⇨Show Comments List.

✦ Choose View⇨Navigation Panels⇨Comments.

No matter which method you use, the Comments List window that shows all the comments in the document appears along the bottom of the Document window. You can see the author of each comment and any notes entered by reviewers. By clicking the plus sign to the left of a comment, you can view more information about it, such as what type of comment it is and the date and time it was created.

If you've clicked the plus sign to the left of the comment to expand the view, it changes to a minus sign, which you can then click to return to the consolidated view showing only the author and the initial portions of any text from the note.

To the right of the plus sign is a check box that you can use to indicate that the comment has been reviewed or to indicate that a certain comment needs further attention. Use these check boxes for your own purposes; their status doesn't export with the document if you send the file to others, so they're for your personal use only.

Changing a comment's review status

Acrobat makes it easy to indicate whether a comment has been reviewed, accepted, or has additional comments attached to it.

To change the status of a comment, follow these steps:

1. **Choose Comments⇨Show Comments List to see the entire list of comments and the status of each one.**

You can also click the Comments tab located on the bottom left side of the screen to display the comments.

2. **In the Comments List, right-click (Windows) or Control-click (Mac) a comment and choose Set Status⇨Review from the contextual menu.**

3. **Select Accepted, Rejected, Cancelled, or Completed, depending on what's appropriate to your situation.**

The comment you modified appears in the list, showing the new status you assigned to it.

Replying to a comment

You can right-click (Windows) or Control-click (Mac) a comment in the Comments List and choose Reply from the contextual menu to add a follow-up note to the comment. This way, new comments can be tied to existing comments. If your documents go through multiple rounds of review, adding a reply allows a secondary or final reviewer to expand on the comments from an initial reviewer. This also allows an author or designer to clearly respond to the suggestions from an editor.

Collapsing or hiding comments

Because the Comments List can become rather large, you can choose to collapse all comments so that only the page number on which comments appear is displayed in the list. To do so, click the Collapse All button in the upper left of the Comments List window; it has a minus sign next to it. To view all comments, click the Expand All button in the same location; this button has a plus sign next to it.

To hide all the comments within a document, click and hold the Show button on the Commenting toolbar and choose Hide All Comments. You can then click the Show button in the Comments toolbar and choose to show comments based upon

◆ Type of comment, such as note, line, or cross out

◆ Reviewer, such as Bob or Jane

◆ Status, such as accepted or rejected

◆ Checked State, which can be checked or unchecked

Use these filtering options to view only those comments that are relevant to you.

Sharing comments

You can share your comments with other reviewers who have access to the same PDF document by following these steps:

1. **Make sure that the Comments List is visible by clicking the Comments tab on the bottom left of the Document window.**

2. **Select the comment that you want to export by clicking it (Shift+click for multiple selections).**

3. **From the Comments List window, choose Options➪Export Selected Comments.**

The Export Comments dialog box appears.

4. **Browse to the location where you want the comments to be saved and give the saved file a new name.**

You now have a file that includes only the comments' information, and not the entire PDF file.

You can share your file with reviewers who have the same PDF file, and they can choose Options➪Import Comments in the Comments List window to add the comments into their document. You can use this method to avoid sending entire PDF files to those who already have the document.

Summarizing comments

You can compile a list of all the comments from a PDF file into a new, separate document. To summarize comments, follow these steps:

1. **From the Comments List window, choose Options➪Summarize Comments.**

The Summarize Options dialog box appears.

2. **Create a listing of the comments with lines connecting them to their locations on the page by selecting the radio button from the top — Document and Connector Lines on a Single Page.**

In the Include section, you can choose which comments should be summarized.

3. **Click the Create PDF Comment Summary button.**

This step creates a new PDF document that simply lists all the comments, as shown in Figure 5-3.

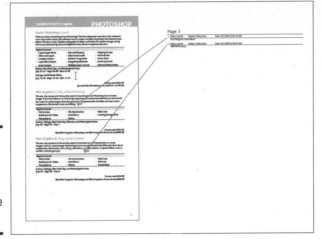

Figure 5-3:
A new PDF document is created, listing all the comments.

Enabling commenting in Adobe Reader

Acrobat 9.0 Professional makes it easy to include users of the free Adobe Reader in a review process. To include Adobe Reader users in a review, choose Comments⇨Enable for Commenting in Adobe Reader. After saving the file, you can share it with users of Adobe Reader, who can then use commenting and markup tools and save their comments into the file. A user of Adobe Acrobat 9.0 Professional must enable commenting in a PDF file before users of Adobe Reader can add comments to a file.

Chapter 6: Securing Your PDF Files

You may think that because you've converted your documents to PDF (Portable Document Format) that they're secure. This isn't quite true because Adobe Acrobat includes tools for changing text and images, as well as extracting them for use in other files. For example, you can use the Select tool (see Chapter 4 of this minibook) to select and copy a passage of text or the Select Object tool to copy or edit graphics.

Applying security provides you with control over who can view, edit, or print the PDF documents you distribute. You can restrict access to certain features, which deters most users from manipulating your files. All Adobe applications recognize and honor security settings applied in Acrobat, but some software ignores Adobe's security settings or can bypass them all together. For this reason, we recommend that you share your most sensitive PDF documents only when you've applied security protection. This way, the only users who can open a file are those who know the password or have the correct certificate, depending upon the type of security applied to the file.

In this chapter, we discuss using security protection to limit access to PDF files and show you how to limit what users can do to the contents of your PDF documents.

Understanding Password Security

By requiring users to enter a password to open and view your PDF files, you limit access to those files so that only certain users can view them. You can also apply security to limit access to certain Acrobat and Adobe Reader features, such as copying text or graphics, editing the file, and printing. Adobe calls this type of security *password security* because it requires a password to either open the document or to change the security that's been applied to the document.

Apply security options to limit the opening or editing of your PDF document, restricting these capabilities to users who have been provided the proper password. This is done by clicking the Secure button on the Tasks toolbar. If the Secure button isn't visible, choose View➪Toolbars➪Tasks.

Click and hold down the Secure button in the Tasks toolbar and choose 2 Encrypt with Password to bring up the Password Security - Settings dialog box.

In the Password Security - Settings dialog box, choose an Acrobat version from the Compatibility drop-down list. The higher the version of Acrobat, the greater the level of security.

Your choice here is based on your needs for security and also the version of Acrobat or Adobe Reader that your audience uses. Lower versions of Acrobat provide more compatibility with the widest number of viewers, as they support much older versions of the free Adobe Reader. In the following list, we explain the compatibility choices before showing you how to enable security in the following sections:

+ **Acrobat 3 and Later:** If the users who receive your PDF files may have older versions of the software, you can choose Acrobat 3 and Later from the Compatibility drop-down list to ensure that the recipients can view the PDF file you're securing. This option provides compatibility for users who may not have updated their software in many years, but the level of security is limited to 40-bit encryption. Although this amount keeps the average user from gaining access to your files, it won't deter a determined hacker from accessing them and can be easily circumvented by a sophisticated user.

+ **Acrobat 5 and Later:** When sharing files with users who have access to Adobe Reader or Adobe Acrobat Version 5 or 6, this option provides expanded security, increasing the security level to 128-bit, which makes the resulting PDF files more difficult to access. Along with the enhanced security, you can also secure the files while still allowing access to the file for visually-impaired users. Earlier versions of security don't provide this option, but it's included when you choose either Acrobat 5- or 6-compatible security.

+ **Acrobat 6 and Later:** Along with the enhanced security offered with Acrobat 5 compatibility, this setting adds the ability to maintain plain text metadata. In short, this option allows for information about the file, such as its author, title, or creation date, to remain visible while the remainder of the file remains secure.

+ **Acrobat 7 and Later:** This choice includes all security options of Acrobat 6 compatibility and also allows you to encrypt file attachments that are part of a PDF file. It uses the *Advanced Encryption Standard,* which is a very high level of encryption, making it unlikely that an unauthorized user can decrypt the file without the password.

✦ **Acrobat 9 and Later:** Choose this option if your audience is using the latest version of Acrobat and you need more advanced security. The encryption improves to 256-bit AES, making the file much more difficult for even the most determined hacker to access.

Applying Password Security to Your PDF Documents

Selecting the Encrypt with Password option from the Secure button in the Acrobat task bar limits access to the PDF file. Only those who know the password can open the file. Documents are only as secure as the passwords that protect them. To guard against discovery of a password, use passwords that are six or more characters in length and include at least one number or symbol. Avoid using words in the dictionary and short passwords. For example, the password `potato` is less secure than `p0tat0`, which mixes numbers and letters.

To apply password security to a file, follow these steps:

1. **With a PDF file open, click and hold the Secure button on the Security taskbar and choose Encrypt with Password.**

Click OK when the dialog box appears, verifying that you want to apply security to this PDF. The Password Security - Settings dialog box appears, as shown in Figure 6-1.

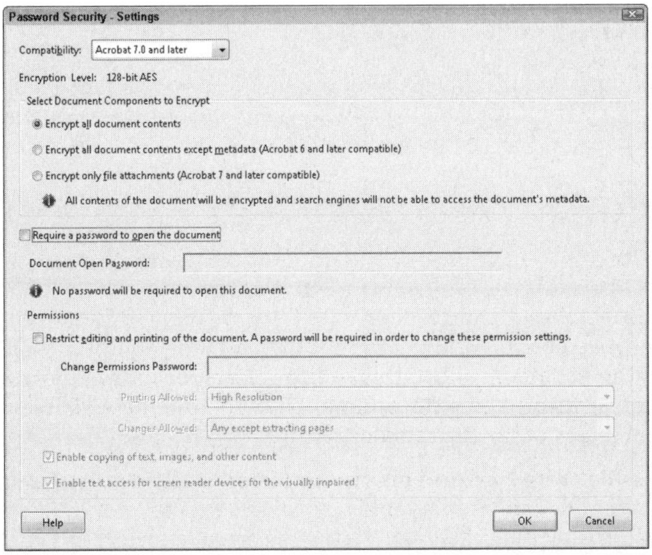

Figure 6-1:
The
Password
Security -
Settings
dialog box.

2. Choose Acrobat 7 and Later from the Compatibility drop-down list.

Although Acrobat 9 and later provides more robust security, few people are using version 9 of Acrobat, making it difficult to distribute the file with this high level of security.

3. Select the Require a Password to Open the Document check box.

4. Enter a password in the Document Open Password text box.

You can also add additional security settings, which we outline in the next section. Or you can use this setting as the only security to be applied to the document.

If password protection is the only security measure you apply to the document, authorized users can access the document by entering a password. Users with the password may also be able to edit or print the document unless you apply additional security measures. We discuss ways to limit the editing and printing of PDF files in the next section.

5. Click the OK button.

6. Confirm the password, click OK again, and the dialog box closes.

7. Save, close, and then reopen the PDF file.

A password dialog box appears asking for the password to access the secured file. Every time a user accesses the file, he or she will be required to enter a password.

Limiting Editing and Printing

In addition to restricting viewing of a PDF file, you can also limit editing and printing, restricting users from making changes to your document. This allows users to view a file but not change it.

To limit editing and printing of your PDF document, follow these steps:

1. With a PDF file open, click and hold the Secure button on the Security taskbar and choose Encrypt with Password.

The Password Security - Settings dialog box opens.

2. In the Permissions area, select the check box labeled Restrict Editing and Printing of the document.

You can now specify a password that will be required for readers to edit the file or change the security settings. (See the previous section.)

With this option selected, you can apply a password for access to features, such as printing or editing. This password can be different than the password used to open the document — in fact, you don't even need to use a document open password if you don't want to, but it's a good idea to use both of these passwords for sensitive data. If you apply a document open password without a permissions password, it's easy for an experienced user to bypass the security in the PDF file.

3. In the Change Permissions Password text box, enter a password.

Users that enter this permissions password when opening the document can change the file or the security settings. The permissions password can also be used to open the file and provides more privileges than the open password.

4. Choose whether users can print the document by selecting from the Printing Allowed drop-down list.

The choices include Low Resolution or High Resolution, or you can prohibit printing by choosing None. The settings you choose here apply to anyone who accesses the document and doesn't know the permissions password.

5. Choose from the Changes Allowed drop-down list (see Figure 6-2) to restrict editing.

For the most security, choose None.

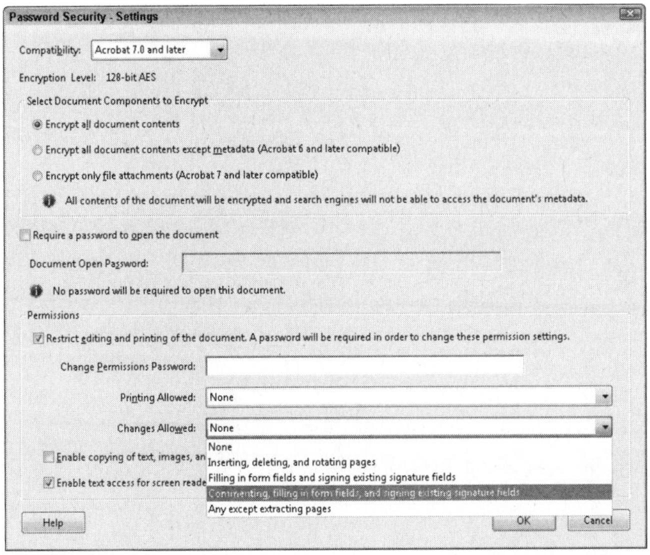

Figure 6-2:
Restrict what users can edit.

Book VIII
Chapter 6

Securing Your
PDF Files

6. **Select the last two check boxes if desired:**

   - *Enable Copying of Text, Images, and Other Content:* When deselected, this option restricts copying and pasting of text and graphics from a PDF file into other documents. Selecting this option lets users extract text and images from a file by using the simple Copy and Paste commands.

   - *Enable Text Access for Screen Reader Devices for the Visually Impaired:* When you choose Acrobat 5 or Later from the Compatibility drop-down list at the top of the dialog box, you can also select this check box to allow visually impaired users to have the PDF file read aloud to them.

7. **When you're satisfied with the settings, click OK.**

Choosing more advanced security settings, and choosing the latest version of compatibility, runs the risk of your file not being visible to many users that may not have upgraded. Always understand your audience and the software versions they're using before distributing files.

Book IX
Contribute CS4

THE GLACIER MOVEMENT PROJECT UPDATE THEIR WEBSITE

Camera ready? Wait a minute, hold it. Ready? Wait for the action...steady...steady...not yet...eeeasy. Hold it. Okay, stay focused. Ready? Not yet...steeeady...eeeasy...

Contents at a Glance

Chapter 1: Getting Started with Contribute CS4

In This Chapter

✔ Figuring out how Contribute works

✔ Combining Contribute and Dreamweaver

✔ Working on blogs

Creating and posting a new Web site or a blog is an exciting new venture, and the real-time nature of the Web opens many doors for presenting content, marketing a product, or simply showcasing your ideas.

The integrity of your site depends largely on the quality, accuracy, and freshness of its content, and in many cases, that responsibility lies in the hands of more than one person. No matter how big or small the site, managing site content needs to be a task that's easy, intuitive, and doesn't require a team of technical geniuses to do it!

Contribute CS4 makes these tasks easy by providing an intuitive workspace from which one or more users can easily create, update, and publish content to a Web site or a blog. If you're already using Dreamweaver CS4 to design and publish Web pages, you'll find many cool options that make setup and site management in Contribute a snap. You can read more about building Web sites and content with Dreamweaver in Book IV.

Introducing Contribute

Contribute is best described as a full-featured content management system (often referred to as a *CMS*), giving you (and selected users) an intuitive workspace and toolset from which you can update a Web site or a blog without getting into the complex nuts and bolts behind it. Figure 1-1 shows the Contribute Start page when you open Contribute.

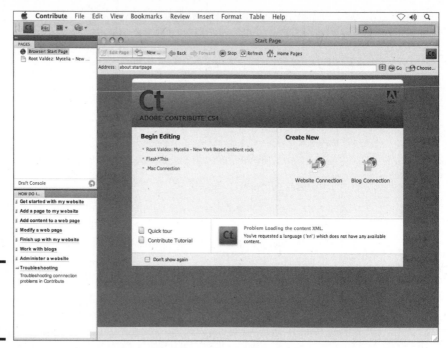

Figure 1-1:
The
Contribute
Start page.

Several content management systems are on the market, many of which are even Web based so that most tasks can be performed through a browser. Contribute offers many advantages over Web-based or third-party content management systems. Here's a look at some key reasons you may want to explore Contribute as a first choice for your site's CMS:

✦ **Ease of use:** Contribute is geared toward users of all experience levels, including experienced Web designers, writers, content publishers, project managers, and even administrative staff.

A simple yet powerful set of tools and features enables users of any level to build new pages, perform updates to existing pages, and publish content to the Web with little or no technical knowledge.

With little or no knowledge about creating or editing Web pages, you can easily add and format text, images, and multimedia as well as publish your work to the Web. In some cases, you may find adding content to a Contribute-enabled Web site is as easy as editing a word processing document!

✦ **Dreamweaver integration:** Sites built in Dreamweaver and managed in Contribute can utilize Dreamweaver-specific features, such as page templates and design notes. If a site utilizes Dreamweaver templates, Contribute makes them available to users so they can build new pages and expand their existing site.

✦ **Simplified Web page design and editing:** Beyond just a simple tweak or text edit, Contribute includes tools for creating more complex Web page layouts, adding images and media, and creating fancy text formatting. Contribute includes an all-in-one page editor and a browser window where you can edit, publish, and preview your work. You find many of the same tools that appear in Dreamweaver CS4, but further simplified for a nonintimidating workspace.

✦ **User management:** Contribute controls who can edit a Web site and how, by allowing you to add users to a project and to assign each user a specific role. A user's role determines what tasks he's allowed to perform and what files he has access to.

For instance, you can allow certain types of users to perform all tasks, such as creating and publishing content, while others can write or edit content without the ability to publish final drafts. This gives you lots of control over content flow and screening, especially when several people are working on a single site.

To access and edit a Contribute-enabled site, contributors are issued a *key,* which contains a predefined role for that user as well as the credentials needed to connect to and edit your Web site or blog. Other participants in your project must also have Contribute CS4 installed to receive and activate keys.

✦ **Rollback support:** Contribute enables you to revert to previous versions of your pages if necessary — a feature that can be quite handy when many people collaborate on a Web site.

Combining Dreamweaver and Contribute

If you've already used Book IV to get started with Dreamweaver CS4 or are already using Dreamweaver to build Web sites, you're off to a good start. Contribute can take advantage of many of the cool features of Dreamweaver sites, such as page templates.

Templates become available as starter pages (as shown in Figure 1-2) if and when you choose to add new pages to an existing Web site. You can easily build new pages from Dreamweaver templates, which we discuss in Chapter 4 of this minibook.

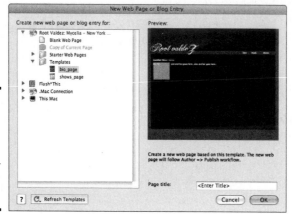

Figure 1-2:
You can easily build new pages from Dreamweaver templates.

In addition, you can enable an existing Dreamweaver site for Contribute use directly from its Manage Site panel.

Working with Blogs

Blogs (short for we*blogs*) are one of the most popular methods of communicating and sharing ideas, and are a tool for both the average Web user as well as media professionals. Chances are someone you know has a blog, as well as your favorite news reporter or celebrity. Blogs are most commonly provided as services (free or paid) by a number of online services.

If you maintain a blog, Contribute makes it easy to update and add content to your Blogger, WordPress, Roller, TypePad, or other hosted blog account. This gives you the ability to manage your blog within Contribute and take advantage of its extensive toolset, providing an alternative to editing your blog in a browser.

You can easily create or view existing blog posts (as shown in Figure 1-3), use the Contribute text editing tools to add and format text, images, and even add multimedia (such as videos and Flash movies) with ease. This is a great alternative to the sometimes limited and clunky Web-based tools that your blog provider may offer.

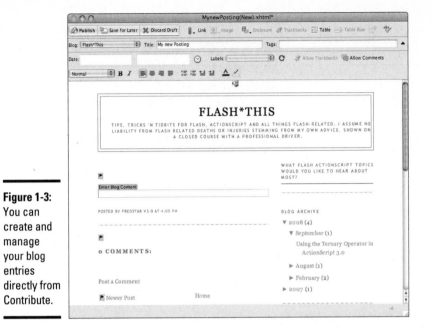

Figure 1-3:
You can
create and
manage
your blog
entries
directly from
Contribute.

Chapter 2: Getting Connected

In This Chapter

✓ Creating connections to Web sites

✓ Creating users and distributing keys

✓ Setting up Dreamweaver sites for use with Contribute

✓ Exploring the Contribute workspace

*I*f you read Chapter 1 in this minibook, you know a little bit more about what Contribute CS4 can do. Time to create your first connection. In this chapter, you discover how to create users and connect contributors through the distribution of keys. You also take a look at setting up an existing Dreamweaver site project to take full advantage of the close workflow between Contribute and Dreamweaver.

You need an active Internet connection before you can create connections, manage users, and perform most other tasks in Contribute. Although you can work offline to edit existing drafts, you can publish those drafts until you're reconnected to the Internet.

Contribute CS4 gives you the same features and tools used to manage Web sites to manage your blog or hosted blog solution. This chapter focuses on Web sites, and Chapter 3 of this minibook details connecting to and managing a blog.

Setting Up a Web Site Connection

Before you manage a Web site, first set up a new connection between the Web site and Contribute. A *connection* lets you access the files on your Web server through Contribute, and from Contribute, you can edit and add pages, send additional connection keys to other Contribute users, and set up user roles. (Connection keys and user roles are covered later in this chapter.)

The initial connection to a Web site or a blog typically establishes you as the administrator of the project and allows you to decide who else can connect and edit content on your site. However, connections can also be created instantly from keys, which we discuss later in this chapter. This allows contributors who aren't necessarily administrators to publish and work with content in the same project with limited capabilities.

Gathering the necessary information

To create a connection to a Web site, make sure that you have the following pieces of information handy:

✦ **A Web address:** This is the location of the Web site or folder where your pages are located, such as `http://www.mywebsite.com` or `http://www.mywebsite.com/myproject`.

✦ **An FTP address:** This is either a numerical address or a Web address (such as `ftp.mywebsite.com`) that points to your Web server and account where your public Web site is located.

✦ **An ID and password:** Generally, a Web site's files and account are protected with an ID and a password, which you need along with the FTP address to gain access to them.

You can get this information from your IT (Information Technology) department or Web site administrator. If you set up your own Web site with a Web hosting provider, these details are most likely provided in a confirmation e-mail or a receipt at the time of purchase.

Creating a new connection

After you have the information you need, you're ready to create a new connection. This can be done from the Start page or the Edit menu.

To create a connection from the Start page or the Edit menu:

1a. **Click the Create Connection button on the left side of the Start page when you launch Contribute.**

1b. **Choose Edit⇨My Connections and click the New button.**

The Create Connection dialog box appears, as shown in Figure 2-1, and asks what type of project you want to connect to.

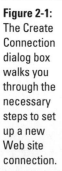

Figure 2-1:
The Create Connection dialog box walks you through the necessary steps to set up a new Web site connection.

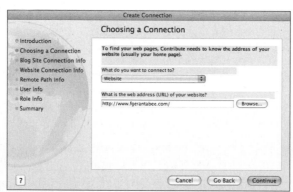

2. **Choose Website from the drop-down list.**

3. **Enter the Web address (or *URL*) of your site (such as** http://www.
   mywebsite.com) **and click the Next or Continue button.**

   Always provide the http:// prefix before your Web address. The trailing
   slash (/) is optional.

   After you click the Next or Continue button, the Website Connection Info
   screen appears.

4. **From the How Do You Connect to Your Web Server drop-down list,
   choose FTP, as shown in Figure 2-2.**

   FTP is the most common option.

5. **Enter the FTP address (such as** ftp.mywebsite.com) **in the What Is the
   Name of Your FTP Server? text box.**

6. **In the following two text boxes, enter the username and password
   (respectively) as provided by your IT department, Web site manager,
   or hosting company and then click the Next or Continue button.**

Figure 2-2:
If you
have your
connection
information
available,
you can
enter it
to allow
Contribute
to download/
upload files.

Your connection information is tested. Upon verification, you continue
to the User Info screen. *Note:* If you receive a connection error, make
sure to check and edit your connection information.

7. **Enter your full name and e-mail address and then click the Next or
   Continue button.**

   Your name and e-mail are used to identify you to other users on your
   project and to keep track of who's connected and editing drafts.

   After you click Continue, the Summary screen appears, confirming the
   creation of your new connection.

8. **Review the information and click the Done or Finish button to exit the
   dialog box.**

To create a connection from the Edit menu (Windows) or Contribute menu (Mac):

1. **Choose Edit⇨My Connections (Windows) or Contribute⇨ My Connections (Mac).**

    The My Connections dialog box appears.

2. **Click the Create button in the upper-left corner.**

3. **Follow Steps 2 through 8 in the preceding steps list to create your new connection.**

 Choose Edit (Windows)/Contribute (Mac)⇨My Connections and select the Don't Connect to Any Site at Startup check box shown at the bottom of the My Connections dialog box. This prevents Contribute from automatically connecting to your last project and speeds up Contribute when launched.

Administering a Web Site

After you establish a new Web site connection, you can administer that Web site by defining new roles, setting workflow preferences, and creating connection keys so that other Contribute users can also connect to your site project.

Understanding preset user roles

Each contributor to your Web site or blog is assigned a role that determines what tasks he can perform and what files he has access to. This information is set in the connection keys you create and distribute, and creates a workflow in which each participant has a set level of responsibility and control.

Contribute contains three predefined roles that you can select from when adding users:

✦ **Administrator:** This user has the utmost control over a Web site, including creating connection keys, assigning roles, editing page content, and publishing page content to a Web site or a blog.

   To avoid the *too many cooks in the kitchen* scenario, creation of additional administrators should be limited and granted only to project managers, site administrators, and other top-level participants in your project.

✦ **Publisher:** A publisher has the ability to edit and create existing Web site content, add new pages, and publish drafts to the live Web site. This role is typically granted to trusted content managers and writers, and can be used to publish and moderate content developed by writers.

Book IX
Chapter 2

Getting Connected

✦ **Writer:** This role is ideal for contributing writers or limited participants who require the basic ability to add and edit content. Writers can create and save drafts, which are then published to the Web site by a publisher or an administrator.

Creating custom roles

In each Web site project, the choice and assignment of each type of role varies based on the number of contributors and the workflow that's been established for your specific project.

In certain cases, you may find that the predefined roles provided by Contribute don't cover every type of user your project may need. For cases like this, Contribute lets you create new custom roles that fit the needs of your workflow.

Follow these steps to create a custom role:

1. **Choose Edit⇨Administer Websites (Windows) or Contribute⇨ Administer Websites (Mac) and select a Web site to manage.**

    The Users and Roles screen in the Administer Website dialog box appears.

2. **To the right of the Users and Roles list, click the Create New Role button, as shown in Figure 2-3.**

Figure 2-3: You can manage and add users, or give different users different capabilities from the Administer Website dialog box.

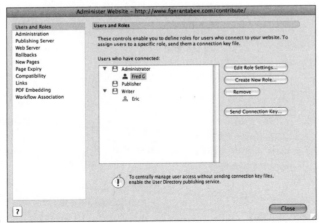

The Create New Role dialog box appears.

3. **Base your new role on either the publisher or writer role and then enter a name for the custom role.**

For this example, select Writer and enter **Guest Writer** for your new role.

4. **Click OK to close the dialog box and create the role.**

The Users and Roles screen displays your new role, and you can edit settings for that role. For now, you can leave the default settings and send a connection key (which we discuss in the "Creating and sending connection keys" section) to a user who will assume that role.

To edit settings for a new/existing role:

1. **Choose Edit⇨Administer Websites (Windows) or Contribute⇨ Administer Websites (Mac) and select a Web site to manage.**

The Users and Roles screen in the Administer Website dialog box appears.

2. **Select the role you want to edit and click the Edit Role Settings button on the right.**

The Edit Settings dialog box appears, which allows you to create settings for your new role in a variety of categories.

In Chapter 5 of this minibook, you take a deeper look into enabling or disabling certain tasks for specific roles and how drafts are reviewed and published.

3. **Click OK to exit the Edit Setting dialog box and return to the administration panel.**

Creating and sending connection keys

Connection keys are small files that can be e-mailed or transferred ondisc to other Contribute users to allow for easy, one-step setup and connection to your Web site project. These keys contain connection information (such as FTP info and credentials) as well as the user's role and capabilities within your project.

To create a connection key:

1. **Choose Edit⇨Administer Websites (Windows) or Contribute⇨ Administer Websites (Mac) and select a Web site (connection) from the list.**

The Administer Website dialog box appears. When the dialog box appears, you see the Users and Roles screen by default.

2. **Click the Send Connection Key button on the right.**

The Send Connection Key dialog box appears, from which you can choose to send the Web site connection information as part of the key.

3. **Leave the Would You Like to Send the Current Connection Settings? radio button set to Yes and click the Next or Continue button.**

Don't select the Include my FTP Username and Password check box unless you're certain that this information won't compromise other files on your Web server. Only select this if you're using a controlled FTP account with limited access to this project.

After you click Next or Continue, the Role Info screen appears, allowing you to assign a role to the new user who will receive the key. The default roles are administrator, publisher, and writer. See the earlier section, "Understanding preset user roles," for details about each role.

4. **For this example, select a role and click the Next or Continue button.**

The Connection Key Info screen appears.

5. **Choose a delivery method for the new key and encrypt it with a password.**

Leave the default option, Send in E-Mail, selected. Select a password and enter it twice in the provided type-in fields. Remember to document and pass this information to the recipient of your new key — she can't use the key without it.

6. **Click the Next or Continue button to advance to the Summary screen and click the Done or Finish button to complete the process.**

Because you chose to e-mail your key, the default e-mail application on your system launches with a new message containing installation instructions and the attached key.

7. **Enter your recipient's e-mail address and send the message.**

8. **Return to Contribute and click Close to exit the Administer Website dialog box.**

When exiting the Administer Website dialog box, you may get an alert dialog box reminding you that you haven't set a password for your administrator account. For the most security, we recommend that you set a password from the Administration screen of the Administer Websites dialog box.

Connecting with a Key

If you're joining an existing Contribute Web site project as a new user, the site's administrator can send you a key with the information you need to connect to the Web site and your role that's been defined for you within the project. You may receive this key by e-mail, or it may be given to you as a stand-alone file on a hard drive or CD.

To connect to an existing Web site with a connection key:

1. Do one of the following:

- *If the key was received via e-mail,* save the attached `.stc` key file to your hard drive.

- *If the key is on a hard drive or CD,* copy the `.stc` key file to an easy-to-find location on your computer.

2. Double-click the key file to open Contribute and begin the setup process.

The Import Connection Key dialog box appears.

3. Enter your name and e-mail address in the fields, as shown in Figure 2-4.

Figure 2-4:
You can easily connect to a Contribute Web site with a key sent via e-mail.

> Import Connection Key: Root Valdez: Mycelia – New York Bas...
>
> **You are setting up a Contribute connection key to:**
> http://www.fgerantabee.com/contribute/
>
> What is your name?
>
> Eric
>
> What is your e-mail address?
>
> erowse@aquent.com
>
> What is the connection key password?
>
> ••••
>
> (i) Contact the sender of the connection key if you don't know the password.
>
> (?)   (Cancel)   (OK)

This helps other users identify you when you create and send drafts.

4. Enter the password given to you by the site administrator to unlock the key.

Contribute sets up the connection for you, and the Web site appears by choosing Edit⇨My Connections (Windows) or Contribute⇨ My Connections (Mac). By default, the home page for the new site appears in the browser window so you can create drafts right away.

Make sure to ask the administrator for the password assigned to your key, or you can't use it!

Using Contribute with Dreamweaver Sites

If you've already created a site definition in Dreamweaver CS4 to manage your Web site project, you want to be aware of some important options that can give you a head start as you manage your site in Contribute.

The details of setting up a site definition in Dreamweaver CS4 are covered in Book IV, Chapter 3. For now, this section focuses on the options you need specifically for Contribute.

The Dreamweaver Site Definition dialog box creates a new Web site project in which you store your Web pages and assets (such as images and video) as well as take advantage of Dreamweaver-specific features, such as page templates and site reports.

You can use the special category provided in Dreamweaver's Site Definition dialog box to enable a site for Contribute users. This enables useful features, such as *Design Notes,* which lets multiple users on a project exchange notes, and *Check In/Check Out,* which lets other users know when you're working on a file and prevents the file from being edited. This option also enables you to use the Contribute Rollback feature (if enabled). Rollback is discussed in detail in Chapter 5 of this minibook.

About Dreamweaver templates

After you set up a site definition in Dreamweaver, you can create and store templates as part of your Web site files. Templates create reusable Web pages that you can duplicate and customize, all while maintaining a consistent look and feel from page to page. Templates restrict editing to very specific portion of a page, dubbed *editable regions,* which prevents important page elements (such as menus and logos) from being accidentally removed or changed.

The best part about templates is that any changes made in the original template update all pages based on that template. If a Web site created in Dreamweaver includes templates, Contribute can easily create new pages based on those templates. Templates are definitely worth trying because they help you save time and maintain a consistent look throughout your site. Although templates are beyond the scope of this book, check out *Dreamweaver CS4 For Dummies* (Wiley Publishing) by Janine Warner for additional help with Dreamweaver CS4 features.

To enable an existing Dreamweaver site for Contribute users:

1. **Open Dreamweaver CS4 and choose Site⇨Manage Sites.**

The Manage Sites dialog box appears.

2. **Select the site definition that you want to work with and click the Edit button.**

The Site Definition dialog box appears.

3. **Click the Advanced tab at the top of the dialog box to view the advanced options for your site definition and then click the Contribute category shown on the left to view the Contribute options screen.**

4. **Click the Enable Contribute Compatibility check box, as shown in Figure 2-5.**

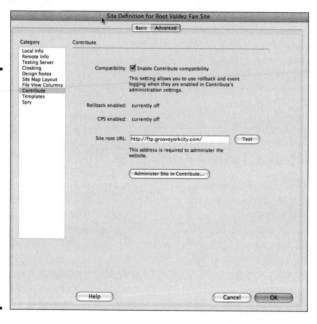

Figure 2-5:
You can enable your Web site project for use with Contribute CS4 in the Advanced view in Dreamweaver's Site Definition dialog box.

5. **When a dialog box notifies you that Design Notes and Check In/Out will be enabled, click OK.**

The Contribute Site Settings dialog box appears.

6. **Type your name in the Check Out Name text box, type your e-mail address in the E-Mail Address text box, and click OK.**

This identifies you to other Contribute users when editing pages in this project.

If you haven't specified an FTP address, as shown in the site root URL, make sure to do so before working with your site in Contribute. This allows Dreamweaver to connect to your Web site and to upload necessary files for Contribute to use. If you've already enabled FTP access in the Remote Info category of the Site Definition dialog box, this information is added automatically here.

7. **Click OK to exit the Site Definition dialog box and click the Done or OK button again to exit the Manage Sites dialog box.**

Checking Out the Contribute Workspace

After you set up a connection (or two), you're ready to become familiar with the workspace and tools. Depending on the task at hand, you have access to a variety of panels, tools, and menus that let you control connections, monitor drafts, and create and edit page content.

Beginning at the Start page

Like most other Adobe CS4 applications, Contribute displays the Start page when you open the program. The Start page is a helpful launching point for most basic tasks in Contribute, such as creating connections to blogs and Web sites, editing pages in existing connections, and even displaying some handy links to online resources and tutorials.

You can disable display of the Start page by clicking the Don't Show Again check box at the bottom of the Start page when the Start page is visible. You can reopen it at any point by choosing View➪Home Pages➪Contribute Start Page.

Editing pages in the Browser/Document Editor window

The central part of your workspace is the Browser/Document Editor, which lets you view, edit, and publish Web pages. This window acts in part as a Web browser, allowing you to browse Web sites and pages, and instantly preview drafts and view published pages.

When you open an existing connection, you can edit, save, and publish drafts directly in this window. When editing a draft, the toolbar changes at the top to display text formatting, image, and media tools, as shown in Figure 2-6.

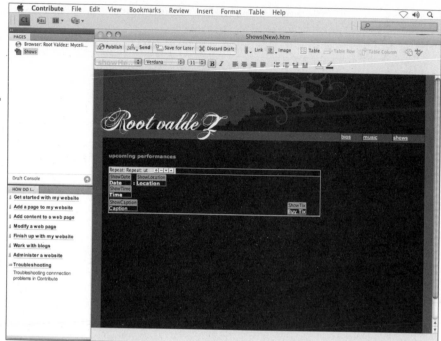

Figure 2-6:
The
Browser/
Document
Editor
window
(right)
changes
appearance
when you're
viewing
your Web
site or
editing a
draft.

To understand the Browser/Document Editor a little better, it helps to see it in action. To view the different modes, follow these steps:

1. **Do either of the following:**

- From the Start page, click and open an existing site or blog connection under the Begin Editing column.

  Or

- Choose View➪Home Pages and select one of your existing connections.

  The main page of your Web site or blog connection appears in the Document window in Browser mode.

2. **In Browser mode, do the following tasks:**

- Click browser controls at the top including Refresh, Back/Forward, and Stop buttons.

- Browse to other pages or Web sites by typing a Web address in the address bar at the top and clicking the Go button.

- Start a connection to a new Web site or blog by typing its address in the address bar and clicking the Go button. Contribute alerts you that the new location isn't one of your existing connections. You can click the New Connection button that appears at the top of the browser to create a new connection to the Web site or the blog you visited.

3. **With an existing connection and home page visible, click the Edit Page button in the upper-left corner of the browser window to edit an existing page.**

   The top of the window changes to display page-editing tools.

   You see buttons at the top of the window for creating hyperlinks, adding images, formatting text, and working with *drafts* (pages you're currently editing).

4. **Click the New button to create a new draft.**

   A draft is any page (new or existing) that you're currently editing, that hasn't been published (copied) to the live Web site.

   Both editing an existing page and starting a new draft create a draft of a page. If you want, you can leave this draft open in the Browser/Document Editor so you can explore some additional panels in the following section.

Navigating with the Pages panel and the Draft Console

After you open an existing connection, you can view and navigate between drafts with the Pages panel. This panel displays any pages you're currently editing, and you can jump to and view a draft in the Browser/Document Editor window on the right.

In addition to the Pages panel, you can view any drafts you're working on or reviewing in the Draft Console, which is just a click away at the bottom of the Pages panel.

To view and manage your current drafts:

1. **Open an existing connection and click the Edit Page button at the top of the browser window to begin editing a new draft.**

   On the left, you see your connection shown with a globe icon to the left, and your current draft is listed below it.

2. **At the bottom of the Pages panel, click the Draft Console link.**

   The Draft Console opens in the browser window on the right. You see a listing of all drafts you're currently editing or reviewing or any drafts you've received or recently acted on.

3. **Select your draft from the Pages panel on the left to exit the Draft Console.**

4. **(Optional) To delete a draft, click the Discard Draft button at the top of the Browser/Document Editor toolbar.**

   When the Are You Sure You Want to Discard This Draft and Lose All Your Changes? dialog box appears, click Yes or OK to close the draft without saving it.

Finding help in the How Do I panel

You have to love an application that gives you what you need to help you understand it even better. The How Do I panel, shown in Figure 2-7, provides integrated help topics in the form of short step-by-step instructions — right inside the panel!

This panel appears directly on the lower-left corner of your screen, and you can also collapse or expand it by choosing View➪Sidebar.

Figure 2-7:
The How Do I panel displays helpful step-by-step instructions on how to complete common tasks.

To find out more about a listed topic, click it directly in the panel. A list of subtopics appears, each of which you can click to receive step-by-step instructions on how to accomplish a specific task. Use the Back and Topics buttons at the top of the panel to return to a previous topic listing, or to return to the main topics listing.

You can collapse the side panels to icon view, including the Pages and How Do I panel by clicking the small double arrows at the top of the panel group or by choosing View➪Sidebar. These two techniques also expand the side panels if the panel group is already collapsed.

Chapter 3: Creating Drafts and Editing Page Content

In This Chapter

✔ Working with drafts in Contribute

✔ Editing your existing pages

✔ Styling pages with CSS

✔ Formatting your text

✔ Adding images to pages

✔ Organizing your content with lists

✔ Creating hyperlinks to new pages

✔ Editing and publishing blog entries

*A*fter you create a connection to a Web site (which we discuss in Chapter 2), you're ready to start editing pages and creating new content. You discover how to create and save drafts from existing Web site pages and even how to add new pages to your site.

Contribute CS4 gives you lots of tools for creating and styling text, adding photos and graphics, and even adding interactive content, such as Flash movies and video. You can apply many of these same techniques to editing and publishing entries to popular online blogs, such as Blogspot, TypePad, WordPress, and more.

This chapter starts off with the basics about drafts and working with CSS. Then you discover how to edit text, images, and links. The last sections of this chapter introduce you to tools for updating your blog.

Introducing Drafts

A key part of working in Contribute CS4 is the concept of creating, saving, and publishing drafts. A *draft* is a temporary copy of an existing or new page that's saved until it's ready to be published back to a live Web site. Your drafts contain any edits you've made as well as any new content you've created.

Drafts are edited in the Browser/Document Editor window, and you can create and manage several drafts at once. Each page that you edit from one of your connected Web sites or blogs automatically becomes a draft and appears in your Pages panel on the left as well as the Browser/Document Editor window's Draft Console.

Editing Existing Pages

You can choose to modify and update any existing page from one of your connected Web sites by using the Edit Page button that appears on the top of the browser. You can navigate to and create a draft from any page on a connected Web site.

When you choose to edit a page or work on an existing draft, the browser goes into Document Editor mode to display the tools you need to add and format text, insert images, create hyperlinks, and save and publish your draft. You can see the toolbar in Figure 3-1.

Figure 3-1:
The Document Editor toolbar features lots of familiar formatting buttons and menus.

The Document Editor's tools will be familiar to Dreamweaver users, but if you've ever used any popular word processing program (such as Microsoft Word), you'll find many familiar buttons for fine-tuning colors, paragraph formatting, and layout.

Starting and saving a draft

Follow these steps to view the Document Editor toolbar and explore the editing workspace:

1. **Do either of the following:**

- From the Contribute Start page (choose View⇨Home Pages⇨ Contribute Start Page), click and select an existing Web site connection from the Begin Editing column.

  Or

- Choose View⇨Home Pages and select an existing connection from the list.

  The home page of the selected connection appears in the browser window.

2. **Click the Connect button on the left side of the Browser toolbar to connect to the Web site.**

After Contribute successfully connects to the Web site, the Edit Page and New buttons replace the Connect button on the browser toolbar.

3. **Use any hyperlinks or navigation shown in the page to navigate to the page you want to edit.**

If you want to edit the current home page, simply leave it displayed in the browser.

4. **Click the Edit Page button on the Browser toolbar.**

A dialog box displays a progress bar while Contribute connects to your Web site. After a successful connection is made, Contribute creates a new draft from the page you've chosen to edit, which appears in the Pages panel on the left.

The Document Editor toolbar replaces the Browser toolbar at the top of the window.

5. **Take a moment to explore the editing tools.**

You see some familiar buttons, such as the B and I buttons (for creating bold and italic text, respectively), buttons to create numbered lists, and a font (typeface) selector.

Above these buttons, you see additional buttons for creating hyperlinks, inserting images, and creating tables for displaying spreadsheet-style information. You find details about how to use these tools in later sections of this chapter.

6. **Click the Save for Later button on the toolbar at the top so you can continue working on it later.**

The draft is available the next time you connect to this Web site, even if you close and reopen Contribute.

Contribute CS4 stores all drafts in a special directory on your computer. The drafts will be in different places depending on whether you're using Contribute CS4 on Windows or Mac.

Reopening an existing draft

If you've saved a draft from a previous Contribute session, you can reopen it in a couple of different ways to continue editing where you left off:

✦ **Locate your draft in the Pages panel** on the left side of the workspace. Click to open it in the Browser/Document Editor window.

✦ **At the bottom of the Pages panel, click the Draft Console link,** shown in Figure 3-2, to open the Draft Console in the Browser. Your draft should appear at the top of the page in the Drafts I'm Editing box. Click to open it for editing in the Browser/Document Editor.

Figure 3-2:
Switch to current drafts or open previously edited ones with the Pages panel or the Draft Console.

You may not be able to edit the selected draft until you click the Connect button at the top of the Browser. Connections are generally left open until Contribute is closed, so you may need to reconnect if you're reopening the application.

Working with Cascading Style Sheets

A crucial part of creating and styling content for Web pages involves the understanding and the use of *Cascading Style Sheets (CSS)*. CSS is a language that works within Web pages to style content and create page layouts. CSS is considered the standard method of formatting Web pages and is utilized in popular Web page editing programs, such as Dreamweaver.

How Cascading Style Sheets work

CSS works within your existing Web pages by creating *rules* (often referred to as *styles*), each of which can contain formatting information, such as color, typeface, margins, and size. For example, a rule may be created that specifies that any text to which it's applied should appear red, bold, and with the Arial font.

The beauty of CSS rules, or styles, is that when created, they can be easily applied to any number of items on a page. If you modify the original rule, anything using that rule automatically updates to reflect those changes.

✔ **A CSS rule** contains properties, such as color, font, and font size. Each property has

a value assigned to it, such as red, Arial, and 12 point.

✔ **A style sheet** is a collection of several CSS rules and is typically written directly into a Web page or stored in a separate .css file, often referred to as an external or attached style sheet. A basic page typically uses a single style sheet, but complex pages or Web sites may use several style sheets at once.

If you're new to CSS, check out *CSS Web Design For Dummies* by Richard Mansfield for an in-depth look at how CSS works.

Contribute can apply CSS rules (or *styles*) from an existing style sheet, or create new ones as you format text or page elements within a draft. Contribute makes use of style sheets from any pages that you edit, and displays existing rules, or *styles* in the Style drop-down list that appears on the Document Editor toolbar. You can apply existing styles with the Style drop-down list or create new ones by using the text formatting tools on selected text in a page.

Applying an existing style

Follow these steps to apply and create styles in a draft:

1. **Connect to an existing Web site and open an existing draft in the Document Editor.**

See the earlier section, "Reopening an existing draft," for details.

2. **Select a piece of text or other element on the page.**

3. **From the Style drop-down list in the lower-left corner of the Document Editor toolbar, select a style to apply it to the selected text or page element.**

The Style drop-down list displays a number of generic styles (such as Normal and Heading 1) as well as any styles already included in the page you're editing. Each style listed previews the formatting it contains, including colors, size, and typeface.

It's that easy!

You can save lots of time and keep a consistent look across your pages by using a previously created style sheet. Every standard Web page editing application, such as Dreamweaver, includes the ability to create and apply style sheets to Web pages.

Creating new styles

Contribute lets you create your own reusable styles and apply them throughout your page. You can accomplish this by simply formatting text in your page with the Document Editor's toolbar.

To create and apply your own styles:

1. **Select some text or a page element within the draft you're editing.**

2. **Use the Document Editor toolbar to format an element on your page.**

For example, click the B (bold) button to bold the selected text, as shown in Figure 3-3. Choose a new font size (for example, 24) from the Font Size drop-down list to change the size of the selected text. The specifics of styling different elements, such as text and images, are explained later in this chapter.

Style menu

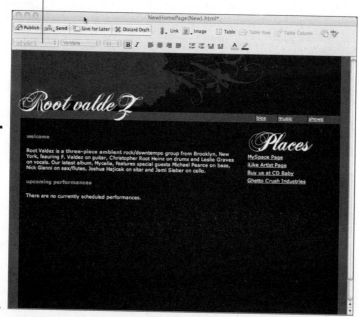

Figure 3-3: Formatting a selected piece of text creates a new, reusable style, shown in the menu on the top left.

3. **In the lower-left corner of the toolbar, locate the Style drop-down list.**

   Notice that the Style drop-down list has added a new, generically named style to the list (such as style1) that includes the choices you just made. A new CSS rule, or style, has been created that you can now reuse again in your page.

4. **Select a different piece of text or element on your page.**

5. **Select the new style that was created in the last steps from the Style drop-down list to apply it to the selected text.**

   The original text you selected and the next text both appear formatted exactly the same way. You can apply this same formatting many more times to other text just by reselecting the same rule from the Style drop-down list.

Renaming and deleting styles

You can rename styles that you've created in your page to make them easier to identify. This allows you to replace the generic names automatically assigned by Contribute. You can also delete styles when they're no longer in use, or if you want to re-create them.

✦ **To rename an existing style,** choose Rename Style from the bottom of the Style drop-down list. When the Rename Style dialog box appears, as shown in Figure 3-4, select the style you want to rename from the Style drop-down list, type a new name in the New Style Name text field, and click OK.

Figure 3-4:
Use the Rename Style dialog box to assign a more user-friendly name to styles you've created in your page.

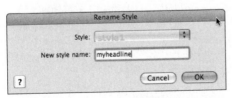

✦ **To delete a style,** choose Delete Style from the bottom of the Style drop-down list. When the Delete Style dialog box appears, select the style you want to delete from the Style drop-down list and click OK.

Contribute doesn't allow you to rename or delete the original styles that were included in the original page. These styles don't show as options in either the Rename Style or Delete Style dialog boxes, allowing you to select only the styles that you've created.

Formatting Text

Some of your most common tasks when editing a draft include adding, styling, or editing text. After a page is converted to a draft and ready for editing, you can type directly in the Document Editor window, select text, copy and paste, or use the buttons and the menus on the Document Editor toolbar to apply color, change font size, and more.

Before you can view and use the Document Editor toolbar, create or open an existing draft, as I discuss in the previous section.

To add and style text in the Document Editor window:

1. **With a draft open, click and select some text inside your page.**

If you don't have any text to work with, click to position your cursor and type a few words directly into the page.

You can copy and paste text from e-mail messages, text files, or Word documents directly into the draft. Copy text from another application and choose Edit⇨Paste from the Contribute menu to paste the text at your current cursor location.

2. **Click and select some text on the page to edit or style it in the following ways, with the Document Editor toolbar:**

- *To add bold or italic:* Click the B button once to apply boldface to the selected text. Click the I button to also apply italic to the same text.

- *To change the font or font size:* The Font and Font Size drop-down lists on the toolbar are located directly to the left of the B and I buttons. Click the Font drop-down list and select a typeface (for example, Arial) to apply it to the selected text. Click the Font Size drop-down list and choose a new type size (in points) to apply it to the selected text.

- *To change the text color:* Locate the Text Color button () in the lower-right corner of the toolbar. Click it to open the Swatches panel. Using the Eyedropper tool that appears, click and choose a color from the Swatches panel to apply it to the selected text.

- *To highlight text:* Locate the Highlight Color button, which sits directly to the right of the Text Color button. Click it to open the Swatches panel and select a color to apply a highlight to the selected text.

You may have noticed that cryptic-looking code that appears on the Swatches panel when you select a color. This is referred to as a *hexadecimal code,* which is how Web browsers understand color. Hexadecimal code is basically a binary representation of RGB (Red, Green, Blue) that you can find used in many other applications, such as Dreamweaver, Fireworks, and Photoshop.

3. **(Optional) To add space between lines, press Enter (Return on a Mac).**

   Contribute works a lot like your favorite word processor when it comes to creating space between lines of text. You can use the Enter/Return key to create either full paragraphs or line breaks.

   - *To create a new paragraph (hard return),* press the Enter/Return key.
   - *To create a line break (soft return) and force text to a new line,* hold down the Shift key and press the Enter/Return key.

4. **Choose File⇨Save to save your edits.**

Adding Images

Creating great Web pages is about more than just gobs of text. Although text-based information is key, illustrations, photos, and icons help complete the story and create compelling content.

Contribute CS4 lets you add image files to a page from a variety of places, including your computer, the Web site you're working on, and directly from the Web. Contribute (and the Web in general) supports the use of three Web-ready image formats: JPEG, GIF, and PNG (8 or 24). You can create these formats in most popular image-editing programs, such as Fireworks and Photoshop.

See Book II for information on preparing graphics for the Web in Photoshop. Or if Fireworks is your program of choice, flip to Book V.

Inserting an image

To add an image to your page, do the following:

1. **Open an existing draft for editing.**

   See the previous section, "Reopening an existing draft," earlier in this chapter for details.

2. **Click and place your cursor at a specific location inside your page where you want the image to be placed.**

3. **Click the Image button at the top of the Document Editor toolbar.**

4. **From the drop-down list that appears, choose the location where you want to grab your image.**

   You can select a file from your hard drive (From My Computer), from the currently active Web site's existing images folder (From Website), or from a location on the Web (From Internet).

5. **Select the image you want to insert by using the steps that correspond to the option you chose in Step 4:**

   - *If you chose From My Computer,* the Select Image dialog box appears. Browse and select a JPEG, a GIF, or a PNG file from your hard drive and click Choose/Select.

   - *If you chose From Website,* the Choose Image on Website dialog box appears. Use the file browser on the left side of the dialog box to browse for images in your Web site. Select an image to preview it on the right and click Open.

   - *If you chose From Internet, the Browse for Image dialog box appears. Enter a Web site or a page URL in the address bar at the top and locate an image on the page or Web site you browse to. Select the image and click OK.*

   The image you selected is placed on the page, as shown in Figure 3-5. You can see that this image sits very close to the text on the page and could use some padding. The next section explains how to adjust image placement if needed.

Figure 3-5:
An image can be placed on your page from your computer, the Web site, or directly from the Web.

Adjusting a placed image

After you place an image, you may want to adjust its appearance by changing its size, adding a border, or adding some padding around it. Contribute includes some basics, such as image size and alignment, as well as more advanced tools for rotating, sharpening, and adjusting the brightness of an image.

To adjust an image you've placed on the page:

1. **Double-click the image to open the Image Properties dialog box, as shown in Figure 3-6.**

2. **Type a value (in pixels) in the Display Width and/or Display Height boxes to change the dimensions of the image.**

To avoid image stretching or distortion, make sure that you leave the Constrain Proportions check box on the Image Properties dialog box selected. This guarantees that changes made to the width will automatically and proportionally adjust the height, and vice versa. It's generally not a good idea to resize images in this way — instead, use an application, such as Photoshop or Fireworks, to resize an image.

3. **Type a value (in pixels) in the Horizontal Padding and/or Vertical Padding to add space around your image and push it away from any neighboring text (for example, 10).**

4. **Apply a border to your image by typing a value (in pixels) into the Border text box (for example, 2).**

Note: The border of an image picks up the default page text color.

5. **In the Description (ALT Text) text field, enter a short description for your image.**

Adding ALT (alternate) text is an important step for making images accessible to screen readers (such as those used by the visually impaired) as well as describing an image to search engines.

6. **Choose how to align your image from the Alignment drop-down list.**

Image alignment is always relative to surrounding text, so choosing a Left alignment also allows text to wrap around it to the right.

Figure 3-6: Double-click an image to edit its properties, including borders, alignment, and alternate text.

Image Properties	
Image file:	file:/// (Choose...)
Display width:	200 Pixels ⬍ (Reset Display Size)
Display height:	200 Pixels ⬍ ☑ Constrain proportions
Horizontal padding:	pixels Alignment: Left ⬍
Vertical padding:	pixels Border: pixels

Description (ALT text):

A beautiful sunset image

This description is used by tools that read web pages to people with visual disabilities.

[?]   (Apply) (Cancel) (OK)

7. **Click OK to exit the dialog box and apply your changes.**

   Leave the image selected.

8. **Use the image-editing buttons at the bottom-left corner of the toolbar to scale, rotate, sharpen, and even adjust the brightness of your image.**

   Experiment with these buttons to see how they affect your image.

Creating Lists to Organize Content

Formatting your text with lists is an easy way to organize related items on a page. Alternately, you can use indenting to visually create an order of importance for different blocks of text.

To create a list:

1. **Position your cursor on a page where you want to insert the list.**

   For best results, put your cursor on a new line or press the Enter/Return key to create a new paragraph first.

2. **Press either the Bulleted List or Numbered List buttons on the Document Editor toolbar to begin the list and create your first list item.**

3. **Type in text or add an image to your list item and press Enter/Return to create additional list items.**

   You can create a list from existing items on a page if each item is already separated by paragraphs. Select all the items and press the Bulleted List or Numbered List button to create a new list and automatically add each paragraph item as a new list item.

Creating Hyperlinks

Hyperlinks (or simply *links*) are what gets you places on the Web. Hyperlinks can be used to navigate from one page to another in a Web site, to jump among different Web sites, or to download files and send e-mails.

You can create hyperlinks easily and quickly by using Contribute toolbars and menus, which enable you to link to other pages on your site, to outside Web sites, or to e-mail addresses. You can even link to different sections within the same page, which is handy for pages with lots of content.

Linking to another Web site

To create a hyperlink to another Web site:

1. **Open an existing draft and select some text on the page that you want to add a link to.**

2. **Click the Insert Link button at the top of the Document Editor toolbar.**

3. **Select Browse to Web Page from the drop-down list that appears.**

4. **When the Insert Link dialog box appears, as shown in Figure 3-7, type the Web address of the Web site you want to link to in the Web Address (URL) text field (for example** http://www.wiley.com**).**

If you're unsure of the exact Web address and want to look for it online, click the Browse button below the Web Address (URL) text field.

Figure 3-7:
Click the
Link button
and choose
Browse to
Web Page
to link to
another
Web site.

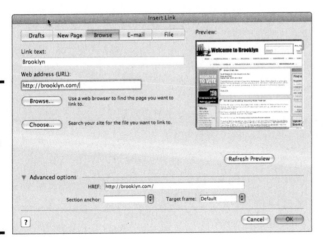

If you chose to look for a Web address online by clicking the Browse button, use the Browse to Link dialog box that appears as you would use a normal browser. When you get to the address you want to use, click OK.

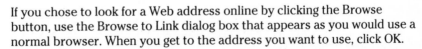

Make sure to include the full http:// prefix when manually typing in a Web address. Without it, the link produces a Page Not Found error when you click it in a browser.

5. **In the Insert Link dialog box, click the OK button to create the link and return to your draft.**

Get in touch! Linking to e-mail addresses

Just as you can link to Web addresses and pages, you can create hyperlinks that go directly to e-mail addresses. E-mail links behave differently from other links; however, when a user clicks an e-mail link, it opens the default e-mail program on his computer (such as Mac Mail or Outlook) and automatically creates a new message addressed to the e-mail recipient you selected.

To create a link to an e-mail address, select some text on a page and click the Insert Link button on the Document Editor toolbar. Select the E-Mail Address option from the drop-down list. Verify the link text in the Link Text field and enter the e-mail address (such as **myname@ mysite.com**) in the E-Mail Address text field. Click OK to create the link.

Linking to a page within your site

You can also link to a page that's already part of your Web site. This is especially useful for linking up brand-new pages you've created with existing ones on your Web site.

To link to an existing page in your Web site:

1. **Open an existing draft and select some text or an image on the page that you want to add a link to.**

2. **Click the Insert Link button at the top of the Document Editor toolbar.**

3. **Select Browse to Web Page from the drop-down list that appears.**

   The Insert Link dialog box appears.

4a. **Choose a button to browse to and select a file from your Web site.**

   The Choose File or Blog Entry dialog box appears.

   Or

4b. **Use the file browser on the left side of the dialog box to browse your Web site and select the page you want to link to. Click Open to choose the page.**

5. **When you're returned to the Insert Link dialog box, click OK to create the link and return to your draft.**

Editing Blog Entries

The weblog, or *blog,* has inarguably become one of the most popular forms of online communication in recent years. From personal online diaries to political commentaries and technical tutorials, the blog gives a forum to anyone who wants one.

Blogs can be created manually with Web-based software, such as WordPress. Commonly, bloggers subscribe to plug-and-play service providers, such as TypePad or Blogger. No matter how you blog, Contribute CS4 provides you the same great tools you use for your Web site to manage your blog.

Creating a blog connection

The first step to managing your blog is to create a connection to your blog or blog account. You follow a very similar set of steps as you do to create a Web site connection.

Before you move forward, make sure that you have any necessary account information (such as ID and password) for your blog or hosted blog solution.

Follow these steps to create a blog connection:

1. **Choose View⇨Home Pages⇨Contribute Start Page to open the Start page.**

2. **Under Create New, choose Blog Connection.**

   The Create Connection dialog box appears.

3. **Leave the What Do You Want to Connect To? drop-down list set to Blogs.**

4. **From the Who Hosts Your Blog? drop-down list, select your blog hosting company (for example, Blogger).**

   If you're using a blog service other than the one listed, you're prompted to provide the URL of your blog.

5. **Click Next or Continue to move to the Blog Site Connection screen.**

6. **Type your username or login in the Username text field and enter your password in the Password text field.**

7. **Click Done or Finish to exit the dialog box and create the blog connection.**

   The connection appears on the Start page, under View⇨Home Pages, and in the My Connections dialog box.

Creating and posting a blog entry

After you establish a connection to a blog, you can easily view your blog, edit existing entries, or create and publish new entries. The Document Editor toolbar provides many of the same tools and menus for formatting text, inserting media, and creating hyperlinks. Because you're editing entries and not *pages,* you see some minor differences in the menu and button options geared specifically for blogs. For example, in Figure 3-8, you see the Blog selector drop-down list, the Title field, and the Tags field for easy selection, titling, and topic tagging.

Figure 3-8:
Edit existing
blog entries
or create
new ones
in the
Document
Editor
toolbar.

To edit an existing blog entry:

1. **Connect to your blog by selecting it from the Start page (under the Begin Editing column), or choose View⇨Home Pages and select your blog from the menu.**

   After your blog loads in the Browser, you see an Entries drop-down list in the lower-right corner of the toolbar. This conveniently lists all your active blog entries.

2. **Click the Entries menu and choose the entry you want to edit from the pop-up menu, as shown in Figure 3-9.**

   The entry appears in the Browser window, and you see the Edit Entry and Delete Entry buttons appear on the top of the toolbar.

3. **Click the Edit Entry button to switch to the Document Editor.**

   A draft of your entry is created, and the Document Editor toolbar appears at the top. You see all the same buttons and menus you need to format text, add images, and create links. You see additional text fields and menus that allow you to modify the entry's title, labels, creation date, and more.

4. **Use the techniques covered in the "Working with Cascading Style Sheets," "Inserting an image," and "Creating Hyperlinks" sections earlier in this chapter to edit and style the contents of your blog entry.**

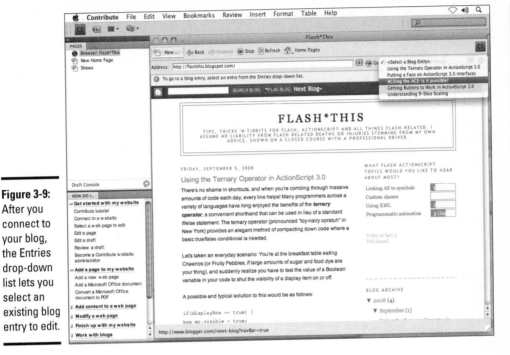

Figure 3-9:
After you connect to your blog, the Entries drop-down list lets you select an existing blog entry to edit.

When editing most blog entries, you can't edit certain portions of your blog, such as navigation and global page elements. Most blog services allow you to edit only the contents of the blog without affecting the overall layout and look.

5. **Click the Labels drop-down list and easily select and apply labels you've used for past blog posts.**

The Labels drop-down list on the Document Editor toolbar is a handy way to easily reassign labels (keywords) that you've given to previous blog posts.

6. **(Optional) If you want to save any changes you've made and pick up editing at a later point, click the Save for Later button at the top of the toolbar to save this draft.**

You can reopen it later from the Draft Console or the Pages panel.

7. **(Optional) If you change your mind and decide to delete your draft, click the Discard Draft button to discard the current draft without saving any changes.**

Certain features of your blog are visible only when viewing the blog in a browser and may not appear in the Document Editor. This may include polls, widgets, or add-ons that are provided and managed by your blog host.

Chapter 4: Creating New Pages and Advanced Content

In This Chapter

✔ Creating new pages

✔ Inserting Microsoft Word and Excel documents

✔ Building tables to display content

✔ Creating new pages from Dreamweaver templates

✔ Inserting Flash movies and video files

*W*hen it's time to expand your Web site and add brand new content, Contribute lets you easily create new pages and link them with your existing site. You can create new pages from existing ones, from Dreamweaver templates, or even from one of Contribute's themed starter pages. Whichever option you choose, Contribute enables you to get up and running quickly.

If you're looking to edit existing pages, not to add new ones, flip to Chapter 3 of this minibook.

To make your pages even more exciting, you can add interactive elements, such as Flash movies, which are video files with the same simplicity that you add images and text. In this chapter, you find the how-to you need to make it happen.

Adding New Pages

You can start fresh with a new page and add content from the ground up by using the Document Editor toolbar. You can create new pages in a variety of ways:

+ From blank pages

+ By duplicating existing pages on your site

+ From a collection of themed starter pages that are packaged with Contribute

In some cases, you may just want a new, blank page, and Contribute lets you create those too!

If you want to create a new page from a template, see "Working with Dreamweaver Templates" later in this chapter.

After you create new pages and add them to your site, you can link them together or link to them from pages on your existing Web site to bring it all together.

Starting a new page

Follow these steps to create a new blank page:

1. **Open an existing Web site connection by selecting it from the Contribute Start Page, or by choosing View⊅Home Pages and selecting your connection.**

    Your Web site's home page displays in the browser.

2. **Click the New button at the top of the Browser/Document Editor toolbar.**

    The New Web Page or Blog Entry dialog box appears, as shown in Figure 4-1. Under the Create New Web Page or Blog Entry For list, you see your site and blog connections listed, with options for different types of new pages you can create for each. You can create blank pages, duplicate an existing page, or choose from starter pages in a variety of themed categories.

Figure 4-1:
Create
a new
page for
your Web
site from
existing
pages,
templates,
or a blank
page.

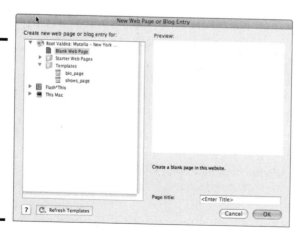

3. **Select the type of new page you want to create (for example, Blank Web Page).**

    You can preview the appearance of duplicated pages, starter pages, or templates; select one and view a thumbnail preview on the right side of the New Web Page or Blog Entry dialog box.

4. **Type a title for your new page in the Page Title text field and click OK to create the new page.**

The new page appears in your Document Editor as a brand-new draft.

5. **Type and format text, add images, or paste content from other pages as needed.**

Chapter 3 of this minibook explains how to do basic tasks, such as formatting text, adding images, and more. This chapter explains more advanced tasks, such as enabling visitors to download files, organizing data into tables, and embedding video.

Linking among new drafts

If you've created several brand-new pages for a Web site, you may want to add hyperlinks among these new drafts so they're already linked together when you publish them to your Web site. Chapter 3 of this minibook explains how to link drafts to other pages or other Web sites. Here you explore the process of getting new pages linked together before they're published so they're ready to go.

You can even link among drafts on different Web site connections or to blog entries you've recently published.

1. **Open a new or existing draft in the Document Editor window.**

2. **Select an image or line of text to create a hyperlink with.**

3. **Click the Link button on the Document Editor toolbar and select Drafts and Recent pages from the drop-down list that appears.**

The Insert Link dialog box appears, and the Drafts category is visible. Any unpublished drafts appear listed below the Select a Page to Link To column.

4. **Click to select the draft you want to link to.**

5. **At the bottom of the dialog box, click the Advanced Options arrow to expand it.**

If you're linking to a draft from another Web site or from your current Web site to a blog entry, you may want to open that site in a new window when the link is clicked.

6. **From the Target Frame drop-down list, select New Window.**

This makes sure that the selected page opens in a new browser window or a new tab so that the page you're linking from remains in the background in the original browser window.

7. **Click OK to create the link and exit the dialog box.**

If you publish a draft that contains a link to an unpublished draft, you receive a warning in the Publish New Linked Pages dialog box. A link to an unpublished draft may cause a broken link and a browser error page. It's best to only publish a page if the page you're linking to is also being (or has been) published. The Publish New Linked Pages dialog box, however, can remedy the problem by publishing the linked page for you.

Adding Content from External Applications

Very often you prepare content for a Web site page in an outside application. If you're like many people who work in collaborative environments, it's likely that you've created or received Web page content in Microsoft Word or Excel documents. Or, you may want to offer content to your visitors as a downloadable PDF (Portable Document Format). The following sections walk you through the steps.

Inserting Microsoft Word and Excel content

If you're using Contribute in Windows, you can instantly insert Microsoft Word and Excel documents into an existing or new draft to save lots of time! (This is much better than cutting and pasting this content into a Web page.)

To insert the contents of a Word or Excel document to your draft:

1. **In a new or existing draft, click the page where you want to insert the contents of your Word or Excel document.**

2. **Choose Insert⇨Microsoft Office Document.**

   The Open dialog box appears.

3. **Choose the Microsoft Word or Excel document you want to use and click Open.**

   The Insert Microsoft Office Document dialog box appears.

4. **Click Insert the Contents of the Document into This Page and then click OK to insert the contents of the document.**

Adding downloadable PDF documents

Adobe's PDF (Portable Document Format) file format has become a standard for delivering digital content in both print and Web communities. PDF files can be generated from Adobe Acrobat, and a number of other applications and can display text, graphics, forms, and even media.

If necessary, you can embed or link to a PDF file from your page in a few simple steps — here's how:

1. **In a new or existing draft, click to position your cursor on the page.**

2. **Choose Insert⇨PDF Document.**

   The Insert PDF Document dialog box appears.

3. **Select where you want to insert a PDF document from: From My Computer, From Website, or From Internet.**

   For example, choose From My Computer to insert a PDF document from your hard drive. If choosing a document from your hard drive, the Open dialog box appears.

4. **Browse and select the PDF file you want to insert, select it, and click the Open/Choose/OK button.**

5. **In the Insert PDF Document dialog box, choose how you want the PDF added to your page.**

   Contribute can create a link to the PDF document to allow your users to download the document from your Web page, or you can insert it as an embedded object to display in the page.

6. **Do one of the following:**

   - *Select Create a Link to the PDF Document and click OK.* A new hyperlink is created at your cursor position. When this page is published, the PDF file you selected is uploaded to the Web site and users can click this new link to download it to their hard drive.

   - *Choose Insert the PDF as an Embedded Object and click OK.* This opens a warning dialog box, warning you that this content isn't accessible (visible to screen readers and other devices that assist the visually impaired). Click OK to proceed, and the document is added to the page. Click Cancel only if you decide not to embed the PDF.

Due to the physical dimensions of an embedded PDF document, it can take up lots of space and displace other content within your page. Avoid this method of including PDFs unless you're creating a page dedicated to that PDF.

Building Tables

Tables have been a fixture in Web pages for a long time and were initially designed to display spreadsheet-style data and organize lots of content in a grid-style layout. Because Web pages have no predefined layout method, many Web designers actually use tables as a way of creating entire page layouts. (Although as tools for Cascading Style Sheets [CSS] improve, CSS is the preferred way to create page layouts.)

You can add tables to your drafts to include new content or to assist in laying out page elements.

Adding a new table to a Web page

To add a table to your page:

1. **In a new or existing draft, position your cursor on the page where you want the table to be inserted.**

2. **Click the Table button at the top of the Document Editor toolbar.**

The Insert Table dialog box appears, as shown in Figure 4-2.

Figure 4-2:
The Insert
Table
dialog box.

3. **In the Number of Rows text field, type the number of rows your table should have; in the Number of Columns text field, type the number of columns you want your table to have.**

4. **Under the Options section of the dialog box, set the table width by selecting the Specific Width radio button and typing a width (in pixels).**

Note: If you want your table to fit to its contents, leave the Default Width radio button selected.

5. **In the Border Thickness text field, enter a border width in pixels.**

This creates a beveled border around all cells in your table. To remove this border, set the Border Thickness to zero (this is standard if you're using your table to create a page layout).

6. **Set the cell padding and cell spacing of your table by typing a value (in pixels) in both the Cell Padding and Cell Spacing text fields.**

   Cell padding determines the padding around each cell's contents, and cell spacing determines the distance between cells in the table.

7. **To set the top row or left column as a header, click the Top or Left button under Header.**

   If you're using your table to display spreadsheet-style information, such as a calendar of events, a company phone directory, or an inventory list, you can set the top row, left column, or both to act as headers. Header rows or columns display their contents in bold type and tell browsers that those cells describe the content of the column/row under them.

8. **Click OK to exit the dialog box and add the new table to the page.**

Filling the table with content

After you set up a table, you can add content to table cells by following these steps:

1. **Click and place your cursor inside a table cell.**

2. **Type or paste text, insert images, or create lists, using the techniques in Chapter 3 of this minibook.**

   Table cells can contain just about any type of content.

3. **Select the table cell and use the Document Editor toolbar as you would on any other page content to format the cell's contents.**

   After you create a table and add content, you can format individual cells and their contents by selecting one or more cells and using the Document Editor toolbar. If you need a refresher on formatting text or images, flip to Chapter 3 of this minibook.

Modifying table properties

You can modify the properties of the table. Format just a cell, a row, or a column or apply changes to the entire table.

You can select just part of a table in the following ways:

+ **To select a cell in your table,** hold down the Ctrl (Windows) or Shift (Mac) key and click anywhere within the cell. A black border appears around the cell.

+ **To select multiple cells,** click and drag across several cells at once to select them.

✦ **To select an entire column,** move your pointer slightly above the top of the column until a downward arrow appears and click to select the entire column.

✦ **To select an entire row,** move your pointer over the left edge of the table next to the row and click to select the entire row.

After you select a portion of the table, you can add a background color to a selected cell by clicking the Highlight Color button on the Document Editor toolbar. Choose a color from the color selector that appears. To change the color, size, or font of text in one or more selected cells, use the text formatting buttons and menus on the toolbar.

To modify the properties of your entire table:

1. **Move your cursor directly over any edge or gridline of your table until the double arrows appear; click to select the entire table.**

2. **Right-click the selected table and choose Table Properties from the contextual menu, or press Shift+Ctrl+T (Windows) or Shift+⌘+T (Mac).**

   The Table Properties dialog box appears. From this dialog box, you can modify many of the settings you chose when you created the table (such as the number of rows and columns), as well as add a background color and a border color. For example, click the color swatch next to Background Color and choose a background color for your table.

3. **Modify table properties to your liking.**

4. **Click OK to apply your changes and exit the dialog box.**

Adding rows and columns

If you need to add rows and columns to a table to add more content, you can do this from a number of places in Contribute:

✦ **To add columns to your table,** click inside a cell in any column in your table and click the Table Column button on the Document Editor toolbar. A new column is added to the right of the one in which your cursor is positioned.

✦ **To add rows to your table,** click inside a cell in any row in your table and click the Table Row button on the Document Editor toolbar. A new row is added below the one in which your cursor is positioned.

Working with Dreamweaver Templates

An advantage to the close relationship between Contribute and Dreamweaver is the ability to use cool features, such as Dreamweaver templates. For any site you create in Dreamweaver, you can build *templates* — master pages from which many other pages can easily be created.

Templates contain all the common items you need for your site (such as your logo and navigation buttons) and allow you to customize select portions of the page in any copies you create from them. This ensures consistency across all or several pages throughout your Web site, and you can create several templates to accommodate different types of pages.

Understanding editable regions

Every page template created in Dreamweaver contains *editable regions* — specific areas of the page that can be modified in every page based on that template.

For example, you may create a product page where only the title, photo, and price can be customized for each new page and product. Areas outside editable regions, however, can't be edited in these pages, preventing others from accidentally modifying the look of your page or deleting important items.

Creating template-based pages

If you're managing a Dreamweaver site in Contribute, any templates created for that site are available for you to use. Templates appear in the New Web Page or Blog Entry dialog box so that you can create new pages from them when you decide to add to your site.

Before you can use templates, establish a connection to a Dreamweaver-enabled web site, as we describe in Chapter 2 of this minibook.

To create and edit a new page from a Dreamweaver template:

1. **Open an existing connection to a Dreamweaver-enabled Web site.**

2. **At the top of the browser, click the New button to create a new page and edit it as a draft.**

   The New Web Page or Blog Entry dialog box appears, with your Web site and blog connections listed on the left.

3. **Under your current Web site connection, locate the Templates folder and expand it if necessary by clicking the arrow directly to the left of it.**

Any templates created for this site in Dreamweaver are listed.

4. **Select a template and enter a title for your page in the Page Title text field at the bottom of the dialog box, as shown in Figure 4-3.**

Figure 4-3:
If your Web site uses Dreamweaver templates, these are listed in the New Web Page or Blog Entry dialog box.

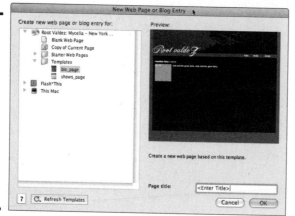

5. **Click OK to create the new page.**

A new page appears in the Document Editor page based on that template. Any editable regions in this page appear as boxes with tabs — you can edit the content within these regions to make this page unique.

Move your pointer around the page outside the editable regions and you'll see your cursor appears with the sign, letting you know that you can't edit these portions of the page.

6. **Edit or add contents to the editable regions shown.**

To test how the feature works, add and format some text or insert some images, as shown in Figure 4-4. You'll find the process is just the same as editing any other draft.

7. **(Optional) If you want to save this draft and continue editing later, click the Save for Later button at the top of the Document Editor toolbar.**

If you're the original creator or designer of the site and want to give yourself or your users the ability to customize more portions of the page, edit the page in Dreamweaver to include more editable regions.

Working with Dreamweaver Templates **825**

Book IX
Chapter 4

Creating New Pages
and Advanced
Content

Figure 4-4:
Editable regions determine what areas of a template-based page can be edited and are shown on the page with a distinctive border and tab.

Working with repeating regions

Dreamweaver templates can include a handy and flexible feature — *repeating regions;* these regions are portions of a template that can be duplicated as necessary to accommodate more items of the same type on a single page.

For example, you may create a calendar page that displays dates for events and happenings around town. Instead of creating a fixed number of possible entries, you can create a repeating region that you can duplicate each time you need a new date. Repeating regions can include any page elements, such as tables, lists, or images, and most important, editable regions that specify the parts of the repeating region you can modify.

Repeating regions in a template can be duplicated, removed, and rearranged by using a built-in toolbar that appears in any page based on that template. Before using this feature, make sure that you're connected to a Dreamweaver-enabled site and that a template that includes repeating regions is available.

To work with repeating regions in a template-based page:

1. **Connect to a Dreamweaver-enabled Web site that contains templates.**

2. **At the top of the browser, click the New button to create a new page and edit it as a draft.**

The New Web Page or Blog Entry dialog box appears, with your Web site and blog connections listed on the left.

3. **Under your current Web site connection, locate the Templates folder and expand it if necessary by clicking the arrow directly to the left of it.**

    Any templates created for this site in Dreamweaver are listed.

4. **Select a template that contains repeating regions (ask the Web site designer or administrator if you're unsure) and enter a title for your page in the Page Title text field at the bottom of the dialog box.**

5. **Click OK to create the new page.**

    A new page appears in the Document Editor page based on that template. You see at least one repeating region, which appears with a small toolbar that includes buttons for arranging, adding, and removing repeating regions.

6. **Click the Add Region (+) button at the top of the repeating region set.**

    This creates another copy of the repeating region below the original.

7. **Edit content in the editable regions contained in each repeating region to customize it, as shown in Figure 4-5.**

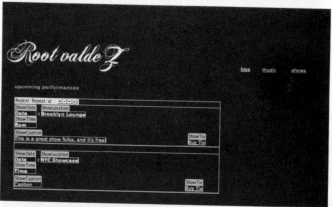

Figure 4-5:
Repeating regions can be duplicated, individually modified, and rearranged in a template-based page with the special toolbar that appears above the region set.

8. **Click within a repeating region that you want to move to a different position; click the up and down arrows above the region set to reposition the region higher or lower (respectively) in the stack.**

To remove an unwanted repeating region, click anywhere within the repeating region and click the Remove (–) button to remove the region from the stack.

9. **Continue editing the contents of your repeating region set or click the Save for Later button at the top of the Document toolbar to save the draft and edit it at a later time.**

Adding Interactive Content

These days, Web pages and blogs include so much more than just text and image content. As a matter of fact, you'd be hard pressed to find a site that doesn't include some type of animation, video, or built-in widgets to attract visitors and keep them engaged.

Contribute CS4 makes it easy to add this content to your pages or blogs, giving you lots of ways to keep your visitors happy and get your message heard.

Adding Flash movies

Adobe Flash movies are one of the most popular types of interactive content on the Web, allowing designers to create eye-catching animation, sophisticated games, and mini-applications that can easily be added to Web pages or included in blog entries.

Flash files, or *movies* are created in Adobe Flash CS4 and saved with an .swf file extension. If you want to read more about creating Flash movies, see Book VII.

Follow these steps to add Flash movies to your page:

1. **From the Pages panel, click the Draft Console link at the bottom to locate and open an existing draft for editing.**

2. **Position your cursor on the page at the point where you want to insert your Flash movie.**

3. **Choose Insert➪SWF and from the submenu that appears, select the option that best fits the location of your Flash file.**

   The submenu displays the three locations where you can add a Flash movie (SWF file) from. To add a movie from your hard drive, choose From My Computer, as shown in Figure 4-6. To add a movie from your Web site, choose From Website. If a Flash movie is located on another Web site that you want to use, choose From Internet.

As with images and other content you may add, make sure that you have permission to include a Flash movie if it's located on another Web site.

A warning dialog appears, reminding you that SWF files aren't accessible by screen readers, which are used by the visually impaired to decipher Web page content.

4. Click OK to proceed if you're ready to insert your file and do one of the following, depending on your choice in Step 3:

- *If you chose to insert a file from your computer,* the Open dialog box appears — browse and select a Flash SWF file from your hard drive and then click the Open or Choose button.

- *If you chose to add an existing Flash movie from your Web site,* the Choose SWF File from Website dialog box appears. Locate the file within your Web site folder displayed on the left side of the dialog box and click Open.

The new movie is inserted, as shown in Figure 4-7, and begins to play automatically within your page.

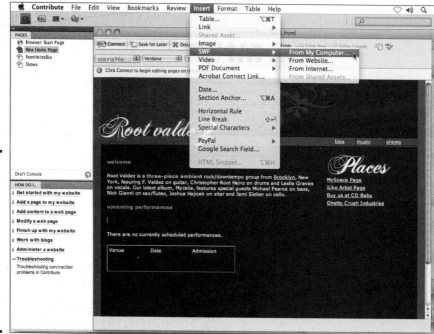

Figure 4-6:
Choose Insert⇨ SWF⇨ From My Computer to locate and place a Flash movie from your hard drive.

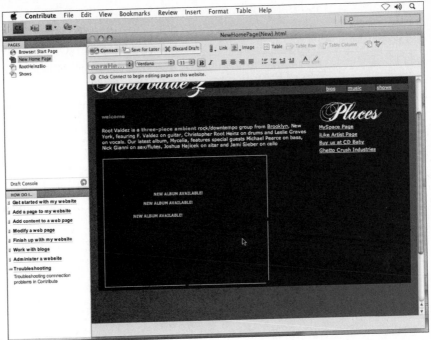

Figure 4-7:
Add a Flash
movie to
enhance
the look and
feel of your
page.

Some Web sites or blogs may not support the use or addition of Flash content. Make sure to check with your Web site or blog host if you're unsure.

Adding video content

Web video (such as QuickTime, Flash, and Windows Media video) parallels most any other type of content as the most popular form of entertainment on the Web. With Web sites like YouTube, Google Video, and most every television network delivering content through their Web sites, video is an important way to boost the online experience.

Contribute lets you add video in popular formats, such as Flash (.flv), QuickTime (.mov), Windows Media (.wmv), and MPEG (.mpg, .mp4).

Follow these steps to add video to your page:

1. **From the Pages panel, click the Draft Console link at the bottom to locate and open an existing draft for editing.**

2. **Position your cursor on the page at the point where you want to insert your video file.**

3. **Choose Insert⇨Video and from the submenu that appears, select the option that best fits the location of your file.**

   To add a movie from your hard drive, choose From My Computer. To add a movie from your Web site, choose From Website. To add a movie from another Web site, choose From Internet.

4. **Do one of the following, depending on your choice in Step 3:**

   - *If you chose to insert a file from your hard drive,* the Open dialog box appears — browse and select a video file from your hard drive and then click the Open or Choose button.

   - *If you chose to add an existing video file from your Web site,* the Choose SWF File from Website dialog box appears. Locate the file within your Web site folder displayed on the left side of the dialog box and click Open.

   The new movie is inserted in the page. ***Note:*** Not all video file formats play automatically when added.

Chapter 5: Managing Roles and Drafts

In This Chapter

✔ Working with user roles

✔ Administering site features

✔ Using the Rollback feature

✔ Reviewing drafts from other contributors

✔ Using the Draft Console

✔ Spell checking pages

✔ Publishing final drafts to your Web site

A fter you work on a draft, create a new page, or add content to an existing page, you're ready to submit your page for final review and publishing. Depending on your role within a Web site, you may be reviewing drafts from several other users, or you may simply be submitting drafts for final review by an administrator or a publisher.

If you're a site administrator, you can assign roles, tasks, and different levels of controls to others within a Web site project. In addition, you can set up useful Contribute features, such as Rollback, which allow you to revert to older versions of a page in certain crucial situations.

This chapter explains some basic tasks for administrators, including managing user roles and rolling back a page to a previous version. You also find out how to review and publish drafts, or submit drafts for review, depending on the abilities your user role allows.

Managing User Roles

User roles are the heart of the Contribute workflow, and each user within your project can be given different tasks and abilities based on the part he plays within the development and growth of your site.

Contribute offers three default user roles: administrator, publisher and writer, each of which has different levels of control over aspects of your Web site, such as editing, publishing, setting up Contribute features, and user management. You can invite others to join your project by sending connection keys and assigning a role at that time. If necessary, you can create custom roles or modify the default ones to more closely meet the needs and workflow requirements of your project. All these topics are introduced in Chapter 2 of this minibook.

In this section, you discover how to define abilities for each user role (custom or built-in), and these include anything from the ability to publish a draft to what types of formatting can be applied to text.

User abilities fall into several categories, and to best understand and see what's possible, you first need to modify an existing role. The following steps explain how:

1. **Choose Edit⟿Administer Websites (Windows) or Contribute⟿ Administer Websites (Mac) and select the Web site (connection) you want to administer.**

The Administer Website dialog box appears, displaying the Users and Roles screen.

2. **In the list of users and roles shown, select a role or user within that role that you want to modify, for example the Writer role, and click the Edit Role Settings button.**

Modifying a role or a user assigned to it has the same effect. Settings applied to a role will affect all users who fall within that role.

The Edit Role Settings dialog box appears. User abilities are broken down into eight categories displayed on the left. Table 5-1 explains what each category does.

3. **In the General category, which appears by default, enter a description in the Role Description text box.**

For example, you might add a line after the existing text that reads *This user can edit styles but not upload images beyond 100K.*

4. **Make any other changes to the categories that you desire.**

The following bullets offer examples of changes you might make:

- *Select the Editing category from the left.* Select the Require ALT Text for Images check box. This improves accessibility for your Web site by making sure that contributors add support text used by screen readers and other assist devices.

- *Select the New Pages category on the left, as shown in Figure 5-1.* To make sure your user uses templates only you've provided or blank pages, deselect the Use Built-In Starter Pages check box. This prevents the use of pages with themes that may not match the existing look and feel of your Web site.

- *Select the New Images category on the left.* Select the Reject Images That Exceed Max File Size radio button. In the text field that appears to its right, type **100**. This rejects any images the user adds if she exceeds 100K in file size.

5. **Click OK to exit the Edit User Settings dialog box.**

6. **Select another role to edit if desired, or if you're done, click OK again to exit the Administer Website dialog box.**

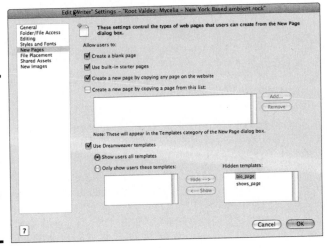

Figure 5-1:
The Edit
User
Settings
dialog box
controls
what a user
in a specific
role can do
(or not do)!

Table 5-1	Categories in the Edit Role Settings Dialog Box
Category	*What You Find Here*
General	This controls the overall description of the role and the default home page for users who log in with this role.
Folder/File Access	Here you can specify what directories or files the user role is limited to editing. This is ideal if you have writers dedicated to content in a specific section of the site. By default, users can edit any page in any directory.

(continued)

Table 5-1 *(continued)*

Category	What You Find Here
Editing	Sets how the page is formatted while the user edits content. The default settings are generally fine, but in some cases, you may want to limit a user from inserting add-ons (such as PayPal buttons or Google search boxes), which can be done by selecting the appropriate radio button or check boxes.
Styles and Fonts	This category controls how users format text in a page. You can restrict the creation of new styles and formatting, or allow users to only apply basic formatting, such as size and color.
New Pages	You can give users the ability to create and add new pages to your Web site, and even restrict the type of pages they create. For instance, to make sure that all new pages are consistent, you can allow users to only add new pages based on existing Dreamweaver templates.
File Placement	Here you can control where new files (such as images and video files) are added to the Web site. By default, new files are stored in the same folder as the page that uses them, but you can filter them into specific folders, such as a dedicated images folder, if necessary.
Shared Assets	You can set images, video files, and Flash movies to be *shared assets* — files that are available on the server for every user to work with. This is especially useful for common items, such as company logos and other branding graphics.
New Images	Here you can set some basic limitations on images that users can add to pages. For instance, you can prevent users from uploading images that exceed a certain file size, or have Contribute reduce the physical size (dimensions) of an image if it's larger than a specified width and height.

Administering Your Web Site

In addition to managing users, many options are available to administrators for adding or modifying features to a Contribute-enabled Web site. You can enable useful features, such as Rollback, determining when pages expire, and so on.

Setting up the basics: Your e-mail and link settings

If you're a new administrator, check the e-mail and link settings to make sure that they're accurate. As you continue to work in Contribute, knowing where these settings are is helpful because you may need to update them occasionally. Follow these steps:

1. **Choose Edit ➪ Administer Websites (Windows) or Contribute ➪ Administer Websites (Mac) and select a Web site connection to manage.**

The Administer Website dialog box appears.

2. **Select the Administration category on the left.**

3. **In the Contact E-Mail Address text field, type or modify your e-mail address where other contributors can reach you.**

4. **Select the Links category from the left.**

Here you can set how links are created in a page.

5. **Make sure that the Write Links Relative to the Current Page option is selected.**

6. **Click OK to exit the Administer Websites dialog box and apply the new settings to your Web site.**

Retrieving previous page versions with Rollback

The Contribute CS4 *Rollback feature* is a powerful tool that lets you revert to previously saved versions of pages. This is useful in the event that you need to retrieve some information previously deleted from a page or to restore a page to an older version.

With Rollback enabled, Contribute keeps a copy of a certain number (which you control) of previously published pages so that you can revert to any of those versions if necessary. To use Rollback, you (or another administrator) must first enable it in the Administer Websites dialog box.

To enable Rollback for a Web site:

1. **Choose Edit ➪ Administer Websites (Windows) or Contribute ➪ Administer Websites (Mac) and select a Web site connection to manage.**

The Administer Website dialog box appears.

2. **Select the Rollbacks category on the left.**

3. **Select the Enable Rollbacks check box, as shown in Figure 5-2.**

4. **Type in or use the up/down arrows to set a number of previous versions to keep.**

If you're unsure how many to keep at this point, leave the default number set at 3.

5. **Click the Close button to exit the dialog box.**

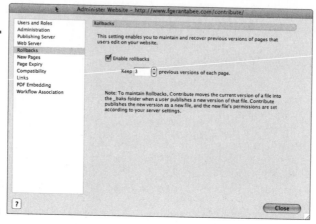

Figure 5-2:
Rollbacks give you the ability to save and revert to an older version of a published page if necessary.

After you enable Rollback, it's easy enough to call up a previously-published version of a page. To roll back to a previous version of a page or asset:

1. **Open an existing connection and browse to the page you want to roll back in the browser window.**

2. **Choose File⇨Actions⇨Roll Back to Previous Version.**

   The Roll Back Page dialog box appears, as shown in Figure 5-3, and recently published versions of the page you selected appear listed at the top of the dialog box.

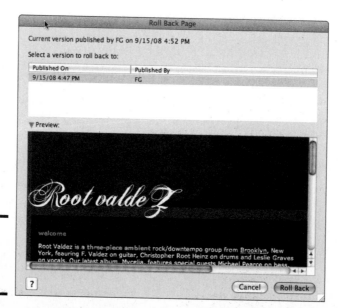

Figure 5-3:
The Roll Back Page dialog box.

The number of versions depends on the number of rollback versions enabled for your Web site, as well as the overall number of times the page has been revised.

3. **Select a previous version of the published page from the list.**

Each version is displayed next to its publish date and publisher. You can also select a version to see a preview of it in the bottom portion of the dialog box.

4. **Click the Roll Back button after you select the version you want to use.**

The page you selected replaces the currently published version of the page on the Web site.

Reviewing and Publishing Drafts

The Contribute workflow enables a single user to create and publish his or her own drafts. Often, however, many contributors to a project need a single point person to manage and approve their work.

The administrator and publisher roles (or any custom roles based on them) have the power to receive and review drafts from writers before they're published to the Web site. A typical workflow may be as follows:

1. Writer (or a similar role) selects a draft for editing and makes changes. They may also (if their role allows) create a new page and submit it for publishing. (Creating and editing drafts is covered in Chapter 3 of this minibook.)

2. The writer sends the draft for review by using the Document toolbar's Send for Review button.

3. An administrator or a publisher receives the draft on login, or sees it listed in the Draft Console.

4. The administrator or the publisher reviews the draft in the Document Editor window, makes any adjustments (if necessary), and publishes the draft to the Web site.

Reviewing drafts in the Draft Console

The Draft Console displays in the Browser/Document Editor window and allows users to see their unpublished drafts, or if their role allows publishing, any action items or received drafts that require review and final publishing.

To open and select drafts from the Draft Console:

1. **Open and connect to an existing Web site.**

2. **Locate the Pages panel on the left side of your workspace and click the Draft Console link at the bottom to open the Draft Console in your Browser/Document Editor window.**

   Your action items appear in four different boxes: Drafts I'm Editing, Drafts I'm Reviewing, Received Drafts, Drafts Acted On. See Figure 5-4.

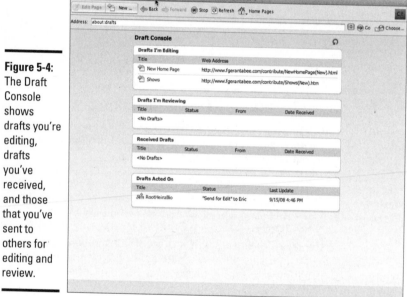

Figure 5-4: The Draft Console shows drafts you're editing, drafts you've received, and those that you've sent to others for editing and review.

Note: Administrators or publishers have more options than writers (or users based on writer).

3. **Select a draft to review and/or publish.**

   If you've received a draft from another user, it appears in the Received Drafts box; if you want to open a draft you've created, select it from the Drafts I'm Editing box.

Submitting drafts for review

If you're a writer or any user who can't publish drafts directly, you'll need to send your drafts for review to another user who has the ability to publish those drafts.

In some cases, you can send drafts simply to have another set of eyes look over your work and make sure that nothing obvious was missed or incorrectly added. Users in any role can send drafts for review to other users in a Contribute site project.

To send a draft for review to another user:

1. **With the draft open in the Document Editor window, click the Send button at the top.**

   The Send dialog box appears.

   You can choose to send the draft for review by e-mail or directly to another Contribute user. Leave the default (Another Contribute User) selected.

2. **Enter helpful notes to the recipient in the Description of Changes text box if you want.**

3. **Select a user from the list shown on the dialog box.**

   You can send drafts to a specific user or to all users within a specific role.

4. **Click the Send button at the bottom to close the dialog box.**

   If you're the user who sent the draft, the draft appears listed in the Drafts Acted On box in the Draft Console. If you're the recipient of the draft, it appears in the Received Drafts box in the Draft Console next time you connect to the Web site.

   If you're the recipient of a draft, you can select the received draft from your Draft Console to open it for editing/publishing in the Browser/ Document Editor window. You can even make changes and forward it to yet another user in the workflow.

Running a spell check

Contribute's built-in spell checker makes it easy to give your page a once-over for spelling or grammar before sending it for final publishing.

To spell check a draft:

1. **With a draft open in the Document Editor window, click the Check Spelling button at the top of the toolbar.**

   The Check Spelling dialog box appears and highlights (if any) spelling or grammar mistakes it finds.

2. **Click the Close button when the spell check is complete, or if you want to discontinue using the spell check.**

Publishing a draft

After a draft has been edited, reviewed, and submitted, post it to the Web site. If you're an administrator or a publisher (or any user with the ability to publish drafts), you can select a draft and easily publish it to the *live* Web site for the world to see. This is one of the most crucial parts of the process, but it's also the simplest!

To publish a draft:

1. **After you connect to a Web site, locate the Pages panel on the left and click the Draft Console link at the bottom to open the Draft Console.**

2. **From any of the boxes shown on the Draft Console, click to select and open a draft in the Document Editor window.**

3. **If everything looks good, click the Publish button at the top of the Document Editor toolbar to publish the page.**

   A dialog box appears to let you know the page has been successfully published, as shown in Figure 5-5.

4. **Click OK.**

   Contribute switches to the browser window and displays your new page directly from the Web site.

Figure 5-5: Click the Publish button in the Document Editor toolbar and wait to receive a confirmation message letting you know that your page has been published.

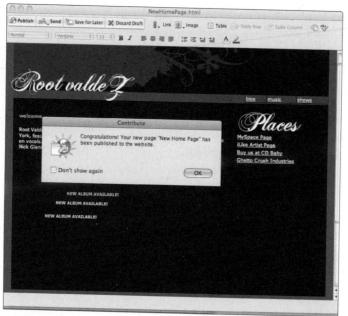

If the page you're publishing isn't linked to any other pages on your Web site, Contribute displays a warning dialog box. If you want the page to be available from other pages on your site, follow the steps shown in the section on creating hyperlinks in Chapter 3 in this minibook, or in the section on linking among new drafts in Chapter 4 of this minibook.

Index

Numbers

A

B

Q

R

Notes

Notes

Notes

Notes

BUSINESS, CAREERS & PERSONAL FINANCE

Accounting For Dummies, 4th Edition*
978-0-470-24600-9

Bookkeeping Workbook For Dummies†
978-0-470-16983-4

Commodities For Dummies
978-0-470-04928-0

Doing Business in China For Dummies
978-0-470-04929-7

E-Mail Marketing For Dummies
978-0-470-19087-6

Job Interviews For Dummies, 3rd Edition*†
978-0-470-17748-8

Personal Finance Workbook For Dummies*†
978-0-470-09933-9

Real Estate License Exams For Dummies
978-0-7645-7623-2

Six Sigma For Dummies
978-0-7645-6798-8

Small Business Kit For Dummies, 2nd Edition*†
978-0-7645-5984-6

Telephone Sales For Dummies
978-0-470-16836-3

BUSINESS PRODUCTIVITY & MICROSOFT OFFICE

Access 2007 For Dummies
978-0-470-03649-5

Excel 2007 For Dummies
978-0-470-03737-9

Office 2007 For Dummies
978-0-470-00923-9

Outlook 2007 For Dummies
978-0-470-03830-7

PowerPoint 2007 For Dummies
978-0-470-04059-1

Project 2007 For Dummies
978-0-470-03651-8

QuickBooks 2008 For Dummies
978-0-470-18470-7

Quicken 2008 For Dummies
978-0-470-17473-9

Salesforce.com For Dummies, 2nd Edition
978-0-470-04893-1

Word 2007 For Dummies
978-0-470-03658-7

EDUCATION, HISTORY, REFERENCE & TEST PREPARATION

African American History For Dummies
978-0-7645-5469-8

Algebra For Dummies
978-0-7645-5325-7

Algebra Workbook For Dummies
978-0-7645-8467-1

Art History For Dummies
978-0-470-09910-0

ASVAB For Dummies, 2nd Edition
978-0-470-10671-6

British Military History For Dummies
978-0-470-03213-8

Calculus For Dummies
978-0-7645-2498-1

Canadian History For Dummies, 2nd Edition
978-0-470-83656-9

Geometry Workbook For Dummies
978-0-471-79940-5

The SAT I For Dummies, 6th Edition
978-0-7645-7193-0

Series 7 Exam For Dummies
978-0-470-09932-2

World History For Dummies
978-0-7645-5242-7

FOOD, GARDEN, HOBBIES & HOME

Bridge For Dummies, 2nd Edition
978-0-471-92426-5

Coin Collecting For Dummies, 2nd Edition
978-0-470-22275-1

Cooking Basics For Dummies, 3rd Edition
978-0-7645-7206-7

Drawing For Dummies
978-0-7645-5476-6

Etiquette For Dummies, 2nd Edition
978-0-470-10672-3

Gardening Basics For Dummies*†
978-0-470-03749-2

Knitting Patterns For Dummies
978-0-470-04556-5

Living Gluten-Free For Dummies†
978-0-471-77383-2

Painting Do-It-Yourself For Dummies
978-0-470-17533-0

HEALTH, SELF HELP, PARENTING & PETS

Anger Management For Dummies
978-0-470-03715-7

Anxiety & Depression Workbook For Dummies
978-0-7645-9793-0

Dieting For Dummies, 2nd Edition
978-0-7645-4149-0

Dog Training For Dummies, 2nd Edition
978-0-7645-8418-3

Horseback Riding For Dummies
978-0-470-09719-9

Infertility For Dummies†
978-0-470-11518-3

Meditation For Dummies with CD-ROM, 2nd Edition
978-0-471-77774-8

Post-Traumatic Stress Disorder For Dummies
978-0-470-04922-8

Puppies For Dummies, 2nd Edition
978-0-470-03717-1

Thyroid For Dummies, 2nd Edition†
978-0-471-78755-6

Type 1 Diabetes For Dummies*†
978-0-470-17811-9

---

* Separate Canadian edition also available
† Separate U.K. edition also available

Available wherever books are sold. For more information or to order direct: U.S. customers visit www.dummies.com or call 1-877-762-2974.

WILEY

INTERNET & DIGITAL MEDIA

AdWords For Dummies
978-0-470-15252-2

Blogging For Dummies, 2nd Edition
978-0-470-23017-6

**Digital Photography All-in-One
Desk Reference For Dummies, 3rd Edition**
978-0-470-03743-0

Digital Photography For Dummies, 5th Edition
978-0-7645-9802-9

**Digital SLR Cameras & Photography
For Dummies, 2nd Edition**
978-0-470-14927-0

**eBay Business All-in-One Desk Reference
For Dummies**
978-0-7645-8438-1

eBay For Dummies, 5th Edition*
978-0-470-04529-9

eBay Listings That Sell For Dummies
978-0-471-78912-3

Facebook For Dummies
978-0-470-26273-3

The Internet For Dummies, 11th Edition
978-0-470-12174-0

Investing Online For Dummies, 5th Edition
978-0-7645-8456-5

iPod & iTunes For Dummies, 5th Edition
978-0-470-17474-6

MySpace For Dummies
978-0-470-09529-4

Podcasting For Dummies
978-0-471-74898-4

**Search Engine Optimization
For Dummies, 2nd Edition**
978-0-471-97998-2

Second Life For Dummies
978-0-470-18025-9

**Starting an eBay Business For Dummies,
3rd Edition†**
978-0-470-14924-9

GRAPHICS, DESIGN & WEB DEVELOPMENT

**Adobe Creative Suite 3 Design Premium
All-in-One Desk Reference For Dummies**
978-0-470-11724-8

**Adobe Web Suite CS3 All-in-One Desk
Reference For Dummies**
978-0-470-12099-6

AutoCAD 2008 For Dummies
978-0-470-11650-0

**Building a Web Site For Dummies,
3rd Edition**
978-0-470-14928-7

**Creating Web Pages All-in-One Desk
Reference For Dummies, 3rd Edition**
978-0-470-09629-1

**Creating Web Pages For Dummies,
8th Edition**
978-0-470-08030-6

Dreamweaver CS3 For Dummies
978-0-470-11490-2

Flash CS3 For Dummies
978-0-470-12100-9

Google SketchUp For Dummies
978-0-470-13744-4

InDesign CS3 For Dummies
978-0-470-11865-8

**Photoshop CS3 All-in-One
Desk Reference For Dummies**
978-0-470-11195-6

Photoshop CS3 For Dummies
978-0-470-11193-2

Photoshop Elements 5 For Dummies
978-0-470-09810-3

SolidWorks For Dummies
978-0-7645-9555-4

Visio 2007 For Dummies
978-0-470-08983-5

Web Design For Dummies, 2nd Edition
978-0-471-78117-2

Web Sites Do-It-Yourself For Dummies
978-0-470-16903-2

Web Stores Do-It-Yourself For Dummies
978-0-470-17443-2

LANGUAGES, RELIGION & SPIRITUALITY

Arabic For Dummies
978-0-471-77270-5

Chinese For Dummies, Audio Set
978-0-470-12766-7

French For Dummies
978-0-7645-5193-2

German For Dummies
978-0-7645-5195-6

Hebrew For Dummies
978-0-7645-5489-6

Ingles Para Dummies
978-0-7645-5427-8

Italian For Dummies, Audio Set
978-0-470-09586-7

Italian Verbs For Dummies
978-0-471-77389-4

Japanese For Dummies
978-0-7645-5429-2

Latin For Dummies
978-0-7645-5431-5

Portuguese For Dummies
978-0-471-78738-9

Russian For Dummies
978-0-471-78001-4

Spanish Phrases For Dummies
978-0-7645-7204-3

Spanish For Dummies
978-0-7645-5194-9

Spanish For Dummies, Audio Set
978-0-470-09585-0

The Bible For Dummies
978-0-7645-5296-0

Catholicism For Dummies
978-0-7645-5391-2

The Historical Jesus For Dummies
978-0-470-16785-4

Islam For Dummies
978-0-7645-5503-9

**Spirituality For Dummies,
2nd Edition**
978-0-470-19142-2

NETWORKING AND PROGRAMMING

ASP.NET 3.5 For Dummies
978-0-470-19592-5

C# 2008 For Dummies
978-0-470-19109-5

Hacking For Dummies, 2nd Edition
978-0-470-05235-8

Home Networking For Dummies, 4th Edition
978-0-470-11806-1

Java For Dummies, 4th Edition
978-0-470-08716-9

**Microsoft® SQL Server™ 2008 All-in-One
Desk Reference For Dummies**
978-0-470-17954-3

**Networking All-in-One Desk Reference
For Dummies, 2nd Edition**
978-0-7645-9939-2

**Networking For Dummies,
8th Edition**
978-0-470-05620-2

SharePoint 2007 For Dummies
978-0-470-09941-4

**Wireless Home Networking
For Dummies, 2nd Edition**
978-0-471-74940-0